General editors:
William C. Carroll, Boston University
Brian Gibbons, University of Münster
Tiffany Stern, University of Oxford

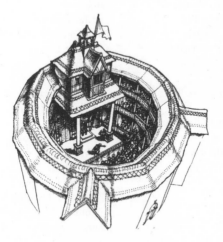

Reconstruction of an Elizabethan theatre
by C. Walter Hodges

NEW MERMAIDS

NEW MERMAIDS

FOUR REVENGE TRAGEDIES

THE SPANISH TRAGEDY
THE REVENGER'S TRAGEDY
'TIS PITY SHE'S A WHORE
THE WHITE DEVIL

Introduction by Janet Clare

methuen | drama

LONDON • NEW YORK • OXFORD • NEW DELHI • SYDNEY

METHUEN DRAMA
Bloomsbury Publishing Plc
50 Bedford Square, London, WC1B 3DP, UK
1385 Broadway, New York, NY 10018, USA

BLOOMSBURY, METHUEN DRAMA and the Methuen Drama logo are
trademarks of Bloomsbury Publishing Plc

First published in 2014 by Methuen Drama
Reprinted by Bloomsbury Methuen Drama 2015, 2019

A catalogue record for this book is available from the British Library.

A catalog record for this book is available from the Library of Congress.

ISBN: PB: 978-1-4081-5960-6
ePDF: 978-1-4725-7358-2
eBook: 978-1-4725-7357-5

Series: New Mermaids

Typeset by Country Setting, Kingsdown, Kent CT14 8ES
Printed and bound in Great Britain

To find out more about our authors and books visit www.bloomsbury.com
and sign up for our newsletters.

CONTENTS

ACKNOWLEDGEMENTS

This anthology of *Four Revenge Tragedies* brings together the texts and commentaries from individual plays of revenge in the current New Mermaid series: *The Spanish Tragedy*, edited by J.R. Mulryne with introduction and notes by Andrew Gurr; *The Revenger's Tragedy*, edited by Brian Gibbons; *The White Devil*, edited by Christina Luckyj; and *'Tis Pity She's a Whore*, edited by Martin Wiggins. Francis Bacon's essay 'Of Revenge' has been included in an appendix, as a point of reference for early modern ideas about the forms and the justice of revenge. A full critical and scholarly introduction is a valuable feature of the single New Mermaid editions. In the Introduction to the present anthology, I have sought to explore the theatrical, rhetorical, and ideological aspects of these revenge tragedies, all of which have different takes on revenge, and to respond to the question of why revenge continued to exert such a strong appeal as a motive and motif of drama performed on the English stage from the 1580s to the 1630s. The Notes on the Texts are taken from the original single editions and placed at the end of the collection.

I am grateful to Brian Gibbons, Margaret Bartley and Emily Hockley, who read the Introduction at different stages and made incisive comments. Claire Cooper has kept a supportive overview at Bloomsbury, while Margaret Berrill has been an exemplary proofreader and Simon Trussler has seen the volume to press with great care and efficiency.

JANET CLARE

INTRODUCTION

Revenge Tragedies

Revenge plays were among the most popular theatrical productions in the early modern period. Revivals and re-printings, parodies and re-workings, all indicate that revenge exerted a considerable fascination upon the early modern theatre-going public. Then and now, plays of revenge acknowledge the human capacity for acts of savagery and violence. Wrongs committed demand vengeance and vengeance breeds further vengeance, escalating violence and consuming all parties in a domino effect of hatred and retaliation. Audiences enjoy fantasies of violence, and if the violence can be construed as just, pleasure in shocking entertainment can be rationalized. Such is the trans-cultural and trans-historical appeal of plays like *The Spanish Tragedy* and *The Revenger's Tragedy*. At the same time revenge plays belong to their age, evidenced in their constructions of nationality, race and gender and in their specific questioning of the pillars of Elizabethan and Jacobean society, church and state.

The plays included in this collection of revenge tragedies were written and performed over some thirty years. Thomas Kyd's *The Spanish Tragedy*,[1] the earliest of the plays, was probably first seen in one of the new amphitheatres on the Bankside in Southwark in the late 1580s;[2] the latest, John Ford's *'Tis Pity She's a Whore*, composed in the 1620s and first published in 1633, was performed in the Phoenix, also known as the Cockpit, one of the more gentrified indoor theatres, which had been converted from an arena for fighting cocks. During this time, playhouse production, dramatic styles and audience taste naturally underwent change, yet *The Spanish Tragedy* continued to be remarkably popular on stage and in print.[3] Indeed, it was last published in the early modern period in 1633, the same year as the first printed version of *'Tis Pity*. Ford's play of tragic love and revenge presented its audience with a daringly

---

1 Although ten extant editions of the play were published between 1592 and 1633 the author's name does not appear on any of the title pages. The anonymous publication of plays was common in the Elizabethan period.

2 The Rose owned by Philip Henslowe was constructed in 1587. From 1592 to 1597 Henslowe kept records of his financial transactions; he first records a performance of *The Spanish Tragedy* in 1592.

3 According to Henslowe, there were twenty-nine performances of *The Spanish Tragedy* between 1592 and 1597, an impressive number in early modern terms, only exceeded by Christopher Marlowe's *Jew of Malta* and a lost play, *The Wise Man of West Chester*. See Lukas Erne, *Beyond The Spanish Tragedy*, 2001, p. 95.

sympathetic treatment of incest.[4] Yet 'Tis Pity is also backward-looking, indebted for its portrayal of young love and the roles of friars and nurses to Shakespeare's Romeo and Juliet. The Revenger's Tragedy was an early Jacobean play performed by Shakespeare's company, the King's Men, sometime before 1607 when it was first published. The passage of time between this revenge play and The Spanish Tragedy is immediately apparent. In place of a formal structure with a choric commentary between the acts and the hero's rhetorical displays of grief and loss, The Revenger's Tragedy is ironic and playful in its treatment of conventions and colloquial in its dialogue. Like The Revenger's Tragedy, John Webster's The White Devil, composed a few years later, is located in an Italian ducal court where sexual corruption, court intrigue and revenge are all inter-connected. In such a setting, revenge is as much motivated by an oppor-tunistic defence of family honour, violent fantasies and misogyny, as it is by the desire for retributive justice, a dominant theme in The Spanish Tragedy and Shakespeare's Hamlet.

Chronology

One of the earliest revenge tragedies in English Gorboduc was performed during the Christmas revels of the Inner Temple in 1562. Academic interest in Latin revenge tragedy is manifest in the publication in English of Seneca his Ten Tragedies (1581). In 1587 the Rose playhouse was built on the Bankside and The Spanish Tragedy, written by the former scrivener Thomas Kyd (1555–94), was performed there by Strange's Men in 1592. Dates of first performance of early modern plays are often difficult to determine. In the case of The Spanish Tragedy the records of Philip Henslowe, owner of the Rose, help to document performance. The Spanish Tragedy was enormously popular on stage and in print, well beyond Kyd's lifetime. It was revised in 1601–2 and the additions are attributed by some scholars to Shakespeare. Kyd's dramatic output is small although he is thought to have written a version of Hamlet from which Shakespeare's Hamlet is an adaptation.

The Revenger's Tragedy was performed by the King's Men at the Globe. For many years the play was thought to be the work of Cyril Tourneur, the author of another revenge play, The Atheist's Tragedy, and more recently it has been attributed to Thomas Middleton. Since neither attribution is beyond doubt, the play's authorship is treated here as anonymous.

---

4 For an examination of incest and its representation on stage, see Richard McCabe, *Incest, Drama and Nature's Law, 1550-1700*, 1993.

John Webster (*c.* 1580–1634) appears to have begun his career collaborating with other playwrights, including Thomas Middleton and Thomas Dekker. The plays by which he is now remembered are *The White Devil* and *The Duchess of Malfi*. *The White Devil* was performed at the open-air Red Bull playhouse, located in Clerkenwell, by Queen Anne's Men sometime between 1609 and 1612, when the play was published. According to James Wright, a late seventeenth-century theatrical historian, the clientele of the Red Bull was more citizen than gentry. The play was not an immediate theatrical success. Webster complained in his address to the reader that since it was acted in a dull time of winter it wanted 'a full and understanding auditory' (l. 4). Webster's second tragedy of horror, *The Duchess of Malfi*, was performed by the King's Men at both the Globe and their indoor theatre, the Blackfriars.

John Ford (1586–post 1640) had a career which spanned the Jacobean and Caroline periods. Like other early modern playwrights, notably John Marston, Ford had legal training and was admitted to one of the Inns of Court. He began his career as playwright collaborating with Dekker and William Rowley before producing work for the King's Men at the Blackfriars, including the tragedies, *Love's Sacrifice* (*c.* 1630) and *The Broken Heart* (*c.* 1632), for which, along with *'Tis Pity*, he is chiefly known. During the later Jacobean and Caroline periods several of the playing companies moved away from the large amphitheatres to indoor theatres. The Cockpit (or Phoenix) theatre was built in 1616 and *'Tis Pity* was staged there sometime before 1633 by Queen Henrietta's Men, the company whose patron was the consort of Charles I.

Theatre of Revenge

Spectacle

Revenge tragedies are visceral in their displays of horror and violence. The popular theatre of the English Renaissance violated the classical convention, imitated in English academic drama, that violent acts of revenge should be reported, not enacted on the stage. In the academic Inns of Court play *Gorboduc* (1562), following the tradition of revenge tragedies written by the Roman dramatist Seneca, the Queen's revenge on her younger son for the murder of her older son is reported – at great length – by one of the women of her Privy Chamber.[5] In contrast, playwrights writing for the new purpose-built, public theatres – with their large stages and much greater audience capacity – evidently recognized the potential for visual impact. Revenge, variously motivated by a

---

5 *Gorboduc* IV.ii, in *Two Tudor Tragedies*, ed. William Tydeman, 1992.

burning sense of injustice, duty to kin, slighted honour, malice and envy, provided an occasion for spectacular and ingenious acts of violence and cruelty. Audiences brought to the theatre not only memories of other revenge plays but other cultural practices: state executions, the heads of traitors displayed on London Bridge, and blood sports such as bear-baiting.[6] Both the place of execution and the platform where plays were performed were in the early modern period known as the scaffold.[7] The ritualized 'justice' of the private avenger could be said to correspond to the theatre of punishment orchestrated by the state and witnessed by the audience in the public execution of – and brutal punishments meted out to – felons and alleged traitors.

Hieronimo's revenge in *The Spanish Tragedy* comes to fruition not in a public arena, but in the private space of the court and during its enter-tainment. The scenario of characters expecting festivity and the audience anticipating murder creates dramatic tension and irony which are effec-tively replicated in other plays. In *The Revenger's Tragedy*, Vindice kills the Duke's son, Lussurioso, during a court masque, muttering in his ear, 'Tell nobody' (V.iii.83). Duke Bracciano in *The White Devil* is killed by a poisoned helmet he puts on in preparation for fighting at the barriers during his wedding celebrations. Various revenge plots are either foiled or materialize during Soranzo's birthday feast in *'Tis Pity*. But none of these scenes conveys quite the same shocking denouement as Hieronimo's staging of *Soliman and Perseda*. Here, Kyd constructs multiple layers of theatricality. The off-stage audience watches the Chorus watching the Spanish court watching what they think is a play, but is in fact a ritual display of revenge. The on-stage audience of the Duke of Castile and the Viceroy applaud the supposed fictional murder of the characters whom their children are impersonating. Hieronimo stipulates that *Soliman and Perseda* should be performed in '*sundry languages*' (IV.iv.10 s.d.) and in the violent, supposedly linguistic chaos of court theatricals Hieronimo plays his murderous part. Spectacle caps spectacle. As the audience take in the scene of murder, Hieronimo draws back a curtain and demands that the audience fix on the spectacle of Horatio's corpse strung up like a common criminal.

Stage images in *The Revenger's Tragedy* are both garish and witty. The play opens with a torchlit procession as the decadent ducal family pass by with the self-proclaimed revenger, Vindice, as sardonic onlooker and

---

6 See Andreas Höfele, *Stage, Stake and Scaffold: Humans and Animals in Shakespeare's Theatre*, 2011, pp. 1-15.

7 See Molly Smith, *Breaking Boundaries: Politics and Play in the Drama of Shakespeare and his Contemporaries*, 1998, pp. 17-40.

commentator.[8] Vindice holds the skull of his murdered love, a striking and visual use of the relic which a revenger might carry with him as an emblem of his mission.[9] Similarly, Hieronimo carries a napkin soaked in the blood of his murdered son.[10] In *The Revenger's Tragedy* nine years have elapsed since the poisoning of Gloriana, and all the while Vindice has been infiltrating the court and waiting for the moment to kill her murderer. Revenge for Vindice does entail justice, with a sense of exactitude as he seeks to make the manner of the Duke's death reflect the original crime, turning murder into a kind of mimetic art. The Duke's death is gruesomely witty as he kisses the poisoned skull hidden behind a mask, believing it to be a country woman. Vindice had commented earlier that he will avenge Gloriana 'after no common action' and certainly the form of his revenge is blackly comic as he handles the reconstructed Gloriana like a ventriloquist's dummy:

VINDICE

> Madam, his Grace will not be absent long.
> Secret? Ne'er doubt us madam. 'Twill be worth
> Three velvet gowns to your ladyship. Known?
> Few ladies respect that; disgrace? A poor thin shell!
> 'Tis the best grace you have to do it well ...

III.v.43–7

'Gloriana' becomes an accomplice, figuratively taking part in her own revenge, although the grotesque image of the skull turned again into a sexual object prompts one of Vindice's rare moments of introspection: 'And now methinks I could e'en chide myself / For doting on her beauty' (III.v.68–9). As token of revenge and *momento mori* the skull acquires a moral symbolism. Once it has been instrumental in exacting revenge, Vindice abandons it, suggesting both fulfilment and liberation.

There is no tragic avenger in *The White Devil*. Revengeful motivation is dispersed among the characters, often of a very shady kind. It is first ignited through crimes of passion as Brachiano and Vittoria contrive to remove Isabella, Brachiano's wife, and Camillo, Vittoria's husband, as obstacles to their relationship. As Isabella's brother, Francisco, Duke of

---

8 Leo Salingar considers the abstract nature of corruption in the play in '*The Revenger's Tragedy* and the Morality Tradition', reprinted in R.V. Holdsworth, *Three Jacobean Revenge Tragedies*, 1990.

9 Michael Neill examines the motifs of macabre art as they appear in early modern drama in *Issues of Death: Mortality and Identity in English Renaissance Tragedy*, 1997, pp. 51–101.

10 For discussion of revenge and remembrance, see John Kerrigan, *Revenge Tragedy: Aeschylus to Armageddon*, 1996, pp. 170–92.

Florence, assumes the position of family avenger although his role and tactics are far from heroic. He rejects active engagement, scorning as he says 'to wear a sword and prate of wrong' (IV.iii.58). Instead, he hires killers to restore the family honour and settle his political rivalry with Brachiano. *The White Devil* treats vengeance primarily as political calculation and introduces aspects of earlier revenge plays only to reject them. Francisco demands to see his sister's face and he conjures up her ghost to spur him into action. But unlike the talismanic force of Horatio's corpse in *The Spanish Tragedy* or Gloriana's skull in *The Revenger's Tragedy*, the fleeting image of Isabella's ghost has little effect on audience or avenger. Francisco remains unmoved by its appearance. It is Lodovico, Francisco's henchman, who appropriates or misappropriates the role of avenger, adopting the familiar tactics of disguise and exulting as he accomplishes his task. In the final act, Webster translates stereotypical images of the Italian proclivity for disguise and secrecy into brilliantly sinister theatre. Having played no direct part in the murder of Brachiano – it is Lodovico who poisons the helmet – Francisco dressed as a Moor silently witnesses Brachiano's prolonged and agonizing death, while Lodovico and Gasparo, disguised as Capuchin monks, profess to bring their victim the last rites and then attend him 'with a crucifix and hallowed candle'. Ritual is mocked as murderers take on sacral roles in this blasphemous parody, characteristic of the anti-Catholicism of a play where a Cardinal is more intent on indicting a glamorous courtesan than attending to spiritual affairs.

Locating *'Tis Pity* in the city of Parma, Ford also exploits the literary and cultural stereotype of Italians settling their rivalries and sexual jealousies through private vengeance. The play moves towards a spectacular denouement as Annabella's husband and her lover/brother compete to take revenge on one other. In one of the most visually arresting moments of early modern theatre, Giovanni enters the Banquet on cue, as Soranzo asks where he is, '*with a heart upon his dagger*' (V.vi.8). This is a shockingly literal realization of the familiar amatory image of the heart pierced by love's arrow.[11] The image of Giovanni as crazed, exulting revenger gives way to an image of him as victim when, at Vasques' signal, the banditti – mercenary killers – enter and put him to death.

Rhetoric
Violent action engenders violent language. Giovanni's rhetoric is self-intoxicated, marked by boasting paradox, as he exults in the glory of a deed which has 'Darkened the midday sun, made noon as night' (V.vi.21).

11 See Marion Lomax, *Stage Images and Traditions: Shakespeare to Ford*, 1987, pp. 171–2.

There is the same tormented logic, though now given a lethal turn, to his claim that the heart he has ripped from Annabella's body entombs his own heart as there was to his earlier reasoning, in conversation with the Friar, that incestuous love is natural because one womb 'gave both us life and birth' and therefore he and Annabella should be 'one soul, one flesh, one love, one heart, one all' (I.i.28–34). The poetic intensity of Giovanni's casuistic hyperbole is highlighted by the ordinary if brutal language in the streets of Parma and by the dialogue between the lovers with its easy, affectionate exchanges and tragic premonitions of death.

In *The White Devil* it is Lodovico who utters the exultant language of the avenger. As a banished and murderous nobleman, hired by Francisco, his revenge on Brachiano and the Corombona family has no real motivation in justice. He pays lip service to the notion of righting a wrong when he refers to his love for Isabella, but this feeling is never mentioned again. Indeed, in Francisco's pact with Lodovico there is a perversion of the ritual and language of revenge as duty: 'You have ta'en the sacrament to prosecute / Th' intended murder' (IV.iii.72–3). It is an indication of the state's moral bankruptcy or perhaps recognition of what has become a well-worn dramatic idiom that a notorious murderer perversely supplies the passionate sense of integrity associated with earlier stage avengers:

> I do glory yet
> That I can call this act mine own: for my part,
> The rack, the gallows, and the torturing wheel
> Shall be but sound sleeps to me. Here's my rest –
> 'I limbed this night-piece and it was my best'.
>
> V.vi.289–93

There is something in the language suggestive of earlier avengers in that 'rest' can only come with the satisfaction of revenge, but the context is quite different. Here revenge has become a self-gratifying form of compensation for the status of outlaw.

The inflated language of revenge is complemented by the rhetoric of loss, reparation and retribution, notably in *The Spanish Tragedy*. When Hieronimo discovers Horatio's murder, his soliloquy, through elaborate conceits – his eyes are 'fountains fraught with tears' (III.ii.1) – conveys his distracted passion and overwhelming sorrow.[12] Hieronimo's grief

---

12 A few years later, Jonson has the dabbling poet Matheo admiringly quote the speech to the braggart Bobadilla in *Every Man in His Humour* (I.iii.107–12), a play for the Chamberlain's Men, attesting to its renown.

emanates not only from loss but from a sense of injustice as his son's murderers intercept his pleas to the King of Spain. Feeling is conveyed in highly patterned declamatory rhetoric. In the final scene, for example, as he pulls back the curtain to reveal his son's corpse, Hieronimo impresses his emotions on his audience, on- and off-stage:

> See here my show, look on this spectacle.
> Here lay my hope, and here my hope hath end;
> Here lay my heart, and here my heart was slain;
> Here lay my treasure, here my treasure lost;
> Here lay my bliss, and here my bliss bereft;
> But hope, heart, treasure, joy, and bliss,
> All fled, failed, died, yea, all decayed with this.
> From forth these wounds came breath that gave me life;
> They murdered me that made these fatal marks.
> The cause was love, whence grew this mortal hate[.]
>   (IV.iv.89–98)

The figures of repetition, alliteration and anamnesis (recital of matters past), convey depths of suffering also communicated in the disruption of logical patterns of thought. Horatio's death compels Hieronimo to proclaim his own death. The ritualized lament contains moments of explanatory paradox – 'the cause was love, whence grew this mortal hate' – though the overall impact depends on formalized, reiterative expressions of grief.

The idiom of *The Revenger's Tragedy* represents a very different theatre poetry. Vindice's anatomizing of the vices of the court which opens the play has a feverish quality, as does his temptation of his sister in the guise of Piato. When he alludes to his murdered love Gloriana he has moments of lyricism, but otherwise the dramatic language is colloquial and informal with the dialogue often mordantly ironic. An aside like Spurio's, on seeing his father's corpse – 'Old dad dead?' (V.i.112) – captures brilliantly the indifference and casualness characters display towards the lives of others, in this instance using an idiom that seems astonishingly modern and natural. On the other hand, the play's sheer theatricality is manifest in the frequent use of asides, indicating endemic levels of deceit and manipulation.

Revenge and Justice

Acts of revenge were outlawed by the state and by Christian teaching. The lawyer and statesman Francis Bacon in his essay 'Of Revenge' reluctantly concedes that 'The most tolerable sort of revenge, is for those wrongs which there is no law to remedy'. Even so, Bacon qualified the statement: 'let a man take heed, the revenge be such as there is no law to punish; else a man's enemy is still before hand, and it is two for one'.[13] The corrupt state – although circumspectly never named the English state – where wrongs cannot be remedied by the law – is a recurring location for revenge plays. Revenge does not necessarily put the law out of office, as Bacon affirms at another point, because in *The Spanish Tragedy* and *The Revenger's Tragedy*, for example, the law is seen to have no authority in the first place. Then the code of revenge becomes a close approximation to the law: vigilantism, a rough justice, or as Bacon declared, a 'wild justice', on the brink of anarchy.

Early revenge plays grapple with the ethics of revenge. Once Hieronimo's appeals for justice from the King are rejected, his dilemma is represented through conflicting classical and Christian imperatives. Holding a book, he delivers a soliloquy (III.xiii): whether the book is the Bible or the plays of Seneca is left unclear, since he quotes from both. The soliloquy opens with '*Vindicta mihi*' – the familiar dictum that revenge is God's – and alludes to other biblical injunctions against self-appointed revenge. Hieronimo recognizes that Heaven will not 'suffer murder un-repaid' and, moreover, 'mortal men may not appoint their time'. On the other hand, Seneca's influential revenge plays offer a different precedent: 'strike and strike home where wrong is offered thee'.[14] The debate comes down on the side of classical revenge as Hieronimo vows to revenge his son's death, awaiting his opportunity, resting in 'unrest' and 'dissembling quiet in unquietness'. The paradoxes neatly capture the avenger's inner tension before the quiescence brought by the act of revenge.

Hieronimo's quest for institutional justice is thwarted by his son's murderers, not the head of state. In *The Revenger's Tragedy* there is no question that Vindice will ever receive justice since the oppressor is the ruler, and in this situation Vindice can only appoint himself judge and executioner. The Duke is a tyrant by his own admission, pardoning his son because it becomes the judge to 'nod at crimes' when he has com-mitted 'greater himself and lives' (II.iii.123–4). Whether Vindice too turns tyrant in his quest to rid the state of the ducal family is a moral question that the play leaves open.[15] Vindice himself has no qualms and identifies completely with the moral rectitude of his role. Standing over the dying

13 The essay is printed as an appendix in the present volume.
14 For a discussion of the relationship between Renaissance tragedy and that of Seneca, see Gordon Braden, *Renaissance Tragedy and the Senecan Tradition: Anger's Privilege*, 1985. John Kerrigan also discusses 'exchanges with antiquity' in part 2 of *Revenge Tragedy*.
15 R.A. Foakes argues that we see moral degeneracy in Vindice's role in 'The Art of Cruelty: Hamlet and Vindice', *Shakespeare Survey 26*, 1973, pp. 21–42.

Duke he says to his brother, 'We dread not death to quittance injuries' (III.v.195) and once the Duke is dead, he announces that he will cut his sons down. His sense of moral justification is his undoing as, not satisfied with ensuring that his victims identify him, he incriminates himself by disclosing the part he has played in the assassinations. Antonio orders his execution. Knowing he has played his part to the end, Vindice almost nonchalantly accepts death: ''Tis time to die when we are ourselves our foes' (V.iii.113). He is the obsessive revenger with little identity outside this role, demonstrating Bacon's maxim that a man that 'studieth revenge' keeps his wounds green.

For protagonists like Hieronimo and Vindice the act of revenge is one of closure, figuratively and literally, as they make reparation for the past and seal their act of retribution with their own deaths. The same might be said for Giovanni, who at the close of *'Tis Pity*, presents his murder of Annabella and Soranzo and his own death in terms of just revenge. The Cardinal admonishes him to think on his life and 'call for mercy', an injunction which Giovanni rejects in favour of justice: 'Mercy? Why, I have found it in this justice' (V.vi.100). But there is no original crime which his alleged revenge aims to counter. This purely rhetorical appropriation of justice seems to be yet another example of Giovanni's self-fashioning world-view.

The law and its processes in *The White Devil* are a sham, not because, as in earlier revenge plays, the legal system is impervious to calls for justice, but because those in power manipulate it against their opponents. Vittoria is brought to trial on the flimsiest of evidence, and since Cardinal Monticelso acts as judge and jury, the trial is rigged against her from the start. Francisco, as Duke of Florence, acts extra-legally to avenge a murder committed in Rome. In wreaking private revenge against Vittoria and Brachiano, Francisco represents the stage Machiavel, a role which combines cunning and ruthlessness. While his henchman Lodovico is punished, Francisco suffers no retribution. Apart from aristocratic privilege, Francisco's easy evasion of the law corresponds to contemporary perceptions of the differences in the operation of law between the Italian city states. The traveller, Fynes Moryson, for example, had commented that in Italy malefactors could easily escape from the jurisdiction of one principality to another[16] (which is what we see with the banditti in *'Tis Pity*). Brachiano's young son, Giovanni, in the play's final lines moralizes that guilty men should remember that 'their black deeds / Do lean on

16 *Unpublished Chapters of Fynes moryson's Itinary Being a Survey of the Conditions of Europe at the End of the Sixteenth-Century*, 1903, p. 137.

crutches, made of slender reeds', but there is no suggestion that Francisco or any of his class will be toppled.

Linda Woodbridge has discussed the idea of revenge in what she describes as a 'golden age of revenge plays' as resistance to an unjust regime.[17] However, the divorce of revenge from justice in some revenge tragedies demonstrates the different dramatic uses of revenge, as characters employ the term as a rationale for acts of gratuitously violent retaliation, self-gratification or envy. Here revenge becomes another instrument of tyranny enabling the powerful to prey on the weak with impunity.

Revenge: Class, Gender and Power

Part of the appeal of revenge drama lies in the ways in which perceived wrong and injustice lead to the challenging of hierarchies based on social position and gender. Avengers such as Hieronimo and Vindice are of lower social status than their adversaries and in rising against the corrupt state they become rebels. In *The White Devil* blood evokes ideas of family and pedigree as well as passion and the spilling of life blood. Vittoria Corombona puns as she is dying, 'my greatest sin lay in my blood. / Now my blood pays for't' (V.vi.236–7). She does not belong to an aristocratic family and has dared socially to climb, first by marrying the Cardinal's nephew and then as mistress and wife of Brachiano. Her death, along with that of her brother, is part of the internal logic of the play in which the aristocratic ruling class are viciously resentful of the lower-caste family that dares to enter their order.

From the beginning of *The Spanish Tragedy* both rank and gender inform the practice of revenge. As niece to the King of Spain, Bel-Imperia has already demonstrated her independence by loving – below her social status – the knight Don Andrea. In picking Horatio as a lover to assist in her revenge for Don Andrea's death in battle, she shows the same indifference to caste. Lorenzo and Balthazar, on the other hand, insist on seeing the relationship as an affront to class hierarchy; and the pair cruelly pun on Horatio's seeming aspiration as they hang up his body: 'Although his life were still ambitious proud, / Yet is he at the highest now he is dead' (II.iv.60–1). Since he is a prince, Lorenzo has no difficulty in convincing the King that his loyal servant Hieronimo is mad. The social positions of the characters are deeply embedded in the play, so much so that C.L. Barber has claimed that Hieronimo, as a high civil servant and former advocate, was a figure with whom the middle-class London audience would identify.[18] Certainly, when the play came to be enlarged in 1602,

---

17 *English Revenge Drama: Money, Resistance, Equality*, 2010, pp. 167–88.
18 See C.L. Barber, *Creating Elizabethan Tragedy: The Theater of Marlowe and Kyd*, 1988, p. 135.

it was Hieronimo's part to which additions were made, attesting again to the great popularity of the role.

In the unnamed Italian state of *The Revenger's Tragedy* social relations are much less nuanced than in the Spain of *The Spanish Tragedy* and the family piety of the latter is largely absent. Vindice is cast as a social malcontent as well as an avenger.[19] There is some mystery surrounding his father's death. In dialogue with his mother, he refers obliquely to it as caused by a failed court career:[20] 'Surely I think he died / Of discontent, the nobleman's consumption' (I.i.125–6), with a characteristic pun on consumption. Indeed, the characters in *The Revenger's Tragedy* are consumed by – and motivated by – discontent and envy. Spurio sees his seduction by the Duchess as revenge against his father for the exclusion resulting from his illegitimate conception. The Duchess seduces Spurio to get even with her husband for not pardoning her son for rape. Her sons conspire against Lussurioso, as heir to the Dukedom, and against each other. The only bond in the play devoid of self-interest or power struggle is that between Vindice and Hippolito.

Generally the social role of women limited their sphere of action. Women did not carry weapons, were physically weaker and ideologically constrained.[21] Yet, on the stage there were female characters who demanded and achieved revenge, not only verbally but also physically. At Vittoria Corombona's rigged trial, Cardinal Monticelso picks on her lower status, scorning her impecunious family and claiming that her kin failed to pay her marriage dowry. At the climax of this travesty of a trial, on the other hand, her angry, frustrated outburst shifts the emphasis onto her sex, 'A rape, a rape', followed by 'Yes, you have ravished Justice, / Forced her to do your pleasure'. Woman's revenge is poor, she declares, since it 'dwells but in the tongue' (IV.ii.273–84). Nonetheless, her voice of resistance strikes home and her male detractors move to contain the threat. 'She's turned fury' responds the Cardinal, brushing away her impassioned denunciation. Bacon compares vengeful individuals to the malevolence of witches, an analogy which conforms with and confirms the widely held view that the role of female avenger is aberrant. Indeed, in early modern ideologies of gender the energies of female revenge were seen as actually unnatural.

---

19 For socio-political readings of the play see J.W. Lever, *The Tragedy of State,* 1987, pp. 28–36, and Jonathan Dollimore, *Radical Tragedy: Religion, Ideology and Power in the Drama of Shakespeare and his Contemporaries,* 3rd edn, 2004.

20 The point is put as a question and could be an insinuation to his mother that his father's death might have been more sinister than suicide (an interesting link with other revenge tragedies – *Hamlet, Hoffman* and *Antonio's Revenge* – in which a son avenges the father).

21 Alison Findlay identifiesd the impulse to revenge as feminine in *A Feminist Perspective on Renaissance Drama,* 1999, p. 50.

Accordingly, the female avenger is demonized in *'Tis Pity*. As Soranzo's discarded mistress, Hippolita finds her reputation destroyed and seeks revenge. Appearing at the birthday banquet where multiple revenges are brewing, disguised as a masque performer, she intends to expose Soranzo's past and poison him. Betrayed by Vasques, her plot backfires and she drinks the poisoned wine intended for Soranzo. The response of the witnesses to her aborted revenge is particularly striking as an instance of the prejudice against female avengers. They celebrate the 'wonderful justice' (IV.i.85) that has foiled her plans. Although Soranzo has used her and broken his promises to her, no one recognizes that Hippolita might have some grievance against him. Even Annabella can only comment that 'It is a fearful sight' (99).

Remarkably, in *The Spanish Tragedy*, Hieronimo can only begin to shape his revenge plot when empowered by Bel-Imperia. 'For what's a play without a woman in it' (IV.i.97), Hieronimo asks as he apportions parts and – against the all-male acting convention – includes Bel-Imperia among his actors. Like any male avenger, Bel-Imperia acts her murderous part, stabbing Balthazar, before turning the knife on herself, and employing conventional rhetoric: '*thus she would revenge / Thy treacheries on thee, ignoble prince: / And on herself she would be thus revenged*' (IV.iv. 65–7), thereby avenging the deaths of her two lovers, Don Andrea and Horatio. Such a noble female revenger is exceptional. Women in *The Revenger's Tragedy* are regarded as either angels or whores. Gloriana's 'purer part' resists the Duke's lust at the expense of her life, Castiza successfully repulses Lussurioso, whereas Antonio's wife commits suicide rather than live in dishonour to a chorus of praise from the men present. Yet the Duchess sleeps with her stepson and Graziana would prostitute her daughter. Although Vindice recognizes that women are being victimized, he is caught up in the misogynistic world the play projects, encapsulated in his aside, 'Wives are but made to go to bed and feed' (I.i.131).

A number of scholars have treated early modern revenge tragedy as a genre or sub-genre of tragedy with identifiable conventions and motifs.[22] The various plays in this collection reveal, however, that there is no set pattern or formula. As a motive in drama, revenge is remarkably adaptable. It impinges on other dramatic concerns: conflicts of kin and status; gender inequality; social corruption; and the perversion of justice. For audience and reader, the enduring fascination of these plays is that they present a unique world in which dark fantasies of revenge are played out.

---

22 See Fredson Bowers's pioneering study, *Elizabethan Revenge Tragedy*, 1940, and Charles A. Hallet and Elaine S. Hallet, *The Revenger's Madness: A Study of Revenge Tragedy Motifs*, 1980.

FURTHER READING

General Works on Revenge Tragedy

Eileen Jorge Allman, *Jacobean Revenge Tragedy and the Politics of Virtue*, 1999

Fredson Bowers, *Elizabethan Revenge Tragedy 1587–1642*, 1940

Gordon Braden, *Renaissance Tragedy and the Senecan Tradition: Anger's Privilege*, 1985

Nicholas Brooke, *Horrid Laughter in Jacobean Tragedy*, 1979

Ronald Broude, 'Revenge and Revenge Tragedy in Renaissance England', *Renaissance Quarterly* 28 (1975), 30–58

Rachel Bushnell, *Tragedies of Tyrants: Political Thought and Theater in the English Renaissance*, 1990

Janet Clare, *Revenge Tragedies of the Renaissance*, 2006

Jonathan Dollimore, *Radical Tragedy: Religion, Ideology and Power in the Drama of Shakespeare and his Contemporaries*, 3rd edn, 2004

Charles A. Hallett and Elaine S. Hallett, *The Revenger's Madness: A Study of Revenge Tragedy Motifs*, 1980

Eugene D. Hill, 'Revenge Tragedy', in Arthur F. Kinney, ed., *A Companion to Renaissance Drama*, 2002, pp. 326–35

Roger Holdsworth, ed., *Three Jacobean Revenge Tragedies*, 1990

John Kerrigan, *Revenge Tragedy: Aeschylus to Armageddon*, 1996

Michael Neil, 'English Revenge Tragedy', in Rebecca Bushell, ed., *A Companion to Tragedy*, 2005, pp. 328–50

Thomas Rist, *Revenge Tragedy and the Drama of Commemoration in Reforming England*, 2008

Stevie Simkin, ed., *Revenge Tragedy*, 2001

Linda Woodbridge, *English Revenge Drama: Money, Resistance, Equality*, 2010

Rowland Wymer, 'Jacobean Tragedy', in Michael Hattaway, ed., *A Companion to Renaissance Literature and Culture*, 2000, pp. 545–55

The Spanish Tragedy

J.R. Mulryne and Andrew Gurr, eds., *The Spanish Tragedy*, New Mermaids, 2009

Clara Calvo and Jesús Tronch, eds., *The Spanish Tragedy*, Arden Early Modern Drama, 2013

Philip Edwards, ed., *The Spanish Tragedy*, The Revels Plays, 1959

Jonathan Bate, 'The Performance of Revenge: *Titus Andronicus* and *The Spanish Tragedy*', in Francois Laroque, ed., *The Show Within: Dramatic and Other Insets. English Renaissance Drama (1550–1642)*, 2 vols, 1992, II, pp. 267–83

Lukas Erne, *Beyond 'The Spanish Tragedy': A Study of the Works of Thomas Kyd*, 2001

Frederick Kiefer, 'Creating a Christian Revenger: *The Spanish Tragedy* and its Progeny *vs Hamlet*', *Shakespeare Yearbook* 13 (2002), 159–80

Daniel T. Kline, 'The Circulation of the Letter in Kyd's *The Spanish Tragedy*', in Lloyd Edward Kermode, Jason Scott-Warren, Martine van Elk, eds., *Tudor Drama before Shakespeare, 1485–1590: New Directions for Research, Criticism, and Pedagogy*, 2004, pp. 229–47

Scott McMillin, 'The Book of Seneca in *The Spanish Tragedy*', *Studies in English Literature* 14 (1974), 201–8

Molly Smith, 'The Theatre and the Scaffold: Death as Spectacle in *The Spanish Tragedy*', *Studies in English Literature* 32 (1992), 217–32

Warren Stevenson, 'Shakespeare's Hand in *The Spanish Tragedy*', *Studies in English Literature* 8 (1968), 307–21

The Revenger's Tragedy

Brian Gibbons, ed., *The Revenger's Tragedy*, New Mermaids, 2008

R.A. Foakes, ed., *The Revenger's Tragedy*, The Revels Plays, 1980

Karin S. Coddon, '"For Show or Useless Property": Necrophilia and *The Revenger's Tragedy*', *English Literary History* 61 (1994), 71–88

R.A. Foakes, 'The Art of Cruelty: Hamlet and Vindice', *Shakespeare Survey* 26, 1973, pp. 21–32

Chris McMahon, *Family and the State in Early Modern Revenge Drama: Economics of Vengeance*, 2012

J. Panek, 'The Mother as Bawd in *The Revenger's Tragedy* and *A Mad World, My Masters*', *Studies in English Literature* 43 (2003), 415–38

L.G. Salingar, '*The Revenger's Tragedy* and the Morality Tradition', repr. in R.V. Holdsworth, ed., *Three Jacobean Revenge Tragedies*, 1990

The White Devil

Christina Luckyj, ed., *The White Devil*, New Mermaids, 2008

John Russell Brown, ed., *The White Devil*, The Revels Plays, 1964

K.M. Carey, 'The Aesthetics of Immediacy and Hypermediation: the Dumb Shows in Webster's *The White Devil*: the Functions Then and Now of an Unfamiliar Stage "Language"', *New Theatre Quarterly* 23 (2007), 73–80

Richard Cave, *Text and Performance: 'The White Devil' and 'The Duchess of Malfi'*, 1988

Inga-Stina Ekeblad (Ewbank), 'The "Impure Art" of John Webster', *Review of English Studies* 9 (1958), 253–67

Harold Jenkins, 'The Tragedy of Revenge in Shakespeare and Webster', *Shakespeare Survey 14*, 1961, pp. 45–55

E. Williamson, 'The Domestication of Religious Objects in *The White Devil*', *Studies in English Literature* 47 (2007), 473–90

Martin Wiggins, 'Conjuring the Ghosts of *The White Devil*', *Review of English Studies* 48 (1997), 448–70

'Tis Pity She's a Whore

Martin Wiggins, ed., *'Tis Pity She's a Whore*, New Mermaids, 2003

Sonia Masai, ed., *'Tis Pity She's a Whore*, Arden Early Modern Drama, 2011

Derek Roper, ed., *'Tis Pity She's a Whore*, The Revels Plays, 1975

D.M. Bergeron, 'Brother–Sister Relationships in Ford's 1633 Plays', in D.K. Anderson, ed., *'Concord in Discord': The Plays of John Ford, 1586–1986*, 1986

Dorothy M. Farr, *John Ford and the Caroline Theatre*, 1979

Lisa Hopkins, *John Ford's Political Theatre*, 1994

Richard McCabe, *Incest, Drama and Nature's Law, 1550–1700*, 1993

S.B. Mintz, 'The Power of "Parity" in Ford's *'Tis Pity She's a Whore*', *Journal of English and Germanic Philology* 102 (2003), 269–91

M. Neill, ed., *John Ford: Critical Re-Visions*, 1988

ABBREVIATIONS

General

Abbott	E. A. Abbott, *A Shakespearian Grammar*, 1869
OED	J.A. Simpson and E.S.C. Weiner, general eds, *The Oxford English Dictionary*, 2nd edn, 1989
N&Q	*Notes and Queries*
l.	left
r.	right
s.d.	stage direction
s.p.	speech prefix
Tilley	Morris Palmer Tilley, *A Dictionary of the Proverbs in England in the Sixteenth and Seventeenth Centuries*, 1950

Shakespeare quotations are taken from *The Riverside Shakespeare*, ed. G. Blakemore Evans, 1974, unless otherwise indicated.

The Spanish Tragedy

1592	the octavo-in-fours edition of *The Spanish Tragedy* printed in 1592
1594	the octavo-in-fours edition of that year
1602	the quarto edition of that year
Edwards	Philip Edwards, ed., *The Spanish Tragedy*, The Revels Plays, 1969
Freeman	Arthur Freeman, *Thomas Kyd: Facts and Problems*, 1967

The usual practice in referring to the seventeenth-century editions of *Dr Faustus* is followed: 'A' indicates substantial agreement between all the A Texts, which are referred to separately on occasion as A1 (1604), A2 (1609), and A3 (1611); the B texts (1616, 1619, 1620, 1624, 1628, and 1631) are similarly distinguished.

The Revenger's Tragedy

EDITIONS OF THE PLAY CITED

Collins	*The Plays and Poems of Cyril Tourneur*, ed. J. Churton Collins, 2 vols, 1878, vol. 1
Dodsley	*A Select Collection of Old English Plays*, published by Robert Dodsley, 12 vols, 1744, vol. 4
Foakes	*The Revenger's Tragedy*, ed. R.A. Foakes, The Revels Plays, 1966

Harrier	*Jacobean Drama*, ed. Richard C. Harrier, 2 vols, 1963, vol. 2
Harrison	*The Revenger's Tragedy*, ed. G.B. Harrison, The Temple Dramatists, 1934
Nicoll	*The Works of Cyril Tourneur*, ed. Allardyce Nicoll, 1930

'Tis Pity She's a Whore

EDITIONS OF THE PLAY CITED

Barker	*'Tis Pity She's a Whore*, ed. Simon Barker, Routledge English Texts, 1997
Dodsley	Robert Dodsley, ed., *A Select Collection of Old Plays*, 1744
Dyce	*The Works of John Ford*, ed. William Gifford, rev. Alexander Dyce, 1869, vol. 1
Gifford	*The Dramatic Works of John Ford*, ed. William Gifford, 1827, vol. 1
Lomax	*'Tis Pity She's a Whore and Other Plays*, ed. Marion Lomax, Oxford English Drama, 1995
Morris	*'Tis Pity She's a Whore*, ed. Brian Morris, The New Mermaids, 1st edn, 1968
Q	the quarto of 1633
Roper	*'Tis Pity She's a Whore*, ed. Derek Roper, The Revels Plays, 1975
Schmitz	'A Critical Edition of John Ford's *'Tis Pitty Shee's a Whore*', ed. Elsie Kemp Schmitz (unpublished Cambridge M.Litt. thesis, 1959)
Weber	*The Dramatic Works of John Ford*, ed. Henry William Weber, 1811, vol. 1

OTHER WORKS

| *First Fruits* | John Florio, *Florio His First Fruites*, 1578 |
| *World* | John Florio, A *Worlde of Wordes*, 1598 |

Other plays of Ford are quoted from the following editions: *The Broken Heart*, ed. T.J.B. Spencer, The Revels Plays, 1980; *The Fancies, Chaste and Noble*, ed. Dominick J. Hart, 1985; *The Sun's Darling*, in *The Dramatic Works of Thomas Dekker*, ed. Fredson Bowers, 1953–61. Shakespeare is quoted from *The Complete Works*, ed. Stanley Wells, Gary Taylor, John Jowett, and William Montgomery, 1986, and the Bible from the King James translation of 1611. Other editions cited are: William Barksted and Lewis Machin, *The Insatiate Countess*, in *Four Jacobean Sex Tragedies*, ed.

Martin Wiggins, 1998; Lording Barry, *Ram Alley*, ed. Peter Corbin and Douglas Sedge, 1981; Thomas Dekker, *The Noble Spanish Soldier*, in *The Dramatic Works*, ed. Bowers; John Marston, *'The Malcontent' and Other Plays*, ed. Keith Sturgess, Oxford English Drama, 1997; John Webster, *The Duchess of Malfi*, ed. Elizabeth M. Brennan, 1993; and *The Fatal Marriage*, ed. S. Brigid Younghughes and Harold Jenkins, 1959 for 1958.

The White Devil

Boklund	Gunnar Boklund, *The Sources of 'The White Devil'*, 1957
Brown	John Russell Brown, ed., *The White Devil*, The Revels Plays, 1960
Dent	R.W. Dent, *John Webster's Borrowing*, 1960
Lucas	F.L. Lucas, ed., *The Complete Works of John Webster*, 1927, vol. 1
NCW	(The New Cambridge Webster) D.C. Gunby, David Carnegie, and Anthony Hammond, eds., *The Works of John Webster*, 1995, vol. 1
Pettie	George Pettie, trans., *The Civile Conversation of M. Steeven Guazzo* (1581), 1925
Thomson	Peter Thomson, 'Webster and the Actor', in *John Webster*, ed. Brian Morris, 1970, pp. 25–44

Quotations are taken from the following New Mermaid texts: *A Chaste Maid in Cheapside*, ed. Alan Brissenden, 1968; *Dr Faustus*, ed. Roma Gill, 1989; *The Revenger's Tragedy*, ed. Brian Gibbons, 1990; *The Duchess of Malfi*, ed. Elizabeth M. Brennan, 1993.

The Spanish Tragedie:

OR,

Hieronimo is mad againe.

Containing the lamentable end of *Don Horatio*, and
Belimperia; with the pittifull death of *Hieronimo*.

Newly correcled, amended, and enlarged wicb new
Addicions of the *Painters* part, and others, as
it hath of late been diuers times acled.

LONDON,
Printed by W. White, for I. White and T. Langley,
and are to be sold at their Shop ouer againft the
Sarazens head without New-gate. 1615.

Title page.

The title page of the eighth quarto (1615). This was the first to have any illustration on it. Most likely it does show the scene of Horatio's murder, roughly as it was staged in the early years, complete with dialogue. See the note to this illustration in R. A. Foakes, *Illustrations of the English Stage 1580–1642*, Stanford, 1985, pp. 104–6.

[DRAMATIS PERSONAE]

[GHOST OF ANDREA
REVENGE
KING OF SPAIN
CYPRIAN, DUKE OF CASTILE, *his brother*
LORENZO, *the Duke's son*
BEL-IMPERIA, *Lorenzo's sister*
GENERAL *of the Spanish Army*

VICEROY OF PORTUGAL
PEDRO, *his brother*
BALTHAZAR, *his son*
ALEXANDRO }
VILLUPPO } *Portuguese noblemen*
AMBASSADOR *of Portugal*

HIERONIMO, *Knight Marshal of Spain*
ISABELLA, *his wife*
HORATIO, *their son*

PEDRINGANO, *servant to Bel-Imperia*
SERBERINE, *servant to Balthazar*
CHRISTOPHIL, *servant to Lorenzo*
BAZULTO, *an old man*

Page *to Lorenzo*, Three Watchmen, Messenger, Deputy, Hangman,
Maid to *Isabella*, Two Portuguese, Servant, Three Citizens,
Portuguese Nobles, Soldiers, Officers, Attendants, Halberdiers

Three Knights, Three Kings, a Drummer *in the first Dumb-show*,
Hymen, Two Torch-bearers *in the second Dumb-show*

In the 'Additions':
PEDRO }
JAQUES } *Hieronimo's servants*
BAZARDO, *a Painter*]

3

ACT I, SCENE i

Enter the Ghost of ANDREA, *and with him* REVENGE

ANDREA

When this eternal substance of my soul
Did live imprisoned in my wanton flesh,
Each in their function serving other's need,
I was a courtier in the Spanish court.
My name was Don Andrea, my descent,   5
Though not ignoble, yet inferior far
To gracious fortunes of my tender youth:
For there in prime and pride of all my years,
By duteous service and deserving love,
In secret I possessed a worthy dame,   10
Which hight sweet Bel-Imperia by name.
But in the harvest of my summer joys
Death's winter nipped the blossoms of my bliss,
Forcing divorce betwixt my love and me.
For in the late conflict with Portingale   15
My valour drew me into danger's mouth,
Till life to death made passage through my wounds.

0   s.d. Andrea's companion is silent, perhaps standing behind the speaker while he
addresses the audience; it has been suggested that their entry was from a trapdoor,
as befitted figures from the underworld, but the octavo's '*Enter*' normally meant
coming onstage through one of the three entrances in the *frons scenae*; they remain
on stage throughout the first two acts, sitting on stools to one side of the main
action. The *1592* text gives them no '*Exeunt*' until the end of Act III, but they do
'*Enter*' for that scene, suggesting that they have exited after their comments at the end
of the second act; as noted elsewhere, scholars have argued that the text of the play
after III.xiii seems different from the earlier part, and more corrupt.

8   *pride* A term denoting not only self-esteem but sexual vigour.

10   The secrecy of this love affair, including the point that Andrea '*possessed*' her, perhaps
meaning sexually, a point developed in line 12's '*harvest*', raises issues about how it
became known, as her second relationship with Horatio also does. Later we learn
that Castile, her father, heard of her love for Andrea and forbade it. Lorenzo claims
to have protected Bel-Imperia from their father's anger over it at II.i.45–8, and
III.x.54–5, and Castile says he has now forgiven her at III.xiv.111–12.

15   *late* recent.

5

When I was slain, my soul descended straight
To pass the flowing stream of Acheron:
But churlish Charon, only boatman there,   20
Said that my rites of burial not performed,
I might not sit amongst his passengers.
Ere Sol had slept three nights in Thetis' lap
And slaked his smoking chariot in her flood,
By Don Horatio, our Knight Marshal's son,   25
My funerals and obsequies were done.
Then was the ferryman of hell content
To pass me over to the slimy strond,
That leads to fell Avernus' ugly waves:
There, pleasing Cerberus with honeyed speech,   30
I passed the perils of the foremost porch.
Not far from hence, amidst ten thousand souls,
Sat Minos, Aeacus, and Rhadamanth,
To whom no sooner 'gan I make approach,
To crave a passport for my wandering ghost,   35
But Minos, in graven leaves of lottery,
Drew forth the manner of my life and death.
'This knight', quoth he, 'both lived and died in love,
And for his love tried fortune of the wars,
And by war's fortune lost both love and life.'   40
'Why then,' said Aeacus, 'convey him hence,
To walk with lovers in our fields of love,
And spend the course of everlasting time
Under green myrtle trees and cypress shades.'
'No, no,' said Rhadamanth, 'it were not well   45
With loving souls to place a martialist:
He died in war, and must to martial fields,
Where wounded Hector lives in lasting pain,

18ff.   Openly borrowed from Virgil's *Aeneid* Book VI, the speech has some resonant
        differences from Virgil, including the location of Elisium that Nashe mocked and
        Marlowe echoed in *Faustus*.
25   *Don Horatio, our Knight Marshal's son* In England the Knight Marshal was the official
        who kept order within a twelve-mile radius of the ruler; the play makes him chief
        magistrate of Spain. Hieronimo is introduced through his legal status.
33   *Minos, Aeacus, and Rhadamanth* the three judges of the underworld, who decided
        where each ghost would have to dwell. Their decision becomes the ghost's 'passport'
        or licence.
36   *graven leaves of lottery* In Virgil Minos draws lots telling Andrea's story (the book of
        fate) from an urn. It says that he went to war in search of 'fortune', but lost.

And Achilles' Myrmidons do scour the plain.'
Then Minos, mildest censor of the three,   50
Made this device to end the difference:
'Send him,' quoth he, 'to our infernal king,
To doom him as best seems his majesty.'
To this effect my passport straight was drawn.
In keeping on my way to Pluto's court,   55
Through dreadful shades of ever-glooming night,
I saw more sights than thousand tongues can tell,
Or pens can write, or mortal hearts can think.
Three ways there were: that on the right-hand side
Was ready way unto the foresaid fields   60
Where lovers live and bloody martialists,
But either sort contained within his bounds.
The left-hand path, declining fearfully,
Was ready downfall to the deepest hell,
Where bloody Furies shakes their whips of steel,   65
And poor Ixion turns an endless wheel;
Where usurers are choked with melting gold,
And wantons are embraced with ugly snakes,
And murderers groan with never-killing wounds,
And perjured wights scalded in boiling lead,   70
And all foul sins with torments overwhelmed.
'Twixt these two ways I trod the middle path,
Which brought me to the fair Elysian green,
In midst whereof there stands a stately tower,
The walls of brass, the gates of adamant.   75
Here finding Pluto with his Proserpine,
I showed my passport, humbled on my knee;
Whereat fair Proserpine began to smile,
And begged that only she might give my doom.
Pluto was pleased, and sealed it with a kiss.   80

55   *Pluto's court* Pluto was the god who ruled the underworld, the Christian hell.
59   *Three ways there were* Virgil has only two; Kyd adds a middle way to Elisium where
     Pluto's court is. In Virgil that was where the damned such as Ixion suffer; this feature
     of the play prompted Nashe's jibe about him finding Elisium in hell.
66   *Ixion* At the play's conclusion Castile is sentenced to replace Ixion on his wheel.
73   In his epistle to *Menaphon* Nashe derided Kyd's deviation from Virgil by locating
     Elisium in the underworld; Marlowe in *Faustus*, written in 1588, seems to have
     picked it up.
76   *Proserpine* daughter of Ceres, goddess of life and agriculture; she became queen of
     the underworld after being kidnapped by Pluto.

Forthwith, Revenge, she rounded thee in th'ear,
And bade thee lead me through the gates of horn,
Where dreams have passage in the silent night.
No sooner had she spoke but we were here,
I wot not how, in twinkling of an eye.   85

REVENGE

Then know, Andrea, that thou art arrived
Where thou shalt see the author of thy death, –
Don Balthazar, the prince of Portingale,
Deprived of life by Bel-Imperia.
Here sit we down to see the mystery,   90
And serve for Chorus in this tragedy.

[handwritten annotations: "Viceroy of Portugal's son."; "narrating the story / as onlookers that's why they're sitting off to the side on stools."]

82   *gates of horn* In Virgil these gates let true visions through, whereas the gates of ivory let in false dreams.
85   *wot* know.
87   *the author of thy death* Andrea's account does not specify Prince Balthazar as the man who killed him, but Revenge's statement, which Bel-Imperia repeats at I.iv.69, motivates her revenge on the prince. The Lord General's account (I.ii.68–72) says that Andrea was killed fighting against Balthazar's men, but does not specify the kind of single combat whereby Horatio defeats Balthazar.
90   *mystery* in the modern sense, something yet to be revealed; Andrea repeats it when he asks about the dumb-show at III.xv.29.

ACT I, SCENE ii

Enter SPANISH KING, GENERAL, CASTILE, HIERONIMO

KING

Now say, Lord General, how fares our camp?

GENERAL

All well, my sovereign liege, except some few

That are deceased by fortune of the war.

KING

But what portends thy cheerful countenance,

And posting to our presence thus in haste? 5

Speak man, hath fortune given us victory?

GENERAL

Victory, my liege, and that with little loss.

KING

Our Portingals will pay us tribute then?

GENERAL

Tribute and wonted homage therewithal.

KING

Then blest be heaven, and guider of the heavens, *Heaven* 10

From whose fair influence such justice flows.

CASTILE

O multum dilecte Deo, tibi militat aether,

Et conjuratae curvato poplite gentes ⎤ 12-14

Succumbunt: recti soror est victoria juris. ⎦

KING

Thanks to my loving brother of Castile. 15

But General, unfold in brief discourse

Your form of battle and your war's success,

That adding all the pleasure of thy news

Unto the height of former happiness,

---

1   *Now ... camp* In *The Alchemist* III.iii.33 (1610) Dol Common quotes this line as a
     greeting to Face.

8   *our Portingals* The king's adjective reminds us that the Lord General has been
     enforcing Spain's new authority over Portugal.

12–14   Castile's Latin asserts 'O greatly beloved of God, for thee the heavens contend, / And
        the united people on bended knee / Do fall; victory is sister to justice.' *1592* has
        'poplito' for *poplite*.

With deeper wage and greater dignity 20
We may reward thy blissful chivalry.

GENERAL   *beside each other?*

Where Spain and Portingale do jointly knit
Their frontiers, leaning on each other's bound,
There met our armies in their proud array:
Both furnished well, both full of hope and fear, 25
Both menacing alike with daring shows,
Both vaunting sundry colours of device,
Both cheerly sounding trumpets, drums and fifes,
Both raising dreadful clamours to the sky,
That valleys, hills, and rivers made rebound, 30
And heaven itself was frighted with the sound.
Our battles both were pitched in squadron form,
Each corner strongly fenced with wings of shot;
But ere we joined and came to push of pike,
I brought a squadron of our readiest shot 35
From out our rearward to begin the fight:
They brought another wing to encounter us.
Meanwhile, our ordnance played on either side,
And captains strove to have their valours tried.
Don Pedro, their chief horsemen's colonel, → *enemy* 40
Did with his cornet bravely make attempt
To break the order of our battle ranks:
But Don Rogero, worthy man of war,
Marched forth against him with our musketeers,
And stopped the malice of his fell approach. 45
While they maintain hot skirmish to and fro,
Both battles join and fall to handy blows,
Their violent shot resembling th'ocean's rage,
When, roaring loud, and with a swelling tide,
It beats upon the rampiers of huge rocks, 50

comparison = Battle + ocean

22–84 An expansion of Andrea's account at I.i.15ff. Villuppo (I.iii.59ff.) and Horatio
(I.iv.9ff.) give variant versions. Horatio identifies Balthazar as killing Andrea when
he is brought down from his horse.
27 *colours of device* heraldic flags.
32 *battles* fighting groups or battalions.
squadron form in a square.
34 *push of pike* the infantryman's weapon, a formidable bladed spear with a shaft long
enough to be set in the ground to outface a cavalry charge.
40 *colonel* a three-syllable word.
41 *cornet* a cavalry squad led by an ensign or 'cornet'.

And gapes to swallow neighbour-bounding lands.
Now while Bellona rageth here and there,
Thick storms of bullets rain like winter's hail,   → metaphor + simile
And shivered lances dark the troubled air.

     Pede pes et cuspide cuspis;   55
     Arma sonant armis, vir petiturque viro.

On every side drop captains to the ground,
And soldiers, some ill-maimed, some slain outright:
Here falls a body scindered from his head,
There legs and arms lie bleeding on the grass,   60
Mingled with weapons and unbowelled steeds,
That scattering overspread the purple plain.
In all this turmoil, three long hours and more,
The victory to neither part inclined,
Till Don Andrea with his brave lanciers   65
In their main battle made so great a breach
That, half dismayed, the multitude retired:
But Balthazar, the Portingales' young prince,
Brought rescue, and encouraged them to stay.
Here-hence the fight was eagerly renewed,   70
And in that conflict was Andrea slain –
Brave man at arms, but weak to Balthazar.
Yet while the prince, insulting over him,
Breathed out proud vaunts, sounding to our reproach,
Friendship and hardy valour joined in one   75
Pricked forth Horatio, our Knight Marshal's son,
To challenge forth that prince in single fight.
Not long between these twain the fight endured,
But straight the prince was beaten from his horse,
And forced to yield him prisoner to his foe: 80
When he was taken, all the rest they fled,
And our carbines pursued them to the death,

---

52   *Bellona* Roman goddess of war; this section of the account echoes Garnier's story of the battle of Thrapsus in *Cornelia*, which Kyd translated from the original French.
54   *dark* a verbal form, 'darken'.
55–6 Latin: 'Foot against foot and lance against lance, arms ring on arms and man is assailed by man.'
59   *scindered 1602* made this the more familiar 'sundered'.
62   *purple* red with imperial blood.
65   *lanciers* a three-syllable variant for 'lancers' in use till the eighteenth century.
70   *Here-hence* As a result.
82   *carbines* the musketeers cited at line 44.

Till, Phoebus waning to the western deep,
Our trumpeters were charged to sound retreat.

KING

Thanks good Lord General for these good news;   85
And for some argument of more to come,
Take this and wear it for thy sovereign's sake.

Give him his chain

But tell me now, hast thou confirmed a peace?

GENERAL

No peace, my liege, but peace conditional,
That if with homage tribute be well paid,   90
The fury of your forces will be stayed:
And to this peace their viceroy hath subscribed,

Give the KING *a paper*

And made a solemn vow that, during life,
His tribute shall be truly paid to Spain.

KING

These words, these deeds, become thy person well.   95
But now, Knight Marshal, frolic with thy king,
For 'tis thy son that wins this battle's prize.

HIERONIMO

Long may he live to serve my sovereign liege,
And soon decay unless he serve my liege.

A tucket afar off

KING

Nor thou, nor he, shall die without reward.   100
What means the warning of this trumpet's sound?

GENERAL

This tells me that your grace's men of war,
Such as war's fortune hath reserved from death,
Come marching on towards your royal seat,
To show themselves before your majesty,   105
For so I gave in charge at my depart.

---

83   *Phoebus* the sun.
       waning 1592 has 'waving', a simple minim error with medial u for n.
       western deep the Atlantic ocean.
92   *viceroy* The play denies Portugal any autonomous king, and Prince Balthazar,
       presumably leader of the Portuguese army, has been captured by the Spanish; the
       Portuguese Viceroy, Balthazar's father, the nearest the play admits to any king of
       Portugal, appears in the next scene; the Viceroy wears a crown at I.iii, and calls
       himself king to his subjects at III.i.1 and 12; *1 Hieronimo* gives Portugal a king.
99   s.d. *A tucket afar off* an offstage cavalry trumpet-call.

Whereby by demonstration shall appear,
That all (except three hundred or few more)
Are safe returned and by their foes enriched.

→ Prince of portingale (handwritten annotation)

The Army enters; BALTHAZAR,
between LORENZO *and* HORATIO, *captive*

KING

A gladsome sight! I long to see them here.   110

They enter and pass by

Was that the warlike prince of Portingale,
That by our nephew was in triumph led?

GENERAL

It was, my liege, the prince of Portingale.

KING

But what was he that on the other side
Held him by th'arm as partner of the prize?   115

HIERONIMO

That was my son, my gracious sovereign,
Of whom, though from his tender infancy
My loving thoughts did never hope but well,
He never pleased his father's eyes till now,
Nor filled my heart with overcloying joys.   120

KING

Go let them march once more about these walls,
That staying them we may confer and talk
With our brave prisoner and his double guard.
Hieronimo, it greatly pleaseth us,
That in our victory thou have a share,   125
By virtue of thy worthy son's exploit.

Enter [the Army] again

Bring hither the young prince of Portingale:
The rest march on, but ere they be dismissed,
We will bestow on every soldier

---

110   s.d. *They enter and pass by* Soldiers marched to the beat of a drum carried by one of
       them; the number depended on how many spare players were available, but would
       not have been more than six or eight, besides the three central figures. They would
       have entered by one of the flanking doors, marched round the flanks of the stage and
       exited by the other flanking door.

116   *That was my son* All the key characters but Bel-Imperia have been set out on the
       stage now; Hieronimo emphasizes his love for his son; the position of Balthazar held
       on each arm by the king's nephew Lorenzo and Horatio anticipates their conflict
       over his capture.

Two ducats, and on every leader ten,   130
That they may know our largess welcomes them.

Exeunt all [the Army] but BALTHAZAR,

LORENZO, HORATIO

Welcome, Don Balthazar, welcome, nephew, → Lorenzo - nephew of the King (duke's son)
And thou, Horatio, thou art welcome too.
Young prince, although thy father's hard misdeeds,
In keeping back the tribute that he owes,   135
Deserve but evil measure at our hands,
Yet shalt thou know that Spain is honourable.

BALTHAZAR

The trespass that my father made in peace
Is now controlled by fortune of the wars;
And cards once dealt, it boots not ask why so.   140
His men are slain, a weakening to his realm,
His colours seized, a blot unto his name,
His son distressed, a corsive to his heart:
Those punishments may clear his late offence.

KING

Ay, Balthazar, if he observe this truce,   145
Our peace will grow the stronger for these wars.
Meanwhile live thou, though not in liberty,
Yet free from bearing any servile yoke;
For in our hearing thy deserts were great,
And in our sight thyself art gracious.   150

BALTHAZAR

And I shall study to deserve this grace.

KING

But tell me, for their holding makes me doubt,
To which of these twain art thou prisoner?

LORENZO

To me, my liege.

HORATIO   To me, my sovereign.

LORENZO

This hand first took his courser by the reins.   155

---

140   *boots not* is pointless.
143   *corsive* corrosive, a poison.
146   *Our peace will grow the stronger* The union of Portugal with Spain was not seen as a
      means to peace by the Dutch or the English; the dispute between Lorenzo and
      Horatio that immediately follows denies the king's expectation.

HORATIO

But first my lance did put him from his horse.

LORENZO

I seized his weapon, and enjoyed it first.

HORATIO

But first I forced him lay his weapons down.

KING

Let go his arm, upon our privilege.

[*They*] *let him go*

Say, worthy prince, to whether didst thou yield?   160

BALTHAZAR

To him in courtesy, to this perforce:
He spake me fair, this other gave me strokes;
He promised life, this other threatened death;
He wan my love, this other conquered me:
And truth to say I yield myself to both.   165

HIERONIMO

But that I know your grace for just and wise,
And might seem partial in this difference,
Enforced by nature and by law of arms
My tongue should plead for young Horatio's right.
He hunted well that was a lion's death,   170
Not he that in a garment wore his skin:
So hares may pull dead lions by the beard.

KING

Content thee, Marshal, thou shalt have no wrong;
And for thy sake thy son shall want no right.
Will both abide the censure of my doom?   175

LORENZO

I crave no better than your grace awards.

HORATIO

Nor I, although I sit beside my right.

---

159   *our privilege* royal authority.
160   *whether* which of the two.
161–5 Balthazar is already willing to befriend Lorenzo against Horatio, but has to concede
       Horatio's conquest.
164   *wan* an alternative pronunciation for 'won'.
172   Hieronimo in citing a familiar proverb (Tilley H165) is less than kind to Lorenzo;
       in his *Strange News* (1592) Nashe quoted this line, saying 'I borrowed this sentence
       [i.e. epigram] out of a Play'.
177   *sit beside my right* not a comment on his physical position, alongside Balthazar, but
       an assertion that he has 'right' on his side.

KING

    Then by my judgment thus your strife shall end:
    You both deserve and both shall have reward.
    Nephew, thou took'st his weapon and his horse,   180
    His weapons and his horse are thy reward.
    Horatio, thou didst force him first to yield,
    His ransom therefore is thy valour's fee:
    Appoint the sum as you shall both agree.
    But nephew, thou shalt have the prince in guard,   185
    For thine estate best fitteth such a guest:
    Horatio's house were small for all his train.
    Yet in regard thy substance passeth his,
    And that just guerdon may befall desert,
    To him we yield the armour of the prince.   190
    How likes Don Balthazar of this device?

BALTHAZAR

    Right well my liege, if this proviso were,
    That Don Horatio bear us company,
    Whom I admire and love for chivalry.

KING

    Horatio, leave him not that loves thee so.   195
    Now let us hence to see our soldiers paid,
    And feast our prisoner as our friendly guest.

                                        Exeunt

---

187   *Horatio's house* Like Andrea, Horatio's social rank is well below that of the king's
       nephew.

189   *guerdon* reward.

190   *the armour* Horatio is given both the prince's ransom and his suit of armour, but not
       the weapons or other fittings given to Lorenzo.

ACT I, SCENE iii

Enter VICEROY, ALEXANDRO, VILLUPPO[, *Attendants*]

VICEROY
Is our ambassador despatched for Spain?
ALEXANDRO
Two days, my liege, are passed since his depart.
VICEROY
And tribute payment gone along with him?
ALEXANDRO
Ay my good lord.
VICEROY
Then rest we here awhile in our unrest,   5
And feed our sorrows with some inward sighs,
For deepest cares break never into tears.
But wherefore sit I in a regal throne?
This better fits a wretch's endless moan.
                                        Falls to the ground
Yet this is higher than my fortunes reach,   10
And therefore better than my state deserves.
Ay, ay, this earth, image of melancholy,
Seeks him whom fates adjudge to misery:
Here let me lie, now am I at the lowest.
    Qui jacet in terra, non habet unde cadat.   15
    In me consumpsit vires fortuna nocendo,
    Nil superest ut jam possit obesse magis.
Yes, Fortune may bereave me of my crown:
Here, take it now; let Fortune do her worst,
She will not rob me of this sable weed: 20
O no, she envies none but pleasant things.
Such is the folly of despiteful chance!

---

6   *our sorrows* The Viceroy is stricken less by the military defeat than by what he
     assumes to be the death of his son; in this he anticipates Hieronimo over Horatio.
9   s.d. *Falls to the ground* Richard II in Shakespeare's play chooses to 'sit upon the
     ground' rather than on his throne when he will 'tell sad stories of the death of kings'.
15–17 'Anyone who throws himself to the ground has no further to fall. Fortune has no
     more power to injure me; nothing more can harm me.' The first line is from Alanus
     de Insulis, while the second echoes Seneca's *Agamemnon*.
20   *this sable weed* his black clothing (as mourning dress).

17

Fortune is blind and sees not my deserts,
So is she deaf and hears not my laments:
And could she hear, yet is she wilful mad,   25
And therefore will not pity my distress.
Suppose that she could pity me, what then?
What help can be expected at her hands,
Whose foot is standing on a rolling stone,
And mind more mutable than fickle winds?   30
Why wail I then, where's hope of no redress?
O yes, complaining makes my grief seem less.
My late ambition hath distained my faith,
My breach of faith occasioned bloody wars,
Those bloody wars have spent my treasure,   35
And with my treasure my people's blood,
And with their blood, my joy and best beloved,
My best beloved, my sweet and only son.
O wherefore went I not to war myself?
The cause was mine, I might have died for both: 40
My years were mellow, his but young and green,
My death were natural, but his was forced.

ALEXANDRO

No doubt, my liege, but still the prince survives.

VICEROY

Survives! ay, where?

ALEXANDRO

In Spain, a prisoner by mischance of war.   45

VICEROY

Then they have slain him for his father's fault.

ALEXANDRO

That were a breach to common law of arms.

VICEROY

They reck no laws that meditate revenge.

---

23   *Fortune* The standard target of laments of this kind; not blindfolded like Justice, but
     blind and deaf to human grief, her constant change is denoted by the rolling sphere
     she stands on in traditional icons. It was usual to blame 'ambition' (33) for the loss
     of blood in war, but the Viceroy also admits to 'My breach of faith' (34) that has
     brought the death of his son.
33   *distained* sullied.
46   *fault* his 'breach of faith'.
48   *They reck no laws* The Viceroy assumes that Spain will ignore justice in revenging his
     'fault'.

ALEXANDRO
>His ransom's worth will stay from foul revenge.

VICEROY
>No, if he lived the news would soon be here.   50

ALEXANDRO
>Nay, evil news fly faster still than good.

VICEROY
>Tell me no more of news, for he is dead.

VILLUPPO
>My sovereign, pardon the author of ill news,
>And I'll bewray the fortune of thy son.

VICEROY
>Speak on, I'll guerdon thee whate'er it be: 55
>Mine ear is ready to receive ill news,
>My heart grown hard 'gainst mischief's battery;
>Stand up I say, and tell thy tale at large.

VILLUPPO
>Then hear that truth which these mine eyes have seen.
>When both the armies were in battle joined,   60
>Don Balthazar, amidst the thickest troops,
>To win renown did wondrous feats of arms:
>Amongst the rest I saw him hand to hand
>In single fight with their Lord General;
>Till Alexandro, that here counterfeits   65
>Under the colour of a duteous friend,
>Discharged his pistol at the prince's back,
>As though he would have slain their general.
>But therewithal Don Balthazar fell down,
>And when he fell, then we began to fly: 70
>But had he lived, the day had sure been ours.

ALEXANDRO
>O wicked forgery! O traitorous miscreant!

VICEROY
>Hold thou thy peace! But now, Villuppo, say,
>Where then became the carcase of my son?

VILLUPPO
>I saw them drag it to the Spanish tents.   75

---

54 *bewray* reveal, uncover (not quite 'betray').
55 *guerdon* reward.
59ff Villuppo's false account is an immediate instance of what Alexandro has called 'foul revenge' (49).

VICEROY

    Ay, ay, my nightly dreams have told me this.

    Thou false, unkind, unthankful, traitorous beast,

    Wherein had Balthazar offended thee,

    That thou shouldst thus betray him to our foes?

    Was't Spanish gold that bleared so thine eyes   80

    That thou couldst see no part of our deserts?

    Perchance because thou art Terceira's lord,

    Thou hadst some hope to wear this diadem,

    If first my son and then myself were slain:

    But thy ambitious thought shall break thy neck.   85

    Ay, this was it that made thee spill his blood,

                     Take the crown and put it on again

    But I'll now wear it till thy blood be spilt.

ALEXANDRO

    Vouchsafe, dread sovereign, to hear me speak.

VICEROY

    Away with him, his sight is second hell;

    Keep him till we determine of his death.   90

               [*Exeunt Attendants with* ALEXANDRO]

    If Balthazar be dead, he shall not live.

    Villuppo, follow us for thy reward.   *Exit* VICEROY

VILLUPPO

    Thus have I with an envious, forged tale

    Deceived the king, betrayed mine enemy,

    And hope for guerdon of my villainy.   *Exit*   95

---

82   *Terceira's lord* Alexandro is identified as lord of the chief city in the Azores, where historically the opposition to Spain's conquest of Portugal was strongest.

86   s.d. *Take the crown* The gesture marks the Viceroy reassuming his authority.

93–5 Villuppo speaks to the audience before following the others offstage, a common way of declaring private villainy.

ACT I, SCENE iv

Enter HORATIO *and* BEL-IMPERIA

BEL-IMPERIA

Signior Horatio, this is the place and hour
Wherein I must entreat thee to relate
The circumstance of Don Andrea's death,
Who, living, was my garland's sweetest flower,
And in his death hath buried my delights.   5

HORATIO

For love of him and service to yourself,
I nill refuse this heavy doleful charge.
Yet tears and sighs, I fear will hinder me.
When both our armies were enjoined in fight,
Your worthy chevalier amidst the thick'st,   10
For glorious cause still aiming at the fairest,
Was at the last by young Don Balthazar
Encountered hand to hand: their fight was long,
Their hearts were great, their clamours menacing,
Their strength alike, their strokes both dangerous.   15
But wrathful Nemesis, that wicked power,
Envying at Andrea's praise and worth,
Cut short his life, to end his praise and worth.
She, she herself, disguised in armour's mask,
(As Pallas was before proud Pergamus)   20
Brought in a fresh supply of halberdiers,
Which paunched his horse, and dinged him to the ground.
Then young Don Balthazar with ruthless rage,
Taking advantage of his foe's distress,
Did finish what his halberdiers begun,   25
And left not till Andrea's life was done.
Then, though too late, incensed with just remorse,

---

7 *nill* will not.
16 *Nemesis* the goddess of retribution, a divine alternative to human revenge.
20 *Pallas* Nemesis in armour behaved like Pallas Athene at Troy.
22 *paunched* disembowelled.
   dinged struck (the word echoing the resonant sound).
24 *Taking advantage* Only Horatio's account of the fight, the third we have heard so far,
   declares that Balthazar ruthlessly killed Andrea when his horse was brought down.

I with my band set forth against the prince,
And brought him prisoner from his halberdiers.

BEL-IMPERIA

Would thou hadst slain him that so slew my love.   30
But then was Don Andrea's carcase lost?

HORATIO

No, that was it for which I chiefly strove,
Nor stepped I back till I recovered him:
I took him up, and wound him in mine arms,
And welding him unto my private tent,   35
There laid him down, and dewed him with my tears,
And sighed and sorrowed as became a friend.
But neither friendly sorrow, sighs nor tears
Could win pale Death from his usurped right.
Yet this I did, and less I could not do: 40
I saw him honoured with due funeral.
This scarf I plucked from off his lifeless arm,
And wear it in remembrance of my friend.

BEL-IMPERIA

I know the scarf, would he had kept it still,
For had he lived he would have kept it still,   45
And worn it for his Bel-Imperia's sake:
For 'twas my favour at his last depart.
But now wear thou it both for him and me,
For after him thou hast deserved it best.
But, for thy kindness in his life and death,   50
Be sure while Bel-Imperia's life endures,
She will be Don Horatio's thankful friend.

HORATIO

And, madam, Don Horatio will not slack
Humbly to serve fair Bel-Imperia.
But now, if your good liking stand thereto,   55
I'll crave your pardon to go seek the prince,
For so the duke your father gave me charge.   *Exit*

32–41   Horatio tells what Andrea has already asserted about his corpse.

35   *welding* wielding, carrying.

42   *This scarf* an emblem of loyalty and love, worn in battle; here it links Horatio to
     Andrea when he is murdered. Hieronimo takes the same emblem for his 'bloody
     handkercher' at II.v.51, the '*bloody napkin*' of III.xiii.85 s.d.

47   *my favour* a lover's gift, the scarf.

54   *to serve* The word normally applies to loyalty in love, but occasionally has a sexual
     innuendo; Balthazar's 'pleasing servitude' (81) is the more conventional usage.

BEL-IMPERIA

    Ay, go Horatio, leave me here alone,
    For solitude best fits my cheerless mood.
    Yet what avails to wail Andrea's death,   60
    From whence Horatio proves my second love?
    Had he not loved Andrea as he did,
    He could not sit in Bel-Imperia's thoughts.
    But how can love find harbour in my breast,
    Till I revenge the death of my beloved?   65
    Yes, second love shall further my revenge.
    I'll love Horatio, my Andrea's friend,
    The more to spite the prince that wrought his end.
    And where Don Balthazar, that slew my love,
    Himself now pleads for favour at my hands,   70
    He shall in rigour of my just disdain
    Reap long repentance for his murderous deed.
    For what was't else but murderous cowardice,
    So many to oppress one valiant knight,
    Without respect of honour in the fight?   75
    And here he comes that murdered my delight.

Enter LORENZO *and* BALTHAZAR

LORENZO

    Sister, what means this melancholy walk?

BEL-IMPERIA

    That for a while I wish no company.

LORENZO

    But here the prince is come to visit you.

BEL-IMPERIA

    That argues that he lives in liberty.   80

BALTHAZAR

    No madam, but in pleasing servitude.

58ff   Bel-Imperia's soliloquy contains the second repetition of the word 'revenge' after Andrea addresses his shadow by his name at I.i.81; the first use is by the Viceroy of Portugal at I.iii.48 when he wrongly assumes Balthazar has been killed by the vengeful Spanish.

65   *Till I revenge* Death in battle, even of a lover, was not normally a matter for revenge; Bel-Imperia's passion for Andrea rules her reason.

73   *murderous cowardice* The other accounts of the battle do not go as far as this.

77–89   This exchange of single-line repartee, a version of the Senecan device of stichomythia, reflects Bel-Imperia's prickly hostility to her brother and his companion.

BEL-IMPERIA

Your prison then belike is your conceit.

BALTHAZAR

Ay, by conceit my freedom is enthralled.

BEL-IMPERIA

Then with conceit enlarge yourself again.

BALTHAZAR

What if conceit have laid my heart to gage?   85

BEL-IMPERIA

Pay that you borrowed and recover it.

BALTHAZAR

I die if it return from whence it lies.

BEL-IMPERIA

A heartless man, and live? A miracle!

BALTHAZAR

Ay lady, love can work such miracles.

LORENZO

Tush, tush, my lord, let go these ambages,   90
And in plain terms acquaint her with your love.

BEL-IMPERIA

What boots complaint, when there's no remedy?

BALTHAZAR

Yes, to your gracious self must I complain,
In whose fair answer lies my remedy,
On whose perfection all my thoughts attend,   95
On whose aspect mine eyes find beauty's bower,
In whose translucent breast my heart is lodged.

BEL-IMPERIA

Alas, my lord, these are but words of course,
And but device to drive me from this place.

She, in going in, lets fall her glove, which HORATIO,
coming out, takes up

HORATIO

Madam, your glove.   100

BEL-IMPERIA

Thanks good Horatio, take it for thy pains.

BALTHAZAR

Signior Horatio stooped in happy time.

90   *ambages* roundabout modes of speech.
98   *words of course* routine (and therefore insincere) lover's praises.

HORATIO

    I reaped more grace than I deserved or hoped.

LORENZO

    My lord, be not dismayed for what is passed,

    You know that women oft are humorous: 105

    These clouds will overblow with little wind;

    Let me alone, I'll scatter them myself.

    Meanwhile let us devise to spend the time

    In some delightful sports and revelling.

HORATIO

    The king, my lords, is coming hither straight,   110

    To feast the Portingale ambassador:

    Things were in readiness before I came.

BALTHAZAR

    Then here it fits us to attend the king,

    To welcome hither our ambassador,

    And learn my father and my country's health.   115

    Enter the Banquet, Trumpets, the KING, *and* AMBASSADOR

KING

    See Lord Ambassador, how Spain entreats

    Their prisoner Balthazar, thy viceroy's son:

    We pleasure more in kindness than in wars.

AMBASSADOR

    Sad is our king, and Portingale laments,

    Supposing that Don Balthazar is slain.   120

BALTHAZAR

    [*Aside*] So am I slain by beauty's tyranny.

    [*To him*] You see, my lord, how Balthazar is slain:

    I frolic with the Duke of Castile's son,

    Wrapped every hour in pleasures of the court,

    And graced with favours of his majesty.   125

KING

    Put off your greetings till our feast be done;

    Now come and sit with us and taste our cheer.

                     [*They*] *sit to the banquet*

    Sit down young prince, you are our second guest;

---

115   s.d. *Enter the Banquet* carried onstage as a table laden with dishes; stools or benches
       would have been brought on too; at 127 they '*sit to the banquet*' to watch Hieronimo's
       'mask' as entertainment.
       Trumpets the standard fanfare to announce a royal entrance.

Brother sit down and nephew take your place;
Signior Horatio, wait thou upon our cup,   130
For well thou hast deserved to be honoured.
Now, lordings, fall to; Spain is Portugal,
And Portugal is Spain, we both are friends,
Tribute is paid, and we enjoy our right.
But where is old Hieronimo, our marshal?   135
He promised us, in honour of our guest,
To grace our banquet with some pompous jest.

> *Enter* HIERONIMO *with a* Drum, *three* KNIGHTS,
> *each* [*with*] *his scutcheon: then he fetches three* KINGS,
> [*the* KNIGHTS] *take their crowns and them captive*

Hieronimo, this masque contents mine eye,
Although I sound not well the mystery.
HIERONIMO
The first armed knight, that hung his scutcheon up,   140
> *He takes the scutcheon and gives it to the* KING
Was English Robert, Earl of Gloucester,
Who when King Stephen bore sway in Albion,
Arrived with five and twenty thousand men
In Portingale, and by success of war
Enforced the king, then but a Saracen,   145
To bear the yoke of the English monarchy.
KING
My lord of Portingale, by this you see
That which may comfort both your king and you,
And make your late discomfort seem the less.
But say, Hieronimo, what was the next?   150
HIERONIMO
The second knight, that hung his scutcheon up,
> *He doth as he did before*
Was Edmund, Earl of Kent in Albion,

---

137   *pompous* stately.
137   s.d. 1 *Drum* a drummer.
137   s.d. 2 *scutcheon* shield; the armorial emblems of the Earls of Kent and Gloucester and
         the Duke of Lancaster would probably have been recognized by at least some of the
         first audiences.
139   *mystery* the word first used by Revenge at I.i.90 is employed more innocently by the
         king; Hieronimo has to explain the dumb-show; all three invasions of the peninsula
         by the three English nobles had a largely mythical status in English history, some of
         them later taken up by the Admiral's company writers as subjects for new plays.

When English Richard wore the diadem;
He came likewise, and razed Lisbon walls,
And took the King of Portingale in fight: 155
For which, and other suchlike service done,
He after was created Duke of York.

KING

This is another special argument,
That Portingale may deign to bear our yoke,
When it by little England hath been yoked.   160
But now Hieronimo, what were the last?

HIERONIMO

The third and last, not least in our account,

Doing as before

Was as the rest a valiant Englishman,
Brave John of Gaunt, the Duke of Lancaster,
As by his scutcheon plainly may appear.   165
He with a puissant army came to Spain,
And took our King of Castile prisoner.

AMBASSADOR

This is an argument for our viceroy,
That Spain may not insult for her success,
Since English warriors likewise conquered Spain,   170
And made them bow their knees to Albion.

KING

Hieronimo, I drink to thee for this device,
Which hath pleased both the ambassador and me;
Pledge me Hieronimo, if thou love the king.

Takes the cup of HORATIO

My lord, I fear we sit but over-long, .   175
Unless our dainties were more delicate:
But welcome are you to the best we have.
Now let us in, that you may be despatched,
I think our council is already set.

Exeunt omnes

169   *insult* brag, vaunt.

ACT I, SCENE v

ANDREA

    Come we for this from depth of underground,
    To see him feast that gave me my death's wound?
    These pleasant sights are sorrow to my soul,
    Nothing but league, and love, and banqueting!

REVENGE

    Be still Andrea, ere we go from hence,   5
    I'll turn their friendship into fell despite,
    Their love to mortal hate, their day to night,
    Their hope into despair, their peace to war,
    Their joys to pain, their bliss to misery.

6–9 Revenge promises the impatient Andrea events to come that the audience can be expected to relish.

ACT II, SCENE i

Enter LORENZO *and* BALTHAZAR

LORENZO

My lord, though Bel-Imperia seem thus coy,
Let reason hold you in your wonted joy:
'In time the savage bull sustains the yoke,
In time all haggard hawks will stoop to lure,
In time small wedges cleave the hardest oak,   5
In time the flint is pierced with softest shower' –
And she in time will fall from her disdain,
And rue the sufferance of your friendly pain.

BALTHAZAR

'No, she is wilder, and more hard withal,
Than beast, or bird, or tree, or stony wall'.   10
But wherefore blot I Bel-Imperia's name?
It is my fault, not she, that merits blame.
My feature is not to content her sight,
My words are rude and work her no delight.
The lines I send her are but harsh and ill,   15
Such as do drop from Pan and Marsyas' quill.
My presents are not of sufficient cost,
And being worthless all my labour's lost.
Yet might she love me for my valiancy;
Ay, but that's slandered by captivity.   20
Yet might she love me to content her sire;
Ay, but her reason masters his desire.
Yet might she love me as her brother's friend;
Ay, but her hopes aim at some other end.
Yet might she love me to uprear her state;   25

---

  1   *coy* the standard word for a seemingly reluctant beloved, as in Marvell's 'To his coy mistress'; it is made a verb at II.iii.3.

3–6 Lorenzo's lines are a fairly direct quotation from Sonnet 47 in Thomas Watson's *Hecatompathia*, published in 1582.

  4   *haggard hawks* wild birds, before they are taught to catch wildfowl by their falconer.

9–10 Balthazar renews Lorenzo's quotation by returning him lines from Watson's next sonnet.

11–28 This standard speech of love with its ay–yet repetitions was often echoed and parodied, for instance by Nathan Field in *A Woman is a Weathercock*, I.ii.345–6.

16 *Pan and Marsyas* gods who unsuccessfully challenged Apollo to a contest in flute playing.

Ay, but perhaps she hopes some nobler mate.
Yet might she love me as her beauty's thrall;
Ay, but I fear she cannot love at all.

LORENZO

My lord, for my sake leave these ecstasies,
And doubt not but we'll find some remedy.   30
Some cause there is that lets you not be loved:
First that must needs be known, and then removed.
What if my sister love some other knight?

BALTHAZAR

My summer's day will turn to winter's night.

LORENZO

I have already found a stratagem,   35
To sound the bottom of this doubtful theme.
My lord, for once you shall be ruled by me:
Hinder me not whate'er you hear or see.
By force or fair means will I cast about
To find the truth of all this question out.   40
Ho, Pedringano!

PEDRINGANO   [*Within*] Signior!

LORENZO   *Vien qui presto.*

Enter PEDRINGANO

PEDRINGANO

Hath your lordship any service to command me?

LORENZO

Ay, Pedringano, service of import.
And not to spend the time in trifling words,
Thus stands the case: it is not long thou know'st,   45
Since I did shield thee from my father's wrath,
For thy conveyance in Andrea's love,
For which thou wert adjudged to punishment.
I stood betwixt thee and thy punishment;
And since, thou know'st how I have favoured thee.   50
Now to these favours will I add reward,

---

27   *beauty's thrall* the *1592* quarto printed 'beauteous' but Jonson quoted this version in
     Poetaster (1601); it is also in *Soliman and Perseda*, IV.iii.6.
41   *Vien qui presto* (Italian). Come here at once; conceivably Lorenzo's liking for Italian
     phrases is meant to mark him as a Machiavellian; nobody else uses this language.
47   *conveyance* secret dealing; this is the first statement that Castile knew about Bel-
     Imperia's love affair with Andrea and acted to stop it.

Not with fair words, but store of golden coin,
And lands and living joined with dignities,
If thou but satisfy my just demand.
Tell truth and have me for thy lasting friend.   55

PEDRINGANO
Whate'er it be your lordship shall demand,
My bounden duty bids me tell the truth,
If case it lie in me to tell the truth.

LORENZO
Then, Pedringano, this is my demand:
Whom loves my sister Bel-Imperia?   60
For she reposeth all her trust in thee –
Speak man, and gain both friendship and reward:
I mean, whom loves she in Andrea's place?

PEDRINGANO
Alas, my lord, since Don Andrea's death,
I have no credit with her as before,   65
And therefore know not if she love or no.

LORENZO
Nay, if thou dally then I am thy foe,   [Draws his sword]
And fear shall force what friendship cannot win.
Thy death shall bury what thy life conceals.
Thou diest for more esteeming her than me.   70

PEDRINGANO
 O, stay, my lord.

LORENZO
Yet speak the truth and I will guerdon thee,
And shield thee from whatever can ensue,
And will conceal whate'er proceeds from thee:
But if thou dally once again, thou diest.   75

PEDRINGANO
If Madam Bel-Imperia be in love –

LORENZO
What, villain, ifs and ands?   [Offers to kill him]

PEDRINGANO
O stay my lord, she loves Horatio.

BALTHAZAR *starts back*

---

67   s.d. (and 77 s.d.) implied. See line 92.
78   s.d. BALTHAZAR *starts back* A stage direction in the original; Balthazar must be shown
     to react to the news, although he does not speak; hence the stage direction.

31

LORENZO
　　What, Don Horatio our Knight Marshal's son?
PEDRINGANO
　　Even him my lord.　　　　　　　　　　　　　　　　80
LORENZO
　　Now say but how know'st thou he is her love,
　　And thou shalt find me kind and liberal:
　　Stand up, I say, and fearless tell the truth.
PEDRINGANO
　　She sent him letters which myself perused,
　　Full-fraught with lines and arguments of love,　　85
　　Preferring him before Prince Balthazar.
LORENZO
　　Swear on this cross that what thou say'st is true,
　　And that thou wilt conceal what thou hast told.
PEDRINGANO
　　I swear to both by him that made us all.
LORENZO
　　In hope thine oath is true, here's thy reward,　　90
　　But if I prove thee perjured and unjust,
　　This very sword whereon thou took'st thine oath,
　　Shall be the worker of thy tragedy.
PEDRINGANO
　　What I have said is true, and shall for me
　　Be still concealed from Bel-Imperia.　　　　　　95
　　Besides, your honour's liberality
　　Deserves my duteous service even till death.
LORENZO
　　Let this be all that thou shalt do for me:
　　Be watchful when, and where, these lovers meet,
　　And give me notice in some secret sort.　　　　100
PEDRINGANO
　　I will my lord.
LORENZO
　　Then shalt thou find that I am liberal.
　　Thou know'st that I can more advance thy state

84　*She sent him letters* This indicates that time has passed; further letters by Bel-Imperia
　　and Pedringano when Hieronimo reads them later become crucial to his revenge.
87　*Swear on this cross* Line 92 shows that Lorenzo presents him with the hilt of his
　　sword; swords were often used to swear oaths, as Hamlet makes Horatio and
　　Marcellus do after they have seen the ghost.
100　*sort* device, trick.

Than she, be therefore wise and fail me not.
Go and attend her as thy custom is,   105
Lest absence make her think thou dost amiss.

                                   Exit PEDRINGANO

Why so: *tam armis quam ingenio*:
Where words prevail not, violence prevails;
But gold doth more than either of them both.
How likes Prince Balthazar this stratagem?   110

BALTHAZAR

Both well, and ill: it makes me glad and sad:
Glad, that I know the hinderer of my love,
Sad, that I fear she hates me whom I love.
Glad, that I know on whom to be revenged,
Sad, that she'll fly me if I take revenge.   115
Yet must I take revenge or die myself,
For love resisted grows impatient.
I think Horatio be my destined plague:
First, in his hand he brandished a sword,
And with that sword he fiercely waged war,   120
And in that war he gave me dangerous wounds,
And by those wounds he forced me to yield,
And by my yielding I became his slave.
Now in his mouth he carries pleasing words,
Which pleasing words do harbour sweet conceits,   125
Which sweet conceits are limed with sly deceits,
Which sly deceits smooth Bel-Imperia's ears,
And through her ears dive down into her heart,
And in her heart set him where I should stand.
Thus hath he ta'en my body by his force,   130
And now by sleight would captivate my soul:
But in his fall I'll tempt the destinies,
And either lose my life, or win my love.

LORENZO

Let's go, my lord, your staying stays revenge.
Do you but follow me and gain your love: 135
Her favour must be won by his remove.   *Exeunt*

107   *tam armis quam ingenio* 'as much by arms as brain'; an apt moment for Lorenzo to
      sheathe his sword again.
115   *if I take revenge* Balthazar follows Bel-Imperia in thinking of revenge; his speech,
      though, in its ponderous conventionality shows how he prefers words to actions, a
      position that Lorenzo utilizes when urging him away.
126   *limed* covered with bird-lime, to trap birds by making their feet stick to the branch.

ACT II, SCENE ii

Enter HORATIO *and* BEL-IMPERIA

HORATIO

Now, madam, since by favour of your love
Our hidden smoke is turned to open flame,
And that with looks and words we feed our thoughts
(Two chief contents, where more cannot be had),
Thus in the midst of love's fair blandishments,   5
Why show you sign of inward languishments?

PEDRINGANO *showeth all to the* PRINCE
and LORENZO, *placing them in secret* [*above*]

BEL-IMPERIA

My heart, sweet friend, is like a ship at sea:
She wisheth port, where riding all at ease,
She may repair what stormy times have worn,
And leaning on the shore, may sing with joy   10
That pleasure follows pain, and bliss annoy.
Possession of thy love is th'only port,
Wherein my heart, with fears and hopes long tossed,
Each hour doth wish and long to make resort;
There to repair the joys that it hath lost,   15
And sitting safe, to sing in Cupid's choir
That sweetest bliss is crown of love's desire.

BALTHAZAR

O sleep mine eyes, see not my love profaned;
Be deaf, my ears, hear not my discontent;
Die, heart, another joys what thou deservest.   20

LORENZO

Watch still mine eyes, to see this love disjoined;
Hear still mine ears, to hear them both lament;
Live, heart, to joy at fond Horatio's fall.

---

2   *hidden smoke* Horatio's metaphor assumes that nobody knows of their love,
    ironically in view of what has just been said in the previous scene.
6   s.d. *in secret* [*above*] The *1592* stage direction does not specify the stage balcony, but
    Balthazar's first speech at line 18 is marked as '*above*'.

BEL-IMPERIA
    Why stands Horatio speechless all this while?
HORATIO
    The less I speak, the more I meditate.   25
BEL-IMPERIA
    But whereon dost thou chiefly meditate?
HORATIO
    On dangers past, and pleasures to ensue.
BALTHAZAR
    On pleasures past, and dangers to ensue.
BEL-IMPERIA
    What dangers and what pleasures dost thou mean?
HORATIO
    Dangers of war and pleasures of our love.   30
LORENZO
    Dangers of death, but pleasures none at all.
BEL-IMPERIA
    Let dangers go, thy war shall be with me,
    But such a war as breaks no bond of peace.
    Speak thou fair words, I'll cross them with fair words;
    Send thou sweet looks, I'll meet them with sweet looks;   35
    Write loving lines, I'll answer loving lines;
    Give me a kiss, I'll countercheck thy kiss:
    Be this our warring peace, or peaceful war.
HORATIO
    But gracious madam, then appoint the field
    Where trial of this war shall first be made.   40
BALTHAZAR
    Ambitious villain, how his boldness grows!
BEL-IMPERIA
    Then be thy father's pleasant bower the field,
    Where first we vowed a mutual amity:
    The court were dangerous, that place is safe.
    Our hour shall be when Vesper gins to rise,   45
    That summons home distressful travellers.
    There none shall hear us but the harmless birds:

34   *cross* meet, with a pun on counter or thwart, as in line 37 '*countercheck*'.
38   *warring peace, or peaceful war* the rhetorical figure of oxymoron.
42   *thy father's pleasant bower* a garden seat, usually covered in branches; gardens were
      commonly the most private places for secret talk in an Elizabethan house.
45   *Vesper* Venus, or the evening star.

Happily the gentle nightingale
Shall carol us asleep ere we be ware,
And singing with the prickle at her breast,   50
Tell our delight and mirthful dalliance.
Till then each hour will seem a year and more.

HORATIO

But, honey sweet, and honourable love,
Return we now into your father's sight:
Dangerous suspicion waits on our delight.   55

LORENZO

Ay, danger mixed with jealious despite
Shall send thy soul into eternal night.

Exeunt

---

50   *singing with the prickle at her breast* Nightingales were thought to stimulate their sad
      singing by pressing their breast against a thorn.
56   *jealious* The spelling of 'jealous' indicates three syllables in speech.

ACT II, SCENE iii

Enter KING *of Spain, Portingale* AMBASSADOR, DON CYPRIAN, *etc.*

KING

    Brother of Castile, to the prince's love
    What says your daughter Bel-Imperia?

CASTILE

    Although she coy it as becomes her kind,
    And yet dissemble that she loves the prince,
    I doubt not, I, but she will stoop in time.   5
    And were she froward, which she will not be,
    Yet herein shall she follow my advice,
    Which is to love him or forgo my love.

KING

    Then, Lord Ambassador of Portingale,
    Advise thy king to make this marriage up,   10
    For strengthening of our late-confirmed league;
    I know no better means to make us friends.
    Her dowry shall be large and liberal:
    Besides that she is daughter and half-heir
    Unto our brother here, Don Cyprian,   15
    And shall enjoy the moiety of his land,
    I'll grace her marriage with an uncle's gift.
    And this it is: in case the match go forward,
    The tribute which you pay shall be released,
    And if by Balthazar she have a son,   20
    He shall enjoy the kingdom after us.

AMBASSADOR

    I'll make the motion to my sovereign liege,

---

5   *stoop* an unintentional pun, meaning both submit and dive in attack, as a hawk does, and as Bel-Imperia will do much later.

6   *froward* perverse.

7   *my advice* her father's wish, the classic parental position in 'forced marriages'.

11   The *1592* text ends this line with a comma, making it possible to link it with either the phrase before or after; this edition links it firmly to the marriage alliance.

16   *the moiety* a half-share.

21   *He shall enjoy the kingdom after us* a promise of unification for the two kingdoms; the king's subsequent warning to his brother (41–50) shows how much of this deal depends on Bel-Imperia's consent to this agreement.

And work it if my counsel may prevail.
KING
Do so, my lord, and if he give consent,
I hope his presence here will honour us   25
In celebration of the nuptial day –
And let himself determine of the time.
AMBASSADOR
Will't please your grace command me aught beside?
KING
Commend me to the king, and so farewell.
But where's Prince Balthazar to take his leave?   30
AMBASSADOR
That is performed already, my good lord.
KING
Amongst the rest of what you have in charge,
The prince's ransom must not be forgot;
That's none of mine, but his that took him prisoner,
And well his forwardness deserves reward: 35
It was Horatio, our Knight Marshal's son.
AMBASSADOR
Between us there's a price already pitched,
And shall be sent with all convenient speed.
KING
Then once again farewell, my lord.
AMBASSADOR
Farewell, my Lord of Castile and the rest.   *Exit*   40
KING
Now, brother, you must take some little pains
To win fair Bel-Imperia from her will:
Young virgins must be ruled by their friends.
The prince is amiable, and loves her well,
If she neglect him and forgo his love,   45
She both will wrong her own estate and ours.
Therefore, whiles I do entertain the prince
With greatest pleasure that our court affords,
Endeavour you to win your daughter's thought:
If she give back, all this will come to naught.   50

Exeunt

---

42   *her will* both brothers are evidently well aware of Bel-Imperia's hostility; 'will' often
     gave a sexual connotation to the concept of irrational desire.
50   *give back* turn her back on them, reject the agreement.

ACT II, SCENE iv

Enter HORATIO, BEL-IMPERIA, *and* PEDRINGANO

HORATIO

Now that the night begins with sable wings
To overcloud the brightness of the sun,
And that in darkness pleasures may be done,
Come Bel-Imperia, let us to the bower,
And there in safety pass a pleasant hour.   5

BEL-IMPERIA

I follow thee my love, and will not back,
Although my fainting heart controls my soul.

HORATIO

Why, make you doubt of Pedringano's faith?

BEL-IMPERIA

No, he is as trusty as my second self.
Go Pedringano, watch without the gate,   10
And let us know if any make approach.

PEDRINGANO

[*Aside*] Instead of watching, I'll deserve more gold
By fetching Don Lorenzo to this match.   *Exit* PEDRINGANO

HORATIO

What means my love?

BEL-IMPERIA   I know not what myself.
And yet my heart foretells me some mischance.   15

HORATIO

Sweet say not so, fair fortune is our friend,
And heavens have shut up day to pleasure us.
The stars thou see'st hold back their twinkling shine,
And Luna hides herself to pleasure us.

BEL-IMPERIA

Thou hast prevailed, I'll conquer my misdoubt,   20
And in thy love and counsel drown my fear.

----

1   *sable* black.
3   *darkness* usually thought of as apt for crime rather than love, appropriately enough
    here.
6   *back* withdraw, a macabre echo of the king's word at the end of the previous scene.
10 *without* outside.
19 *Luna* the moon.

I fear no more, love now is all my thoughts.
Why sit we not? for pleasure asketh ease.

HORATIO

The more thou sit'st within these leafy bowers,
The more will Flora deck it with her flowers.   25

BEL-IMPERIA

Ay, but if Flora spy Horatio here,
Her jealous eye will think I sit too near.

HORATIO

Hark, madam, how the birds record by night,
For joy that Bel-Imperia sits in sight.

BEL-IMPERIA

No, Cupid counterfeits the nightingale,   30
To frame sweet music to Horatio's tale.

HORATIO

If Cupid sing, then Venus is not far:
Ay, thou art Venus or some fairer star.

BEL-IMPERIA

If I be Venus, thou must needs be Mars,
And where Mars reigneth, there must needs be wars.   35

HORATIO

Then thus begin our wars: put forth thy hand,
That it may combat with my ruder hand.

BEL-IMPERIA

Set forth thy foot to try the push of mine.

HORATIO

But first my looks shall combat against thine.

BEL-IMPERIA

Then ward thyself: I dart this kiss at thee.   40

HORATIO

Thus I retort the dart thou threw'st at me.

BEL-IMPERIA

Nay then, to gain the glory of the field,
My twining arms shall yoke and make thee yield.

HORATIO

Nay then, my arms are large and strong withal:

28   *record* renew their musical chords.
34   *Venus . . . Mars* the goddess of love and the god of war, famous lovers.
40   *ward* guard.

Thus elms by vines are compassed till they fall.   45
BEL-IMPERIA
O let me go, for in my troubled eyes
Now may'st thou read that life in passion dies.
HORATIO
O stay a while and I will die with thee,
So shalt thou yield and yet have conquered me.
BEL-IMPERIA
Who's there? Pedringano! We are betrayed!   50

Enter LORENZO, BALTHAZAR, SERBERINE,
PEDRINGANO, *disguised*

LORENZO
My lord, away with her, take her aside.
O sir, forbear, your valour is already tried.
Quickly despatch, my masters.
They hang him in the arbour
HORATIO
What, will you murder me?
LORENZO
Ay, thus, and thus; these are the fruits of love.   55
They stab him
BEL-IMPERIA
O save his life and let me die for him!
O save him, brother, save him, Balthazar:
I loved Horatio, but he loved not me.
BALTHAZAR
But Balthazar loves Bel-Imperia.

45 *elms . . . they fall* a macabre inversion of the usual image, which says that vines (a
    common image for entwining Venus) uphold elm trees.
48 *die with thee* (with a sexual connotation).
50 s.d. *disguised* despite their disguises (masks in the 1615 title-page illustration), Bel-
    Imperia recognizes both her brother and Balthazar at line 57.
53 s.d. *in the arbour* called a 'bower' by Horatio, the title page of the 1615 quarto shows
    it as an arched and leafy framework with Horatio dangling by the neck from the
    centre; Hieronimo later says he found Horatio 'hanging on a tree' (IV.iv.111), either
    because its leafy branches made it seem like one or because it seemed to him like the
    gallows-tree on which Pedringano was executed; Isabella when she cuts it down in
    IV.ii speaks of 'these branches and these loathsome boughs / Of this unfortunate
    and fatal pine' (6–7). The 1615 woodcut may be based on the original staging, since
    it includes a black-masked ('*disguised*') figure dragging Bel-Imperia away. .

LORENZO

    Although his life were still ambitious proud,   60

    Yet is he at the highest now he is dead.

BEL-IMPERIA

    Murder! murder! Help, Hieronimo, help!

LORENZO

    Come, stop her mouth, away with her.

                          Exeunt [*leaving* HORATIO's *body*]

ACT II, SCENE v

Enter HIERONIMO *in his shirt, etc.*

HIERONIMO

What outcries pluck me from my naked bed,
And chill my throbbing heart with trembling fear,
Which never danger yet could daunt before?
Who calls Hieronimo? Speak, here I am.
I did not slumber, therefore 'twas no dream,   5
No, no, it was some woman cried for help,
And here within this garden did she cry,
And in this garden must I rescue her.
But stay, what murderous spectacle is this?
A man hanged up and all the murderers gone,   10
And in my bower to lay the guilt on me.
This place was made for pleasure not for death.
                              He cuts him down
Those garments that he wears I oft have seen –
Alas, it is Horatio, my sweet son!
Oh no, but he that whilom was my son.   15
O was it thou that calledst me from my bed?
O speak, if any spark of life remain:
I am thy father. Who hath slain my son?
What savage monster, not of human kind,
Hath here been glutted with thy harmless blood,   20
And left thy bloody corpse dishonoured here,
For me, amidst this dark and deathful shades,
To drown thee with an ocean of my tears?
O heavens, why made you night to cover sin?
By day this deed of darkness had not been.   25
O earth, why didst thou not in time devour
The vild profaner of this sacred bower?
O poor Horatio, what hadst thou misdone,

1   s.d. *shirt* nightshirt.
1   *naked bed* a transferred epithet.
15 *whilom* formerly.
21 *dishonoured* by being hanged, a criminal's death, as well as covered in blood.
22 *dark and deathful* a reminder of Horatio's praise of darkness at II.iv.3.
27 *vild* vile (with a possible hint of 'wild').

To leese thy life ere life was new begun?
O wicked butcher, whatsoe'er thou wert, 30
How could thou strangle virtue and desert?
Ay me most wretched, that have lost my joy,
In leesing my Horatio, my sweet boy!

Enter ISABELLA

ISABELLA
  My husband's absence makes my heart to throb –
  Hieronimo! 35
HIERONIMO
  Here, Isabella, help me to lament,
  For sighs are stopped and all my tears are spent.
ISABELLA
  What world of grief! My son Horatio!
  O where's the author of this endless woe?
HIERONIMO
  To know the author were some ease of grief, 40
  For in revenge my heart would find relief.
ISABELLA
  Then is he gone? and is my son gone too?
  O, gush out, tears, fountains and floods of tears;
  Blow, sighs, and raise an everlasting storm:
  For outrage fits our cursed wretchedness. 45
HIERONIMO
  Sweet lovely rose, ill plucked before thy time,
  Fair worthy son, not conquered, but betrayed:
  I'll kiss thee now, for words with tears are stayed .
ISABELLA
  And I'll close up the glasses of his sight,
  For once these eyes were only my delight. 50
HIERONIMO
  See'st thou this handkercher besmeared with blood?
  It shall not from me till I take revenge.
  See'st thou those wounds that yet are bleeding fresh?

---

29 *leese* lose.
     new begun a reference to the favour he gained from his victory over Balthazar.
39 *author* Horatio's mother's first thought is what villain did the murder; Hieronimo
     immediately thinks of revenge as a consolation for his grief.
51 *handkercher* possibly the same scarf that Bel-Imperia gave to Andrea, kept by
     Horatio (I.iv.42).

I'll not entomb them till I have revenged.
Then will I joy amidst my discontent,   55
Till then my sorrow never shall be spent.

ISABELLA

The heavens are just, murder cannot be hid:
Time is the author both of truth and right,
And time will bring this treachery to light.

HIERONIMO

Meanwhile, good Isabella, cease thy plaints,   60
Or at the least dissemble them awhile:
So shall we sooner find the practice out,
And learn by whom all this was brought about.
Come Isabel, now let us take him up,

They take him up

And bear him in from out this cursed place.   65
I'll say his dirge, singing fits not this case.
O aliquis mihi quas pulchrum ver educat herbas

HIERONIMO *sets his breast unto his sword*

Misceat, et nostro detur medicina dolori;
Aut, si qui faciunt animis oblivia, succos
Praebeat; ipse metam magnum quaecunque per orbem   70
Gramina Sol pulchras effert in luminis oras;
Ipse bibam quicquid meditatur saga veneni,
Quicquid et herbarum vi caeca nenia nectit:
Omnia perpetiar, lethum quoque, dum semel omnis
Noster in extincto moriatur pectore sensus.   75

---

58   *Time* Isabella expresses the traditional aphorism *veritas filia temporis*, time reveals
      the truth.

66   *his dirge* his funeral hymn, here to be spoken, not sung.

67–80 'Let someone bind for me the herbs that beautiful spring fosters, and let a salve be
       given for our grief; or let him apply juices, if there are any that bring forgetfulness
       to men's minds. I myself shall gather anywhere in the great world whatever plants
       the sun brings forth into the fair regions of light; I myself shall drink whatever drug
       the wise woman devises, and whatever herbs incantation assembles by its secret
       power. I shall face all things, even death, until the moment our every feeling dies in
       this dead breast. And so shall I never again, my life, see those eyes of yours, and has
       everlasting sleep sealed up your light of life? I shall perish with you; thus, thus would
       it please me to go to the shades below. Nonetheless I shall keep myself from yielding
       to a hastened death, lest in that case no revenge should follow your death.' The
       speech is largely a pastiche of lines from Lucretius, Virgil, and Ovid. .
            We are told that '*They take him up*', ready to carry the body offstage, but they must
       set him down again, since Hieronimo holds his sword to his chest while he speaks
       the dirge, and casts it away at the end, before he '*bears the body away*'.

Ergo tuos oculos nunquam, mea vita, videbo,
Et tua perpetuus sepelivit lumina somnus?
Emoriar tecum: sic, sic juvat ire sub umbras.
At tamen absistam properato cedere letho,
Ne mortem vindicta tuam tum nulla sequatur.   80

        Here he throws it from him and bears the body away

ACT II, SCENE vi

ANDREA

Brought'st thou me hither to increase my pain?
I looked that Balthazar should have been slain;
But 'tis my friend Horatio that is slain,
And they abuse fair Bel-Imperia,
On whom I doted more than all the world,   5
Because she loved me more than all the world.

REVENGE

Thou talk'st of harvest when the corn is green:
The end is crown of every work well done;
The sickle comes not till the corn be ripe.
Be still, and ere I lead thee from this place,   10
I'll show thee Balthazar in heavy case.

---

2   *looked* expected.
11 *in heavy case* in deep trouble.

ACT III, SCENE i

Enter VICEROY *of Portingale,* NOBLES, VILLUPPO

VICEROY

    Infortunate condition of kings,
    Seated amidst so many helpless doubts!
    First we are placed upon extremest height,
    And oft supplanted with exceeding heat,
    But ever subject to the wheel of chance;   5
    And at our highest never joy we so,
    As we both doubt and dread our overthrow.
    So striveth not the waves with sundry winds
    As Fortune toileth in the affairs of kings,
    That would be feared, yet fear to be beloved,   10
    Sith fear or love to kings is flattery.
    For instance, lordings, look upon your king,
    By hate deprived of his dearest son,
    The only hope of our successive line.

1 NOBLEMAN

    I had not thought that Alexandro's heart   15
    Had been envenomed with such extreme hate:
    But now I see that words have several works,
    And there's no credit in the countenance.

VILLUPPO

    No, for, my lord, had you beheld the train
    That feigned love had coloured in his looks,   20
    When he in camp consorted Balthazar,
    Far more inconstant had you thought the sun,
    That hourly coasts the centre of the earth,
    Than Alexandro's purpose to the prince.

1–11   A speech based on Seneca's *Agamemnon* 57–73.
   2   *helpless* hopeless, for which there is no help.
   5   *wheel of chance* Fortune's wheel.
  12   *look upon your king* The *1592* text gives him a speech heading 'Viceroy', or '*Vice*', but at line 69 the stage direction calls him 'King'.
  13   *hate* i.e, Alexandro's.
  14   *our successive line* our line of inheritance, succession to the kingship of Portugal.
  19   *train* treachery, the effect of feigned love.
  21   *consorted* kept company with.

VICEROY

No more, Villuppo, thou hast said enough,   25
And with thy words thou slay'st our wounded thoughts.
Nor shall I longer dally with the world,
Procrastinating Alexandro's death:
Go some of you and fetch the traitor forth,
That as he is condemned he may die.   30

Enter ALEXANDRO *with a* NOBLEMAN *and* HALBERTS

2 NOBLEMAN

In such extremes will naught but patience serve.

ALEXANDRO

But in extremes what patience shall I use?
Nor discontents it me to leave the world,
With whom there nothing can prevail but wrong.

2 NOBLEMAN

Yet hope the best.

ALEXANDRO   'Tis Heaven is my hope.   35
As for the earth, it is too much infect
To yield me hope of any of her mould.

VICEROY

Why linger ye? bring forth that daring fiend,
And let him die for his accursed deed.

ALEXANDRO

Not that I fear the extremity of death,   40
For nobles cannot stoop to servile fear,
Do I, O king, thus discontented live.
But this, O this, torments my labouring soul,
That thus I die suspected of a sin,
Whereof, as heavens have known my secret thoughts,   45
So am I free from this suggestion.

VICEROY

No more, I say! to the tortures! when!
Bind him, and burn his body in those flames,
                              They bind him to the stake

---

30   s.d. *HALBERTS* halberdiers.
32–7 Alexandro's view of injustice anticipates Hieronimo's attitude in III.ii.3ff, including
      the only hope being in heaven (line 35).
46   *suggestion* false accusation.
47   *when!* an expression of impatience.

That shall prefigure those unquenched fires
Of Phlegethon prepared for his soul.   50

ALEXANDRO

My guiltless death will be avenged on thee,
On thee, Villuppo, that hath maliced thus,
Or for thy meed hast falsely me accused.

VILLUPPO

Nay, Alexandro, if thou menace me,
I'll lend a hand to send thee to the lake   55
Where those thy words shall perish with thy works –
Injurious traitor, monstrous homicide!

Enter AMBASSADOR

AMBASSADOR

Stay, hold a while,
And here, with pardon of his majesty,
Lay hands upon Villuppo.
VICEROY   Ambassador,   60
What news hath urged this sudden entrance?

AMBASSADOR

Know, sovereign lord, that Balthazar doth live.

VICEROY

What say'st thou? liveth Balthazar our son?

AMBASSADOR

Your highness' son, Lord Balthazar, doth live;
And, well entreated in the court of Spain,   65
Humbly commends him to your majesty.
These eyes beheld, and these my followers;
With these, the letters of the king's commends,
                                        Gives him letters
Are happy witnesses of his highness' health.
                    The VICEROY *looks on the letters, and proceeds*

VICEROY

[*Reads*] 'Thy son doth live, your tribute is received,   70
Thy peace is made, and we are satisfied.
The rest resolve upon as things proposed
For both our honours and thy benefit.'

---

55   *the lake* i.e, of Avernus in hell.
62   *Balthazar doth live* the first good news, a false omen.

AMBASSADOR

    These are his highness' farther articles.

He gives him more letters

VICEROY

    Accursed wretch, to intimate these ills   75

    Against the life and reputation

    Of noble Alexandro! Come, my lord,

    Let him unbind thee that is bound to death,

    To make a quital for thy discontent.

They unbind him

ALEXANDRO

    Dread lord, in kindness you could do no less,   80

    Upon report of such a damned fact.

    But thus we see our innocence hath saved

    The hopeless life which thou, Villuppo, sought

    By thy suggestions to have massacred.

VICEROY

    Say, false Villuppo, wherefore didst thou thus   85

    Falsely betray Lord Alexandro's life?

    Him, whom thou knowest that no unkindness else,

    But even the slaughter of our dearest son,

    Could once have moved us to have misconceived.

ALEXANDRO

    Say, treacherous Villuppo, tell the king,   90

    Wherein hath Alexandro used thee ill?

VILLUPPO

    Rent with remembrance of so foul a deed,

    My guilty soul submits me to thy doom:

    For not for Alexandro's injuries,

    But for reward and hope to be preferred,   95

    Thus have I shamelessly hazarded his life.

VICEROY

    Which, villain, shall be ransomed with thy death,

    And not so mean a torment as we here

    Devised for him who thou said'st slew our son,

---

78   *Let him unbind thee* i.e. let Villuppo, who is now himself 'bound to death' in requital
     of 'thy discontent,' untie him from the stake.

79   s.d. *They unbind him* In *1592* this line comes at the end of line 77, a non-metrical
     addition that ignores the king's order to Villuppo and must have been intended as
     a stage direction.

But with the bitterest torments and extremes   100
That may be yet invented for thine end.

                    ALEXANDRO *seems to entreat*

Entreat me not, go, take the traitor hence.

                      Exit VILLUPPO [*guarded*]

And, Alexandro, let us honour thee
With public notice of thy loyalty.
To end those things articulated here   105
By our great lord, the mighty King of Spain,
We with our Council will deliberate.
Come, Alexandro, keep us company.

                      Exeunt

---

100   *the bitterest torments* i.e. worse than the death by fire on the stake to which Alexandro
       was bound; this order allows Villuppo to be led offstage.

ACT III, SCENE ii

Enter HIERONIMO

HIERONIMO

O eyes, no eyes, but fountains fraught with tears;
O life, no life, but lively form of death;
O world, no world, but mass of public wrongs,
Confused and filled with murder and misdeeds!
O sacred heavens! if this unhallowed deed,   5
If this inhuman and barbarous attempt,
If this incomparable murder thus
Of mine, but now no more my son,
Shall unrevealed and unrevenged pass,
How should we term your dealings to be just,   10
If you unjustly deal with those that in your justice trust?
The night, sad secretary to my moans,
With direful visions wake my vexed soul,
And with the wounds of my distressful son
Solicit me for notice of his death.   15
The ugly fiends do sally forth of hell,
And frame my steps to unfrequented paths,
And fear my heart with fierce inflamed thoughts.
The cloudy day my discontents records,
Early begins to register my dreams   20
And drive me forth to seek the murderer.
Eyes, life, world, heavens, hell, night, and day,
See, search, show, send some man, some mean, that may –
                    A letter falleth

What's here? a letter? tush, it is not so!
A letter written to Hieronimo!   *Red ink* 25
[*Reads*] 'For want of ink, receive this bloody writ.

---

1   Hieronimo's famous first line is a quotation from Petrarch's sonnet 161.
12 *sad secretary* serious confidant.
23 s.d. The pat arrival of the letter emphasizes how Revenge supports the ultimate working-out of vengeance.
25 s.d. probably an authorial note indicating that 'this bloody writ' (line 26) is composed in Bel-Imperia's blood; in *1592* lines 26–31 are headed '*Bel*' as if she should read them.

Me hath my hapless brother hid from thee:
Revenge thyself on Balthazar and him,
For these were they that murdered thy son.
Hieronimo, revenge Horatio's death,   30
And better fare than Bel-Imperia doth.'
What means this unexpected miracle?
My son slain by Lorenzo and the prince!
What cause had they Horatio to malign?
Or what might move thee, Bel-Imperia,   35
To accuse thy brother, had he been the mean?
Hieronimo, beware, thou art betrayed,
And to entrap thy life this train is laid.
Advise thee therefore, be not credulous:
This is devised to endanger thee,   40
That thou by this Lorenzo shouldst accuse,
And he, for thy dishonour done, should draw
Thy life in question, and thy name in hate.
Dear was the life of my beloved son,
And of his death behoves me be revenged: 45
Then hazard not thine own, Hieronimo,
But live t'effect thy resolution.
I therefore will by circumstances try
What I can gather to confirm this writ,
And, hearkening near the Duke of Castile's house,   50
Close if I can with Bel-Imperia,
To listen more, but nothing to bewray.

Enter PEDRINGANO

Now Pedringano!
PEDRINGANO   Now, Hieronimo!
HIERONIMO
Where's thy lady?
PEDRINGANO   I know not; here's my lord.

Enter LORENZO

---

39   *be not credulous* be more sceptical.
48   *by circumstances* by gathering circumstantial evidence.
51   *Close* develop an understanding.
52   *bewray* reveal.
54   *my lord* Pedringano here declares that Lorenzo rather than Bel-Imperia is now his master.

LORENZO
    How now, who's this? Hieronimo?
HIERONIMO   My lord.   55
PEDRINGANO
    He asketh for my lady Bel-Imperia.
LORENZO
    What to do, Hieronimo? The duke my father hath
    Upon some disgrace awhile removed her hence;
    But if it be aught I may inform her of,
    Tell me, Hieronimo, and I'll let her know it.   60
HIERONIMO
    Nay, nay, my lord, I thank you, it shall not need.
    I had a suit unto her, but too late,
    And her disgrace makes me unfortunate.
LORENZO
    Why so, Hieronimo? use me.
HIERONIMO
    O no, my lord, I dare not, it must not be,   65
    I humbly thank your lordship.
LORENZO   Why then, farewell.
HIERONIMO
    My grief no heart, my thoughts no tongue can tell.   *Exit*
LORENZO
    Come hither, Pedringano, see'st thou this?
PEDRINGANO
    My lord, I see it, and suspect it too.
LORENZO
    This is that damned villain Serberine,   70
    That hath, I fear, revealed Horatio's death.
PEDRINGANO
    My lord, he could not, 'twas so lately done;
    And since, he hath not left my company.
LORENZO
    Admit he have not, his condition's such,
    As fear or flattering words may make him false.   75
    I know his humour, and therewith repent
    That e'er I used him in this enterprise.
    But Pedringano, to prevent the worst,
    And 'cause I know thee secret as my soul,

58   *some disgrace* an unspecified trouble.

Here, for thy further satisfaction, take thou this,   80
                                        Gives him more gold
And hearken to me. Thus it is devised:
This night thou must, and prithee so resolve,
Meet Serberine at Saint Luigi's Park –
Thou know'st 'tis here hard by behind the house.
There take thy stand, and see thou strike him sure,   85
For die he must, if we do mean to live.

PEDRINGANO
But how shall Serberine be there, my lord?

LORENZO
Let me alone, I'll send to him to meet
The prince and me, where thou must do this deed.

PEDRINGANO
It shall be done, my lord, it shall be done,   90
And I'll go arm myself to meet him there.

LORENZO
When things shall alter, as I hope they will,
Then shalt thou mount for this: thou know'st my mind.
                                        Exit PEDRINGANO
Che le Ieron!

                            Enter PAGE

PAGE   My lord?

LORENZO   Go, sirrah, to Serberine,
And bid him forthwith meet the prince and me   95
At Saint Luigi's Park, behind the house,
This evening, boy.

PAGE   I go, my lord.

LORENZO
But, sirrah, let the hour be eight o'clock.
Bid him not fail.

PAGE   I fly, my lord.   *Exit*

LORENZO
Now to confirm the complot thou hast cast   100
Of all these practices, I'll spread the watch,

---

88   *Let me alone* Leave it to me.
93   *mount* rise socially (and by implication on the gallows).
94   *Che le Ieron* A summons to his page, either an Italian phrase like the one he uses at
      II.i.41 ('Chi la' means 'Who's there') or else the boy's name, which is never specified.
100   *complot* conspiracy.

Upon precise commandment from the king,
Strongly to guard the place where Pedringano
This night shall murder hapless Serberine.
Thus must we work that will avoid distrust,   105
Thus must we practise to prevent mishap,
And thus one ill another must expulse.
This sly enquiry of Hieronimo
For Bel-Imperia breeds suspicion,
And this suspicion bodes a further ill.   110
As for myself, I know my secret fault;
And so do they, but I have dealt for them.
They that for coin their souls endangered,
To save my life, for coin shall venture theirs:
And better it's that base companions die,   115
Than by their life to hazard our good haps.
Nor shall they live, for me to fear their faith:
I'll trust myself, myself shall be my friend,
For die they shall, slaves are ordained to no other end.   *Exit*

---

106   *practise* plan, scheme.
108   *sly enquiry* It is Lorenzo who is being sly.
116   *hazard our good haps* put our good luck at risk.

ACT III, SCENE iii

Enter PEDRINGANO *with a pistol*

PEDRINGANO

Now, Pedringano, bid thy pistol hold;
And hold on, Fortune! once more favour me;
Give but success to mine attempting spirit,
And let me shift for taking of mine aim!
Here is the gold, this is the gold proposed: 5
It is no dream that I adventure for,
But Pedringano is possessed thereof.
And he that would not strain his conscience
For him that thus his liberal purse hath stretched,
Unworthy such a favour may he fail,   10
And, wishing, want, when such as I prevail.
As for the fear of apprehension,
I know, if need should be, my noble lord
Will stand between me and ensuing harms;
Besides, this place is free from all suspect.   15
Here therefore will I stay and take my stand.

Enter the WATCH

1 WATCH

I wonder much to what intent it is
That we are thus expressly charged to watch.

2 WATCH

'Tis by commandment in the king's own name.

3 WATCH

But we were never wont to watch and ward   20
So near the duke his brother's house before.

2 WATCH

Content yourself, stand close, there's somewhat in't.

Enter SERBERINE

---

4   *let me shift* trust my contrivances.
12   *apprehension* being caught.
20   *watch and ward* patrol and guard.

SERBERINE

    Here, Serberine, attend and stay thy pace,

    For here did Don Lorenzo's page appoint

    That thou by his command shouldst meet with him.   25

    How fit a place, if one were so disposed,

    Methinks this corner is, to close with one.

PEDRINGANO

    Here comes the bird that I must seize upon;

    Now, Pedringano, or never, play the man!

SERBERINE

    I wonder that his lordship stays so long,   30

    Or wherefore should he send for me so late?

PEDRINGANO

    For this, Serberine, and thou shalt ha't.

Shoots the dag

    So, there he lies, my promise is performed.

The WATCH [*come forward*]

1 WATCH

    Hark gentlemen, this is a pistol shot.

2 WATCH

    And here's one slain; stay the murderer.   35

PEDRINGANO

    Now by the sorrows of the souls in hell,

He strives with the WATCH

    Who first lays hand on me, I'll be his priest.

3 WATCH

    Sirrah, confess, and therein play the priest;

    Why hast thou thus unkindly killed the man?

PEDRINGANO

    Why? because he walked abroad so late.   40

3 WATCH

    Come sir, you had been better kept your bed,

    Than have committed this misdeed so late.

2 WATCH

    Come, to the marshal's with the murderer!

27   *close with* have a secret meeting with.

32   s.d. *dag* a large pistol.

38   *unkindly* unnaturally, contrary to human nature.

43   *the marshal's* Hieronimo's house is adjacent to Castile's, and he is Spain's chief judge.

1 WATCH

    On to Hieronimo's! help me here
    To bring the murdered body with us too. 45

PEDRINGANO

    Hieronimo? Carry me before whom you will,
    Whate'er he be I'll answer him and you.
    And do your worst, for I defy you all.

Exeunt

ACT III, SCENE iv

Enter LORENZO *and* BALTHAZAR

BALTHAZAR
How now, my lord, what makes you rise so soon?
LORENZO
Fear of preventing our mishaps too late.
BALTHAZAR
What mischief is it that we not mistrust?
LORENZO
Our greatest ills we least mistrust, my lord,
And inexpected harms do hurt us most.   5
BALTHAZAR
Why tell me Don Lorenzo, tell me man,
If aught concerns our honour and your own.
LORENZO
Nor you nor me, my lord, but both in one;
For I suspect, and the presumption's great,
That by those base confederates in our fault   10
Touching the death of Don Horatio,
We are betrayed to old Hieronimo.
BALTHAZAR
Betrayed, Lorenzo? tush, it cannot be.
LORENZO
A guilty conscience, urged with the thought
Of former evils, easily cannot err: 15
I am persuaded, and dissuade me not,
That all's revealed to Hieronimo.
And therefore know that I have cast it thus –

[*Enter* PAGE]

But here's the page. How now, what news with thee?
PAGE
My lord, Serberine is slain.   20
BALTHAZAR
Who? Serberine, my man?

2   *preventing* anticipating, forestalling.
18   *cast it* made plans.

61

PAGE

Your highness' man, my lord.

LORENZO

Speak page, who murdered him?

PAGE

He that is apprehended for the fact.

LORENZO

Who?   25

PAGE

Pedringano.

BALTHAZAR

Is Serberine slain, that loved his lord so well?
Injurious villain, murderer of his friend!

LORENZO

Hath Pedringano murdered Serberine?
My lord, let me entreat you to take the pains   30
To exasperate and hasten his revenge
With your complaints unto my lord the king.
This their dissension breeds a greater doubt.

BALTHAZAR

Assure thee, Don Lorenzo, he shall die,
Or else his highness hardly shall deny.   35
Meanwhile I'll haste the Marshal-Sessions,
For die he shall for this his damned deed.   *Exit* BALTHAZAR

LORENZO

Why so, this fits our former policy,
And thus experience bids the wise to deal:
I lay the plot, he prosecutes the point;   40
I set the trap, he breaks the worthless twigs,
And sees not that wherewith the bird was limed.
Thus hopeful men, that mean to hold their own,
Must look like fowlers to their dearest friends.
He runs to kill whom I have holp to catch,   45
And no man knows it was my reaching fatch.
'Tis hard to trust unto a multitude,

31 *exasperate* intensify, make harsher.
33 *a greater doubt* fear of the truth becoming known.
36 *I'll haste* Serberine being Balthazar's servant makes his master's speeding of
    Pedringano's punishment an act of revenge.
44 *fowlers* bird-catchers.
46 *my reaching fatch* my successful plot.

Or anyone, in mine opinion,
When men themselves their secrets will reveal.

Enter a MESSENGER *with a letter*

Boy.   50
PAGE
  My lord?
LORENZO
  What's he?
MESSENGER
          I have a letter to your lordship.
LORENZO
  From whence?
MESSENGER   From Pedringano that's imprisoned.
LORENZO
  So he is in prison then?
MESSENGER   Ay, my good lord.
LORENZO
  What would he with us? He writes us here   55
  To stand good lord and help him in distress.
  Tell him I have his letters, know his mind,
  And what we may, let him assure him of.
  Fellow, begone: my boy shall follow thee.
                                              Exit MESSENGER
  This works like wax; yet once more try thy wits.   60
  Boy, go convey this purse to Pedringano,
  Thou knowest the prison, closely give it him,
  And be advised that none be there about.
  Bid him be merry still, but secret;
  And though the Marshal-Sessions be today,   65
  Bid him not doubt of his delivery.
  Tell him his pardon is already signed,
  And thereon bid him boldly be resolved;
  For, were he ready to be turned off
  (As 'tis my will the uttermost be tried)   70
  Thou with his pardon shalt attend him still.
  Show him this box, tell him his pardon's in't,
  But open't not, and if thou lov'st thy life,
  But let him wisely keep his hopes unknown;

73   *and if* (*an if*, an intensitive) if.

63

He shall not want while Don Lorenzo lives. 75
Away!

PAGE   I go my lord, I run.

LORENZO

But sirrah, see that this be cleanly done.

Exit PAGE

Now stands our fortune on a tickle point,
And now or never ends Lorenzo's doubts.
One only thing is uneffected yet, 80
And that's to see the executioner.
But to what end? I list not trust the air
With utterance of our pretence therein,
For fear the privy whispering of the wind
Convey our words amongst unfriendly ears, 85
That lie too open to advantages.
E quel che voglio io, nessun lo sa;
Intendo io: quel mi basterà. *Exit*

78   *tickle point* finely balanced.
87–8 Lorenzo's use of Italian again marks him as a Machiavellian villain; 'And what I want,
      nobody knows; it is enough that I alone understand'.

ACT III, SCENE v

Enter BOY *with the box*

PAGE

My master hath forbidden me to look in this box, and by my
troth 'tis likely, if he had not warned me, I should not have had
so much idle time; for we men's-kind in our minority are like
women in their uncertainty: that they are most forbidden,
they will soonest attempt. So I now. By my bare honesty, here's   5
nothing but the bare empty box. Were it not sin against secrecy,
I would say it were a piece of gentleman-like knavery. I must
go to Pedringano, and tell him his pardon is in this box; nay, I
would have sworn it, had I not seen the contrary. I cannot choose
but smile to think how the villain will flout the gallows, scorn   10
the audience, and descant on the hangman, and all presuming
of his pardon from hence. Will't not be an odd jest, for me to
stand and grace every jest he makes, pointing my finger at this
box, as who would say, 'Mock on, here's thy warrant.' Is't not a
scurvy jest that a man should jest himself to death? Alas, poor   15
Pedringano, I am in a sort sorry for thee, but if I should be
hanged with thee, I cannot weep.   *Exit*

---

3 *in our minority* a metatheatrical joke: the boy playing the page very likely doubled
   Isabella or her maid, so he is 'like women in their uncertainty'.

6 *bare empty box* variously related to Pandora's box or the box of Silenus in Plato's
   Symposium, which Erasmus used to denote the difference between appearance and
   reality.

ACT III, SCENE vi

Enter HIERONIMO *and the* DEPUTY

HIERONIMO

    Thus must we toil in other men's extremes,
    That know not how to remedy our own;
    And do them justice, when unjustly we,
    For all our wrongs, can compass no redress.
    But shall I never live to see the day   5
    That I may come, by justice of the heavens,
    To know the cause that may my cares allay?
    This toils my body, this consumeth age,
    That only I to all men just must be,
    And neither gods nor men be just to me.   10

DEPUTY

    Worthy Hieronimo, your office asks
    A care to punish such as do transgress.

HIERONIMO

    So is't my duty to regard his death
    Who when he lived deserved my dearest blood.
    But come, for that we came for, let's begin,   15
    For here lies that which bids me to be gone.

Enter OFFICERS, BOY, *and* PEDRINGANO,
with a letter in his hand, bound

DEPUTY

    Bring forth the prisoner, for the court is set.

PEDRINGANO

    Gramercy, boy, but it was time to come;
    For I had written to my lord anew
    A nearer matter that concerneth him,   20

1–10   Hieronimo's complaint about doing justice for others is spoken in ignorance of
       Pedringano's involvement in his son's murder.
  16   *here* He touches his heart, or his head; Boas thinks he may touch the bloody
       handkercher, but that would require him to know that it was Pedringano who
       betrayed Horatio to Lorenzo and Balthazar.
  16   s.d. *with a letter in his hand, bound* Pedringano must have his hands bound together
       in front, not behind, so that the letter is clearly visible; he can then more easily
       gesture at the scaffold and the noose, as he does subsequently.

For fear his lordship had forgotten me.
But sith he hath remembered me so well –
Come, come, come on, when shall we to this gear?

HIERONIMO

Stand forth, thou monster, murderer of men,
And here, for satisfaction of the world,   25
Confess thy folly and repent thy fault,
For there's thy place of execution.

PEDRINGANO

This is short work! Well, to your marshalship
First I confess, nor fear I death therefore,
I am the man, 'twas I slew Serberine.   30
But sir, then you think this shall be the place
Where we shall satisfy you for this gear?

DEPUTY

Ay, Pedringano.

PEDRINGANO   Now I think not so.

HIERONIMO

Peace, impudent, for thou shalt find it so:
For blood with blood shall, while I sit as judge,   35
Be satisfied, and the law discharged.
And though myself cannot receive the like,
Yet will I see that others have their right.
Despatch, the fault's approved and confessed,
And by our law he is condemned to die.   40

HANGMAN

Come on sir, are you ready?

PEDRINGANO

To do what, my fine officious knave?

HANGMAN

To go to this gear.

PEDRINGANO

O sir, you are too forward; thou wouldst fain furnish me with
a halter, to disfurnish me of my habit. So I should go out of this   45
gear, my raiment, into that gear, the rope. But, hangman, now
I spy your knavery, I'll not change without boot, that's flat.

---

23   *this gear* The term's recurrence at lines 32, 43 and 46 emphasizes the scaffold's iconic
       function, perhaps because it was a version of the arbour where Horatio was hanged.
45   *to disfurnish me of my habit* The hangman normally took the victim's clothing.
47   *without boot* without any reward, perhaps punning on his footwear.

HANGMAN

Come sir.

PEDRINGANO

So then, I must up?

HANGMAN

No remedy.   50

PEDRINGANO

Yes, but there shall be for my coming down.

HANGMAN

Indeed, here's a remedy for that.

PEDRINGANO

How? Be turned off?

HANGMAN

Ay, truly; come, are you ready? I pray, sir, despatch, the day
goes away.   55

PEDRINGANO

What, do you hang by the hour? If you do, I may chance to break
your old custom.

HANGMAN

Faith, you have reason, for I am like to break your young neck.

PEDRINGANO

Dost thou mock me, hangman? Pray God I be not preserved
to break your knave's pate for this.   60

HANGMAN

Alas, sir, you are a foot too low to reach it, and I hope you will
never grow so high while I am in the office.

PEDRINGANO

Sirrah, dost see yonder boy with the box in his hand?

HANGMAN

What, he that points to it with his finger?

PEDRINGANO

Ay, that companion.   65

HANGMAN

I know him not, but what of him?

---

53   *turned off* The traditional hangman's phrase, pushed off the bench on which he
     stands with the rope round his neck; if the scaffold was the same structure as the
     bower or arbour from which Horatio was hanged, it would have had a bench for
     the lovers to sit on.

63   The game with the box has possible reminiscences of a *Commedia dell'arte* trick in
     which the hangman hangs himself; whatever inspired Kyd to devise this trick, it has
     a macabre point in showing a real hanging on stage.

PEDRINGANO

Dost thou think to live till his old doublet will make thee a
new truss?

HANGMAN

Ay, and many a fair year after, to truss up many an honester
man than either thou or he. 70

PEDRINGANO

What hath he in his box, as thou think'st?

HANGMAN

Faith, I cannot tell, nor I care not greatly. Methinks you should
rather hearken to your soul's health.

PEDRINGANO

Why, sirrah hangman, I take it that that is good for the body is
likewise good for the soul; and it may be, in that box is balm 75
for both.

HANGMAN

Well, thou art even the merriest piece of man's flesh that e'er
groaned at my office door.

PEDRINGANO

Is your roguery become an 'office' with a knave's name?

HANGMAN

Ay, and that shall all they witness that see you seal it with a 80
thief's name.

PEDRINGANO

I prithee, request this good company to pray with me.

HANGMAN

Ay marry sir, this is a good motion; my masters, you see here's
a good fellow.

PEDRINGANO

Nay, nay, now I remember me, let them alone till some other 85
time, for now I have no great need.

HIERONIMO

I have not seen a wretch so impudent!
O monstrous times, where murder's set so light;
And where the soul that should be shrined in heaven,
Solely delights in interdicted things, 90
Still wandering in the thorny passages
That intercepts itself of happiness.
Murder, O bloody monster, God forbid
A fault so foul should 'scape unpunished.

Despatch and see this execution done – 95
This makes me to remember thee, my son.

Exit HIERONIMO

PEDRINGANO
  Nay soft, no haste.
DEPUTY
  Why, wherefore stay you? Have you hope of life?
PEDRINGANO
  Why, ay.
HANGMAN
  As how? 100
PEDRINGANO
  Why, rascal, by my pardon from the king.
HANGMAN
  Stand you on that? then you shall off with this.

He turns him off

DEPUTY
  So, executioner. Convey him hence,
  But let his body be unburied:
  Let not the earth be choked or infect 105
  With that which heaven contemns, and men neglect.

Exeunt

---

106 *contemns* scorns, is contemptuous of.

ACT III, SCENE vii

Enter HIERONIMO

HIERONIMO

    Where shall I run to breathe abroad my woes,
    My woes whose weight hath wearied the earth?
    Or mine exclaims, that have surcharged the air
    With ceaseless plaints for my deceased son?
    The blustering winds, conspiring with my words,   5
    At my lament have moved the leafless trees,
    Disrobed the meadows of their flowered green,
    Made mountains marsh with spring-tides of my tears,
    And broken through the brazen gates of hell.
    Yet still tormented is my tortured soul   10
    With broken sighs and restless passions,
    That winged mount, and hovering in the air,
    Beat at the windows of the brightest heavens,
    Soliciting for justice and revenge;
    But they are placed in those empyreal heights,   15
    Where, counter-mured with walls of diamond,
    I find the place impregnable; and they
    Resist my woes, and give my words no way.

Enter HANGMAN *with a letter*

HANGMAN

    O lord sir, God bless you sir, the man sir,
    Petergade sir, he that was so full of merry conceits –   20
HIERONIMO

    Well, what of him?

    1   *breathe abroad* speak, express.
    6   *leafless trees* Conceivably he gestures to the arbour where Pedringano was hanged,
        stripped of the leaves that were on it when it was the bower where Horatio was killed;
        Isabella later strips branches and leaves from the arbour.
  12 *winged mount* ascend on wings.
  14 *justice and revenge* As Chief Marshal, Hieronimo feels they are the same, and due
        from heaven.
  15 *empyreal* a word sounding like 'imperial', God's realm.
  16 *counter-mured* double-walled, with an inner wall.
  20 *Petergade* the hangman's attempt at Pedringano's name.

HANGMAN

    O lord sir, he went the wrong way, the fellow had a fair
    commission to the contrary. Sir, here is his passport; I pray
    you sir, we have done him wrong.

HIERONIMO

    I warrant thee, give it me.   25

HANGMAN

    You will stand between the gallows and me?

HIERONIMO

    Ay, ay.

HANGMAN

    I thank your Lord Worship.   *Exit* HANGMAN

HIERONIMO

    And yet, though somewhat nearer me concerns,
    I will, to ease the grief that I sustain,   30
    Take truce with sorrow while I read on this.
    'My lord, I writ as mine extremes required,
    That you would labour my delivery;
    If you neglect, my life is desperate,
    And in my death I shall reveal the troth.   35
    You know, my lord, I slew him for your sake;
    And as confederate with the prince and you,
    Won by rewards and hopeful promises,
    I holp to murder Don Horatio too.'
    Holp he to murder mine Horatio?   40
    And actors in th' accursed tragedy
    Wast thou, Lorenzo, Balthazar and thou,
    Of whom my son, my son deserved so well?
    What have I heard, what have mine eyes beheld?
    O sacred heavens, may it come to pass   45
    That such a monstrous and detested deed,
    So closely smothered, and so long concealed,
    Shall thus by this be vengéd or revealed!

22–3   *a fair commission* The hangman thinks the letter was an official order to Pedringano
        to shoot Serberine, which would explain his expectation that he would not be
        hanged.

23   *passport* i.e. his letter, which the hangman thinks would release him from execution.

35   *in my death I shall reveal the troth* As indeed the letter does.

37   *as* Edwards corrects the *1592* 'was', which equally confirms Pedringano's guilt to
        Hieronimo, as his first exclamation on reading the letter says; this second letter
        confirms the truth of Bel-Imperia's first, written in her blood.

Now see I what I durst not then suspect,
That Bel-Imperia's letter was not feigned.   50
Nor feigned she, though falsely they have wronged
Both her, myself, Horatio and themselves.
Now may I make compare, 'twixt hers and this,
Of every accident; I ne'er could find
Till now, and now I feelingly perceive,   55
They did what heaven unpunished would not leave.
O false Lorenzo, are these thy flattering looks?
Is this the honour that thou didst my son?
And Balthazar, bane to thy soul and me,
Was this the ransom he reserved thee for?   60
Woe to the cause of these constrained wars,
Woe to thy baseness and captivity,
Woe to thy birth, thy body and thy soul,
Thy cursed father, and thy conquered self!
And banned with bitter execrations be   65
The day and place where he did pity thee!
But wherefore waste I mine unfruitful words,
When naught but blood will satisfy my woes?
I will go plain me to my lord the king,
And cry aloud for justice through the court,   70
Wearing the flints with these my withered feet,
And either purchase justice by entreats
Or tire them all with my revenging threats.   *Exit*

56   *what heaven unpunished would not leave* The letter is heaven's confirmation:
      Hieronimo now knows he must not leave the crime unpunished.
59   *bane to thy soul* Balthazar's crime will send his soul to hell.
61   *constrained* needless, pointless.
69   *go plain me* level my complaint.
72   *purchase justice by entreats* buy justice by begging.
73   *tire them all* weary the king and court: exactly what Lorenzo was afraid he would do.

ACT III, SCENE viii

Enter ISABELLA *and her* MAID

ISABELLA

    So that, you say, this herb will purge the eye,
    And this the head?
    Ah, but none of them will purge the heart:
    No, there's no medicine left for my disease,
    Nor any physic to recure the dead.   5

                        She runs lunatic

    Horatio! O, where's Horatio?

MAID

    Good madam, affright not thus yourself
    With outrage for your son Horatio:
    He sleeps in quiet in the Elysian fields.

ISABELLA

    Why, did I not give you gowns and goodly things,   10
    Bought you a whistle and a whipstalk too,
    To be revenged on their villainies?

MAID

    Madam, these humours do torment my soul.

ISABELLA

    My soul! poor soul, thou talks of things
    Thou know'st not what – my soul hath silver wings,   15
    That mounts me up unto the highest heavens;
    To heaven, ay, there sits my Horatio,
    Backed with a troop of fiery cherubins,
    Dancing about his newly-healed wounds,
    Singing sweet hymns and chanting heavenly notes,   20
    Rare harmony to greet his innocence,
    That died, ay died a mirror in our days.
    But say, where shall I find the men, the murderers,
    That slew Horatio? Whither shall I run
    To find them out that murdered my son?   *Exeunt*   25

    1   *this herb* a model for Ophelia, Isabella looks for herbal remedies; her hair and
          clothing must be designed to show that she has gone mad.
   10   *give you* To Horatio, not the maid; Isabella speaks to her dead son.
   11   *whipstalk* a whip-handle, used for spinning a child's top.
   21   *greet* weep in welcome.

ACT III, SCENE ix

BEL-IMPERIA *at a window*

BEL-IMPERIA
What means this outrage that is offered me?
Why am I thus sequestered from the court?
No notice? Shall I not know the cause
Of this my secret and suspicious ills?
Accursed brother, unkind murderer,   5
Why bends thou thus thy mind to martyr me?
Hieronimo, why writ I of thy wrongs,
Or why art thou so slack in thy revenge?
Andrea, O Andrea, that thou sawest
Me for thy friend Horatio handled thus,   10
And him for me thus causeless murdered.
Well, force perforce, I must constrain myself
To patience, and apply me to the time,
Till heaven, as I have hoped shall set me free.

Enter CHRISTOPHIL

CHRISTOPHIL
Come, Madam Bel-Imperia, this may not be.   15

Exeunt

2   *sequestered* kept apart, locked away.
3   *No notice* No word to say why she is locked up.
13   *patience* The Christian resource when afflicted; Bel-Imperia no longer believes that
     Hieronimo will take the revenge she desires, so patience must be her only help.

ACT III, SCENE x

Enter LORENZO, BALTHAZAR, *and the* PAGE

LORENZO

    Boy, talk no further, thus far things go well.

    Thou art assured that thou sawest him dead?

PAGE

    Or else my lord I live not.

LORENZO   That's enough.

    As for his resolution in his end,

    Leave that to him with whom he sojourns now.   5

    Here, take my ring and give it Christophil,

    And bid him let my sister be enlarged,

    And bring her hither straight.

                                Exit PAGE

    This that I did was for a policy

    To smooth and keep the murder secret,   10

    Which as a nine-days' wonder being o'erblown,

    My gentle sister will I now enlarge.

BALTHAZAR

    And time, Lorenzo, for my lord the duke,

    You heard, enquired for her yester-night.

LORENZO

    Why, and, my lord, I hope you heard me say   15

    Sufficient reason why she kept away.

    But that's all one. My lord, you love her?

BALTHAZAR   Ay.

LORENZO

    Then in your love beware, deal cunningly,

    Salve all suspicions; only soothe me up;

    And if she hap to stand on terms with us,   20

---

  7   *enlarged* set free.

  9   *policy* Lorenzo hopes that his plan for the murder of Horatio will be merely '*a nine-days' wonder*,' soon to be forgotten; it is working well, so he can now afford to free Bel-Imperia.

 13   *my lord the duke* Castile, Lorenzo's unknowing father.

 19   *Salve* appease, allay.

       only soothe me up keep in confidence only with me.

 20   *if she hap to stand on terms* if by any chance she makes things difficult.

As for her sweetheart, and concealment so,
Jest with her gently: under feigned jest
Are things concealed that else would breed unrest.
But here she comes.

Enter BEL-IMPERIA

Now, sister –
BEL-IMPERIA   Sister? No!
Thou art no brother, but an enemy,   25
Else wouldst thou not have used thy sister so:
First, to affright me with thy weapons drawn,
And with extremes abuse my company;
And then to hurry me, like whirlwind's rage,
Amidst a crew of thy confederates,   30
And clap me up where none might come at me,
Nor I at any, to reveal my wrongs.
What madding fury did possess thy wits?
Or wherein is't that I offended thee?

LORENZO

Advise you better, Bel-Imperia,   35
For I have done you no disparagement;
Unless, by more discretion than deserved,
I sought to save your honour and mine own.

BEL-IMPERIA

Mine honour! why, Lorenzo, wherein is't
That I neglect my reputation so,   40
As you, or any, need to rescue it?

LORENZO

His highness and my father were resolved
To come confer with old Hieronimo,
Concerning certain matters of estate,
That by the viceroy was determined.   45

BEL-IMPERIA

And wherein was mine honour touched in that?

BALTHAZAR

Have patience, Bel-Imperia; hear the rest.

31   *clap me up* lock me away.
38   *I sought… mine own* our joint family honour.
42   *His highness and my father* the king and his brother Castile.
45   *the viceroy* i.e. a matter relating to Portugal.
47   *patience* Balthazar invokes the Christian word most inaptly here.

LORENZO
    Me next in sight as messenger they sent,
    To give him notice that they were so nigh:
    Now when I came, consorted with the prince,   50
    And unexpected, in an arbour there,
    Found Bel-Imperia with Horatio –
BEL-IMPERIA
    How then?
LORENZO
    Why then, remembering that old disgrace,
    Which you for Don Andrea had endured,   55
    And now were likely longer to sustain,
    By being found so meanly accompanied,
    Thought rather, for I knew no readier mean,
    To thrust Horatio forth my father's way.
BALTHAZAR
    And carry you obscurely somewhere else,   60
    Lest that his highness should have found you there.
BEL-IMPERIA
    Even so, my lord? And you are witness
    That this is true which he entreateth of?
    You, gentle brother, forged this for my sake,
    And you, my lord, were made his instrument: 65
    A work of worth, worthy the noting too!
    But what's the cause that you concealed me since?
LORENZO
    Your melancholy, sister, since the news
    Of your first favourite Don Andrea's death,
    My father's old wrath hath exasperate.   70
BALTHAZAR
    And better was't for you, being in disgrace,
    To absent yourself, and give his fury place.
BEL-IMPERIA
    But why had I no notice of his ire?

---

54   *disgrace* Lorenzo uses the term he had previously applied (at III.ii.58) to her liaison with Andrea.
57   *meanly accompanied* the same complaint of low social rank is applied to both Andrea and Horatio.
62   *my lord?* Bel-Imperia asks Balthazar for confirmation of Lorenzo's lie.
70   *exasperate* Lorenzo claims that her grief for Andrea has intensified their father's anger against Bel-Imperia.

LORENZO

    That were to add more fuel to your fire,

    Who burnt like Aetna for Andrea's loss.   75

BEL-IMPERIA

    Hath not my father then enquired for me?

LORENZO

    Sister, he hath, and thus excused I thee.

                            He whispereth in her ear

    But, Bel-Imperia, see the gentle prince;

    Look on thy love, behold young Balthazar,

    Whose passions by thy presence are increased;   80

    And in whose melancholy thou may'st see

    Thy hate, his love; thy flight, his following thee.

BEL-IMPERIA

    Brother, you are become an orator –

    I know not, I, by what experience –

    Too politic for me, past all compare,   85

    Since last I saw you; but content yourself,

    The prince is meditating higher things.

BALTHAZAR

    'Tis of thy beauty, then, that conquers kings;

    Of those thy tresses, Ariadne's twines,

    Wherewith my liberty thou hast surprised;   90

    Of that thine ivory front, my sorrow's map,

    Wherein I see no haven to rest my hope.

BEL-IMPERIA

    To love and fear, and both at once, my lord,

    In my conceit, are things of more import

    Than women's wits are to be busied with.   95

---

75   *Aetna* Mount Etna, a live volcano.

77   s.d. *He whispereth in her ear* This stage direction is perhaps meant to make Lorenzo tell Bel-Imperia something not heard by anyone else; more likely, though, it was designed to make what he says heard by the audience but not by Balthazar; she replies loudly, claiming that Balthazar is 'meditating higher things' than love of her.

89   *Ariadne's* either Ariadne who helped Theseus find the Minotaur with a thread or the weaver Arachne who Athene turned into a spider; Shakespeare's *Troilus and Cressida* V.ii.151 has the same merger of the two names.

91   *my sorrow's map* her forehead, commonly seen (by lovers) as the reflection of grief.

94   *In my conceit* Bel-Imperia, commenting on Balthazar's conventional imagery, says she has more pressing matters in her mind; she is sharper and more ominous to her brother — her Latin on parting at 102–3 is threatening in a deliberately vague way.

BALTHAZAR
  'Tis I that love.
BEL-IMPERIA   Whom?
BALTHAZAR   Bel-Imperia.
BEL-IMPERIA
  But I that fear.
BALTHAZAR   Whom?
BEL-IMPERIA   Bel-Imperia.
LORENZO
  Fear yourself?
BEL-IMPERIA   Ay, brother.
LORENZO   How?
BEL-IMPERIA   As those
  That what they love are loath and fear to lose.
BALTHAZAR
  Then, fair, let Balthazar your keeper be.   100
BEL-IMPERIA
  No, Balthazar doth fear as well as we:
  Et tremulo metui pavidum junxere timorem,
  Et vanum stolidae proditionis opus.   *Exit*
LORENZO
  Nay and you argue things so cunningly,
  We'll go continue this discourse at court.   105
BALTHAZAR
  Led by the loadstar of her heavenly looks,
  Wends poor oppressed Balthazar,
  As o'er the mountains walks the wanderer,
  Incertain to effect his pilgrimage.

                                        Exeunt

102–3 'They yoked cowardly fear to trembling dread, as a fruitless act of stupid treason'.
   106 *loadstar* a magnetic compass, a star to steer by.
   109 *Incertain to effect* Unsure how to manage.

ACT III, SCENE xi

Enter two PORTINGALES, *and* HIERONIMO *meets them*

1 PORTINGALE
 By your leave, sir.
HIERONIMO
 Good leave have you: nay, I pray you go,
 For I'll leave you; if you can leave me, so.
2 PORTINGALE
 Pray you, which is the next way to my lord the duke's?
HIERONIMO
 The next way from me.
1 PORTINGALE   To his house, we mean.   5
HIERONIMO
 O, hard by, 'tis yon house that you see.
2 PORTINGALE
 You could not tell us if his son were there?
HIERONIMO
 Who, my lord Lorenzo?
1 PORTINGALE   Ay, sir.
          He goeth in at one door and comes out at another
HIERONIMO   O, forbear,
 For other talk for us far fitter were.
 But if you be importunate to know   10
 The way to him, and where to find him out,
 Then list to me, and I'll resolve your doubt.
 There is a path upon your left-hand side,
 That leadeth from a guilty conscience
 Unto a forest of distrust and fear,   15
 A darksome place, and dangerous to pass:
 There shall you meet with melancholy thoughts,
 Whose baleful humours if you but uphold,
 It will conduct you to despair and death;
 Whose rocky cliffs when you have once beheld,   20
 Within a hugy dale of lasting night,

---

   4   *to my lord the duke's* i.e. to Castile's palace.
  10   *importunate* insistent.
13–29 Compare Andrea's account of his journey to the underworld, I.i.63–71.
  21   *hugy dale* a precipitous valley.

That, kindled with the world's iniquities,
Doth cast up filthy and detested fumes,
Not far from thence, where murderers have built
A habitation for their cursed souls,   25
There, in a brazen cauldron, fixed by Jove
In his fell wrath upon a sulphur flame,
Yourselves shall find Lorenzo bathing him
In boiling lead and blood of innocents.

I PORTINGALE
  Ha, ha, ha!
HIERONIMO   Ha, ha, ha!   30
  Why, ha, ha, ha! Farewell, good, ha, ha, ha!   *Exit*
2 PORTINGALE
  Doubtless this man is passing lunatic,
  Or imperfection of his age doth make him dote.
  Come, let's away to seek my lord the duke.

                                                  [*Exeunt*]

27   *fell wrath* fatally intense anger.
32   *passing* exceedingly.

ACT III, SCENE xii

Enter HIERONIMO, *with a poniard in one hand,*
and a rope in the other

HIERONIMO

Now sir, perhaps I come and see the king,
The king sees me, and fain would hear my suit:
Why, is not this a strange and seld-seen thing,
That standers-by with toys should strike me mute?
Go to, I see their shifts, and say no more.   5
Hieronimo, 'tis time for thee to trudge:
Down by the dale that flows with purple gore
Standeth a fiery tower; there sits a judge
Upon a seat of steel and molten brass,
And 'twixt his teeth he holds a fire-brand,   10
That leads unto the lake where hell doth stand.
Away, Hieronimo, to him be gone:
He'll do thee justice for Horatio's death.
Turn down this path, thou shalt be with him straight;
Or this, and then thou need'st not take thy breath.   15
This way or that way? Soft and fair, not so:
For if I hang or kill myself, let's know
Who will revenge Horatio's murder then?
No, no! fie, no! pardon me, I'll none of that:
                    He flings away the dagger and halter
This way I'll take, and this way comes the king;   20
                         He takes them up again
And here I'll have a fling at him, that's flat;
And, Balthazar, I'll be with thee to bring,
And thee, Lorenzo! Here's the king; nay, stay,
And here, ay here; there goes the hare away.

---

1   s.d. Hieronimo's knife and rope indicate two means of killing, either his enemies or
    himself; his sane advice to himself here contrasts with the verdict of the Portuguese
    citizens at the end of the previous scene.
4   *toys* trivial things.
5   *shifts* tricks, stratagems.
6   *trudge* take strenuous action (not slowly); at this point Hieronimo is still facing the
    two options for action, suicide or murder.
24 *there goes the hare away* The arrival of Lorenzo and Balthazar with the king prompts
    a pun on Hieronimo's role, hunting the hare/heir.

Enter KING, AMBASSADOR, CASTILE, *and* LORENZO

KING

    Now show, Ambassador, what our viceroy saith: 25

    Hath he received the articles we sent?

HIERONIMO

    Justice, O, justice to Hieronimo.

LORENZO

    Back, see'st thou not the king is busy?

HIERONIMO

    O, is he so?

KING

    Who is he that interrupts our business?   30

HIERONIMO

    Not I. Hieronimo, beware: go by, go by.

AMBASSADOR

    Renowned king, he hath received and read

    Thy kingly proffers, and thy promised league,

    And, as a man extremely overjoyed

    To hear his son so princely entertained,   35

    Whose death he had so solemnly bewailed,

    This for thy further satisfaction

    And kingly love, he kindly lets thee know: .

    First, for the marriage of his princely son

    With Bel-Imperia, thy beloved niece,   40

    The news are more delightful to his soul,

    Than myrrh or incense to the offended heavens.

    In person, therefore, will he come himself,

    To see the marriage rites solemnised;

    And, in the presence of the court of Spain,   45

    To knit a sure, inexplicable band

    Of kingly love, and everlasting league,

---

26   *the articles* the marriage alliance which will unite Spain with Portugal, the royal priority which is going to supplant Hieronimo's plea.

31   *go by go by* This much-quoted phrase, meaning be careful, don't get into trouble, marks Hieronimo's recognition that he will not get justice from the king, let alone revenge; the Ambassador's stately speech that follows about the political situation overrides Hieronimo's personal concern.

46   *inexplicable* (*1594*); *1592*'s '*inexecrable*' does not make much sense; Edwards suggested that the *1594* reading which is better might have been taken from a press correction in a copy of *1592* that has not survived; throughout this final section of *1592* the text seems deficient in a number of places.

Betwixt the crowns of Spain and Portingale,
There will he give his crown to Balthazar,
And make a queen of Bel-Imperia.   50
KING
Brother, how like you this our viceroy's love?
CASTILE
No doubt, my lord, it is an argument
Of honourable care to keep his friend,
And wondrous zeal to Balthazar his son;
Nor am I least indebted to his grace,   55
That bends his liking to my daughter thus.
AMBASSADOR
Now last, dread lord, here hath his highness sent
(Although he send not that his son return)
His ransom due to Don Horatio.
HIERONIMO
Horatio! who calls Horatio?   60
KING
And well remembered, thank his majesty.
Here, see it given to Horatio.
HIERONIMO
Justice, O justice, justice, gentle king!
KING
What is that? Hieronimo?
HIERONIMO
Justice, O, justice! O my son, my son,   65
My son, whom naught can ransom or redeem!
LORENZO
Hieronimo, you are not well-advised.
HIERONIMO
Away, Lorenzo, hinder me no more,
For thou hast made me bankrupt of my bliss.
Give me my son, you shall not ransom him!   70

---

50 The Ambassador's declaration of the Portuguese king's readiness to give his crown
    to Balthazar makes the political case for the marriage completely convincing.
58 *that* in order that.
62 The king's ignorance of Horatio's death is left unexplained, but may be seen as a
    result of Lorenzo's machinations; Castile seems equally unaware of Horatio's death,
    possibly a consequence of the youth's low rank, like Andrea's; Lorenzo later (85–9)
    avoids saying that Horatio is dead, and claims Hieronimo's hysteria is from greed
    over the ransom.

Away! I'll rip the bowels of the earth,
                              He diggeth with his dagger
And ferry over to th' Elysian plains,
And bring my son to show his deadly wounds.
Stand from about me!
I'll make a pickaxe of my poniard,   75
And here surrender up my marshalship:
For I'll go marshal up the fiends in hell,
To be avenged on you all for this.

KING
What means this outrage?
Will none of you restrain his fury?   80

HIERONIMO
Nay, soft and fair: you shall not need to strive,
Needs must he go that the devils drive.   *Exit*

KING
What accident hath happed Hieronimo?
I have not seen him to demean him so.

LORENZO
My gracious lord, he is with extreme pride,   85
Conceived of young Horatio his son,
And covetous of having to himself
The ransom of the young prince Balthazar,
Distract, and in a manner lunatic.

KING
Believe me, nephew, we are sorry for't: 90
This is the love that fathers bear their sons.
But, gentle brother, go give to him this gold,
The prince's ransom; let him have his due.
For what he hath Horatio shall not want:
Haply Hieronimo hath need thereof.   95

LORENZO
But if he be thus helplessly distract,
'Tis requisite his office be resigned,
And given to one of more discretion.

KING
We shall increase his melancholy so.
'Tis best that we see further in it first;   100

---

71   s.d. *his dagger* Hieronimo would wear both the sword that every gentleman carried
      and a dagger; conceivably the same poniard he held at the beginning of the scene.

Till when, ourself will exempt the place.
And brother, now bring in the ambassador,
That he may be a witness of the match
'Twixt Balthazar and Bel-Imperia,
And that we may prefix a certain time,   105
Wherein the marriage shall be solemnised,
That we may have thy lord the viceroy here.

AMBASSADOR

Therein your highness highly shall content
His majesty, that longs to hear from hence.

KING

On, then, and hear you, Lord Ambassador.   110

Exeunt

---

101   *ourself will exempt the place* either 'we will take his place as Marshal,' or 'we will hold
      the post in suspense for him'; either course would save Hieronimo from being
      replaced. Collier suggested the word should be 'execute', which is better metrically
      but does not make a very obvious compositor's misreading.

ACT III, SCENE xiii

Enter HIERONIMO *with a book in his hand*

HIERONIMO
  Vindicta mihi!
  Ay, heaven will be revenged of every ill,
  Nor will they suffer murder unrepaid:
  Then stay, Hieronimo, attend their will,
  For mortal men may not appoint their time.   5
  'Per scelus semper tutum est sceleribus iter.'
  Strike, and strike home, where wrong is offered thee;
  For evils unto ills conductors be,
  And death's the worst of resolution.
  For he that thinks with patience to contend   10
  To quiet life, his life shall easily end.
  'Fata si miseros juvant, habes salutem;
  Fata si vitam negant, habes sepulchrum.'
  If destiny thy miseries do ease,
  Then hast thou health, and happy shalt thou be;   15
  If destiny deny thee life, Hieronimo,
  Yet shalt thou be assured of a tomb;
  If neither, yet let this thy comfort be,
  Heaven covereth him that hath no burial.
  And to conclude, I will revenge his death!   20
  But how? not as the vulgar wits of men,
  With open, but inevitable ills,

---

  1   *Vindicta mihi!* The scene of Hieronimo's decision-making starts with a well-known quotation from the New Testament, Romans 12.19, where God is said to declare that vengeance is exclusive to Him, not ordinary humans. In line 6 Hieronimo counters this biblical injunction with a quotation from the book of Seneca he holds in his hand.

  6   This quotation, 'The safe way with crime is more crime,' Seneca's *Agamemnon* line 155, makes him think that adopting Christian patience will allow Lorenzo after killing Horatio to kill Hieronimo too.

  9   *death's the worst of resolution* the worst that comes from being firmly resolved is death.

12–13   Seneca, *Troades*, 511–12, translated in lines 14–17 following.

 18   *neither* not health or death.

 22   *open, but inevitable* predictable public success.

As by a secret, yet a certain mean,
Which under kindship will be cloaked best.
Wise men will take their opportunity,   25
Closely and safely fitting things to time.
But in extremes advantage hath no time;
And therefore all times fit not for revenge.
Thus therefore will I rest me in unrest,
Dissembling quiet in unquietness,   30
Not seeming that I know their villainies;
That my simplicity may make them think
That ignorantly I will let all slip –
For ignorance, I wot, and well they know,
Remedium malorum iners est.   35
Nor aught avails it me to menace them,
Who, as a wintry storm upon a plain,
Will bear me down with their nobility.
No, no, Hieronimo, thou must enjoin
Thine eyes to observation, and thy tongue   40
To milder speeches than thy spirit affords,
Thy heart to patience, and thy hands to rest,
Thy cap to courtesy, and thy knee to bow,
Till to revenge thou know, when, where and how.

A noise within

How now, what noise? what coil is that you keep?   45

Enter a SERVANT

SERVANT

Here are a sort of poor petitioners,
That are importunate, and it shall please you, sir,
That you should plead their cases to the king.

23   *a certain mean* (like Lorenzo), action hidden yet certain.
24   *kindship* kindness, friendliness.
27–8 'there is no advantage when things are at an extreme, so revenge needs to wait its
      opportunity'.
30   *quiet in unquietness* a pair of oxymorons, pretending calm when he is on edge.
35   (ignorance) 'is a poor antidote to evil,' another quotation from Seneca, *Oedipus*,
      515.
38   *nobility* social elevation, a sarcastic point here.
42   *patience* the Christian virtue must now be used as part of the aim of revenge.
44   s.d. *A noise within* loud voices from the tiring house; at the moment when
      Hieronimo decides what he must do, the petitioners interrupt him; some of the
      'Additions' appear to perform a similar function in holding up the plot at this point.

89

HIERONIMO

    That I should plead their several actions?

    Why, let them enter, and let me see them.   50

Enter three CITIZENS *and an* OLD MAN

1 CITIZEN

    So, I tell you this, for learning and for law,

    There's not any advocate in Spain

    That can prevail, or will take half the pain

    That he will, in pursuit of equity.

HIERONIMO

    Come near, you men, that thus importune me.   55

    [*Aside*] Now must I bear a face of gravity,

    For thus I used, before my marshalship,

    To plead in causes as corregidor. –

    Come on sirs, what's the matter?

2 CITIZEN   Sir, an action.

HIERONIMO

    Of battery?

1 CITIZEN   Mine of debt.

HIERONIMO   Give place.   60

2 CITIZEN

    No sir, mine is an action of the case.

3 CITIZEN

    Mine an *ejectione firmae* by a lease.

HIERONIMO

    Content you sirs, are you determined

    That I should plead your several actions?

1 CITIZEN

    Ay sir, and here's my declaration.   65

2 CITIZEN

    And here is my band.

3 CITIZEN   And here is my lease.

                         They give him papers

HIERONIMO

    But wherefore stands yon silly man so mute,

    With mournful eyes and hands to heaven upreared?

    Come hither, father, let me know thy cause.

---

58   *corregidor* (Spanish) advocate, the chief magistrate of a Spanish town.

62   *ejectione firmae* (*1592 firma*) a writ to remove a tenant before the lease expires.

SENEX

    O worthy sir, my cause, but slightly known,   70
    May move the hearts of warlike Myrmidons
    And melt the Corsic rocks with ruthful tears.

HIERONIMO

    Say, father, tell me what's thy suit?

SENEX

    No sir, could my woes
    Give way unto my most distressful words,   75
    Then should I not in paper, as you see,
    With ink bewray what blood began in me.

HIERONIMO

    What's here? 'The humble supplication
    Of Don Bazulto for his murdered son.'

SENEX

    Ay sir.

HIERONIMO No sir, it was my murdered son,   80
    O my son, my son, O my son Horatio!
    But mine, or thine, Bazulto, be content.
    Here, take my handkercher, and wipe thine eyes,
    Whiles wretched I in thy mishaps may see
    The lively portrait of my dying self.   85

                  He draweth out a bloody napkin

    O no, not this: Horatio, this was thine,
    And when I dyed it in thy dearest blood,
    This was a token 'twixt thy soul and me
    That of thy death revenged I should be.
    But here, take this, and this – what, my purse? –   90
    Ay, this, and that, and all of them are thine;
    For all as one are our extremities.

1 CITIZEN

    O see the kindness of Hieronimo!

2 CITIZEN

    This gentleness shows him a gentleman.

---

71   *Myrmidons* fierce soldiers, followers of Achilles.
72   *Corsic* of Corsica, where Seneca lived in exile; his *Octavia* refers to its 'craggy' rocks.
79   *Don Bazulto* The fourth 'Addition' has sometimes been thought of as a replacement
      for this scene, since the painter who features in it is called 'Bazurdo'.
92   *extremities* Hieronimo has already said that revenge's time suffers from '*extremes*'
      (l. 27); here he says all suffering is the same extreme.

HIERONIMO

    See, see, O see thy shame, Hieronimo,   95
    See here a loving father to his son!
    Behold the sorrows and the sad laments
    That he delivereth for his son's decease!
    If love's effects so strives in lesser things,
    If love enforce such moods in meaner wits,   100
    If love express such power in poor estates –
    Hieronimo, whenas a raging sea
    Tossed with the wind and tide, o'erturneth then
    The upper billows, course of waves to keep,
    Whilst lesser waters labour in the deep,   105
    Then sham'st thou not, Hieronimo, to neglect
    The sweet revenge of thy Horatio?
    Though on this earth justice will not be found,
    I'll down to hell, and in this passion
    Knock at the dismal gates of Pluto's court,   110
    Getting by force, as once Alcides did,
    A troop of Furies and tormenting hags
    To torture Don Lorenzo and the rest.
    Yet lest the triple-headed porter should
    Deny my passage to the slimy strond,   115
    The Thracian poet thou shalt counterfeit:
    Come on, old father, be my Orpheus,
    And if thou canst no notes upon the harp,
    Then sound the burden of thy sore heart's grief,
    Till we do gain that Proserpine may grant   120
    Revenge on them that murdered my son.
    Then will I rent and tear them thus and thus,
    Shivering their limbs in pieces with my teeth.

Tear the papers

1 CITIZEN

    O sir, my declaration!

---

109   *I'll down to hell* where Andrea went.
111   *Alcides* Hercules, whose twelfth labour required to him go to hell and defeat its
        watchdog Cerberus, the 'triple-headed porter' (line 114).
114   *triple-headed porter* Cerberus, the three-headed dog guarding the entrance to Hades,
        and charmed by Orpheus.
115   *strond* see I.i.27–9.
116   *Thracian poet* Orpheus, who descended to the underworld to appeal to Proserpine
        to return his wife Eurydice. He charmed ths shades of the dead with his music.
120   *that Proserpine may grant* We already know that she has granted Andrea's request.

Exit HIERONIMO *and they after*

2 CITIZEN

Save my bond!   125

Enter HIERONIMO

2 CITIZEN

Save my bond!

3 CITIZEN

Alas, my lease! it cost me ten pound,

And you, my lord, have torn the same.

HIERONIMO

That cannot be, I gave it never a wound;

Show me one drop of blood fall from the same: 130

How is it possible I should slay it then?

Tush, no; run after, catch me if you can.

Exeunt all but the OLD MAN

BAZULTO *remains till* HIERONIMO *enters again,*
who, staring him in the face, speaks

HIERONIMO

And art thou come, Horatio, from the depth,

To ask for justice in this upper earth?

To tell thy father thou art unrevenged,   135

To wring more tears from Isabella's eyes,

Whose lights are dimmed with over-long laments?

Go back my son, complain to Aeacus,

For here's no justice; gentle boy be gone,

For justice is exiled from the earth;   140

Hieronimo will bear thee company.

Thy mother cries on righteous Rhadamanth

For just revenge against the murderers.

SENEX

Alas my lord, whence springs this troubled speech?

HIERONIMO

But let me look on my Horatio.   145

Sweet boy, how art thou changed in death's black shade!

Had Proserpine no pity on thy youth,

---

133   Hieronimo addresses the old man as if he were Horatio, as Hamlet addresses his
        father's ghost in the closet scene.

138   *Aeacus* the second underworld judge named by Andrea at I.i.33.

142   *Rhadamanth* the third underworld judge.

But suffered thy fair crimson-coloured spring
With withered winter to be blasted thus?
Horatio, thou art older than thy father;   150
Ah ruthless fate, that favour thus transforms!

SENEX

Ah my good lord, I am not your young son.

HIERONIMO

What, not my son? thou, then, a Fury art,
Sent from the empty kingdom of black night
To summon me to make appearance   155
Before grim Minos and just Rhadamanth,
To plague Hieronimo that is remiss,
And seeks not vengeance for Horatio's death.

SENEX

I am a grieved man, and not a ghost,
That came for justice for my murdered son.   160

HIERONIMO

Ay, now I know thee, now thou nam'st thy son;
Thou art the lively image of my grief:
Within thy face my sorrows I may see.
Thy eyes are gummed with tears, thy cheeks are wan,
Thy forehead troubled, and thy muttering lips   165
Murmur sad words abruptly broken off
By force of windy sighs thy spirit breathes;
And all this sorrow riseth for thy son:
And selfsame sorrow feel I for my son.
Come in old man, thou shalt to Isabel;   170
Lean on my arm: I thee, thou me shalt stay,
And thou, and I, and she, will sing a song,
Three parts in one, but all of discords framed –
Talk not of cords, but let us now be gone,
For with a cord Horatio was slain.   175

Exeunt

150   *older than thy father* The ballad version of *The Spanish Tragedy* mentions Hieronimo's
       'silvered hair'.
153   *a Fury* an avenging spirit.
156   *Minos* the first of the three underworld judges.
174   *cords* the rope that hanged Horatio, and musical chords.

ACT III, SCENE xiv

Enter KING *of* SPAIN, *the* DUKE, VICEROY, *and* LORENZO,
BALTHAZAR, DON PEDRO, *and* BEL-IMPERIA

KING

Go brother, it is the Duke of Castile's cause,
Salute the viceroy in our name.

CASTILE   I go.

VICEROY

Go forth, Don Pedro, for thy nephew's sake,
And greet the Duke of Castile.

PEDRO   It shall be so.

KING

And now to meet these Portuguese,   5
For as we now are, so sometimes were these,
Kings and commanders of the western Indies.
Welcome, brave viceroy, to the court of Spain,
And welcome all his honourable train.
'Tis not unknown to us, for why you come,   10
Or have so kingly crossed the seas:
Sufficeth it, in this we note the troth
And more than common love you lend to us.
So is it that mine honourable niece,
(For it beseems us now that it be known)   15

---

1   *it is the Duke of Castile's cause* Not the king but his brother must pursue the marriage
    of his daughter Bel-Imperia to the Portuguese heir; Castile's paternal role in forcing
    her to marry Balthazar for political reasons, emphasized here, could be the reason
    for Hieronimo killing him in his final act of revenge.
3   *thy nephew* Like the Spanish king, the Portuguese king (viceroy) has a (not historical)
    brother; he may be the Don Pedro of I.ii.40.
6–7 Portugal's control of Brazil by papal decree was a long-running trouble to the
    Spanish, who colonized the rest of central and southern America; Spain's takeover
    of Portugal and all its territories in 1580 was part of what drew Kyd into this play.
11 *crossed the seas* Critics have wrongly mocked Kyd for not knowing that Portugal and
    Spain shared a land frontier; the Duke of Alba's army, however, took a month to get
    from Bajadoz on the Spanish border to Lisbon because the roads were appallingly
    bad, even for horses; travel round the coast by sea was the standard means of access
    for royal parties.
12 *the troth* loyalty, faith, as in romantic love.

Already is betrothed to Balthazar,
And by appointment and our condescent
To-morrow are they to be married.
To this intent we entertain thyself,
Thy followers, their pleasure and our peace.   20
Speak, men of Portingale, shall it be so?
If ay, say so; if not, say flatly no.

VICEROY

Renowned king, I come not as thou think'st,
With doubtful followers, unresolved men,
But such as have upon thine articles   25
Confirmed thy motion and contented me.
Know sovereign, I come to solemnise
The marriage of thy beloved niece,
Fair Bel-Imperia, with my Balthazar –
With thee, my son; whom sith I live to see,   30
Here take my crown, I give it her and thee;
And let me live a solitary life,
In ceaseless prayers,
To think how strangely heaven hath thee preserved.

KING

See brother, see, how nature strives in him!   35
Come, worthy viceroy, and accompany
Thy friend with thine extremities;
A place more private fits this princely mood.

VICEROY

Or here or where your highness thinks it good.
                    Exeunt all but CASTILE *and* LORENZO

CASTILE

Nay stay, Lorenzo, let me talk with you.   40
See'st thou this entertainment of these kings?

LORENZO

I do, my lord, and joy to see the same.

CASTILE

And knowest thou why this meeting is?

---

17   *condescent* agreement, gracious condescension.
31   *Here take my crown* The Portuguese king's withdrawal elevates Balthazar, and so in
     some degree removes him from the scope of Hieronimo's revenge.
35   *nature strives in him* he weeps with joy to see his son alive.
40   *let me talk with you* As Bel-Imperia's brother, Lorenzo must have been thought the
     heir apparent to the Spanish throne, but the play ignores this possibility except when
     Hieronimo calls him 'the hope of Spain' at line 140 in this scene.

LORENZO

    For her, my lord, whom Balthazar doth love,

    And to confirm their promised marriage.   45

CASTILE

    She is thy sister?

LORENZO   Who, Bel-Imperia?

    Ay, my gracious lord, and this is the day

    That I have longed so happily to see.

CASTILE

    Thou wouldst be loath that any fault of thine

    Should intercept her in her happiness.   50

LORENZO

    Heavens will not let Lorenzo err so much.

CASTILE

    Why then, Lorenzo, listen to my words:

    It is suspected and reported too,

    That thou, Lorenzo, wrong'st Hieronimo,

    And in his suits towards his majesty   55

    Still keep'st him back, and seeks to cross his suit.

LORENZO

    That I, my lord – ?

CASTILE

    I tell thee son, myself have heard it said,

    When, to my sorrow, I have been ashamed

    To answer for thee, though thou art my son.   60

    Lorenzo, knowest thou not the common love

    And kindness that Hieronimo hath won

    By his deserts within the court of Spain?

    Or seest thou not the king my brother's care

    In his behalf, and to procure his health?   65

    Lorenzo, shouldst thou thwart his passions,

    And he exclaim against thee to the king,

    What honour were't in this assembly,

    Or what a scandal were't among the kings

    To hear Hieronimo exclaim on thee?   70

    Tell me, and look thou tell me truly too,

    Whence grows the ground of this report in court?

LORENZO

    My lord, it lies not in Lorenzo's power

53–72   Castile takes a while to come to the point; his question at line 72 is that of an honestly
       concerned father.

To stop the vulgar, liberal of their tongues:
A small advantage makes a water-breach,   75
And no man lives that long contenteth all.

CASTILE
Myself have seen thee busy to keep back
Him and his supplications from the king.

LORENZO
Yourself, my lord, hath seen his passions,
That ill beseemed the presence of a king;   80
And for I pitied him in his distress,
I held him thence with kind and courteous words,
As free from malice to Hieronimo
As to my soul, my lord.

CASTILE
Hieronimo, my son, mistakes thee then.   85

LORENZO
My gracious father, believe me so he doth.
But what's a silly man, distract in mind,
To think upon the murder of his son?
Alas, how easy is it for him to err!
But for his satisfaction and the world's,   90
'Twere good, my lord, that Hieronimo and I
Were reconciled, if he misconster me.

CASTILE
Lorenzo, thou hast said; it shall be so;
Go one of you and call Hieronimo.

Enter BALTHAZAR *and* BEL-IMPERIA

BALTHAZAR
Come, Bel-Imperia, Balthazar's content,   95
My sorrow's ease and sovereign of my bliss,
Sith heaven hath ordained thee to be mine;
Disperse those clouds and melancholy looks,
And clear them up with those thy sun-bright eyes,
Wherein my hope and heaven's fair beauty lies.   100

---

75   *advantage* opportunity, weakness.
      a water-breach a gap in a dyke or weir through which water can pour.
79–92 Lorenzo uses his skill at lying to allay his father's worry, although the murder of
      Horatio is evidently known to the court, since Lorenzo says that 'the murder of his
      son' (88) is one reason for Hieronimo's lunacy.
92   *misconster* wilfully misunderstand.

BEL-IMPERIA
  My looks, my lord, are fitting for my love,
  Which new begun, can show no brighter yet.
BALTHAZAR
  New kindled flames should burn as morning sun.
BEL-IMPERIA
  But not too fast, lest heat and all be done.
  I see my lord my father.
BALTHAZAR   Truce, my love;   105
  I will go salute him.
CASTILE   Welcome, Balthazar,
  Welcome brave prince, the pledge of Castile's peace;
  And welcome Bel-Imperia. How now, girl?
  Why com'st thou sadly to salute us thus?
  Content thyself, for I am satisfied;   110
  It is not now as when Andrea lived,
  We have forgotten and forgiven that,
  And thou art graced with a happier love.
  But Balthazar, here comes Hieronimo,
  I'll have a word with him.   115

                Enter HIERONIMO *and a* SERVANT

HIERONIMO
  And where's the duke?
SERVANT   Yonder.
HIERONIMO   Even so:
  What new device have they devised, trow?
  Pocas palabras! mild as the lamb,
  Is't I will be revenged? No, I am not the man.
CASTILE
  Welcome Hieronimo.   120
LORENZO
  Welcome Hieronimo.

---

102   *no brighter* The *1592* text, corrected in *1594*, omits 'no', which destroys the metre.
105   *Truce* Balthazar asks for a temporary cessation of Bel-Imperia's repartee.
109   *sadly* with a serious face; Castile is trying to make peace with his daughter after the
      breach that brought his anger onto her over Andrea, as he acknowledges.
117   *device have they devised* Hieronimo is suspicious of both father and son plotting
      against him.
      trow in truth.
118   *Pocas palabras!* 'few words', an exclamation in Spanish, unlike Lorenzo's Italian.

BALTHAZAR
  Welcome Hieronimo.
HIERONIMO
  My lords, I thank you for Horatio.
CASTILE
  Hieronimo, the reason that I sent
  To speak with you, is this.
HIERONIMO   What, so short?   125
  Then I'll be gone, I thank you for't.
CASTILE
  Nay, stay, Hieronimo – go call him, son.
LORENZO
  Hieronimo, my father craves a word with you.
HIERONIMO
  With me sir? why, my lord, I thought you had done.
LORENZO
  [*Aside*] No, would he had.
CASTILE   Hieronimo, I hear   130
  You find yourself aggrieved at my son
  Because you have not access unto the king,
  And say 'tis he that intercepts your suits.
HIERONIMO
  Why, is not this a miserable thing, my lord?
CASTILE
  Hieronimo, I hope you have no cause,   135
  And would be loath that one of your deserts
  Should once have reason to suspect my son,
  Considering how I think of you myself.
HIERONIMO
  Your son Lorenzo! whom, my noble lord?
  The hope of Spain, mine honourable friend?   140
  Grant me the combat of them, if they dare:
                                    Draws out his sword
  I'll meet him face to face, to tell me so.
  These be the scandalous reports of such
  As love not me, and hate my lord too much.
  Should I suspect Lorenzo would prevent   145

123   *I thank you for Horatio* Hieronimo links all three as responsible for his son's death,
      a warning that all three will suffer from his revenge, as they do.
141   *the combat of them* the right to meet them in a formal fight.

Or cross my suit, that loved my son so well?
My lord, I am ashamed it should be said.

LORENZO

Hieronimo, I never gave you cause.

HIERONIMO

My good lord, I know you did not.

CASTILE   There then pause,
And for the satisfaction of the world,   150
Hieronimo, frequent my homely house,
The Duke of Castile, Cyprian's ancient seat,
And when thou wilt, use me, my son, and it.
But here, before Prince Balthazar and me,
Embrace each other, and be perfect friends.   155

HIERONIMO

Ay marry, my lord, and shall.
Friends, quoth he? see, I'll be friends with you all:
Specially with you, my lovely lord;
For divers causes it is fit for us
That we be friends – the world is suspicious,   160
And men may think what we imagine not.

BALTHAZAR

Why, this is friendly done, Hieronimo.

LORENZO

And thus I hope old grudges are forgot.

HIERONIMO

What else? it were a shame it should not be so.

CASTILE

Come on, Hieronimo, at my request;   165
Let us intreat your company today.
                    Exeunt [*all but* HIERONIMO]

HIERONIMO

Your lordship's to command. – Pha! keep your way:
Chi mi fa più carezze che non suole,
Tradito mi ha, o tradir vuole.   *Exit*

146   *cross* block; Hieronimo is using Lorenzo's guile against him.
158   *my lovely lord* i.e. Lorenzo; Balthazar is as usual a clumsy accessory to the Spanish trickster.
167   *Pha!* an exclamation of disgust, Hieronimo drops into Lorenzo's favoured Italian, his own Machiavellian mode now, for his parting words, saying 'He who gives me more caresses than usual is busy betraying me, or trying to'; much of the Italian in this section of the text is corrupt, and seems to be phonetically transcribed.

ACT III, SCENE xv

Ghost [of ANDREA*] and* REVENGE

ANDREA
   Awake, Erichtho! Cerberus, awake!
   Solicit Pluto, gentle Proserpine;
   To combat, Acheron and Erebus!
   For ne'er by Styx and Phlegethon in hell

     5
   Nor ferried Charon to the fiery lakes
   Such fearful sights, as poor Andrea sees!
   Revenge, awake!
REVENGE
   Awake? for why?
ANDREA
   Awake, Revenge, for thou art ill-advised   10
   To sleep away what thou art warned to watch!
REVENGE
   Content thyself, and do not trouble me.
ANDREA
   Awake, Revenge, if love, as love hath had,
   Have yet the power or prevalence in hell!
   Hieronimo with Lorenzo is joined in league,   15
   And intercepts our passage to revenge:
   Awake, Revenge, or we are woe-begone!

1 Andrea, now called '*Ghost*' in the *1592* text, leaps up from his stool in fury; at the end of the scene, appeased, he resumes his stool when he says (39) '*for I will sit to see the rest*'.
1 *Erichtho* a sorceress and poisoner of Thessaly, one of the Furies according to Ovid; it may be an error for Alecto, who was certainly a Fury.
3 *Acheron and Erebus* the grim river of hell and primeval darkness.
4 *Styx and Phlegethon* rivers of the underworld.
5 A line seems to have been accidentally omitted here, expressing what Andrea witnessed in hell; he thinks Hieronimo's apparent alliance with Lorenzo an appalling monstrosity.
6 *Charon* the ferryman over the river into the underworld; see I.i.20.
17 *woe-begone* stricken with grief (*1592* 'woe degone').

REVENGE

> Thus worldlings ground, what they have dreamed, upon.
> Content thyself, Andrea: though I sleep,
> Yet is my mood soliciting their souls; 20
> Sufficeth thee that poor Hieronimo
> Cannot forget his son Horatio.
> Nor dies Revenge although he sleep awhile,
> For in unquiet, quietness is feigned,
> And slumbering is a common worldly wile. 25
> Behold, Andrea, for an instance how
> Revenge hath slept, and then imagine thou
> What 'tis to be subject to destiny.

Enter a Dumb Show [they act and exeunt]

ANDREA

> Awake, Revenge, reveal this mystery.

REVENGE

> The two first, the nuptial torches bore, 30
> As brightly burning as the mid-day's sun;
> But after them doth Hymen hie as fast,
> Clothed in sable, and a saffron robe,
> And blows them out, and quencheth them with blood,
> As discontent that things continue so. 35

ANDREA

> Sufficeth me; thy meaning's understood;
> And thanks to thee and those infernal powers
> That will not tolerate a lover's woe.
> Rest thee, for I will sit to see the rest.

REVENGE

> Then argue not, for thou hast thy request. 40

Exeunt

---

18 Worldlings ground their beliefs on dreams and fancy.
24 *in unquiet ... feigned* just what Hieronimo said at III.xiii.30.
26 *an instance* an example, an action symbolizing what is in Revenge's mood.
28 s.d. *Dumb Show* a mute 'mask' like the one devised by Hieronimo for the court in I.iv; Revenge explains what the audience has just seen, a bleak inversion of a wedding ceremony, where Hymen as the god of marriage with black covering his normal saffron robes puts out the nuptial torches in pots of blood.

Enter BEL-IMPERIA *and* HIERONIMO

BEL-IMPERIA

    Is this the love thou bear'st Horatio?
    Is this the kindness that thou counterfeits?
    Are these the fruits of thine incessant tears?
    Hieronimo, are these thy passions,
    Thy protestations and thy deep laments,   5
    That thou wert wont to weary men withal?
    O unkind father, O deceitful world!
    With what excuses canst thou show thyself,
    What what . . . .
    From this dishonour and the hate of men? –   10
    Thus to neglect the loss and life of him
    Whom both my letters and thine own belief
    Assures thee to be causeless slaughtered.
    Hieronimo, for shame, Hieronimo,
    Be not a history to after times   15
    Of such ingratitude unto thy son.
    Unhappy mothers of such children then –
    But monstrous fathers, to forget so soon
    The death of those, whom they with care and cost
    Have tendered so, thus careless should be lost.   20
    Myself a stranger in respect of thee,
    So loved his life, as still I wish their deaths;
    Nor shall his death be unrevenged by me,
    Although I bear it out for fashion's sake:
    For here I swear in sight of heaven and earth,   25
    Shouldst thou neglect the love thou shouldst retain
    And give it over and devise no more,

---

  9   The *1592* text gives 'dishonour, and the hate of men,' twice, at lines 9 and 10, an
      obvious case of compositor eyeskip, with most of the first line lost, and the second
      word of line 9 possibly repeated from 8.
17–20 The absence of a verb here has been seen as ungrammatical, but the exclamatory
      form of Bel-Imperia's speech makes one unnecessary.
  20   *tendered* cherished.
  24   *bear it out for fashion's sake* i.e. do what Hieronimo has been doing.

Myself should send their hateful souls to hell,
That wrought his downfall with extremest death.

HIERONIMO

But may it be that Bel-Imperia   30
Vows such revenge as she hath deigned to say?
Why then, I see that heaven applies our drift
And all the saints do sit soliciting
For vengeance on those cursed murderers.
Madam 'tis true, and now I find it so;   35
I found a letter, written in your name,
And in that letter, how Horatio died.
Pardon, O pardon, Bel-Imperia,
My fear and care in not believing it,
Nor think I thoughtless think upon a mean   40
To let his death be unrevenged at full;
And here I vow, so you but give consent,
And will conceal my resolution,
I will ere long determine of their deaths
That causeless thus have murdered my son.   45

BEL-IMPERIA

Hieronimo, I will consent, conceal;
And aught that may effect for thine avail
Join with thee to revenge Horatio's death.

HIERONIMO

On then; whatsoever I devise,
Let me entreat you, grace my practices.   50
For why, the plot's already in mine head.
Here they are.

Enter BALTHAZAR *and* LORENZO

31   *deigned* condescended; Hieronimo is implying that her new dignity as queen of
     Portugal might be found unsuited to the personal act of revenge.
32   *applies our drift* supports our aim.
40   *Nor think I thoughtless think* Do not believe that I am mindlessly prepared to let go.
45   *causeless* Castile tells Hieronimo 'I hope you have no cause' against Lorenzo at
     III.xiv.135 and Lorenzo repeats the word at 148; its judicial sense, used by Othello
     when he thinks he must kill Desdemona, is a heavy term here for the unjustified
     murder which is to be revenged.
49   *devise* This term now becomes the word for machiavellian plotting, as does 'practices'
     in the next line; everything that Hieronimo speaks to Lorenzo and Balthazar from
     here on is packed with his own devious practices.
51   *For why* because.

BALTHAZAR   How now, Hieronimo?
  What, courting Bel-Imperia?
HIERONIMO   Ay, my lord,
  Such courting as, I promise you,
  She hath my heart, but you, my lord, have hers.   55
LORENZO
  But now, Hieronimo, or never,
  We are to entreat your help.
HIERONIMO   My help?
  Why, my good lords, assure yourselves of me,
  For you have given me cause,
  Ay, by my faith have you.
BALTHAZAR   It pleased you   60
  At the entertainment of the ambassador
  To grace the king so much as with a show:
  Now were your study so well furnished,
  As, for the passing of the first night's sport,
  To entertain my father with the like,   65
  Or any such-like pleasing motion,
  Assure yourself it would content them well.
HIERONIMO
  Is this all?
BALTHAZAR
  Ay, this is all.
HIERONIMO
  Why then I'll fit you; say no more.   70
  When I was young I gave my mind
  And plied myself to fruitless poetry:
  Which though it profit the professor naught,
  Yet is it passing pleasing to the world.
LORENZO
  And how for that?
HIERONIMO   Marry, my good lord, thus –   75
  And yet, methinks, you are too quick with us –

---

62 *with a show* It is one of Kyd's neater ironies that Hieronimo gets his chance to
    commit revenge through an innocently generous act of Lorenzo's.

70 *I'll fit you* Another much-quoted phrase of Hieronimo; it means both 'I'll provide
    what you want,' and 'I'll pay you back'.

73 *professor* the one who practises it.

75 *my good lord* the standard form of address Hieronimo uses to Lorenzo, although his
    'good' is more pointed than usual; at III.xiv.158 he calls him 'my lovely lord'.

76 *too quick* too pressing, with a hint of 'quick' meaning alive.

When in Toledo there I studied,
It was my chance to write a tragedy –
See here my lords –   *He shows them a book*
Which long forgot, I found this other day.   80
Now would your lordships favour me so much
As but to grace me with your acting it –
I mean each one of you to play a part –
Assure you it will prove most passing strange
And wondrous plausible to that assembly.   85

BALTHAZAR
What, would you have us play a tragedy?

HIERONIMO
Why, Nero thought it no disparagement,
And kings and emperors have ta'en delight
To make experience of their wits in plays!

LORENZO
Nay, be not angry good Hieronimo,   90
The prince but asked a question.

BALTHAZAR
In faith, Hieronimo, and you be in earnest,
I'll make one.

LORENZO
And I another.

HIERONIMO
Now my good lord, could you entreat   95
Your sister Bel-Imperia to make one?
For what's a play without a woman in it?

BEL-IMPERIA
Little entreaty shall serve me, Hieronimo,
For I must needs be employed in your play.

HIERONIMO
Why, this is well; I tell you lordings,   100
It was determined to have been acted
By gentlemen and scholars too
Such as could tell what to speak.

85   *plausible* (*a*) appealing, worthy of applause, (*b*) realistic.
87   *Nero thought it* the allusion that Heywood remembered twenty years later, in *An Apology for Actors*.
92   *and* if.
97   *without a woman in it* an in-joke, since in Kyd's time boys played all the women's parts such as Bel-Imperia.

BALTHAZAR

    And now it shall be played by princes and courtiers,
    Such as can tell how to speak,   105
    If, as it is our country manner,
    You will but let us know the argument.

HIERONIMO

    That shall I roundly. The chronicles of Spain
    Record this written of a knight of Rhodes:
    He was betrothed, and wedded at the length   110
    To one Perseda, an Italian dame,
    Whose beauty ravished all that her beheld,
    Especially the soul of Soliman,
    Who at the marriage was the chiefest guest.
    By sundry means sought Soliman to win   115
    Perseda's love, and could not gain the same.
    Then gan he break his passions to a friend,
    One of his bashaws whom he held full dear;
    Her had this bashaw long solicited,
    And saw she was not otherwise to be won   120
    But by her husband's death, this knight of Rhodes,
    Whom presently by treachery he slew.
    She, stirred with an exceeding hate therefore,
    As cause of this slew Soliman;
    And to escape the bashaw's tyranny   125
    Did stab herself: and this the tragedy.

LORENZO

    O excellent!

BEL-IMPERIA But say, Hieronimo,
    What then became of him that was the bashaw?

HIERONIMO

    Marry thus: moved with remorse of his misdeeds,
    Ran to a mountain-top and hung himself.   130

BALTHAZAR

    But which of us is to perform that part?

---

107   *the argument* the gist of the story; in *Hamlet* before the play within the play starts the
      worried Claudius asks Hamlet 'Have you heard the argument? Is there no offence in it?'.

111   *Perseda* A play called *Soliman and Perseda* was printed in 1592, the same year as the
      first extant text of *The Spanish Tragedy*. Often thought to be by Kyd, its style is quite
      distinct, though Hieronimo's summary of its 'argument' here is faithful to it;
      Hieronimo's claim to have written it when a student should not be taken as a
      concealed boast about Kyd's own composition.

118   *bashaws* pashas, Turkish officers of high rank.

HIERONIMO

O, that will I my lords, make no doubt of it:
I'll play the murderer, I warrant you,
For I already have conceited that.

BALTHAZAR

And what shall I?   135

HIERONIMO

Great Soliman the Turkish emperor.

LORENZO

And I?

HIERONIMO

Erastus the knight of Rhodes.

BEL-IMPERIA

And I?

HIERONIMO

Perseda, chaste and resolute.   140
And here, my lords, are several abstracts drawn,
For each of you to note your parts,
And act it, as occasion's offered you.
You must provide a Turkish cap,
A black mustachio and a fauchion.   145

Gives a paper to BALTHAZAR

You with a cross like to a knight of Rhodes.

Gives another to LORENZO

And madam, you must attire yourself

He giveth BEL-IMPERIA *another*

Like Phoebe, Flora, or the Huntress,
Which to your discretion shall seem best.
And as for me, my lords, I'll look to one;   150
And, with the ransom that the viceroy sent
So furnish and perform this tragedy,
As all the world shall say Hieronimo
Was liberal in gracing of it so.

BALTHAZAR

Hieronimo, methinks a comedy were better.   155

HIERONIMO

A comedy?

---

145   *fauchion* a broad curved sword or scimitar.
148   *Phoebe, Flora, or the Huntress* the virginal moon, the goddess of flowers and gardens,
       or Diana, goddess of hunting, who had her would-be lover Actaeon killed.
154   *liberal* lavish.

Fie, comedies are fit for common wits:
But to present a kingly troop withal,
Give me a stately-written tragedy,
Tragedia cothurnata, fitting kings,   160
Containing matter, and not common things.
My lords, all this must be performed,
As fitting for the first night's revelling.
The Italian tragedians were so sharp of wit,
That in one hour's meditation   165
They would perform anything in action.

LORENZO

And well it may; for I have seen the like
In Paris, 'mongst the French tragedians.

HIERONIMO

In Paris? mass, and well remembered!
There's one thing more that rests for us to do.   170

BALTHAZAR

What's that, Hieronimo? forget not anything.

HIERONIMO

Each one of us must act his part
In unknown languages,
That it may breed the more variety.
As you, my lord, in Latin, I in Greek,   175
You in Italian; and for because I know
That Bel-Imperia hath practised the French,
In courtly French shall all her phrases be.

158   *a kingly troop* an audience of royalty.
160   *Tragedia cothurnata* the most serious form of Greek drama.
164   *Italian tragedians* a slightly oblique allusion to the *Commedia dell' arte*, comedians
       who would improvise a play out of a short scenario.
173   *In unknown languages* There is some evidence of indecision here, either on Kyd's
       own part or by the editor who prepared the text for the press; Kyd clearly thought
       his chosen languages, Latin, Greek, Italian, and French, would be '*unknown*' and
       incomprehensible to most of his audiences, even though Hieronimo uses Latin and
       Spanish quotations himself and Lorenzo uses Italian exclamations. Kyd's object
       seems to be to create amongst the players a Tower of Babel, an Elizabethan synonym
       for the pagan grandeur of Babylon; but this has little to do with the deaths of the
       participants and does very little for the enactment of the play. Freeman argues that
       the rendering of the whole story in English was an afterthought, to make the story
       more comprehensible to the theatre audience. The statement at the outset of the
       staged play within the play in IV.iv, that this version has been set out '*in sundry
       languages*,' '*for the easier understanding to every public reader*', suggests that what was
       given to the press was a revised text. Edwards and others link this with the evidence
       suggesting that the last section of the play was set from imperfect copy.

BEL-IMPERIA

You mean to try my cunning then, Hieronimo.

BALTHAZAR

But this will be a mere confusion, 180
And hardly shall we all be understood.

HIERONIMO

It must be so, for the conclusion
Shall prove the invention and all was good.
And I myself in an oration,
And with a strange and wondrous show besides, 185
That I will have there behind a curtain,
Assure yourself, shall make the matter known.
And all shall be concluded in one scene,
For there's no pleasure ta'en in tediousness.

BALTHAZAR

[*Aside to* LORENZO] How like you this? 190

LORENZO

Why, thus my lord,
We must resolve to soothe his humours up.

BALTHAZAR

On then Hieronimo, farewell till soon.

HIERONIMO

You'll ply this gear?

LORENZO   I warrant you.

                    Exeunt all but HIERONIMO

HIERONIMO   Why so.

Now shall I see the fall of Babylon, 195
Wrought by the heavens in this confusion.
And if the world like not this tragedy,
Hard is the hap of old Hieronimo.   *Exit*

---

183   *the invention* the idea behind the staging, though of course also Hieronimo's own
      more savage plot.
185   *a strange and wondrous show* Hieronimo plans to have Horatio's body 'discovered'
      as the justification and explanation for his own plot; at the beginning of IV.iii he
      '*knocks up the curtain*' to conceal this show. .
192   *soothe his humours* humour him in his lunacy.
194   *this gear* a reminder of Pedringano's derisive word for the scaffold on which he dies.
195   *the fall of Babylon* the Tower of Babel where the victims act in their 'unknown'
      languages; the Geneva Bible used the term both for the Tower and for the wicked city
      of Babylon; in 1606 Dekker wrote an anti-Catholic play for the same stage that *The
      Spanish Tragedy* was acted on called *The Whore of Babylon*, in which the Whore was
      a female Pope plotting against England's female monarch.

ACT IV, SCENE ii

Enter ISABELLA *with a weapon*

ISABELLA
Tell me no more! O monstrous homicides!
Since neither piety nor pity moves
The king to justice or compassion,
I will revenge myself upon this place
Where thus they murdered my beloved son.   5
She cuts down the arbour
Down with these branches and these loathsome boughs
Of this unfortunate and fatal pine:
Down with them, Isabella, rent them up
And burn the roots from whence the rest is sprung.
I will not leave a root, a stalk, a tree,   10
A bough, a branch, a blossom, nor a leaf,
No, not an herb within this garden-plot.
Accursed complot of my misery,
Fruitless for ever may this garden be!
Barren the earth, and blissless whosoever   15
Imagines not to keep it unmanured!
An eastern wind commixed with noisome airs
Shall blast the plants and the young saplings;
The earth with serpents shall be pestered,
And passengers, for fear to be infect,   20
Shall stand aloof, and, looking at it, tell,
'There, murdered, died the son of Isabel.'
Ay, here he died, and here I him embrace:
See where his ghost solicits with his wounds
Revenge on her that should revenge his death.   25
Hieronimo, make haste to see thy son,
For sorrow and despair hath cited me

---

1   s.d. *with a weapon* an axe or a knife; chopping down the arbour chiefly meant
    lopping its smaller branches with their leaves rather than the main structure, though
    it could have been made to fall before it descended down the trapdoor; the
    Shakespeare company play *A Warning for Fair Women* has a tree chopped down on
    stage after arising through the trapdoor.
13 *complot* accomplice and location.
17 *noisome* noxious.

To hear Horatio plead with Rhadamanth:
Make haste, Hieronimo, to hold excused
Thy negligence in pursuit of their deaths,   30
Whose hateful wrath bereaved him of his breath.
Ah nay, thou dost delay their deaths,
Forgives the murderers of thy noble son,
And none but I bestir me – to no end.
And as I curse this tree from further fruit,   35
So shall my womb be cursed for his sake;
And with this weapon will I wound the breast,
                            She stabs herself
The hapless breast that gave Horatio suck.   [*Exit*]

28   *Rhadamanth* one of the underworld's three judges.
38   s.d. *Exit* With nobody to carry her offstage, she must exit holding her breast, to die
       offstage; the *1592* text gives her no exit, but she must leave here.

ACT IV, SCENE iii

Enter HIERONIMO; *he knocks up the curtain.*
Enter the DUKE OF CASTILE

CASTILE

How now Hieronimo, where's your fellows,
That you take all this pain?

HIERONIMO

O sir, it is for the author's credit
To look that all things may go well.
But, good my lord, let me entreat your grace   5
To give the king the copy of the play:
This is the argument of what we show.

CASTILE

I will, Hieronimo.

HIERONIMO

One thing more, my good lord.

CASTILE

What's that?   10

HIERONIMO

Let me entreat your grace
That, when the train are passed into the gallery,
You would vouchsafe to throw me down the key.

CASTILE

I will, Hieronimo.   *Exit* CASTILE

HIERONIMO

What are you ready, Balthazar?   15
Bring a chair and a cushion for the king.

---

1   s.d. *he knocks up the curtain* At IV.i.185 Hieronimo explains his plan to conceal
    Horatio's body onstage; this trick of his has been used by critics to argue that the
    royal party must have sat on the main stage, since from the balcony they could hardly
    have seen into the central opening, but the Rose *frons scenae* had three angles, and a
    flanking balcony seat on an angle to the central opening would have been sufficient.
13 *the key* It was not uncommon for great dignitaries to lock themselves into their
    auditorium boxes; in 1636 the Duke of Lennox, the king's uncle, quarrelled with the
    Earl of Pembroke, the Lord Chamberlain, over a key to a box at the Blackfriars
    playhouse.
15 *What are you ready* Hieronimo calls up to Balthazar to bring a chair for the king to
    sit on in the so-far-unlocked room; Balthazar appears on the balcony carrying a
    board with the play's title, ready to hang it above the central opening.

114

Enter BALTHAZAR *with a chair*

Well done, Balthazar; hang up the title.
Our scene is Rhodes – what, is your beard on?
BALTHAZAR
Half on, the other is in my hand.
HIERONIMO
Despatch for shame, are you so long?   20

Exit BALTHAZAR

Bethink thyself, Hieronimo,
Recall thy wits, recompt thy former wrongs
Thou has received by murder of thy son;
And lastly, not least, how Isabel,
Once his mother and thy dearest wife,   25
All woe-begone for him, hath slain herself.
Behoves thee then, Hieronimo, to be revenged.
The plot is laid of dire revenge:
On then, Hieronimo, pursue revenge,
For nothing wants but acting of revenge.   30

Exit HIERONIMO

18   *your beard* young Balthazar is half-ready in his role as great Soliman, the Turkish
      emperor, who would have had a large beard.
27–30 *revenge* Hieronimo, acting as if he ignored the horror of his wife dead and the
      comedy of Balthazar's incomplete beard, uses his repetitions to point the audience
      to the acts of murder to come.

ACT IV, SCENE iv

Enter SPANISH KING, VICEROY, *the* DUKE OF CASTILE,
and their train

KING

Now, Viceroy, shall we see the tragedy
Of Soliman the Turkish emperor,
Performed of pleasure by your son the prince,
My nephew Don Lorenzo, and my niece.

VICEROY

Who, Bel-Imperia?   5

KING

Ay, and Hieronimo, our marshal,
At whose request they deign to do't themselves:
These be our pastimes in the court of Spain.
Here, brother, you shall be the book-keeper:
This is the argument of that they show.   10

He giveth him a book

*Gentlemen, this play of Hieronimo, in sundry languages, was
thought good to be set down in English more largely, for the easier
understanding to every public reader.*

Enter BALTHAZAR, BEL-IMPERIA, *and* HIERONIMO

BALTHAZAR

*Bashaw, that Rhodes is ours, yield heavens the honour,
And holy Mahomet, our sacred prophet;
And be thou graced with every excellence
That Soliman can give, or thou desire.
But thy desert in conquering Rhodes is less   15
Than in reserving this fair Christian nymph,
Perseda, blissful lamp of excellence,
Whose eyes compel, like powerful adamant,
The warlike heart of Soliman to wait.*

---

1   *Viceroy* the king graciously tells his visitor what to expect, and passes the written
    'argument,' which he has evidently just read, to his brother, who he asks to assist the
    show.

10 s.d. *Gentlemen ... reader* This insertion is almost unique in early English drama in
    being addressed to the reader, not a character in the play; see note to IV.i.173.

18 *adamant* the magnetic loadstone used for compasses.

KING

    See, Viceroy, that is Balthazar, your son,   20

    That represents the emperor Soliman:

    How well he acts his amorous passion.

VICEROY

    Ay, Bel-Imperia hath taught him that.

CASTILE

    That's because his mind runs all on Bel-Imperia.

HIERONIMO

    Whatever joy earth yields betide your majesty.   25

BALTHAZAR

    Earth yields no joy without Perseda's love.

HIERONIMO

    Let then Perseda on your grace attend.

BALTHAZAR

    She shall not wait on me, but I on her:

    Drawn by the influence of her lights, I yield.

    But let my friend, the Rhodian knight, come forth,   30

    Erasto, dearer than my life to me,

    That he may see Perseda, my beloved.

            Enter [LORENZO *as*] ERASTO

KING

    Here comes Lorenzo; look upon the plot,

    And tell me, brother, what part plays he?

BEL-IMPERIA

    Ah, my Erasto, welcome to Perseda.   35

LORENZO

    Thrice happy is Erasto that thou liv'st –

    Rhodes' loss is nothing to Erasto's joy;

    Sith his Perseda lives, his life survives.

BALTHAZAR

    Ah, bashaw, here is love between Erasto

    And fair Perseda, sovereign of my soul.   40

HIERONIMO

    Remove Erasto, mighty Soliman,

    And then Perseda will be quickly won.

BALTHAZAR

    Erasto is my friend, and while he lives

    Perseda never will remove her love.

HIERONIMO

   Let not Erasto live to grieve great Soliman. 45

BALTHAZAR

   Dear is Erasto in our princely eye.

HIERONIMO

   But if he be your rival, let him die.

BALTHAZAR

   Why, let him die: so love commandeth me.

   Yet grieve I that Erasto should so die.

HIERONIMO

   Erasto, Soliman saluteth thee, 50

   And lets thee wit by me his highness' will

   Which is, thou shouldst be thus employed.

                            Stab him

BEL-IMPERIA   *Ay me,*

   Erasto! see, Soliman, Erasto's slain!

BALTHAZAR

   Yet liveth Soliman to comfort thee.

   Fair queen of beauty, let not favour die, 55

   But with a gracious eye behold his grief,

   That with Perseda's beauty is increased,

   If by Perseda his grief be not released.

BEL-IMPERIA

   Tyrant, desist soliciting vain suits;

   Relentless are mine ears to thy laments, 60

   As thy butcher is pitiless and base,

   Which seized on my Erasto, harmless knight,

   Yet by thy power thou thinkest to command,

   And to thy power Perseda doth obey:

   But were she able, thus she would revenge 65

   Thy treacheries on thee, ignoble prince: *Stab him*

   And on herself she would be thus revenged.   *Stab herself*

KING

   Well said, old marshal, this was bravely done!

HIERONIMO

   But Bel-Imperia plays Perseda well.

VICEROY

   Were this in earnest, Bel-Imperia, 70

   You would be better to my son than so.

59–67   Bel-Imperia's answer in the person of Perseda to Balthazar as her new lover exactly
       replicates her grief for both Andrea and Horatio.

KING

But now what follows for Hieronimo?

HIERONIMO

Marry, this follows for Hieronimo:
Here break we off our sundry languages
And thus conclude I in our vulgar tongue.   75
Haply you think, but bootless are your thoughts,
That this is fabulously counterfeit,
And that we do as all tragedians do:
To die today, for fashioning our scene,
The death of Ajax, or some Roman peer,   80
And in a minute starting up again,
Revive to please to-morrow's audience.
No, princes; know I am Hieronimo,
The hopeless father of a hapless son,
Whose tongue is tuned to tell his latest tale,   85
Not to excuse gross errors in the play.
I see your looks urge instance of these words;
Behold the reason urging me to this:

Shows his dead son

See here my show, look on this spectacle.
Here lay my hope, and here my hope hath end;   90
Here lay my heart, and here my heart was slain;
Here lay my treasure, here my treasure lost;
Here lay my bliss, and here my bliss bereft;
But hope, heart, treasure, joy, and bliss,
All fled, failed, died, yea, all decayed with this.   95
From forth these wounds came breath that gave me life;
They murdered me that made these fatal marks.
The cause was love, whence grew this mortal hate,
The hate, Lorenzo and young Balthazar,
The love, my son to Bel-Imperia.   100

---

72   *what follows for Hieronimo?* Breaking off the 'sundry languages' to tell the audience
     the truth of what they have seen, Hieronimo returns to his formal speech, from line
     76, '*Haply you think, but bootless are your thoughts*' to line 84, '*The hopeless father of
     a hapless son*'; the two 'haps' are opposed, the first meaning 'perhaps', the second
     'unhappy, unfortunate'; he then pulls back the curtain to 'discover' his dead son to
     the watching king who had ignored his plea for justice.

90   *hope* picking up the 'hopeless' of 84.

98–113 Hieronimo tells his story in heavy, measured language, explaining the cause '*as you
        see*'.

But night, the coverer of accursed crimes,
With pitchy silence hushed these traitors' harms
And lent them leave, for they had sorted leisure
To take advantage in my garden-plot
Upon my son, my dear Horatio: 105
There merciless they butchered up my boy,
In black dark night, to pale dim cruel death.
He shrieks, I heard, and yet methinks I hear,
His dismal outcry echo in the air.
With soonest speed I hasted to the noise,   110
Where hanging on a tree I found my son,
Through-girt with wounds, and slaughtered as you see.
And grieved I, think you, at this spectacle?
Speak, Portuguese, whose loss resembles mine:
If thou canst weep upon thy Balthazar,   115
'Tis like I wailed for my Horatio.
And you, my lord, whose reconciled son
Marched in a net, and thought himself unseen
And rated me for brainsick lunacy,
With 'God amend that mad Hieronimo!' –   120
How can you brook our play's catastrophe?
And here behold this bloody handkercher,
Which at Horatio's death I weeping dipped
Within the river of his bleeding wounds:
It as propitious, see I have reserved,   125
And never hath it left my bloody heart,
Soliciting remembrance of my vow
With these, O these accursed murderers:
Which now performed, my heart is satisfied.
And to this end the bashaw I became   130
That might revenge me on Lorenzo's life,
Who therefore was appointed to the part,
And was to represent the knight of Rhodes,
That I might kill him more conveniently.
So, Viceroy, was this Balthazar, thy son –   135
That Soliman which Bel-Imperia
In person of Perseda murdered –
Solely appointed to that tragic part

114   *Portuguese* he addresses the visiting Viceroy or king first, before turning to the second
       father who suffers his own personal disaster, Castile.

That she might slay him that offended her.
Poor Bel-Imperia missed her part in this: 140
For though the story saith she should have died,
Yet I of kindness, and of care to her,
Did otherwise determine of her end;
But love of him whom they did hate too much
Did urge her resolution to be such.   145
And princes, now behold Hieronimo,
Author and actor in this tragedy,
Bearing his latest fortune in his fist:
And will as resolute conclude his part
As any of the actors gone before.   150
And, gentles, thus I end my play:
Urge no more words: I have no more to say.

He runs to hang himself

KING

O hearken, Viceroy! Hold, Hieronimo!
Brother, my nephew and thy son are slain!

VICEROY

We are betrayed! my Balthazar is slain!   155
Break ope the doors, run, save Hieronimo.

[*They break in, and hold* HIERONIMO]

Hieronimo, do but inform the king of these events;
Upon mine honour thou shalt have no harm.

HIERONIMO

Viceroy, I will not trust thee with my life,
Which I this day have offered to my son.   160
Accursed wretch,
Why stayest thou him that was resolved to die?

KING

Speak, traitor; damned, bloody murderer, speak!
For now I have thee I will make thee speak –

---

148   *Bearing his latest fortune in his fist* Hieronimo must hold a rope, though since '*He
      runs to hang himself*' at line 152 it is unlikely the spectacle had an arbour for
      Horatio's body.
153   *Hold, Hieronimo!* wait, stop; the *1592* text has no comma, suggesting that the king
      orders Hieronimo to be taken prisoner, but if he is running to hang himself, ordering
      him to halt is more likely.
156   *Break ope the doors* Castile had locked them into their room on the balcony, as
      Hieronimo asked him to.
158   *thou shalt have no harm* It is not in the Viceroy's power to offer protection for
      Hieronimo.

Why hast thou done this undeserving deed?   165

VICEROY

Why hast thou murdered my Balthazar?

CASTILE

Why hast thou butchered both my children thus?

HIERONIMO

O, good words!

As dear to me was my Horatio

As yours, or yours, or yours, my lord, to you.   170

My guiltless son was by Lorenzo slain,

And by Lorenzo and that Balthazar

Am I at last revenged thoroughly,

Upon whose souls may heavens be yet avenged

With greater far than these afflictions.   175

CASTILE

But who were thy confederates in this?

VICEROY

That was thy daughter Bel-Imperia;

For by her hand my Balthazar was slain:

I saw her stab him.

KING   Why speak'st thou not?

HIERONIMO

What lesser liberty can kings afford   180

Than harmless silence? Then afford it me:

Sufficeth I may not, nor I will not tell thee.

KING

Fetch forth the tortures.

Traitor as thou art, I'll make thee tell.

HIERONIMO   Indeed,

Thou may'st torment me, as his wretched son   185

Hath done in murdering my Horatio,

But never shalt thou force me to reveal

---

167   *both my children* Castile notes the dynastic disaster that the deaths represent for both Spain and Portugal, though his first reaction is personal, like Hieronimo and Bel-Imperia.

174   *heavens be yet avenged* Hieronimo prepares for the announcement by Andrea of the fates of those who have died.

176   *who were thy confederates in this?* Much debated, and used as evidence for a mangled text, since Hieronimo has already given his reason for taking revenge; he refuses to speak, having only glancingly implicated Bel-Imperia, but rulers always suspect conspiracies, and the threat of torture which Hieronimo defies at 187–8 is based on the king's assumption that he must have had accomplices.

The thing which I have vowed inviolate.
And therefore in despite of all thy threats,
Pleased with their deaths, and eased with their revenge,   190
First take my tongue, and afterwards my heart.
                              [*He bites out his tongue*]
KING
O monstrous resolution of a wretch!
See, Viceroy, he hath bitten forth his tongue
Rather than to reveal what we required.
CASTILE
Yet can he write.   195
KING
And if in this he satisfy us not,
We will devise th'extremest kind of death
That ever was invented for a wretch.
                    Then he makes signs for a knife to mend his pen
CASTILE
O, he would have a knife to mend his pen.
VICEROY
Here; and advise thee that thou write the troth.   200
KING
Look to my brother! save Hieronimo!
                    He with a knife stabs the DUKE *and himself*
What age hath ever heard such monstrous deeds?
My brother, and the whole succeeding hope
That Spain expected after my decease!
Go bear his body hence, that we may mourn   205
The loss of our beloved brother's death;
That he may be entombed, whate'er befall:
I am the next, the nearest, last of all.
VICEROY
And thou, Don Pedro, do the like for us;
Take up our hapless son, untimely slain: 210

---

188   *The thing which I have vowed inviolate* Hieronimo has already spoken of his reason
      for taking his revenge on Balthazar and Lorenzo; what else he may wish to keep
      secret has been the subject of much speculation, producing arguments that the text
      is cut and/or corrupt.
201   *my brother* The killing of Castile is thought by some to be an excess, Freeman in
      particular arguing that the last scenes show him benevolent; he, however, is the
      ultimate cause of Andrea's tragic story by rejecting his daughter's love for the man
      at the outset; this may be a reason for Hieronimo's reluctance to pronounce her his
      accomplice; in the play his revenge outdoes hers.

Set me with him, and he with woeful me,
Upon the main-mast of a ship unmanned,
And let the wind and tide haul me along
To Scylla's barking and untamed gulf,
Or to the loathsome pool of Acheron,   215
To weep my want for my sweet Balthazar:
Spain hath no refuge for a Portingale.

> *The trumpets sound a dead march, the* KING *of* SPAIN
> *mourning after his brother's body, and the* VICEROY
> *of* PORTINGALE *bearing the body of his son*

---

214   *Scylla's… gulf* the rock alongside Charybdis the whirlpool; Odysseus had to sail past
       both between Sicily and Italy.
215   *Acheron* the river of the lower world, first mentioned at I.i.19.
217   s.d. Carrying bodies offstage was essential; Castile and Balthazar are carried off in
       state, with royal ceremonial, but Lorenzo, Bel-Imperia, and Hieronimo must be
       carried off too; nothing in the text specifies how.

ACT IV, SCENE v

Ghost [of ANDREA] *and* REVENGE

ANDREA

Ay, now my hopes have end in their effects,
When blood and sorrow finish my desires:
Horatio murdered in his father's bower,
Vild Serberine by Pedringano slain,
False Pedringano hanged by quaint device,   5
Fair Isabella by herself misdone,
Prince Balthazar by Bel-Imperia stabbed,
The Duke of Castile and his wicked son
Both done to death by old Hieronimo,
My Bel-Imperia fallen as Dido fell,   10
And good Hieronimo slain by himself:
Ay, these were spectacles to please my soul.
Now will I beg at lovely Proserpine,
That, by the virtue of her princely doom,
I may consort my friends in pleasing sort,   15
And on my foes work just and sharp revenge.
I'll lead my friend Horatio through those fields
Where never-dying wars are still inured:
I'll lead fair Isabella to that train
Where pity weeps but never feeleth pain: 20
I'll lead my Bel-Imperia to those joys
That vestal virgins and fair queens possess;
I'll lead Hieronimo where Orpheus plays,
Adding sweet pleasure to eternal days.
But say, Revenge, for thou must help, or none,   25
Against the rest how shall my hate be shown?

1–24   Andrea exults in his victories, promising rewards in the beneficent parts of the
        underworld for his friends; Revenge develops his mood, saying that those Andrea
        hated will go to hell, with specific punishments; Castile is to replace Tityus, a giant
        whose liver is constantly devoured by a snake; Lorenzo replaces Ixion, king of
        Thessaly, who tried to seduce Juno, on his perpetually turning wheel; Balthazar is to
        hang round the neck of Chimaera, a three-headed, fire-breathing monster; Serberine
        must replace Sisyphus eternally rolling his stone up the mountain, while Pedringano
        is to boil in the bitter waters of Acheron; critics have understandably questioned
        whether this is justice or vengeance.

REVENGE

This hand shall hale them down to deepest hell,
Where none but Furies, bugs and tortures dwell.

ANDREA

Then, sweet Revenge, do this at my request;
Let me be judge, and doom them to unrest: 30
Let loose poor Tityus from the vulture's gripe,
And let Don Cyprian supply his room;
Place Don Lorenzo on Ixion's wheel,
And let the lover's endless pains surcease –
Juno forgets old wrath, and grants him ease; 35
Hang Balthazar about Chimaera's neck,
And let him there bewail his bloody love,
Repining at our joys that are above;
Let Serberine go roll the fatal stone,
And take from Sisyphus his endless moan; 40
False Pedringano for his treachery,
Let him be dragged through boiling Acheron,
And there live, dying still in endless flames,
Blaspheming gods and all their holy names.

REVENGE

Then haste we down to meet thy friends and foes: 45
To place thy friends in ease, the rest in woes.
For here, though death hath end their misery,
I'll there begin their endless tragedy.

Exeunt

Opposite: the title page of the fourth quarto (1602), the first to include the 'Additions'.

THE
Spanish Tragedie:

Containing the lamen-

t, table end of *Don Horatio, and Bel-imperia:*
with the pitifull death of olde
Hieronimo.

Newly corrected, amended, and enlarged with
new additions of the Painters part, and
others, as it hath of late been
diuers times acted.

Imprinted at London by W. W. for
T. Pauier, and are to be solde at the
figne of the Carte and Parrats
neare the Exchange.
1602

THE ADDITIONS

Scenes added to *The Spanish Tragedy* in the edition of 1602

First Addition
between II.v.45 and 46

[For outrage fits our cursed wretchedness.]
Ay me, Hieronimo, sweet husband speak.

HIERONIMO
He supped with us tonight, frolic and merry,
And said he would go visit Balthazar
At the duke's palace: there the prince doth lodge.
He had no custom to stay out so late,   5
He may be in his chamber; some go see.
Roderigo, ho!

Enter PEDRO *and* JAQUES

ISABELLA
Ay me, he raves. Sweet Hieronimo!

HIERONIMO
True, all Spain takes note of it.
Besides, he is so generally beloved   10
His majesty the other day did grace him
With waiting on his cup: these be favours
Which do assure he cannot be short-lived.

ISABELLA
Sweet Hieronimo!

HIERONIMO
I wonder how this fellow got his clothes?   15
Sirrah, sirrah, I'll know the truth of all:
Jaques, run to the Duke of Castile's presently,
And bid my son Horatio to come home:
I and his mother have had strange dreams tonight.
Do you hear me, sir?

JAQUES   Ay, sir.

HIERONIMO   Well sir, begone.   20
Pedro, come hither: knowest thou who this is?

PEDRO
Too well, sir.

HIERONIMO
    Too well? Who? Who is it? Peace, Isabella:
    Nay, blush not, man.
PEDRO   It is my lord Horatio.
HIERONIMO
    Ha, ha! Saint James, but this doth make me laugh,   25
    That there are more deluded than myself.
PEDRO
    Deluded?
HIERONIMO
    Ay, I would have sworn myself within this hour
    That this had been my son Horatio,
    His garments are so like.   30
    Ha! are they not great persuasions?
ISABELLA
    O, would to God it were not so!
HIERONIMO
    Were not, Isabella? Dost thou dream it is?
    Can thy soft bosom entertain a thought
    That such a black deed of mischief should be done   35
    On one so pure and spotless as our son?
    Away, I am ashamed.
ISABELLA   Dear Hieronimo,
    Cast a more serious eye upon thy grief:
    Weak apprehension gives but weak belief.
HIERONIMO
    It was a man, sure, that was hanged up here;   40
    A youth, as I remember: I cut him down.
    If it should prove my son now after all –
    Say you, say you, light! Lend me a taper,
    Let me look again. O God!
    Confusion, mischief, torment, death and hell,   45
    Drop all your stings at once in my cold bosom,
    That now is stiff with horror; kill me quickly:
    Be gracious to me, thou infective night,
    And drop this deed of murder down on me;
    Gird in my waste of grief with thy large darkness,   50
    And let me not survive to see the light
    May put me in the mind I had a son.
ISABELLA
    O, sweet Horatio. O, my dearest son!

HIERONIMO

How strangely had I lost my way to grief!
[Sweet lovely rose, ill plucked before thy time,]

Second Addition

replacing III.ii.65 and part of 66

[LORENZO

Why so, Hieronimo? use me.]
HIERONIMO

Who, you, my lord?
I reserve your favour for a greater honour;
This is a very toy my lord, a toy.
LORENZO

All's one, Hieronimo, acquaint me with it.
HIERONIMO

I'faith, my lord, 'tis an idle thing.   5
I must confess, I ha' been too slack,
Too tardy. Too remiss unto your honour.
LORENZO

How now, Hieronimo?
HIERONIMO

In troth, my lord, it is a thing of nothing,
The murder of a son, or so: 10
A thing of nothing, my lord.
[LORENZO   Why then, farewell.]

Third Addition

between III.xi.1 and 2

[1 PORTINGALE

By your leave, sir.]
HIERONIMO

'Tis neither as you think, nor as you think,
Nor as you think: you're wide all:
These slippers are not mine, they were my son Horatio's.
My son, and what's a son? A thing begot
Within a pair of minutes, thereabout: 5
A lump bred up in darkness, and doth serve

To ballace these light creatures we call women;
And, at nine moneths' end, creeps forth to light.
What is there yet in a son
To make a father dote, rave or run mad?   10
Being born, it pouts, cries, and breeds teeth.
What is there yet in a son? He must be fed,
Be taught to go, and speak. Ay, or yet?
Why might not a man love a calf as well?
Or melt in passion o'er a frisking kid,   15
As for a son? Methinks a young bacon
Or a fine little smooth horse-colt
Should move a man as much as doth a son:
For one of these in very little time
Will grow to some good use, whereas a son,   20
The more he grows in stature and in years,
The more unsquared, unbevelled he appears,
Reckons his parents among the rank of fools,
Strikes care upon their heads with his mad riots,
Makes them look old before they meet with age: 25
This is a son:
And what a loss were this, considered truly?
Oh, but my Horatio
Grew out of reach of these insatiate humours:
He loved his loving parents,   30
He was my comfort, and his mother's joy,
The very arm that did hold up our house:
Our hopes were stored up in him,
None but a damned murderer could hate him.
He had not seen the back of nineteen year,   35
When his strong arm unhorsed the proud Prince Balthazar,
And his great mind, too full of honour,
Took him unto mercy,
That valiant but ignoble Portingale.
Well, heaven is heaven still,   40
And there is Nemesis and Furies,
And things called whips,
And they sometimes do meet with murderers:
They do not always 'scape, that's some comfort.
Ay, ay, ay, and then time steals on: 45
And steals, and steals, till violence leaps forth
Like thunder wrapped in a ball of fire,

And so doth bring confusion to them all.
[Good leave have you: nay, I pray you go,]

Fourth Addition
between III.xii and xiii

Enter JAQUES *and* PEDRO

JAQUES
I wonder, Pedro, why our master thus
At midnight sends us with our torches' light,
When man and bird and beast are all at rest,
Save those that watch for rape and bloody murder?
PEDRO
O Jaques, know thou that our master's mind   5
Is much distraught since his Horatio died,
And now his aged years should sleep in rest,
His heart in quiet; like a desperate man,
Grows lunatic and childish for his son:
Sometimes, as he doth at his table sit,   10
He speaks as if Horatio stood by him;
Then starting in a rage, falls on the earth,
Cries out 'Horatio, where is my Horatio?'
So that with extreme grief and cutting sorrow,
There is not left in him one inch of man: 15
See, where he comes.

Enter HIERONIMO

HIERONIMO
I pry through every crevice of each wall,
Look on each tree, and search through every brake,
Beat at the bushes, stamp our grandam earth,
Dive in the water, and stare up to heaven,   20
Yet cannot I behold my son Horatio.
How now, who's there, sprites, sprites?
PEDRO
We are your servants that attend you, sir.
HIERONIMO
What make you with your torches in the dark?

PEDRO
    You bid us light them, and attend you here.   25
HIERONIMO
    No, no, you are deceived, not I, you are deceived:
    Was I so mad to bid you light your torches now?
    Light me your torches at the mid of noon,
    Whenas the sun-god rides in all his glory:
    Light me your torches then.
PEDRO   Then we burn daylight.   30
HIERONIMO
    Let it be burnt: night is a murderous slut,
    That would not have her treasons to be seen;
    And yonder pale-faced Hecate there, the moon,
    Doth give consent to that is done in darkness;
    And all those stars that gaze upon her face,   35
    Are aglets on her sleeve, pins on her train;
    And those that should be powerful and divine,
    Do sleep in darkness when they most should shine.
PEDRO
    Provoke them not, fair sir, with tempting words:
    The heavens are gracious, and your miseries   40
    And sorrow makes you speak you know not what.
HIERONIMO
    Villain, thou liest, and thou doest naught
    But tell me I am mad: thou liest, I am not mad.
    I know thee to be Pedro, and he Jaques.
    I'll prove it to thee, and were I mad, how could I?   45
    Where was she that same night when my Horatio
    Was murdered? She should have shone: search thou the book.
    Had the moon shone, in my boy's face there was a kind of grace,
    That I know (nay, I do know) had the murderer seen him,
    His weapon would have fallen and cut the earth,   50
    Had he been framed of naught but blood and death.
    Alack, when mischief doth it knows not what,
    What shall we say to mischief?

Enter ISABELLA

ISABELLA
    Dear Hieronimo, come in a-doors.
    O, seek not means so to increase thy sorrow.   55

HIERONIMO
    Indeed, Isabella, we do nothing here;
    I do not cry; ask Pedro, and ask Jaques;
    Not I indeed, we are very merry, very merry.
ISABELLA
    How? be merry here, be merry here?
    Is not this the place, and this the very tree,   60
    Where my Horatio died, where he was murdered?
HIERONIMO
    Was – do not say what: let her weep it out.
    This was the tree, I set it of a kernel,
    And when our hot Spain could not let it grow,
    But that the infant and the human sap   65
    Began to wither, duly twice a morning
    Would I be sprinkling it with fountain water.
    At last it grew, and grew, and bore and bore,
    Till at length
    It grew a gallows, and did bear our son.   70
    It bore thy fruit and mine: O wicked, wicked plant.
                    One knocks within at the door
  See who knock there.
PEDRO   It is a painter, sir.
HIERONIMO
    Bid him come in, and paint some comfort,
    For surely there's none lives but painted comfort.
    Let him come in. One knows not what may chance: 75
    God's will that I should set this tree – but even so
    Masters ungrateful servants rear from naught,
    And then they hate them that did bring them up.

                 Enter the PAINTER

PAINTER
    God bless you, sir.
HIERONIMO
    Wherefore? why, thou scornful villain,   80
    How, where, or by what means should I be blessed?
ISABELLA
    What wouldst thou have, good fellow?
PAINTER   Justice, madam.
HIERONIMO
    O ambitious beggar, wouldst thou have that

That lives not in the world?
Why, all the undelved mines cannot buy   85
An ounce of justice, 'tis a jewel so inestimable:
I tell thee,
God hath engrossed all justice in his hands,
And there is none, but what comes from him.

PAINTER
O then I see   90
That God must right me for my murdered son.

HIERONIMO
How, was thy son murdered?

PAINTER
Ay sir, no man did hold a son so dear.

HIERONIMO
What, not as thine? that's a lie
As massy as the earth: I had a son,   95
Whose least unvalued hair did weigh
A thousand of thy sons: and he was murdered.

PAINTER
Alas sir, I had no more but he.

HIERONIMO
Nor I, nor I: but this same one of mine
Was worth a legion: but all is one.   100
Pedro, Jaques, go in a-doors: Isabella go,
And this good fellow here and I
Will range this hideous orchard up and down,
Like to two lions reaved of their young.
Go in a-doors, I say.   105
                    Exeunt [ISABELLA, PEDRO, JAQUES]
                    The PAINTER *and he sits down*
Come, let's talk wisely now. Was thy son murdered?

PAINTER
Ay sir.

HIERONIMO
So was mine. How dost take it? Art thou not sometimes mad?
Is there no tricks that comes before thine eyes?

PAINTER
O Lord, yes sir.   110

HIERONIMO
Art a painter? Canst paint me a tear, or a wound, a groan, or a
sigh? Canst paint me such a tree as this?

PAINTER

Sir, I am sure you have heard of my painting, my name's
Bazardo.

HIERONIMO

Bazardo! afore God, an excellent fellow! Look you sir, do you   115
see, I'd have you paint me in my gallery, in your oil colours
matted, and draw me five years younger than I am. Do you see
sir, let five years go, let them go, like the marshal of Spain. My
wife Isabella standing by me, with a speaking look to my son
Horatio, which should intend to this or some such like purpose: 120
'God bless thee, my sweet son': and my hand leaning upon his
head, thus, sir, do you see? may it be done?

PAINTER

Very well sir.

HIERONIMO

Nay, I pray mark me sir. Then sir, would I have you paint me this
tree, this very tree. Canst paint a doleful cry?   125

PAINTER

Seemingly, sir.

HIERONIMO

Nay, it should cry: but all is one. Well sir, paint me a youth run
through and through with villains' swords, hanging upon this
tree. Canst thou draw a murderer?

PAINTER

I'll warrant you sir, I have the pattern of the most notorious   130
villains that ever lived in all Spain.

HIERONIMO

O, let them be worse, worse: stretch thine art, and let their
beards be of Judas his own colour, and let their eyebrows jutty
over: in any case observe that. Then sir, after some violent noise,
bring me forth in my shin, and my gown under mine arm, with   135
my torch in my hand, and my sword reared up thus: and with
these words:

What noise is this? who calls Hieronimo?

May it be done?

PAINTER

Yea sir.   140

HIERONIMO

Well sir, then bring me forth, bring me through alley and alley,
still with a distracted countenance going along, and let my hair
heave up my night-cap. Let the clouds scowl, make the moon dark,

the stars extinct, the winds blowing, the bells tolling, the owl
shrieking, the toads croaking, the minutes jarring, and the clock   145
striking twelve. And then at last, sir, starting, behold a man hanging: and tottering, and tottering as you know the wind will weave
a man, and I with a trice to cut him down. And looking upon
him by the advantage of my torch, find it to be my son Horatio.
There you may show a passion, there you may show a passion.   150
Draw me like old Priam of Troy, crying 'The house is a-fire, the
house is a-fire as the torch over my head!' Make me curse, make
me rave, make me cry, make me mad, make me well again, make
me curse hell, invocate heaven, and in the end leave me in a
trance; and so forth.   155

PAINTER

And is this the end?

HIERONIMO

O no, there is no end: the end is death and madness! As I am never
better than when I am mad, then methinks I am a brave fellow,
then I do wonders: but reason abuseth me, and there's the torment,
there's the hell. At the last, sir, bring me to one of the murderers,   160
were he as strong as Hector, thus would I tear and drag him up
and down.

> *He beats the* PAINTER *in, then comes out again*
> *with a book in his hand*

Fifth Addition

replacing IV.iv.168–90

[CASTILE

Why hast thou butchered both my children thus?]

HIERONIMO

But are you sure they are dead?

CASTILE   Ay, slave, too sure.

HIERONIMO

What, and yours too?

VICEROY

Ay, all are dead, not one of them survive.

HIERONIMO

Nay then, I care not, come, and we shall be friends:

Let us lay our heads together; 5
See here's a goodly noose will hold them all.

VICEROY

O damned devil, how secure he is.

HIERONIMO

Secure, why dost thou wonder at it?
I tell thee Viceroy, this day I have seen revenge,
And in that sight am grown a prouder monarch 10
Than ever sat under the crown of Spain:
Had I as many lives as there be stars,
As many heavens to go to as those lives,
I'd give them all, ay, and my soul to boot,
But I would see thee ride in this red pool. 15

CASTILE

Speak, who were thy confederates in this?

VICEROY

That was thy daughter Bel-Imperia,
For by her hand my Balthazar was slain:
I saw her stab him.

HIERONIMO   Oh, good words:
As dear to me was my Horatio, 20
As yours, or yours, or yours, my lord, to you.
My guiltless son was by Lorenzo slain,
And by Lorenzo, and that Balthazar,
Am I at last revenged thoroughly,
Upon whose souls may heavens be yet revenged 25
With greater far than these afflictions.
Methinks since I grew inward with revenge,
I cannot look with scorn enough on death.

KING

What, dost thou mock us, slave? Bring tortures forth.

HIERONIMO

Do, do, do, and meantime I'll torture you. 30
You had a son, as I take it: and your son
Should ha' been married to your daughter:
Ha, was't not so? You had a son too,
He was my liege's nephew. He was proud,
And politic. Had he lived, he might ha' come 35
To wear the crown of Spain, I think 'twas so:
'Twas I that killed him; look you, this same hand,

'Twas it that stabbed his heart; do you see, this hand?
For one Horatio, if you ever knew him, a youth,
One that they hanged up in his father's garden,   40
One that did force your valiant son to yield,
While your more valiant son did take him prisoner.

VICEROY

Be deaf my senses, I can hear no more.

KING

Fall heaven, and cover us with thy sad ruins.

CASTILE

Roll all the world within thy pitchy cloud.   45

HIERONIMO

Now do I applaud what I have acted
      Nunc iners cadat manus.
Now to express the rupture of my part,
[First take my tongue, and afterwards my heart.]

THE
REVENGERS
TRAGÆDIE.

As it hath beene sundry times Acted,
by the Kings Maiesties
Seruants.

AT LONDON
Printed by G. E l d, and are to be sold at his
house in Fleete-lane at the signe of the
Printers-Presse.
1 6 0 8.

DRAMATIS PERSONAE

THE DUKE

DUCHESS

LUSSURIOSO *the Duke's son by an earlier marriage*

SPURIO *the Duke's bastard*

AMBITIOSO *the Duchess' eldest son* 5

SUPERVACUO *the Duchess' second son*

YOUNGEST SON *the Duchess' third son*

VINDICE
HIPPOLITO } brothers

CASTIZA *their sister* 10

GRATIANA *their widowed mother*

ANTONIO *An elderly noble*

PIERO *a noble*

DONDOLO *a servant to Castiza*

Nobles, Lords, Gentlemen, Judges, Officers, Prison-Keeper, 15
Servants

Most of the names are Italian words which appear in John Florio's dictionary *A Worlde of Wordes* (1598): *lussurioso*, lecherous; *spurio*, bastard; *ambitioso*, ambitious; *supervacuo*, superfluous; vain; *vindice*, a revenger of wrongs; *dondolo*, a gull or fool; *piato* (role assumed by Vindice), flat, squat, cowered down, hidden; *nencio* and *sordido* (servants of Lussurioso), a fool and a covetous wretch. *Gratiana* derives from *gratia*, grace; *Castiza* from *casta*, chaste.

ACT I, SCENE i

Enter VINDICE *[carrying a skull]; [then] the* DUKE, DUCHESS,
LUSSURIOSO *his son,* SPURIO *the bastard, with a train,*
pass over the stage with torchlight

VINDICE

Duke: royal lecher: go, grey haired Adultery,
And thou his son, as impious steeped as he:
And thou his bastard true-begot in evil:
And thou his duchess that will do with devil:
Four ex'lent characters! – Oh that marrowless age   5
Would stuff the hollow bones with damned desires,
And 'stead of heat kindle infernal fires
Within the spendthrift veins of a dry duke,
A parched and juiceless luxur. Oh God! One
That has scarce blood enough to live upon,   10
And he to riot it like a son and heir?
Oh the thought of that
Turns my abused heart-strings into fret.
Thou sallow picture of my poisoned love,
My study's ornament, thou shell of Death,   15
Once the bright face of my betrothed lady,
When life and beauty naturally filled out
These ragged imperfections;

---

0   s.d. *his son* ed. (her son Q)

4   *do* copulate

5–6   *marrowless . . . bones* Vindice (as T. S. Eliot said of Webster) is much obsessed by death and
      sees the skull beneath the skin. The spectator sees a proud courtly procession but Vindice
      sees instead that age withers the body, the bone marrow no longer produces the healthy
      blood of youth. In place of fertile passion the frenzy of mortal sin goads the Duke, who
      ignores these warnings of approaching death and judgement

7   *infernal fires* The damned suffer the fires of hell, and a burning sensation is a symptom of
      various venereal diseases

8   *dry* withered and sterile

11   *like . . . heir* The prodigal son is a stock type in dramatic satire of city and Court at this
      period; ambitious courtiers in fact spent huge sums to promote their interests at court. The
      new king, James, also indulged in lavish expenditure

13   *fret* anger (and with a musical pun, as in *Hamlet* III.ii.370–2: 'Call me what instrument you
      will, though you fret me you cannot play upon me')

14   Vindice addresses a skull, the 'sallow picture' of his poisoned love

When two heaven-pointed diamonds were set
In those unsightly rings – then 'twas a face   20
So far beyond the artificial shine
Of any woman's bought complexion
That the uprightest man – if such there be,
That sin but seven times a day – broke custom
And made up eight with looking after her.   25
Oh she was able to ha' made a usurer's son
Melt all his patrimony in a kiss,
And what his father fifty years told
To have consumed, and yet his suit been cold;
But oh accursed palace!   30
Thee when thou wert apparelled in thy flesh,
The old duke poisoned,
Because thy purer part would not consent
Unto his palsy-lust; for old men lustful
Do show like young men angry-eager, violent,   35
Out-bid like their limited performances –
Oh 'ware an old man hot and vicious:
'Age as in gold, in lust is covetous'.
Vengeance, thou Murder's quit-rent, and whereby
Thou show'st thyself tenant to Tragedy,   40
Oh keep thy day, hour, minute, I beseech,
For those thou hast determined. Hum, who e'er knew
Murder unpaid? Faith, give Revenge her due,
She's kept touch hitherto – be merry, merry,

19–20 The diamond ring's durability is ironically contrasted to the eyes of his spiritually bright but
       tragically short-lived beloved. Vindice is imaginatively preoccupied with eyes and eye sock-
       ets; see I.iii.9
   20 *unsightly* (i) unseeing, (ii) ugly
   22 *bought complexion* face made up with cosmetics
   25 *after* at
   27 *patrimony* property or estates inherited from ancestors
   28 *told* counted up, amassed
   29 *cold* unsuccessful
 34–6 i.e. the lust of old men is like the violence of young men, limited in performance
   35 *angry-eager* apparently a compound adjective
   36 *Out-bid* inadequate, out-bidden by others who are stronger
   39 *quit-rent* rent paid by a tenant in lieu of service: hence, vengeance as murder's due
   42 *determined* chosen, condemned
 42–3 *Hum ... unpaid?* alluding to the proverb 'Murder will out, murder cannot be hid (see
       IV.ii.203 below)

Advance thee, oh thou terror to fat folks   45
To have their costly three-piled flesh worn off
As bare as this – for banquets, ease and laughter
Can make great men, as greatness goes by clay,
But wise men, little, are more great than they.

Enter [his] brother HIPPOLITO

HIPPOLITO
Still sighing o'er Death's vizard?
VINDICE   Brother welcome,   50
What comfort bring'st thou? How go things at Court?
HIPPOLITO
In silk and silver brother: never braver.
VINDICE   Puh,
Thou play'st upon my meaning, prithee say
Has that bald madam, Opportunity,
Yet thought upon's, speak, are we happy yet?   55
Thy wrongs and mine are for one scabbard fit.
HIPPOLITO
It may prove happiness?
VINDICE   What is't may prove?
Give me to taste.
HIPPOLITO   Give me your hearing then.
You know my place at Court.
VINDICE   Ay, the duke's chamber.
But 'tis a marvel thou'rt not turned out yet!   60
HIPPOLITO
Faith I have been shoved at, but 'twas still my hap
To hold by the duchess' skirt, you guess at that –

---

46 *three-piled* finest velvet (having the thickest pile). Compare the clothing image of line 31
    above
48 *by clay* in terms merely of flesh
49 *little* of low rank. Foakes compares the proverb 'Wisdom is better than riches' (Tilley T 3ll)
    s.d. *his* ed. (*her* Q)
51 *things* affairs. Hippolito's satiric answer makes 'things' become the dehumanized fops at
    Court who 'go' about dressed lavishly in silk and silver
54 *Opportunity* Also known as Occasion (see 98–100 below). Occasion was depicted as a
    woman with a long forelock standing on a turning wheel, bearing a razor in her hand: her
    forelock had to be seized. She shared emblems of fickleness with Fortune (see *Henry V* III.vi
    for Fluellen's account of Fortune)

Whom such a coat keeps up can ne'er fall flat –
But to the purpose.
Last evening predecessor unto this,   65
The duke's son warily enquired for me,
Whose pleasure I attended: he began
By policy to open and unhusk me
About the time and common rumour:
But I had so much wit to keep my thoughts   70
Up in their built houses, yet afforded him
An idle satisfaction without danger.
But the whole aim and scope of his intent
Ended in this: conjuring me in private
To seek some strange digested fellow forth   75
Of ill-contented nature, either disgraced
In former times, or by new grooms displaced
Since his step-mother's nuptials: such a blood,
A man that were for evil only good;
To give you the true word some base-coined pandar.   80

VINDICE

I reach you, for I know his heat is such,
Were there as many concubines as ladies
He would not be contained, he must fly out.
I wonder how ill-featured, vile proportioned
That one should be, if she were made for woman,   85
Whom at the insurrection of his lust
He would refuse for once: heart, I think none;

68–9   i.e. artfully to sound me out on recent events and what people are saying about them

70–1   *keep . . . houses* keep my real opinions to myself

72   *idle satisfaction* token answer

75   *strange digested* of unusual, odd or melancholic disposition. The malcontent is a type in drama of the time (see Marston's play of 1603 called *The Malcontent*). Melancholy was associated with madness as well as dark moods: it was believed to be physiological, though it might also be triggered by frustrated ambition or injustice

78   *step-mother's nuptials* This is oddly specific, as if the dramatist meant to remind spectators of *Hamlet* (although there it is a step-*father*, Claudius, who marries the hero's mother, Gertrude)

80   *base-coined* The association of begetting children and coining money is memorably expressed in *Measure for Measure* II.iv.45–6, which may be in the dramatist's memory here

81   *reach* understand

84–7   i.e. there's no woman his lust would refuse, however ugly

Next to a skull, though more unsound than one,
Each face he meets he strongly dotes upon.

HIPPOLITO

Brother y'ave truly spoke him!   90
He knows not you, but I'll swear you know him.

VINDICE

And therefore I'll put on that knave for once,
And be a right man then, a man o' the time,
For to be honest is not to be i' the world.
Brother I'll be that strange composed fellow.   95

HIPPOLITO

And I'll prefer you brother.

VINDICE   Go to then,
The small'st advantage fattens wronged men.
It may point out Occasion; if I meet her
I'll hold her by the fore-top fast enough
Or like the French mole heave up hair and all.   100
I have a habit that will fit it quaintly –
Here comes our mother.

[*Enter* GRATIANA *and* CASTIZA]

HIPPOLITO   And sister.
VINDICE   We must coin.
Women are apt you know to take false money,
But I dare stake my soul for these two creatures,
Only excuse excepted, that they'll swallow   105
Because their sex is easy in belief.

GRATIANA

What news from Court son Carlo?
HIPPOLITO   Faith mother,

---

88 *unsound* diseased, with pun as in *Measure for Measure* I.ii.55–7: 'Nay, not (as one would
    say) healthy; but so sound as things that are hollow. Thy bones are hollow.' The bones
    are affected by syphilis: the conceit being that hollow things give off a hollow *sound*
92 *put on* disguise myself as
96 *prefer* recommend
100 *French mole* The mole undermines a lawn as syphilis (the French disease, prover-
    bially) causes hair to fall out
101 *habit* costume
102 *coin* feign (with subsequent pun on 'make money')
107 *Carlo* Presumably the author changed the character's name to 'Hippolito' in the
    course of composition, but forgot to cancel it here

'Tis whispered there the duchess' youngest son
Has played a rape on Lord Antonio's wife.

GRATIANA

On that religious lady!   110

CASTIZA

Royal blood monster! He deserves to die,
If Italy had no more hopes but he.

VINDICE

Sister y'ave sentenced most direct, and true,
The law's a woman, and would she were you.
Mother I must take leave of you.

GRATIANA   Leave for what?   115

VINDICE

I intend speedy travel.

HIPPOLITO

That he does madam.

GRATIANA   Speedy indeed!

VINDICE

For since my worthy father's funeral,
My life's unnatural to me, e'en compelled,
As if I lived now when I should be dead.   120

GRATIANA

Indeed he was a worthy gentleman
Had his estate been fellow to his mind.

VINDICE

The duke did much deject him.

GRATIANA   Much?

VINDICE   Too much.

And through disgrace oft smothered in his spirit
When it would mount. Surely I think he died   125
Of discontent, the nobleman's consumption.

GRATIANA

Most sure he did.

VINDICE   Did he? 'Lack, – you know all,

---

111 *Royal blood monster* i.e. the Youngest Son
114 *the law's a woman* Justice is conventionally represented as a blindfold woman hold-
     ing a sword and scales
118–20 The analogy with Hamlet seems clear and deliberate

You were his midnight secretary.

GRATIANA   No,

He was too wise to trust me with his thoughts.

VINDICE

[*Aside*] I' faith then father thou wast wise indeed,   130

'Wives are but made to go to bed and feed'. –

Come mother, sister; you'll bring me onward, brother?

HIPPOLITO

I will.

VINDICE

[*Aside*] I'll quickly turn into another.

Exeunt

128   *midnight secretary* most private confidante
134   *turn into another* adopt my disguise

[ACT I, SCENE ii]

Enter the old DUKE, LUSSURIOSO *his son, the* DUCHESS,
[SPURIO] *the bastard, the duchess' two sons* AMBITIOSO *and*
SUPERVACUO, *the third her youngest brought out with*
OFFICERS *for the* [*trial for*] *rape,* [*and*] *two* JUDGES

DUKE

Duchess it is your youngest son, we're sorry,
His violent act has e'en draw blood of honour
And stained our honours,
Thrown ink upon the forehead of our state
Which envious spirits will dip their pens into   5
After our death, and blot us in our tombs.
For that which would seem treason in our lives
Is laughter when we're dead. Who dares now whisper
That dares not then speak out, and e'en proclaim
With loud words and broad pens our closest shame.   10

1 JUDGE

Your Grace hath spoke like to your silver years
Full of confirmed gravity; for what is it to have
A flattering false insculption on a tomb
And in men's hearts reproach? The 'bowelled corpse
May be cered in, but, with free tongue I speak –   15
'The faults of great men through their cere cloths break'.

DUKE

They do, we're sorry for't, it is our fate,
To live in fear and die to live in hate.
I leave him to your sentence: doom him, lords,
The fact is great – whilst I sit by and sigh.   20

DUCHESS

[*Kneels*] My gracious lord I pray be merciful
Although his trespass far exceed his years;

---

4   *Thrown . . .forehead* Compare other allusions to the forehead at lines 33, 107,175,
    and 200, and at I.iii.8 and II.ii.163 below
10 *closest* most secret
13 *insculption* inscription carved into stone
14 *'bowelled* disembowelled and embalmed
15 *cered* sealed up in waxed (cered) cloth
20 *fact* crime

Think him to be your own as I am yours,
Call him not son-in-law: the law I fear
Will fall too soon upon his name and him.   25
Temper his fault with pity.
LUSSURIOSO   Good my lord,
Then 'twill not taste so bitter and unpleasant
Upon the judge's palate; for offences
Gilt o'er with mercy show like fairest women,
Good only for their beauties, which washed off,   30
No sin is uglier.
AMBITIOSO   I beseech your Grace,
Be soft and mild, let not relentless law
Look with an iron forehead on our brother.
SPURIO
[*Aside*] He yields small comfort yet – hope he shall die;
And if a bastard's wish might stand in force,   35
Would all the Court were turned into a corse.
DUCHESS
No pity yet? Must I rise fruitless then –
A wonder in a woman – are my knees
Of such low metal that without respect –
1 JUDGE
Let the offender stand forth,   40
'Tis the duke's pleasure that impartial doom
Shall take fast hold of his unclean attempt.
A rape! Why 'tis the very core of lust,
Double adultery.
YOUNGEST SON   So sir.
2 JUDGE   And which was worse,
Committed on the Lord Antonio's wife,   45
That general-honest lady. Confess my lord:
What moved you to't?

24   *son-in-law* step-son
36   *corse* an early form of 'corpse'
37   *rise fruitless* i.e. because she has kneeled in vain, with a pun on 'rise' = swell in
     pregnancy
38–9 *are . . . respect* i.e. is not my birth noble enough to deserve respect for my plea, espe-
     cially when it is made kneeling?
41   *doom* judgement
42   *fast* ed. (first Q)
46   *general-honest* wholly virtuous. For other composite forms see cruel-wise (line 70)
     and old-cool (line 74)

YOUNGEST SON   Why flesh and blood my lord:
    What should move men unto a woman else?

LUSSURIOSO
    Oh do not jest thy doom, trust not an axe
    Or sword too far; the law is a wise serpent   50
    And quickly can beguile thee of thy life.
    Though marriage only has made thee my brother
    I love thee so far: play not with thy death.

YOUNGEST SON
    I thank you troth, good admonitions faith,
    If I'd the grace now to make use of them.   55

1 JUDGE
    That lady's name has spread such a fair wing
    Over all Italy that if our tongues
    Were sparing toward the fact, judgement itself
    Would be condemned and suffer in men's thoughts.

YOUNGEST SON
    Well then 'tis done, and it would please me well   60
    Were it to do again. Sure she's a goddess
    For I'd no power to see her and to live;
    It falls out true in this for I must die.
    Her beauty was ordained to be my scaffold,
    And yet methinks I might be easier ceas'd;   65
    My faults being sport, let me but die in jest.

1 JUDGE
    This be the sentence—

DUCHESS
    Oh keep't upon your tongue, let it not slip,
    Death too soon steals out of a lawyer's lip,
    Be not so cruel-wise.

1 JUDGE   Your Grace must pardon us,   70
    'Tis but the justice of the law.

DUCHESS   The law
    Is grown more subtle than a woman should be.

SPURIO
    [*Aside*] Now, now he dies, rid 'em away.

DUCHESS
    [*Aside*] Oh what it is to have an old-cool duke

57–8   *our tongues . . . fact* we punished the crime lightly
  65 *ceas'd* put a stop to (Dodsley's emendation 'sess'd' = judged)

To be as slack in tongue as in performance.   75

1 JUDGE
Confirmed, this be the doom irrevocable.

DUCHESS
Oh!

1 JUDGE   Tomorrow early–

DUCHESS   Pray be abed my lord.

1 JUDGE
Your Grace much wrongs yourself.

AMBITIOSO   No 'tis that tongue.
Your too much right does do us too much wrong.

1 JUDGE
Let that offender–

DUCHESS   Live, and be in health.   80

1 JUDGE
Be on a scaffold–

DUKE   Hold, hold, my lord.

SPURIO [*Aside*]   Pox on't.
What makes my dad speak now?

DUKE
We will defer the judgement till next sitting,
In the meantime let him be kept close prisoner:
Guard bear him hence.

AMBITIOSO [*Aside*]   Brother this makes for thee,   85
Fear not, we'll have a trick to set thee free.

YOUNGEST SON
[*Aside*] Brother I will expect it from you both,
And in that hope I rest.

SUPERVACUO   Farewell, be merry.
                  Exit [YOUNGEST SON] *with a guard*

SPURIO
Delayed, deferred, nay then if judgement have
Cold blood, flattery and bribes will kill it.   90

DUKE
About it then my lords with your best powers,
More serious business calls upon our hours.
              Exeunt; [*all but the*] DUCHESS

---

75 *performance* sexual performance
79 *too much right* too strict application of the law, or too great privilege as a judge

DUCHESS
 Was't ever known step-duchess was so mild
 And calm as I? Some now would plot his death
 With easy doctors, those loose living men,   95
 And make his withered Grace fall to his grave
 And keep church better.
 Some second wife would do this, and dispatch
 Her double loathed lord at meat and sleep.
 Indeed 'tis true an old man's twice a child,   100
 Mine cannot speak! One of his single words
 Would quite have freed my youngest dearest son
 From death or durance, and have made him walk
 With a bold foot upon the thorny law,
 Whose prickles should bow under him; but 'tis not: 105
 And therefore wedlock faith shall be forgot.
 I'll kill him in his forehead, hate there feed –
 That wound is deepest though it never bleed;

[Enter SPURIO]

 And here comes he whom my heart points unto,
 His bastard son, but my love's true-begot;   110
 Many a wealthy letter have I sent him
 Swelled up with jewels, and the timorous man
 Is yet but coldly kind;
 That jewel's mine that quivers in his ear,
 Mocking his master's chillness and vain fear –   115
 H'as spied me now.
SPURIO   Madam? Your Grace so private?
 My duty on your hand.
DUCHESS
 Upon my hand sir, troth I think you'd fear
 To kiss my hand too if my lip stood there.
SPURIO
 Witness I would not madam.   *[He kisses her]*
DUCHESS   'Tis a wonder,   120
 For ceremony has made many fools.

 95 *easy* compliant
 103 *durance* imprisonment
 117 *My duty . . . hand* In token of dutiful respect I kiss your hand

It is as easy way unto a duchess
As to a hatted dame, if her love answer,
But that by timorous honours, pale respects,
Idle degrees of fear, men make their ways   125
Hard of themselves. What have you thought of me?

SPURIO

Madam I ever think of you, in duty,
Regard and—

DUCHESS   Puh, upon my love I mean.

SPURIO

I would 'twere love, but 'tis a fouler name than lust;
You are my father's wife, your Grace may guess now   130
What I could call it.

DUCHESS   Why th'art his son but falsely,
'Tis a hard question whether he begot thee.

SPURIO

I' faith 'tis true too; I'm an uncertain man
Of more uncertain woman; may be his groom
O' the stable begot me – you know I know not.   135
He could ride a horse well, a shrewd suspicion – marry!
He was wondrous tall, he had his length i' faith
For peeping over half-shut holiday windows:
Men would desire him 'light. When he was afoot
He made a goodly show under a penthouse,   140

---

123   *hatted dame* Women of the lower class wore hats
125   *Idle* foolish
134–5   Spurio's speculations about his paternity recall the bastard Edmund in *King Lear* who claims (I.ii.12–15) that his father's unlawful act of begetting him 'in the lusty stealth of nature' endowed him with
    'More composition and fierce quality,
    Than doth within a dull, stale, tired bed
    Go to th'creating a whole tribe of fops,
    Got 'tween asleep and wake'
136   *ride* The verb often carried a sexual sense (= have sexual intercourse with)
137–42   Given the context, further sexual innuendoes are to be assumed here, the general sense being that he went out to attract merchants' and citizens' wives, showing off and making their husbands jealous
139   *'light* alight from his horse
140   *penthouse* awning over shop windows ('your hat penthouse-like o'er the shop of your eyes' – *Love's Labour's Lost* III.i.17–18) or any sloping-roofed subsidiary building

And when he rid his hat would check the signs
And clatter barbers' basins.

DUCHESS   Nay, set you a horseback once
You'll ne'er 'light off.

SPURIO   Indeed I am a beggar.

DUCHESS

That's more the sign thou art great – but to our love.
Let it stand firm both in thought and mind   145
That the duke was thy father: as no doubt then
He bid fair for't, thy injury is the more;
For had he cut thee a right diamond,
Thou had'st been next set in the dukedom's ring,
When his worn self like age's easy slave   150
Had dropped out of the collet into the grave.
What wrong can equal this? Canst thou be tame
And think upon't?

SPURIO   No, mad and think upon't.

DUCHESS

Who would not be revenged of such a father,
E'en in the worst way? I would thank that sin   155
That could most injury him, and be in league with it.
Oh what a grief 'tis that a man should live
But once i' the world, and then to live a bastard,
The curse o' the womb, the thief of Nature,
Begot against the seventh commandment   160
Half damned in the conception by the justice
Of that unbribed everlasting law.

SPURIO

Oh I'd a hot backed devil to my father.

DUCHESS

Would not this mad e'en Patience, make blood rough?
Who but an eunuch would not sin, his bed   165
By one false minute disinherited?

141–2 He deliberately clattered the suspended shop signs and barbers' basins.
       (Presumably this arrogant behaviour was intended to make the shopkeepers jealous
       as well as to insult them. Mockery of citizens is typical in satiric plays of this time.)
142–3 Mocking Spurio's exuberant speech with a proverb
148–9 *diamond . . . ring* This recalls the image in I.i.19–20
151   *collet* socket, setting for a precious stone in a ring
164   *blood* i.e. temper

SPURIO

    Ay, there's the vengeance that my birth was wrapped in,

    I'll be revenged for all: now hate begin,

    I'll call foul incest but a venial sin.

DUCHESS

    Cold still: in vain then must a duchess woo?   170

SPURIO

    Madam I blush to say what I will do.

DUCHESS

    Thence flew sweet comfort, earnest and farewell.

                                         [*She kisses him*]

SPURIO

    Oh one incestuous kiss picks open hell.

DUCHESS

    Faith now old duke, my vengeance shall reach high,

    I'll arm thy brow with woman's heraldry.   *Exit*   175

SPURIO

    Duke, thou did'st do me wrong and by thy act

    Adultery is my nature.

    Faith if the truth were known I was begot

    After some gluttonous dinner – some stirring dish

    Was my first father; when deep healths went round   180

    And ladies' cheeks were painted red with wine,

    Their tongues as short and nimble as their heels

    Uttering words sweet and thick; and when they rose

    Were merrily disposed to fall again.

    In such a whispering and withdrawing hour,   185

    When base male bawds kept sentinel at stair-head

    Was I stol'n softly – oh damnation met

    The sin of feasts, drunken adultery.

    I feel it swell me; my revenge is just,

    I was begot in impudent wine and lust.   190

    Stepmother I consent to thy desires,

    I love thy mischief well but I hate thee,

    And those three cubs thy sons, wishing confusion

---

175 *woman's heraldry* i.e. the cuckold's horns which proverbially sprouted on the betrayed husband's forehead

178–88 Cf. Marston, *The Malcontent* III.ii.24–49, especially 'When in an Italian lascivious palace, a lady guardianless, / Left to the push of all allurement . . . / Her veins fill'd high with heating delicates, / Soft rest, sweet music, amorous masquerers, / Lascivious banquets, sin itself gilt o'er'

Death and disgrace may be their epitaphs.
As for my brother, the duke's only son,   195
Whose birth is more beholding to report
Than mine, and yet perhaps as falsely sown
– Women must not be trusted with their own–
I'll loose my days upon him, hate all I!
Duke on thy brow I'll draw my bastardy: 200
For indeed a bastard by nature should make cuckolds
Because he is the son of a cuckold maker.   *Exit*

---

195 *only son* i.e. Lussurioso
196 *birth . . . report* legitimacy is more firmly claimed
200 Cf. line 175 above

ACT I, SCENE iii

Enter VINDICE *and* HIPPOLITO, VINDICE *in disguise to
attend Lord* LUSSURIOSO *the duke's son*

VINDICE

What brother, am I far enough from myself?

HIPPOLITO

As if another man had been sent whole
Into the world and none wist how he came.

VINDICE

It will confirm me bold – the child o' the Court;
Let blushes dwell i' the country. Impudence,   5
Thou goddess of the palace, mistress of mistresses,
To whom the costly-perfumed people pray,
Strike thou my forehead into dauntless marble,
Mine eyes to steady sapphires; turn my visage
And if I must needs glow let me blush inward   10
That this immodest season may not spy
That scholar in my cheeks, fool bashfulness,
That maid in the old time whose flush of grace
Would never suffer her to get good clothes.
Our maids are wiser and are less ashamed –   15
Save Grace the bawd I seldom hear grace named!

HIPPOLITO

Nay brother you reach out o' the verge now –

[*Enter* LUSSURIOSO]

'Sfoot, the duke's son! Settle your looks.

VINDICE

Pray let me not be doubted.

HIPPOLITO

My lord.

LUSSURIOSO Hippolito? – [*To Vindice*] Be absent, leave us.   20
                                        [VINDICE *withdraws*]

---

1 *far . . . myself* sufficiently well disguised
13 The mother's name, Gratiana, means 'grace'
17 i.e. now you are going too far

HIPPOLITO

My lord, after long search, wary enquiries
And politic siftings I made choice of yon fellow
Whom I guess rare for many deep employments:
This our age swims within him; and if Time
Had so much hair I should take him for Time,   25
He is so near kin to this present minute.

LUSSURIOSO

'Tis enough,
We thank thee: yet words are but great men's blanks;
Gold though it be dumb does utter the best thanks.

                                                              [*Gives him money*]

HIPPOLITO

Your plenteous honour – an ex'lent fellow my lord.   30

LUSSURIOSO

So, give us leave–

                                                              [*Exit* HIPPOLITO]

    [*To* VINDICE]   Welcome, be not far off,
We must be better acquainted. Push, be bold
With us, thy hand.

VINDICE   With all my heart i' faith!
How dost sweet musk-cat? When shall we lie together?

LUSSURIOSO

[*Aside*] Wondrous knave!   35
Gather him into boldness: 'sfoot the slave's
Already as familiar as an ague
And shakes me at his pleasure. – Friend I can
Forget myself in private, but elsewhere
I pray do you remember me.   40

24–5 *Time . . . hair* Time was proverbially bald: see Tilley T 311

28   *words . . . blanks* i.e. words come cheap. *Blanks* may mean a document or bill with
      spaces left to be filled in, or metal not yet stamped to give it value as currency (as
      Foakes suggests)

34   *musk-cat* paramour, courtesan. Cf. Jonson, *Every Man Out of His Humour* II.i.97:
      'He sleepes with a muske-cat every night.' Here a homosexual affair is implied

36   *Gather . . . boldness* This phrase is obscure. *OED* 'gather' vt 16e records a rare mean-
      ing, 'chide or reprove'. Given the sense of the general context, where Lussurioso
      realizes he made an error (lines 31–3) in supposing Vindice to be shy, the sense
      may be 'he must be accounted bold'

39   *Forget myself* be familiar

40   i.e. kindly show me due respect

VINDICE

Oh very well sir – I conster myself saucy!

LUSSURIOSO

What hast been – of what profession?

VINDICE

A bone setter.

LUSSURIOSO

A bone setter!

VINDICE

A bawd my lord. One that sets bones together.   45

LUSSURIOSO

[*Aside*] Notable bluntness!

Fit, fit for me, e'en trained up to my hand. –

Thou hast been scrivener to much knavery then?

VINDICE

Fool to abundance sir; I have been witness

To the surrenders of a thousand virgins   50

And not so little;

I have seen patrimonies washed apieces,

Fruit fields turned into bastards,

And in a world of acres

Not so much dust due to the heir 'twas left to   55

As would well gravel a petition.

LUSSURIOSO

[*Aside*] Fine villain! Troth I like him wondrously,

He's e'en shaped for my purpose. – Then thou know'st

In the world strange lust?

VINDICE   Oh Dutch lust! Fulsome lust!

Drunken procreation, which begets so many drunkards;   60

Some father dreads not, gone to bed in wine,

---

41 *conster* construe, consider

48 *scrivener* secretary, assistant

49 *Fool* Q's reading means 'voluntary dupe' (Nicoll). Collins in his 1878 edition conjectures *'Sfoot*, and some such expletive (*Pooh, Push*) is orthographically possible

52 *patrimonies washed apieces* estates dissolved or broken up by drunken profligacy. (The metaphor associates drinking with flooding.)

53 *Fruit fields . . . bastards* i.e. fruit fields sold to pay for maintaining bastards, sexual profligacy being another threat to maintaining estates. County gentry selling out to city merchants are often a topic of satiric comment in plays of the time, especially Middleton's city comedies

56 *gravel* Sand would be strewn on a petition to dry the ink

59 *Dutch* i.e. proverbially excessive, Gargantuan

To slide from the mother and cling the daughter-in-law;
Some uncles are adulterous with their nieces,
Brothers with brothers' wives – Oh hour of incest!
Any kin now next to the rim o' the sister   65
Is man's meat in these days, and in the morning,
When they are up and dressed and their mask on,
Who can perceive this, save that eternal eye
That sees through flesh and all? Well – if anything be damned
It will be twelve o'clock at night: that twelve   70
Will never 'scape;
It is the Judas of the hours, wherein
Honest salvation is betrayed to sin.

LUSSURIOSO
In troth it is too; but let this talk glide.
It is our blood to err though hell gaped loud: 75
Ladies know Lucifer fell, yet still are proud!
Now sir, wert thou as secret as thou'rt subtle
And deeply fathomed into all estates
I would embrace thee for a near employment,
And thou should'st swell in money and be able   80
To make lame beggars crouch to thee.

VINDICE   My lord?
Secret? I ne'er had that disease o' the mother,
I praise my father! Why are men made close
But to keep thoughts in best? I grant you this:
Tell but some woman a secret over night,   85
Your doctor may find it in the urinal i' the morning;
But, my lord–

LUSSURIOSO   So, thou'rt confirmed in me
And thus I enter thee.

                              [*Gives him money*]

VINDICE   This Indian devil
Will quickly enter any man: but a usurer,
He prevents that by entering the devil first!   90

LUSSURIOSO
Attend me, I am past my depth in lust
And I must swim or drown. All my desires

82 *disease o' the mother* i.e. of talking too much, with a possible pun on 'the mother', a
    term for a form of hysteria, as in *King Lear* II.iv.56
87 *in me* in my confidence
88 *Indian devil* silver and gold from the Indies

Are levelled at a virgin not far from Court,
To whom I have conveyed by messenger
Many waxed lines full of my neatest spirit,   95
And jewels that were able to ravish her
Without the help of man: all which and more
She, foolish-chaste, sent back, the messengers
Receiving frowns for answers.
VINDICE   Possible?
'Tis a rare phoenix whoe'er she be.   100
If your desires be such, she so repugnant:
In troth my lord I'd be revenged and marry her.
LUSSURIOSO
Push; the dowry of her blood and of her fortunes
Are both too mean – good enough to be bad withal.
I'm one of that number can defend   105
Marriage is good; yet rather keep a friend.
Give me my bed by stealth – there's true delight;
What breeds a loathing in't but night by night?
VINDICE
A very fine religion!
LUSSURIOSO   Therefore thus:
I'll trust thee in the business of my heart   110
Because I see thee well experienced
In this luxurious day wherein we breathe:
Go thou and with a smooth enchanting tongue
Bewitch her ears and cozen her of all grace;
Enter upon the portion of her soul,   115
Her honour, which she calls her chastity,
And bring it into expense, for honesty
Is like a stock of money laid to sleep
Which, ne'er so little broke, does never keep.

---

95 *waxed lines* sealed letters
    neatest most intense
98 *foolish-chaste* Cf. composite adjectives in I.ii.46 and n.
101 *repugnant* resisting
106 *friend* mistress
115 A bride brings to her husband a financial dowry (*portion*); she also brings a
     spiritual dowry, virtue, and its corresponding social/cultural value, honour
117 *bring . . . expense* make her spend it

VINDICE

    You have given 't the tang i' faith my lord;   120
    Make known the lady to me and my brain
    Shall swell with strange invention: I will move it
    Till I expire with speaking and drop down
    Without a word to save me; – but I'll work–

LUSSURIOSO

    We thank thee and will raise thee; receive her name.   125
    It is the only daughter to Madam Gratiana
    The late widow.

VINDICE [*Aside*]   Oh, my sister, my sister!

LUSSURIOSO

    Why dost walk aside?

VINDICE

    My lord I was thinking how I might begin,
    As thus – 'oh lady' – or twenty hundred devices: 130
    Her very bodkin will put a man in.

LUSSURIOSO

    Ay, or the wagging of her hair.

VINDICE

    No, that shall put you in my lord.

LUSSURIOSO

    Shall't? Why content: dost know the daughter then?

VINDICE

    Oh ex'lent well by sight.

LUSSURIOSO   That was her brother   135
    That did prefer thee to us.

VINDICE   My lord I think so,
    I knew I had seen him somewhere.

LUSSURIOSO

    And therefore prithee let thy heart to him
    Be as a virgin, close.

VINDICE   Oh my good lord.

LUSSURIOSO

    We may laugh at that simple age within him–   140

VINDICE

    Ha! Ha! Ha!

    120 *given 't* ed. (gint Q)
          given 't the tang caught the flavour, got it right
    122 *move it* make it work
    131 *put a man in* provide an opening for seduction

LUSSURIOSO

    Himself being made the subtle instrument

    To wind up a good fellow.

VINDICE   That's I my lord.

LUSSURIOSO

    That's thou.

    To entice and work his sister.

VINDICE   A pure novice!   145

LUSSURIOSO

    'Twas finely managed.

VINDICE   Gallantly carried:

    A pretty-perfumed villain!

LUSSURIOSO   I've bethought me.

    If she prove chaste still and immoveable,

    Venture upon the mother, and with gifts

    As I will furnish thee, begin with her.   150

VINDICE

    Oh fie, fie, that's the wrong end my lord.

    'Tis mere impossible that a mother by any gifts

    Should become a bawd to her own daughter!

LUSSURIOSO

    Nay then I see thou'rt but a puny

    In the subtle mystery of a woman: 155

    Why 'tis held now no dainty dish: the name

    Is so in league with age that nowadays

    It does eclipse three quarters of a mother.

VINDICE

    Does 't so my lord?

    Let me alone then to eclipse the fourth.   160

LUSSURIOSO

    Why well said; come I'll furnish thee: but first

    Swear to be true in all.

VINDICE   True?

LUSSURIOSO   Nay but swear!

VINDICE

    Swear?

    I hope your honour little doubts my faith.

---

143   *wind up* set up, recruit (with the implication of embolden)

152–3 This is what happens in Machiavelli's comedy *Mandragola*

LUSSURIOSO

    Yet, for my humour's sake, 'cause I love swearing—   165

VINDICE

    'Cause you love swearing, 'slud I will.

LUSSURIOSO   Why enough:

    Ere long look to be made of better stuff.

VINDICE

    That will do well indeed my lord.

LUSSURIOSO   Attend me.   [*Exit*]

VINDICE

    Oh,

    Now let me burst, I've eaten noble poison!   170

    We are made strange fellows, brother, innocent villains:

    Wilt not be angry when thou hear'st on't, think'st thou?

    I' faith thou shalt. Swear me to foul my sister!

    Sword I durst make a promise of him to thee,

    Thou shalt dis-heir him, it shall be thine honour;   175

    And yet, now angry froth is down in me,

    It would not prove the meanest policy

    In this disguise to try the faith of both;

    Another might have had the self-same office,

    Some slave that would have wrought effectually,   180

    Ay and perhaps o'erwrought 'em: therefore I,

    Being thought travelled, will apply myself

    Unto the self-same form, forget my nature,

    As if no part about me were kin to 'em,

    So touch 'em – though I durst almost for good   185

    Venture my lands in heaven upon their blood.

---

167   i.e. expect promotion as your prompt reward

182   *travelled* on a journey abroad

[ACT I, SCENE iv]

Enter the discontented lord ANTONIO (*whose wife the
duchess' youngest son ravished*); *he discovering* [*her dead body*]
to certain Lords and [*to* PIERO *and*] HIPPOLITO

ANTONIO

Draw nearer lords and be sad witnesses
Of a fair comely building newly fallen,
Being falsely undermined. Violent rape
Has played a glorious act: behold my lords
A sight that strikes man out of me.   5

PIERO

That virtuous lady!

ANTONIO   Precedent for wives!

HIPPOLITO

The blush of many women, whose chaste presence
Would e'en call shame up to their cheeks
And make pale wanton sinners have good colours—

ANTONIO

Dead!   10
Her honour first drank poison, and her life,
Being fellows in one house, did pledge her honour.

PIERO

Oh grief of many!

ANTONIO   I marked not this before:
A prayer book the pillow to her cheek;
This was her rich confection, and another   15
Placed in her right hand with a leaf tucked up,
Pointing to these words:

---

0 s.d. Presumably a traverse curtain, hung across the central part of the tiring-house wall, is drawn to reveal the dead woman: her pose is emblematic and its significance is explained by the lords who gather round it. Its pose is like that of Imogen, who falls asleep, leaving a book open at a significant place, in *Cymbeline* II.ii. See also the discussion in Marion Lomax, *Stage Images and Traditions, Shakespeare to Ford* (1987)

s.d.2 *her dead body* ed. (the body of her dead Q)

15 *confection* a term for a medicinal means of preservation, here transferred to a religious sense

Melius virtute mori, quam per dedecus vivere.
True and effectual it is indeed.

HIPPOLITO

My lord since you invite us to your sorrows   20
Let's truly taste 'em, that with equal comfort
As to ourselves we may relieve your wrongs:
We have grief too that yet walks without tongue:
Curae leves loquuntur, majores stupent.

ANTONIO

You deal with truth my lord.   25
Lend me but your attentions and I'll cut
Long grief into short words: last revelling night,
When torchlight made an artificial noon
About the Court, some courtiers in the masque
Putting on better faces than their own,   30
Being full of fraud and flattery, amongst whom
The duchess' youngest son – that moth to honour –
Filled up a room; and with long lust to eat
Into my wearing, amongst all the ladies
Singled out that dear form, who ever lived   35
As cold in lust as she is now in death –
Which that step-duchess' monster knew too well –
And therefore in the height of all the revels,
When music was heard loudest, courtiers busiest,
And ladies great with laughter – Oh vicious minute!   40
Unfit, but for relation, to be spoke of –
Then with a face more impudent than his vizard
He harried her amidst a throng of pandars
That live upon damnation of both kinds
And fed the ravenous vulture of his lust.   45

18   'Better die virtuous than live dishonoured.' This classical Roman principle inspired
     the tragic resolve of the noble Lucrece, who committed suicide to purify the family
     honour after being raped by Tarquin – a tale which Shakespeare treated in his
     poem *The Rape of Lucrece*
24   'Lesser cares can speak, greater cares are silent'. Nicoll notes this as a recollection of
     Seneca, *Hippolytus*
29   *masque* Q (mask)
32   *moth* The youngest son destroys Antonio's honour as a moth eats away fabric.
     Antonio refers to his honour as clothing ('my wearing', line 34)
37   *step-duchess' monster* ed. (step Duchess-Monster Q)
39   *heard* ed. (hard Q)
41   *for relation* except for the necessity of informing you

Oh death to think on't! She, her honour forced,
Deemed it a nobler dowry for her name
To die with poison than to live with shame.
HIPPOLITO
A wondrous lady of rare fire compact,
She's made her name an empress by that act.   50
PIERO
My lord what judgement follows the offender?
ANTONIO
Faith none my lord, it cools and is deferred.
PIERO
Delay the doom for rape?
ANTONIO
Oh you must note who 'tis should die –
The duchess' son. She'll look to be a saver: 55
'Judgement in this age is near kin to favour'.
HIPPOLITO
Nay then, step forth thou bribeless officer;   [*Draws sword*]
I bind you all in steel to bind you surely,
Here let your oaths meet, to be kept and paid
Which else will stick like rust and shame the blade.   60
Strengthen my vow, that if at the next sitting
Judgement speak all in gold and spare the blood
Of such a serpent, e'en before their seats
To let his soul out, which long since was found
Guilty in heaven.
ALL   We swear it and will act it.   65
ANTONIO
Kind gentlemen I thank you in mine ire.
HIPPOLITO
'Twere pity
The ruins of so fair a monument
Should not be dipped in the defacer's blood.
PIERO
Her funeral shall be wealthy, for her name   70
Merits a tomb of pearl. My lord Antonio

---

50   *empress* There may be a pun on 'impress' = emblem
65   Ironically recalling I.iii.161–6 above

For this time wipe your lady from your eyes;
No doubt our grief and yours may one day court it
When we are more familiar with Revenge.

ANTONIO

That is my comfort gentlemen, and I joy   75
In this one happiness above the rest,
Which will be called a miracle at last,
That being an old man I'd a wife so chaste.

Exeunt

ACT II, SCENE i

Enter CASTIZA *the sister*

CASTIZA

How hardly shall that maiden be beset
⌈Whose only fortunes are her constant thoughts,⌉ ✍
That has no other child's-part but her honour
That keeps her low and empty in estate.
Maids and their honours are like poor beginners: 5
Were not sin rich there would be fewer sinners:
Why had not virtue a revenue? Well,
I know the cause: 'twould have impoverished hell.

[*Enter* DONDOLO]

How now Dondolo.

DONDOLO

Madonna, there is one as they say a thing of flesh and blood, a   10
man I take him, by his beard, that would very desirously mouth
to mouth with you.

CASTIZA

What's that?

DONDOLO

Show his teeth in your company.

CASTIZA

I understand thee not.   15

DONDOLO

Why, speak with you Madonna.

CASTIZA

Why, say so madman and cut off a great deal of dirty way. Had
it not been better spoke, in ordinary words, that one would
speak with me?

DONDOLO

Ha, ha, that's as ordinary as two shillings; I would strive a little   20
to show myself in my place. A gentleman-usher scorns to use
the phrase and fancy of a servingman.

---

1   *beset* besieged, surrounded by men of hostile intent
3   *child's-part* inheritance

CASTIZA

Yours be your own sir: go direct him hither.

[*Exit* DONDOLO]

I hope some happy tidings from my brother
That lately travelled, whom my soul affects.   25
Here he comes.

Enter VINDICE *her brother disguised*

VINDICE

Lady the best of wishes to your sex:
Fair skins and new gowns.

[*Gives her a letter*]

CASTIZA   Oh they shall thank you sir–
Whence this?

VINDICE   Oh from a dear and worthy friend,
Mighty!

CASTIZA   From whom?

VINDICE   The duke's son.

CASTIZA   Receive that!   30

A box o' the ear to [VINDICE] *her brother*

I swore I'd put anger in my hand
And pass the virgin limits of myself
To him that next appeared in that base office,
To be his sin's attorney. Bear to him
That figure of my hate upon thy cheek   35
Whilst 'tis yet hot, and I'll reward thee for 't;
Tell him my honour shall have a rich name
When several harlots shall share his with shame:
Farewell, commend me to him in my hate!   *Exit*

VINDICE

It is the sweetest box that e'er my nose came nigh: 40
The finest drawn-work cuff that e'er was worn:
I'll love this blow forever, and this cheek
Shall still henceforward take the wall of this.
Oh I'm above my tongue! Most constant sister,
In this thou hast right honourable shown;   45

23 *own* ed. (one Q)
25 *affects* loves
41 *drawn-work cuff* a pun on (i) the decorated cuff of her sleeve, (ii) the blow or cuff
    round the ear she gave him which has decorated his cheek (Foakes)
43 *take the wall* take precedence over

Many are called by their honour that have none,
Thou art approved forever in my thoughts.
It is not in the power of words to taint thee.
And yet for the salvation of my oath,
As my resolve in that point, I will lay   50
Hard siege unto my mother, though I know
A siren's tongue could not bewitch her so.

[*Enter* GRATIANA]

Mass, fitly, here she comes: thanks my disguise:
Madam good afternoon.
GRATIANA   Y'are welcome sir.
VINDICE
The next of Italy commends him to you: 55
Our mighty expectation, the duke's son.
GRATIANA
I think myself much honoured that he pleases
To rank me in his thoughts.
VINDICE   So may you lady:
One that is like to be our sudden duke –
The crown gapes for him every tide – and then   60
Commander o'er us all; do but think on him,
How blest were they now that could pleasure him,
E'en with anything almost.
GRATIANA   Ay, save their honour.
VINDICE
Tut, one would let a little of that go too
And ne'er be seen in't: ne'er be seen in't, mark you,   65
I'd wink and let it go–
GRATIANA   Marry but I would not.
VINDICE
Marry but I would I hope; I know you would too
If you'd that blood now which you gave your daughter;
To her indeed 'tis, this wheel comes about;
That man that must be all this perhaps ere morning –   70
For his white father does but mould away –
Has long desired your daughter.
GRATIANA   Desired?

55   *next of Italy* i.e. next in succession to the Duke
65   *in't* i.e. losing honour

175

VINDICE

Nay but hear me:
He desires now that will command hereafter
Therefore be wise; I speak as more a friend   75
To you than him. Madam I know y'are poor,
And 'lack the day,
There are too many poor ladies already;
Why should you vex the number? 'Tis despised.
Live wealthy, rightly understand the world   80
And chide away that foolish country girl
Keeps company with your daughter, chastity.

GRATIANA

Oh fie, fie, the riches of the world cannot hire a mother to such
a most unnatural task.

VINDICE

No, but a thousand angels can.   85
Men have no power, angels must work you to it,
The world descends into such base born evils
That forty angels can make four score devils.
There will be fools still I perceive, still fools.
Would I be poor, dejected, scorned of greatness,   90
Swept from the palace, and see other daughters
Spring with the dew o'the Court, having mine own
So much desired and loved – by the duke's son?
No, I would raise my state upon her breast
And call her eyes my tenants; I would count   95
My yearly maintenance upon her cheeks,
Take coach upon her lip, and all her parts
Should keep men after men and I would ride

---

79   *vex* aggravate the problem by increasing the number
85   *angels* gold coins
90   *dejected* lowly
94–9 The daughter's physical attractions are itemized and fancifully imagined as parts of
an estate, each part yielding rents to pay for the mother's extravagant way of life.
This is an ironic use of a rhetorical scheme, the poetical catalogue of the charms of
a woman from head to foot: see Andrew Marvell's poem 'To His Coy Mistress' for a
comic-hyperbolic version, in which each part of the body is valued in terms of the
time needed to admire it as it deserves:
    'An hundred years should go to praise
    Thine eyes, and on thy forehead gaze.
    Two hundred to adore each breast . . .'
98   *ride* with a bawdy innuendo, as at I.ii.136

In pleasure upon pleasure.
You took great pains for her, once when it was,   100
Let her requite it now, though it be but some.
You brought her forth, she may well bring you home.

GRATIANA

Oh heavens, this overcomes me!

VINDICE

[*Aside*] Not, I hope, already?

GRATIANA

[*Aside*] It is too strong for me. Men know, that know us,   105
We are so weak their words can overthrow us.
He touched me nearly, made my virtues bate
When his tongue struck upon my poor estate.

VINDICE

[*Aside*] I e'en quake to proceed, my spirit turns edge,
I fear me she's unmothered, yet I'll venture –   110
'That woman is all male whom none can enter!'
What think you now lady, speak, are you wiser?
What said advancement to you? Thus it said:
The daughter's fall lifts up the mother's head:
Did it not madam? But I'll swear it does   115
In many places. Tut, this age fears no man –
' 'Tis no shame to be bad, because 'tis common'.

GRATIANA

Ay that's the comfort on't.

VINDICE   The comfort on't!
I keep the best for last; can these persuade you
To forget heaven – and–

                                        [*Gives her gold*]

GRATIANA   Ay, these are they –
VINDICE   Oh!   120

GRATIANA

That enchant our sex; these are the means

---

100 *pains* i.e. in childbirth as well as those taken in careful upbringing
101 *but some* i.e. only in part
107 *bate* become depressed, weaken
109 *turns edge* becomes blunt or dull
116 *places*, ed. (places. Q)
117 *'tis common* Perhaps recalling *Hamlet* I.ii.72–4: Gertrude: 'Thou know'st 'tis common,
     all that lives must die,/Passing through nature to eternity.' Hamlet: 'Ay, madam, it is
     common.'

That govern our affections. That woman will
Not be troubled with the mother long
That sees the comfortable shine of you;
I blush to think what for your sakes I'll do.   125

VINDICE

[*Aside*] Oh suffering heaven with thy invisible finger
E'en at this instant turn the precious side
Of both mine eyeballs inward, not to see myself.

GRATIANA

Look you sir.

VINDICE   Holla.

GRATIANA   Let this thank your pains.

VINDICE

Oh you're a kind madam.   130

GRATIANA

I'll see how I can move.

VINDICE   Your words will sting.

GRATIANA

If she be still chaste I'll ne'er call her mine.

VINDICE

[*Aside*] Spoke truer than you meant it.

GRATIANA

Daughter Castiza.

[*Enter* CASTIZA]

CASTIZA   Madam.

VINDICE   Oh she's yonder.

Meet her.   135

Troops of celestial soldiers guard her heart:

123 *the mother* Punning on the senses (i) a mother's sense of duty, (ii) hysteria, as at I.iii.82
125 *blush* another emphasis on this sign of modest or guilty shame (See IV.iv.44.)
126 *invisible finger* Probably, taken with other references to supernatural omens in the play (the blazing star, V.iii.16; the thunder, IV.ii.156, 195), the dramatist has in mind the Book of Daniel, chapter 5, the story of Belshazzar, who (with a thousand of his lords) made a great feast and praised the gods of gold and silver, brass, iron, wood, and stone while drinking wine. Then 'came forth fingers of a man's hand' and wrote on the wall. The king saw this and trembled. Daniel, called to interpret the words (Mene, Mene, Tekel, Upharsin), declared that they announced God's judgement that Belshazzar's rule was found wanting and his kingdom would be divided. The same night Belshazzar the king was slain and Darius the Median took his kingdom. The phrase 'the finger of God' occurs in Exodus 8 : 19 and Luke 11 : 20

Yon dam has devils enough to take her part.

CASTIZA

Madam what makes yon evil-officed man
In presence of you?

GRATIANA   Why?

CASTIZA   He lately brought
Immodest writing sent from the duke's son   140
To tempt me to dishonourable act.

GRATIANA

Dishonourable act? Good honourable fool,
That wouldst be honest 'cause thou wouldst be so,
Producing no one reason but thy will;
And 't 'as a good report, prettily commended –   145
But pray by whom? Mean people, ignorant people!
The better sort I'm sure cannot abide it,
And by what rule should we square out our lives
But by our betters' actions? Oh if thou knew'st
What 'twere to lose it, thou would never keep it: 150
But there's a cold curse laid upon all maids,
Whilst others clip the sun they clasp the shades!
Virginity is paradise, locked up.
You cannot come by yourselves without fee,
And 'twas decreed that man should keep the key: 155
Deny advancement, treasure, the duke's son!

CASTIZA

I cry you mercy; lady I mistook you,
Pray did you see my mother? Which way went you?
Pray God I have not lost her.

VINDICE [*Aside*]   Prettily put by.

GRATIANA

Are you as proud to me as coy to him?   160
Do you not know me now?

CASTIZA   Why are you she?
The world's so changed, one shape into another,
It is a wise child now that knows her mother.

---

147 *better* i.e. superior in wealth and rank. Note this attempt to suppress the moral con-
     notation
154 i.e. you cannot take full possession of yourselves without paying a fee to have the
     treasure unlocked
163 A proverb listed by Tilley (C 309)

VINDICE
    [*Aside*] Most right i' faith.
GRATIANA   I owe your cheek my hand
    For that presumption now, but I'll forget it;   165
    Come you shall leave those childish 'haviours
    And understand your time; fortunes flow to you –
    What, will you be a girl?
    If all feared drowning that spy waves ashore
    Gold would grow rich and all the merchants poor.   170
CASTIZA
    It is a pretty saying of a wicked one.
    But methinks now
    It does not show so well out of your mouth–
    Better in his.
VINDICE [*Aside*] Faith bad enough in both.
    Were I in earnest – as I'll seem no less–   175
    I wonder lady your own mother's words
    Cannot be taken, nor stand in full force.
    'Tis honesty you urge: what's honesty?
    'Tis but heaven's beggar; and what woman is
    So foolish to keep honesty   180
    And be not able to keep herself? No,
    Times are grown wiser and will keep less charge.
    A maid that has small portion now intends
    To break up house and live upon her friends;
    How blest are you: you have happiness alone;   185
    Others must fall to thousands, you to one
    Sufficient in himself to make your forehead
    Dazzle the world with jewels, and petitionary people
    Start at your presence.
GRATIANA   Oh if I were young
    I should be ravished!
    CASTIZA   Ay, to lose your honour.   190
VINDICE
    'Slid, how can you lose your honour
    To deal with my lord's grace?
    He'll add more honour to it by his title;

187   *forehead* See I.ii.4 and n.

Your mother will tell you how.

GRATIANA   That I will.

VINDICE

Oh think upon the pleasure of the palace,   195
Secured ease and state; the stirring meats
Ready to move out of the dishes
That e'en now quicken when they're eaten,
Banquets abroad by torchlight, musics, sports,
Bare-headed vassals that had ne'er the fortune   200
To keep on their own hats, but let horns wear 'em;
Nine coaches waiting – hurry, hurry, hurry–

CASTIZA

Ay, to the devil!

VINDICE

[*Aside*] Ay, to the devil. – To the duke by my faith!

GRATIANA

Ay, to the duke. Daughter you'd scorn to think o' the devil an   205
you were there once.

VINDICE

[*Aside*] True, for most there are as proud as he for his heart,
i' faith–
Who'd sit at home in a neglected room
Dealing her short-lived beauty to the pictures   210
That are as useless as old men, when those
Poorer in face and fortune than herself
Walk with a hundred acres on their backs –
Fair meadows cut into green foreparts – oh,
It was the greatest blessing ever happened to women   215
When farmers' sons agreed, and met again,
To wash their hands and come up gentlemen.

198   *quicken* enliven, with a play on the sense 'make pregnant'
199   *musics* (Q) The plural form makes sense, signifying pieces of music performed.
        OED cites a usage in Sidney, *Arcadia* (OED sb 4)
200   *bare-headed vassals* Hats were not worn by men at court
201   *horns* antlers used as hatracks, with a glance at the horns sprouted by a cuckold
211   *useless* i.e. in terms of sensuous pleasure
213   i.e. their clothes cost as much as a hundred acres of land
214   *green foreparts* (i) the park in front of a manor-house, (ii) an ornamental part of a
        woman's dress, covering the breast
217   i.e. exchange their honest working lives as farmers for the foppish existence of
        gentlemen in town and at court

The commonwealth has flourished ever since.
Lands that were mete by the rod – that labour's spared –
Tailors ride down and measure 'em by the yard.   220
Fair trees, those comely foretops of the field,
Are cut to maintain head-tires: much untold.
All thrives but Chastity, she lies a-cold.
Nay shall I come nearer to you: mark but this:
Why are there so few honest women but because 'tis the poorer   225
profession? That's accounted best that's best followed, least in
trade, least in fashion, and that's not honesty, believe it; and do
but note the low and dejected price of it:
'Lose but a pearl, we search and cannot brook it;
But that once gone, who is so mad to look it?'   230

GRATIANA
Troth he says true.

CASTIZA   False! I defy you both:
I have endured you with an ear of fire,
Your tongues have struck hot irons on my face;
Mother, come from that poisonous woman there.

GRATIANA
Where?   235

CASTIZA
Do you not see her? She's too inward then:
Slave perish in thy office; you heavens please
Henceforth to make the mother a disease
Which first begins with me; yet I've outgone you.   *Exit*

VINDICE
[*Aside*] Oh angels clap your wings upon the skies   240
And give this virgin crystal plaudities!

219   *mete by the rod* measured in rods (the customary measuring unit for land)
219–20   The destruction of tradition is ironically imaged in the different scales of measure-
         ment used by the farming gentry and merchant tailors. Even when the city tailor
         buys a manor in the country he retains the acquisitive attitudes of the shopkeeper
         instead of adopting the values of conservation and continuity associated with keep-
         ing a country estate
220   *yard* the unit of measure for cloth, the cloth-yard
221   *foretops* front lock of hair arranged ornamentally
222   *head-tires* head-dresses
228   *low* ed. (loue Q)
229   *brook it* bear its loss

GRATIANA

    Peevish, coy, foolish! But return this answer:
    My lord shall be most welcome when his pleasure
    Conducts him this way; I will sway mine own:
    Women with women can work best alone.   *Exit*   245

VINDICE

    Indeed I'll tell him so.
    Oh more uncivil, more unnatural
    Than those base-titled creatures that look downward,
    Why does not heaven turn black or with a frown
    Undo the world? Why does not earth start up   250
    And strike the sins that tread upon it? Oh,
    Were't not for gold and women there would be no damnation.
    Hell would look like a lord's great kitchen without fire in't;
    But 'twas decreed before the world began
    That they should be the hooks to catch at man.   *Exit*   255

[ACT II, SCENE ii]

Enter LUSSURIOSO *with* HIPPOLITO *Vindice's brother*

LUSSURIOSO
I much applaud
Thy judgement, thou art well read in a fellow,
And 'tis the deepest art to study man.
I know this which I never learned in schools,
The world's divided into knaves and fools.   5
HIPPOLITO
[*Aside*] Knave in your face my lord – behind your back!
LUSSURIOSO
And I much thank thee that thou hast preferred
A fellow of discourse, well mingled,
And whose brain time hath seasoned.
HIPPOLITO   True my lord,
We shall find season once I hope. – [*Aside*] Oh villain,   10
To make such an unnatural slave of me! – But–

[*Enter* VINDICE *disguised*]

LUSSURIOSO
Mass here he comes.
HIPPOLITO
[*Aside*] And now shall I have free leave to depart.
LUSSURIOSO
Your absence – leave us.
HIPPOLITO
[*Aside*] Are not my thoughts true?   15
I must remove; but brother you may stay.
Heart, we are both made bawds a new found way!   *Exit*
LUSSURIOSO
Now, we're an even number: a third man's dangerous,
Especially her brother. Say, be free,
Have I a pleasure toward?
VINDICE   Oh my lord.   20
LUSSURIOSO
Ravish me in thine answer: art thou rare,

Hast thou beguiled her of salvation
And rubbed hell o'er with honey? Is she a woman?

INDICE
  In all but in desire.

USSURIOSO   Then she's in nothing –
  I bate in courage now.

INDICE   The words I brought   25
  Might well have made indifferent honest naught;
  A right good woman in these days is changed
  Into white money with less labour far.
  Many a maid has turned to Mahomet
  With easier working. I durst undertake,   30
  Upon the pawn and forfeit of my life
  With half those words to flat a Puritan's wife,
  But she is close and good; yet 'tis a doubt
  By this time – oh the mother, the mother!

USSURIOSO
  I never thought their sex had been a wonder   35
  Until this minute: what fruit from the mother?

INDICE
  [*Aside*] Now must I blister my soul, be forsworn,
  Or shame the woman that received me first.
  I will be true; thou liv'st not to proclaim;
  Spoke to a dying man shame has no shame.   40
  My lord.

USSURIOSO Who's that?

INDICE   Here's none but I my lord.

USSURIOSO
  What would thy haste utter?

INDICE   Comfort.

USSURIOSO   Welcome.

INDICE
  The maid being dull, having no mind to travel
  Into unknown lands, what did me I straight
  But set spurs to the mother; golden spurs   45
  Will put her to a false gallop in a trice.

---

26 *indifferent honest naught* a person of average virtue wicked
28 *white* silver
29 Many a virgin has been converted with less difficulty to the worship of Mahomet
44 *did me I* did I do

LUSSURIOSO

    Is't possible that in this
    The mother should be damned before the daughter?

VINDICE

    Oh that's good manners my lord: the mother for her age must
    go foremost you know.   50

LUSSURIOSO

    Thou'st spoke that true! But where comes in this comfort?

VINDICE

    In a fine place my lord. The unnatural mother
    Did with her tongue so hard beset her honour
    That the poor fool was struck to silent wonder;
    Yet still the maid like an unlighted taper   55
    Was cold and chaste, save that her mother's breath
    Did blow fire on her cheeks. The girl departed
    But the good ancient madam, half mad, threw me
    These promising words which I took deeply note of:
    'My lord shall be most welcome,' –

LUSSURIOSO   Faith I thank her!   60

VINDICE

    'When his pleasure conducts him this way' –

LUSSURIOSO

    That shall be soon i' faith!

VINDICE   'I will sway mine own' –

LUSSURIOSO

    She does the wiser, I commend her for't.

VINDICE

    'Women with women can work best alone.'

LUSSURIOSO

    By this light and so they can; give 'em their due, men are not   65
    comparable to 'em.

VINDICE

    No that's true, for you shall have one woman knit more in a
    hour than any man can ravel again in seven and twenty year.

LUSSURIOSO

    Now my desires are happy, I'll make 'em freemen now.
    Thou art a precious fellow, faith I love thee,   70

    57   *blow . . . cheeks* made her blush
            cheeks ed. (checkes Q)
    68   *ravel* unravel

Be wise and make it thy revenue: beg, leg!
What office couldst thou be ambitious for?
VINDICE
Office my lord! Marry if I might have my wish I would have
one that was never begged yet.
LUSSURIOSO
Nay then thou canst have none.   75
VINDICE
Yes my lord, I could pick out another office yet, nay and keep a
horse and drab upon it.
LUSSURIOSO
Prithee good bluntness tell me—
VINDICE
Why I would desire but this my lord: to have all the fees behind
the arras, and all the farthingales that fall plump about twelve   80
o'clock at night upon the rushes.
LUSSURIOSO
Thou'rt a mad apprehensive knave: dost think to make any
great purchase of that?
VINDICE
Oh 'tis an unknown thing my lord; I wonder 't 'as been missed
so long!   85
LUSSURIOSO
Well this night I'll visit her, and 'tis till then
A year in my desires. Farewell, attend,
Trust me with thy preferment.   *Exit*
VINDICE   My loved lord.—
Oh shall I kill him o' the wrong-side now? No,
Sword thou wast never a back-biter yet.   90
I'll pierce him to his face, he shall die looking upon me;

71   *beg, leg* beg and bow in a servile manner
77   *drab* mistress
79   *fees* Ironically proposing a new tax on love-making. There was enough
      room between the hangings and the wall for people to conceal themselves
      – thus Polonius hides behind the arras in Hamlet's mother's bedchamber
      and is killed there by Hamlet
80   *farthingales* hooped petticoats *plump* (adv) with an abrupt fall (*OED* adv
      2), implying that they are dropped with impatient haste
81   *rushes* These were strewn on the floors of houses and theatre stages
82   *mad apprehensive* witty, crazy
89   Perhaps recalling *Hamlet* III.iii.73: 'Now might I do it pat'

Thy veins are swelled with lust, this shall unfill 'em;
Great men were gods if beggars could not kill 'em.
Forgive me heaven to call my mother wicked,
Oh lessen not my days upon the earth!   95
I cannot honour her; by this I fear me
Her tongue has turned my sister into use.
I was a villain not to be forsworn
To this our lecherous hope, the duke's son;
For lawyers, merchants, some divines and all,   100
Count beneficial perjury a sin small.
It shall go hard yet but I'll guard her honour
And keep the ports sure.

Enter HIPPOLITO

HIPPOLITO
Brother how goes the world? I would know news
Of you, but I have news to tell you.   105
VINDICE
What, in the name of knavery?
HIPPOLITO   Knavery faith:
This vicious old duke's worthily abused,
The pen of his bastard writes him cuckold!
VINDICE
His bastard?
HIPPOLITO   Pray believe it; he and the duchess
By night meet in their linen, they have been seen   110
By stair-foot pandars.
VINDICE   Oh sin foul and deep,
Great faults are winked at when the duke's asleep.
See, see, here comes the Spurio—

[*Enter* SPURIO *with two men*]

HIPPOLITO   Monstrous luxur!

95   Alluding to Exodus 20:12
98   *use* the gold of virginity sold, made current
101 *beneficial perjury* Apparently alluding to equivocation. Father Garnet, a Jesuit
     implicated in the Gunpowder Plot, claimed the right to make ambiguous answers
     under interrogation in order not to incriminate himself. This made the topic one of
     current scandulous interest. See *Macbeth* II.iii.8–11

VINDICE

    Unbraced: two of his valiant bawds with him.

    Oh there's a wicked whisper; hell is in his ear.   115

    Stay, let's observe his passage—

                                      [They retire]

SPURIO

    Oh but are you sure on't?

SERVANT

    My lord most sure on't, for 'twas spoke by one

    That is most inward with the duke's son's lust;

    That he intends within this hour to steal   120

    Unto Hippolito's sister, whose chaste life

    The mother has corrupted for his use.

SPURIO

    Sweet word, sweet occasion, faith then brother

    I'll disinherit you in as short time

    As I was when I was begot in haste,   125

    I'll damn you at your pleasure: precious deed!

    After your lust oh 'twill be fine to bleed!

    Come let our passing out be soft and wary.

                      Exeunt [SPURIO *and two men*]

VINDICE

    Mark, there, there, that step! Now to the duchess;

    This their second meeting writes the duke cuckold   130

    With new additions, his horns newly revived;

    Night, thou that look'st like funeral herald's fees

    Torn down betimes i' the morning, thou hang'st fitly

    To grace those sins that have no grace at all.

    Now 'tis full sea abed over the world,   135

    There's juggling of all sides. Some that were maids

    E'en at sunset are now perhaps i' the toll-book;

114   *Unbraced* not fully or properly dressed

131   *additions* in the sense (ironic) of honours: his coat of arms is crested with cuckold's
      horns

132   *funeral herald's fees* Collins supposes fees = phease, hangings of black cloth put up
      for a funeral. Foakes suggests the additional allusion to the high fees charged by
      heralds for the display of escutcheons and other trappings exhibiting the dead
      person's noble lineage

135   *full sea* high tide. See other water images at I.iii.52, 91–2

136   *juggling* deception

137   *toll-book* Strictly speaking, the toll-book listed horses for sale at a fair. Here it is
      used ironically

This woman in immodest thin apparel
Lets in her friend by water, here a dame
Cunning, nails leather hinges to a door   140
To avoid proclamation.
Now cuckolds are a-coining, apace, apace, apace, apace!
And careful sisters spin that thread i' the night
That does maintain them and their bawds i' the day.

HIPPOLITO

You flow well brother.

VINDICE   Puh I'm shallow yet,   145
Too sparing and too modest; shall I tell thee,
If every trick were told that's dealt by night
There are few here that would not blush outright.

HIPPOLITO

I am of that belief too.

VINDICE   Who's this comes?

[*Enter* LUSSURIOSO]

The duke's son up so late! Brother fall back   150
And you shall learn some mischief. – My good lord.

LUSSURIOSO

Piato, why the man I wished for, come,
I do embrace this season for the fittest
To taste of that young lady.

VINDICE [*Aside*]   Heart and hell!

HIPPOLITO

[*Aside*] Damned villain!   155

---

140 *leather hinges* i.e. to reduce noise and evade detection. Compare *The Malcontent*
      I.vii.38–41, *The Atheist's Tragedy* I.iv.146
141 *proclamation* public exposure
142 *a-coining* being coined. For the metaphor of coining for begetting see *Measure for
      Measure* II.iv.45–6
143 *sisters* OED cites a 1550 usage, 'sisters of the Bank' (i.e. Bankside) = prostitutes
      spin that thread like silk worms, their own bodies are a luxurious source of profit
150 *The duke's* ed. (*Vind.* The Dukes Q) This is the first line of the page on D4v in Q,
      but the catchword on D4 has no speech prefix for Vindice. Perhaps Q caught the
      s.p. from the final line on D4:' *Vind.* Whose this comes'. I assume the catchword is
      correct
152 *Piato* Florio defines the Italian as (i) hidden, (ii) plated, (iii) pleader. The connota-
      tion of deception seems appropriate

VINDICE
   [*Aside*] I ha' no way now to cross it, but to kill him.
LUSSURIOSO
   Come, only thou and I.
VINDICE   My lord, my lord.
LUSSURIOSO
   Why dost thou start us?
VINDICE
   I'd almost forgot – the bastard!
LUSSURIOSO   What of him?
VINDICE
   This night, this hour – this minute, now–   160
LUSSURIOSO
   What? What?
VINDICE   Shadows the duchess–
LUSSURIOSO   Horrible word.
VINDICE
   And like strong poison eats
   Into the duke your father's forehead.
LUSSURIOSO   Oh!
VINDICE
   He makes horn royal.
LUSSURIOSO   Most ignoble slave!
VINDICE
   This is the fruit of two beds.
LUSSURIOSO   I am mad.   165
VINDICE
   That passage he trod warily.
LUSSURIOSO   He did!
VINDICE
   And hushed his villains every step he took.
LUSSURIOSO
   His villains! I'll confound them.
VINDICE
   Take 'em finely, finely now.

164 *horn royal* a royal cuckold; but perhaps 'royal' carries the sense 'riotously, extremely'
     as in the phrase 'sport royal' *(Twelfth Night* II.iii.172). There may be a recollection
     of the term *horn-mad* = enraged, or of *royal antlers,* the branch of a stag's horns
     above the brow-antler (*OED*)

LUSSURIOSO

    The duchess' chamber door shall not control me.   170

                Exeunt [LUSSURIOSO *and* VINDICE]

HIPPOLITO

    Good, happy, swift, there's gunpowder i' the Court,

    Wildfire at midnight! In this heedless fury

    He may show violence to cross himself:

    I'll follow the event.   *Exit*

170   *control* prevent
173   i.e. he may become violent and so thwart his own aims

[ACT II, SCENE iii]

[The DUKE *and* DUCHESS *discovered in bed.] Enter again*
*[*LUSSURIOSO *and* VINDICE *disguised]*

LUSSURIOSO
  Where is that villain?
VINDICE
  Softly my lord and you may take 'em twisted.
LUSSURIOSO
  I care not how!
VINDICE   Oh 'twill be glorious,
  To kill 'em doubled, when they're heaped – be soft my lord.
LUSSURIOSO
  Away! My spleen is not so lazy – thus, and thus,   5
  I'll shake their eyelids ope and with my sword
  Shut 'em again for ever: villain! Strumpet!
                                    [They approach the bed]
DUKE
  You upper guard defend us!
DUCHESS   Treason, treason!
DUKE
  Oh take me not in sleep,
  I have great sins, I must have days,   10
  Nay months dear son, with penitential heaves,
  To lift 'em out and not to die unclear;
  Oh thou wilt kill me both in heaven and here.
LUSSURIOSO
  I am amazed to death.
DUKE   Nay villain, traitor,

---

0 s.d. The scene may have been played as a night scene, the characters carrying lighted torches, as
       stage convention dictated. In other plays of the time s.d.'s have the wording '*bed put forth*'.
       The bed, with drawn curtains concealing the occupants, could be pushed on stage
       through the doors in the tiring-house wall. *In Romeo & Juliet*, after the heroine
       swallows a potion there is the s.d. '*She falls upon her bed within the curtains*' (IV.iii),
       where a bed may have been 'put forth' or where a curtain across an opening in the
       tiring-house facade, suggesting a curtained four-poster bed, was used. It is impor-
       tant in the present scene that both occupants be discovered as if in bed, as the
       dialogue shows
2–4   Compare *Hamlet* III.iii.88–95

Worse than the foulest epithet, now I'll grip thee   15
E'en with the nerves of wrath, and throw thy head
Amongst the lawyers. Guard!

Enter NOBLES *and sons* [AMBITIOSO *and*
SUPERVACUO *with* HIPPOLITO]

NOBLE
How comes the quiet of your Grace disturbed?
DUKE
This boy that should be myself after me
Would be myself before me, and in heat   20
Of that ambition bloodily rushed in
Intending to depose me in my bed.
NOBLE
Duty and natural loyalty forfend!
DUCHESS
He called his father villain and me strumpet,
A word that I abhor to 'file my lips with.   25
AMBITIOSO
That was not so well done brother!
LUSSURIOSO   I am abused:
I know there's no excuse can do me good.
VINDICE
[*Aside to* HIPPOLITO] 'Tis now good policy to be from sight;
His vicious purpose to our sister's honour
Is crossed beyond our thought.
HIPPOLITO   You little dreamed   30
His father slept here?
VINDICE   Oh 'twas far beyond me.
But since it fell so – without frightful word –
Would he had killed him, 'twould have eased our swords.
                    [*Exeunt* VINDICE *and* HIPPOLITO *stealthily*]
DUKE
Be comforted our duchess, he shall die.

25 *'file* defile
33 *eased our swords* saved us the trouble
    s.d. ed. (*dissemble a flight* Q)

LUSSURIOSO
    Where's this slave-pandar now? Out of mine eye,   35
    Guilty of this abuse.

Enter SPURIO *with his villains*

SPURIO   Y'are villains, fablers,
    You have knaves' chins and harlots' tongues, you lie,
    And I will damn you with one meal a day!
SERVANT
    Oh good my lord!
SPURIO   'Sblood you shall never sup.
SERVANT
    Oh I beseech you sir!
SPURIO   To let my sword   40
    Catch cold so long and miss him!
SERVANT   Troth my lord,
    'Twas his intent to meet there.
SPURIO   Heart he's yonder!
    Ha? What news here? Is the day out o' the socket,
    That it is noon at midnight, the Court up?
    How comes the guard so saucy with his elbows?   45
LUSSURIOSO
    The bastard here?
    Nay then the truth of my intent shall out –
    My lord and father, hear me.
DUKE   Bear him hence.
LUSSURIOSO
    I can with loyalty excuse–
DUKE
    Excuse? To prison with the villain: 50
    Death shall not long lag after him.

---

43   *day . . . socket* Compare I.iv.27–8 'torchlight made an artificial noon'. The regular
     place of the sun is compared to a torch fixed in its wall-socket. The blaze of many
     torches (brought in by the assembling company) makes the scene as bright as day,
     and furthermore, with such unnatural crimes, ominous perturbations in the heav-
     ens might well be expected (see *Macbeth* II.i.4–5 and II.iv.4–11). There may also be
     a submerged link with the skull–eye–eye-socket–diamond–collet images earlier

SPURIO
　[*Aside*] Good i' faith, then 'tis not much amiss.
LUSSURIOSO
　Brothers my best release lies on your tongues,
　I pray persuade for me.
AMBITIOSO　　　　　　　It is our duties:
　Make yourself sure of us.
SUPERVACUO　　　　　　We'll sweat in pleading.　　　　　55
LUSSURIOSO
　And I may live to thank you.
　　　　　　　　　　　Exeunt [LUSSURIOSO *and guards*]
AMBITIOSO [*Aside*]　　　　No, thy death
　Shall thank me better.
SPURIO [*Aside*]　　　　He's gone – I'll after him,
　And know his trespass, seem to bear a part
　In all his ills – but with a Puritan heart.　　　　　*Exit*
AMBITIOSO
　Now brother let our hate and love be woven　　　　60
　So subtly together that in speaking
　One word for his life, we may make three for his death;
　The craftiest pleader gets most gold for breath.
SUPERVACUO
　Set on, I'll not be far behind you brother.
DUKE
　Is't possible a son should　　　　　　　　65
　Be disobedient as far as the sword?
　It is the highest, he can go no farther.
AMBITIOSO
　My gracious lord take pity.
　　DUKE　　　　　　　　Pity, boys?
AMBITIOSO
　Nay we'd be loth to move your grace too much:
　We know the trespass is unpardonable,　　　　　70
　Black, wicked and unnatural.
SUPERVACUO
　In a son, oh monstrous!
AMBITIOSO　　　　　　Yet my lord
　A duke's soft hand strokes the rough head of law

59　*Puritan* hypocritical

And makes it lie smooth.
DUKE   But my hand shall ne'er do't.
AMBITIOSO
That as you please my lord.
SUPERVACUO   We must needs confess   75
Some father would have entered into hate
So deadly-pointed, that before his eyes
He would ha' seen the execution sound
Without corrupted favour.
AMBITIOSO   But my lord,
Your Grace may live the wonder of all times   80
In pard'ning that offence which never yet
Had face to beg a pardon.
DUKE   Honey how's this?
AMBITIOSO
Forgive him good my lord, he's your own son,
And – I must needs say – 'twas the vilelier done.
SUPERVACUO
He's the next heir; yet this true reason gathers;   85
None can possess that dispossess their fathers.
Be merciful–
DUKE [*Aside*]   Here's no stepmother's wit:
I'll try 'em both upon their love and hate.
AMBITIOSO
Be merciful – although–
DUKE   You have prevailed,
My wrath like flaming wax hath spent itself,   90
I know 'twas but some peevish moon in him:
Go, let him be released.
SUPERVACUO [*Aside*]   'Sfoot how now brother?
AMBITIOSO
Your Grace doth please to speak beside your spleen;
I would it were so happy.
DUKE   Why, go release him.
SUPERVACUO
Oh my good lord I know the fault's too weighty   95

77   *deadly-pointed* i.e. fatally dangerous (as of a weapon)
78   *sound* i.e. secure. Compare III.iv. 26 (Nicoll)
91   *moon* fit of lunacy

And full of general loathing, too inhuman,
Rather by all men's voices worthy death.

DUKE

'Tis true too.
Here then receive this signet; doom shall pass.
Direct it to the judges. He shall die   100
Ere many days – make haste.

AMBITIOSO   All speed that may be.
We could have wished his burden not so sore,
We knew your Grace did but delay before.

     Exeunt [AMBITIOSO *and* SUPERVACUO]

DUKE

Here's envy with a poor thin cover o'er it,
Like scarlet hid in lawn, easily spied through;   105
This their ambition by the mother's side
Is dangerous and for safety must be purged.
I will prevent their envies, sure it was
But some mistaken fury in our son
Which these aspiring boys would climb upon;   110
He shall be released suddenly.

      Enter NOBLES

1 NOBLE

Good morning to your Grace.

DUKE   Welcome my lords.

      [*The* NOBLES *kneel*]

2 NOBLE

Our knees shall take away the office of our feet for ever,
Unless your Grace bestow a father's eye
Upon the clouded fortunes of your son.   115
And in compassionate virtue grant him that
Which makes e'en mean men happy: liberty.

DUKE

[*Aside*] How seriously their loves and honours woo
For that which I am about to pray them do. –

---

99 *signet* The word was used for King James I's own seal (*OED*)
104 *o'er it* ed. (or't Q)
105 Scarlet cloth would show through the fine linen worn over it

198

Rise my lords, your knees sign his release: 120
We freely pardon him.

1 NOBLE

We owe your Grace much thanks, and he much duty.

Exeunt [NOBLES]

DUKE

It well becomes that judge to nod at crimes
That does commit greater himself and lives.
I may forgive a disobedient error   125
That expect pardon for adultery,
And in my old days am a youth in lust.
Many a beauty have I turned to poison
In the denial, covetous of all;
Age hot, is like a monster to be seen: 130
My hairs are white and yet my sins are green.   [*Exit*]

---

120 *Rise my lords* ed. (Which, rise my lords Q)
128 i.e. I have poisoned many a beauty who denied my suit – I desire every one of
      them

ACT III[, SCENE i]

Enter AMBITIOSO *and* SUPERVACUO

SUPERVACUO
Brother let my opinion sway you once;
I speak it for the best to have him die
Surest and soonest; if the signet come
Unto the judge's hands, why then his doom
Will be deferred till sittings and court-days, 5
Juries and further; faiths are bought and sold,
Oaths in these days are but the skin of gold.
AMBITIOSO
In troth 'tis true too.
SUPERVACUO   Then let's set by the judges
And fall to the officers; 'tis but mistaking
The duke our father's meaning, and where he named 10
'Ere many days' 'tis but forgetting that
And have him die i' the morning.
AMBITIOSO   Excellent!
Then am I heir – duke in a minute!
SUPERVACUO [*Aside*]   Nay,
And he were once puffed out, here is a pin
Should quickly prick your bladder.
AMBITIOSO   Blest occasion! 15
He being packed we'll have some trick and wile
To wind our younger brother out of prison
That lies in for the rape; the lady's dead
And people's thoughts will soon be buried.
SUPERVACUO
We may with safety do't and live and feed: 20
The duchess' sons are too proud to bleed.
AMBITIOSO
We are i' faith to say true. Come let's not linger –
I'll to the officers, go you before

---

14 *puffed out* i.e. killed, blown out like a candle flame
15 *Blest* ed. (Blast Q)
16 *packed* got rid of

And set an edge upon the executioner.
SUPERVACUO
    Let me alone to grind him.   *Exit*
AMBITIOSO   Meet; farewell.   25
    I am next now, I rise just in that place
    Where thou'rt cut off – upon thy neck kind brother;
    The falling of one head lifts up another.   *Exit*

---

24   *set . . . executioner* sharpen the axe. There is a subsidiary sense: urge the officer to put him quickly to death

[ACT III, SCENE ii]

Enter with the NOBLES LUSSURIOSO *from prison*

LUSSURIOSO
My lords,
I am so much indebted to your loves
For this, oh this delivery.
NOBLE   But our duties
My lord unto the hopes that grow in you.
LUSSURIOSO
If e'er I live to be myself I'll thank you.   5
Oh liberty thou sweet and heavenly dame!
But hell, for prison, is too mild a name!

Exeunt

[ACT III, SCENE iii]

Enter AMBITIOSO *and* SUPERVACUO *with* OFFICERS

AMBITIOSO
    Officers, here's the duke's signet, your firm warrant,
    Brings the command of present death along with it
    Unto our brother the duke's son; we are sorry
    That we are so unnaturally employed
    In such an unkind office, fitter far   5
    For enemies than brothers.
SUPERVACUO   But you know
    The duke's command must be obeyed.
1 OFFICER
    It must and shall my lord – this morning then,
    So suddenly?
AMBITIOSO   Ay alas poor good soul,
    He must breakfast betimes, the executioner   10
    Stands ready to put forth his cowardly valour.
2 OFFICER
    Already?
SUPERVACUO
    Already i' faith; oh sir destruction hies,
    And that is least impudent, soonest dies.
1 OFFICER
    Troth you say true my lord; we take our leaves.   15
    Our office shall be sound, we'll not delay
    The third part of a minute.
AMBITIOSO   Therein you show
    Yourselves good men and upright officers;
    Pray let him die as private as he may,
    Do him that favour, for the gaping people   20
    Will but trouble him at his prayers
    And make him curse and swear and so die black.
    Will you be so far kind?
1 OFFICER   It shall be done my lord.

---

  9   *poor good soul* ed. (poor-good-soul Q)
 16   *sound* reliably, properly carried out
 22   *so die black* die in sin, hence damned

AMBITIOSO

    Why we do thank you; if we live to be,

    You shall have a better office.

2 OFFICER   Your good lordship.   25

SUPERVACUO

    Commend us to the scaffold in our tears.

1 OFFICER

    We'll weep and do your commendations.

                              Exeunt [OFFICERS]

AMBITIOSO

    Fine fools in office!

SUPERVACUO   Things fall out so fit!

AMBITIOSO

    So happily! Come brother ere next clock

    His head will be made serve a bigger block.   30

                                Exeunt

---

30   *block* (i) execution block, (ii) hat-size

[ACT III, SCENE iv]

Enter [YOUNGEST SON *and his prison* KEEPER]

YOUNGEST SON
  Keeper.
KEEPER My lord.
YOUNGEST SON   No news lately from our brothers?
  Are they unmindful of us?
KEEPER
  My lord a messenger came newly in
  And brought this from 'em.
                              [*He gives him a letter*]
YOUNGEST SON   Nothing but paper comforts?
  I looked for my delivery before this;   5
  Had they been worth their oaths – prithee be from us;
                              [*Exit* KEEPER]
  Now, what say you forsooth? Speak out I pray.
                              [*He reads out the*] *letter*
  'Brother be of good cheer' –
  'Slud it begins like a whore with good cheer!
  'Thou shall not be long a prisoner' –   10
  Not five and thirty year like a bankrupt, I think so!
  'We have thought upon a device to get thee out by a trick' –
  By a trick! Pox o' your trick and it be so long a-playing.
  'And so rest comforted, be merry and expect it suddenly' –
  Be merry, hang merry, draw and quarter merry, I'll be mad!   15
  Is't not strange that a man should lie in a whole month for a
  woman? Well, we shall see how sudden our brothers will be in
  their promise, I must expect still a trick: I shall not be long a
  prisoner. How now, what news?

                      [*Enter* KEEPER]

KEEPER
  Bad news my lord, I am discharged of you.   20

___

  15 *hang ... quarter* Hanging, disembowelling, and cutting in quarters was the punish-
       ment for treason in England at the time
       Perhaps a s.d. should be added: *Tears up the letter* (see line 57 below)
  16 *lie in* the usual term for a woman's confinement at childbirth

YOUNGEST SON

Slave, call'st thou that bad news! I thank you brothers.

KEEPER

My lord 'twill prove so; here come the officers

Into whose hands I must commit you.   [*Exit*]

YOUNGEST SON

Ha, officers? What, why?

[*Enter* OFFICERS]

1 OFFICER

You must pardon us my lord,   25

Our office must be sound, here is our warrant,

The signet from the duke; you must straight suffer.

YOUNGEST SON

Suffer? I'll suffer you to be gone, I'll suffer you

To come no more – what would you have me suffer?

2 OFFICER

My lord those words were better changed to prayers,   30

The time's but brief with you; prepare to die.

YOUNGEST SON

Sure 'tis not so.

3 OFFICER   It is too true my lord.

YOUNGEST SON

I tell you 'tis not, for the duke my father

Deferred me till next sitting, and I look

E'en every minute, threescore times an hour   35

For a release, a trick, wrought by my brothers.

1 OFFICER

A trick my lord? If you expect such comfort

Your hope's as fruitless as a barren woman:

Your brothers were the unhappy messengers

That brought this powerful token for your death.   40

YOUNGEST SON

My brothers! No, no!

2 OFFICER   'Tis most true my lord.

---

26 *sound* See III.iii.16 and n.

34 *sitting* session of the law-courts

YOUNGEST SON

    My brothers to bring a warrant for my death:

    How strange this shows!

3 OFFICER   There's no delaying time.

YOUNGEST SON

    Desire 'em hither, call 'em up, my brothers –

    They shall deny it to your faces!

1 OFFICER   My lord,   45

    They're far enough by this, at least at Court,

    And this most strict command they left behind 'em

    When grief swum in their eyes: they showed like brothers,

    Brim-full of heavy sorrow; but the duke

    Must have his pleasure.

YOUNGEST SON   His pleasure?   50

1 OFFICER

    These were their last words which my memory bears:

    'Commend us to the scaffold in our tears'.

YOUNGEST SON

    Pox dry their tears: what should I do with tears?

    I hate 'em worse than any citizen's son

    Can hate salt water. Here came a letter now,   55

    New bleeding from their pens, scarce stinted yet –

    Would I'd been torn in pieces when I tore it –

    Look you officious whoresons, words of comfort:

    'Not long a prisoner'.

1 OFFICER

    It says true in that sir, for you must suffer presently.   60

YOUNGEST SON

    A villainous Duns upon the letter: knavish exposition!

    Look you then here sir: 'We'll get thee out by a trick' says he.

---

  52 Italic in Q

53 ff. The Youngest Son introduces a strong element of farce into the melodramatic atmosphere, strongly indebted as it is here to *Richard III*, where the reciprocal effects of melodrama and farce are vividly apparent. Sympathetic theatrical interpretation of *The Revenger's Tragedy* confounds hostile critics of the farcical element in the play

  54 *worse ... water* Citizens, as mere land-lubbers, find the sea and voyages by sea frightening. Possibly there is an allusion (as Foakes suggests) to press-gangs enforcing civilians to serve in the navy

  61 *Duns* The medieval scholastic philosopher Duns Scotus, known for his hairsplitting distinctions, is here invoked by the exasperated Youngest Son on hearing this sophistical interpretation of 'not long'. *Duns* came to be a common proverbial term for fool, surviving in the modern word *dunce*

2 OFFICER

    That may hold too sir, for you know a trick is commonly four
    cards, which was meant by us four officers.

YOUNGEST SON

    Worse and worse dealing.

1 OFFICER   The hour beckons us,   65

    The headsman waits: lift up your eyes to heaven.

YOUNGEST SON

    I thank you faith, good pretty wholesome counsel!
    I should look up to heaven as you said
    Whilst he behind cozens me of my head!
    Ay, that's the trick.

3 OFFICER   You delay too long my lord.   70

YOUNGEST SON

    Stay good authority's bastards: since I must
    Through brothers' perjury die, oh let me venom
    Their souls with curses.

1 OFFICER   Come 'tis no time to curse.

YOUNGEST SON

    Must I bleed then without respect of sign? Well –
    My fault was sweet sport which the world approves;   75
    I die for that which every woman loves.

Exeunt

---

74   G.B. Harrison remarks that medical bleeding had to be done under favourable astrological
      conditions.

[ACT III, SCENE v]

Enter VINDICE [*disguised*] *with* HIPPOLITO *his brother*

VINDICE
  Oh sweet, delectable, rare, happy, ravishing!
HIPPOLITO
  Why what's the matter brother?
VINDICE   Oh 'tis able
  To make a man spring up and knock his forehead
  Against yon silver ceiling.
HIPPOLITO   Prithee tell me
  Why may not I partake with you? You vowed once   5
  To give me share to every tragic thought.
VINDICE
  By th' Mass I think I did too:
  Then I'll divide it to thee. The old duke,
  Thinking my outward shape and inward heart
  Are cut out of one piece – for he that prates his secrets,   10
  His heart stands o' the outside – hires me by price
  To greet him with a lady
  In some fit place veiled from the eyes o' the Court,
  Some darkened blushless angle that is guilty
  Of his forefathers' lusts, and great folks' riots;   15
  To which I easily, to maintain my shape,
  Consented, and did wish his impudent Grace
  To meet her here in this unsunned lodge
  Wherein 'tis night at noon, and here the rather
  Because unto the torturing of his soul   20
  The bastard and the duchess have appointed
  Their meeting too in this luxurious circle –
  Which most afflicting sight will kill his eyes
  Before we kill the rest of him.

---

 4 *silver ceiling* the sky (with punning allusions to the real sky above the open-air
    Globe Theatre where the play was performed, and to the canopy over the stage
    which was painted to suggest the heavens)
14 *guilty* in the sense of having witnessed guilty acts
19 *night at noon* i.e. with an ominous implication

HIPPOLITO

    'Twill i' faith, most dreadfully digested. 25

    I see not how you could have missed me brother.

VINDICE

    True, but the violence of my joy forgot it.

HIPPOLITO

    Ay; but where's that lady now?

VINDICE   Oh at that word

    I'm lost again, you cannot find me yet,

    I'm in a throng of happy apprehensions! 30

    He's suited for a lady: I have took care

    For a delicious lip, a sparkling eye:

    You shall be witness brother,

    Be ready, stand with your hat off. *Exit*

HIPPOLITO

    Troth I wonder what lady it should be. 35

    Yet 'tis no wonder now I think again

    To have a lady stoop to a duke, that stoops unto his men:

    'Tis common to be common, through the world,

    And there's more private common shadowing vices

    Than those who are known both by their names and prices. 40

    'Tis part of my allegiance to stand bare

    To the duke's concubine – and here she comes.

Enter VINDICE *with the skull of his love dressed up in tires*

VINDICE

    Madam, his Grace will not be absent long.

    Secret? Ne'er doubt us madam. 'Twill be worth

    Three velvet gowns to your ladyship. Known? 45

    Few ladies respect that; disgrace? A poor thin shell!

    'Tis the best grace you have to do it well;

    I'll save your hand that labour, I'll unmask you.

                      [VINDICE *reveals the skull*]

HIPPOLITO

    Why brother, brother.

---

25   *digested* worked out, planned (*OED* lists a usage in chemistry (1607), meaning 'bring to maturity by the action of heat'.)

VINDICE

Art thou beguiled now? Tut a lady can   50
At such, all hid, beguile a wiser man.
Have I not fitted the old surfeiter
With a quaint piece of beauty? Age and bare bone
Are e'er allied in action. Here's an eye
Able to tempt a great man – to serve God;   55
A pretty hanging lip, that has forgot now to dissemble.
Methinks this mouth should make a swearer tremble,
A drunkard clasp his teeth, and not undo 'em
To suffer wet damnation to run through 'em.
Here's a cheek keeps her colour, let the wind go whistle: 60
Spout rain, we fear thee not, be hot or cold
All's one with us. And is not he absurd
Whose fortunes are upon their faces set,
That fear no other God but wind and wet?

HIPPOLITO

Brother y'ave spoke that right.   65
Is this the form that, living, shone so bright?

VINDICE

The very same.
And now methinks I could e'en chide myself
For doting on her beauty, though her death
Shall be revenged after no common action.   70
Does the silkworm expend her yellow labours
For thee? For thee does she undo herself?
Are lordships sold to maintain ladyships
For the poor benefit of a bewitching minute?
Why does yon fellow falsify highways   75

51 *all hid* the game of hide-and-seek, and a call in the game
58 *clasp* clench
59 *wet damnation* alcoholic drink (inducing the sin of drunkenness)
64 Wind and rain are enemies to cosmetics. Recalling *King Lear* III.ii.1 and
    14–15; III.ii. in general and III.iv, especially III.iv.101–9, and see *The
    Revenger's Tragedy* IV.ii.218–19
71 *yellow* the colour of gold – hence, producing luxury, very costly – as well as
    the colour of the silkworm's cocoon
75 *fellow ... highways* An obscure expression: *fellow* may stand for
    'good-fellow', i.e. thief, and *falsify* may mean 'make unsafe', together giving
    the sense 'turn highwayman'. The idea may be that he tricks travellers into
    taking the wrong road in order to hold them up and rob them. One inter-
    pretation reads *highways* as the moral path of virtue which the fellow
    perverts and corrupts, *falsifies*

And put his life between the judge's lips
To refine such a thing, keeps horse and men
To beat their valours for her?
Surely we're all mad people and they,
Whom we think are, are not: we mistake those. 80
'Tis we are mad in sense, they but in clothes.

HIPPOLITO

Faith and in clothes too we, give us our due.

VINDICE

Does every proud and self-affecting dame
Camphor her face for this, and grieve her maker
In sinful baths of milk, when many an infant starves 85
For her superfluous outside – all for this?
Who now bids twenty pound a night, prepares
Music, perfumes and sweetmeats? All are hushed,
Thou may'st lie chaste now! It were fine methinks
To have thee seen at revels, forgetful feasts 90
And unclean brothels; sure 'twould fright the sinner
And make him a good coward, put a reveller
Out of his antic amble
And cloy an epicure with empty dishes.
Here might a scornful and ambitious woman 95
Look through and through herself; see, ladies, with false forms
You deceive men but cannot deceive worms.
Now to my tragic business. Look you brother,
I have not fashioned this only for show
And useless property, no – it shall bear a part 100
E'en in it own revenge. This very skull,
Whose mistress the duke poisoned with this drug,
The mortal curse of the earth, shall be revenged
In the like strain and kiss his lips to death.

76 risk the death penalty
77 *refine* lavish finery and luxury upon
84 *Camphor* aromatic base for cosmetics
86 *superfluous outside* excessively pampered appearance or exterior
93 *antic amble* grotesque motion (Both words are perhaps remembering *Hamlet*, where the Prince adopts an 'antic disposition' and scorns the affectations of women, telling Ophelia 'You jig and amble' – see *Hamlet* I.v.172, III.i.144.)
100 *property* i.e. theatrical stage accessory (Presumably it could be the same skull used to represent Yorick's skull in the Globe's *Hamlet*.)
101 *it own* an Elizabethan form of the genitive (Abbott, *Shakespearean Grammar* 228)

As much as the dumb thing can, he shall feel;   105
What fails in poison we'll supply in steel.

HIPPOLITO

Brother I do applaud thy constant vengeance,
The quaintness of thy malice, above thought.

VINDICE

So 'tis laid on: now come and welcome duke,
I have her for thee. I protest it brother,   110
Methinks she makes almost as fair a sign
As some old gentlewoman in a periwig.
Hide thy face now for shame, thou hadst need have a mask
    now.
'Tis vain when beauty flows, but when it fleets
This would become graves better than the streets.   115

HIPPOLITO

You have my voice in that. Hark, the duke's come.

                                              [*Noises within*]

VINDICE

Peace – let's observe what company he brings
And how he does absent 'em, for you know
He'll wish all private. Brother fall you back a little
With the bony lady.

HIPPOLITO   That I will.   [*He retires*]

VINDICE   So, so–   120
Now nine years' vengeance crowd into a minute.

                [*Enter the* DUKE *and* GENTLEMEN]

DUKE

You shall have leave to leave us, with this charge.
Upon your lives, if we be missed by the duchess
Or any of the nobles, to give out
We're privately rid forth.

VINDICE   Oh happiness!   125

DUKE

With some few honourable gentlemen, you may say:
You may name those that are away from Court.

108   *quaintness* witty ingenuity
118   *absent* send away

213

GENTLEMAN

Your will and pleasure shall be done my lord.

[*Exeunt* GENTLEMEN]

VINDICE

Privately rid forth?

He strives to make sure work on't. [*Advances*] Your good Grace.   130

DUKE

Piato! Well done. Hast brought her? What lady is't?

VINDICE

Faith my lord a country lady, a little bashful at first as most of
them are, but after the first kiss my lord the worst is past with
them: your Grace knows now what you have to do. She's somewhat a grave look with her, but–   135

DUKE

I love that best, conduct her.

VINDICE

[*Aside*] Have at all.

DUKE

In gravest looks the greatest faults seem less:
Give me that sin that's robed in holiness.

VINDICE

[*Aside*] Back with the torch; brother raise the perfumes.   140

DUKE

How sweet can a duke breathe? Age has no fault.
Pleasure should meet in a perfumed mist.
Lady, sweetly encountered: I came from Court,
I must be bold with you – oh! What's this? Oh!

[*He kisses the skull*]

VINDICE

Royal villain, white devil!

DUKE   Oh!

VINDICE   Brother,   145

Place the torch here that his affrighted eyeballs
May start into those hollows. Duke, dost know
Yon dreadful vizard? View it well; 'tis the skull
Of Gloriana, whom thou poisonedst last.

---

134   *She's* ed. (sha's Q) = She has
135   *grave look* Punning on the senses (i) serious expression, (ii) look of a corpse
138–9   Possibly recalling Angelo's soliloquy in *Measure for Measure* II.ii.164 ff.
145   *white* fair-seeming
147   *hollows* eye-sockets in the skull

DUKE

Oh 't 'as poisoned me! 150

VINDICE

Didst not know that till now?

DUKE What are you two?

VINDICE

Villains all three! The very ragged bone
Has been sufficiently revenged.

DUKE

Oh Hippolito – call treason!

[*Falls*]

HIPPOLITO

Yes my good lord. Treason, treason, treason! 155

Stamping on him

DUKE

Then I'm betrayed.

VINDICE

Alas poor lecher: in the hands of knaves
A slavish duke is baser than his slaves.

DUKE

My teeth are eaten out.

VINDICE Hadst any left?

HIPPOLITO

I think but few. 160

VINDICE

Then those that did eat are eaten.

DUKE Oh my tongue!

VINDICE

Your tongue? 'Twill teach you to kiss closer
Not like a slobbering Dutchman. You have eyes still:
Look, monster, what a lady hast thou made me
My once betrothed wife.

DUKE Is it thou villain? 165

Nay then—

VINDICE 'Tis I, 'tis Vindice, 'tis I!

161 Compare Hamlet's remark about the dead Polonius being 'Not where he eats, but
where 'a is eaten' (*Hamlet* IV.iii.19)

163 *slobbering* ed. (Flobbering Q). *OED* records 'flober' meaning 'to befoul', but the
more likely sense, 'slobber', was at this time conveyed by '*slabber*'. A MS form of
slabbering could have been misread, 'f' and long 's' being very similar
Dutchman proverbial for drunkenness and general physical grossness

HIPPOLITO

    And let this comfort thee. Our lord and father
    Fell sick upon the infection of thy frowns
    And died in sadness. Be that thy hope of life.

DUKE   Oh!

VINDICE

    He had his tongue, yet grief made him die speechless.   170
    Puh, 'tis but early yet; now I'll begin
    To stick thy soul with ulcers; I will make
    Thy spirit grievous sore, it shall not rest
    But like some pestilent man, toss in thy breast.
    Mark me, duke,   175
    Thou'rt a renowned, high, and mighty cuckold!

DUKE   Oh!

VINDICE

    Thy bastard, thy bastard rides a-hunting in thy brow.

DUKE

    Millions of deaths!

VINDICE   Nay to afflict thee more,
    Here in this lodge they meet for damned clips:
    Those eyes shall see the incest of their lips.   180

DUKE

    Is there a hell besides this, villains?

VINDICE   Villain?

    Nay heaven is just, scorns are the hires of scorns,
    I ne'er knew yet adulterer without horns.

HIPPOLITO

    Once ere they die 'tis quitted.

                                [*Noises within*]

VINDICE   Hark the music,
    Their banquet is prepared, they're coming–   185

DUKE

    Oh kill me not with that sight.

VINDICE

    Thou shalt not lose that sight for all thy dukedom.

DUKE

    Traitors, murderers!

---

177   *rides* with a sexual meaning, as in I.ii.136
       brow Where the cuckold's horns sprout. Associated with reputation and honour
179   *clips* embraces

VINDICE

    What, is not thy tongue eaten out yet?

    Then we'll invent a silence. Brother, stifle the torch.   190

DUKE

    Treason! Murder!

VINDICE

    Nay faith, we'll have you hushed now with thy dagger.

    Nail down his tongue, and mine shall keep possession

    About his heart; if he but gasp he dies,

    We dread not death to quittance injuries. Brother,   195

    If he but wink, not brooking the foul object

    Let our two other hands tear up his lids

    And make his eyes, like comets, shine through blood.

    When the bad bleeds, then is the tragedy good.

HIPPOLITO

    Whist brother, music's at our ear: they come.   200

Enter [SPURIO] *the bastard meeting the* DUCHESS

SPURIO

    Had not that kiss a taste of sin 'twere sweet.

DUCHESS

    Why there's no pleasure sweet but it is sinful.

SPURIO

    True, such a bitter sweetness fate hath given;

    Best side to us, is the worst side to heaven.

DUCHESS

    Push, come, 'tis the old duke thy doubtful father –   205

    The thought of him rubs heaven in thy way;

192–4 Vindice's directions make precise and clear that the brothers station themselves on either side of the Duke, their daggers pointing at his treacherous tongue and false heart. The stage image has ironic and emblematic aptness. See also below IV.iv. 0 s.d. and n .

196 *object* objection

198 *The Atheist's Tragedy* contains several references to the significance of portents in the heavens as signs of divine anger, especially IV.iii.164–7:

            'How can earth endure

        The burden of this wickedness without

        An earthquake, or the angry face of Heav'n

        Be not enflam'd with lightning?'

206 *rubs* pushes (from the term in the game of bowls meaning to knock a bowl into an opponent's way)

But I protest by yonder waxen fire,
Forget him or I'll poison him.

SPURIO

Madam you urge a thought which ne'er had life.
So deadly do I loathe him for my birth   210
That, if he took me hasped within his bed,
I would add murder to adultery
And with my sword give up his years to death.

DUCHESS

Why, now thou'rt sociable: let's in and feast.
Loudest music sound: pleasure is banquet's guest.   215

Exeunt [SPURIO *and* DUCHESS]

DUKE

I cannot brook –

[VINDICE *and* HIPPOLITO *kill the* DUKE]

VINDICE   The brook is turned to blood.

HIPPOLITO

Thanks to loud music.

VINDICE   'Twas our friend indeed;
'Tis state, in music for a duke to bleed.
The dukedom wants a head, though yet unknown;
As fast as they peep up let's cut 'em down.   220

Exeunt

207   *waxen fire* torch or candle
216   Punning on the verb meaning 'put up with' and noun 'stream'
219   though *his death* is not yet public knowledge

[ACT III, SCENE vi]

Enter the duchess' two sons AMBITIOSO *and* SUPERVACUO

AMBITIOSO

    Was not his execution rarely plotted?

    We are the duke's sons now.

SUPERVACUO

    Ay, you may thank my policy for that.

AMBITIOSO

    Your policy for what?

SUPERVACUO

    Why was't not my invention brother   5

    To slip the judges, and, in lesser compass,

    Did not I draw the model of his death,

    Advising you to sudden officers

    And e'en extemporal execution?

AMBITIOSO

    Heart 'twas a thing I thought on too.   10

SUPERVACUO

    You thought on't too! 'Sfoot slander not your thoughts

    With glorious untruth: I know 'twas from you.

AMBITIOSO

    Sir I say 'twas in my head.

[SUPERVACUO]   Ay, like your brains then:

    Ne'er to come out as long as you lived.

AMBITIOSO

    You'd have the honour on't forsooth that your wit   15

    Led him to the scaffold.

SUPERVACUO   Since it is my due

    I'll publish't – but I'll ha't, in spite of you.

AMBITIOSO

    Methinks y'are much too bold, you should a little

    Remember us brother, next to be honest duke.

---

  6 *slip* evade

     in lesser compass of smaller importance or scope (The next line exploits the other

     sense of *compass*, a geometrical instrument.)

8–9 recommending to you officers to carry out sudden – even summary – execution

12 *from you* not in your mind

13 s.p. ed. (*Spu.* Q)

19 i.e. that I am next in line for the honour of becoming duke

SUPERVACUO

    [*Aside*] Ay, it shall be as easy for you to be duke   20

    As to be honest, and that's never i' faith.

AMBITIOSO

    Well, cold he is by this time, and because

    We're both ambitious be it our amity,

    And let the glory be shared equally.

SUPERVACUO

    I am content to that.   25

AMBITIOSO

    This night our younger brother shall out of prison:

    I have a trick.

SUPERVACUO   A trick? Prithee what is't?

AMBITIOSO

    We'll get him out by a wile.

SUPERVACUO   Prithee what wile?

AMBITIOSO

    No sir you shall not know it till it be done,

    For then you'd swear 'twere yours.   30

        [*Enter an* OFFICER *with a bleeding head in his hand*]

SUPERVACUO

    How now, what's he?

AMBITIOSO   One of the officers.

SUPERVACUO

    Desired news.

AMBITIOSO   How now my friend?

OFFICER

    My lords, under your pardon, I am allotted

    To that desertless office to present you

    With the yet bleeding head—

SUPERVACUO [*Aside*]   Ha! Ha! Excellent!   35

AMBITIOSO [*Aside*]

    All's sure our own – brother canst weep thinkst thou?

    'Twould grace our flattery much; think of some dame,

---

21 *honest* Punning on the senses 'honourable' and 'virtuous'

22 *he* i.e. Lussurioso

'Twill teach thee to dissemble.

SUPERVACUO   I have thought –
  Now for yourself.
AMBITIOSO   Our sorrows are so fluent
  Our eyes o'erflow our tongues; words spoke in tears   40
  Are like the murmurs of the waters, the sound
  Is loudly heard but cannot be distinguished.
SUPERVACUO
  How died he pray?
OFFICER   Oh full of rage and spleen.
SUPERVACUO
  He died most valiantly then: we're glad
  To hear it.
OFFICER   We could not woo him once to pray.   45
AMBITIOSO
  He showed himself a gentleman in that,
  Give him his due.
OFFICER   But in the stead of prayer
  He drew forth oaths.
SUPERVACUO   Then did he pray dear heart,
  Although you understood him not.
OFFICER   My lords,
  E'en at his last – with pardon be it spoke –   50
  He cursed you both.
SUPERVACUO   He cursed us? 'Las, good soul.
AMBITIOSO
  It was not in our powers, but the duke's pleasure.
  [*Aside*] Finely dissembled o' both sides! Sweet fate,
  Oh happy opportunity!

Enter LUSSURIOSO

LUSSURIOSO   Now my lords–
AMBITIOSO & SUPERVACUO   Oh!
LUSSURIOSO
  Why do you shun me brothers? You may come nearer now,   55
  The savour of the prison has forsook me,
  I thank such kind lords as yourselves I'm free.

45   *woo* ed. (woe Q)

221

AMBITIOSO
    Alive!
SUPERVACUO   In health!
AMBITIOSO   Released!
    We were both e'en amazed with joy to see it.
LUSSURIOSO
    I am much to thank you.   60
SUPERVACUO
    Faith we spared no tongue unto my lord the duke.
AMBITIOSO
    I know your delivery, brother,
    Had not been half so sudden but for us.
SUPERVACUO
    Oh how we pleaded.
LUSSURIOSO   Most deserving brothers;
    In my best studies I will think of it.   *Exit*   65
AMBITIOSO
    Oh death and vengeance!
SUPERVACUO   Hell and torments!
AMBITIOSO
    Slave! Cam'st thou to delude us?
OFFICER   Delude you my lords?
SUPERVACUO
    Ay villain: where's this head now?
OFFICER   Why here my lord;
    Just after his delivery you both came
    With warrant from the duke to behead your brother.   70
AMBITIOSO
    Ay, our brother, the duke's son.
OFFICER   The duke's son
    My lord, had his release before you came.
AMBITIOSO
    Whose head's that, then?
OFFICER   His, whom you left command for –
    Your own brother's.
AMBITIOSO   Our brother's? Oh furies!
SUPERVACUO
    Plagues!
AMBITIOSO   Confusions!
SUPERVACUO   Darkness!
AMBITIOSO   Devils!   75

SUPERVACUO
   Fell it out so accursedly?
AMBITIOSO   So damnedly?
SUPERVACUO
   Villain I'll brain thee with it!
OFFICER   Oh my good lord!
SUPERVACUO
   The devil overtake thee!
AMBITIOSO   Oh fatal–
SUPERVACUO
   Oh prodigious to our bloods!
AMBITIOSO   Did we dissemble?
SUPERVACUO
   Did we make our tears women for thee?   80
AMBITIOSO
   Laugh and rejoice for thee?
SUPERVACUO
   Bring warrant for thy death?
AMBITIOSO
   Mock off thy head?
SUPERVACUO
   You had a trick, you had a wile forsooth.
AMBITIOSO
   A murrain meet 'em! There's none of these wiles that ever   85
   come to good. I see now there is nothing sure in mortality but
   mortality.
   Well, no more words – shalt be revenged i' faith.
   Come throw off clouds now brother; think of vengeance
   And deeper settled hate. Sirrah sit fast: 90
   We'll pull down all, but thou shalt down at last.

                                        Exeunt

---

85   *murrain* plague
90   *Sirrah* i.e. Lussurioso

ACT IV, SCENE i

Enter LUSSURIOSO *with* HIPPOLITO

LUSSURIOSO
Hippolito—
HIPPOLITO
My lord:
Has your good lordship aught to command me in?
LUSSURIOSO
I prithee leave us.
HIPPOLITO   How's this! Come, and leave us?
LUSSURIOSO
Hippolito.   5
HIPPOLITO
Your honour, I stand ready for any dutious employment.
LUSSURIOSO
Heart, what mak'st thou here?
HIPPOLITO [*Aside*]   A pretty lordly humour:
He bids me to be present; to depart;
Something has stung his honour.
LUSSURIOSO   Be nearer, draw nearer;
You're not so good methinks, I'm angry with you.   10
HIPPOLITO
With me my lord? I'm angry with myself for't.
LUSSURIOSO
You did prefer a goodly fellow to me:
'Twas wittily elected, 'twas – I thought
He'd been a villain, and he proves a knave!
To me a knave!
HIPPOLITO   I chose him for the best my lord: 15
'Tis much my sorrow if neglect in him
Breed discontent in you.
LUSSURIOSO   Neglect? 'Twas will: judge of it:
Firmly to tell of an incredible act
Not to be thought, less to be spoken of,

---

3 *aught* ed. (ought Q)
14 *He'd* ed. (Had Q)

'Twixt my stepmother and the bastard – oh,   20
Incestuous sweets between 'em!

HIPPOLITO   Fie my lord.

LUSSURIOSO

I, in kind loyalty to my father's forehead,
Made this a desperate arm, and in that fury
Committed treason on the lawful bed
And with my sword e'en razed my father's bosom,   25
For which I was within a stroke of death.

HIPPOLITO

Alack, I'm sorry. [*Aside*] 'Sfoot, just upon the stroke
Jars in my brother: 'twill be villainous music!

Enter VINDICE [*disguised*]

VINDICE

My honoured lord.

LUSSURIOSO

Away prithee, forsake us: hereafter we'll not know thee.   30

VINDICE

Not know me my lord? Your lordship cannot choose.

LUSSURIOSO

Begone I say, thou art a false knave.

VINDICE

Why, the easier to be known my lord.

LUSSURIOSO

Push, I shall prove too bitter with a word,
Make thee a perpetual prisoner   35
And lay this iron-age upon thee.

VINDICE [*Aside*]   Mum,
For there's a doom would make a woman dumb.
Missing the bastard next him, the wind's come about;
Now 'tis my brother's turn to stay, mine to go out.   *Exit* VINDICE

---

22 *forehead* See III.v.177 and n.
25 *razed* grazed
28 *Jars* interrupts discordantly
36 *iron-age* (i) imprisonment in iron fetters, (ii) fettering lasting an Age of Iron, the
    last and worst of the mythical four Ages (Gold, Silver, and Brass being the first
    three)
38 *come* ed. (comes Q)

LUSSURIOSO
    Has greatly moved me.
HIPPOLITO   Much to blame i' faith.   40
LUSSURIOSO
    But I'll recover, to his ruin. 'Twas told me lately,
    I know not whether falsely, that you'd a brother.
HIPPOLITO
    Who I? Yes my good lord, I have a brother.
LUSSURIOSO
    How chance the Court ne'er saw him? Of what nature?
    How does he apply his hours?
HIPPOLITO   Faith to curse Fates   45
    Who, as he thinks, ordained him to be poor;
    Keeps at home full of want and discontent.
LUSSURIOSO
    There's hope in him, for discontent and want
    Is the best clay to mould a villain of.
    Hippolito, wish him repair to us.   50
    If there be aught in him to please our blood
    For thy sake we'll advance him, and build fair
    His meanest fortunes; for it is in us
    To rear up towers from cottages.
HIPPOLITO
    It is so my lord; he will attend your honour,   55
    But he's a man in whom much melancholy dwells.
LUSSURIOSO
    Why the better: bring him to Court.
HIPPOLITO
    With willingness and speed. [*Aside*] Whom he cast off
    E'en now, must now succeed. Brother disguise must off;
    In thine own shape now I'll prefer thee to him.   60
    How strangely does himself work to undo him.   *Exit*
LUSSURIOSO
    This fellow will come fitly; he shall kill
    That other slave that did abuse my spleen
    And made it swell to treason. I have put

50   *repair* make his way
51   *blood* desire, temper (with allusion to Lussurioso's boasted proud breeding)
59   *succeed* be the successor
61   *himself . . him* he strives to achieve his own undoing

Much of my heart into him; he must die. 65
He that knows great men's secrets, and proves slight,
That man ne'er lives to see his beard turn white.
Ay, he shall speed him: I'll employ the brother,
Slaves are but nails to drive out one another.
He being of black condition, suitable 70
To want and ill content, hope of preferment
Will grind him to an edge.

The NOBLES *enter*

1 NOBLE
Good days unto your honour.
LUSSURIOSO   My kind lords,
  I do return the like.
2 NOBLE   Saw you my lord the duke?
LUSSURIOSO
  My lord and father: is he from Court? 75
1 NOBLE
  He's sure from Court – but where, which way his pleasure took,
  we know not nor can we hear on't.

[*Enter other* NOBLES]

LUSSURIOSO
  Here come those should tell – saw you my lord and father?
3 NOBLE
  Not since two hours before noon my lord, and then he privately
  rid forth. 80
LUSSURIOSO
  Oh he's rode forth.
1 NOBLE   'Twas wondrous privately.
2 NOBLE
  There's none i' the Court had any knowledge on't.

66 *slight* not trustworthy
68 *speed* i.e. kill
    the ed. (thee Q)
70 *black* melancholic
73, 74, 76 s.p. ed. (1., 2., 1. Q)
79 s.p. ed. (3. Q)
81 *rode* (rod Q)

227

LUSSURIOSO

His Grace is old, and sudden, 'tis no treason
To say the duke my father has a humour
Or such a toy, about him; what in us   85
Would appear light, in him seems virtuous.

3 NOBLE

'Tis oracle my lord.

Exeunt

[ACT IV, SCENE ii]

Enter VINDICE *and* HIPPOLITO (VINDICE *out of his disguise*)

HIPPOLITO

So, so, all's as it should be, y'are yourself.

VINDICE

How that great villain puts me to my shifts!

HIPPOLITO

He that did lately in disguise reject thee
Shall, now thou art thyself, as much respect thee.

VINDICE

'Twill be the quainter fallacy; but brother,   5
'Sfoot, what use will he put me to now, think'st thou?

HIPPOLITO

Nay you must pardon me in that, I know not;
H'as some employment for you, but what 'tis
He and his secretary the devil knows best.

VINDICE

Well I must suit my tongue to his desires   10
What colour soe'er they be, hoping at last
To pile up all my wishes on his breast.

HIPPOLITO

Faith brother he himself shows the way.

VINDICE

Now the duke is dead the realm is clad in clay,
His death being not yet known, under his name   15
The people still are governed; well, thou his son
Art not long-lived, thou shalt not 'joy his death:
To kill thee then I should most honour thee,
For 'twould stand firm in every man's belief
Thou'st a kind child, and only diedst with grief.   20

HIPPOLITO

You fetch about well; but let's talk in present.
How will you appear in fashion different,
As well as in apparel, to make all things possible?
If you be but once tripped we fall for ever.

---

2   *shifts* (i) tricks, (ii) disguises
21 *in present* i.e. in terms of the present

It is not the least policy to be doubtful;   25
You must change tongue – familiar was your first.
VINDICE
Why I'll bear me in some strain of melancholy
And string myself with heavy sounding wire
Like such an instrument that speaks
Merry things sadly.
HIPPOLITO   Then 'tis as I meant,   30
I gave you out at first in discontent.
VINDICE
I'll turn myself, and then–

[*Enter* LUSSURIOSO]

HIPPOLITO   'Sfoot here he comes –
Hast thought upon't?
VINDICE   Salute him, fear not me.
LUSSURIOSO
Hippolito.
HIPPOLITO
Your lordship.   35
LUSSURIOSO
What's he yonder?
HIPPOLITO
'Tis Vindice my discontented brother,
Whom, 'cording to your will I've brought to Court.
LUSSURIOSO
Is that thy brother? Beshrew me a good presence;
I wonder h'as been from the Court so long.   40
Come nearer.
HIPPOLITO
Brother: Lord Lussurioso the duke's son.
LUSSURIOSO
Be more near to us: welcome, nearer yet.
VINDICE
How don you? God you god den.
                    [VINDICE] *snatches off his hat and* [*bows*] *to him*
LUSSURIOSO   We thank thee.
How strangely such a coarse, homely salute   45

25   It is not the worst policy to anticipate trouble

Shows in the palace, where we greet in fire –
Nimble and desperate tongues! Should we name
God in a salutation 'twould ne'er be 'stood on't – heaven!
Tell me, what has made thee so melancholy.

VINDICE

Why going to law.   50

LUSSURIOSO

Why, will that make a man melancholy?

VINDICE

Yes, to look long upon ink and black buckram. I went me to law
in *anno quadragesimo secundo*, and I waded out of it in *anno
sextagesimo tertio*.

LUSSURIOSO

What, three and twenty years in law?   55

VINDICE

I have known those that have been five and fifty, and all about
pullin and pigs.

LUSSURIOSO

May it be possible such men should breathe to vex the terms so
much?

VINDICE

'Tis food to some my lord. There are old men at the present   60
that are so poisoned with the affectation of law words, having
had many suits canvassed, that their common talk is nothing
but Barbary Latin; they cannot so much as pray, but in law, that
their sins may be removed with a writ of Error, and their souls
fetched up to heaven with a sasarara.   65

LUSSURIOSO

It seems most strange to me;
Yet all the world meets round in the same bent:
Where the heart's set, there goes the tongue's consent.
How dost apply thy studies fellow?

---

    48   *'twould . . . on't* it would never be understood as such
    53   *anno . . . secundo* forty-second
 53–4   *anno . . . tertio* sixty-third
    57   *pullin* poultry
    58   *terms* the four terms in the year when the law-courts sit
    63   *Barbary* barbarous
    65   *sasarara* i.e. certiorari, a writ issued by a superior court when a plaintiff claims
         injustice from a lower court

VINDICE

Study? Why, to think how a great rich man lies a-dying, and a 70
poor cobbler tolls the bell for him; how he cannot depart the
world, and see the great chest stand before him; when he lies
speechless, how he will point you readily to all the boxes, and
when he is past all memory, as the gossips guess, then thinks he
of forfeitures and obligations. Nay, when to all men's hearings 75
he whirls and rattles in the throat, he's busy threatening his
poor tenants; and this would last me now some seven years
thinking, or thereabouts! But I have a conceit a-coming in picture upon this, I draw it myself, which i' faith la I'll present to
your honour; you shall not choose but like it for your lordship 80
shall give me nothing for it.

LUSSURIOSO

Nay you mistake me then,
For I am published bountiful enough;
Let's taste of your conceit.

VINDICE

In picture my lord? 85

LUSSURIOSO

Ay, in picture.

VINDICE

Marry this it is: 'A usuring father to be boiling in hell, and his
son and heir with a whore dancing over him'.

HIPPOLITO

[*Aside*] H'as pared him to the quick.

LUSSURIOSO

The conceit's pretty i' faith – but take't upon my life 'twill ne'er 90
be liked.

VINDICE

No? Why I'm sure the whore will be liked well enough!

HIPPOLITO

[*Aside*] Ay, if she were out o' the picture he'd like her then
himself.

VINDICE

And as for the son and heir, he shall be an eyesore to no young 95
revellers, for he shall be drawn in cloth of gold breeches.

---

87   *usuring . . . hell* the punishment traditionally believed to apply to usurers

LUSSURIOSO

    And thou hast put my meaning in the pockets

    And canst not draw that out. My thought was this:

    To see the picture of a usuring father

    Boiling in hell – our rich men would ne'er like it.   100

VINDICE

    Oh true, I cry you heartily mercy; I know the reason: for some

    of 'em had rather be damned indeed than damned in colours.

LUSSURIOSO

    [*Aside*] A parlous melancholy! H'as wit enough

    To murder any man, and I'll give him means.

    I think thou art ill-moneyed?

VINDICE   Money! Ho, ho.   105

    'T 'as been my want so long 'tis now my scoff;

    I've e'en forgot what colour silver's of!

LUSSURIOSO

    [*Aside*] It hits as I could wish.

VINDICE   I get good clothes

    Of those that dread my humour, and for table room

    I feed on those that cannot be rid of me.   110

LUSSURIOSO

    [*Giving* VINDICE *money*] Somewhat to set thee up withal.

VINDICE

    Oh mine eyes!

LUSSURIOSO   How now man?

VINDICE   Almost struck blind!

    This bright unusual shine to me seems proud:

    I dare not look till the sun be in a cloud.

LUSSURIOSO

    [*Aside*] I think I shall affect his melancholy;   115

    How are they now?

VINDICE   The better for your asking.

LUSSURIOSO

    You shall be better yet if you but fasten

    Truly on my intent. Now y'are both present

    I will unbrace such a close private villain

    Unto your vengeful swords, the like ne'er heard of   120

    Who hath disgraced you much and injured us.

102 *colours* (i) in a painting, (ii) in mere seeming, appearance
115 *affect* like

HIPPOLITO
　Disgraced us my lord?
LUSSURIOSO　　　　　　　Ay, Hippolito.
　I kept it here till now that both your angers
　Might meet him at once.
VINDICE　　　　　　　I'm covetous
　To know the villain.
LUSSURIOSO　　　You know him – that slave pandar　　125
　Piato, whom we threatened last
　With irons in perpetual prisonment.
VINDICE
　[*Aside*] All this is I!
HIPPOLITO　　　Is't he my lord?
LUSSURIOSO　　　　　　　I'll tell you–
　You first preferred him to me.
VINDICE [*Aside*]　　　　　Did you brother?
HIPPOLITO
　I did indeed.
LUSSURIOSO　And the ungrateful villain　　　130
　To quit that kindness strongly wrought with me,
　Being as you see a likely man for pleasure,
　With jewels to corrupt your virgin sister.
HIPPOLITO
　Oh villain!
VINDICE　　He shall surely die that did it.
LUSSURIOSO
　I, far from thinking any virgin harm,　　　135
　Especially knowing her to be as chaste
　As that part which scarce suffers to be touched,
　The eye, would not endure him–
VINDICE　　　　　　　Would you not my lord?
　'Twas wondrous honourably done.
LUSSURIOSO
　But with some fine frowns kept him out.
VINDICE　　　　　　　　　Out slave!　　140
LUSSURIOSO
　What did me he but in revenge of that
　Went of his own free will to make infirm
　Your sister's honour, whom I honour with my soul

140　*fine* ed. (five Q)

234

For chaste respect; and, not prevailing there —
As 'twas but desperate folly to attempt it —   145
In mere spleen, by the way, waylays your mother,
Whose honour being a coward as it seems,
Yielded by little force.

VINDICE   Coward indeed.

LUSSURIOSO

He, proud of this advantage, as he thought,
Brought me these news for happy; but I —   150
Heaven forgive me for't —

VINDICE   What did your honour?

LUSSURIOSO

In rage pushed him from me,
Trampled beneath his throat, spurned him and bruised;
Indeed I was too cruel, to say truth.

HIPPOLITO

Most nobly managed.   155

VINDICE

[*Aside*] Has not heaven an ear? Is all the lightning wasted?

LUSSURIOSO

If I now were so impatient in a modest cause,
What should you be?

VINDICE   Full mad: he shall not live
To see the moon change.

LUSSURIOSO   He's about the palace.
Hippolito, entice him this way, that thy brother   160
May take full mark of him.

HIPPOLITO

Heart! That shall not need my lord,
I can direct him so far.

LUSSURIOSO   Yet for my hate's sake
Go, wind him this way; I'll see him bleed myself.

149   *this* ed. (their Q)
156   *Is . . . wasted* Compare the discussion about thunder's intervention in human
      affairs in Tourneur, *The Atheist's Tragedy* II. iv. 140–55, or in Chettle, *Tragedy of
      Hoffman* I.i, where Hoffman has thunder's support:
          'Ill acts move some, but myne's a cause that's right
                  Thunder and Lightning
          See the powers of heaven in apparitions/ . . . incensed'
164   *wind* entice, draw

HIPPOLITO
  [*Aside*] What now brother?   165
VINDICE
  [*Aside*] Nay e'en what you will; y'are put to't, brother?
HIPPOLITO
  [*Aside*] An impossible task I'll swear,
  To bring him hither that's already here.   *Exit* HIPPOLITO
LUSSURIOSO
  Thy name? I have forgot it.
VINDICE   Vindice my lord.
LUSSURIOSO
  'Tis a good name, that.
VINDICE   Ay, a revenger.   170
LUSSURIOSO
  It does betoken courage, thou shouldst be valiant
  And kill thine enemies.
VINDICE   That's my hope my lord.
LUSSURIOSO
  This slave is one.
VINDICE   I'll doom him.
LUSSURIOSO   Then I'll praise thee.
  Do thou observe me best and I'll best raise thee.

Enter HIPPOLITO

VINDICE
  Indeed I thank you.
LUSSURIOSO   Now Hippolito,   175
  Where's the slave pandar?
HIPPOLITO   Your good lordship would have
  A loathsome sight of him, much offensive?
  He's not in case now to be seen my lord,
  The worst of all the deadly sins is in him:
  That beggarly damnation, drunkenness.   180
LUSSURIOSO
  Then he's a double slave.
VINDICE [*Aside*]   'Twas well conveyed,

174 *observe* serve, follow
178 *in case* in a condition (and punning on the sense case = mask, disguise, costume, as
     in *Measure for Measure* II.iv.12–13)

Upon a sudden wit.
LUSSURIOSO   What, are you both
Firmly resolved? I'll see him dead myself!
VINDICE
Or else let not us live.
LUSSURIOSO   You may direct
Your brother to take note of him.
HIPPOLITO   I shall.   185
LUSSURIOSO
Rise but in this and you shall never fall.
VINDICE
Your honour's vassals.
LUSSURIOSO [*Aside*]   This was wisely carried;
Deep policy in us makes fools of such:
Then must a slave die, when he knows too much.
                              Exit LUSSURIOSO
VINDICE
Oh thou almighty patience 'tis my wonder,   190
That such a fellow, impudent and wicked,
Should not be cloven as he stood
Or with a secret wind burst open!
Is there no thunder left, or is't kept up
In stock for heavier vengeance? [*Thunder*] There it goes!   195
HIPPOLITO
Brother we lose ourselves.
VINDICE   But I have found it,
'Twill hold, 'tis sure, thanks, thanks to any spirit
That mingled it 'mongst my inventions.
HIPPOLITO
What is't?
VINDICE   'Tis sound and good, thou shalt partake it,
I'm hired to kill myself.
HIPPOLITO   True.
VINDICE   Prithee mark it;   200
And the old duke being dead but not conveyed —
For he's already missed too – and you know
Murder will peep out of the closest husk —

196   *found it* thought up a solution

237

HIPPOLITO
  Most true!
VINDICE   What say you then to this device:
  If we dressed up the body of the duke—   205
HIPPOLITO
  In that disguise of yours!
VINDICE   Y'are quick, y'ave reached it.
HIPPOLITO
  I like it wondrously.
VINDICE
  And being in drink, as you have published him,
  To lean him on his elbow as if sleep had caught him –
  Which claims most interest in such sluggish men.   210
HIPPOLITO
  Good yet; but here's a doubt.
  We thought by th' duke's son to kill that pandar,
  Shall, when he is known, be thought to kill the duke.
VINDICE
  Neither, oh thanks! It is substantial; for that disguise being on
  him, which I wore, it will be thought I, which he calls the   215
  pandar, did kill the duke and fled away in his apparel, leaving
  him so disguised to avoid swift pursuit.
HIPPOLITO
  Firmer and firmer.
VINDICE   Nay doubt not, 'tis in grain,
  I warrant it hold colour.
HIPPOLITO   Let's about it.
VINDICE
  But by the way too, now I think on't, brother,   220
  Let's conjure that base devil out of our mother.

                                              Exeunt

---

209 The idea of arranging the corpse in a life-like way ingeniously varies the device of
     the bony lady in III.v, which in turn reversed the image of the dead wife of Antonio
     in I.iv
212 *We* ed. (Me Q)
218 i.e. it is sound and will hold firmly. (For the metaphor of colour being fast-dyed
     rather than soluble, on the mere surface, see *Twelfth Night* I.v.237–8.) Another
     instance of the images of painting, especially face-painting, which abound in the
     play. Male as well as female courtiers used face-paint in the Jacobean period

[ACT IV, SCENE iii]

Enter the DUCHESS *arm in arm with the bastard* [SPURIO]:
he seemeth lasciviously to her; after them enter
SUPERVACUO *running with a rapier: his brother*
[AMBITIOSO] *stops him*

SPURIO
    Madam unlock yourself; should it be seen
    Your arm would be suspected.
DUCHESS
    Who is't that dares suspect or this, or these?
    May not we deal our favours where we please?
SPURIO
    I'm confident you may.

                              Exeunt [SPURIO *and* DUCHESS]
AMBITIOSO   'Sfoot brother hold!   5
SUPERVACUO
    Wouldst let the bastard shame us?
AMBITIOSO   Hold, hold brother!
    There's fitter time than now.
SUPERVACUO   Now, when I see it!
AMBITIOSO
    'Tis too much seen already.
SUPERVACUO   Seen and known:
    The nobler she's, the baser is she grown.
AMBITIOSO
    If she were bent lasciviously – the fault   10
    Of mighty women that sleep soft – Oh death
    Must she needs choose such an unequal sinner
    To make all worse?
SUPERVACUO
    A bastard! The duke's bastard! Shame heaped on shame!
AMBITIOSO
    Oh our disgrace!   15

---

3   *this, or these* Presumably she gives him further caresses or kisses
6   *Wouldst* (Woult Q)
10 *bent lasciviously* determined to be lascivious

Most women have small waist the world throughout,
But their desires are thousand miles about.
SUPERVACUO
Come, stay not here, let's after and prevent:
Or else they'll sin faster than we'll repent.

Exeunt

16   *waist* ed. (waste Q)
18–19   Uncorrected copies reverse the order of these lines; corrected copies misplace
Exeunt after line 18

[ACT IV, SCENE iv]

Enter VINDICE *and* HIPPOLITO *bringing out their mother*
[GRATIANA,] *one by one shoulder, and the other by the other,*
with daggers in their hands

VINDICE

Oh thou for whom no name is bad enough!

GRATIANA

What means my sons? What, will you murder me?

VINDICE

Wicked, unnatural parent!

HIPPOLITO   Fiend of women!

GRATIANA

Oh! Are sons turned monsters? Help!

VINDICE   In vain.

GRATIANA

Are you so barbarous, to set iron nipples   5

Upon the breast that gave you suck?

VINDICE   That breast

Is turned to quarled poison.

GRATIANA

Cut not your days for't: am not I your mother?

VINDICE

Thou dost usurp that title now by fraud,

For in that shell of mother breeds a bawd.   10

GRATIANA

A bawd! Oh name far loathsomer than hell!

HIPPOLITO

It should be so, knew'st thou thy office well.

GRATIANA

I hate it.

---

  0   s.d. The brothers, either side of their mother, daggers drawn, present a visual paral-
       lel to their seizing of the Duke: see III.v.192–4 and n. Their interrogation of their
       mother recalls *Hamlet* III.iv

  3   *parent* ed. (parents Q)

  7   *quarled* curdled

  8   *Cut . . . days* i.e. do not shorten your life. (See II.ii.95 where Exodus 20:12 is
       invoked.)

 12 *knewst* Q corrected (knowst Q uncorrected)   *office* maternal duty

VINDICE
    Ah is't possible, thou only – you powers on high,
    That women should dissemble when they die?   15
GRATIANA
    Dissemble?
VINDICE   Did not the duke's son direct
    A fellow of the world's condition hither
    That did corrupt all that was good in thee,
    Made thee uncivilly forget thyself
    And work our sister to his lust?
GRATIANA   Who, I?   20
    That had been monstrous! I defy that man
    For any such intent. None lives so pure
    But shall be soiled with slander –
    Good son believe it not.
VINDICE   Oh I'm in doubt
    Whether I'm myself or no!   25
    Stay – let me look again upon this face:
    Who shall be saved when mothers have no grace?
HIPPOLITO
    'Twould make one half despair.
VINDICE   I was the man:
    Defy me now! Let's see: do't modestly.
GRATIANA
    Oh hell unto my soul.   30
VINDICE
    In that disguise, I, sent from the duke's son,
    Tried you, and found you base metal
    As any villain might have done.
GRATIANA   Oh no:
    No tongue but yours could have bewitched me so.

14 *thou only* ed. (printed in italic in Q). Swinburne, cited by Nicoll, suggested that the
    line originally read 'Ah ist possible Thou onely God on hie'. Either in the playhouse
    or the printinghouse this was emended, 'Thou onely God' being crossed out and
    'you powers' written in above. The compositor misunderstood the MS and printed
    'thou onely'. Nicoll emends with a compromise, 'Ah ist possible, you [heavenly]
    powers on hie', to restore metre, accepting Swinburne's conjecture. A number of
    playscripts at this time witness deference to the new (1606) Act to Restrain the
    Abuses of Players, which forbade direct references to the Deity
32 Alluding to the proving or testing of precious metals for purity. Gold was assayed
    or tried with a touchstone and stamped if found true

VINDICE

    Oh nimble in damnation, quick in tune: 35
    There is no devil could strike fire so soon!
    I am confuted in a word.

GRATIANA   Oh sons

    Forgive me, to myself I'll prove more true;
    You that should honour me, I kneel to you.

                         [*She kneels and weeps*]

VINDICE

    A mother to give aim to her own daughter!   40

HIPPOLITO

    True brother: how far beyond nature 'tis,
    Though many mothers do't!

VINDICE

    Nay and you draw tears once, go you to bed;
    Wet will make iron blush and change to red:
    Brother it rains, 'twill spoil your dagger, house it.   45

HIPPOLITO

    'Tis done.

VINDICE

    I' faith 'tis a sweet shower, it does much good;
    The fruitful grounds and meadows of her soul
    Has been long dry. Pour down, thou blessed dew.
    Rise mother; troth this shower has made you higher.   50

GRATIANA

    Oh you heavens,
    Take this infectious spot out of my soul!
    I'll rinse it in seven waters of mine eyes;

---

39   In a society where parental authority was so strong, a parent's submission to a child
      was a deep and disturbing breach of custom. See *King Lear* and Lear's mock-kneeling
      to Regan and Goneril, his daughters, II.iv.154–5, and his later contrition with
      Cordelia, V.iii.10–11

40   *give aim* i.e. guide her daughter to seduce someone

41   *'tis* Q corrected (to't Q uncorrected)

44   *wet . . . iron . . . red* Q corrected 2 (Wet . . . you . . . red Q corrected 1; Wee . . . you
      Q uncorrected) This line exists in three states, and it is difficult to be sure of their
      order. I suppose Vindice to be talking to his dagger. Tempered steel is susceptible to
      rusting (Othello says 'Keep up your bright swords, for the dew will rust them'
      (I.ii.59)), but the added conceit is that the dagger-blade will reflect the mother's
      shame, expressed in tears and blushes

45   *it rains* Referring to Gratiana's tears

52   *infectious* infected

Make my tears salt enough to taste of grace;
To weep is to our sex naturally given,   55
But to weep truly – that's a gift from heaven!

VINDICE

Nay I'll kiss you now; kiss her, brother,
Let's marry her to our souls, wherein's no lust,
And honourably love her.

HIPPOLITO   Let it be.

VINDICE

For honest women are so seld and rare,   60
'Tis good to cherish those poor few that are.
Oh you of easy wax, do but imagine
Now the disease has left you, how leprously
That office would have clinged unto your forehead.
All mothers that had any graceful hue   65
Would have worn masks to hide their face at you.
It would have grown to this, at your foul name
Green-coloured maids would have turned red with shame.

HIPPOLITO

And then, our sister full of hire and baseness–

VINDICE

There had been boiling lead again!   70
The duke's son's great concubine!
A drab of state, a cloth o' silver slut,
To have her train borne up and her soul
Trail i' the dirt: great!

HIPPOLITO   To be miserably great:
Rich, to be eternally wretched.   75

VINDICE

Oh common madness:
Ask but the thriving'st harlot in cold blood,
She'd give the world to make her honour good.

60   *seld* ed. (sild Q) = rare
63–4 *leprously . . . forehead* See *Hamlet* III.iv.42–4:
                'takes off the rose
           From the fair forehead of an innocent love
           And sets a blister there'
68   *Green-coloured* very young, inexperienced
69   *hire* payment for services as a whore
71   *The duke's* Q corrected (dukes Q uncorrected)
74   *To be* Q corrected (Too Q uncorrected)

Perhaps you'll say, but only to the duke's son
In private – why, she first begins with one   80
Who afterward to thousand proves a whore:
'Break ice in one place it will crack in more'.

GRATIANA

Most certainly applied!

HIPPOLITO

Oh brother you forgot our business.

VINDICE

And well remembered: joy's a subtle elf,   85
I think man's happiest when he forgets himself.
Farewell once dried, now holy-watered mead:
Our hearts wear feathers that before wore lead.

GRATIANA

I'll give you this: that one I never knew
Plead better for, and 'gainst the devil, than you.   90

VINDICE

You make me proud on't.

HIPPOLITO

Commend us in all virtue to our sister.

VINDICE

Ay for the love of heaven, to that true maid.

GRATIANA

With my best words.

VINDICE   Why that was motherly said.

                Exeunt [VINDICE *and* HIPPOLITO]

GRATIANA

I wonder now what fury did transport me,   95
I feel good thoughts begin to settle in me.
Oh with what forehead can I look on her
Whose honour I've so impiously beset –
And here she comes.

           [*Enter* CASTIZA]

---

82   This sententious remark is not cited as proverbial in Tilley but its meaning is clear:
      chastity is proverbially cold as ice
97   *forehead* See lines 63–4 and n. above

CASTIZA

 Now mother you have wrought with me so strongly   100
 That what for my advancement, as to calm
 The trouble of your tongue, I am content—

GRATIANA

 Content to what?

CASTIZA   To do as you have wished me,
 To prostitute my breast to the duke's son
 And put myself to common usury.   105

GRATIANA

 I hope you will not so.

CASTIZA   Hope you I will not?
 That's not the hope you look to be saved in.

GRATIANA

 Truth but it is.

CASTIZA Do not deceive yourself:
 I am, as you, e'en out of marble wrought:
 What would you now, are ye not pleased yet with me? 110
 You shall not wish me to be more lascivious
 Than I intend to be.

GRATIANA   Strike not me cold.

CASTIZA

 How often have you charged me on your blessing
 To be a cursed woman! When you knew
 Your blessing had no force to make me lewd   115
 You laid your curse upon me. That did more –
 The mother's curse is heavy; where that fights,
 Sons set in storm and daughters lose their lights.

GRATIANA

 Good child, dear maid, if there be any spark
 Of heavenly intellectual fire within thee,   120
 Oh let my breath revive it to a flame:
 Put not all out with woman's wilful follies,
 I am recovered of that foul disease
 That haunts too many mothers: kind, forgive me,

---

109 *marble* i.e. impervious to shame (See I.iii.8, 'dauntless marble'.)

118 i.e. sons and daughters end in damnation (punning on sons / *suns* and on *lights*:
  (i) spiritual guidance, (ii) heavenly bodies, sun, moon, stars)

124 *kind, forgive* ed. (kind forgive Q). The comma emphasizes that kind is a term of
  address, 'kind one'. The mother commends her daughter as loving, as close kin, and
  as natural (not unnatural)

Make me not sick in health. If then   125
My words prevailed when they were wickedness,
How much more now when they are just and good!

CASTIZA
I wonder what you mean: are not you she
For whose infect persuasions I could scarce
Kneel out my prayers, and had much ado   130
In three hours' reading to untwist so much
Of the black serpent as you wound about me?

GRATIANA
'Tis unfruitful, held tedious, to repeat what's past:
I'm now your present mother.

CASTIZA   Push, now 'tis too late.

GRATIANA
Bethink again, thou know'st not what thou say'st.   135

CASTIZA
No – deny advancement, treasure, the duke's son?

GRATIANA
Oh see, I spoke those words, and now they poison me:
What will the deed do then?
Advancement? True: as high as shame can pitch;
For treasure? Who e'er knew a harlot rich   140
Or could build by the purchase of her sin
An hospital to keep their bastards in?
The duke's son! Oh when women are young courtiers
They are sure to be old beggars;
To know the miseries most harlots taste   145
Thou'd'st wish thyself unborn when thou art unchaste.

CASTIZA
Oh mother let me twine about your neck
And kiss you till my soul melt on your lips:
I did but this to try you.

GRATIANA   Oh speak truth!

CASTIZA
Indeed I did not; for no tongue has force   150
To alter me from honest.
If maidens would, men's words could have no power;

125   *sick in health* i.e. spiritually distressed though physically well
131   *reading* i.e. in devotional works and prayers
133   *held* Q (child conj. Collins)

A virgin honour is a crystal tower
Which being weak is guarded with good spirits:
Until she basely yields no ill inherits. 155

GRATIANA

Oh happy child! Faith and thy birth hath saved me.
'Mongst thousand daughters happiest of all others!
Be thou a glass for maids, and I for mothers.

Exeunt

---

158 *Be* ed. (Buy Q)
    glass i.e. image of perfection (Compare *Hamlet* III.i.153 'glass of fashion'.)

[ACT V, SCENE i]

Enter VINDICE *and* HIPPOLITO [*with the* DUKE'*s corpse*]

VINDICE

So, so, he leans well; take heed you wake him not brother.

HIPPOLITO

I warrant you, my life for yours.

VINDICE

That's a good lay, for I must kill myself! [*Points to corpse*]
Brother that's I: that sits for me: do you mark it. And I must
stand ready here to make away myself yonder; I must sit to be   5
killed, and stand to kill myself – I could vary it not so little as
thrice over again, 't 'as some eight returns like Michaelmas
Term.

HIPPOLITO

That's enow, o' conscience.

VINDICE

But sirrah does the duke's son come single?   10

HIPPOLITO

No, there's the hell on't, his faith's too feeble to go alone. He
brings flesh-flies after him that will buzz against supper time,
and hum for his coming out.

VINDICE

Ah the fly-flop of vengeance beat 'em to pieces! Here was the
sweetest occasion, the fittest hour to have made my revenge   15
familiar with him – shown him the body of the duke his father,

---

    0 s.d. The corpse is arranged as if asleep, as lines 41–3 indicate. Macabre comedy was
       made, in the 1988 Swan Theatre production, of the fact that rigor mortis had set in
       and the corpse was far from pliant
    3 *lay* bet
    7 *returns* i.e. various ways of describing it. A return, technically speaking, was a
       report on a writ or court order: hence, *returns* meant also the days such reports
       were made. Michaelmas term had eight such days (Foakes)
   12 *flesh-flies* Hamlet calls the sycophantic courtier Osric a 'water-fly' (*Hamlet* V.ii.82).
       Flesh-flies lay their eggs in putrefying flesh, and hence serve as metaphors for those
       who live off court corruption
   16 *shown* ed. (show Q). The past tense is required following 'to have made', and note
       line 18's *slain*, which is part of the same construction

and how quaintly he died like a politician in hugger-mugger –
made no man acquainted with it, and in catastrophe slain him
over his father's breast! And oh I'm mad to lose such a sweet
opportunity.   20

HIPPOLITO

Nay push, prithee be content! There's no remedy present; may
not hereafter times open in as fair faces as this?

VINDICE

They may if they can paint so well.

HIPPOLITO

Come now, to avoid all suspicion let's forsake this room and be
going to meet the duke's son.   25

VINDICE

Content, I'm for any weather. Heart, step close, here he comes!

Enter LUSSURIOSO

HIPPOLITO

My honoured lord.

LUSSURIOSO

Oh me – you both present.

VINDICE

E'en newly my lord, just as your lordship entered now. About
this place we had notice given he should be, but in some loath-   30
some plight or other.

HIPPOLITO

Came your honour private?

LUSSURIOSO

Private enough for this: only a few
Attend my coming out.

HIPPOLITO [*Aside*]   Death rot those few!

LUSSURIOSO

Stay – yonder's the slave.   35

VINDICE

Mass there's the slave indeed my lord.
[*Aside*] 'Tis a good child, he calls his father slave!

---

17   *died* Q corrected (did Q uncorrected)
     like ... hugger-mugger i.e. like a machiavel in some secret intrigue. See *Hamlet*
     IV.v.83–4: 'we have done but greenly/In hugger-mugger to inter him'
23   *paint* i.e. use face-paint: see IV.ii.218 and n .

LUSSURIOSO

    Ay, that's the villain, the damned villain! Softly,

    Tread easy.

VINDICE   Puh, I warrant you my lord,

    We'll stifle in our breaths.

LUSSURIOSO   That will do well.   40

    Base rogue thou sleepest thy last! [*Aside*] 'Tis policy

    To have him killed in's sleep, for if he waked

    He would betray all to them.

VINDICE   But my lord –

LUSSURIOSO

    Ha? What say'st?

VINDICE

    Shall we kill him now he's drunk?

LUSSURIOSO   Ay, best of all.   45

VINDICE

    Why then he will ne'er live to be sober.

LUSSURIOSO

    No matter: let him reel to hell.

VINDICE

    But being so full of liquor I fear he will put out all the fire!

LUSSURIOSO

    Thou art a mad breast!

VINDICE

    [*Aside*] And leave none to warm your lordship's gols withal. –   50

    For he that dies drunk falls into hell fire like a bucket o' water:

    qush, qush.

LUSSURIOSO

    Come, be ready, nake your swords, think of your wrongs: this

    slave has injured you.

VINDICE

    Troth so he has, and he has paid well for't.   55

LUSSURIOSO

    Meet with him now.

---

39   *Puh* Q (Push *Harrier*)

45   Recalling *Hamlet* III.iii.84–92: such a death ensuring damnation

49   *breast* Q corrected (beast Q uncorrected)

50   *gols* hands

52   *qush* splash

53   *nake* Q corrected (make Q uncorrected) = unsheathe

VINDICE

You'll bear us out my lord?

LUSSURIOSO

Puh, am I a lord for nothing think you? Quickly now!

VINDICE

Sa, sa, sa, thump! [*He stabs the corpse*] There he lies!

LUSSURIOSO

Nimbly done. Ha! Oh, villains, murderers,   60

'Tis the old duke my father!

VINDICE [*Aside*]   That's a jest.

LUSSURIOSO

What, stiff and cold already?

Oh pardon me to call you from your names,

'Tis none of your deed; that villain Piato

Whom you thought now to kill has murdered him   65

And left him thus disguised.

HIPPOLITO   And not unlikely.

VINDICE

Oh rascal, was he not ashamed

To put the duke into a greasy doublet?

LUSSURIOSO

He has been cold and stiff – who knows how long?

VINDICE

[*Aside*] Marry that do I!   70

LUSSURIOSO

No words, I pray, of anything intended!

VINDICE

Oh my lord.

HIPPOLITO

I would fain have your lordship think that we have small reason

to prate.

LUSSURIOSO

Faith thou sayest true. I'll forthwith send to Court   75

For all the nobles, bastard, duchess, all –

How here by miracle we found him dead

And, in his raiment, that foul villain fled.

57   *bear us out* support us

63   *from your names* far from what you deserve

VINDICE
> That will be the best way my lord, to clear us all; let's cast about
> to be clear.   80
LUSSURIOSO
> Ho! Nencio, Sordido, and the rest!

Enter all [his ATTENDANTS]

1 ATTENDANT
> My lord.
2 ATTENDANT
> My lord.
LUSSURIOSO
> Be witnesses of a strange spectacle.
> Choosing for private conference that sad room   85
> We found the duke my father 'gealed in blood.
1 ATTENDANT
> My lord the duke! Run, hie thee Nencio,
> Startle the Court by signifying so much.   [*Exit* ATTENDANT]
VINDICE
> [*Aside*] Thus much by wit a deep revenger can:
> When murder's known, to be the clearest man.   90
> We're furthest off, and with as bold an eye
> Survey his body as the standers-by.
LUSSURIOSO
> My royal father, too basely let blood
> By a malevolent slave!
HIPPOLITO[*Aside*]   Hark!
> He calls thee slave again.
VINDICE [*Aside*]   H'as lost, he may!   95
LUSSURIOSO
> Oh sight, look hither, see, his lips are gnawn
> With poison!
VINDICE   How? His lips? By the Mass, they be!
LUSSURIOSO
> Oh villain – Oh rogue – Oh slave – Oh rascal!
HIPPOLITO
> [*Aside*] Oh good deceit! – He quits him with like terms.

82, 83, 87 s.p. ed. (1., 2., 1. Q)
86   *'gealed in blood* covered in congealed blood
91   *furthest* Q (fordest)

253

[*Enter* AMBITIOSO *and* SUPERVACUO *with* NOBLES]

1 [NOBLE]
  Where?   100
2 [NOBLE]
  Which way?
AMBITIOSO
  Over what roof hangs this prodigious comet
  In deadly fire?
LUSSURIOSO   Behold, behold my lords:
  The duke my father's murdered by a vassal
  That owes this habit, and here left disguised.   105

[*Enter the* DUCHESS *and* SPURIO]

DUCHESS
  My lord and husband!
2 NOBLE   Reverend majesty.
1 NOBLE
  I have seen these clothes often attending on him.
VINDICE
  [*Aside*] That nobleman has been in the country, for he does
  not lie.
SUPERVACUO
  [*Aside*] Learn of our mother – let's dissemble too!   110
  I am glad he's vanished: so I hope are you?
AMBITIOSO
  [*Aside*] Ay, you may take my word for't.
SPURIO   Old dad dead?
  I, one of his cast sins will send the fates
  Most hearty commendations by his own son;
  I'll tug in the new stream till strength be done.   115

100, 101 s.p. ed. (1., 2. Q) and throughout scene
102 *prodigious comet* A commonplace in Elizabethan drama is the idea that commotions in the heavens presage doom; cf. I *Henry VI* I.i.2–3:
    'Comets, importing change of times and states,
    Brandish your crystal tresses in the sky'
105 *owes* owns

LUSSURIOSO
    Where be those two that did affirm to us
    My lord the duke was privately rid forth?
1 NOBLE
    Oh pardon us my lords, he gave that charge
    Upon our lives, if he were missed at Court,
    To answer so. He rode not anywhere,   120
    We left him private with that fellow, here.
VINDICE
    [*Aside*] Confirmed.
LUSSURIOSO
    Oh heavens, that false charge was his death.
    Impudent beggars! Durst you to our face
    Maintain such a false answer? Bear him straight   125
    To execution.
1 NOBLE   My lord!
LUSSURIOSO   Urge me no more.
    In this, the excuse may be called half the murder.
VINDICE
    [*Aside*] You've sentenced well.
LUSSURIOSO   Away, see it be done.
                            [*Exit* 1 NOBLE *under guard*]
VINDICE
    [*Aside*] Could you not stick? See what confession doth.
    Who would not lie when men are hanged for truth?   130
HIPPOLITO
    [*Aside*] Brother, how happy is our vengeance!
VINDICE [*Aside*]   Why, it hits
    Past the apprehension of indifferent wits.
LUSSURIOSO
    My lord let post horse be sent
    Into all places to entrap the villain.
VINDICE
    [*Aside*] Post horse! Ha, ha.   135
2 NOBLE
    My lord we're something bold to know our duty.
    Your father's accidentally departed,
    The titles that were due to him meet you.

129   *stick* i.e. keep quiet
136, 147, 149, 151, 153, 156, 161 s.p. ed. (*Nob.* or *Nobl.*

255

LUSSURIOSO
  Meet me? I'm not at leisure my good lord,
  I've many griefs to dispatch out o' the way –   140
  [*Aside*] Welcome sweet titles! – Talk to me my lords
  Of sepulchres and mighty emperors' bones,
  That's thought for me.
VINDICE
  [*Aside*] So, one may see by this how foreign markets go:
  Courtiers have feet o' the nines and tongues o' the twelves: 145
  They flatter dukes, and dukes flatter themselves.
2 NOBLE
  My lord it is your shine must comfort us.
LUSSURIOSO
  Alas I shine in tears like the sun in April.
2 NOBLE
  You're now my lord's Grace.
LUSSURIOSO
  My lord's Grace? I perceive you'll have it so.   150
2 NOBLE
  'Tis but your own.
LUSSURIOSO
  Then heavens give me grace to be so.
VINDICE
  [*Aside*] He prays well for himself!
3 NOBLE   Madam all sorrows
  Must run their circles into joys; no doubt but time
  Will make the murderer bring forth himself.   155
VINDICE
  [*Aside*] He were an ass then i' faith!
3 NOBLE   In the mean season
  Let us bethink the latest funeral honours
  Due to the duke's cold body; and, withal,
  Calling to memory our new happiness
  Spread in his royal son – lords, gentlemen,   160
  Prepare for revels!
VINDICE [*Aside*]   Revels!
3 NOBLE   Time hath several falls:
  Griefs lift up joys, feasts put down funerals.

145 *feet . . . twelves* (flattering) tongues three sizes larger than their feet
161 *falls* changes or disguises (Nicoll)

LUSSURIOSO

    Come then my lords, my favours to you all.

    [*Aside*] The duchess is suspected foully bent;

    I'll begin dukedom with her banishment. 165

                  Exeunt [LUSSURIOSO,] NOBLES, *and* DUCHESS

HIPPOLITO

    [*Aside*] Revels.

VINDICE [*Aside*]   Ay that's the word. We are firm yet:

    Strike one strain more and then we crown our wit.

                  Exeunt [VINDICE *and* HIPPOLITO]

SPURIO

    Well, have the fairest mark –

    So said the duke when he begot me –

    And if I miss his heart or near about 170

    Then have at any – a bastard scorns to be out.   [*Exit*]

SUPERVACUO

    Not'st thou that Spurio, brother?

AMBITIOSO

    Yes I note him, to our shame.

SUPERVACUO

    He shall not live: his hair shall not grow much longer. In this

    time of revels tricks may be set afoot. Seest thou yon new 175

    moon? It shall outlive the new duke by much: this hand shall

    dispossess him: then we're mighty.

    A masque is treason's licence: that build upon –

    'Tis murder's best face, when a vizard's on! *Exit* SUPERVACUO

AMBITIOSO

    Is't so? 'Tis very good: 180

    And do you think to be duke then, kind brother?

    I'll see fair play: drop one, and there lies t'other. *Exit* AMBITIOSO

---

167 s.d. ed. (*Exeu.* Bro. Q)

178 *masque* An entertainment at feasts involving dance and face-masks and often dis-
      guise. In the Jacobean Court, highly elaborate in costume, scenery, music, and
      dance, and having a dramatic text. Such masques would end in 'revels', a general
      dance. The masques presented here are simple in form, though they might have
      been lavishly dressed

180 *'Tis* ed. ('ts Q)

[ACT V, SCENE ii]

Enter VINDICE *and* HIPPOLITO *with* PIERO *and other* LORDS

VINDICE

    My lords be all of music! Strike old griefs
    Into other countries
    That flow in too much milk and have faint livers,
    Not daring to stab home their discontents.
    Let our hid flames break out as fire, as lightning,   5
    To blast this villainous dukedom vexed with sin:
    Wind up your souls to their full height again.

PIERO

    How?

1 LORD Which way?

3 LORD   Any way! Our wrongs are such,
    We cannot justly be revenged too much.

VINDICE

    You shall have all enough. Revels are toward,   10
    And those few nobles that have long suppressed you
    Are busied to the furnishing of a masque
    And do affect to make a pleasant tale on't.
    The masquing suits are fashioning; now comes in
    That which must glad us all: we to take pattern   15
    Of all those suits, the colour, trimming, fashion,
    E'en to an undistinguished hair almost.
    Then entering first, observing the true form,
    Within a strain or two we shall find leisure
    To steal our swords out handsomely,   20
    And when they think their pleasure sweet and good,
    In midst of all their joys they shall sigh blood!

PIERO

    Weightily, effectually!

---

    3 *flow . . . milk* are effeminate
       have faint livers lack courage (The liver was believed to be the seat of courage.)
    7 *Wind up* brace yourselves for action
 8, 24 s.p. ed. (1., 3. Q)
   13 *affect* desire
   17 *undistinguished hair* i.e. down to the smallest detail; 'undistinguished' = too small
       to pick out or distinguish
   19 *strain or two* few bars of music

3 LORD

Before the other maskers come—

VINDICE

We're gone, all done and past. 25

PIERO

But how for the duke's guard?

VINDICE   Let that alone:

By one and one their strengths shall be drunk down.

HIPPOLITO

There are five hundred gentlemen in the action

That will apply themselves and not stand idle.

PIERO

Oh let us hug your bosoms!

VINDICE   Come my lords, 30

Prepare for deeds, let other times have words.

Exeunt

---

24   *the other* ed. (the tother Q)
27   i.e. they will be rendered powerless by being made drunk
28   *five hundred gentlemen* An implausibly large number for such a small-scale secret operation as actually takes place, and Vindice's jesting allusion (at V.iii.125) to incriminating them ('we could have nobles clipped') seems to imply a smallish number

[ACT V, SCENE iii]

*In a dumb show: the possessing of the young duke
[LUSSURIOSO] with all his NOBLES; then sounding music,
a furnished table is brought forth, then enters [LUSSURIOSO]
and his NOBLES to the banquet. A blazing star appeareth*

1 NOBLE

Many harmonious hours and choicest pleasures
Fill up the royal numbers of your years.

LUSSURIOSO

My lords we're pleased to thank you – though we know
'Tis but your duty now to wish it so.

1 NOBLE

That shine makes us all happy.   5

3 NOBLE

His Grace frowns?

2 NOBLE

Yet we must say he smiles.

1 NOBLE   I think we must.

LUSSURIOSO

[*Aside*] That foul incontinent duchess we have banished:
The bastard shall not live. After these revels
I'll begin strange ones: he and the stepsons   10
Shall pay their lives for the first subsidies;
We must not frown so soon, else 't 'ad been now.

1 NOBLE

My gracious lord please you prepare for pleasure;

---

0   s.d. 1 *possessing* installation as duke. This is the first of two successive dumb-shows; all
exit after the first and re-enter for the second
s.d. 2 [LUSSURIOSO] ed. (*the Duke* Q)
s.d. 4 *blazing star* Not referred to in the dialogue until line 16, so this could be an
anticipatory s.d. However, the star's appearance just as the banquet begins would be
aptly ominous and increase audience expectation

1, 5 s.p. ed. (*Nob.* Q)
5   *shine* i.e. warmth of ducal favour. If the blazing star is already visible to the audience but not to the nobles, this would have an ironic effect
11   *subsidies* penalties (used at the time to refer to financial grants to the king by
Parliament)
12   *else . . . now* otherwise I'd be doing it now (i.e. I must not show displeasure and so
forewarn my enemies)

The masque is not far off.
LUSSURIOSO   We are for pleasure:
Beshrew thee what art thou? Madest me start!   15
Thou hast committed treason! – A blazing star!
1 NOBLE
A blazing star! Oh where my lord?
LUSSURIOSO   Spy out.
2 NOBLE
See see my lords, a wondrous dreadful one!
LUSSURIOSO
I am not pleased at that ill-knotted fire,
That bushing-flaring star. Am not I duke?   20
It should not quake me now. Had it appeared
Before it, I might then have justly feared:
But yet they say, whom art and learning weds,
When stars wear locks they threaten great men's heads.
Is it so? You are read my lords.
1 NOBLE   May it please your Grace,   25
It shows great anger.
LUSSURIOSO   That does not please our Grace.
2 NOBLE
Yet here's the comfort my lord: many times
When it seems most, it threatens farthest off.
LUSSURIOSO
Faith and I think so too.
1 NOBLE   Beside my lord,
You're gracefully established with the loves   30
Of all your subjects; and for natural death,
I hope it will be threescore years a-coming.
LUSSURIOSO
True – no more but threescore years?

---

16 The line may be delivered so as to show that the blazing star is at first mistaken for
   a stage-effect connected to the masque (this seems exactly in the spirit of the
   dramatist's stagecraft)
20 *bushing* a term used of a comet's 'tail' (*OED*)
22 *Believe it. I* 'it' = my installation as duke
24 *wear* (were Q).
   wear locks i.e. the shooting or falling is marked by fiery trails. For their ominous
   significance see V.i.102 and n.
25 *read* learned, well-read

261

1 NOBLE
Fourscore I hope my lord.
2 NOBLE   And fivescore I.
3 NOBLE
But 'tis my hope my lord you shall ne'er die.   35
LUSSURIOSO
Give me thy hand: these others I rebuke:
He that hopes so, is fittest for a duke.
Thou shalt sit next me. Take your places, lords,
We're ready now for sports, let 'em set on. [*Looks at blazing star*]
You thing! We shall forget you quite anon.   40
3 NOBLE
I hear 'em coming my lord.

Enter the masque of revengers (the two brothers [VINDICE *and*
HIPPOLITO] *and two* LORDS *more)*

LUSSURIOSO   Ah 'tis well!
[*Aside*] Brothers, and bastard, you dance next in hell!

The revengers dance.
At the end [*they*] *steal out their swords and these four kill the four*
at the table, in their chairs. It thunders

VINDICE
Mark; thunder! Dost know thy cue, thou big-voiced crier?
Duke's groans are thunder's watchwords.
HIPPOLITO
So my lords, you have enough.   45
VINDICE
Come let's away – no lingering.
HIPPOLITO   Follow – go!
                              Exeunt [*all but* VINDICE]
VINDICE
No power is angry when the lustful die:

---

43   Compare Chettle, *The Tragedy of Hoffman* I.i, where Hoffman responds to thun-
     der's insistent peals, demanding that he execute revenge: 'againe I come, I come, I
     come'

When thunder claps, heaven likes the tragedy.   *Exit*

LUSSURIOSO

Oh, oh.

> *Enter the other masque of intended murderers, stepsons*
> [AMBITIOSO *and* SUPERVACUO], *bastard* [SPURIO], *and a*
> *fourth man coming in dancing.* [LUSSURIOSO] *recovers a little in*
> *voice and groans, calls 'A guard! Treason!' at which they all start*
> *out of their measure, and turning towards the table they find*
> *them all to be murdered*

[handwritten margin note: Lussurioso almost dead]

SPURIO

Whose groan was that?

LUSSURIOSO   Treason. A guard.   50

AMBITIOSO

How now! All murdered!

SUPERVACUO   Murdered!

4 NOBLE

And those his nobles?

AMBITIOSO   [*Aside*] Here's a labour saved:

I thought to have sped him. 'Sblood – how came this?

[SUPERVACUO]

Then I proclaim myself. Now I am duke.

AMBITIOSO

Thou duke! Brother thou liest.

                                    [*Stabs* SUPERVACUO]

SPURIO   Slave! So dost thou.   55

                                    [*Stabs* AMBITIOSO]

4 NOBLE

Base villain, hast thou slain my lord and master?

                                    [*Stabs* SPURIO]

Enter the first men [VINDICE, HIPPOLITO, *and two* LORDS]

---

49   s.d. 3 [LUSSURIOSO] ed. (*the Duke* Q)

   s.d. 4–5 *start . . . measure* break off their dance

52   s.p. ed. (4. Q) and throughout scene

54   s.p. [SUPERVACUO] ed. (*Spu.* Q)

VINDICE

Pistols, treason, murder, help, guard! My lord the duke!

[*Enter* ANTONIO *and guard*]

HIPPOLITO

Lay hold upon these traitors!

LUSSURIOSO

Oh.

VINDICE

Alas the duke is murdered.

HIPPOLITO   And the nobles.   60

VINDICE

Surgeons, surgeons! – [*Aside*] heart, does he breathe so long?

ANTONIO

A piteous tragedy, able to make

An old man's eyes bloodshot.

LUSSURIOSO

Oh.

VINDICE

Look to my lord the duke. [*Aside*] A vengeance throttle him! –   65

Confess thou murderous and unhallowed man,

Didst thou kill all these?

4 NOBLE   None but the bastard, I.

VINDICE

How came the duke slain then?

4 NOBLE   We found him so.

LUSSURIOSO

Oh villain.

VINDICE

Hark.

LUSSURIOSO [Those in the masque did murder us.]   70

VINDICE

Law! You now sir:

Oh marble impudence – will you confess now?

4 NOBLE

'Sblood, 'tis all false!

ANTONIO   Away with that foul monster

Dipped in a prince's blood.

58   *these* ed. (this Q)

4 NOBLE   Heart 'tis a lie.

ANTONIO

    Let him have bitter execution.   75

                               [*Exit* 4 NOBLE *guarded*]

VINDICE

    [*Aside*] New marrow! No I cannot be expressed. –

    How fares my lord the duke?

LUSSURIOSO   Farewell to all:

    He that climbs highest has the greatest fall.

    My tongue is out of office.

VINDICE   Air, gentlemen, air.

    [*Whispers*] Now thou'lt not prate on't, 'twas Vindice murdered

        thee!   80

LUSSURIOSO

    Oh.

VINDICE

    [*Whispers*] Murdered thy father!

LUSSURIOSO   Oh.

VINDICE [*Whispers*]   And I am he!

    Tell nobody. – [LUSSURIOSO *dies*] So, so. The duke's departed.

ANTONIO

    It was a deadly hand that wounded him;

    The rest, ambitious who should rule and sway   85

    After his death, were so made all away.

VINDICE

    My lord was unlikely.

HIPPOLITO   Now the hope

    Of Italy lies in your reverend years.

VINDICE

    Your hair will make the silver age again,

    When there was fewer, but more honest men.   90

ANTONIO

    The burden's weighty and will press age down:

    May I so rule that heaven may keep the crown.

VINDICE

    The rape of your good lady has been 'quited

---

87   *unlikely* unpromising

With death on death.

ANTONIO   Just is the law above.
But of all things it puts me most to wonder   95
How the old duke came murdered.

VINDICE   Oh my lord.

ANTONIO
It was the strangeliest carried: I not heard of the like.

HIPPOLITO
'Twas all done for the best my lord.

VINDICE
All for your Grace's good. We may be bold
To speak it now: 'twas somewhat wittily carried   100
Though we say it. 'Twas we two murdered him!

ANTONIO
You two?

VINDICE
None else i' faith my lord. Nay 'twas well managed.

ANTONIO
Lay hands upon those villains.

VINDICE   How? On us?

ANTONIO
Bear 'em to speedy execution.   105

VINDICE
Heart! Was't not for your good my lord?

ANTONIO
My good! Away with 'em! Such an old man as he!
You that would murder him would murder me!

VINDICE
Is't come about?

HIPPOLITO   'Sfoot brother you begun.

VINDICE
May not we set as well as the duke's son?   110
Thou hast no conscience: are we not revenged?
Is there one enemy left alive amongst those?

---

105   *to* ed. (two Q)

108   Thus Antonio provides an illustration of the general law propounded by
      Machiavelli: 'He who is the cause of another becoming powerful is ruined; because
      that predominance has been brought about either by astuteness or else by force,
      and both are distrusted by him who has been raised to power' – *The Prince*, trans.
      W. K. Marriott (1908), ch. 3

'Tis time to die when we are ourselves our foes.
When murderers shut deeds close this curse does seal 'em:
If none disclose 'em, they themselves reveal 'em!   115
This murder might have slept in tongueless brass
But for ourselves, and the world died an ass.
Now I remember too; here was Piato
Brought forth a knavish sentence once:
No doubt – said he – but time   120
Will make the murderer bring forth himself.
'Tis well he died, he was a witch!
And now my lord, since we are in for ever
This work was ours, which else might have been slipped;
And if we list we could have nobles clipped   125
And go for less than beggars. But we hate
To bleed so cowardly: we have enough –
I' faith we're well – our mother turned, our sister true,
We die after a nest of dukes! Adieu.
                        Exeunt [VINDICE *and* HIPPOLITO *guarded*]
ANTONIO
How subtly was that murder closed! Bear up   130
Those tragic bodies; 'tis a heavy season.
Pray heaven their blood may wash away all treason.
                                                        [*Exeunt*]

FINIS

---

114   *murderers* ed. (murders Q)
122   *witch* Because, evidently, he could prophesy
125   *nobles clipped* Punning on (i) the clipping of gold coins called 'nobles', (ii) the
      beheading of noblemen who took part in the plot
128   *turned* converted
130   *closed* disclosed
132   s.d. *Exeunt* ed. (*Exit.* Q)

·TIS
Pitty Shees a Whore

Acted by the *Queenes* Maiesties Seruants, at *The Phœnix* in
Drury-Lane.

LONDON.
Printed by *Nicholas Okes* for *Richard
Collins*, and are to be sold at his shop
in *Pauls* Church-yard, at the signe
of the three Kings. 1633.

[COMMENDATORY VERSE]

To my Friend, the Author.

With admiration I beheld this Whore
Adorned with beauty, such as might restore
(If ever being as thy Muse hath famed)
Her Giovanni, in his love unblamed.   5
The ready Graces lent their willing aid;
Pallas herself now played the chambermaid
And helped to put her dressings on: secure
Rest thou, that thy name herein shall endure
To th' end of age; and Annabella be   10
Gloriously fair, even in her infamy.

THOMAS ELLICE

This does not appear in all copies of Q.

6   *The . . . Graces* in classical mythology, the three daughters of Jupiter, who both personified and bestowed beauty and charm.

7   *Pallas* surname of Athena, classical goddess of wisdom.

12 THOMAS ELLICE born in 1607, a member of Gray's Inn from 1626 and, along with his elder brother Robert a member of Ford's literary circle; see Mary Hobbs, 'Robert and Thomas Ellice, Friends of Ford and Davenant', *N&Q* NS 21 (1974), 292–3.

[DEDICATORY EPISTLE]

To the truly noble, John, Earl of Peterborough,
Lord Mordaunt, Baron of Turvey.

My Lord,

Where a truth of merit hath a general warrant, there love is but a
debt, acknowledgment a justice. Greatness cannot often claim virtue 5
by inheritance; yet in this yours appears most eminent, for that
you are not more rightly heir to your fortunes, than glory shall be
to your memory. Sweetness of disposition ennobles a freedom of
birth; in both, your lawful interest adds honour to your own name,
and mercy to my presumption. Your noble allowance of these first 10
fruits of my leisure in the action, emboldens my confidence of
your as noble construction in this presentment; especially since my
service must ever owe particular duty to your favours, by a particular engagement. The gravity of the subject may easily excuse the
lightness of the title; otherwise I had been a severe judge against 15
mine own guilt. Princes have vouchsafed grace to trifles, offered from
a purity of devotion; your lordship may likewise please to admit into
your good opinion, with these weak endeavours, the constancy of
affection from the sincere lover of your deserts in honour,

JOHN FORD 20

1–2   *John . . . Turvey* John Mordaunt (*c.* 1599–1642), a court favourite, created 1st Earl of
         Peterborough in 1628.
8   *freedom* distinction.
10–12 *Your . . . presentment* Mordaunt had enjoyed seeing the play in performance ('in the
         action'), which led Ford to dedicate to him the printed version ('this presentment').
14–15 *gravity . . . lightness* playing on (*a*) seriousness versus levity and (*b*) physical heaviness
         versus lightness; 'the lightness of the title' also carries an implication of sexual
         licentiousness (with reference to its use of the word 'whore').
15–16 *otherwise . . . guilt* Ford himself would not have approved the use of a licentious title
         in a less serious play.

THE PERSONS OF THE PLAY

ANNABELLA, *Florio's daughter*
GIOVANNI, *Annabella's brother*
SIGNOR FLORIO, *a citizen of Parma*
PUTANA, *Annabella's tutoress*
FRIAR BONAVENTURA, *Giovanni's tutor and confessor*   5
LORD SORANZO, *a nobleman, Annabella's suitor*
VASQUES, *Soranzo's Spanish servant*
GRIMALDI, *a Roman gentleman and soldier, Annabella's suitor*
SIGNOR DONADO, *a citizen of Parma*
BERGETTO, *Donado's nephew, Annabella's suitor*   10
POGGIO, *Bergetto's servant*
HIPPOLITA, *Soranzo's former paramour*
RICHARDETTO, *Hippolita's husband, believed dead; disguised*
    as a physician
PHILOTIS, *Richardetto's niece*   15
THE CARDINAL, *the Pope's Nuncio*
His Servant
Officers of the watch, Ladies, Banditti, Attendants

The action takes place in Parma

The Persons of the Play ed. (Q's list of 'The Actors' Names' appears in the Appendix).

1   ANNABELLA The dialogue indicates that her hair is blonde (II.v.52–3), which was considered exceptionally beautiful in the period.

2   GIOVANNI The name is pronounced with four syllables (rather than three as in modern Italian).

4   PUTANA From the sixteenth-century Italian word *puttana*, defined in *World* as 'a whore, a harlot, a strumpet, a quean'.

5   FRIAR BONAVENTURA Named after the philosopher and theologian, St Bonaventure (1221–74); he became head of the Franciscan order in 1257, in succession to John of Parma (c. 1209–57), and became a Cardinal in 1273. If the character is portrayed as a Franciscan like his namesake (and like most other friars in English Renaissance drama), then his habit will be grey; the other possibilities are black (Dominican) or white (Carmelite).

7   VASQUES His name 'indicates that he is the only Spaniard' (Lomax).

8   GRIMALDI Perhaps the name draws associations from the Italian word *grimaldelli*, defined in *World* as 'a kind of darting weapon'.

9   DONADO The dialogue indicates that he is bearded (II.iv.21).

11 POGGIO Named after the Florentine scholar and historian, Gian Francesco Poggio Bracciolini (1380–1459), who was the subject of a sardonic epigram (I. 20) by Jacopo Sannazaro.

12   HIPPOLITA Named after two characters in classical mythology: Hippolyta the Amazon queen conquered by Theseus, and Hippolyte, the lustful Queen of Iolcus who fell in love with Peleus and, when he refused to enter an adulterous relationship with her, avenged herself by accusing him of trying to seduce her.

15   PHILOTIS From the Greek word *philotes* (= love, affection). Ford had made extensive use of significant Greek names in *The Broken Heart*, probably written soon before *'Tis Pity She's a Whore*.

19   *Parma* A city in Lombardy, about 220 miles north of Rome. It had been an independent state since 1545 (see note to I.ii.75–6), and in Ford's time was known as a flourishing mercantile centre; compare *The Fatal Marriage* (1620s), 972–3: 'a richer treasure . . . / Than Parma's custom comes to by the year'.

[ACT I, SCENE i]

Enter FRIAR *and* GIOVANNI

FRIAR

Dispute no more in this, for know, young man,
These are no school-points: nice philosophy
May tolerate unlikely arguments,
But Heaven admits no jest. Wits that presumed
On wit too much by striving how to prove   5
There was no God, with foolish grounds of art
Discovered first the nearest way to hell,
And filled the world with devilish atheism.
Such questions, youth, are fond, for better 'tis
To bless the sun, than reason why it shines;   10
Yet he thou talk'st of is above the sun.
No more! I may not hear it.

GIOVANNI   Gentle father,
To you I have unclasped my burdened soul,
Emptied the storehouse of my thoughts and heart,
Made myself poor of secrets, have not left   15
Another word untold which hath not spoke
All what I ever durst or think, or know;
And yet is here the comfort I shall have?
Must I not do what all men else may – love?

FRIAR

Yes, you may love, fair son.

---

1   *young man* Giovanni's name implies youth in Italian.
2   *school-points* issues in a university disputation (used to train students in the practice of logical reasoning.
     nice over-precise.
4   *Heaven* a periphrasis for God, here respectful, sometimes merely polite; the word is capitalized when used in this sense
     admits tolerates.
4–5 *Wits . . . much* Clever people whose intellect made them arrogantly presumptuous.
6   *grounds of art* scholarly proofs.
9   *fond* foolish, pointless.
11   *he . . . of* God.
17   *All what* Everything.
     durst dared.
     or . . . or either . . . or.

275

GIOVANNI   Must I not praise   20
That beauty which, if framed anew, the gods
Would make a god of if they had it there,
And kneel to it, as I do kneel to them?

FRIAR
Why, foolish madman!
GIOVANNI   Shall a peevish sound,
A customary form, from man to man,   25
Of brother and of sister, be a bar
'Twixt my perpetual happiness and me?
Say that we had one father, say one womb
(Curse to my joys!) gave both us life and birth:
Are we not therefore each to other bound   30
So much the more by nature, by the links
Of blood, of reason (nay, if you will have't,
Even of religion), to be ever one,
One soul, one flesh, one love, one heart, one all?

FRIAR
Have done, unhappy youth, for thou art lost.   35

GIOVANNI
Shall then, for that I am her brother born,
My joys be ever banished from her bed?
No, father: in your eyes I see the change
Of pity and compassion; from your age,
As from a sacred oracle, distils   40
The life of counsel. Tell me, holy man,
What cure shall give me ease in these extremes?

FRIAR
Repentance, son, and sorrow for this sin;
For thou hast moved a majesty above
With thy unrangèd almost blasphemy.   45

21–2   *the gods . . . there* Giovanni speaks in terms of the classical gods, who are neither
       omnipresent nor omniscient: they exist in a definite location ('there') and their
       appreciation of beauty is dependent on its physical presence. The wording accord-
       ingly establishes his distance from the Friar's Christian discourse.
24   *peevish* (*a*) meaningless; (*b*) spiteful.
25   *A customary . . . man* terminology which carries only the authority of human custom
       (rather than divine law).
32   *blood* Giovanni means 'consanguinity', but the word also carries the relevant
       secondary meaning, 'lust'.
35   *unhappy* ill-fated.
45   *unrangèd* limitless.
       almost Whether the word qualifies 'unrangèd' or 'blasphemy' is ambiguous.

GIOVANNI

O, do not speak of that, dear confessor.

FRIAR

Art thou, my son, that miracle of wit
Who once, within these three months, wert esteemed
A wonder of thine age, throughout Bologna?
How did the university applaud   50
Thy government, behaviour, learning, speech,
Sweetness, and all that could make up a man!
I was proud of my tutelage, and chose
Rather to leave my books than part with thee:
I did so – but the fruits of all my hopes   55
Are lost in thee, as thou art in thyself.
O Giovanni! Hast thou left the schools
Of knowledge, to converse with lust and death?
For death waits on thy lust. Look through the world,
And thou shalt see a thousand faces shine   60
More glorious than this idol thou ador'st:
Leave her, and take thy choice; 'tis much less sin,
Though in such games as those they lose that win.

GIOVANNI

It were more ease to stop the ocean
From floats and ebbs, than to dissuade my vows.   65

FRIAR

Then I have done, and in thy wilful flames
Already see thy ruin: Heaven is just.
Yet hear my counsel.

GIOVANNI   As a voice of life.

---

49   *A wonder . . . age* i.e. a precociously brilliant student.
     Bologna ed. (*Bononia* Q); a city in the Papal States, about 50 miles from Parma,
     where the play is set; it was the seat of Italy's oldest university, founded in the twelfth
     century. The university owed its association with free-thinking, relevant to Giovanni,
     in part to the philosopher Pietro Pomponazzi (1462–1525), who there wrote his
     treatise (published 1516) denying the immortality of the soul.
51   *government* self-discipline.
58   *death* spiritual death.
60–1 *shine . . . glorious* appear more beautiful.
62–3 *'tis . . . win* The Friar's proposal is a compromise: because he is committed to celibacy
     (as both academic and friar), any sexual relationship is in his eyes a loser's game, but
     most are less sinful than the incest Giovanni desires.
65   *floats and ebbs* high and low tides.
     vows wishes, promises.
66   *wilful flames* self-willed heat (of sexuality).

FRIAR

> Hie to thy father's house, there lock thee fast
> Alone within thy chamber, then fall down   70
> On both thy knees, and grovel on the ground.
> Cry to thy heart, wash every word thou utter'st
> In tears, and, if't be possible, of blood.
> Beg Heaven to cleanse the leprosy of lust
> That rots thy soul. Acknowledge what thou art,   75
> A wretch, a worm, a nothing. Weep, sigh, pray
> Three times a day, and three times every night.
> For seven days' space do this; then if thou find'st
> No change in thy desires, return to me:
> I'll think on remedy. Pray for thyself   80
> At home, whilst I pray for thee here. Away,
> My blessing with thee. We have need to pray.

GIOVANNI

> All this I'll do, to free me from the rod
> Of vengeance; else I'll swear my fate's my God.

> *Exeunt*

[ACT I, SCENE ii]

Enter GRIMALDI *and* VASQUES *ready to fight*

VASQUES

> Come sir, stand to your tackling. If you prove craven I'll make
> you run quickly.

---

69 *Hie* Go speedily.

73 *tears . . . of blood* tears expressing the most absolute penitence.

74 *leprosy* a disfiguring disease which eats away the skin, leaving red lesions; it was often
used as a metaphor for moral or sexual corruption.

·

0   s.d. *ready to fight* The phrase probably refers only to Vasques: both men are armed,
but the ensuing dialogue indicates that Grimaldi is initially unwilling to fight, so
only Vasques' sword is drawn.

1   *stand . . . tackling* stand and fight (tackling = weapons); a variant of the military
command 'stand to arms' (= prepare for combat).

1–2 prose ed. (Come . . . *Crauen,* / I'le . . . quickly Q).

GRIMALDI

Thou art no equal match for me.

VASQUES

Indeed I never went to the wars to bring home news, nor cannot play the mountebank for a meal's meat, and swear I got my 5
wounds in the field. See you these grey hairs? They'll not flinch
for a bloody nose! Wilt thou to this gear?

GRIMALDI

Why, slave, think'st thou I'll balance my reputation with a cast-
suit? Call thy master, he shall know that I dare –

VASQUES

Scold like a cotquean, that's your profession, thou poor shadow 10
of a soldier. I will make thee know my master keeps servants thy
betters in quality and performance. Comest thou to fight, or
prate?

GRIMALDI

Neither with thee. I am a Roman and a gentleman, one that
have got mine honour with expense of blood. 15

VASQUES

You are a lying coward and a fool. Fight, or by these hilts I'll
kill thee.

[GRIMALDI *draws his sword*]

3   *no equal* Grimaldi is a gentleman, Vasques a servant; the inequality is underlined by
     Grimaldi's use of the familiar 'thou' pronoun (whereas Vasques at first uses the more
     respectful 'you').
4–6 *I never . . . field* Vasques goads Grimaldi with an accusation of cowardice and
     mendacity. Mountebanks (itinerant medicine pedlars) were notorious for telling
     exaggerated lies about their wares, and Vasques suggests that Grimaldi's claims of
     military honour are in the same category: that he was never at the wars as a com-
     batant, only a reporter, and has lied about his wounds to make himself a welcome
     guest at Florio's table. (The scene apparently takes place during an all-male dinner –
     here a midday meal – for the three suitors; see also lines 100–1 below.)
7   *gear* the matter in hand (i.e. the fight between them).
8   *balance* equate.
8–9 *cast-suit* a base person who wears cast-off clothes.
10   *cotquean* low-born housewife.
     your profession the category of person in which you belong.
11   *shadow* unreal image.
11–12 *servants thy betters* servants, who are your betters.
14–15 prose ed. (Neither . . . thee, / I . . . got / Mine . . . blood Q).
15   *expense of blood* shedding of his own blood.
16   *by these hilts* An asseveration, but also referring to Grimaldi's undrawn sword, with
     its hilt pointing forward; the plural, *hilts,* may suggest that he is armed with rapier
     and dagger, the latter used for parrying (though compare II.vi.72 and note).

Brave, my lord! You'll fight.

GRIMALDI

Provoke me not, for if thou dost –

VASQUES

Have at you!   20

They fight; GRIMALDI *hath the worst*

Enter FLORIO, DONADO, SORANZO

FLORIO

What mean these sudden broils so near my doors?
Have you not other places but my house
To vent the spleen of your disordered bloods?
Must I be haunted still with such unrest
As not to eat or sleep in peace at home?   25
Is this your love, Grimaldi? Fie, 'tis naught.

DONADO

And, Vasques, I may tell thee 'tis not well
To broach these quarrels. You are ever forward
In seconding contentions.

Enter above ANNABELLA *and* PUTANA

FLORIO   What's the ground?

SORANZO

That, with your patience, signors, I'll resolve: 30
This gentleman, whom fame reports a soldier
(For else I know not) rivals me in love
To Signor Florio's daughter, to whose ears
He still prefers his suit, to my disgrace,
Thinking the way to recommend himself   35
Is to disparage me in his report.
But know, Grimaldi, though maybe thou art

18   *Brave . . . lord* If 'Brave' is an adjective (as punctuated here), the line is a sarcastic
     taunt; if it is a verb, however, the sense is 'How dare you challenge my lord!'
21   *sudden* rash, violent.
23   *spleen* a fit of anger or proud temper.
26   *naught* worthless.
29   *seconding* stirring up.
     the ground the cause of the argument.
29   s.d. *above* on the stage balcony.
     resolve explain, clarify.
32   *else* otherwise. Soranzo says, provocatively that Grimaldi's reputation ('fame') is the
     only soldierly thing about him.
34   *prefers* advances.

My equal in thy blood, yet this bewrays
A lowness in thy mind, which, wert thou noble,
Thou wouldst as much disdain as I do thee   40
For this unworthiness. [*To* FLORIO] And on this ground
I willed my servant to correct this tongue,
Holding a man so base no match for me.

VASQUES

And had not your sudden coming prevented us, I had let my
gentleman blood under the gills. [*To* GRIMALDI] I should have   45
wormed you, sir, for running mad.

GRIMALDI

I'll be revenged, Soranzo.

VASQUES

On a dish of warm broth to stay your stomach – do, honest
innocence, do! Spoon-meat is a wholesomer diet than a
Spanish blade.   50

GRIMALDI

Remember this.

SORANZO   I fear thee not, Grimaldi.

Exit GRIMALDI

FLORIO

My lord Soranzo, this is strange to me,
Why you should storm, having my word engaged:
Owing her heart, what need you doubt her ear?
Losers may talk by law of any game.   55

---

38   *bewrays* reveals, exposes (implying that the thing revealed is shameful).

42   *this* Q; other editors, assuming that Soranzo is still speaking to Grimaldi, have
     emended to 'thy'. The recurrence of the word 'ground', however, suggests to me that
     he is addressing Florio in conclusion to his answer to the question Florio asked in
     line 29, 'What's the ground?' The Q reading's unusual wording (as distinct from, say,
     'his') conveys his disdainful contempt for his rival.

44   *had not* ed. (had Q).

44–5 *let . . . gills* The metaphor is of a Renaissance doctor drawing off infected blood to
     cure the patient. A man's gills are the fleshy area under his jaw: Vasques is saying he
     would have cut Grimaldi's throat. The phrase may also suggest that Grimaldi has
     become red-faced with anger or exertion.

46   *wormed . . . mad* To worm a dog was to cut its lytta, a ligament under its tongue, as a
     preventative against rabies ('running mad'); Grimaldi has also 'run mad' with anger.

48   *stay your stomach* (*a*) satisfy your appetite; (*b*) check your aggression.

49   *Spoon-meat* Liquid food typically eaten by invalids and toothless people.

49–50 *a Spanish blade* Vasques' sword.

53   *engaged* pledged.

54   *Owing* Possessing.

55   The winner of a game should magnanimously allow the losers to express their dis-
     appointment or resentment; proverbial (Tilley, L. 458).

VASQUES

Yet the villainy of words, Signor Florio, may be such as would
make any unspleened dove choleric. Blame not my lord in this.

FLORIO

Be you more silent.
I would not for my wealth my daughter's love
Should cause the spilling of one drop of blood.   60
Vasques, put up. Let's end this fray in wine.

Exeunt [FLORIO, DONADO, SORANZO, *and* VASQUES]

PUTANA

How like you this, child? Here's threatening, challenging, quar-
relling, and fighting, on every side, and all is for your sake. You
had need look to yourself, charge, you'll be stolen away sleeping
else shortly.   65

ANNABELLA

But tut'ress, such a life gives no content
To me: my thoughts are fixed on other ends.
Would you would leave me.

PUTANA

Leave you? No marvel else! Leave me no leaving, charge, this is
love outright. Indeed, I blame you not, you have choice fit for   70
the best lady in Italy.

ANNABELLA

Pray do not talk so much.

PUTANA

Take the worst with the best – there's Grimaldi the soldier,
a very well-timbered fellow: they say he is a Roman, nephew
to the Duke Monferrato; they say he did good service in the   75

---

56   *villainy* ed. (villaine Q).
57   *make . . . choleric* In contemporary psychology, choler was the 'humour' (bodily
      fluid) which caused anger when an excessive amount was present in the blood-
      stream. It was believed that doves' livers did not secrete gall (thought to be a form
      of choler); thus to make a dove choleric is to enrage even the mildest of creatures.
56–8 prose ed. (Yet . . . such, / As . . . Chollerick, / Blame . . . this Q).
61   *put up* sheathe your sword.
67   *ends* matters.
69–71 prose ed. (Leaue . . . (Chardge) / This . . . haue / Choyce . . . Italy Q).
69   *No marvel else!* No wonder [you want me to do so]! Putana assumes that Annabella
      wishes to be left alone for sexual reasons.
74   *well-timbered* well-built. (The metaphor is of a house.)
75   *Duke Monferrato* ed. (Duke *Mount Ferratto* Q). Monferrato was a small, strategically
      important state in north-west Italy, which was annexed to the state of Mantua in
      1536, and became a duchy in 1574.

wars against the Milanese. But faith, charge, I do not like him,
an't be for nothing but for being a soldier: one amongst twenty
of your skirmishing captains but have some privy maim or
other that mars their standing upright. I like him the worse. He
crinkles so much in the hams – though he might serve if there   80
were no more men. Yet he's not the man I would choose.

ANNABELLA

Fie, how thou pratest.

PUTANA

As I am a very woman, I like Signor Soranzo well: he is wise;
and what is more, rich; and what is more than that, kind; and
what is more than all this, a nobleman. Such a one, were I the   85
fair Annabella myself, I would wish and pray for. Then he is
bountiful; besides he is handsome; and, by my troth, I think
wholesome – and that's news in a gallant of three-and-twenty.
Liberal, that I know; loving, that you know; and a man sure,
else he could never ha' purchased such a good name with   90
Hippolita the lusty widow in her husband's lifetime. An 'twere
but for that report, sweetheart, would a were thine! Commend
a man for his qualities, but take a husband as he is a plain-

---

75–6   the wars . . . Milanese Parma was part of the Duchy of Milan until annexed to the
        Papal States in 1512; it was later incorporated into the Duchy of Piacenza and Parma
        in 1545. Milan still pressed its claim to Parma, and recaptured Piacenza in 1547; war
        followed in 1551–2.
76   Milanese ed. (Millanoys Q).
77   an't if it.
77–8   one . . . twenty . . . but have there is not one amongst twenty . . . who do not have.
78   privy maim hidden wound.
79   mars . . . upright makes them impotent (playing on the usual meaning of 'standing
        upright'; but, since the wound is 'privy', the sexual sense is dominant).
80   crinkles . . . in the hams (a) bows obsequiously; (b) shrinks from his (sexual)
        purpose .
83   very true.
        Signor Soranzo Putana (ignorantly?) 'demotes' Soranzo, who is everywhere else
        addressed as 'Lord Soranzo', to 'Signor' (a polite term of address, similar to the
        modern English 'Mister').
88   wholesome uninfected by venereal disease.
89   Liberal Generous, especially with money; that Putana says she knows this implies
        that he has bribed her to promote his suit (compare II.vi.14–21, where she cadges
        money from Donado for similar alleged services).
        a man i.e. not impotent.
90   good name high regard.
92   would a were 'a' is the unstressed form of 'he'.
93   qualities skills, accomplishments.

sufficient, naked man: such a one is for your bed, and such a
one is Signor Soranzo, my life for't.   95

ANNABELLA

Sure the woman took her morning's draught too soon.

Enter BERGETTO *and* POGGIO

PUTANA

But look, sweetheart, look what thing comes now: here's another
of your ciphers to fill up the number. O, brave old ape in a
silken coat! Observe.

BERGETTO

Didst thou think, Poggio, that I would spoil my new clothes,   100
and leave my dinner to fight?

POGGIO

No sir, I did not take you for so arrant a baby.

BERGETTO

I am wiser than so; for I hope, Poggio, thou never heard'st of an
elder brother that was a coxcomb, didst, Poggio?

POGGIO

Never indeed sir, as long as they had either land or money left   105
them to inherit.

BERGETTO

Is it possible, Poggio? O monstrous! Why, I'll undertake, with a
handful of silver, to buy a headful of wit at any time. But, sirrah,
I have another purchase in hand: I shall have the wench, mine

---

96   *took . . . soon* started drinking alcohol too early in the day; a 'morning's draught' was
literally a drink of wine or beer taken in the morning, often before work, so
Annabella is probably speaking jocularly rather than with irritation (especially if
the scene takes place around mid-day, as it seems to).

96   s.d. Bergetto and Poggio enter on the main stage, with Annabella and Putana looking
down on them from above.

97–9   prose ed. (But . . . now: / Here's . . . number: / Oh . . . obserue Q).

98   *ciphers* nonentities
brave finely clad.

98–9   *ape . . . coat* i.e. a fool dressed in finery.

100–1   prose ed. (Did'st . . . my / New . . . fight Q).

101   *leave my dinner* All Florio's other guests broke off their meal because of the fight
between Grimaldi and Vasques; Bergetto has stayed behind to finish his.

103–4   prose ed. (I . . . thou / Neuer . . . Coxcomb, / Did'st *Poggio?* Q).

104   *elder brother* Implying an heir (with reference to himself as Donado's heir).
coxcomb fool.

uncle says. I will but wash my face, and shift socks, and then   110
have at her i'faith! – Mark my pace, Poggio.

                                 [He walks affectedly]

POGGIO

Sir, I have seen an ass and a mule trot the Spanish pavan with a
better grace, I know not how often.

                               Exeunt [BERGETTO *and* POGGIO]

ANNABELLA

This idiot haunts me too.

PUTANA

Ay, ay, he needs no description. The rich magnifico that is   115
below with your father, charge, Signor Donado, his uncle, for
that he means to make this his cousin a golden calf, thinks that
you will be a right Israelite and fall down to him presently; but
I hope I have tutored you better. They say a fool's bauble is a
lady's playfellow; yet you having wealth enough, you need not   120
cast upon the dearth of flesh at any rate: hang him, innocent!

                      Enter GIOVANNI

ANNABELLA

But see, Putana, see; what blessed shape
Of some celestial creature now appears?
What man is he, that with such sad aspect
Walks careless of himself?

PUTANA   Where?

ANNABELLA   Look below.   125

PUTANA

O, 'tis your brother, sweet –

ANNABELLA   Ha!

110   *shift* change.
111   *Mark my pace* Watch how I walk.
112   *the Spanish pavan* a slow, stately dance.
115   *magnifico* wealthy man.
117   *golden calf* Alluding to the idol worshipped by the Israelites in the wilderness
      (Exodus 32); Donado is said to expect that Bergetto's riches will make Annabella
      'fall down to' him (meaning both worship him and accept him as a sexual partner
      in marriage), even though he is a 'mooncalf' (= a simpleton).
118   *presently* immediately.
119–20   *a fool's . . . playfellow* Proverbial (Tilley, F. 528); 'bauble' means both a professional
      fool's stick with a carved head, and a penis.
121   *cast . . . flesh* take decisions (literally, calculate) based on a shortage of male suitors
      (literally, penises); implying that she need not consider taking someone like Bergetto
      as her husband.

PUTANA   'Tis your brother.

ANNABELLA

    Sure 'tis not he: this is some woeful thing

    Wrapped up in grief, some shadow of a man.

    Alas, he beats his breast, and wipes his eyes

    Drowned all in tears; methinks I hear him sigh.   130

    Let's down, Putana, and partake the cause;

    I know my brother, in the love he bears me,

    Will not deny me partage in his sadness.

    My soul is full of heaviness and fear.

              Exeunt [from above ANNABELLA *and* PUTANA]

GIOVANNI

    Lost, I am lost: my fates have doomed my death.   135

    The more I strive, I love; the more I love,

    The less I hope. I see my ruin, certain.

    What judgement or endeavours could apply

    To my incurable and restless wounds

    I throughly have examined, but in vain.   140

    O that it were not in religion sin

    To make our love a god, and worship it!

    I have even wearied Heaven with prayers, dried up

    The spring of my continual tears, even starved

    My veins with daily fasts: what wit or art   145

    Could counsel, I have practised. But alas,

    I find all these but dreams, and old men's tales

    To fright unsteady youth: I'm still the same.

    Or I must speak, or burst. 'Tis not, I know,

    My lust, but 'tis my fate that leads me on.   150

    Keep fear and low, faint-hearted shame with slaves!

    I'll tell her that I love her, though my heart

    Were rated at the price of that attempt.

             Enter ANNABELLA *and* PUTANA

---

131   *partake* be told (and so share).

133   *partage* a share.

140   *throughly* thoroughly.

145   *wit* intellect.

151   *Keep fear and . . . shame* May fear and . . . shame dwell.

152–3   *though . . . attempt* though attempting it should cost me my heart.

153   *rated* valued.

153   s.d. ed. (after line 154a in Q).

O me! She comes.

ANNABELLA   Brother.

GIOVANNI [*Aside*]   If such a thing
As courage dwell in men, ye heavenly powers,   155
Now double all that virtue in my tongue.

ANNABELLA

Why brother, will you not speak to me?

GIOVANNI

Yes; how d'ee, sister?

ANNABELLA

Howsoever I am, methinks you are not well.

PUTANA

Bless us, why are you so sad, sir?   160

GIOVANNI

Let me entreat you leave us awhile, Putana.
Sister, I would be private with you.

ANNABELLA

Withdraw, Putana.

PUTANA

I will. [*Aside*] If this were any other company for her, I should
think my absence an office of some credit; but I will leave   165
them together.   *Exit*

GIOVANNI

Come sister, lend your hand, let's walk together.
I hope you need not blush to walk with me;
Here's none but you and I.

ANNABELLA   How's this?

GIOVANNI

Faith, I mean no harm.   170

ANNABELLA

Harm?

GIOVANNI

No, good faith; how is't with 'ee?

---

158   *d'ee* do you (a contraction often used by Ford).

164   *I will* printed on a separate line in Q.

165   *an office . . . credit* a favour deserving reward (with the ironic secondary meaning, 'post of honour').

168   Annabella would have cause to blush with sexual modesty if walking alone with any man but her brother.

ANNABELLA [*Aside*]

    I trust he be not frantic. [*To him*] I am very well, brother.

GIOVANNI

    Trust me, but I am sick; I fear so sick

    'Twill cost my life.   175

ANNABELLA

    Mercy forbid it! 'Tis not so, I hope.

GIOVANNI

    I think you love me, sister.

ANNABELLA

    Yes, you know I do.

GIOVANNI

    I know't, indeed. – You're very fair.

ANNABELLA

    Nay then, I see you have a merry sickness.   180

GIOVANNI

    That's as it proves. The poets feign, I read,

    That Juno for her forehead did exceed

    All other goddesses; but I durst swear

    Your forehead exceeds hers, as hers did theirs.

ANNABELLA

    Troth, this is pretty!

GIOVANNI   Such a pair of stars   185

    As are thine eyes would, like Promethean fire,

    If gently glanced, give life to senseless stones.

ANNABELLA

    Fie upon 'ee!

GIOVANNI

    The lily and the rose, most sweetly strange,

    Upon your dimpled cheeks do strive for change.   190

---

173   *frantic* deranged.

       prose ed. (I . . . franticke— /1 . . . brother Q).

179   *You're* ed. (/are Q) *fair* beautiful.

181   *The poets* ed. (they Poets Q).

182   *Juno* the classical goddess of marriage, twin sister and wife of Jupiter.

186   *Promethean fire* a life-giving force; in classical mythology, Prometheus stole fire from heaven and, in some versions of the story, used it to animate the first human beings. Ford may be recalling Shakespeare's usage in *Love's Labour's Lost* (IV.iii.325), where Promethean fire is also an attribute of beautiful women's eyes. The whole passage plays on the two principal meanings of 'glance', to look swiftly and to strike obliquely (here against a stone, producing sparks).

189   *strange* in opposition (to one another).

190   *change* interchange; Annabella is blushing and blanching by turns.

Such lips would tempt a saint; such hands as those
Would make an anchorite lascivious.

ANNABELLA
D'ee mock me, or flatter me?

GIOVANNI
If you would see a beauty more exact
Than art can counterfeit or nature frame,   195
Look in your glass, and there behold your own.

ANNABELLA
O, you are a trim youth.

GIOVANNI
Here.   *Offers his dagger to her*

ANNABELLA What to do?

GIOVANNI   And here's my breast: strike home.
Rip up my bosom: there thou shalt behold   200
A heart in which is writ the truth I speak.
Why stand 'ee?

ANNABELLA   Are you earnest?

GIOVANNI   Yes, most earnest.
You cannot love?

ANNABELLA   Whom?

GIOVANNI   Me. My tortured soul
Hath felt affliction in the heat of death.
O, Annabella, I am quite undone: 205
The love of thee, my sister, and the view
Of thy immortal beauty hath untuned
All harmony both of my rest and life.
Why d'ee not strike?

ANNABELLA   Forbid it, my just fears.
If this be true, 'twere fitter I were dead.   210

GIOVANNI
True, Annabella? 'Tis no time to jest.
I have too long suppressed the hidden flames
That almost have consumed me. I have spent
Many a silent night in sighs and groans,
Ran over all my thoughts, despised my fate,   215

192   *anchorite* a hermit or religious recluse; a byword for the absence of sexual desire.
196   *glass* mirror.
197   *trim* handsome.
202   *stand* hesitate.
204   *affliction . . . death* suffering so intense that it resembles or threatens death.
215   *despised* attempted to defy.

Reasoned against the reasons of my love,
Done all that smoothed-cheek Virtue could advise,
But found all bootless: 'tis my destiny
That you must either love, or I must die.

ANNABELLA
Comes this in sadness from you?   220
                                    Let some mischief
GIOVANNI
Befall me soon, if I dissemble aught.

ANNABELLA
You are my brother, Giovanni.
                                    You
GIOVANNI
My sister, Annabella. I know this,
And could afford you instance why to love   225
So much the more for this, to which intent
Wise Nature first in your creation meant
To make you mine; else't had been sin and foul
To share one beauty to a double soul.
Nearness in birth or blood doth but persuade   230
A nearer nearness in affection.
I have asked counsel of the holy Church,
Who tells me I may love you; and 'tis just
That, since I may, I should; and will, yes will.
Must I now live, or die?
                                    Live. Thou hast won
ANNABELLA   235
The field, and never fought: what thou hast urged,
My captive heart had long ago resolved.
I blush to tell thee (but I'll tell thee now),
For every sigh that thou hast spent for me,
I have sighed ten; for every tear shed twenty;   240
And not so much for that I loved, as that
I durst not say I loved, nor scarcely think it.

GIOVANNI
Let not this music be a dream, ye gods,
For pity's sake I beg 'ee!

217 *smoothed-cheek* dean-shaven (implying either youth and inexperience or slippery
     persuasiveness); the term may also be a misprint for 'smooth-cheeked'.
218 *bootless* useless, ineffectual.
220 *in sadness* sincerely, earnestly.
221 *aught* anything, in any respect.
222–8 Giovanni offers her an argument ('afford…instance') in favour of incest: having already
     established that they are physically alike in beauty, he argues that they must also have a
     corresponding affinity of souls which, in neoplatonic philosophy, was the origin of love.

290

She kneels

ANNABELLA   On my knees,
Brother, even by our mother's dust, I charge you,
Do not betray me to your mirth or hate: 245
Love me, or kill me, brother.

He kneels

GIOVANNI   On my knees,
Sister, even by my mother's dust I charge you,
Do not betray me to your mirth or hate:
Love me, or kill me, sister.

ANNABELLA
You mean good sooth then?

GIOVANNI   In good troth I do,   250
And so do you, I hope. Say: I'm in earnest.

ANNABELLA
I'll swear't, and I.

GIOVANNI   And I, and by this kiss –   *Kisses her*
Once more. [*Kisses her*] Yet once more. [*Kisses her*] Now let's
   rise, by this

[*They rise*]

I would not change this minute for Elysium.
What must we now do?

ANNABELLA   What you will.

GIOVANNI   Come then: 255
After so many tears as we have wept,
Let's learn to court in smiles, to kiss and sleep.

Exeunt

[ACT I, SCENE iii]

Enter FLORIO *and* DONADO

FLORIO

Signor Donado, you have said enough,
I understand you, but would have you know

250   *good sooth* truthfully.
254   *change* exchange.
      Elysium in classical mythology, the posthumous destination of the virtuous; the
      pagan equivalent of heaven.
255   *What you will* Whatever you like (with a sexual implication).

I will not force my daughter 'gainst her will.
You see I have but two, a son and her;
And he is so devoted to his book,　　　　　　　　　　5
As, I must tell you true, I doubt his health.
Should he miscarry, all my hopes rely
Upon my girl. As for worldly fortune,
I am, I thank my stars, blessed with enough.
My care is how to match her to her liking:　　　　10
I would not have her marry wealth, but love;
And if she like your nephew, let him have her.
Here's all that I can say.
DONADO　　　　　　　　Sir, you say well,
Like a true father, and for my part, I,
If the young folks can like ('twixt you and me),　　15
Will promise to assure my nephew presently
Three thousand florins yearly during life,
And, after I am dead, my whole estate.
FLORIO
'Tis a fair proffer, sir. Meantime your nephew
Shall have free passage to commence his suit.　　20
If he can thrive, he shall have my consent.
So for this time I'll leave you, signor.　　　　*Exit*
DONADO　　　　　　　　　　Well,
Here's hope yet, if my nephew would have wit;
But he is such another dunce, I fear
He'll never win the wench. When I was young　　25
I could have done't, i' faith, and so shall he
If he will learn of me.

　　　　　Enter BERGETTO *and* POGGIO

　　　　　And in good time
He comes himself.

7　*miscarry* die prematurely, without continuing the family line.
16　*presently* now.
17　*Three thousand florins* Roughly equivalent to £250; a substantial but not lavish annual income for a landed gentleman.
20　*free passage* access to speak to Annabella.
27　s.d. ed.; after line 28 in Q.
27　*in good time* at the appropriate moment, 'as if on cue'.

POGGIO

How now, Bergetto, whither away so fast?

BERGETTO

O uncle, I have heard the strangest news that ever came out of   30
the mint – have I not, Poggio?

POGGIO

Yes indeed, sir.

DONADO

What news, Bergetto?

BERGETTO

Why, look ye uncle, my barber told me just now that there is a
fellow come to town, who undertakes to make a mill go without   35
the mortal help of any water or wind, only with sandbags! And
this fellow hath a strange horse, a most excellent beast I'll assure
you, uncle, my barber says, whose head, to the wonder of all
Christian people, stands just behind where his tail is. Is't not
true, Poggio?   40

POGGIO

So the barber swore, forsooth.

DONADO

And you are running thither?

29   s.p. *POGGIO* Q. The implied stage action has Bergetto rushing across the stage, a man
        with his mind on the fairground and anxious to get there quickly, while Poggio
        follows calling after: he may just be struggling to keep up (the verb *to podge*, which
        is echoed in his name, means to dawdle), or he may be giving Bergetto a gentle hint
        not to rush rudely past his uncle. All other editors since Weber reassign the line to
        Donado, primarily because it is uncharacteristic for Poggio to address his master by
        name; but this makes good enough sense either as a lapse of courtesy in the haste of
        the moment or a calculated way of getting Bergetto's attention and so forestalling the
        faux pas he is about to commit.

30–1   *news . . . mint* the newest news. The reference to the mint is double-edged: Bergetto
        means it to suggest the news's authenticity (in that the mint is the source of the
        currency), but minting is also a process of fabrication.

34   *uncle,* ed. (uncle? Q).

35–6   *to make . . . sandbags* This probably refers to a perpetual motion machine.

37–9   *a strange horse . . . tail is* A famous fairground fraud: punters were charged to see this
        wondrous animal, which turned out to be an ordinary horse with its tail tied to a
        manger (where its head would normally be).

41   *barber* Barbers were notorious purveyors of false news, so the line can be played
        with sardonic irony, introducing the possibility that Poggio is somewhat brighter
        than Bergetto.
        forsooth truly.

42   *thither* ed. (hither Q).

BERGETTO

Ay, forsooth, uncle.

DONADO

Wilt thou be a fool still? Come, sir, you shall not go. You have
more mind of a puppet-play than on the business I told ye.   45
Why, thou great baby, wilt never have wit, wilt make thyself a
May-game to all the world?

POGGIO

Answer for yourself, master.

BERGETTO

Why, uncle, should I sit at home still, and not go abroad to see
fashions like other gallants?   50

DONADO

To see hobby-horses! What wise talk, I pray, had you with
Annabella, when you were at Signor Florio's house?

BERGETTO

O, the wench: Uds sa' me, uncle, I tickled her with a rare speech,
that I made her almost burst her belly with laughing.

DONADO

Nay, I think so; and what speech was't?   55

BERGETTO

What did I say, Poggio?

POGGIO

Forsooth, my master said that he loved her almost as well as he
loved parmesan, and swore – I'll be sworn for him – that she
wanted but such a nose as his was, to be as pretty a young
woman as any was in Parma.   60

DONADO

O gross!

BERGETTO

Nay uncle, then she asked me whether my father had any more

---

45 *puppet-play* another traditional fairground entertainment.
46 *wilt . . . wilt* ed. (wu't . . . wu't Q).
47 *May-game* laughing-stock.
49 *still* constantly.
    abroad out of doors.
51 *hobby-horses* trivial pastimes; but the word also meant 'prostitutes', so Donado may
    alternatively suspect that Bergetto has ulterior motives for going out, which would
    compromise his suit to Annabella.
53 *Uds sa' me* an oath, minced from 'God save me'.
58 *parmesan* (Q Parmasent). Probably an Italian style of drinking (*OED* B.2) rather
    than an absurd reference to parmesan cheese (though the latter tends to raise a
    bigger laugh in the modern theatre).

children than myself; and I said, 'No, 'twere better he should
have had his brains knocked out first.'

DONADO

This is intolerable. 65

BERGETTO

Then said she, 'Will Signor Donado your uncle leave you all his
wealth?'

DONADO

Ha! That was good, did she harp upon that string?

BERGETTO

Did she harp upon that string? Ay, that she did. I answered,
'Leave me all his wealth? Why, woman, he hath no other wit; 70
if he had, he should hear on't to his everlasting glory and
confusion. I know,' quoth I, 'I am his white boy, and will not be
gulled.' And with that she fell into a great smile, and went away.
Nay, I did fit her.

DONADO

Ah, sirrah, then I see there is no changing of nature. Well, 75
Bergetto, I fear thou wilt be a very ass still.

BERGETTO

I should be sorry for that, uncle.

DONADO

Come, come you home with me. Since you are no better a
speaker, I'll have you write to her after some courtly manner,
and enclose some rich jewel in the letter. 80

BERGETTO

Ay marry, that will be excellent.

DONADO

Peace, innocent!
Once in my time I'll set my wits to school;
If all fail, 'tis but the fortune of a fool.

BERGETTO

Poggio, 'twill do, Poggio! 85

Exeunt

71 *glory* He means 'shame'; this kind of ignorant misapplication of words had been a
    common source of comedy in drama since Shakespeare's time.
72 *white boy* a term of endearment for a favourite child.
73 *gulled* duped, conned (i.e. deprived of his inheritance by fraud).
74 *fit her* answer her aptly.
75–6 prose ed. (Ah . . . nature, / Well . . . still Q).
80 *enclose . . . letter* Envelopes were not used in the seventeenth century: the paper of
    the letter itself will be folded around the jewel to make a small packet, and then
    sealed with wax.

ACT II[, SCENE i]

Enter GIOVANNI *and* ANNABELLA, *as from their chamber*

GIOVANNI
Come, Annabella, no more sister now
But love, a name more gracious. Do not blush,
Beauty's sweet wonder, but be proud to know
That yielding thou hast conquered, and inflamed
A heart whose tribute is thy brother's life.   5

ANNABELLA
And mine is his. O, how these stol'n contents
Would print a modest crimson on my cheeks,
Had any but my heart's delight prevailed!

GIOVANNI
I marvel why the chaster of your sex
Should think this pretty toy called maidenhead   10
So strange a loss, when, being lost, 'tis nothing,
And you are still the same.

ANNABELLA   'Tis well for you;
Now you can talk.

GIOVANNI   Music as well consists
In th'ear, as in the playing.

ANNABELLA   O, you're wanton!
Tell on't, you're best, do.

GIOVANNI   Thou wilt chide me, then.   15
Kiss me. [*They kiss*] So. Thus hung Jove on Leda's neck

---

0   s.d. *as from* This wording in seventeenth-century stage directions usually indicates
    some significant action by the characters; see Alan C. Dessen, *Elizabethan Stage
    Conventions and Modem Interpreters* (Cambridge, 1984), pp. 31–3. In this case,
    Giovanni and Annabella might be rearranging their clothes to suggest that they have
    come 'from their chamber' (= bedroom; i.e. from 'chambering' = sex).

4   *yielding* giving up her virginity.

6   *contents* pleasures.

10 *toy* a trivial thing.
    maidenhead virginity (literally, a woman's hymen, pierced in her first sexual encounter).

11 *nothing* (*a*) an insignificant thing; (*b*) a vagina.

13–14 *Music . . . playing* Implying that you don't have to experience something directly to
    understand it (with reference to Giovanni's inability to share Annabella's female
    experience of losing her virginity).

16 *Thus . . . Leda's neck* In classical mythology, the god Jupiter (also known as Jove)
    visited the woman Leda in the shape of a swan, and fathered twins on her.

And sucked divine ambrosia from her lips.
I envy not the mightiest man alive,
But hold myself, in being king of thee,
More great than were I king of all the world.   20
But I shall lose you, sweetheart.

ANNABELLA   But you shall not.

GIOVANNI
You must be married, mistress.

ANNABELLA   Yes, to whom?

GIOVANNI
Someone must have you.

ANNABELLA   You must.

GIOVANNI   Nay, some other.

ANNABELLA
Now prithee do not speak so without jesting:
You'll make me weep in earnest.

GIOVANNI   What, you will not!   25
But tell me, sweet, canst thou be dared to swear
That thou wilt live to me, and to no other?

ANNABELLA
By both our loves I dare; for didst thou know,
My Giovanni, how all suitors seem
To my eyes hateful, thou wouldst trust me then.   30

GIOVANNI
Enough, I take thy word. Sweet, we must part.
Remember what thou vowst: keep well my heart.

ANNABELLA
Will you be gone?

GIOVANNI   I must.

ANNABELLA
When to return?

GIOVANNI   Soon.

ANNABELLA   Look you do.

GIOVANNI   Farewell.   *Exit*

17   *ambrosia* the food of the classical gods; hence a byword for anything with a super-
      latively pleasant taste.
25   *weep in earnest* truly cry; possibly she has feigned tears during the preceding jocular
      banter.
27   *live to me* live faithful to me.
33–4 lineation ed. (Will . . . must. / When . . . Soone. / Looke . . . Farewell Q) The first
      verse line is incomplete, perhaps indicating a stunned pause from Annabella after
      Giovanni's 'I must.'

ANNABELLA

Go where thou wilt, in mind I'll keep thee here,   35
And where thou art, I know I shall be there.
Guardian!

Enter PUTANA

PUTANA

Child, how is't, child? Well, thank Heaven, ha?

ANNABELLA

O guardian, what a paradise of joy
Have I passed over!   40

PUTANA

Nay, what a paradise of joy have you passed under! Why, now I
commend thee, charge. Fear nothing, sweetheart: what though
he be your brother? Your brother's a man I hope, and I say still,
if a young wench feel the fit upon her, let her take anybody,
father or brother, all is one.   45

ANNABELLA

I would not have it known for all the world.

PUTANA

Nor I indeed, for the speech of the people; else 'twere nothing.

FLORIO (*within*)

Daughter Annabella!

ANNABELLA

O me, my father! [*Calls off-stage*] Here, sir! [*To* PUTANA] Reach
my work.   50

[PUTANA *passes her a piece of needlework*]

FLORIO (*Within*)

What are you doing?

ANNABELLA   So, let him come now.

Enter FLORIO, RICHARDETTO *like a doctor of physic,
and* PHILOTIS *with a lute in her hand*

40   *passed over* travelled through.
41   *passed under* Referring to the conventional 'missionary' sexual position, with the
     man on top of the woman.
44   *the fit* sexual desire.
47   *the speech of the people* vulgar, censorious gossip.
51   s.d. *Within* Off-stage.
     s.d. *like a doctor of physic* disguised as a medical doctor (as distinct from a holder of
     a university doctorate); the disguise includes 'a broad beard' (II.vi.78), probably
     adopted the better to cover his face. Richardetto remains disguised in public until
     V.vi.145.

FLORIO
    So hard at work, that's well: you lose no time.
    Look, I have brought you company: here's one,
    A learned doctor, lately come from Padua,
    Much skilled in physic; and for that I see   55
    You have of late been sickly, I entreated
    This reverend man to visit you some time.
ANNABELLA
    You're very welcome, sir.
RICHARDETTO   I thank you, mistress.
    Loud fame in large report hath spoke your praise
    As well for virtue as perfection;   60
    For which I have been bold to bring with me
    A kinswoman of mine, a maid, for song
    And music, one perhaps will give content.
    Please you to know her?
ANNABELA   They are parts I love,
    And she for them most welcome.
PHILOTIS   Thank you, lady.   65
FLORIO
    Sir, now you know my house, pray make not strange;
    And if you find my daughter need your art,
    I'll be your paymaster.
RICHARDETTO   Sir, what I am
    She shall command.
FLORIO   You shall bind me to you.
    Daughter, I must have confidence with you   70
    About some matters that concerns us both.

---

  52   *lose* waste.
52–7 lineation ed. (prose in Q).
  54   *Padua* a city in the state of Venice, about 80 miles north east of Parma; its university
       included one of the leading medical schools in Europe. In reality, as is established in
       the next scene, Richardetto has come from the opposite direction, from Leghorn
       (see note to II.ii.74).
  55   *for that* because.
  59   *large* extensive; full and free.
  64   *parts* talents, accomplishments.
  66   *make not strange* either 'don't stay away (i.e. Florio issues a standing invitation to
       'the Doctor'), or 'don't behave too formally'; 'strange' means 'like a stranger'.
  67   *art* medical skill.
  69   *bind . . . you* i.e. in bonds of gratitude.
  70   *confidence* private talk. Ford perhaps recalls the Nurse's usage in *Romeo and Juliet*
       (II.iii.118), which Shakespeare may originally have intended as a malapropism.

Good master Doctor, please you but walk in,
We'll crave a little of your cousin's cunning.
I think my girl hath not quite forgot
To touch an instrument; she could have done't.   75
We'll hear them both.
RICHARDETTO   I'll wait upon you, sir.

Exeunt

[ACT II, SCENE ii]

Enter SORANZO *in his study, reading a book*

SORANZO
'Love's measure is extreme, the comfort pain,
The life unrest, and the reward disdain.'
What's here? Look't o'er again. 'Tis so, so writes
This smooth licentious poet in his rhymes;
But Sannazar, thou liest, for had thy bosom   5
Felt such oppression as is laid on mine,
Thou wouldst have kissed the rod that made the smart.

73   *cunning* skill.
75   *touch an instrument* play a musical instrument; but 'instrument' could also mean
      'penis', so there is a bawdy undertone unintended by Florio, but relevant to the
      context now that Annabella is no longer a virgin.
      could have done used to be able to do.

 0   s.d. In the original production, the 'study' may have been represented by scenery set
      out in the 'discovery space' (a curtained alcove at the back of the stage). Many
      previous editors assume that Soranzo writes down his poetical contradiction of
      Sannazaro, and supply a stage direction at line 9. (The first to do so was Gifford in
      1827.) If so, he needs to have writing materials to hand, but Ford provides no
      attendant to carry them on for him; he will probably also need something to lean on
      as he writes. The likeliest solution is a desk in the 'study', probably set side-on to
      avoid his having to turn his back on the audience. Instead of a conventional
      entrance, he may have been 'discovered' in the study, i.e. the discovery-space curtain
      would be drawn to reveal him already there.
 1   s.p. SORANZO ed. (not in Q).
 5   *Sannazar* Jacopo Sannazaro (*c.* 1456–1530), Neapolitan humanist and love poet
      (hence 'licentious' in line 4). His Italian and Latin poems contain much about the
      pains of love, but nothing that corresponds precisely with the epigrammatic lines
      Soranzo quotes. In seventeenth-century England he was best known for his six-line
      Latin eulogy of Venice (*Epigrams*, I. 36), for which the city rewarded him with 600
      crowns (as mentioned in lines 14–15).

To work then, happy Muse, and contradict
What Sannazar hath in his envy writ.
'Love's measure is the mean, sweet his annoys,   10
His pleasures life, and his reward all joys.'
Had Annabella lived when Sannazar
Did in his brief encomium celebrate
Venice, that queen of cities, he had left
That verse which gained him such a sum of gold,   15
And for one only look from Annabel
Had writ of her, and her diviner cheeks.
O, how my thoughts are –

VASQUES (*Within*)

Pray forbear! In rules of civility, let me give notice on't: I shall
be taxed of my neglect of duty and service.   20

SORANZO

What rude intrusion interrupts my peace?
Can I be nowhere private?

VASQUES (*Within*)

Troth, you wrong your modesty.

SORANZO

What's the matter, Vasques, who is't?

Enter HIPPOLITA [*dressed in black*] *and* VASQUES

HIPPOLITA

'Tis I: 25
Do you know me now? Look, perjured man, on her
Whom thou and thy distracted lust have wronged.
Thy sensual rage of blood hath made my youth
A scorn to men and angels; and shall I
Be now a foil to thy unsated change?   30
Thou know'st, false wanton, when my modest fame

---

8   *Muse* Conventionally invoked by poets as an inspiring agency; from the nine Muses
    of classical mythology, patron goddesses of the arts.
9   *envy* malice.
10 *mean* norm.
    annoys troubles.
14 *left* abandoned.
20 *taxed of* reprimanded for.
28 *rage of blood* lustful frenzy.
30 *foil . . . unsated change* A foil is a thin sheet of metal on which a jewel is mounted to
    set off its lustre by contrast; Hippolita is saying that, having changed lovers even
    though his sexual appetite is not 'sated' (fully satisfied), Soranzo now uses her as the
    foil to his new love, Annabella.

Stood free from stain or scandal, all the charms
Of hell or sorcery could not prevail
Against the honour of my chaster bosom.
Thine eyes did plead in tears, thy tongue in oaths   35
Such, and so many, that a heart of steel
Would have been wrought to pity, as was mine;
And shall the conquest of my lawful bed,
My husband's death urged on by his disgrace,
My loss of womanhood, be ill rewarded   40
With hatred and contempt? No! Know, Soranzo,
I have a spirit doth as much distaste
The slavery of fearing thee as thou
Dost loathe the memory of what hath passed.

SORANZO

Nay, dear Hippolita –

HIPPOLITA   Call me not dear,   45
Nor think with supple words to smooth the grossness
Of my abuses. 'Tis not your new mistress,
Your goodly Madam Merchant, shall triumph
On my dejection: tell her thus from me,
My birth was nobler, and by much more free.   50

SORANZO

You are too violent.

HIPPOLITA   You are too double
In your dissimulation. Seest thou this,
This habit, these black mourning weeds of care?
'Tis thou art cause of this, and hast divorced
My husband from his life and me from him,   55
And made me widow in my widowhood.

SORANZO

Will you yet hear?

39   *urged on* partly induced.
40   *womanhood* womanly attributes (here, sexual fidelity to her husband).
42   *distaste* dislike.
48   *Madam Merchant* Annabella; Florio is either a merchant or a member of the merchant class, which is socially lower than Hippolita's.
48–9   *triumph . . . dejection* exult in my being humiliated.
50   *free* honourable.
51   *double* duplicitous.
53   *weeds* clothes.
56   *widow in my widowhood* doubly a widow, both because her husband is dead and because Soranzo has not kept his promise to be her second husband (see below, lines 69–71).

HIPPOLITA   More of thy perjuries?
Thy soul is drowned too deeply in those sins:
Thou need'st not add to th'number.

SORANZO   Then I'll leave you;
You are past all rules of sense.

HIPPOLITA   And thou of grace.   60

VASQUES
Fie, mistress, you are not near the limits of reason: if my lord
had a resolution as noble as virtue itself, you take the course to
unedge it all. Sir, I beseech you do not perplex her. Griefs, alas,
will have a vent; I dare undertake Madam Hippolita will now
freely hear you.   65

SORANZO
Talk to a woman frantic! Are these the fruits of your love?

HIPPOLITA
They are the fruits of thy untruth, false man!
Didst thou not swear, whilst yet my husband lived,
That thou wouldst wish no happiness on earth
More than to call me wife? Didst thou not vow,   70
When he should die, to marry me? For which
The devil in my blood, and thy protests,
Caused me to counsel him to undertake
A voyage to Leghorn, for that we heard
His brother there was dead and left a daughter   75
Young and unfriended, who with much ado

---

63   *unedge* make blunt (like a sword)
      perplex torment.
64   *will . . . vent* must be spoken.
65   *freely* without interrupting.
66   *Are . . . love?* This could be spoken to either Vasques or Hippolita, but in either case
      it carries implications about Soranzo's relationship with the former. If to Vasques,
      it means 'Is your love to me so unprofitable that I end up having to reason with a
      deranged woman?', and it is suggestive that he speaks not of Vasques' duty but his
      love (implying a more personal relationship than is usual between master and servant,
      though not necessarily a sexual one). If he is speaking to Hippolita, however, it
      means 'So this is how your love for me ends up', with a kind of forced reasonableness
      that is obviously crass in the circumstances; in this case, the whole line shows him
      first rejecting and then submitting to Vasques' recommendation, suggesting the
      servant's unusually dominant role in their relationship.
72   *protests* solemn affirmations, vows (to marry her).
74   *Leghorn* a coastal town in Tuscany (after 1606, a city) about 80 miles south of Parma;
      the journey between the two would take a traveller through dangerous mountain
      districts.
76   *unfriended* with nobody to support her.

I wished him to bring hither. He did so,
And went, and, as thou know'st, died on the way.
Unhappy man to buy his death so dear
With my advice! Yet thou for whom I did it   80
Forget'st thy vows, and leav'st me to my shame.

SORANZO
Who could help this?

HIPPOLITA   Who? Perjured man, thou couldst,
If thou hadst faith or love.

SORANZO   You are deceived:
The vows I made, if you remember well,
Were wicked and unlawful, 'twere more sin   85
To keep them than to break them; as for me,
I cannot mask my penitence. Think thou
How much thou hast digressed from honest shame
In bringing of a gentleman to death
Who was thy husband. Such a one as he,   90
So noble in his quality, condition,
Learning, behaviour, entertainment, love,
As Parma could not show a braver man.

VASQUES
You do not well, this was not your promise.

SORANZO
I care not: let her know her monstrous life.   95
Ere I'll be servile to so black a sin
I'll be a corpse. Woman, come here no more,
Learn to repent and die; for by my honour
I hate thee and thy lust. You have been too foul.   [*Exit*]

VASQUES
This part has been scurvily played.   100

HIPPOLITA
How foolishly this beast contemns his fate,
And shuns the use of that which I more scorn
Than I once loved, his love! But let him go:

---

88   *digressed . . . shame* deviated from proper behaviour (inhibited from wrongdoing
        by shame); Hippolita is now 'shameless'.
91   *quality* social position or personal disposition
        condition personal qualities.
92   *entertainment* hospitality (considered a mark of nobility).
93   *braver* finer.
101   *contemns* contemptuously disregards, scorns.

My vengeance shall give comfort to his woe.

She offers to go away

VASQUES

Mistress, mistress, Madam Hippolita! Pray, a word or two.   105

HIPPOLITA

With me, sir?

VASQUES

With you if you please.

HIPPOLITA

What is't?

VASQUES

I know you are infinitely moved now, and you think you have
cause: some I confess you have, but, sure, not so much as you   110
imagine.

HIPPOLITA

Indeed!

VASQUES

O you were miserably bitter, which you followed even to the
last syllable; faith, you were somewhat too shrewd. By my life,
you could not have took my lord in a worse time since I first   115
knew him; tomorrow you shall find him a new man.

HIPPOLITA

Well, I shall wait his leisure.

VASQUES

Fie, this is not a hearty patience: it comes sourly from you.
Troth, let me persuade you for once.

HIPPOLITA [*Aside*]

I have it, and it shall be so. Thanks opportunity!   120
[*To him*] Persuade me to what?

VASQUES

Visit him in some milder temper. O, if you could but master a
little your female spleen, how might you win him!

HIPPOLITA

He will never love me. Vasques, thou hast been a too trusty
servant to such a master, and I believe thy reward in the end will   125
fall out like mine.

104   *his woe* the woe he has caused her.
113   *followed* maintained.
114   *shrewd* aggressively harsh, scolding.
118   *hearty* sincere, heartfelt.
123   *spleen* bitter passion.

VASQUES

So perhaps too.

HIPPOLITA

Resolve thyself, it will. Had I one so true, so truly honest, so
secret to my counsels, as thou hast been to him and his, I should
think it a slight acquittance not only to make him master of all   130
I have, but even of myself.

VASQUES

O, you are a noble gentlewoman!

HIPPOLITA

Wilt thou feed always upon hopes? Well, I know thou art wise,
and seest the reward of an old servant daily what it is.

VASQUES

Beggary and neglect.   135

HIPPOLITA

True; but Vasques, wert thou mine, and wouldst be private to
me and my designs, I here protest myself, and all what I can else
call mine, should be at thy dispose.

VASQUES [*Aside*]

Work you that way, old mole? Then I have the wind of you. [*To
her*] I were not worthy of it, by any desert that could lie within   140
my compass. If I could –

HIPPOLITA

What then?

VASQUES

I should then hope to live in these my old years with rest and
security.

---

129   *and his* Probably referring to Vasques' prior relationship with Soranzo's dead father
       (see V.vi.112–16).

130   *acquittance* repayment.

130–1   *master . . . of myself* her husband.

137   *all what* everything.

138   *dispose* disposal.

139   *mole* Vasques imagines Hippolita's plotting in terms of a mole's underground
       burrowing; but a relevant secondary sense alludes to the animal's supposed blindness
       (as Hippolita is blind to Vasques' own motives).
       I have . . . you Vasques describes himself in terms of a predator upwind of its prey
       (= Hippolita), and so able to track it by scent.

HIPPOLITA

    Give me thy hand. Now promise but thy silence,   145
    And help to bring to pass a plot I have,
    And here in sight of Heaven, that being done,
    I make thee lord of me and mine estate.

VASQUES

    Come, you are merry: this is such a happiness that I can neither
    think or believe.   150

HIPPOLITA

    Promise thy secrecy, and 'tis confirmed.

VASQUES

    Then here I call our good genii for witnesses, whatsoever your
    designs are, or against whomsoever, I will not only be a special
    actor therein, but never disclose it till it be effected.

HIPPOLITA

    I take thy word, and with that, thee for mine.   155
    Come then, let's more confer of this anon.
    On this delicious bane my thoughts shall banquet;
    Revenge shall sweeten what my griefs have tasted.

                                        Exeunt

---

145   *Give me thy hand* This may mean more than simply shaking hands on a bargain:
        since the joining of hands also had a specific matrimonial significance (see note to
        III.vi.52 s.d.) which is activated by the terms of Hippolita's offer to Vasques, it also
        underlines how absolutely they have committed themselves to each other in and
        through the plot against Soranzo.
149–50 prose ed. (Come . . . merry, / This . . . can / Neither . . . beleeue Q).
  149   *merry* only joking.
  152   *good genii* guardian angels; Ford had probably read in Robert Burton's *Anatomy of
        Melancholy* (1621) that 'every man hath a good and a bad angel attending of him in
        particular all his life', and that these spirits were known as *genii* (Clarendon edn,
        1989–, vol. 1, p. 191).
        for witnesses ed. (foe-witnesses Q).
  158   *bane* poison.

[ACT II, SCENE iii]

Enter RICHARDETTO *and* PHILOTIS

RICHARDETTO
    Thou seest, my lovely niece, these strange mishaps,
    How all my fortunes turn to my disgrace,
    Wherein I am but as a looker-on
    Whiles others act my shame and I am silent.
PHILOTIS
    But, uncle, wherein can this borrowed shape   5
    Give you content?
RICHARDETTO   I'll tell thee, gentle niece:
    Thy wanton aunt in her lascivious riots
    Lives now secure, thinks I am surely dead
    In my late journey to Leghorn for you,
    As I have caused it to be rumoured out.   10
    Now would I see with what an impudence
    She gives scope to her loose adultery,
    And how the common voice allows hereof:
    Thus far I have prevailed.
PHILOTIS   Alas, I fear
    You mean some strange revenge.
RICHARDETTO   O, be not troubled: 15
    Your ignorance shall plead for you in all.
    But to our business: what, you learnt for certain
    How Signor Florio means to give his daughter

---

    0   s.d. It is possible that Richardetto does not wear his disguise in private with Philotis.
         If so, the costume and false beard need to be seen on stage in this scene, not only
         because Philotis refers to the disguise ('this borrowed shape') in line 5 but also to
         show the audience that this is the same character as the Doctor who appeared in II.i
         (rather than the same actor doubling another role). He might, for example, be taking
         off the beard as he enters (in which case he will need to put it hastily back on when
         Grimaldi arrives later in the scene).
    4   *act my shame* Because in reality Richardetto is planning revenge, his 'shame' (as an
         unavenged cuckold) is only a fiction in which other people unwittingly participate,
         like actors performing a play.
    8   *secure* unsuspecting, with a false sense of security.
   13   *how . . . allows* how public opinion responds.
   16   Richardetto saves her from becoming an accessory in his criminal plans (and so
         legally liable for them) by not telling her what they are.
   18   *How* That.

In marriage to Soranzo?

PHILOTIS   Yes, for certain.

RICHARDETTO

But how find you young Annabella's love   20
Inclined to him?

PHILOTIS   For aught I could perceive,
She neither fancies him or any else.

RICHARDETTO

There's mystery in that which time must show.
She used you kindly?

PHILOTIS   Yes.

RICHARDETTO   And craved your company?

PHILOTIS

Often.

RICHARDETTO 'Tis well: it goes as I could wish.   25
I am the Doctor now, and, as for you,
None knows you; if all fail not we shall thrive.
But who comes here?

Enter GRIMALDI

             I know him: 'tis Grimaldi,
A Roman and a soldier, near allied
Unto the Duke of Monferrato; one   30
Attending on the Nuncio of the Pope
That now resides in Parma, by which means
He hopes to get the love of Annabella.

GRIMALDI

Save you, sir.

---

24   *used* behaved towards, treated.

28   s.d. Q places Grimaldi's entrance here, but it is hard to make sense of this in staging the scene: it seems to indicate that Grimaldi walks uninvited and unannounced into what the preceding dialogue suggests to be Richardetto's private chamber, a discourtesy the audience would be particularly likely to notice after Hippolita's bursting in on Soranzo in the previous scene; he is then ignored for six lines while Richardetto explains who he is. Possibly Richardetto's 'Who comes here?' is in response to a knock at the door; he would then look through a spy-hole or lattice in the door to see the caller, talk briefly to Philotis about him (perhaps while donning his disguise; see note to 0 s.d.), and then open the door for Grimaldi to enter after line 33.

31   *Nuncio* A permanent representative of the Pope at a foreign court, with both political and ecclesiastical powers.

32   *by which means* i.e. by playing on his association with an influential person .

34   *Save you* A greeting (worn down from 'God save you').

RICHARDETTO And you, sir.

GRIMALDI   I have heard
Of your approvèd skill, which through the city   35
Is freely talked of, and would crave your aid.

RICHARDETTO
For what, sir?

GRIMALDI   Marry sir, for this –
But I would speak in private.

RICHARDETTO   Leave us, cousin.

Exit PHILOTIS

GRIMALDI
I love fair Annabella, and would know
Whether in arts there may not be receipts   40
To move affection.

RICHARDETTO   Sir, perhaps there may,
But these will nothing profit you.

GRIMALDI   Not me?

RICHARDETTO
Unless I be mistook, you are a man
Greatly in favour with the Cardinal.

GRIMALDI
What of that?

RICHARDETTO   In duty to his grace,   45
I will be bold to tell you, if you seek
To marry Florio's daughter, you must first
Remove a bar 'twixt you and her.

GRIMALDI   Who's that?

RICHARDETTO
Soranzo is the man that hath her heart,
And while he lives, be sure you cannot speed.   50

GRIMALDI
Soranzo! What, mine enemy, is't he?

RICHARDETTO
Is he your enemy?

GRIMALDI   The man I hate
Worse than confusion. I'll kill him straight.

---

40   *arts* Grimaldi's unusual plural is perhaps intended to flatter Richardetto with omni-
      competence. Dyce and some other editors, suspecting a misprint, emend to 'art'.
40–1 *receipts . . . affection* love-philtres ('receipts' = recipes).
50   *speed* succeed.
53   lineation ed. (Worse . . . Confusion; / I'le . . . streight Q).

RICHARDETTO
Nay, then, take mine advice:
Even for his grace's sake the Cardinal,   55
I'll find a time when he and she do meet,
Of which I'll give you notice, and to be sure
He shall not 'scape you, I'll provide a poison
To dip your rapier's point in: if he had
As many heads as Hydra had, he dies.   60
GRIMALDI
But shall I trust thee, Doctor?
RICHARDETTO   As yourself,
Doubt not in aught. [*Aside*] Thus shall the fates decree,
By me Soranzo falls, that ruined me.

Exeunt

[ACT II, SCENE iv]

Enter DONADO [*with a letter*], BERGETTO *and* POGGIO

DONADO
Well sir, I must be content to be both your secretary and your
messenger myself: I cannot tell what this letter may work, but
as sure as I am alive, if thou come once to talk with her, I fear
thou wilt mar whatsoever I make.
BERGETTO
You 'make', uncle? Why, am not I big enough to carry mine own   5
letter, I pray?

55   This line (presented as a parenthesis in Q) could qualify either the preceding or, as
      here punctuated, the following line. In the former case, Richardetto presumptuously
      recommends that Grimaldi should accept his advice for the Cardinal's sake; in the
      latter, he offers to help plan the murder as a favour to the Cardinal through Grimaldi,
      reflecting not only his disingenuous humility in the rest of the exchange but also
      his facade of not being personally concerned in the crime.
59–60 *if he ... Hydra had* no matter how hard he is to kill. The Hydra was a many-headed
      venomous monster in classical mythology, which grew two new heads for every one
      that was cut off.

1   *secretary* Donado has written the letter himself

DONADO

Ay, ay, carry a fool's head o'thy own. Why thou dunce, wouldst
thou write a letter, and carry it thyself?

BERGETTO

Yes, that I would, and read it to her with my own mouth; for
you must think, if she will not believe me myself when she   10
hears me speak, she will not believe another's handwriting. O,
you think I am a blockhead, uncle! No, sir, Poggio knows I have
indited a letter myself, so I have.

POGGIO

Yes truly, sir, I have it in my pocket.

DONADO

A sweet one no doubt, pray let's see't.   15

[POGGIO *gives* BERGETTO *the letter*]

BERGETTO

I cannot read my own hand very well, Poggio. Read it, Poggio.

DONADO

Begin.

POGGIO (*Reads*)

'Most dainty and honey-sweet mistress, I could call you fair,
and lie as fast as any that loves you; but my uncle being the
elder man, I leave it to him as more fit for his age and the colour   20
of his beard. I am wise enough to tell you I can board where I see
occasion: or if you like my uncle's wit better than mine, you shall
marry me; if you like mine better than his, I will marry you in
spite of your teeth; so commending my best parts to you, I rest

Yours upwards and downwards, or you may choose,   25

Bergetto.'

---

7   *a fool's . . . own* Proverbial (Tilley, G. 519).

13   *indited* composed.

16   prose ed. (I . . . *Poggio,* / Reads . . . *Poggio* Q).
     hand handwriting.

19   *fast* firmly, utterly.

20–1   *the colour of his beard* Probably just a periphrasis for age; it is tempting to suppose
     a latent pun on 'white lie', but *OED* does not record the term in use before 1741.

21   *board* 'chat up', make sexual advances (to Annabella); an alternative might be 'bourd'
     (= jest).

22   *occasion* opportunity.
     or either (= 'on the one hand').

23–4   *in spite of your teeth* whether you like it or not (literally, notwithstanding your
     resistance).

BERGETTO

Ah, ha! Here's stuff, uncle!

DONADO

Here's stuff indeed to shame us all. Pray whose advice did you take in this learned letter?

POGGIO

None, upon my word, but mine own.   30

BERGETTO

And mine, uncle, believe it nobody's else; 'twas mine own brain, I thank a good wit fot't.

DONADO

Get you home, sir, and look you keep within doors till I return.

BERGETTO

How! That were a jest indeed; I scorn it i' faith.

DONADO

What, you do not!   35

BERGETTO

Judge me, but I do now.

POGGIO

Indeed, sir, 'tis very unhealthy.

DONADO

Well, sir, if I hear any of your apish running to motions and fopperies till I come back, you were as good no: look to't.   *Exit*

BERGETTO

Poggio, shall's steal to see this horse with the head in's tail?   40

POGGIO

Ay, but you must take heed of whipping.

BERGETTO

Dost take me for a child, Poggio? Come, honest Poggio.

Exeunt

28–9   prose ed. (Here's . . . all, / Pray . . . Letter? Q).
   37   Probably addressed to Donado (Poggio usually calls Bergetto 'master' rather than 'sir').
   38   *apish* foolish (literally, like a monkey imitating a human being)
          motions puppet-shows.
   39   *you . . . no* you'll regret it (literally, you had better not have done so).
   41   *take . . . whipping* beware beating (as a punishment for disobedience).
   42   prose ed. (Dost . . . *Poggio,* / Come . . . *Poggio* Q).

[ACT II, SCENE v]

Enter FRIAR *and* GIOVANNI

FRIAR

    Peace! Thou hast told a tale whose every word
    Threatens eternal slaughter to the soul;
    I'm sorry I have heard it. Would mine ears
    Had been one minute deaf before the hour
    That thou camest to me! O young man cast away,   5
    By the religious number of mine order,
    I day and night have waked my aged eyes
    Above my strength, to weep on thy behalf;
    But Heaven is angry, and be thou resolved,
    Thou art a man remarked to taste a mischief.   10
    Look for't: though it come late, it will come sure.

GIOVANNI

    Father, in this you are uncharitable.
    What I have done I'll prove both fit and good:
    It is a principle, which you have taught
    When I was yet your scholar, that the frame   15
    And composition of the mind doth follow
    The frame and composition of the body;
    So where the body's furniture is beauty,
    The mind's must needs be virtue; which allowed,
    Virtue itself is reason but refined,   20
    And love the quintessence of that; this proves
    My sister's beauty, being rarely fair,
    Is rarely virtuous; chiefly in her love,
    And chiefly in that love, her love to me;
    If hers to me, then so is mine to her;   25
    Since in like causes are effects alike.

4   *one . . . hour* struck deaf the moment before the time.
5   *cast away* damned (literally, discarded).
6   *number* company, group of people.
10 *remarked* marked out.
12 *uncharitable* lacking in Christian love for one's fellow men (see also note on *charity*,
     IV.i.56).
15 *frame* ed. (Fame Q).
18 *furniture* accoutrement.
21 *quintessence* a stage of refinement beyond essence; hence, the purest manifestation.

FRIAR

O ignorance in knowledge! Long ago,
How often have I warned thee this before!
Indeed, if we were sure there were no Deity,
Nor heaven nor hell, then to be led alone   30
By Nature's light – as were philosophers
Of elder times – might instance some defence;
But 'tis not so. Then, madman, thou wilt find
That Nature is in Heaven's positions blind.

GIOVANNI

Your age o'errules you; had you youth like mine,   35
You'd make her love your heaven, and her divine.

FRIAR

Nay, then I see thou'rt too far sold to hell;
It lies not in the compass of my prayers
To call thee back. Yet let me counsel thee:
Persuade thy sister to some marriage.   40

GIOVANNI

Marriage? Why, that's to damn her: that's to prove
Her greedy of variety of lust.

FRIAR

O fearful! If thou wilt not, give me leave
To shrive her, lest she should die unabsolved.

GIOVANNI

At your best leisure, father; then she'll tell you   45
How dearly she doth prize my matchless love.
Then you will know what pity 'twere we two
Should have been sundered from each other's arms.
View well her face, and in that little round
You may observe a world of variety: 50
For colour, lips, for sweet perfumes, her breath;

30–2 *led alone ... times* guided by empirical reasoning alone, without the benefit of divine
      revelation, like the pre-Christian Greek philosophers.
  34 *Nature ... blind* empiricism ('Nature') is ignorant about the 'positions' affirmed by
      God; 'positions' usually meant statements for academic disputation, but the Friar's
      point is that God's 'positions' are not debatable but absolute.
41–2 If she marries, Annabella will show herself not to be satisfied with the one man she
      already has; this desire for multiple lovers ('variety of lusts') will be unchaste and so
      will damn her.
  44 *shrive her* hear her confession and grant her absolution of her sins.
49–58 This passage draws on the Renaissance poetic form of the blazon, which described
      a woman in a catalogue of her beauties from head to toe.

For jewels, eyes; for threads of purest gold,
Hair; for delicious choice of flowers, cheeks;
Wonder in every portion of that throne.
Hear her but speak, and you will swear the spheres   55
Make music to the citizens in heaven;
But father, what is else for pleasure framed
Lest I offend your ears shall go unnamed.

FRIAR

The more I hear, I pity thee the more,
That one so excellent should give those parts   60
All to a second death. What I can do
Is but to pray; and yet I could advise thee,
Wouldst thou be ruled.

GIOVANNI   In what?

FRIAR   Why, leave her yet.
The throne of mercy is above your trespass;
Yet time is left you both –

GIOVANNI   To embrace each other;   65
Else let all time be struck quite out of number.
She is like me, and I like her resolved.

FRIAR

No more: I'll visit her. This grieves me most,
Things being thus, a pair of souls are lost.

Exeunt

54 *throne* Giovanni treats his sister with the veneration due to God or a king.
55 *the spheres* In the Ptolemaic theory of the universe, between Earth and heaven there were seven planets (including the sun and moon) fixed to concentric crystal spheres; their harmonious rotation was thought to produce a beautiful melody.
57 *what . . . framed* Annabella's private parts; Giovanni is heterodox in saying that they were created by God ('framed') for pleasure rather than procreation.
60 *parts* abilities, skills
61 *a second death* damnation.
62 *but* only.
64 God's power to exercise mercy is greater than the sin Giovanni and Annabella have committed; in Christian theology, all sins except despair of mercy can be forgiven if the sinner repents.
65 *Yet* Still.
66 *number* sequence.

[ACT II, SCENE vi]

Enter FLORIO, DONADO, ANNABELLA, PUTANA

FLORIO

Where's Giovanni?

ANNABELLA   Newly walked abroad,

And, as I heard him say, gone to the Friar,

His reverend tutor.

FLORIO   That's a blessed man,

A man made up of holiness; I hope

He'll teach him how to gain another world.   5

DONADO

Fair gentlewoman, here's a letter sent

To you from my young cousin. I dare swear

He loves you in his soul; would you could hear

Sometimes what I see daily, sighs and tears,

As if his breast were prison to his heart!   10

FLORIO

Receive it, Annabella.

ANNABELLA   Alas, good man!

[*She takes the letter, but does not read it*]

DONADO

What's that she said?

PUTANA

An't please you, sir, she said, 'Alas, good man!' [*Aside to* DONADO]

Truly, I do commend him to her every night before her first

sleep, because I would have her dream of him; and she hearkens   15

to that most religiously.

---

5   *gain another world* achieve a place in heaven.

7   *cousin* kinsman.

11   s.d. It is unclear when Annabella opens the letter; inside it she will find the jewel
       mentioned at I.iii.81.

14–15   *first sleep* sleep during the first part of the night (after which a person might wake
           and take drink before sleeping again). The first sleep was thought to be associated
           with dreams, especially, in young women, erotic ones; compare Lording Barry, *Ram
           Alley*, 1483–6: 'When maids awaked from their first sleep, / Deceived with dreams,
           began to weep / And think, if dreams such pleasures know, / What sport the sub-
           stance then would show.'

DONADO [*Aside to* PUTANA]

Say'st so? Godamercy, Putana, there's something for thee, [*Gives
her money*] and prithee do what thou canst on his behalf; sha'
not be lost labour, take my word for't.

PUTANA [*Aside to* DONADO]

Thank you most heartily, sir; now I have a feeling of your mind,   20
let me alone to work.

ANNABELLA

Guardian!

PUTANA

Did you call?

ANNABELLA

Keep this letter.

DONADO

Signor Florio, in any case bid her read it instantly.   25

FLORIO

Keep it, for what? Pray read it me here right.

ANNABELLA

I shall, sir.   *She reads*

DONADO

How d'ee find her inclined, signor?

FLORIO

Troth sir, I know not how; not all so well
As I could wish.   30

ANNABELLA

Sir, I am bound to rest your cousin's debtor.
The jewel I'll return; for if he love,
I'll count that love a jewel.

DONADO   Mark you that?
Nay, keep them both, sweet maid.

ANNABELLA   You must excuse me:
Indeed I will not keep it.

---

17   *Godamercy* Thank you.
18   *prithee* please.
20   *feeling . . . mind* understanding of your intentions (punning on the tangible reward
     she has just received).
26   *read it me* oblige me by reading it (silently), *not* read it (aloud) to me; Florio uses the
     grammatical inflection known as the ethical dative, common in the seventeenth
     century but now obsolete, which is used to imply indirect involvement in an action.
     here right straight away.

318

FLORIO   Where's the ring,   35
   That which your mother in her will bequeathed,
   And charged you on her blessing not to give't
   To any but your husband? Send back that.
ANNABELLA
   I have it not.
FLORIO   Ha! 'Have it not', where is't?
ANNABELLA
   My brother in the morning took it from me,   40
   Said he would wear't today.
FLORIO   Well, what do you say
   To young Bergetto's love? Are you content
   To match with him? Speak.
DONADO   There's the point indeed.
ANNABELLA [*Aside*]
   What shall I do? I must say something now.
FLORIO
   What say? Why d'ee not speak?
ANNABELLA   Sir, with your leave;   45
   Please you to give me freedom.
FLORIO   Yes you have't.
ANNABELLA
   Signor Donado, if your nephew mean
   To raise his better fortunes in his match,
   The hope of me will hinder such a hope.
   Sir, if you love him, as I know you do,   50
   Find one more worthy of his choice than me;
   In short, I'm sure I sha' not be his wife.

35–8   Perhaps Florio infers from Annabella's polite words (lines 31–3) that she is genuinely
       interested in Bergetto.

43   *match with* marry.

45   *What say?* What do you say?

46   *Please . . . freedom* Punctuation as in Q; some other editors (beginning with Gifford
     in 1827) end the line with a question mark. This is not a necessary intervention,
     since Annabella may be using 'please' in the sense *OED* 3c, implying 'May it please
     you'; its effect is to make her appear less forward, more uncertain with her father
     than if, as here and in Q, the line is played as a statement,
     have't ed. (haue Q).

49   i.e. he is wasting his time.

DONADO

    Why, here's plain dealing; I commend thee for't,
    And all the worst I wish thee, is Heaven bless thee!
    Your father yet and I will still be friends,   55
    Shall we not, Signor Florio?

FLORIO   Yes, why not?

Enter BERGETTO *and* POGGIO

    Look, here your cousin comes.

DONADO [*Aside*]

    O coxcomb, what doth he make here?

BERGETTO

    Where's my uncle, sirs?

DONADO

    What's the news now?   60

BERGETTO

    Save you, uncle, save you. You must not think I come for nothing,
    masters; and how, and how is't? What, you have read my letter?
    Ah, there I – tickled you i' faith!

POGGIO

    But 'twere better you had tickled her in another place.

BERGETTO

    Sirrah! [*To* ANNABELLA] Sweetheart, I'll tell thee a good jest,   65
    and riddle what 'tis.

---

53   *plain dealing* frank honesty.
56   s.d. ed.; after line 59 in Q.
58   *what . . . here?* what's he doing here?.
59   *sirs* This must be addressed to Florio and Donado, the only two men already on
    stage when Bergetto and Poggio enter; probably the scene should be staged in such
    a way that Bergetto cannot initially see Donado's face.
63   *I – tickled* Q's dash may be intended to indicate inarticulacy, as Bergetto gropes for
    the right word.
64–5   *But . . . Sweetheart* This passage is open to many different interpretations in
    performance; which is chosen will depend on the director's and actors' broader
    understanding of the two characters and the relationship between them. If 'Sirrah'
    is taken to be spoken to Poggio, as punctuated here, then Poggio's preceding remark
    can be spoken aloud; Bergetto's response need not mean that he recognizes the
    inappropriateness of the bawdy reference to heavy petting – he could just be irritated
    at the interruption. Other editors take Q's 'Sirrah *Sweetheart*' to be an inept form of
    address to Annabella, and accordingly make Poggio's line an aside, either spoken to
    Bergetto (Dyce) or directly to the audience (Lomax).
66   *riddle* guess.

ANNABELLA

You say you'd tell me.

BERGETTO

As I was walking just now in the street, I met a swaggering
fellow would needs take the wall of me; and because he did
thrust me, I very valiantly called him rogue. He hereupon bade   70
me draw. I told him I had more wit than so; but when he saw
that I would not, he did so maul me with the hilts of his rapier,
that my head sung whilst my feet capered in the kennel.

DONADO [*Aside*]

Was ever the like ass seen?

ANNABELLA

And what did you all this while?   75

BERGETTO

Laugh at him for a gull, till I see the blood run about mine ears,
and then I could not choose but find in my heart to cry till a
fellow with a broad beard – they say he is a newcome doctor –
called me into this house, and gave me a plaster – look you, here
'tis – and, sir, there was a young wench washed my face and   80
hands most excellently; i'faith I shall love her as long as I live
for't. Did she not, Poggio?

POGGIO

Yes, and kissed him too.

---

69   *take . . . me* The ruffian forced Bergetto away from the wall and towards the middle
     of the street. The preferred walking position in seventeenth-century city streets was
     alongside the wall, because the drainage gutter or 'kennel' ran down the middle,
     making that part of the street not only wet but filthy; it was considered polite to step
     aside from the wall for someone of higher rank than yourself, whereas 'taking the
     wall' was considered offensive and sometimes provoked street-fights.

72   *hilts* Probably a colloquial rather than an ignorant usage, though it is not recorded
     in *OED*.

76   *gull* fool.

77–80   *here 'tis* This moment is open to two distinct stagings, depending on whether or not
     Bergetto's 'plaster' (a bandage, larger than a modern sticking plaster) is already visible
     to the audience and characters. Nobody remarks on it when he enters (unless this is
     a latent secondary meaning of Donado's 'coxcomb' in line 59), which might be out
     of politeness or might be because they actually cannot see it In the latter case
     Bergetto is probably wearing a hat, which he now removes to show the bandage.
     Alternatively, 'here 'tis' could be played as a comically fatuous line drawing attention
     to something that is already obvious.

BERGETTO

Why la now, you think I tell a lie, uncle, I warrant.

DONADO

Would he that beat thy blood out of thy head had beaten some   85
wit into it, for I fear thou never wilt have any.

BERGETTO

O, uncle, but there was a wench would have done a man's heart
good to have looked on her. By this light, she had a face methinks worth twenty of you, Mistress Annabella.

DONADO [*Aside*]

Was ever such a fool born?   90

ANNABELLA

I am glad she liked you, sir.

BERGETTO

Are you so? By my troth, I thank you, forsooth.

FLORIO

Sure 'twas the Doctor's niece that was last day with us here.

BERGETTO

'Twas she, 'twas she!

DONADO

How do you know that, simplicity?   95

BERGETTO

Why, does not he say so? If I should have said no, I should have
given him the lie, uncle, and so have deserved a dry beating
again: I'll none of that.

FLORIO

A very modest, well-behaved young maid as I have seen.

DONADO

Is she indeed?   100

FLORIO

Indeed she is, if I have any judgement.

---

84   *la now* an emphatic expression with no particular meaning.

87   *O, uncle* This could be played either as an indication of Bergetto's irrepressibility (as
punctuated here) or a response to Donado's previous comment ('O uncle!').

91   *liked* pleased.

97   *given . . . the lie* To tell someone they were lying ('give the lie') was a grave insult
which usually led to a duel.
    dry hard, severe.

101   lineation ed. (Indeed / Shee . . . Judgement Q).

DONADO

Well, sir, now you are free: you need not care for sending letters
now, you are dismissed; your mistress here will none of you.

BERGETTO

No? Why, what care I for that? I can have wenches enough in
Parma for half-a-crown apiece, cannot I, Poggio?   105

POGGIO

I'll warrant you, sir.

DONADO

Signor Florio,
I thank you for your free recourse you gave
For my admittance; and to you, fair maid,
That jewel I will give you 'gainst your marriage.   110
[*To* BERGETTO] Come, will you go, sir?

BERGETTO

Ay, marry will I. Mistress, farewell, mistress; I'll come again tomorrow; farewell, mistress.

> *Exeunt* DONADO, BERGETTO, *and* POGGIO

> *Enter* GIOVANNI

FLORIO

Son where have you been? What, alone, alone, still, still?
I would not have it so: you must forsake   115
This over-bookish humour. Well, your sister
Hath shook the fool off.

GIOVANNI   'Twas no match for her.

FLORIO

'Twas not indeed, I meant it nothing less.
Soranzo is the man I only like:
Look on him, Annabella! Come, 'tis supper-time,   120

---

105   *half-a-crown apiece* Half-a-crown (2*s*. 6*d*.) was about twice the going rate for
      prostitutes in mid-seventeenth-century England; Bergetto is probably not speaking
      from experience.
107–11   lineation ed. (prose in Q).
108   *recourse* access.
110   *'gainst* in anticipation of (with the expectation that the jewel will be worn on the
      wedding day, hence Giovanni's reaction at line 125–6).
114–17   *Son . . . off* lineation ed. (prose in Q).
116   *humour* quirk of personality.
117   *match* appropriate marriage.
119   *the man . . . like* my preferred candidate among the suitors.

And it grows late.   *Exit*

GIOVANNI
  Whose jewel's that?

ANNABELLA
  Some sweetheart's.

GIOVANNI   So I think.

ANNABELLA   A lusty youth,
  Signor Donado, gave it me to wear
  Against my marriage.

GIOVANNI   But you shall not wear it: 125
  Send it him back again.

ANNABELLA   What, you are jealous?

GIOVANNI
  That you shall know anon, at better leisure.
  Welcome, sweet night! The evening crowns the day.

                                              Exeunt

122–7   Putana is still present on stage during this exchange.
123–6   *A . . . again* lineation ed. (A . . . me / To . . . Marriage. / But . . . againe Q).
123–4   *A lusty . . . Donado* The passage is open to two distinct interpretations. As punctuated
        here, Annabella ironically calls old Donado a youth, expecting Giovanni's complicity
        in the joke and not yet recognizing how far the gift of the ring has irritated him.
        Alternatively, 'a lusty youth' could be the teasing fiction and 'Signor Donado' the
        harmless truth; this interpretation requires a stronger pause after 'youth', in which
        her playfulness evaporates as she realizes she may have gone too far.

ACT III[, SCENE i]

Enter BERGETTO *and* POGGIO

BERGETTO

Does my uncle think to make me a baby still? No, Poggio, he
shall know I have a sconce now.

POGGIO

Ay, let him not bob you off like an ape with an apple.

BERGETTO

'Sfoot, I will have the wench, if he were ten uncles, in despite of
his nose, Poggio.   5

POGGIO

Hold him to the grindstone, and give not a jot of ground: she
hath in a manner promised you already.

BERGETTO

True, Poggio, and her uncle the Doctor swore I should marry
her.

POGGIO

He swore, I remember.   10

BERGETTO

And I will have her, that's more. Didst see the codpiece-point
she gave me, and the box of marmalade?

POGGIO

Very well, and kissed you, that my chops watered at the sight on't.

---

2   *sconce* brain, intellect (literally, head).
3   *let . . . apple* don't let him make a fool of you. To bob someone off was to get rid of
    them (fob them off) with a trifling bribe, as an ape will be easily satisfied with an
    apple (supposedly its favourite food; bananas were little known in England at the
    time).
4   *'Sfoot* a strong oath, contracted from 'by God's foot'.
    the wench Philotis, not Annabella.
6–9 prose ed. (Hold . . . ground, / Shee . . . already. / True . . . Doctor / Swore . . . her Q).
8   s.p. *BERGETTO* ed. (line attributed to Poggio in Q).
11 *codpiece-point* a lace for fastening a codpiece (a decorative pouch worn by a man
    over his genitals; no longer fashionable when the play was written).
12 *box* a small receptacle.
    marmalade any kind of fruit preserve; commonly made with plums, dates, and
    quinces.
13 *chops* mouth. The word usually referred to the outside of the mouth, so not only
    salivation but drooling is probably implied.

There's no way but to clap up a marriage in hugger-mugger.

BERGETTO

I will do't, for I tell thee, Poggio, I begin to grow valiant, me-   15
thinks, and my courage begins to rise.

POGGIO

Should you be afraid of your uncle?

BERGETTO

Hang him, old doting rascal, no: I say I will have her.

POGGIO

Lose no time, then.

BERGETTO

I will beget a race of wise men and constables, that shall cart   20
whores at their own charges, and break the Duke's peace ere I
have done myself. Come away!

Exeunt

[ACT III, SCENE ii]

Enter FLORIO, GIOVANNI, SORANZO, ANNABELLA,
PUTANA, *and* VASQUES

FLORIO

My lord Soranzo, though I must confess
The proffers that are made me have been great
In marriage of my daughter, yet the hope
Of your still-rising honours have prevailed
Above all other jointures. Here she is;   5

14   *clap up* arrange hastily .
in hugger-mugger secretly.
20   *constables* local officers of justice. Bergetto takes literally the usually ironic proverb
(Tilley, C. 616) that they were especially intelligent. Since his name as Ford originally
found it was spelt Bargetto, it may be relevant that the Italian equivalent of a constable
was called a *bargello* (defined in *World* as 'a captain of sergeants').
20–1   *cart . . . charges* administer justice to prostitutes at their own expense (rather than
having it paid for out of the public purse; a sign of a rich man's public-spirited
munificence). Public exhibition in a cart drawn through the streets was a common
punishment for whores.

4   *have* has (governed by 'hope', not 'honours').
5   *jointures* gifts of property made to a woman by her fiancé as part of the marriage
contract (here, offered by prospective fiancés).

She knows my mind. Speak for yourself to her;
And hear you, daughter, see you use him nobly.
For any private speech I'll give you time;
Come, son, and you the rest, let them alone,
Agree as they may.

SORANZO   I thank you, sir.   10

GIOVANNI [*Aside to* ANNABELLA]

Sister, be not all woman: think on me.

SORANZO

Vasques!

VASQUES

My lord?

SORANZO

Attend me without.

Exeunt all but SORANZO *and* ANNABELLA

ANNABELLA

Sir, what's your will with me?   15

SORANZO

Do you not know what I should tell you?

ANNABELLA   Yes,

You'll say you love me.

SORANZO   And I'll swear it, too;

Will you believe it?

ANNABELLA   'Tis not point of faith.

Enter GIOVANNI *above*

SORANZO

Have you not will to love?

ANNABELLA   Not you.

SORANZO   Whom then?

ANNABELLA

That's as the Fates infer.

9–10   *let . . . may* leave them alone in order that they may agree.
  11   *all woman* i.e. inconstant; women were proverbially subject to irrational change,
         particularly in sexual matters.
  14   *without* outside.
  16   *should* may be about to.
16–18   lineation ed. (Doe . . . you? / Yes . . . mee. / And . . . it? / 'Tis . . . faith Q).
  18   *point of faith* a doctrine or article of belief essential for salvation; Annabella is saying,
         'I don't have to believe it.'
  20   *infer* cause to happen.

327

GIOVANNI [*Aside*] Of those I'm regent now. 20
SORANZO
  What mean you, sweet?
ANNABELLA To live and die a maid.
SORANZO
  O, that's unfit.
GIOVANNI [*Aside*]
  Here's one can say that's but a woman's note.
SORANZO
  Did you but see my heart, then would you swear –
ANNABELLA
  That you were dead.
GIOVANNI [*Aside*] That's true, or somewhat near it. 25
SORANZO
  See you these true love's tears?
ANNABELLA No.
GIOVANNI [*Aside*] Now she winks.
SORANZO
  They plead to you for grace.
ANNABELLA Yet nothing speak.
SORANZO
  O grant my suit!
ANNABELLA What is't?
SORANZO To let me live –
ANNABELLA
  Take it.
SORANZO – Still yours.
ANNABELLA That is not mine to give.
GIOVANNI [*Aside*]
  One such another word would kill his hopes. 30
SORANZO
  Mistress, to leave those fruitless strifes of wit,
  I know I have loved you long, and loved you truly;
  Not hope of what you have, but what you are

---

20 *regent* ruler.
23 *but . . . note* only a woman's song, not the truth (in that Annabella is no longer a virgin); contrast Giovanni's next aside.
26 *winks* closes her eyes (so that she cannot see tears which would otherwise be in plain sight). Since the whole exchange sardonically deflates Soranzo's conventional romantic metaphors by literalizing them (e.g. seeing his heart), this line may be ironic rather than an indication that Soranzo really is weeping.
31 *strifes of wit* banter (implying an aggressive edge).

Have drawn me on; then let me not in vain
Still feel the rigour of your chaste disdain. 35
   I'm sick, and sick to th' heart.
ANNABELLA   Help, aqua-vitae!
SORANZO
   What mean you?
ANNABELLA   Why, I thought you had been sick!
SORANZO
   Do you mock my love?
GIOVANNI [*Aside*]   There, sir, she was too nimble.
SORANZO [*Aside*]
   'Tis plain, she laughs at me!
   [*To* ANNABELLA]   These scornful taunts
Neither become your modesty, or years. 40
ANNABELLA
   You are no looking-glass, or, if you were,
   I'd dress my language by you.
GIOVANNI [*Aside*]   I'm confirmed.
ANNABELLA
   To put you out of doubt, my lord, methinks
   Your common sense should make you understand
   That if I loved you, or desired your love, 45
   Some way I should have given you better taste;
   But since you are a nobleman, and one
   I would not wish should spend his youth in hopes,
   Let me advise you here to forbear your suit,
   And think I wish you well I tell you this. 50
SORANZO
   Is't you speak this?
ANNABELLA   Yes, I myself. Yet know –
   Thus far I give you comfort – if mine eyes
   Could have picked out a man amongst all those
   That sued to me, to make a husband of,
   You should have been that man. Let this suffice. 55

36   *sick ... heart* (*a*) mortally ill; (*b*) love-sick.
     aqua-vitae distilled alcoholic liquor, taken medicinally.
38   *nimble* quick-witted.
39–50   lineation ed. (prose in Q).
42   *dress ... by you* order ... according to your example. The phrase plays on the image
     of dressing one's hair at a mirror.
46   *given ... taste* been nicer to you.
50   *I ... this* since I tell you this.

Be noble in your secrecy, and wise.

GIOVANNI

[*Aside*] Why, now I see she loves me.

ANNABELLA   One word more:

As ever virtue lived within your mind,

As ever noble courses were your guide,

As ever you would have me know you loved me,   60

Let not my father know hereof by you.

If I hereafter find that I must marry,

It shall be you or none.

SORANZO   I take that promise.

ANNABELLA

O, O my head!

SORANZO   What's the matter, not well?

ANNABELLA

O, I begin to sicken!

GIOVANNI [*Aside*]   Heaven forbid!   *Exit from above*   65

SORANZO

Help, help, within there, ho!

Look to your daughter, Signor Florio.

Enter FLORIO, GIOVANNI, PUTANA

FLORIO

Hold her up, she swoons.

GIOVANNI

Sister, how d'ee?

ANNABELLA   Sick, brother, are you there?

FLORIO

Convey her to her bed instantly, whilst I send for a physician –   70

quickly I say!

PUTANA

Alas, poor child!

Exeunt [FLORIO, ANNABELLA, GIOVANNI, PUTANA];

SORANZO *remains*

Enter VASQUES

VASQUES

My lord.

SORANZO

O Vasques, now I doubly am undone.

66   s.p. *SORANZO* ed. (attributed to Giovanni in Q).

Both in my present and my future hopes: 75
She plainly told me that she could not love,
And thereupon soon sickened, and I fear
Her life's in danger.

VASQUES [*Aside*]

By'r Lady sir, and so is yours, if you knew all. [*Aloud*] 'Las, sir,
I am sorry for that. Maybe 'tis but the maid's sickness, an over-   80
flux of youth – and then, sir, there is no such present remedy as
present marriage. But hath she given you an absolute denial?

SORANZO

She hath and she hath not. I'm full of grief,
But what she said I'll tell thee as we go.

                                                                    Exeunt

[ACT III, SCENE iii]

Enter GIOVANNI *and* PUTANA

PUTANA

O sir, we are all undone, quite undone, utterly undone, and
shamed forever! Your sister, O your sister!

GIOVANNI

What of her? For heaven's sake speak, how does she?

PUTANA

O that ever I was born to see this day!

GIOVANNI

She is not dead, ha, is she?   5

PUTANA

Dead! No, she is quick; 'tis worse, she is with child. You know
what you have done, Heaven forgive 'ee! 'Tis too late to repent,
now Heaven help us!

---

81   *youth* a pubescent readiness for sex; the condition could be dangerous in excess
      ('overflux').
82   *present* immediate.

1-2   prose ed. (Oh . . . vndone, / And . . . sister Q).
  6   *quick* alive (but also implying 'quick with child', pregnant).
6–8   prose ed. (Dead? . . . childe, / You . . . 'ee, / 'Tis . . . vs Q).
7–8   *'Tis . . . us* There is an element of comic confusion in Putana's panic: in orthodox
      theology, heaven would help people only if they did repent.

GIOVANNI

With child? How dost thou know't?

PUTANA

How do I know't? Am I at these years ignorant what the mean-   10
ings of qualms and water-pangs be, of changing of colours,
queasiness of stomachs, pukings, and another thing that I could
name? Do not, for her and your credit's sake, spend the time in
asking how and which way 'tis so; she is quick, upon my word.
If you let a physician see her water you're undone.   15

GIOVANNI

But in what case is she?

PUTANA

Prettily amended: 'twas but a fit, which I soon espied, and she
must look for often henceforward.

GIOVANNI

Commend me to her; bid her take no care,
Let not the doctor visit her, I charge you;   20
Make some excuse till I return. O me,
I have a world of business in my head!
Do not discomfort her.
How do this news perplex me! If my father
Come to her, tell him she's recovered well,   25
Say 'twas but some ill diet. D'ee hear, woman?
Look you to't.

PUTANA

I will, sir.

Exeunt

10   *at these years* at my age.
11–12   *qualms . . . pukings* symptoms of pregnancy, including suddenly feeling faint
('qualms'), frequent need to urinate ('water-pangs'), nausea ('queasiness of stomachs'),
and morning sickness ('pukings').
12   *another thing* Probably Annabella has stopped menstruating.
13   *credit's* reputation's.
15   *water* urine. Examination of a patient's water was a usual method of medical diag-
nosis in the seventeenth century.
16   *case* condition, state.
17   *amended* recovered, feeling better.
espied realized.
19   *take no care* not to worry.
22   *business* things to do.
23–5   lineation ed. (Doe . . . mee! / If . . . well, Q).
24   *do* does (colloquial usage).

[ACT III, SCENE iv]

Enter FLORIO *and* RICHARDETTO [*disguised as the Doctor*]

FLORIO
And how d'ee find her, sir?
RICHARDETTO   Indifferent well:
I see no danger, scarce perceive she's sick,
But that she told me she had lately eaten
Melons, and as she thought, those disagreed
With her young stomach.
FLORIO   Did you give her aught?   5
RICHARDETTO
An easy surfeit-water, nothing else.
You need not doubt her health; I rather think
Her sickness is a fullness of her blood –
You understand me?
FLORIO   I do – you counsel well –
And once within these few days will so order't   10
She shall be married, ere she know the time.
RICHARDETTO
Yet let not haste, sir, make unworthy choice:
That were dishonour.
FLORIO   Master Doctor, no,
I will not do so neither. In plain words,

1   *Indifferent* Moderately.
3–5   Melons must be eaten at the correct stage of ripeness; when over-ripe, they are likely
      to cause gastric ailments. The supposed cause of Annabella's illness corresponds
      with Richardetto's erroneous diagnosis (line 8).
6   *easy surfeit-water* mild indigestion remedy.
8   *fullness of her blood* sexual ripeness (compare III.ii.81 and note). This was believed
      to be an ailment of female virgins; the usual remedy was for the young woman to have
      sex as soon as possible. It is ambiguous whether Richardetto, who is only posing as
      a physician, makes an honestly mistaken diagnosis; it is possible that he recognizes
      the signs of pregnancy but conceals them in order to inveigle Soranzo into a humili-
      ating marriage to an unchaste woman.
10   *once* at some point.
11   *ere . . . time* before she reaches the crucial point of her illness (i.e. the stage when
      continued abstinence from sex will be dangerous); there is probably a latent second-
      ary meaning, unintended by Florio, referring to pregnancy ('the time' being the
      period of confinement before giving birth).

My lord Soranzo is the man I mean.   15
RICHARDETTO
  A noble and a virtuous gentleman.
FLORIO
  As any is in Parma. Not far hence
  Dwells Father Bonaventure, a grave friar,
  Once tutor to my son; now at his cell
  I'll have 'em married.
RICHARDETTO   You have plotted wisely.   20
FLORIO
  I'll send one straight to speak with him tonight.
RICHARDETTO
  Soranzo's wise, he will delay no time.
FLORIO
  It shall be so.

Enter FRIAR *and* GIOVANNI

FRIAR   Good peace be here and love!
FLORIO
  Welcome, religious friar, you are one
  That still bring blessing to the place you come to.   25
GIOVANNI
  Sir, with what speed I could, I did my best
  To draw this holy man from forth his cell
  To visit my sick sister, that with words
  Of ghostly comfort in this time of need
  He might absolve her, whether she live or die.   30
FLORIO
  'Twas well done, Giovanni: thou herein
  Hast showed a Christian's care, a brother's love.
  [*To the* FRIAR] Come, father, I'll conduct you to her chamber,
  And one thing would entreat you.
FRIAR   Say on, sir.

---

21   lineation ed. (I'le . . . straight / To . . . to night Q).
23   Richardetto plays no part in the rest of the scene. It is possible that he exits here
     without witnessing the Friar's arrival; thus in the next scene he unwittingly gives
     Grimaldi wrong information about the marriage arrangements.
25   *still* always.
29   *ghostly* spiritual.

FLORIO

    I have a father's dear impression,   35
    And wish, before I fall into my grave,
    That I might see her married, as 'tis fit.
    A word from you, grave man, will win her more
    Than all our best persuasions.

FRIAR   Gentle sir,

    All this I'll say, that Heaven may prosper her.   40

Exeunt

[ACT III, SCENE v]

Enter GRIMALDI

GRIMALDI

    Now if the Doctor keep his word, Soranzo,
    Twenty to one you miss your bride. I know
    'Tis an unnoble act, and not becomes
    A soldier's valour; but in terms of love,
    Where merit cannot sway, policy must.   5
    I am resolved: if this physician
    Play not on both hands, then Soranzo falls.

Enter RICHARDETTO [*disguised as the Doctor, with a box*]

RICHARDETTO

    You are come as I could wish.
    This very night Soranzo, 'tis ordained, must be affied
    To Annabella, and for aught I know,   10
    Married.

35   *a father's dear impression* This may mean a loving notion typical of fathers; or Florio
       may instead be saying that he bears the reproduced image ('impression') of his own
       father, and wants Annabella married so that she can 'print off' further 'impressions'
       by producing grandchildren (which is all the more important to him in view of the
       anxieties about Giovanni's health which he expresses at I.iii.5–8).

  4 *terms of* matters relating to.
  5 *policy* devious cunning. The word had strongly negative connotations, which add
       emphasis to Grimaldi's point that all's fair in love.
  7 *Play . . . on both hands* Act duplicitously.
8–11 *You . . . Married* lineation ed. (prose in Q).
  9 *affied* betrothed. A betrothal was the final stage before the formal solemnization of
       marriage, and was a legally binding contract.

GRIMALDI How!

RICHARDETTO   Yet your patience:
The place, 'tis Friar Bonaventure's cell.
Now I would wish you to bestow this night
In watching thereabouts. 'Tis but a night.
If you miss now! Tomorrow I'll know all.   15

GRIMALDI
Have you the poison?

RICHARDETTO   Here 'tis in this box.
Doubt nothing, this will do't; in any case,
As you respect your life, be quick and sure.

GRIMALDI
I'll speed him.

RICHARDETTO   Do. Away, for 'tis not safe
You should be seen much here. Ever my love.   20

GRIMALDI
And mine to you.   *Exit*

RICHARDETTO
So, if this hit, I'll laugh and hug revenge,
And they that now dream of a wedding-feast
May chance to mourn the lusty bridegroom's ruin.
But to my other business: 25
[*Calls*] Niece Philotis!

Enter PHILOTIS

PHILOTIS   Uncle?

RICHARDETTO   My lovely niece,
You have bethought 'ee?

PHILOTIS   Yes, and, as you counselled,
Fashioned my heart to love him; but he swears
He will tonight be married, for he fears
His uncle else, if he should know the drift,   30
Will hinder all, and call his coz to shrift.

---

12   *Friar* ed. (Fryars Q).
13   *bestow* spend.
15   *If . . . now* You should act at once: there will never be a better opportunity.
19   *speed him* kill him (literally, see him off on his journey).
22   *hit* succeed, 'come off'.
      hug revenge i.e. having achieved it.
25–7   lineation ed. (But . . . *Philotis*. / Vnkle. / My . . . bethought 'ee. /Yes . . . counsel'd Q).
31   *call . . . shrift* make him repent ('his coz' = Donado's kinsman, i.e. Bergetto).

RICHARDETTO

    Tonight? Why, best of all. But let me see,
    I – ha – yes, – so it shall be: in disguise
    We'll early to the Friar's, I have thought on't.

            Enter BERGETTO *and* POGGIO

PHILOTIS

    Uncle, he comes.

RICHARDETTO   Welcome, my worthy coz.   35

BERGETTO

    Lass, pretty lass; come buss, lass. [*Kisses her*] Aha, Poggio!

PHILOTIS

    There's hope of this yet.

RICHARDETTO

    You shall have time enough. Withdraw a little:
    We must confer at large.

BERGETTO [*To* PHILOTIS]

    Have you not sweetmeats, or dainty devices for me?   40

PHILOTIS

    You shall enough, sweetheart.

BERGETTO

    Sweetheart! Mark that, Poggio. By my troth, I cannot choose
    but kiss thee once more for that word 'sweetheart'. [*Kisses her*]
    Poggio, I have a monstrous swelling about my stomach, what-
    soever the matter be.   45

---

33   *I – ha – yes, – so* Richardetto mutters to himself as he turns things over in his mind.
      Most editors since Dodsley have interpreted Q's 'I' as signifying 'Ay' rather than the
      personal pronoun, and have modernized accordingly; one cannot rationally decide
      between the two when the dialogue is calculatedly incoherent; I have accordingly
      opted to retain the Q reading. In performance, the two words sound the same.

36   *buss* kiss.

37   s.p. PHILOTIS Q. This is Philotis' crucial line. Her previous remarks on the subject of
      her relationship with Bergetto (lines 27–8) suggest that she has accepted her im-
      pending marriage primarily in deference to Richardetto; now she speaks on her own
      account after having enjoyed the kiss. As an expression of emergent sexual feeling,
      it is matched by Bergetto's response to their next kiss (see note on line 44 below); the
      effect is to humanize the relationship in preparation for the events of III.vii and
      IV.ii. Nonetheless, many previous editors have followed the nineteenth-century
      tradition of reassigning the line to either Richardetto (Gifford) or Poggio (Schmitz).

38–9 *Withdraw . . . at large* By 'at large', Richardetto may mean either 'at length' or 'as a
      group'; either way, Bergetto will need to give his full attention, so he must 'withdraw'
      (stop kissing Philotis).

44   *a monstrous swelling* i.e. an erection ('stomach' here means his abdomen).

POGGIO

You shall have physic for't, sir.

RICHARDETTO

Time runs apace.

BERGETTO

Time's a blockhead! [*Kisses her*]

RICHARDETTO

Be ruled: when we have done what's fit to do,

Then you may kiss your fill, and bed her too.   50

Exeunt

[ACT III, SCENE vi]

Enter the FRIAR *in his study, sitting in a chair,*
ANNABELLA *kneeling and whispering to him,*
a table before them and wax-lights;
she weeps, and wrings her hands.

FRIAR

I am glad to see this penance, for, believe me,

You have unripped a soul so foul and guilty

As, I must tell you true, I marvel how

The earth hath borne you up. But weep, weep on:

These tears may do you good. Weep faster yet,   5

Whiles I do read a lecture.

---

 0   s.d. In the original production, the 'study' would again have been set in the discovery
      space (see note to II.ii.0 s.d.) and the traverse curtain drawn to show the characters
      already in position. (There is no other way literally to '*Enter . . . sitting*' and '*kneel-
      ing*'.) The statement that this is the Friar's study (i.e. in his cell) seems to be
      contradicted by the reference in line 45 to Soranzo's waiting 'below', which suggests
      that the action takes place in Annabella's room at home, where Florio escorted the
      Friar in III.iv. (Barker suggests that, alternatively, 'in his study' may not be an indic-
      ation of location at all, and may instead refer to 'the way the Friar is observed wrapped
      up in his contemplation of damnation'.) If the intended location is indeed Florio's
      house, then this is especially significant in that the scene's events obviate the original
      plan for Soranzo and Annabella to go to the Friar's cell (see note to line 42).
      wax-lights candles or tapers.
 2   *unripped* disclosed.
 6   *Whiles* Whilst.
      read a lecture deliver an admonitory speech.

ANNABELLA   Wretched creature!

FRIAR

Ay, you are wretched, miserably wretched,
Almost condemned alive. There is a place –
List, daughter! – in a black and hollow vault,
Where day is never seen. There shines no sun,   10
But flaming horror of consuming fires,
A lightless sulphur, choked with smoky fogs
Of an infected darkness. In this place
Dwell many thousand thousand sundry sorts
Of never-dying deaths: there damnèd souls   15
Roar without pity; there are gluttons fed
With toads and adders; there is burning oil
Poured down the drunkard's throat, the usurer
Is forced to sup whole draughts of molten gold;
There is the murderer forever stabbed,   20
Yet can he never die; there lies the wanton
On racks of burning steel, whiles in his soul
He feels the torment of his raging lust.

ANNABELLA

Mercy, O mercy!

FRIAR   There stands these wretched things
Who have dreamt out whole years in lawless sheets   25
And secret incests, cursing one another.
Then you will wish each kiss your brother gave
Had been a dagger's point; then you shall hear
How he will cry, 'O, would my wicked sister
Had first been damned, when she did yield to lust!'   30

8–23   These lines are imitated from a passage in Thomas Nashe's *Pierce Penniless* (1592),
where hell is described as 'a place of horror, stench, and darkness, where men see
meat, but can get none, or are ever thirsty and ready to swelt for drink, yet have not
the power to taste the cool streams that run at their feet; where . . . he that was a
great drunkard here on earth hath his penance assigned him to carouse himself
drunk with dishwash and vinegar, and surfeit four times a day with sour ale and
small beer; as so of the rest, the usurer to swallow molten gold, the glutton to eat
nothing but toads, and the murderer to be still stabbed with daggers, but never die'
(Nashe, *Works*, ed. McKerrow, i. 218). Ford had previously imitated this passage in
Christ's Bloody Sweat (1613).

9   *List* Listen.

13   *infected* contaminated.

25   *dreamt . . . years* Refers to a long period of moral insensibility (the incestuous liaison
having the same relation to reality as does a dream).
lawless sheets Metonymic for an unlawful sexual relationship.

But soft, methinks I see repentance work
New motions in your heart. Say, how is't with you?

ANNABELLA

Is there no way left to redeem my miseries?

FRIAR

There is: despair not. Heaven is merciful,
And offers grace even now. 'Tis thus agreed: 35
First, for your honour's safety, that you marry
The Lord Soranzo; next, to save your soul,
Leave off this life, and henceforth live to him.

ANNABELLA

Ay me!

FRIAR   Sigh not. I know the baits of sin
Are hard to leave. O, 'tis a death to do't.   40
Remember what must come! Are you content?

ANNABELLA

I am.

FRIAR

I like it well; we'll take the time. Who's near us there?

Enter FLORIO, GIOVANNI

FLORIO

Did you call, father?

FRIAR

Is Lord Soranzo come?

FLORIO   He stays below.   45

FRIAR

Have you acquainted him at full?

---

 32   *motions* mental impulses.
36–7   *First . . . next* Probably referring to simple chronological sequence rather than
       implying an order of priority.
 38   *live to him* live as a faithful wife to Soranzo.
 40   *'tis . . . do't* it is intensely difficult and painful to tear oneself away from a sinful
       lifestyle (leading on to the implication that this metaphorical death is trivial com-
       pared with the absolute spiritual death suffered by those who fail to do so).
 41   *what must come* Implying hell, if she does not carry through her repentance to the
       end.
 42   *the time* the immediate opportunity (to have Soranzo and Annabella affianced).
       This supersedes the original betrothal plans which Florio mentioned to Richardetto
       in III.iv, and Richardetto to Grimaldi in III.v.
 45   *stays below* waits downstairs.
46–9   lineation ed.(Haue . . . full? / I . . . ouer-ioy'd./ And . . . neere./ My . . . falshood,/I . . .
       him Q).

FLORIO   I have,
And he is overjoyed.
FRIAR   And so are we.
Bid him come near.
GIOVANNI [*Aside*]   My sister weeping, ha!
I fear this friar's falsehood. [*Aloud*] I will call him.   *Exit*
FLORIO
Daughter, are you resolved?
ANNABELLA   Father, I am.   50

     Enter GIOVANNI, SORANZO, *and* VASQUES

FLORIO
My lord Soranzo, here
Give me your hand; for that I give you this.
        [*He joins* SORANZO*'s and* ANNABELLA*'s hands*]
SORANZO
Lady, say you so too?
ANNABELLA   I do, and vow
To live with you and yours.
FRIAR   Timely resolved:
My blessing rest on both! More to be done,   55
You may perform it on the morning sun.

             Exeunt

[ACT III, SCENE vii]

Enter GRIMALDI *with his rapier drawn, and a dark lantern*

GRIMALDI
'Tis early night as yet, and yet too soon
To finish such a work. Here I will lie
To listen who comes next.   *He lies down*

---

52   s.d. The joining of hands (known in the period as 'handfasting') formally signifies
      the couple's betrothal.
53–4 *I do . . . yours* lineation ed. (one line in Q).

0   s.d. a *dark lantern* a sealed lantern with a slide or shutter enabling a beam of light to
     be shown or hidden at will; it enabled a person (usually a criminal) to move about
     at night without attracting attention.

Enter BERGETTO *and* PHILOTIS *disguised, and after*
RICHARDETTO [*disguised as the Doctor*] *and* POGGIO

BERGETTO

We are almost at the place, I hope, sweetheart.

GRIMALDI [*Aside*]

I hear them near, and heard one say 'sweetheart':   5
'Tis he. Now guide my hand, some angry Justice,
Home to his bosom. [*Aloud*] Now have at you, sir!

Strikes BERGETTO *and exit*

BERGETTO

O help, help, here's a stitch fallen in my guts! O for a flesh-
tailor quickly! Poggio!

PHILOTIS

What ails my love?   10

BERGETTO

I am sure I cannot piss forward and backward, and yet I am
wet before and behind. Lights, lights, ho lights!

PHILOTIS

Alas, some villain here has slain my love!

RICHARDETTO

O, Heaven forbid it! Raise up the next neighbours instantly,
Poggio, and bring lights.   15

Exit POGGIO

How is't, Bergetto? Slain? It cannot be; are you sure you're hurt?

BERGETTO

O, my belly seethes like a porridge-pot. Some cold water, I shall
boil over else! My whole body is in a sweat, that you may wring
my shirt – feel here. Why, Poggio!

Enter POGGIO *with* OFFICERS, *and lights and halberds*

POGGIO

Here. Alas, how do you?   20

---

3   s.d. *disguised* They are probably wearing masks.
      after following them.
6   *Justice* a god or other supernatural force of justice.
7   s.d. *Strikes* Runs him through with the poisoned rapier.
8   *a stitch fallen* The phrase was normally used of a burst seam in an article of clothing
      (hence Bergetto's periphrasis for a surgeon, 'a flesh-tailor').
8–9   Prose ed. (Oh . . . gutts, / Oh . . . *Poggio* Q).
14–16 prose ed. (Oh . . . neighbours / Instantly . . . lights, / How . . . slaine? / It . . . hurt? Q).
19   s.d. *halberds* long-handled weapons combining an axe-blade and spear-head, carried
      by officers of the watch (who policed the city at night).

RICHARDETTO

Give me a light. What's here? All blood! O, sirs,
Signor Donado's nephew now is slain!
Follow the murderer with all the haste
Up to the city, he cannot be far hence.
Follow, I beseech you.

OFFICERS   Follow, follow, follow!   25

Exeunt OFFICERS

RICHARDETTO [*To* PHILOTIS]

Tear off thy linen, coz, to stop his wounds.
[*To* BERGETTO] Be of good comfort, man.

BERGETTO

Is all this mine own blood? Nay then, goodnight with me.
Poggio, commend me to my uncle, dost hear? Bid him for my
sake make much of this wench. O, I am going the wrong way   30
sure, my belly aches so! O, farewell, Poggio – O – O –   *Dies*

PHILOTIS

O, he is dead!

POGGIO   How! Dead?

RICHARDETTO   He's dead indeed.
'Tis now too late to weep. Let's have him home,
And with what speed we may find out the murderer.

POGGIO

O my master, my master, my master!   *Exeunt*   35

[ACT III, SCENE viii]

Enter VASQUES *and* HIPPOLITA

HIPPOLITA

Betrothed?

VASQUES

I saw it.

HIPPOLITA

And when's the marriage-day?

---

24   *the city* Parma's central administrative district.
26   *linen* petticoats (usable as makeshift bandages).
30   *make much of* treat generously.

VASQUES   Some two days hence.

HIPPOLITA

Two days? Why man, I would but wish two hours
To send him to his last and lasting sleep;   5
And Vasques, thou shalt see, I'll do it bravely.

VASQUES

I do not doubt your wisdom, nor, I trust, you my secrecy: I am
infinitely yours.

HIPPOLITA

I will be thine in spite of my disgrace.
So soon? O wicked man, I durst be sworn   10
He'd laugh to see me weep.

VASQUES

And that's a villainous fault in him.

HIPPOLITA

No, let him laugh: I'm armed in my resolves.
Be thou still true.

VASQUES

I should get little by treachery against so hopeful a preferment   15
as I am like to climb to.

HIPPOLITA

Even to my bosom, Vasques: let my youth
Revel in these new pleasures. If we thrive,
He now hath but a pair of days to live.

Exeunt

---

5   *his last ... sleep* death
7–8   prose ed. (I ... secresie, / I ... yours Q).
9   *disgrace* This may refer either to the disgrace that will follow her open involvement
     in a plot against Soranzo, or the disgrace that comes from a woman of her rank
     marrying a servant.
15   *against* compared with.
     preferment promotion.
17–18 *my youth ... new pleasures* This could refer either to Soranzo and his marriage to
     Annabella or to herself and her forthcoming liaison with Vasques.

[ACT III, SCENE ix]

Enter FLORIO, DONADO [*weeping*], RICHARDETTO
[*disguised as the Doctor*], POGGIO, *and* OFFICERS

FLORIO
    'Tis bootless now to show yourself a child,
    Signor Donado: what is done, is done.
    Spend not the time in tears, but seek for justice.

RICHARDETTO
    I must confess, somewhat I was in fault,
    That had not first acquainted you what love,   5
    Passed 'twixt him and my niece; but as I live,
    His fortune grieves me as it were mine own.

DONADO
    Alas, poor creature, he meant no man harm,
    That I am sure of.

FLORIO   I believe that too;
    But stay, my masters, are you sure you saw   10
    The murderer pass here?

OFFICER
    An it please you sir, we are sure we saw a ruffian with a naked
    weapon in his hand all bloody, get into my lord Cardinal's
    grace's gate: that we are sure of, but for fear of his grace – bless
    us! – we durst go no further.   15

DONADO
    Know you what manner of man he was?

OFFICER
    Yes, sure I know the man, they say a is a soldier. [*To* FLORIO]
    He that loved your daughter, sir, an't please ye, 'twas he for
    certain.

FLORIO
    Grimaldi, on my life!

OFFICER   Ay, ay, the same.   20

RICHARDETTO
    The Cardinal is noble: he no doubt
    Will give true justice.

DONADO
    Knock, someone, at the gate.

---

  1   *bootless* useless, pointless.

POGGIO
> I'll knock, sir.   POGGIO *knocks*

SERVANT (*Within*)
> What would 'ee?   25

FLORIO
> We require speech with the lord Cardinal
> About some present business. Pray inform
> His grace that we are here.

Enter CARDINAL *and* GRIMALDI

CARDINAL
> Why, how now, friends! What saucy mates are you
> That know nor duty nor civility?   30
> Are we a person fit to be your host?
> Or is our house become your common inn,
> To beat our doors at pleasure? What such haste
> Is yours, as that it cannot wait fit times?
> Are you the masters of this commonwealth,   35
> And know no more discretion? O, your news
> Is here before you: you have lost a nephew,
> Donado, last night by Grimaldi slain.
> Is that your business? Well sir, we have knowledge on't:
> Let that suffice.

GRIMALDI [*Kneeling*] In presence of your grace,   40
> In thought I never meant Bergetto harm;
> But, Florio, you can tell with how much scorn
> Soranzo, backed with his confederates,
> Hath often wronged me. I to be revenged,
> For that I could not win him else to fight,   45
> Had thought by way of ambush to have killed him,
> But was unluckily therein mistook,

---

27   *present* urgent.
29   *mates* an insulting epithet, implying low social status in those addressed.
30   *nor . . . nor* neither . . . nor.
34   *fit times* It is still night-time.
35   *the masters of this commonwealth* Not the political rulers but the municipal authorities responsible for policing the community.
39   *on't* of it.
40   *In . . . grace* an affirmation of truthfulness, often used to strengthen a solemn oath.
41   *In thought* In the conception of the crime. This was not an admissible defence in English law.
45   *else* by any other means.

Else he had felt what late Bergetto did.
And though my fault to him were merely chance,
Yet humbly I submit me to your grace,   50
To do with me as you please.

CARDINAL   Rise up, Grimaldi.

                                    [GRIMALDI *rises*]

You citizens of Parma, if you seek
For justice, know, as Nuncio from the Pope,
For this offence I here receive Grimaldi
Into his Holiness' protection.   55
He is no common man, but nobly born
Of princes' blood, though you, sir Florio,
Thought him too mean a husband for your daughter.
If more you seek for, you must go to Rome,
For he shall thither. Learn more wit, for shame.   60
Bury your dead. Away, Grimaldi; leave 'em.

                        Exeunt CARDINAL *and* GRIMALDI

DONADO

Is this a churchman's voice? Dwells Justice here?

FLORIO

Justice is fled to heaven and comes no nearer.
Soranzo, was't for him? O impudence!
Had he the face to speak it, and not blush?   65
Come, come, Donado, there's no help in this
When cardinals think murder's not amiss.
Great men may do their wills, we must obey,
But Heaven will judge them for't another day.

                                            Exeunt

---

49 *him* Bergetto.
58 *mean* lowly.
60 *wit* common sense.
63 In classical mythology, Astraea, the goddess of justice, left the earth at the start of the
    iron age, driven away by human murderousness, and was placed in the heavens as
    the constellation of Virgo. The idea, best known from Ovid, *Metamorphoses* 1.150,
    became a Renaissance commonplace, which the Cardinal's behaviour is taken to
    illustrate.

[ACT IV, SCENE i]

A banquet. Hautboys. Enter the FRIAR, GIOVANNI,
ANNABELLA, PHILOTIS, SORANZO, DONADO,
FLORIO, RICHARDETTO [*disguised as the Doctor*],
PUTANA, *and* VASQUES

FRIAR

These holy rites performed, now take your times
To spend the remnant of the day in feast.
Such fit repasts are pleasing to the saints
Who are your guests, though not with mortal eyes
To be beheld. Long prosper in this day,   5
You happy couple, to each other's joy!

SORANZO

Father, your prayer is heard. The hand of goodness
Hath been a shield for me against my death,
And, more to bless me, hath enriched my life
With this most precious jewel, such a prize,   10
As earth hath not another like to this.
Cheer up, my love; and gentlemen, my friends,
Rejoice with me in mirth. This day we'll crown
With lusty cups to Annabella's health.

GIOVANNI [*Aside*]

O, torture! Were the marriage yet undone,   15
Ere I'd endure this sight, to see my love
Clipped by another, I would dare confusion
And stand the horror of ten thousand deaths.

---

  0   s.d. *Hautboys* Wind instruments with a shrill, reedy sound, usually played in a
        consort; the ancestor of the modern oboe.
3–5   *the saints . . . beheld* The invisible presence of the saints (which might include angels
        and the blessed dead in heaven as well as canonized persons) is invoked as a sign of
        divine favour towards the marriage.
  5   *in this day* as a result of the marriage.
  7   *The hand of goodness* God's providential action (to which he attributes the failure of
        Grimaldi's murder plot).
 10   *this . . . jewel* Annabella.
 17   *Clipped* Embraced.
       confusion destruction.

VASQUES

    Are you not well, sir?

GIOVANNI   Prithee fellow, wait,

    I need not thy officious diligence.   20

FLORIO

    Signor Donado, come: you must forget

    Your late mishaps, and drown your cares in wine.

SORANZO

    Vasques!

VASQUES   My lord?

SORANZO   Reach me that weighty bowl.

    Here, brother Giovanni, here's to you:

    Your turn comes next, though now a bachelor.   25

    Here's to your sister's happiness and mine!

                    [SORANZO *drinks, and offers* GIOVANNI *the goblet*]

GIOVANNI

    I cannot drink.

SORANZO   What?

GIOVANNI   'Twill indeed offend me.

ANNABELLA

    Pray, do not urge him if he be not willing.

                     [*Sounds are heard off-stage*]

FLORIO

    How now, what noise is this?

VASQUES

    O, sir, I had forgot to tell you: certain young maidens of Parma,   30
    in honour to Madam Annabella's marriage, have sent their
    loves to her in a masque, for which they humbly crave your
    patience and silence.

SORANZO

    We are much bound to them, so much the more

    As it comes unexpected. Guide them in.   35

---

   19   *wait* see to your duties as an attendant.

   23   *bowl* goblet.

   27   *offend* cause physical unease (*OED* 7), rather than offence in the modern sense;
       Giovanni is attempting to refuse politely.

   32   *masque* an entertainment at an aristocratic wedding (or other formal occasion)
       involving dancing by masked performers; in Ford's time (though not in the play),
       masques also incorporated elaborate dramatic narrative and spectacular scenery.

 34–5 lineation ed. (prose in Q).

Hautboys. Enter HIPPOLITA *and Ladies*
in [masks and] white robes, with garlands of willow.
Music and a dance.

SORANZO

    Thanks, lovely virgins. Now might we but know

    To whom we have been beholding for this love,

    We shall acknowledge it.

HIPPOLITA   Yes, you shall know:

    [*Unmasks*] What think you now?

ALL   Hippolita!

HIPPOLITA   'Tis she,

    Be not amazed; nor blush, young lovely bride: 40

    I come not to defraud you of your man.

    [*To* SORANZO] 'Tis now no time to reckon up the talk

    What Parma long hath rumoured of us both.

    Let rash report run on: the breath that vents it

    Will, like a bubble, break itself at last.   45

    [*To* ANNABELLA]

    But now to you, sweet creature: lend's your hand.

    Perhaps it hath been said that I would claim

    Some interest in Soranzo, now your lord.

    What I have right to do, his soul knows best;

    But in my duty to your noble worth,   50

    Sweet Annabella, and my care of you,

    Here take Soranzo; take this hand from me.

    I'll once more join what by the holy Church

    Is finished and allowed. Have I done well?

SORANZO

    You have too much engaged us.

HIPPOLITA   One thing more: 55

    That you may know my single charity,

---

35 s.d. *garlands of willow* associated with forsaken women (hence appropriate to
    Hippolita's view of her own situation)
    dance ed. (the word is repeated at the right-hand margin in Q).

37 *love* act of kindness.

44 *report* gossip.

46 *lend's* lend us (= me).

48 *lord* husband.

54 *allowed* approved.

55 *engaged us* put us in your debt.

Freely I here remit all interest
I e'er could claim, and give you back your vows;
And to confirm't – [*To* VASQUES] reach me a cup of wine –
My lord Soranzo, in this draught I drink   60
Long rest t'ee! [*Aside to* VASQUES] Look to it, Vasques.

VASQUES [*Aside to* HIPPOLITA]   Fear nothing.
                              He gives her a poisoned cup; she drinks

SORANZO
Hippolita, I thank you, and will pledge
This happy union as another life. Wine there!

VASQUES
You shall have none, neither shall you pledge her.

HIPPOLITA
How!   65

VASQUES
Know now, mistress she-devil, your own mischievous treachery
hath killed you. I must not marry you.

HIPPOLITA
Villain!

ALL
What's the matter?

VASQUES
Foolish woman, thou art now like a firebrand, that hath kindled   70
others and burnt thyself. *Troppo sperare inganna*, thy vain hope
hath deceived thee: thou art but dead. If thou hast any grace,
pray.

---

56 *single* sincere (also implying celibate).
    charity disinterested love for one's fellow human beings (broader than the modern
    sense of the word). Charity was named as the principal Christian virtue in the 1568
    and King James translations of 1 Corinthians 13.
57 *remit* renounce.
62 *pledge* drink from the same cup as a mark of respect.
63 lineation ed. (This . . . life, / Wine there Q).
    union the union between him and Annabella which Hippolita has effected by joining
    their hands.
66–7 prose ed. (Know . . . treachery / Hath . . . you Q).
70–1 *like . . . thyself* Imitated from First *Fruits* (I2^r): 'He is like a brand of fire, kindleth
    others and burneth himself.'
71 *Troppo . . . inganna* 'To hope too much deceives' (Italian). The idea was proverbial
    (Tilley, H. 608); Ford took the Italian version from First *Fruits* (I1^v).
    inganna ed. (*niganna* Q).
72 *but dead* as good as dead.
    grace the divine power which enables a person to overcome original sin and act
    virtuously.

HIPPOLITA
Monster!

VASQUES
Die in charity, for shame! [*To the others*] This thing of malice, 75
this woman, had privately corrupted me with promise of
marriage, under this politic reconciliation to poison my lord,
whiles she might laugh at his confusion on his marriage-day.
I promised her fair, but I knew what my reward should have
been, and would willingly have spared her life but that I was 80
acquainted with the danger of her disposition, and now have
fitted her a just payment in her own coin. There she is, she hath
yet – [*To* HIPPOLITA] – and end thy days in peace, vile woman.
As for life, there's no hope: think not on't.

ALL
Wonderful justice! 85

RICHARDETTO
Heaven, thou art righteous.

HIPPOLITA   O, 'tis true,
I feel my minute coming. Had that slave
Kept promise – O, my torment! – thou this hour
Hadst died, Soranzo. – Heat above hell-fire! –
Yet ere I pass away – cruel, cruel flames! – 90
Take here my curse amongst you: may thy bed
Of marriage be a rack unto thy heart. –
Burn, blood, and boil in vengeance! O my heart,
My flame's intolerable! – May'st thou live

75   *Die . . . shame* Die speaking well of others, rather than ill. Vasques makes ironic
      reference back to Hippolita's mendaciously claiming charity at line 56 (lineation
      ed.; printed on a separate line in Q).
77   *marriage* ed. (malice Q).
      politic cunningly deceitful.
79–80 *I knew . . . been* She would have broken her promise and let Vasques be executed for
      the murder.
80–1 *would . . . disposition* She is too vicious by nature to be allowed to live.
83   *yet . . . and end* ed. (yet – – and end Q). The two long dashes probably indicate
      illegible words in the copy. Roper suggests that the original text may have read
      something like 'she hath yet a minute to live. [*To* HIPPOLITA] Repent, and end thy
      days in peace'; this might usefully be adopted in production.
87   *minute* the moment of death.
89   *Heat* The perceived symptoms of poisoning in this period included an intense
      burning sensation throughout the body; Ford portrayed the same effects at the end
      of his later tragedy, *Love's Sacrifice* (1632), when Fernando is poisoned.
94   *My flame's intolerable* She imagines herself turning to flame, causing intolerable
      pain.

To father bastards, may her womb bring forth   95
Monsters, and die together in your sins,
Hated, scorned and unpitied! – O – O!   *Dies*

FLORIO

Was e'er so vile a creature?

RICHARDETTO   Here's the end
Of lust and pride.

ANNABELLA   It is a fearful sight.

SORANZO

Vasques, I know thee now a trusty servant,   100
And never will forget thee. Come, my love,
We'll home, and thank the heavens for this escape.
Father and friends, we must break up this mirth:
It is too sad a feast.

DONADO   Bear hence the body.

FRIAR [*Aside to* GIOVANNI]

Here's an ominous change.   105
Mark this, my Giovanni, and take heed!
I fear the event: that marriage seldom's good,
Where the bride-banquet so begins in blood.

Exeunt [*with the body*]

[ACT IV, SCENE ii]

Enter RICHARDETTO *and* PHILOTIS

RICHARDETTO

My wretched wife, more wretched in her shame
Than in her wrongs to me, hath paid too soon

---

96   *Monsters* Deformed children (then considered ominous rather than unfortunate).
105   *change* i.e. from rejoicing to death.
107   *event* subsequent outcome.
108   *bride-banquet* wedding breakfast.
    s.d. Vasques is the only servant present on stage (the text provides for no other attendants), so it is probably he who carries off Hippolita's body in an ironic visual conclusion to their duplicitous marital agreement. Single-handedly moving a 'corpse' is a cumbersome process which would give the actors of Richardetto and Philotis a moment to prepare for their immediate re-entry at the start of the next scene.

The forfeit of her modesty and life;
And I am sure, my niece, though vengeance hover,
Keeping aloof yet from Soranzo's fall,   5
Yet he will fall, and sink with his own weight.
I need not – now my heart persuades me so –
To further his confusion: there is one
Above begins to work; for, as I hear,
Debates already 'twixt his wife and him   10
Thicken and run to head. She, as 'tis said,
Slightens his love, and he abandons hers:
Much talk I hear. Since things go thus, my niece,
In tender love and pity of your youth,
My counsel is that you should free your years   15
From hazard of these woes by flying hence
To fair Cremona, there to vow your soul
In holiness a holy votaress.
Leave me to see the end of these extremes.
All human worldly courses are uneven: 20
No life is blessed but the way to heaven.

PHILOTIS

Uncle, shall I resolve to be a nun?

RICHARDETTO

Ay, gentle niece, and in your hourly prayers
Remember me, your poor unhappy uncle.
Hie to Cremona now, as fortune leads,   25
Your home your cloister, your best friends your beads.
Your chaste and single life shall crown your birth:
Who dies a virgin lives a saint on earth.

3   *life* the promiscuous life she led.
8   *further his confusion* act to advance his destruction.
8–9 *one Above* God.
10 *Debates* Quarrels, disputes.
11 *run to head* develop towards a point of crisis, 'like a ripe boil ready to burst' (Morris).
12 *Slightens* Depreciates, contemptuously rejects.
16 *flying* fleeing.
17 *Cremona* a city about 30 miles north of Parma, part of the state of Milan; it was notable for its many nunneries.
18 *votaress* nun.
19 *extremes* desperate events.
20 *uneven* morally irregular.
25 *Hie* Go swiftly.
26 *beads* rosary beads, used by Roman Catholics to count prayers.
28 *lives* ed. (liue Q).

PHILOTIS
    Then farewell world, and worldly thoughts adieu!
    Welcome, chaste vows, myself I yield to you.   30

Exeunt

[ACT IV, SCENE iii]

Enter SORANZO, *unbraced* [*with his sword drawn*],
and ANNABELLA *dragged in*

SORANZO
    Come, strumpet, famous whore! Were every drop
    Of blood that runs in thy adulterous veins
    A life, this sword – dost see't? – should in one blow
    Confound them all. Harlot, rare, notable harlot,
    That with thy brazen face maintain'st thy sin,   5
    Was there no man in Parma to be bawd
    To your loose, cunning whoredom else but I?
    Must your hot itch and pleurisy of lust,
    The heyday of your luxury, be fed
    Up to a surfeit, and could none but I   10
    Be picked out to be cloak to your close tricks,
    Your belly-sports? Now I must be the dad
    To all that gallimaufry that's stuffed

30   *yield* A young woman would also 'yield' in giving up her virginity (compare II.i.4),
      so the use of the word in this context gives Philotis' situation additional poignancy.

  0   s.d. *unbraced* with his clothes unfastened; not fully dressed.
  1   *famous* i.e. infamous.
  4   *Confound* Destroy.
  5   *maintain'st* either (*a*) persist in or (*b*) defend.
  6   *bawd* brothel-keeper, pimp; Soranzo pays for his wife's upkeep as a pimp supports
      a prostitute, both for other men's sexual use.
  7   *else but* other than.
8–10   *Must . . . surfeit* Are you so incapable of controlling your sexual appetite.
  8   *pleurisy* (*a*) a feverish disease, alluding metaphorically to the heat of lust; (*b*) excess.
  9   *heyday . . . luxury* the highest pitch of lecherous excitement (referring, presumably,
      to the female orgasm).
 11   *cloak* cover, disguise
      close secret.
 13   *gallimaufry* a hodge-podge of different materials; here used as a metaphor for a bastard.

In thy corrupted bastard-bearing womb?
Why must I?
ANNABELLA Beastly man, why, 'tis thy fate: 15
I sued not to thee, for – but that I thought
Your over-loving lordship would have run
Mad on denial – had ye lent me time
I would have told 'ee in what case I was;
But you would needs be doing.
SORANZO   Whore of whores!   20
Darest thou tell me this?
ANNABELLA   O yes, why not?
You were deceived in me: 'twas not for love
I chose you, but for honour. Yet know this:
Would you be patient yet and hide your shame,
I'd see whether I could love you.
SORANZO   Excellent quean!   25
Why, art thou not with child?
ANNABELLA   What needs all this,
When 'tis superfluous? I confess I am.
SORANZO
Tell me by whom.
ANNABELLA Soft, sir, 'twas not in my bargain;
Yet somewhat, sir, to stay your longing stomach
I'm content t' acquaint you with. The man,   30
The more than man that got this sprightly boy –
For 'tis a boy, that's for your glory, sir,
Your heir shall be a son –
SORANZO   Damnable monster!
ANNABELLA
Nay, an you will not hear, I'll speak no more.

18 *on denial* at her refusal to marry him.
19 *case* condition.
20 *would . . . doing* couldn't wait.
24 *patient* stoical.
25 *quean* sexually promiscuous woman.
28 *'twas . . . bargain* I didn't agree to tell you *that*.
29 *somewhat* something.
  stay . . . stomach The primary sense is 'satisfy your hungry appetite (for information)', but 'longing' was also used of cravings in pregnancy, creating an ironic twist: Annabella has just been found to be pregnant, but it is Soranzo who has the unusual appetitive craving.
32 *that's . . . glory* ed. (that for glory Q).

356

SORANZO
    Yes, speak, and speak thy last.
ANNABELLA   A match, a match: 35
    This noble creature was in every part
    So angel-like, so glorious, that a woman
    Who had not been but human as was I,
    Would have kneeled to him, and have begged for love.
    You – why you are not worthy once to name   40
    His name without true worship, or indeed,
    Unless you kneeled, to hear another name him.
SORANZO
    What was he called?
ANNABELLA   We are not come to that.
    Let it suffice that you shall have the glory
    To father what so brave a father got.   45
    In brief, had not this chance fall'n out as't doth,
    I never had been troubled with a thought
    That you had been a creature; but for marriage,
    I scarce dream yet of that.
SORANZO
    Tell me his name!
ANNABELLA   Alas, alas, there's all.   50
    Will you believe?
SORANZO   What?
ANNABELLA   You shall never know.
SORANZO
    How!
ANNABELLA Never: if you do, let me be cursed.
SORANZO
    Not know it, strumpet! I'll rip up thy heart
    And find it there.
ANNABELLA   Do, do.
SORANZO   And with my teeth

---

35   *A match, a match* It's a deal.
37–9   *a woman . . . love* Annabella was only human, but even a woman who was above
       that frailty would have been overpowered by his beauty.
42   *another* someone else.
45   *To father* To bear the name and play the part of a father in all except the biological sense.
       brave excellent.
48   *been a creature* existed.
       but for marriage were it not for the fact that I am married to you.

Tear the prodigious lecher joint by joint.   55

ANNABELLA

Ha, ha, ha, the man's merry.

SORANZO   Dost thou laugh?

Come, whore, tell me your lover, or by truth

I'll hew thy flesh to shreds! Who is't?

ANNABELLA (*Sings*)

Che morte più dolce che morire per amore?

SORANZO

Thus will I pull thy hair, and thus I'll drag   60

Thy lust-belepered body through the dust.

Yet tell his name.

ANNABELLA (*Sings*)

Morendo in grazia a lui, morirei senza dolore.

SORANZO

Dost thou triumph? The treasure of the earth

Shall not redeem thee. Were there kneeling kings   65

Did beg thy life, or angels did come down

To plead in tears, yet should not all prevail

Against my rage. Dost thou not tremble yet?

ANNABELLA

At what? To die? No, be a gallant hangman:

I dare thee to the worst, strike, and strike home.   70

---

55   *prodigious* unnatural and monstrous.
59   What death is sweeter than to die for love? (Italian). This and the next Italian line
      (63) are copied directly from consecutive sayings in the section of *First Fruits*
      devoted to 'amorous talk' (D1^V); there, both refer to a man's love for a woman.
      più ed. (*pluis* Q).
61   *lust-belepered* made leprous through lust.
63   Dying in favour with him, I would die without pain. (Italian).
      a lui ed. (*Lei* Q) *Lei* is the feminine pronoun, whereas Annabella, of course, is
      speaking of a man (*lui*). There is no certain evidence about whether Ford
      understood Italian: he never, so far as is known, used an Italian vernacular source,
      and the language is represented in his other plays only by two words of *The Fancies,
      Chaste and Noble* ('*Signor mio*', I.ii.35) and a passage of 'cod' Italian in *The Sun's
      Darling* (II.i.179-81), which might anyway have been written by his collaborator,
      Thomas Dekker. It is possible that he simply copied *lei* directly from *First Fruits*, not
      realizing the error of gender.
      morirei ed. (*morire* Q uncorrected; *morirere* Q corrected).
64   *triumph* exult.
69   *hangman* In killing a woman, unequal to him in strength, Soranzo will be like an
      executioner, whose victims are unable to defend themselves; the insult turns on the
      fact that the job was considered the basest kind of honest work, far beneath an
      aristocrat's dignity.

I leave revenge behind, and thou shall feel't.

SORANZO

Yet tell me ere thou diest, and tell me truly,
Knows thy old father this?

ANNABELLA   No, by my life.

SORANZO

Wilt thou confess, and I will spare thy life?

ANNABELLA

My life! I will not buy my life so dear.   75

SORANZO

I will not slack my vengeance.

Enter VASQUES

VASQUES   What d'ee mean, sir?

SORANZO

Forbear, Vasques: such a damnèd whore
Deserves no pity.

VASQUES   Now the gods forfend!
And would you be her executioner, and kill her in your rage
too? O, 'twere most unmanlike! She is your wife. What faults   80
hath been done by her before she married you, were not against
you. Alas poor lady, what hath she committed which any lady
in Italy in the like case would not? Sir, you must be ruled by
your reason and not by your fury: that were unhuman and
beastly.   85

SORANZO

She shall not live.

VASQUES

Come, she must. You would have her confess the authors of
her present misfortunes, I warrant 'ee. 'Tis an unconscionable
demand, and she should lose the estimation that I, for my part,
hold of her worth, if she had done it. Why sir, you ought not of 90
all men living to know it. Good sir, be reconciled. Alas, good
gentlewoman!

ANNABELLA

Pish, do not beg for me: I prize my life

71 I . . . *behind* There will be someone left alive to avenge my death (meaning the lover
    whose identity Soranzo does not know).
76 *slack* put off, delay.
78 *forfend* forbid.
87 *the authors of* those responsible for.
88 *unconscionable* unreasonably excessive.

359

As nothing. If the man will needs be mad,
Why, let him take it.

SORANZO   Vasques, hear'st thou this?   95

VASQUES

Yes, and commend her for it: in this she shows the nobleness of
a gallant spirit, and beshrew my heart but it becomes her rarely.
[*Aside to* SORANZO] Sir, in any case smother your revenge: leave
the scenting-out your wrongs to me. Be ruled, as you respect
your honour, or you mar all. [*Aloud*] Sir, if ever my service were   100
of any credit with you, be not so violent in your distractions.
You are married now: what a triumph might the report of this
give to other neglected suitors! 'Tis as manlike to bear extremities, as godlike to forgive.

SORANZO

O Vasques, Vasques, in this piece of flesh,   105
This faithless face of hers, had I laid up
The treasure of my heart!
[*To* ANNABELLA]   Hadst thou been virtuous,
Fair, wicked woman, not the matchless joys
Of life itself had made me wish to live
With any saint but thee. Deceitful creature,   110
How hast thou mocked my hopes, and in the shame
Of thy lewd womb even buried me alive!
I did too dearly love thee.

VASQUES (*Aside* [*to* SORANZO]) This is well;
Follow this temper with some passion, be brief and moving: 'tis
for the purpose.   115

SORANZO [*To* ANNABELLA]

Be witness to my words thy soul and thoughts,

---

    97   *beshrew* may evil befall
              but unless.
  100   *your honour* ed. (hour honour Q).
  101   *credit with* value to.
              distractions deranged fits.
102–3   *You . . . suitors* As a winner in the marriage game, Soranzo should not give losers the
              opportunity to gloat; contrast Florio's views at I.ii.55.
103–4   *bear extremities* put up with others' egregious behaviour.
114–15   prose ed. (Follow . . . passion, / Bee . . . purpose Q).
  114   *Follow . . . passion* Vasques tells Soranzo how to play it next: having toned down
              ('tempered') his rage against Annabella, he should now show her the strong emotion
              she provokes in him.
  116   Let your soul and thoughts be witness to my words.

And tell me, didst not think that in my heart
I did too superstitiously adore thee?

ANNABELLA

I must confess, I know you loved me well.

SORANZO

And wouldst thou use me thus? O Annabella,   120
Be thou assured, whatsoe'er the villain was
That thus hath tempted thee to this disgrace,
Well he might lust, but never loved like me;
He doted on the picture that hung out
Upon thy cheeks, to please his humorous eye,   125
Not on the part I loved, which was thy heart,
And, as I thought, thy virtues.

ANNABELLA   O my lord!
These words wound deeper than your sword could do.

VASQUES

Let me not ever take comfort, but I begin to weep myself, so much
I pity him. Why, madam, I knew when his rage was overpassed   130
what it would come to.

SORANZO

Forgive me, Annabella. Though thy youth
Hath tempted thee above thy strength to folly,
Yet will not I forget what I should be,
And what I am, a husband: in that name   135
Is hid divinity. If I do find
That thou wilt yet be true, here I remit
All former faults, and take thee to my bosom.

VASQUES

By my troth, and that's a point of noble charity.

ANNABELLA [*Kneeling*]

Sir, on my knees –

SORANZO   Rise up, you shall not kneel.   140

---

118   *did . . . thee* worshipped you like a pagan idol.
121   *thou* ed. (thus Q).
125   *humorous* capricious.
133   *above thy strength* beyond your powers of resistance.
135–6 *a husband . . . divinity* An orthodox notion of the time, which drew biblical authority
       from Ephesians 5. 22–3: 'Wives, submit yourselves unto your own husbands, as unto
       the Lord. For the husband is the head of the wife, even as Christ is the head of the
       church.' The point of the analogy here is that Soranzo will exercise the divine
       prerogative of forgiveness if Annabella repents.
137   *remit* forgive, pardon.

Get you to your chamber; see you make no show
Of alteration. I'll be with you straight.
My reason tells me now that 'tis as common
To err in frailty as to be a woman.
Go to your chamber.   145

Exit ANNABELLA

VASQUES

So, this was somewhat to the matter. What do you think of your
heaven of happiness now, sir?

SORANZO

I carry hell about me: all my blood
Is fired in swift revenge.

VASQUES

That may be, but know you how, or on whom? Alas, to marry a   150
great woman, being made great in the stock to your hand, is a
usual sport in these days; but to know what ferret it was that
haunted your cunny-berry, there's the cunning.

SORANZO

I'll make her tell herself, or –

VASQUES

Or what? You must not do so. Let me yet persuade your suffer-   155
ance a little while: go to her, use her mildly, win her, if it be
possible, to a voluntary, to a weeping tune. For the rest, if all hit,

---

141–2   *see . . . alteration* now that you are penitent, let there be no backsliding.
143–4   Ford was probably recalling *Hamlet* I.ii.146: 'frailty, thy name is woman'.
  146   *to the matter* pertinent, relevant.
  151   *great* pregnant.
         great . . . hand The phrase contains complex and significant word-play around the
         multiple meanings of 'stock'. The primary sense is 'handed over to you already
         pregnant' ('stock' = body), with the latent, ironic suggestion that Soranzo has been
         spared the pro-creative drudgery of begetting an heir. A similar implication comes
         from 'stock' as (*a*) a handle (which is now the right size to fit Soranzo's hand) and
         (*b*) the stem of a plant into which a graft is inserted. The word could also mean
         'rabbit-hole' (anticipating 'cunny-berry' later in the sentence).
  152   *ferret* ed. (*Secret* Q).
         cunny-berry (*a*) rabbit ('cony') burrow; (*b*) vagina ('cunny').
  153   *cunning* intelligent, artful skill .
155–6   *sufferance* toleration.
  157   *voluntary* a spontaneous part of a musical performance, chosen by the performer
         rather than prescribed by the score; the musical equivalent of an ad lib (here applied
         to Annabella's penitence).
         if all hit if everything comes off (perhaps with a latent pun on archery, developed in
         'mark').

I will not miss my mark. Pray sir, go in. The next news I tell you
shall be wonders.

SORANZO

Delay in vengeance gives a heavier blow.   *Exit*   160

VASQUES

Ah, sirrah, here's work for the nonce! I had a suspicion of a bad
matter in my head a pretty whiles ago; but after my madam's
scurvy looks here at home, her waspish perverseness and loud
fault-finding, then I remembered the proverb, that where hens
crow and cocks hold their peace there are sorry houses. 'Sfoot,   165
if the lower parts of a she-tailor's cunning can cover such a
swelling in the stomach, I'll never blame a false stitch in a shoe
whiles I live again. Up, and up so quick? And so quickly too?
'Twere a fine policy to learn by whom; this must be known.

Enter PUTANA [*weeping*]

And I have thought on't: here's the way, or none. [*To* PUTANA]   170
What, crying, old mistress? Alas, alas, I cannot blame 'ee. We
have a lord, Heaven help us, is so mad as the devil himself, the
more shame for him.

PUTANA

O Vasques, that ever I was born to see this day! Doth he use
thee so too sometimes, Vasques?   175

VASQUES

Me! Why, he makes a dog of me; but if some were of my mind,
I know what we would do. As sure as I am an honest man, he

158   *mark* target.
161   *the nonce* the present occasion.
164–5   *where ... houses* domestic life is unsatisfactory when the wife dominates her husband
        (which was considered contrary to the natural order of things). The proverb (Tilley,
        H. 778) is closely adapted from *First Fruits* (11ᵛ).
166–7   *lower ... stomach* A 'she-tailor' is probably a male tailor who makes clothing *for*
        women, rather than one who is a woman herself. His 'cunning', in the sense of 'skill',
        is metonymic for its product, i.e. the dress he makes; the 'lower parts' of that dress
        might be artfully designed to conceal ('cover') the outward signs of pregnancy.
        Vasques also puns on 'cunning' in its usual modern sense, with 'lower parts' imply-
        ing baseness.
168   *Up ... quickly* The passage works as a cascade of meaning from word to word: 'up'
        means pregnant (referring to the physical swelling of the stomach); 'quick' means
        both pregnant and rapidly; and the latter sense is then picked up in 'quickly'.
169   s.d. ed. (after 'or none.' in Q).
172   *mad* angry.
174–5   prose ed. (O ... day, / Doth ... *Vasques?* Q).

will go near to kill my lady with unkindness. Say she be with
child, is that such a matter for a young woman of her years to
be blamed for?   180

PUTANA

Alas, good heart, it is against her will full sore.

VASQUES

I durst be sworn, all his madness is for that she will not confess whose 'tis, which he will know, and when he doth know it,
I am so well acquainted with his humour that he will forget all
straight. Well, I could wish she would in plain terms tell all, for   185
that's the way indeed.

PUTANA

Do you think so?

VASQUES

Foh, I know't, provided that he did not win her to't by force. He
was once in a mind that you could tell, and meant to have
wrung it out of you, but I somewhat pacified him for that. Yet   190
sure you know a great deal.

PUTANA

Heaven forgive us all, I know a little, Vasques.

VASQUES

Why should you not? Who else should? Upon my conscience,
she loves you dearly, and you would not betray her to any
affliction for the world.   195

PUTANA

Not for all the world, by my faith and troth, Vasques.

VASQUES

'Twere pity of your life if you should; but in this you should
both relieve her present discomforts, pacify my lord, and gain
yourself everlasting love and preferment.

PUTANA

Dost think so, Vasques?   200

VASQUES

Nay, I know't. Sure 'twas some near and entire friend.

PUTANA

'Twas a dear friend indeed; but –

184   *humour* characteristic temperament.
        that as to be able to say that.
188   *provided . . . force* Everything will be all right so long as Soranzo finds out before
        resorting to violence; Putana is being given the opportunity to forestall such an
        eventuality.
201   *entire* intimate.

VASQUES

But what? Fear not to name him: my life between you and danger.
Faith, I think 'twas no base fellow.

PUTANA

Thou wilt stand between me and harm?   205

VASQUES

Ud's pity, what else? You shall be rewarded too. Trust me.

PUTANA

'Twas even no worse than her own brother.

VASQUES

Her brother Giovanni, I warrant 'ee?

PUTANA

Even he, Vasques. As brave a gentleman as ever kissed fair lady.
O, they love most perpetually.   210

VASQUES

A brave gentleman indeed; why, therein I commend her choice.
[*Aside*] Better and better. [*To her*] You are sure 'twas he?

PUTANA

Sure; and you shall see he will not be long from her, too.

VASQUES

He were to blame if he would. But may I believe thee?

PUTANA

Believe me! Why, dost think I am a Turk or a Jew! No, Vasques,   215
I have known their dealings too long to belie them now.

VASQUES

Where are you? There within, sirs!

Enter BANDITTI

PUTANA

How now, what are these?

206 *Ud's pity* an oath, minced from 'God's pity'·
   what else? of course!
208 *'ee*. Q. The punctuation could be modernized as a question mark or an exclamation
   mark (the two symbols were not differentiated in the early seventeenth century):
   the latter would signal shock at what Putana is saying, whereas the former would
   show a punctilious concern to make absolutely sure. Either version is possible, but
   as a question the line is more in keeping with the gentle way in which Vasques has
   drawn the information out of Putana so far.
214 *to blame* blameworthy.
215 *a Turk or a Jew* Implying a person unworthy of belief, not to be trusted; in effect,
   Putana avers her story 'as I am a Christian' (Turks and Jews being the principal non-
   Christian races known to early seventeenth-century Europe).
217 s.d. *BANDITTI* Members of an organized gang of robbers such as operated in the
   mountains and forests of Italy.

VASQUES

You shall know presently. Come sirs, take me this old damnable
hag, gag her instantly, and put out her eyes. Quickly, quickly!   220

[The BANDITTI *tie up* PUTANA]

PUTANA

Vasques, Vasques!

VASQUES

Gag her I say! 'Sfoot, d'ee suffer her to prate? What, d'ee fumble
about? Let me come to her. I'll help your old gums, you toad-
bellied bitch! [*He gags* PUTANA] Sirs, carry her closely into the
coal-house and put out her eyes instantly. If she roars, slit her   225
nose. D'ee hear? Be speedy and sure.

Exeunt [BANDITTI] *with* PUTANA

Why, this is excellent and above expectation! Her own brother?
O horrible! To what a height of liberty in damnation hath the
devil trained our age! Her brother, well! There's yet but a beginning. I must to my lord, and tutor him better in his points of   230
vengeance. Now I see how a smooth tale goes beyond a smooth
tail.

Enter GIOVANNI

But soft, what thing comes next? Giovanni! As I would wish.
My belief is strengthened: 'tis as firm as winter and summer.

GIOVANNI

Where's my sister?   235

VASQUES

Troubled with a new sickness, my lord; she's somewhat ill.

GIOVANNI

Took too much of the flesh, I believe.

219–20   prose ed. (You . . . presently, / Come . . . *hagge,* / Gag . . . quickly Q).
   219   *presently* immediately.
223–4   *toad-bellied* a general term of opprobrium and abuse; compare Thomas Dekker, *The
      Noble Spanish Soldier* (1622), IV.ii.179: 'Sirrah, you sarsaparilla rascal toad-guts'.
   228   *liberty* licentiousness.
   229   *trained* tempted, enticed.
231–2   *how a smooth . . . tail* how a plausible lie overcomes a wanton woman (literally, a
      well-lubricated, easily penetrated vagina). Ford is probably recalling *The Duchess of
      Malfi:* 'What cannot a neat knave with a smooth tale / Make a woman believe?'
      (I.ii.258–9).
   232   s.d. ed. (after 'next?' in Q).
   234   *as firm . . . summer* as certain as the interchange of the seasons.
   237   *took . . . flesh* over-indulged in (*a*) meat and (*b*) sex ('flesh' = penis); the latter sense
      is, of course, unintended by Giovanni, though heard by Vasques.

VASQUES

Troth sir, and you I think have e'en hit it; but my virtuous lady –

GIOVANNI

Where's she?   [*Gives him money*]

VASQUES

In her chamber; please you visit her? She is alone. Your liber-   240
ality hath doubly made me your servant, and ever shall, ever –

                                         Exit GIOVANNI

Enter SORANZO

Sir, I am made a man. I have plied my cue with cunning and
success. I beseech you, let's be private.

SORANZO

My lady's brother's come; now he'll know all.

VASQUES

Let him know't: I have made some of them fast enough. How   245
have you dealt with my lady?

SORANZO

Gently, as thou hast counselled. O, my soul
Runs circular in sorrow for revenge!
But Vasques, thou shalt know –

VASQUES

Nay, I will know no more, for now comes your turn to know.   250
I would not talk so openly with you. Let my young master take
time enough, and go at pleasure: he is sold to death, and the
devil shall not ransom him. Sir, I beseech you, your privacy.

SORANZO

No conquest can gain glory of my fear.

                                          Exeunt

238   Prose ed. (Troth . . . it, / But . . . *Lady* Q).   *hit it* correctly identified the reason.
240–1   *liberality* generosity in tipping.
242   *made a man* a man who has been entirely successful (in seventeenth-century idiom,
        'a made man'; a misprint is not impossible).
242–3   *plied . . . success* played my part effectively. The metaphor is of an actor giving cue-
        lines that prompt his fellow-performers to speak (here, to utter the incriminating
        information that Vasques wants to know).
245   *fast* secure; referring to Putana, whom Vasques has just silenced and imprisoned.
245–6   prose ed. (Let . . . enough, / How . . . Lady ? Q).
248   *Runs circular* Moves without getting anywhere (like an animal tied to a stake).
250   *know* be told.
251   *openly* publicly.
254   No matter what success ('conquest') Vasques has achieved, it will be unable to
        overcome ('gain glory of') Soranzo's fear.
        s.d. ed. (*Exit.* Q).

ACT V[, SCENE i]

Enter ANNABELLA *above,*
[*with a letter written in blood*]

ANNABELLA

Pleasures farewell, and all ye thriftless minutes
Wherein false joys have spun a weary life;
To these my fortunes now I take my leave.
Thou precious Time, that swiftly ridest in post
Over the world to finish up the race   5
Of my last fate, here stay thy restless course
And bear to ages that are yet unborn
A wretched, woeful woman's tragedy.
My conscience now stands up against my lust
With depositions charactered in guilt,   10

Enter FRIAR [*below*]

And tells me I am lost. Now I confess,
Beauty that clothes the outside of the face
Is cursed if it be not clothed with grace.
Here like a turtle, mewed up in a cage

---

1   *thriftless* (spiritually) unprofitable.
4–8 Time's riding 'in post' refers partly to the speed with which events move towards
     the play's destructive climax. Some earlier tragic heroes, such as Marlowe's Doctor
     Faustus, wish for time to stop in order to avert their doom; Annabella, however,
     accepts its inevitability and simply wants Time, conceived as a 'post' (messenger), to
     stop and collect her story for delivery to future times.
9–10 Annabella imagines her conscience as her prosecutor in a trial, armed with depo-
     sitions (formal written testimony, accepted as evidence in court in the absence of a
     witness); the ink with which these documents are written ('charactered') is her own
     moral guilt, so they substantiate the case against her in their medium as well as their
     content. Given the concern with unconventional writing media (also the blood with
     which Annabella has written her letter; and see note on 'gall' to V.iii.75), 'guilt' may
     also pun on 'gilt', suggesting gold lettering, 'as of words deserving display' (Roper).
10   *depositions* ed. (dispositions Q).
     grace both moral virtue and the favour of God which enables it (compare note to
     IV.i.72).
14   *turtle* turtle-dove, an emblem of wedded constancy in English folklore because it
     took only a single mate in its lifetime. Thus Annabella is 'unmated' in her captivity,
     even though her husband has access to her, because her original partner, Giovanni,
     does not
     mewed up confined (sometimes in preparation for slaughter).

Unmated, I converse with air and walls,   15
And descant on my vile unhappiness.
O Giovanni, that hast had the spoil
Of thine own virtues and my modest fame,
Would thou hadst been less subject to those stars
That luckless reigned at my nativity!   20
O, would the scourge due to my black offence
Might pass from thee, that I alone might feel
The torment of an uncontrolled flame!

FRIAR [*Aside*]
What's this I hear?

ANNABELLA   That man, that blessed friar,
Who joined in ceremonial knot my hand   25
To him whose wife I now am, told me oft
I trod the path to death, and showed me how.
But they who sleep in lethargies of lust
Hug their confusion, making Heaven unjust,
And so did I.

FRIAR [*Aside*] Here's music to the soul!   30

ANNABELLA
Forgive me, my good genius, and this once
Be helpful to my ends: let some good man
Pass this way, to whose trust I may commit
This paper double-lined with tears and blood;
Which being granted, here I sadly vow   35
Repentance, and a leaving of that life
I long have died in.

FRIAR   Lady, Heaven hath heard you,
And hath by providence ordained that I

15   *Unmated* Without a mate.
      converse with keep company with (but also implying 'have sex with', here suggesting
      enforced celibacy).
16   *descant on* discourse at large about.
17   *had the spoil* (*a*) destroyed; (*b*) plundered.
23   *an uncontrolled flame* the fire of hell.
25   *ceremonial knot* bonds of matrimony.
29   *making . . . unjust* supposing that divine law is unjust (because arbitrarily restrictive).
31   *genius* guardian angel; see note to II.ii.152.
32   *ends* purposes.
34   *double-lined . . . blood* The paper is written ('lined', i.e. with lines of script) in her
      blood, but her penitent tears have also dropped on to the page, making it 'double-
      lined'.
35   *sadly* solemnly, seriously.
37   *died* died spiritually.

Should be his minister for your behoof.

ANNABELLA

Ha, what are you?

FRIAR   Your brother's friend the friar,   40
Glad in my soul that I have lived to hear
This free confession 'twixt your peace and you.
What would you, or to whom? Fear not to speak.

ANNABELLA

Is Heaven so bountiful? Then I have found
More favour than I hoped. Here, holy man.   45

                    Throws [down the] letter

Commend me to my brother, give him that,
That letter; bid him read it and repent.
Tell him that I – imprisoned in my chamber,
Barred of all company, even of my guardian,
Who gives me cause of much suspect – have time   50
To blush at what hath passed. Bid him be wise,
And not believe the friendship of my lord.
I fear much more than I can speak. Good father,
The place is dangerous, and spies are busy:
I must break off. You'll do't?

FRIAR   Be sure I will,   55
And fly with speed. My blessing ever rest
With thee, my daughter. Live to die more blessed.   *Exit*

ANNABELLA

Thanks to the heavens, who have prolonged my breath
To this good use. Now I can welcome death.   *Exit*

---

39   *behoof* benefit, advantage.
42   *peace* quiet (here implying privacy).
49   *my guardian* Putana.
50   *Who* The absence of whom.
       suspect suspicion, anxiety.
52   *not believe* mistrust.

[ACT V, SCENE ii]

Enter SORANZO *and* VASQUES

VASQUES

Am I to be believed now? First, marry a strumpet that cast
herself away upon you but to laugh at your horns? To feast on
your disgrace, riot in your vexations, cuckold you in your bride-
bed, waste your estate upon panders and bawds?

SORANZO

No more, I say no more!   5

VASQUES

A cuckold is a goodly tame beast, my lord.

SORANZO

I am resolved; urge not another word.
My thoughts are great, and all as resolute
As thunder. In meantime I'll cause our lady
To deck herself in all her bridal robes,   10
Kiss her, and fold her gently in my arms.
Begone. Yet hear you, are the banditti ready
To wait in ambush?

VASQUES

Good sir, trouble not yourself about other business than your
own resolution: remember that time lost cannot be recalled.   15

SORANZO

With all the cunning words thou canst, invite
The states of Parma to my birthday's feast.
Haste to my brother-rival and his father,
Entreat them gently, bid them not to fail.
Be speedy and return.   20

---

1   *Am . . . now?* prose ed. (printed on a separate line in Q).
2   *but* only.
     horns Said to grow on cuckolds' foreheads.
3   *riot in* revel in, derive disorderly pleasure from.
8   *great* pregnant; the metaphor was commonly used of someone hatching a revenge
     plot (compare *Othello*, I.iii.395–6).
10 *deck* clothe.
15 *time . . . recalled* Proverbial (Tilley, T. 332).
17 *states* senior government figures, dignitaries.

VASQUES

Let not your pity betray you till my coming back: think upon
incest and cuckoldry.

SORANZO

Revenge is all the ambition I aspire;
To that I'll climb or fall. My blood's on fire!

Exeunt

[ACT V, SCENE iii]

Enter GIOVANNI

GIOVANNI

Busy opinion is an idle fool,
That, as a school-rod keeps a child in awe,
Frights the unexperienced temper of the mind.
So did it me, who, ere my precious sister
Was married, thought all taste of love would die   5
In such a contract; but I find no change
Of pleasure in this formal law of sports.
She is still one to me, and every kiss
As sweet and as delicious as the first
I reaped when yet the privilege of youth
Entitled her a virgin. O, the glory   10
Of two united hearts like hers and mine!
Let poring bookmen dream of other worlds:

21–2   prose ed. (Let . . . backe, / Thinke . . . *Cuckoldry* Q).
  23   *aspire* wish for.

1–3   Giovanni's point is that what common consensus ('opinion') teaches people to
      believe and expect is contradicted by actual experience.
  1   *Busy* Meddlesome, interfering
      idle ineffectual.
  2   *school-rod* a bundle of birch-twigs used as an instrument of corporal punishment,
      but more commonly displayed as a threat, 'For terror, not to use' (Shakespeare,
      Measure for Measure, I.iii.26).
  7   *in . . . sports* as a result of the legalization (by marriage) of Annabella's sexual activity.
  8   *one* the same as she was.
10–11 *when . . . virgin* when she was still a virgin. The point is expressed in quasi-legal
      terms, with 'virgin' a title bestowed on Annabella ('Entitled') by legal right or
      prerogative ('privilege').
  13 *bookmen* scholars.

My world and all of happiness is here,
And I'd not change it for the best to come.   15
A life of pleasure is Elysium.

Enter FRIAR

Father, you enter on the jubilee
Of my retired delights. Now I can tell you,
The hell you oft have prompted is nought else
But slavish and fond superstitious fear,   20
And I could prove it, too –
FRIAR   Thy blindness slays thee.

Gives the letter

Look there, 'tis writ to thee.
GIOVANNI
From whom?
FRIAR
Unrip the seals and see.

[GIOVANNI *opens and reads the letter*]
The blood's yet seething hot, that will anon   25
Be frozen harder than congealèd coral.
Why d'ee change colour, son?
GIOVANNI   'Fore heaven, you make
Some petty devil factor 'twixt my love
And your religion-masked sorceries.
Where had you this?
FRIAR   Thy conscience, youth, is seared,   30
Else thou wouldst stoop to warning.
GIOVANNI   'Tis her hand,
I know't, and 'tis all written in her blood.
She writes I know not what. Death? I'll not fear

17   *jubilee* time of celebration.
18   *retired* private.
19   *prompted* spoken of.
21   *I could prove it* The choice of words ('could' rather than 'can') is interesting, perhaps
     suggesting that he cannot be bothered.
25–6 These lines may be spoken as an aside while Giovanni reads.
26   *congealèd coral* ed. (congeal'd Corrall Q). Coral was thought to be an undersea plant
     which hardened when exposed to the air.
28   *factor* intermediary (in carrying the letter from Annabella, Giovanni's 'love'); Ford
     uses the word similarly in *The Broken Heart*, II.i.10.
30   *seared* cauterized (and so rendered insensible).
31   *stoop to warning* restrain your own impulses in heeding and obeying the warning
     you have been given.

An armèd thunderbolt aimed at my heart.
She writes we are discovered. Pox on dreams   35
Of low faint-hearted cowardice! Discovered?
The devil we are! Which way is't possible?
Are we grown traitors to our own delights?
Confusion take such dotage; 'tis but forged!
This is your peevish chattering, weak old man.   40

Enter VASQUES

Now, sir, what news bring you?

VASQUES

My lord, according to his yearly custom keeping this day a feast
in honour of his birthday, by me invites you thither. Your
worthy father, with the Pope's reverend Nuncio and other mag-
nificoes of Parma, have promised their presence. Will't please   45
you to be of the number?

GIOVANNI

Yes, tell them I dare come.

VASQUES

Dare come?

GIOVANNI

So I said; and tell him more, I will come.

VASQUES

These words are strange to me.   50

GIOVANNI

Say I will come.

VASQUES

You will not miss?

GIOVANNI

Yet more? I'll come! Sir, are you answered?

VASQUES

So I'll say. My service to you.   *Exit*

FRIAR

You will not go, I trust.

GIOVANNI   Not go! For what?   55

---

38 Giovanni assumes that he and Annabella are the only ones who know, forgetting
Putana (and also the Friar).

39 *dotage* nonsense (literally, senile ramblings).

40 s.d. ed. (after line 41 in Q).

52 *miss* fail to come.

FRIAR

    O do not go! This feast, I'll gage my life,
    Is but a plot to train you to your ruin.
    Be ruled, you sha' not go.

GIOVANNI   Not go? Stood Death

    Threat'ning his armies of confounding plagues,
    With hosts of dangers hot as blazing stars,   60
    I would be there. Not go! Yes, and resolve
    To strike as deep in slaughter as they all,
    For I will go.

FRIAR   Go where thou wilt; I see

    The wildness of thy fate draws to an end,
    To a bad, fearful end. I must not stay   65
    To know thy fall: back to Bologna I
    With speed will haste, and shun this coming blow.
    Parma, farewell; would I had never known thee,
    Or aught of thine! Well, young man, since no prayer
    Can make thee safe, I leave thee to despair.   *Exit*   70

GIOVANNI

    Despair or tortures of a thousand hells,
    All's one to me: I have set up my rest.
    Now, now, work serious thoughts on baneful plots:
    Be all a man, my soul; let not the curse
    Of old prescription rend from me the gall   75
    Of courage, which enrols a glorious death.
    If I must totter like a well-grown oak,
    Some under-shrubs shall in my weighty fall
    Be crushed to splits; with me they all shall perish.   *Exit*

56   *gage* stake, wager.
57   *train* allure, entice.
60   *blazing stars* comets, thought to be a portent of death.
69   *aught of thine* i.e Giovanni   *young man* ed. (*Youngman* Q).
71   s.p. GIOVANNI ed. (missing in Q).
72   *set . . . rest* committed myself to my final venture, staked my all. In the card game primero, the 'rest' was a stake held in reserve; to 'set up' your rest was to make a final wager which, if lost, would put you out of the game.
73   *baneful* destructive.
75   *prescription* prescribed social behaviour (such as not murdering people at parties)
     gall The primary sense is 'aggression', from the bodily fluid which supposedly induced this; but Giovanni imagines it in terms of an organ (the gall-bladder) being ripped out of his body. 'Gall' also referred to a secretion from the oak tree (compare line 77) that was used in making ink (hence the next line's suggestion of its 'enrolling' his death, writing it down in the roll of honour).
79   *splits* splinters.

[ACT V, SCENE iv]

Enter SORANZO, VASQUES *and* BANDITTI

SORANZO

You will not fail, or shrink in the attempt?

VASQUES

I will undertake for their parts. [*To the* BANDITTI] Be sure, my
masters, to be bloody enough, and as unmerciful as if you were
preying upon a rich booty on the very mountains of Liguria.
For your pardons, trust to my lord; but for reward you shall   5
trust none but your own pockets.

ALL THE BANDITTI

We'll make a murder.

SORANZO [*Giving them money*]

Here's gold, here's more; want nothing. What you do
Is noble and an act of brave revenge.
I'll make ye rich banditti, and all free.   10

ALL [THE BANDITTI]

Liberty! Liberty!

VASQUES

Hold, take every man a vizard. When ye are withdrawn, keep as
much silence as you can possibly. You know the watchword, till
which be spoken, move not; but when you hear that, rush in like
a stormy flood. I need not instruct ye in your own profession.   15

ALL [THE BANDITTI]

No, no, no.

VASQUES

In, then. Your ends are profit and preferment. Away!

Exeunt BANDITTI

---

   2   *undertake . . . parts* guarantee that they will play their parts efficiently.
   4   *Liguria* a mountainous region of north-western Italy between Parma and Genoa.
5–10   *pardons . . . free* Banditti were thought often to be banished men (like the outlaws in
       The Two Gentlemen of Verona) who would welcome the opportunity to return to
       civil society as free men if a pardon were offered them.
   8   *want* lack.
 8–9   lineation ed. (prose in Q).
  12   *vizard* mask.
  17   *ends* purposes.
       s.d. *Exeunt* ed. (*Exit* Q).

SORANZO

The guests will all come, Vasques?

VASQUES

Yes, sir, and now let me a little edge your resolution. You see
nothing is unready to this great work but a great mind in you.　20
Call to your remembrance your disgraces, your loss of honour,
Hippolita's blood, and arm your courage in your own wrongs:
so shall you best right those wrongs in vengeance which you
may truly call your own.

SORANZO

'Tis well: the less I speak, the more I burn,　25
And blood shall quench that flame.

VASQUES

Now you begin to turn Italian! This beside, when my young
incest-monger comes, he will be sharp set on his old bit. Give
him time enough; let him have your chamber and bed at liberty;
let my hot hare have law ere he be hunted to his death, that if it　30
be possible he may post to hell in the very act of his damnation.

Enter GIOVANNI

SORANZO

It shall be so; and see, as we would wish,
He comes himself first.
[*To* GIOVANNI]　　Welcome, my much-loved brother.
Now I perceive you honour me; you're welcome.
But where's my father?

GIOVANNI　　　　　　With the other states,　35
Attending on the Nuncio of the Pope
To wait upon him hither. How's my sister?

SORANZO

Like a good housewife, scarcely ready yet;

19　*Yes, sir* prose ed. (printed on a separate line in Q)
　　edge sharpen (like a sword); compare.
27　*you . . . Italian* In becoming more vindictive, Soranzo is living up to his nationality:
　　among the perceived national characteristics of the Italians was vengefulness.
28　*sharp . . . old bit* keen for sex with his former paramour.
30　*hare* supposed to have an excessive sexual appetite *law* a head-start.
31　*post* ride swiftly.
　　in . . . damnation If killed while committing a mortal sin, without time to repent,
　　Giovanni will go directly to hell.
35　*father* father-in-law (= Florio).
38　*good* typical – here meaning one who is idle and wastes time; a relevant secondary
　　sense of 'housewife', in Soranzo's mouth though not in Giovanni's ears, is 'hussy',
　　promiscuous woman.

377

You're best walk to her chamber.

GIOVANNI   If you will.

SORANZO

I must expect my honourable friends.   40

Good brother, get her forth.

GIOVANNI   You are busy, sir.   *Exit*

VASQUES

Even as the great devil himself would have it! Let him go and
glut himself in his own destruction.   *Flourish*

Hark, the Nuncio is at hand. Good sir, be ready to receive him.

Enter CARDINAL, FLORIO, DONADO, RICHARDETTO
[*disguised as the Doctor*], *and Attendants*

SORANZO [*To the* CARDINAL]

Most reverend lord, this grace hath made me proud   45

That you vouchsafe my house; I ever rest

Your humble servant for this noble favour.

CARDINAL

You are our friend, my lord. His Holiness

Shall understand how zealously you honour

Saint Peter's vicar in his substitute: 50

Our special love to you.

SORANZO   Signors, to you

My welcome, and my ever best of thanks

For this so memorable courtesy.

Pleaseth your grace to walk near?

CARDINAL   My lord, we come

To celebrate your feast with civil mirth,   55

As ancient custom teacheth. We will go.

SORANZO

Attend his grace, there! Signors, keep your way.

Exeunt

---

40   *expect* await.
43   s.d. *Flourish* A fanfare of trumpets played upon the arrival of an important
      personage (here, the Cardinal).
45   *this grace* the honour the Cardinal does Soranzo in visiting his feast.
46   *vouchsafe* deign to visit.
50   *Saint Peter's vicar* the Pope (St Peter was thought to be the first Pope; his successors
      were thus considered his 'vicars', substitute representatives).
57   *keep your way* carry on in the direction you're going.

[ACT V, SCENE v]

Enter GIOVANNI *and* ANNABELLA *lying on a bed*

GIOVANNI

What, changed so soon? Hath your new sprightly lord
Found out a trick in night-games more than we
Could know in our simplicity? Ha, is't so?
Or does the fit come on you to prove treacherous
To your past vows and oaths?

ANNABELLA   Why should you jest   5
At my calamity, without all sense
Of the approaching dangers you are in?

GIOVANNI

What danger's half so great as thy revolt?
Thou art a faithless sister, else thou know'st
Malice, or any treachery beside,   10
Would stoop to my bent brows. Why, I hold fate
Clasped in my fist, and could command the course
Of time's eternal motion hadst thou been
One thought more steady than an ebbing sea.
And what? You'll now be honest, that's resolved?   15

ANNABELLA

Brother, dear brother, know what I have been,
And know that now there's but a dining-time
'Twixt us and our confusion. Let's not waste
These precious hours in vain and useless speech.

---

 0   s.d. In the original production, the bed would probably have been pushed out on to
     the stage through the discovery space with Annabella (and perhaps Giovanni)
     already on it. In view of Soranzo's comment that she is 'scarcely ready yet' (V.iv.38),
     it is possible that Annabella is not yet fully dressed. If she is (as her reference to 'gay
     attires' at line 20 suggests), then she is wearing the 'bridal robes' which Soranzo
     mentioned earlier (V.ii.10).
 1   *changed* Referring to her disposition, not her clothes.
1–3 *Hath . . . simplicity?* Giovanni wants to know if Soranzo's love-making is more
     exciting than his own.
 4   *the fit* a capricious impulse.
 6   *calamity* distress.
 8   *revolt* disloyalty.
11   *stoop . . . brows* submit on seeing me frown.
18   *confusion* destruction.

Alas, these gay attires were not put on   20
But to some end; this sudden solemn feast
Was not ordained to riot in expense:
I that have now been chambered here alone,
Barred of my guardian, or of any else,
Am not for nothing at an instant freed   25
To fresh access. Be not deceived, my brother:
This banquet is an harbinger of death
To you and me; resolve yourself it is,
And be prepared to welcome it.
GIOVANNI   Well then,
The schoolmen teach that all this globe of earth   30
Shall be consumed to ashes in a minute.
ANNABELLA
So I have read too.
GIOVANNI   But 'twere somewhat strange
To see the waters burn. Could I believe
This might be true, I could believe as well
There might be hell or heaven.
ANNABELLA   That's most certain.   35
GIOVANNI
A dream, a dream; else in this other world
We should know one another.
ANNABELLA   So we shall.
GIOVANNI
Have you heard so?

---

21   *solemn* (*a*) ceremonious; (*b*) lavish.
22   *riot in expense* waste money.
25–6 *freed . . . access* allowed visitors again after her imprisonment.
30–3 The belief that the world would end in a conflagration of purging fire was as old as
      the Stoic philosophers of ancient Greece, but its principal biblical authority was
      Revelation 21.1: 'And I saw a new heaven and a new earth; for the first heaven and
      the first earth were passed away; and there was no more sea'; see also 2 Peter 3.10.
      Scholastic philosophers (known as 'schoolmen') attempted to rationalize this notion:
      the classic statement is that of Thomas Aquinas in *Summa Theologica* 3. 74. Giovanni
      astutely locates one of the holes in the case which had previously puzzled St
      Augustine (*City of God* 20.16): whereas the Stoics had taught that the seas would
      gradually dry up in the heat, the idea of a destruction that is instantaneous and
      absolute ('all this globe . . . consumed to ashes in a minute') entails believing that
      water will burn.
37–41 lineation ed. (Wee . . . another. / So . . . shall. / Haue . . . so? / For certaine. / But . . .
      thinke, / That . . . there, / You . . . mee. / May . . . another, / Prate . . . laugh, / Or . . .
      here? / I . . . that Q).

ANNABELLA   For certain.
GIOVANNI   But d'ee think
 That I shall see you there, you look on me;
 May we kiss one another, prate or laugh,   40
 Or do as we do here?
ANNABELLA   I know not that,
 But, good, for the present, what d'ee mean
 To free yourself from danger? Some way think
 How to escape. I'm sure the guests are come.
GIOVANNI
 Look up, look here: what see you in my face?   45
ANNABELLA
 Distraction and a troubled countenance.
GIOVANNI
 Death, and a swift repining wrath. Yet look:
 What see you in mine eyes?
ANNABELLA   Methinks you weep.
GIOVANNI
 I do indeed: these are the funeral tears
 Shed on your grave; these furrowed up my cheeks   50
 When first I loved and knew not how to woo.
 Fair Annabella, should I here repeat
 The story of my life, we might lose time.
 Be record all the spirits of the air,
 And all things else that are, that day and night,   55
 Early and late, the tribute which my heart
 Hath paid to Annabella's sacred love
 Hath been these tears, which are her mourners now.
 Never till now did Nature do her best
 To show a matchless beauty to the world,   60
 Which in an instant, ere it scarce was seen,
 The jealous Destinies required again.
 Pray, Annabella, pray. Since we must part,
 Go thou white in thy soul to fill a throne

40   *prate* talk casually.
42   *good* A vocative term of address (like the modern 'dear'), often used by Ford.
     mean intend to do.
47   *repining* angrily discontented.
54   *spirits of the air* In hermetic philosophy 'middle spirits', neither angels nor devils,
     whose bodies were made of air; they could hear human speech but not read
     thoughts.
62   *required again* demanded the return of (in death).

Of innocence and sanctity in heaven. 65
Pray, pray, my sister.

ANNABELLA   Then I see your drift.
Ye blessed angels, guard me!

GIOVANNI   So say I.
Kiss me. [*They kiss*] If ever after-times should hear
Of our fast-knit affections, though perhaps
The laws of conscience and of civil use 70
May justly blame us, yet when they but know
Our loves, that love will wipe away that rigour
Which would in other incests be abhorred.
Give me your hand. How sweetly life doth run
In these well-coloured veins! How constantly 75
These palms do promise health! But I could chide
With Nature for this cunning flattery.
Kiss me again. Forgive me.

ANNABELLA   With my heart.   [*They kiss*]

GIOVANNI
Farewell.

ANNABELLA Will you be gone?

GIOVANNI   Be dark, bright sun,
And make this midday night, that thy gilt rays 80
May not behold a deed will turn their splendour
More sooty than the poets feign their Styx!
One other kiss, my sister.

ANNABELLA   What means this?

GIOVANNI
To save thy fame, and kill thee in a kiss.   *Stabs her*
Thus die, and die by me, and by my hand. 85
Revenge is mine; honour doth love command.

ANNABELLA
O brother, by your hand?

GIOVANNI   When thou art dead
I'll give my reasons for't; for to dispute

---

68   *after-times* future ages.
70   *civil use* the customary practice of civilization.
72   *rigour* passionate extremity.
77   *cunning flattery* It is flattering in that the apparent healthiness of her hand belies
      her imminent fate (i.e. death).
82   *Styx* Principal river of the classical underworld, with poisonous black waters.
84   *fame* reputation.

With thy (even in thy death) most lovely beauty,
Would make me stagger to perform this act   90
Which I most glory in.

ANNABELLA

Forgive him, Heaven – and me my sins. Farewell,
Brother, unkind, unkind. – Mercy, great Heaven!
– O – O!   *Dies*

GIOVANNI

She's dead. Alas, good soul. The hapless fruit   95
That in her womb received its life from me,
Hath had from me a cradle and a grave.
I must not dally. This sad marriage-bed,
In all her best, bore her alive and dead.
Soranzo, thou hast missed thy aim in this: 100
I have prevented now thy reaching plots
And killed a love, for whose each drop of blood
I would have pawned my heart. Fair Annabella,
How over-glorious art thou in thy wounds,
Triumphing over infamy and hate!   105
Shrink not, courageous hand; stand up, my heart,
And boldly act my last and greater part!

Exit with the body

[ACT V, SCENE vi]

A banquet [is set out]. Enter CARDINAL, FLORIO, DONADO,
SORANZO, RICHARDETTO [*disguised as the Doctor*],
VASQUES, *and Attendants; they take their places [at the table]*

VASQUES [*Aside to* SORANZO]

Remember sir, what you have to do: be wise and resolute.

90   *stagger* hesitate.
93   *unkind* (*a*) cruel; (*b*) unnatural (literally, unlike the behaviour expected of a kinsman).
95   *hapless* unfortunate, luckless.
101   *prevented* forestalled.
      reaching subtle and cunning.
104   *over-glorious* superlatively beautiful.

·

  0   s.d. *take their places* sit at the table.

SORANZO [*Aside to* VASQUES]
　　Enough, my heart is fixed.
　　[*To* CARDINAL]　　　　　Pleaseth your grace
　　To taste these coarse confections? Though the use
　　Of such set entertainments more consists
　　In custom than in cause, yet, reverend sir,　　　　　　　　5
　　I am still made your servant by your presence.
CARDINAL
　　And we your friend.
SORANZO
　　But where's my brother Giovanni?

Enter GIOVANNI *with a heart upon his dagger*

GIOVANNI
　　Here, here, Soranzo, trimmed in reeking blood
　　That triumphs over death, proud in the spoil　　　　　　10
　　Of love and vengeance! Fate, or all the powers
　　That guide the motions of immortal souls
　　Could not prevent me.
CARDINAL　　　　　　　　What means this?
FLORIO
　　Son Giovanni!
SORANZO [*Aside*] Shall I be forestalled?
GIOVANNI
　　Be not amazed: if your misgiving hearts　　　　　　　　15
　　Shrink at an idle sight, what bloodless fear
　　Of coward passion would have seized your senses,
　　Had you beheld the rape of life and beauty
　　Which I have acted? My sister, O my sister!
FLORIO
　　Ha! What of her?
GIOVANNI　　　　　The glory of my deed　　　　　　　　20
　　Darkened the midday sun, made noon as night.
　　You came to feast, my lords, with dainty fare.
　　I came to feast too, but I digged for food
　　In a much richer mine than gold or stone

3-5　*the use ... cause* formal entertainments like this are held more because of the inertia
　　of custom than for any good reason.
9　*trimmed* covered (literally, decorated). *reeking* steaming.
16　*idle* mere.
18　*rape* violent theft.
24　*stone* precious stones, jewels.

Of any value balanced. 'Tis a heart,   25
A heart, my lords, in which is mine entombed.
Look well upon't; d'ee know't?
VASQUES
What strange riddle's this?
GIOVANNI
'Tis Annabella's heart, 'tis. Why d'ee startle?
I vow 'tis hers: this dagger's point ploughed up   30
Her fruitful womb, and left to me the fame
Of a most glorious executioner.
FLORIO
Why, madman, art thyself?
GIOVANNI
Yes father, and, that times to come may know
How as my fate I honoured my revenge,   35
List, father: to your ears I will yield up
How much I have deserved to be your son.
FLORIO
What is't thou say'st?
GIOVANNI   Nine moons have had their changes,
Since I first throughly viewed and truly loved
Your daughter and my sister.
FLORIO   How! Alas,   40
My lords, he's a frantic madman!
GIOVANNI   Father, no.
For nine months' space in secret I enjoyed
Sweet Annabella's sheets; nine months I lived
A happy monarch of her heart and her.
Soranzo, thou know'st this: thy paler cheek   45
Bears the confounding print of thy disgrace,
For her too fruitful womb too soon bewrayed
The happy passage of our stol'n delights,
And made her mother to a child unborn.

25   *balanced* calculated .
39   *throughly* thoroughly.
40–1 *How . . . madman* lineation ed. (one line in Q).
45   *paler cheek* It is not clear whether he means paler than his own (which is covered in
     blood) or Florio's (which may be blushing in shame at Giovanni's revelations).
47   *bewrayed* revealed.
48   *passage* The word implies both a sequence of events and a mutual interchange of
     amorous experience between lovers; Ford was probably recalling Shakespeare's
     Prologue to *Romeo and Juliet* ('The fearful passage of their death-marked love').

CARDINAL
   Incestuous villain!
FLORIO   O, his rage belies him!   50
GIOVANNI
   It does not, 'tis the oracle of truth:
   I vow it is so.
SORANZO   I shall burst with fury.
   Bring the strumpet forth!
VASQUES
   I shall, sir.   *Exit*
GIOVANNI   Do, sir. Have you all no faith
   To credit yet my triumphs? Here I swear   55
   By all that you call sacred, by the love
   I bore my Annabella whilst she lived,
   These hands have from her bosom ripped this heart.

Enter VASQUES

   Is't true or no, sir?
VASQUES   'Tis most strangely true.
FLORIO
   Cursed man! Have I lived to –   *Dies*
CARDINAL   Hold Up, Florio.   60
   [*To* GIOVANNI] Monster of children, see what thou hast done,
   Broke thy old father's heart! Is none of you
   Dares venture on him?
GIOVANNI   Let 'em! O, my father,
   How well his death becomes him in his griefs!
   Why, this was done with courage; now survives   65
   None of our house but I, gilt in the blood
   Of a fair sister and a hapless father.

---

50   *rage* frenzy.
58   s.d. ed. (after line 60a in Q).
60   *Hold up, Florio* The words are ambiguous, their sense depending on whether the
      Cardinal already recognizes that Florio is dead. As here punctuated, the Cardinal
      offers encouragement to Florio in the belief that he is still alive; dramatic irony thus
      cuts against the Cardinal, making him yet another character wrong-footed by
      Giovanni's actions in this and the previous scene. Without the comma, the Cardinal
      would be ordering attendants to show Giovanni the dead body (hence 'see what
      thou hast done' in the next line).
66   *gilt* covered; but in performance, assonance may also convey the implication of
      blood-guilt.
67   *hapless* unlucky, ill-fated.

SORANZO
Inhuman scorn of men, hast thou a thought
T' outlive thy murders?
GIOVANNI   Yes, I tell thee yes;
For in my fists I bear the twists of life.   70
Soranzo, see this heart which was thy wife's:
Thus I exchange it royally for thine,   [*Stabs him*]
And thus, and thus. Now brave revenge is mine.
VASQUES
I cannot hold any longer. You sir, are you grown insolent in
your butcheries? Have at you!   75
                    [VASQUES *and* GIOVANNI] *fight*
GIOVANNI
Come, I am armed to meet thee.
VASQUES
No, will it not be yet? If this will not, another shall. – Not yet? I
shall fit you anon. – [*Calls offstage*] Vengeance!

          Enter BANDITTI [*all masked and armed*]

GIOVANNI
Welcome! Come more of you, whate'er you be,
I dare your worst. –   80
            [*The* BANDITTI *surround and wound him*]
O, I can stand no longer; feeble arms,
Have you so soon lost strength?
VASQUES
Now you are welcome, sir! Away, my masters, all is done. Shift
for yourselves; your reward is your own; shift for yourselves.

70   *twists* woven threads. Giovanni alludes to the thread representing a human life which
     was spun, woven, and cut by the Fates of classical mythology, whom he earlier
     claimed to rule (III.ii.20).
72   s.d. In order to be able to use his dagger on Soranzo, Giovanni must by this point
     have removed the heart from it; it was probably still on the dagger (or else held in
     his other hand) moments before when he referred to it as 'this heart' (71). The
     question of when to remove it and what to do with it is open to any number of
     inventive solutions in performance. (In the 1991–2 RSC production, for example,
     Giovanni physically placed the organ in Soranzo's hands before stabbing him,
     making the exchange of one heart for another a semi-literal one; in Griffi's film
     version he uses Soranzo's own dagger.) Alternatively, Giovanni may have more than
     one weapon (e.g. rapier as well as dagger), and uses the other on Soranzo here.
77   *will . . . yet?* Giovanni is taking a long time to die.
78   *fit you* deal with you.
     Vengeance The watchword to call in the banditti (see V.iv.13–14).
83–4 prose ed. (Now . . . Sir, / Away . . . done, / Shift . . . owne, / Shift . . . selues Q).
84   *Shift for yourselves* Every man for himself.

387

BANDITTI

    Away, away!   *Exeunt* BANDITTI   85

VASQUES

    How d'ee, my lord? See you this? How is't?

SORANZO

    Dead, but in death well pleased, that I have lived

    To see my wrongs revenged on that black devil.

    O Vasques, to thy bosom let me give

    My last of breath: let not that lecher live – O!   *Dies*   90

VASQUES

    The reward of peace and rest be with him, my ever dearest lord

    and master.

GIOVANNI

    Whose hand gave me this wound?

VASQUES

    Mine, sir, I was your first man. Have you enough?

GIOVANNI

    I thank thee: thou hast done for me   95

    But what I would have else done on myself.

    Art sure thy lord is dead?

VASQUES   O impudent slave,

    As sure as I am sure to see thee die.

CARDINAL

    Think on thy life and end, and call for mercy.

GIOVANNI

    Mercy? Why, I have found it in this justice.   100

CARDINAL

    Strive yet to cry to heaven.

GIOVANNI   O, I bleed fast.

    Death, thou art a guest long looked-for: I embrace

    Thee and thy wounds. O, my last minute comes.

    Where'er I go, let me enjoy this grace,

    Freely to view my Annabella's face.   *Dies*   105

DONADO

    Strange miracle of justice!

CARDINAL

    Raise up the city! We shall be murdered all!

89–90   *give . . . breath* i.e. in a dying instruction.
91–2   prose ed. (The . . . him, / My . . . Maister Q).
95–8   lineation ed. (prose in Q).
  98   *thee* ed. (the Q).

VASQUES

    You need not fear, you shall not. This strange task being ended,
    I have paid the duty to the son which I have vowed to the father.

CARDINAL

    Speak, wretched villain, what incarnate fiend   110
    Hath led thee on to this?

VASQUES

    Honesty, and pity of my master's wrongs. For know, my lord, I
    am by birth a Spaniard, brought forth my country in my youth
    by Lord Soranzo's father, whom, whilst he lived I served faith-
    fully; since whose death I have been to this man, as I was to   115
    him. What I have done was duty, and I repent nothing but that
    the loss of my life had not ransomed his.

CARDINAL

    Say, fellow, know'st thou any yet unnamed
    Of counsel in this incest?

VASQUES

    Yes, an old woman, sometimes guardian to this murdered lady.   120

CARDINAL

    And what's become of her?

VASQUES

    Within this room she is, whose eyes after her confession I caused
    to be put out, but kept alive, to confirm what from Giovanni's
    own mouth you have heard. Now, my lord, what I have done
    you may judge of, and let your own wisdom be a judge in your   125
    own reason.

CARDINAL

    Peace! First, this woman, chief in these effects,
    My sentence is that forthwith she be ta'en
    Out of the city, for example's sake,
    There to be burnt to ashes.

DONADO   'Tis most just.   130

---

115   *this man* Soranzo.
119   *Of counsel* Complicit.
120   *sometimes* formerly.
127   *this woman* It is unclear whether this means Putana or the dead Annabella, who is
      more obviously 'chief [i.e. principal] in these effects'. Either way, the Cardinal focuses
      the primary blame on a character who has been disempowered either by gender or
      rank: Annabella's body is given an admonitory cremation but Giovanni's is spared;
      or, alternatively, the servant Putana is made a scapegoat as the 'chief' criminal when
      she was really only an accomplice.

CARDINAL

Be it your charge, Donado, see it done.

DONADO

I shall.

VASQUES

What for me? If death, 'tis welcome. I have been honest to the
son as I was to the father.

CARDINAL

Fellow, for thee: since what thou didst was done   135
Not for thyself, being no Italian,
We banish thee for ever, to depart
Within three days; in this we do dispense
With grounds of reason, not of thine offence.

VASQUES

'Tis well: this conquest is mine, and I rejoice that a Spaniard   140
outwent an Italian in revenge.   *Exit*

CARDINAL

Take up these slaughtered bodies, see them buried;
And all the gold and jewels, or whatsoever,
Confiscate by the canons of the Church,
We seize upon to the Pope's proper use.   145

[RICHARDETTO *takes off his disguise*]

RICHARDETTO

Your grace's pardon: thus long I lived disguised
To see the effect of pride and lust at once
Brought both to shameful ends.

CARDINAL

What, Richardetto, whom we thought for dead?

DONADO

Sir, was it you –

RICHARDETTO   Your friend.

138–9   *dispense . . . offence* The Cardinal grants Vasques a legal dispensation (in commuting
the death penalty to banishment) in recognition of the nature of his motives
('reason'), but this does not diminish the gravity of the offence itself.

140–1   *I rejoice . . . revenge* Vasques takes it as a point of national pride that he has outdone
an Italian in a field where Italians were considered pre-eminent. It is unclear whether
the particular Italian he has in mind is Giovanni or Soranzo (who begins 'to turn
Italian' at V.iv.27); if the latter, then the previously devoted servant is showing a new
independence of mind now that his obligations to the Soranzo family are done.

143   *all the . . . jewels* Florio, Giovanni, and Soranzo have all died without heirs to inherit
their property.

145   *proper* personal.

CARDINAL   We shall have time   150
  To talk at large of all; but never yet
  Incest and murder have so strangely met.
  Of one so young, so rich in Nature's store,
  Who could not say, 'Tis pity she's a whore?

                              Exeunt [with the bodies]

                    FINIS

151   *at large* in full.
153   *Nature's store* The gifts of abundant Nature. The image was often used in connection
       with beautiful women; compare William Barksted and Lewis Machin, *The Insatiate
       Countess,* IV.ii.182: 'Thou abstract drawn from Nature's . . . storehouse'.

[PRINTER'S AFTERWORD]

The general commendation deserved by the actors in
their presentment of this tragedy may easily excuse
such few faults as are escaped in the printing: a common charity may allow him the ability of spelling,
whom a secure confidence assures that he cannot   5
ignorantly err in the application of sense.

2   *presentment* presentation on stage.
3   *faults . . . escaped* uncorrected misprints.
3–6 *a common . . . sense* if you accept that a person understands the meaning of the words
    he uses, it is only fair to assume that he knows how to spell them.

APPENDIX

List of Characters from the 1633 Quarto

THE SCENE

Parma

THE ACTORS' NAMES

Bonaventura,	A Friar
A Cardinal,	Nuncio to the Pope
Soranzo,	A Nobleman
Florio,	A Citizen of *Parma*
Donado,	Another Citizen
Grimaldi,	A Roman Gentleman
Giovanni,	Son to *Florio*
Bergetto,	Nephew to *Donado*
Richardetto,	A supposed Physician
Vasques,	Servant to *Soranzo*
Poggio,	Servant to *Bergetto*
Banditti	

Women

Annabella,	Daughter to *Florio*
Hippolita,	Wife to *Richardetto*
Philotis,	His Niece
Putana,	Tutoress to *Annabella*

This list is authorial: it shares its distinctive layout with similar lists in four other Ford Quartos (*The Broken Heart, Love's Sacrifice, Perkin Warbeck,* and *The Lady's Trial*) from various different printers and publishers. Ford tended to order his characters hierarchically, here with churchmen at the top and women at the bottom. Within this structure three factors determine the characters' precise positioning: social standing (so that Soranzo, an aristocrat, is above the gentlemen, who are in turn above the servants); age (so that Florio and Donado are above Giovanni); and moral worth (so that the Friar, though technically junior to the Cardinal, stands at the head). Richardetto's lowly place is especially intriguing.

THE
WHITE DIVEL,

OR,

The Tragedy of *Paulo Giordano
Urſini*, Duke of *Brachiano*,

With

The Life and Death of Vittoria
Corombona the famous
Venetian Curtizan.

Acted by the Queenes Maieſties Seruants.

Written by IOHN WEBSTER.

Non inferiora ſecutus.

LONDON,
Printed by *N.O.* for *Thomas Archer*, and are to be ſold
at his Shop in Popes head Pallace, neere the
Royall Exchange. 1612.

[DRAMATIS PERSONAE]

[MONTICELSO, a Cardinal; afterwards Pope PAUL IV

FRANCISCO DE' MEDICI, Duke of Florence; in the fifth act disguised
    for a Moor, under the name of MULINASSAR

BRACHIANO, otherwise PAULO GIORDANO URSINI, Duke of Brachiano;
    husband to Isabella and in love with Vittoria

GIOVANNI, his son, by Isabella

LODOVICO or LODOWICK, an Italian Count, but decayed

ANTONELLI and GASPARO, his friends, and dependants of the Duke of
    Florence

CAMILLO, husband to Vittoria

HORTENSIO, one of Brachiano's officers

MARCELLO, an attendant of the Duke of Florence, and brother to
    Vittoria

FLAMINEO, his brother; secretary to Brachiano

CARDINAL OF ARRAGON

DOCTOR JULIO, a conjuror

*CHRISTOPHERO, his assistant

*GUID-ANTONIO

*FERNESE

*JACQUES, a Moor, servant to Giovanni

ISABELLA, sister to Francisco de' Medici, and wife to Brachiano

VITTORIA COROMBONA, a Venetian Lady, first married to Camillo,
    afterwards to Brachiano

CORNELIA, mother to Vittoria, Flamineo and Marcello

ZANCHE, a Moor; servant to Vittoria

MATRON of the House of Convertites

CARLO

PEDRO

AMBASSADORS	CHANCELLOR
PHYSICIANS	REGISTER
COURTIERS	PAGE
LAWYERS	ARMOURER
OFFICERS	CONJUROR
ATTENDANTS	CONCLAVIST]

---

* non-speaking parts or 'ghost characters'

TO THE READER

In publishing this tragedy, I do but challenge to myself that liberty, which other men have ta'en before me; not that I affect praise by it, for, *nos haec novimus esse nihil,* only since it was acted, in so dull a time of winter, presented in so open and black a theatre, that it wanted (that which is the only grace and setting out of a tragedy) 5 a full and understanding auditory: and that since that time I have noted, most of the people that come to that play-house, resemble those ignorant asses (who visiting stationers' shops, their use is not to enquire for good books, but new books) I present it to the general view with this confidence: 10

> *Nec rhoncos metues, maligniorum,*
> *Nec scombris tunicas, dabis molestas.*

If it be objected this is no true dramatic poem, I shall easily confess it, – *non potes in nugas dicere plura meas: ipse ego quam dixi,* – willingly, and not ignorantly, in this kind have I faulted: for 15 should a man present to such an auditory, the most sententious tragedy that ever was written, observing all the critical laws, as height of style, and gravity of person; enrich it with the sententious *Chorus,* and as it were liften death, in the passionate and weighty

---

1   *challenge* claim
3   *nos . . . nihil* 'We know these things are nothing' (Martial XIII, 2); Webster probably borrowed this quotation and that at ll. 14–15 from Dekker's preface to *Satiromastix* (1602).
4   *open . . . theatre* The Red Bull, the playhouse in which *The White Devil* was first performed in February or March 1612, was unroofed and thus open to the weather, which may have been quite 'black', or overcast on the occasion.
6   *understanding auditory* i.e. an appreciative audience (possibly in contrast to those simply 'standing under' the stage, in the yard); like his contemporaries, Webster commends the ear, not the eye (cf. his character of 'An Excellent Actor': 'Sit in a full theatre, and you will think you see so many lines drawn from the circumference of so many ears, while the actor is the centre.')
11–12 *Nec . . . molestas* 'You [the poet's book] will not fear the sneers of the malicious, nor supply wrappers for mackerel' (Martial IV, 86).
14–15 *non . . . dixi* 'You cannot say more against my trifles than I have said myself' (Martial XIII, 2).
15   *willingly . . . faulted* Thus Webster aligns his play not with the compressive simplicity of classical theatre but with the episodic multiplicity of native English drama.
18   *sententious* full of maxims and *sententiae,* as in the tragedies of Seneca

Nuntius: yet after all this divine rapture, *O dura messorum ilia,* the   20
breath that comes from the uncapable multitude is able to poison
it, and ere it be acted, let the author resolve to fix to every scene,
this of Horace,

> *Haec hodie porcis comedenda relinques.*

To those who report I was a long time in finishing this tragedy, I   25
confess I do not write with a goose-quill, winged with two feathers, and if they will needs make it my fault, I must answer them
with that of Euripides to Alcestides, a tragic writer: Alcestides
objecting that Euripides had only in three days composed three
verses, whereas himself had written three hundred: 'Thou tell'st   30
truth', (quoth he), 'but here's the difference: thine shall only be
read for three days, whereas mine shall continue three ages'.

Detraction is the sworn friend to ignorance: for mine own part
I have ever truly cherished my good opinion of other men's worthy
labours, especially of that full and heightened style of Master   35
Chapman, the laboured and understanding works of Master
Jonson: the no less worthy composures of the both worthily excellent Master Beaumont, and Master Fletcher: and lastly (without
wrong last to be named) the right happy and copious industry of
Master Shakespeare, Master Dekker, and Master Heywood, wishing   40
what I write may be read by their light: protesting, that, in the
strength of mine own judgement, I know them so worthy, that
though I rest silent in my own work, yet to most of theirs I dare
(without flattery) fix that of Martial:

> *non norunt, haec monumenta mori.*   45

19–20 *lifen ... Nuntius* i.e. make death come alive in the report of the passionate and
serious messenger

20 *O ... ilia* 'O strong stomachs of harvesters' (Horace, *Epodes* III, 4; alluding to
peasants' love of garlic)

24 *Haec ... relinques* 'What you leave will go today to feed the pigs' (Horace, *Epistles* I,
vii, 19)

25–7 *I ... feathers* Webster published nothing between 1605 and 1612, when *The White
Devil* appeared; he may indeed have laboured over his first independent dramatic
effort.

28–32 In the original story (told by Valerius Maximus), the poet Alcestis writes a hundred
verses in three days; Webster probably borrowed his version from L. Lloyd, *Linceus
Spectacles* (1607).

36 *understanding* intellectual

45 *non ... mori* 'These monuments do not know death' (Martial X, ii, 12; comparing
literature with ruined tombs).

THE TRAGEDY OF PAULO
GIORDANO URSINI DUKE OF
BRACHIANO, AND VITTORIA
COROMBONA

[ACT I, SCENE i]

Enter Count LODOVICO, ANTONELLI *and* GASPARO

LODOVICO
  Banished?
ANTONELLI It grieved me much to hear the sentence.
LODOVICO
  Ha, ha, O Democritus, thy gods
  That govern the whole world: courtly reward,
  And punishment. Fortune's a right whore:
  If she give ought, she deals it in small parcels,   5
  That she may take away all at one swoop.
  This 'tis to have great enemies, God quite them.
  Your wolf no longer seems to be a wolf
  Than when she's hungry.
GASPARO   You term those enemies
  Are men of princely rank.
LODOVICO   O I pray for them.   10
  The violent thunder is adored by those
  Are pashed in pieces by it.

---

  0   s.d. The three men may enter and react together to a previous offstage sentence, or
       (probably more effective theatrically) Antonelli and Gasparo may enter to hand
       Lodovico his decree of banishment, visually re-enacting the confrontation between
       social forces and the anarchic individual. Not only does Webster choose to open
       and close the play with Lodovico, he also sets him up as an analogue to the desper-
       ate Brachiano of I.ii.
1–4   ed. (Banisht ... to / heare ... sentence / LODO ... Gods / That ... re- / ward ...
       whore Q – lineation altered to make room for ornamental first letter)
  2   *Democritus, thy gods* Webster is here borrowing from Guevara's *Diall of Princes*
       (trans. North 1557), which attributes to Pliny and Democritus the view that 'there
       were two gods, which governed the universal world: ... reward and punishment'.
  5   *parcels* portions
  6   *swoop* stroke
  7   *quite* requite
 12   *pashed* dashed

ANTONELLI   Come my lord,
  You are justly doomed; look but a little back
  Into your former life: you have in three years
  Ruined the noblest earldom—
GASPARO   Your followers   15
  Have swallowed you like mummia, and being sick
  With such unnatural and horrid physic
  Vomit you up i'th'kennel—
ANTONELLI   All the damnable degrees
  Of drinkings have you staggered through. One citizen
  Is lord of two fair manors, called you master   20
  Only for caviar.
GASPARO   Those noblemen
  Which were invited to your prodigal feasts,
  Wherein the phoenix scarce could scape your throats,
  Laugh at your misery, as fore-deeming you
  An idle meteor which, drawn forth the earth,   25
  Would be soon lost i'th'air.
ANTONELLI   Jest upon you
  And say you were begotten in an earthquake,
  You have ruined such fair lordships.
LODOVICO   Very good,
  This well goes with two buckets, I must tend
  The pouring out of either.
GASPARO   Worse than these,   30
  You have acted certain murders here in Rome,
  Bloody and full of horror.

  16 *mummia* a medicine made from dead flesh, difficult to swallow but thought to
       produce excellent results
  18 *kennel* gutter
  19 *you* (you, you Q)
  19–21 i.e. a citizen, though richer than you, was prepared to humble himself in order to
       get your gifts
  23 *phoenix* legendary bird and rare delicacy. Since only one phoenix lived at one time,
       the new bird rose from the ashes of the old.
  25 *idle* worthless
       meteor a luminous body seen temporarily in the sky and supposed to emerge from
       a lower region or corrupt source; an evil omen
  29–30 *This . . . either* Lodovico uses the image of two buckets alternately drawing from a
       common well to caricature the alternation of Antonelli's and Gasparo's attacks as
       mechanical and composed of mere proverbs. The image may be reinforced visually,
       with Antonelli and Gasparo on either side of Lodovico (NCW I.ii.29–30 n.).
  31 *acted* carried out

LODOVICO   'Las they were flea-bitings:
   Why took they not my head then?
GASPARO   O my lord
   The law doth sometimes mediate, thinks it good
   Not ever to steep violent sins in blood.   35
   This gentle penance may both end your crimes
   And in the example better these bad times.
LODOVICO
   So, but I wonder then some great men scape
   This banishment; there's Paulo Giordano Orsini,
   The Duke of Brachiano, now lives in Rome,   40
   And by close panderism seeks to prostitute
   The honour of Vittoria Corombona:
   Vittoria, she that might have got my pardon
   For one kiss to the Duke.
ANTONELLI   Have a full man within you.
   We see that trees bear no such pleasant fruit   45
   There where they grew first, as where they are new set.
   Perfumes, the more they are chafed, the more they render
   Their pleasing scents; and so affliction
   Expresseth virtue fully, whether true,
   Or else adulterate.
LODOVICO   Leave your painted comforts.   50
   I'll make Italian cut-works in their guts
   If ever I return.
GASPARO   O sir.
LODOVICO   I am patient.
   I have seen some ready to be executed
   Give pleasant looks, and money, and grown familiar
   With the knave hangman; so do I, I thank them,   55
   And would account them nobly merciful
   Would they dispatch me quickly.

36   *This gentle penance* i.e. banishment
41   *close* secret
44   *Have . . . you* i.e. be the complete and self-sufficient man
46   *they* ed. (the Q)
      new set transplanted
50   *painted* false, artificial
51   *Italian cut-works* openwork embroidery, an Italian fashion
55   *knave* menial servant; base rogue

ANTONELLI   Fare you well,
  We shall find time I doubt not to repeal
  Your banishment.   *Sennet* [*sounds*]
LODOVICO   I am ever bound to you:
  This is the world's alms; pray make use of it;   60
  Great men sell sheep, thus to be cut in pieces,
  When first they have shorn them bare and sold their fleeces.

                                                              Exeunt

[ACT I, SCENE ii]

Enter BRACHIANO, CAMILLO, FLAMINEO, VITTORIA
  COROMBONA [*and* ATTENDANTS *with torches*]

BRACHIANO
  Your best of rest.
VITTORIA   Unto my lord the Duke
  The best of welcome. More lights, attend the Duke.
                            [*Exeunt* VITTORIA *and* CAMILLO]

BRACHIANO
  Flamineo.
FLAMINEO   My lord.
BRACHIANO   Quite lost Flamineo.
FLAMINEO
  Pursue your noble wishes, I am prompt
  As lightning to your service, O my lord!   5
  (*Whispers*) The fair Vittoria, my happy sister
  Shall give you present audience. [*Aloud*] Gentlemen,

---

  59   s.d. *Sennet* ed. (Enter Senate Q) a set of notes sounded on the trumpet to announce
       a ceremonial entrance (that of Vittoria, Brachiano and attendants in the following
       scene). The trumpeters may have appeared on the stage.
  60   Previous editors have taken 'alms' to refer to the cynical adage that follows, but it is
       possible that Lodovico is giving Gasparo and Antonelli money to repeal his banish-
       ment, at the same time cynically referring to them as hangmen (l. 55).
       make use of it earn interest on it (NCW I.i.60 n.)

 0–9   Vittoria passes over the stage in a blaze of light (cf. III.ii.294). In a typical stroke of
       dramaturgy, Webster first crowds and illuminates the stage only to empty and
       (imaginatively, in an outdoor theatre) darken it: a public, ceremonial world quickly
       gives way to the private intensity of Brachiano's illicit passion.
   6   s.d. (*Whispers*) ed. (whisper r. margin opposite l. 7 in Q)

Let the caroche go on, and 'tis his pleasure
You put out all your torches and depart.

[Exeunt ATTENDANTS *with torches]*

BRACHIANO

Are we so happy?

FLAMINEO   Can't be otherwise?   10

Observed you not tonight, my honoured lord,
Which way so e'er you went she threw her eyes?
I have dealt already with her chamber-maid
Zanche the Moor, and she is wondrous proud
To be the agent for so high a spirit.   15

BRACHIANO

We are happy above thought, because 'bove merit.

FLAMINEO

'Bove merit! We may now talk freely: 'bove merit; what is't you
doubt? Her coyness, that's but the superficies of lust most women
have. Yet why should ladies blush to hear that named, which they
do not fear to handle? O they are politic; they know our desire is   20
increased by the difficulty of enjoying, whereas satiety is a blunt,
weary and drowsy passion. If the buttery-hatch at court stood
continually open there would be nothing so passionate crowding,
nor hot suit after the beverage.

BRACHIANO

O but her jealous husband—   25

FLAMINEO

Hang him, a gilder that hath his brains perished with quicksilver
is not more cold in the liver. The great barriers moulted not

---

  8 *caroche* luxurious coach for town use
 15 i.e. to help you because of your outstanding desire and high rank
 17 *talk freely* As Flamineo relaxes with Brachiano on a stage now cleared of observers,
     his speech acquires the metrical looseness of prose.
 21 *whereas* ed. (where a Q)
 22 *buttery-hatch* the half-door over which were served food and drink from the
     buttery
26–7 *gilder . . . liver* Gilders used a mixture of gold and mercury to gild objects, then later
     drew off the mercury with heat, thereby inhaling the fumes, causing mercury poi-
     soning; the symptoms include tremors, insanity and general torpor (or reduction
     in body heat). Flamineo compares Camillo to gilders because he is so lacking in
     passion. The liver was supposedly the seat of the passions.
27–8 *great barriers . . . hairs* During barriers, a martial tournament fought with short
     swords or pikes across a low railing (cf. V.iii), the feathers in the helmets of combat-
     ants would often be struck off. As the challengers at barriers lose feathers, so Camillo's
     sexual encounters have given him syphilis, which causes hair loss and impotence.

more feathers than he hath shed hairs by the confession of his
doctor. An Irish gamester that will play himself naked, and then
wage all downward, at hazard, is not more venturous. So unable   30
to please a woman that like a Dutch doublet all his back is
shrunk into his breeches.
Shroud you within this closet, good my lord;
Some trick now must be thought on to divide
My brother-in-law from his fair bed-fellow.   35

BRACHIANO

O should she fail to come!

FLAMINEO

I must not have your lordship thus unwisely amorous; I myself
have loved a lady and pursued her with a great deal of under-
age protestation, whom some three or four gallants that have
enjoyed would with all their hearts have been glad to have been   40
rid of. 'Tis just like a summer bird-cage in a garden: the birds
that are without, despair to get in, and the birds that are within
despair and are in a consumption for fear they shall never get
out: away, away my lord—

Enter CAMILLO [BRACHIANO *withdraws*]

See, here he comes; this fellow by his apparel   45
Some men would judge a politician,
But call his wit in question, you shall find it

29–30 *An Irish gamester ... venturous* According to Richard Stanyhurst's *Description of
        Irelande* in Holinshed's *Chronicles*, some 'wild Irish' would gamble away their
        clothes until they were stark naked, then pawn their fingernails, toenails and even
        their testicles, which they lost or redeemed at the courtesy of the winner. The sense
        here is that Camillo has pawned his virility.

31–2   *Dutch doublet ... breeches* Like a Dutch doublet, which was close fitting except for
        its large breeches, Camillo's 'back' (manhood) has withered or shrunk.

33   *Shroud you ... closet* It is unlikely that Brachiano actually disappears from the audi-
        ence's view here (or at l. 44), since the effectiveness of Flamineo's cross-talk would be
        heightened by Brachiano's visibility. The actor may simply retreat to a different part of
        the stage, crouching, perhaps, behind an arras or door; later in the scene, Cornelia is
        likewise visible to the audience but invisible to the other characters. The stage direction
        for Brachiano's entrance at l. 179 thus registers his coming forward to centre stage.

38–9   *under-age protestation* inexperienced or immature declaration of love

45–6   *his apparel ... politician* Camillo appears dressed in the long robes of a counsellor
        of state or an old man (NCW I.ii.47 n.)

Merely an ass in's foot-cloth. [*To* CAMILLO] How now, brother,
What, travailing to bed to your kind wife?

CAMILLO

I assure you brother, no. My voyage lies   50
More northerly, in a far colder clime;
I do not well remember, I protest,
When I last lay with her.

FLAMINEO   Strange you should lose your count.

CAMILLO

We never lay together but ere morning
There grew a flaw between us.

FLAMINEO   'T had been your part   55
To have made up that flaw.

CAMILLO   True, but she loathes
I should be seen in't.

FLAMINEO   Why sir, what's the matter?

CAMILLO

The Duke your master visits me, I thank him,
And I perceive how like an earnest bowler
He very passionately leans that way   60
He should have his bowl run.

FLAMINEO   I hope you do not think–

CAMILLO

That noblemen bowl booty? 'Faith his cheek

---

48 *foot-cloth* a large and richly ornamented cloth laid over the back of a horse, hanging
    down to the ground on either side, considered a mark of dignity (here, adorning
    an ass)

48–9 ed. (cloath/How . . . wife? Q)

49 *travailing* archaic form of 'travelling', containing both the straightforward sense of
    'journeying' and the more sardonic sense of 'labouring, exerting yourself' (with
    another disparaging glance at Camillo's futile exertions as a lover)

52–3 ed. (I do not well . . . her / Strange Q)

53 *lose your count* a bawdy pun, again at Camillo's expense. 'Count' was a variant
    spelling of (and probably close in pronunciation to) 'cunt'.

55 *flaw* a sudden storm or squall (which would part two ships which 'lay together'
    after a 'voyage'), or, figuratively, a passionate outburst; also a breach or crack (with
    a bawdy allusion to the female genitals; cf. *A Chaste Maid in Cheapside* I.i.29)

56–7 ed. (Trew . . . in't / Why Q)

62 *bowl booty* a term from the game of bowls: to conspire with another player in order
    to victimize a third player; hence, to play the game falsely so as to gain a desired
    object. (Camillo suspects Brachiano and Flamineo are conspiring against him to
    win Vittoria.)

Hath a most excellent bias, it would fain
Jump with my mistress.

FLAMINEO   Will you be an ass
Despite your Aristotle, or a cuckold   65
Contrary to your ephemerides
Which shows you under what a smiling planet
You were first swaddled?

CAMILLO   Pew wew, sir tell not me
Of planets nor of ephemerides.
A man may be made cuckold in the day-time   70
When the stars' eyes are out.

FLAMINEO   Sir, God boy you,
I do commit you to your pitiful pillow
Stuffed with horn-shavings.

CAMILLO   Brother–

FLAMINEO   God refuse me
Might I advise you now your only course
Were to lock up your wife.

CAMILLO   'Twere very good.   75

FLAMINEO
Bar her the sight of revels.

CAMILLO   Excellent.

FLAMINEO
Let her not go to church, but like a hound
In leon at your heels.

CAMILLO   'Twere for her honour.

FLAMINEO
And so you should be certain in one fortnight,
Despite her chastity or innocence,   80

62–4   *his cheek . . . mistress* Camillo goes on to compare Brachiano's cheek (buttock) to
       the bowl itself, whose off-centre weighting (bias) causes it to run in an oblique line
       towards the 'mistress', the smaller white ball at which the bowls are aimed.
   64 *Jump with* lie with. When one bowl touches another one or the 'mistress', it is said
       to 'kiss' it. Camillo wants to suggest Brachiano's overtly sexual motives.
63–4   ed. (Hath . . . mistress / Will . . . asse Q)
   65 *your* ed. (you Q) *Aristotle* philosophical learning
   66 *ephemerides* astrological tables showing predicted positions of heavenly bodies on
       successive days
   71 *God boy you* God be with you (ironically dismissive)
   73 *horn-shavings* Horns were supposed to grow on the foreheads of men whose wives
       were unfaithful.
   78 *leon* leash

To be cuckolded, which yet is in suspense:
This is my counsel and I ask no fee for't.

CAMILLO

Come, you know not where my nightcap wrings me.

FLAMINEO

Wear it o'th'old fashion, let your large ears come through, it
will be more easy; nay, I will be bitter: bar your wife of her   85
entertainment: women are more willingly and more gloriously
chaste, when they are least restrained of their liberty. It seems
you would be a fine capricious mathematically jealous coxcomb, take the height of your own horns with a Jacob's staff
afore they are up. These politic enclosures for paltry mutton   90
makes more rebellion in the flesh than all the provocative
electuaries doctors have uttered since last Jubilee.

CAMILLO

This doth not physic me.

FLAMINEO

It seems you are jealous. I'll show you the error of it by a
familiar example: I have seen a pair of spectacles fashioned   95
with such perspective art that, lay down but one twelve pence
o'th'board, 'twill appear as if there were twenty; now should you
wear a pair of these spectacles, and see your wife tying her shoe,
you would imagine twenty hands were taking up of your wife's
clothes, and this would put you into a horrible causeless fury.   100

CAMILLO

The fault there, sir, is not in the eyesight—

---

83   *my nightcap ... me* i.e. my nightcap pinches me (because of the cuckold's horns
      sprouting from my forehead)
84   *large ears* ass's ears (cf. l. 83)
89   *Jacob's staff* instrument used for measuring height or distance
90–1 *politic ... flesh* Flamineo's punning is based on 'mutton', slang for loose woman. As
      the enclosure of common land by rich men leads to peasant uprisings, so putting
      restraints on loose women leads to their sexual rebellion.
91–2 *provocative electuaries* aphrodisiacs
   92 *uttered* issued, supplied
      Jubilee a year (first instituted by the Pope in 1300) of remission from sin by papal
      indulgence through various acts of piety. The 'last Jubilee' before the play's per-
      formance was 1600.
   96 *perspective art* the skill of constructing a picture or figure so as to produce some
      fantastic optical effect. These spectacles were cut into facets so as to multiply the
      image twentyfold.
   99 *wife's* ed. (wives Q)

FLAMINEO

True, but they that have the yellow jaundice, think all objects they look on to be yellow. Jealousy is worser, her fits present to a man, like so many bubbles in a basin of water, twenty several crabbed faces; many times makes his own shadow his cuckold-maker.   105

Enter [VITTORIA] COROM[BON]A

See she comes; what reason have you to be jealous of this creature? What an ignorant ass or flattering knave might he be counted, that should write sonnets to her eyes, or call her brow the snow of Ida, or ivory of Corinth, or compare her hair to the blackbird's bill, when 'tis liker the blackbird's feather. This is all: 110
be wise; I will make you friends and you shall go to bed together; marry look you, it shall not be your seeking, do you stand upon that by any means; walk you aloof, I would not have you seen in't. [*Aside*] Sister, my lord attends you in the banqueting-house – [*Aloud*] your husband is wondrous discontented.   115

VITTORIA

I did nothing to displease him, I carved to him at supper-time.

FLAMINEO

You need not have carved him in faith, they say he is a capon already. I must now seemingly fall out with you. [*Aloud*] Shall a

103   *worser* worse
105   s.d. ed. (Enter Coroma l. margin; asterisk after -maker Q)
109   *Ida* sacred mountain near Troy, usually associated with the green groves in which Paris lived as a shepherd
      ivory of Corinth Corinth was famous for excessive luxury.
110   *blackbird's bill ... feather* The blackbird's bill is yellow, its feathers black; in sonneteering convention fair-haired women were considered more beautiful than dark-haired women.
111   *friends* lovers
113   *walk ... aloof* Flamineo removes Camillo to a safe distance. He thus jokes privately with Vittoria at Camillo's expense, possibly in stage whispers (cf. 6 above).
115–44   I have added dashes to those already in the copy text in order to clarify Flamineo's cross-talk. Up to l. 130, Flamineo's jokes depend on remarks which Vittoria (and Brachiano) can hear and Camillo cannot; the double meaning of l. 132 depends on Camillo's ignorance of Flamineo's asides. After l. 132, since Flamineo has promised Vittoria's sexual favours to Brachiano and Camillo, his lines apply equally well to both men.
116   *carved* shown great courtesy; made seductive advances – 'by signalling with the fingers' (Lucas, p. 209)
117   *carved* castrated
      capon a castrated cock; a eunuch

gentleman so well descended as Camillo [*Aside*] a lousy slave
that within this twenty years rode with the black-guard in the   120
Duke's carriage 'mongst spits and dripping-pans–

CAMILLO

Now he begins to tickle her.

FLAMINEO

An excellent scholar – one that hath a head filled with calves'
brains without any sage in them – come crouching in the hams to
you for a night's lodging – that hath an itch in's hams, which like   125
the fire at the glass-house hath not gone out this seven years – Is
he not a courtly gentleman? – When he wears white satin one
would take him by his black muzzle to be no other creature than a
maggot – You are a goodly foil, I confess, well set out – but
covered with a false stone, yon counterfeit diamond.   130

CAMILLO

He will make her know what is in me.

FLAMINEO

Come, my lord attends you; thou shalt go to bed to my lord.

CAMILLO

Now he comes to't.

FLAMINEO

With a relish as curious as a vintner going to taste new wine, I
am opening your case hard.   135

CAMILLO

A virtuous brother o' my credit.

FLAMINEO

He will give thee a ring with a philosopher's stone in it.

---

120 *black-guard* lowest menial servants of a noble household; scullions and kitchen-
knaves
122 *tickle* excite agreeably, arouse
123–4 *calves'... them* Calves' brains unseasoned by the culinary herb sage are a metaphor
for the brains of a dolt unseasoned by wisdom.
124 *crouching... hams* in a servile, bowing position
125 *itch in's hams* irritation in the thighs and buttocks
126 *glass-house* the glass factory in which fires were always kept burning; in Webster
metaphorically associated with sexual organs
129 *foil* setting of a jewel
135 *case* legal case; and punning on the sense, the female genitals
137 *philosopher's stone* miraculous substance sought by alchemists which would turn
base metals into precious ones, cure disease and prolong life; here also a bawdy
reference to the testicle (stone)

CAMILLO

Indeed I am studying alchemy.

FLAMINEO

Thou shalt lie in a bed stuffed with turtles' feathers, swoon in
perfumed linen like the fellow was smothered in roses, so   140
perfect shall be thy happiness, that as men at sea think land and
trees and ships go that way they go, so both heaven and earth
shall seem to go your voyage. Shalt meet him, 'tis fixed, with
nails of diamonds to inevitable necessity.

VITTORIA

[*Aside*] How shall's rid him hence?   145

FLAMINEO

[*Aside*] I will put breese in's tail, set him gadding presently. [*To*
CAMILLO] I have almost wrought her to it, I find her coming,
but might I advise you now for this night I would not lie with
her, I would cross her humour to make her more humble.

CAMILLO

Shall I? Shall I?   150

FLAMINEO

It will show in you a supremacy of judgement.

CAMILLO

True, and a mind differing from the tumultuary opinion, for
quae negata grata.

FLAMINEO

Right, you are the adamant shall draw her to you, though you
keep distance off.   155

CAMILLO

A philosophical reason.

FLAMINEO

Walk by her o' the nobleman's fashion, and tell her you will lie
with her at the end of the progress.

139   *turtles'* turtle doves', emblems of fidelity in love
145   i.e. how shall we get rid of him?
146   *breese* gadflies
147   *coming* well inclined; sexually receptive
152   *tumultuary* irregular, confused
153   *quae negata grata* what is denied is desired
154   *adamant* magnet
156   *philosophical* wise; scientific
158   *progress* a state procession. Camillo might parade himself before Vittoria during
        these speeches (NCW I.ii.160 n.).

CAMILLO

Vittoria, I cannot be induced or as a man would say incited—

VITTORIA

To do what sir?   160

CAMILLO

To lie with you tonight; your silkworm useth to fast every third day, and the next following spins the better. Tomorrow at night I am for you.

VITTORIA

You'll spin a fair thread, trust to't.

FLAMINEO

But do you hear, I shall have you steal to her chamber about   165
midnight.

CAMILLO

Do you think so? Why look you brother, because you shall not think I'll gull you, take the key, lock me into the chamber, and say you shall be sure of me.

FLAMINEO

In truth I will, I'll be your jailer once;   170
But have you ne'er a false door?

CAMILLO

A pox on't, as I am a Christian tell me tomorrow how scurvily she takes my unkind parting.

FLAMINEO

I will.

CAMILLO

Didst thou not mark the jest of the silkworm? Good night; in   175
faith I will use this trick often.

FLAMINEO

Do, do, do.

Exit CAMILLO

So now you are safe. Ha ha ha, thou entanglest thyself in thine own work like a silkworm.

---

164   *thread* punning on the sense 'semen'
168   *gull* deceive
172   *scurvily* sourly
175   *mark* ed. (make Q)
179   s.d. ed. (*Enter Brachiano* Q). See 33n. above.

[BRACHIANO *comes forward*]

Come sister, darkness hides your blush; women are like cursed   180
dogs, civility keeps them tied all daytime, but they are let loose
at midnight; then they do most good or most mischief. My
lord, my lord—

BRACHIANO

Give credit: I could wish time would stand still
And never end this interview this hour,   185
But all delight doth itself soon'st devour.

> ZANCHE *brings out a carpet, spreads it and lays on it*
> *two fair cushions*

> *Enter* CORNELIA [*listening*]

Let me into your bosom, happy lady,
Pour out instead of eloquence my vows;
Loose me not madam, for if you forgo me
I am lost eternally.   190

VITTORIA

Sir in the way of pity I wish you heart-whole.

BRACHIANO

You are a sweet physician.

VITTORIA

Sure sir a loathed cruelty in ladies
Is as to doctors many funerals:
It takes away their credit.

180 *cursed* vicious; (often of women) shrewish
184 *Give credit* i.e. trust me (addressed either to Vittoria or to Flamineo)
186 s.d. The compositor squeezed this stage direction into the text space available
     beside Brachiano's speech. While we cannot therefore be certain of the exact posi-
     tion of the stage direction in the copy, Zanche's actions (and Cornelia's entrance)
     are especially significant if they occur as Brachiano addresses Vittoria. Brachiano's
     courtly vows are thus immediately counterbalanced by the overtly sexual nature of
     the lovers' encounter suggested by the placing of cushions and also by the presence
     of an outsider and critic (Cornelia, perhaps wearing a crucifix). The staging recalls
     that of the morality play, with Vice (Flamineo and Zanche) and Virtue (Cornelia)
     present as observers, probably framing the lovers on either side.
189 *loose* release; lose (in modern sense)
189–90 ed. (one line in Q)
194–5 ed. (Is . . . credit / Excellent Q)

BRACHIANO   Excellent creature.   195
  We call the cruel fair, what name for you
  That are so merciful?   [*They embrace*]
ZANCHE   See now they close.
FLAMINEO
  Most happy union.
CORNELIA
  [*Aside*] My fears are fall'n upon me, O my heart!
  My son the pander: now I find our house   200
  Sinking to ruin. Earthquakes leave behind,
  Where they have tyrannized, iron, or lead, or stone,
  But, woe to ruin, violent lust leaves none.
BRACHIANO
  What value is this jewel?
VITTORIA   'Tis the ornament
  Of a weak fortune.   205
BRACHIANO
  In sooth I'll have it; nay I will but change
  My jewel for your jewel.
FLAMINEO   Excellent,
  His jewel for her jewel; well put in Duke.
BRACHIANO
  Nay let me see you wear it.
VITTORIA   Here sir.
BRACHIANO
  Nay lower, you shall wear my jewel lower.   210
FLAMINEO
  That's better; she must wear his jewel lower.

---

197 *close* come together
204 *jewel* Brachiano presumably fingers a gem worn by Vittoria, and then offers one of his own, as in a formal betrothal ceremony in which tokens were exchanged before witnesses; 'jewel' signifies both married chastity or 'maidenhead' and the sexual organ – hence the subsequent word-play. Brachiano encourages Vittoria to pin his jewel at the base of her dress's V-shaped bodice, over her pudendum (NCW I.ii.205–12 n.).
208 *put in* make a claim; also with a sexual innuendo
209 *Here* ed. (Heare Q)

VITTORIA

    To pass away the time I'll tell your Grace
    A dream I had last night.

BRACHIANO   Most wishedly.

VITTORIA

    A foolish idle dream:
    Methought I walked about the mid of night,   215
    Into a church-yard, where a goodly yew-tree
    Spread her large root in ground; under that yew,
    As I sat sadly leaning on a grave,
    Checkered with cross-sticks, there came stealing in
    Your Duchess and my husband; one of them   220
    A pick-axe bore, th'other a rusty spade,
    And in rough terms they gan to challenge me,
    About this yew.

BRACHIANO   That tree.

VITTORIA   This harmless yew.

    They told me my intent was to root up
    That well-grown yew, and plant i'th'stead of it   225
    A withered blackthorn, and for that they vowed
    To bury me alive: my husband straight
    With pick-axe gan to dig, and your fell Duchess
    With shovel, like a fury, voided out
    The earth and scattered bones. Lord, how methought   230
    I trembled, and yet for all this terror
    I could not pray.

FLAMINEO   No, the devil was in your dream.

VITTORIA

    When to my rescue there arose, methought,
    A whirlwind which let fall a massy arm

214–37 By recounting her dream, Vittoria physically disengages herself from Brachiano's
        sexual overtures, perhaps walking about the stage as she imaginatively re-enacts it
        (NCW I.ii.216 n.). When she has finished, Brachiano reasserts control by renewing
        his embrace.

  219 *cross-sticks* May mean any of the following: wooden crosses sticking out of graves;
        the 'chequered pattern of light and shade' created by the overhanging branches of
        the yew tree against the night sky (Brown, I.ii.236 n.); criss-crossed osiers protect-
        ing the grave; devices used by witches to raise tempests.

  225 *yew* traditionally associated with death (cf. IV.iii.120), here an ambiguous symbol.
        Isabella and Camillo would think of 'That well-grown yew' as Camillo himself, the
        deserving husband, or perhaps as Brachiano, still uncorrupted; Vittoria's obvious
        pun on 'you' and the end of the dream clearly suggest Brachiano as the yew.

From that strong plant, 235
And both were struck dead by that sacred yew
In that base shallow grave that was their due.

FLAMINEO
Excellent devil.
She hath taught him in a dream
To make away his Duchess and her husband. 240

BRACHIANO
Sweetly shall I interpret this your dream:
You are lodged within his arms who shall protect you
From all the fevers of a jealous husband,
From the poor envy of our phlegmatic Duchess;
I'll seat you above law and above scandal, 245
Give to your thoughts the invention of delight
And the fruition; nor shall government
Divide me from you longer than a care
To keep you great: you shall to me at once
Be dukedom, health, wife, children, friends, and all. 250

CORNELIA
[*Approaching them*] Woe to light hearts, they still fore-run
our fall.

FLAMINEO
What fury raised thee up? Away, away–

Exit ZANCHE

CORNELIA
What make you here, my lord, this dead of night?
Never dropped mildew on a flower here,
Till now.

FLAMINEO I pray will you go to bed then, 255
Lest you be blasted?

CORNELIA   O that this fair garden
Had with all poisoned herbs of Thessaly
At first been planted, made a nursery

---

247   *government* i.e. governing my dukedom
252   *fury* in classical mythology one of the avenging deities, dread goddesses with snakes
     twined in their hair
     s.d. Flamineo's direction to Zanche provides an early hint of their illicit relation-
     ship of which Cornelia later shows open disapproval (V.i.175).
254–5 *Never . . . now* ed. (one line in Q)
257   *with* ed. (not in Q)
     Thessaly the special home of witches and poisonous herbs

For witchcraft; rather than a burial plot
For both your honours.

VITTORIA [*Kneeling*]   Dearest mother hear me.   260

CORNELIA

O thou dost make my brow bend to the earth
Sooner than nature. See the curse of children.
In life they keep us frequently in tears,
And in the cold grave leave us in pale fears.

BRACHIANO

Come, come, I will not hear you.

VITTORIA   Dear my lord.   265

CORNELIA

Where is thy Duchess now, adulterous Duke?
Thou little dreamed'st this night she is come to Rome.

FLAMINEO

How? Come to Rome!

VITTORIA   The Duchess–

BRACHIANO   She had been better–

CORNELIA

The lives of princes should like dials move,
Whose regular example is so strong,   270
They make the times by them go right or wrong.

FLAMINEO

So, have you done?

CORNELIA   Unfortunate Camillo.

VITTORIA

I do protest if any chaste denial,
If anything but blood could have allayed
His long suit to me–

CORNELIA [*Kneeling*] I will join with thee,   275
To the most woeful end e'er mother kneeled,
If thou dishonour thus thy husband's bed,

259   *than* ed. (not in Q)
260   s.d. Vittoria probably kneels at this point, as she pleads with her mother, whose
      'brow bend[s] to the earth'; at l. 275, Cornelia clearly indicates that she kneels to join
      Vittoria. Vittoria's kneeling posture – a traditional show of respect for authority –
      softens 'the curse of children' of which Cornelia accuses her daughter.
264   *leave* ed. (leaves Q)
274   *blood* her reciprocated sexual passion, life itself (Vittoria's own death or Brachiano's
      suicide) or bloodshed (crimes which Brachiano is prepared to commit to win her)

Be thy life short as are the funeral tears
In great men's.
BRACHIANO   Fie, fie, the woman's mad.
CORNELIA
Be thy act Judas-like, betray in kissing;   280
May'st thou be envied during his short breath,
And pitied like a wretch after his death.
VITTORIA
O me accursed.   *Exit*
FLAMINEO
Are you out of your wits? My lord,
I'll fetch her back again!
BRACHIANO   No, I'll to bed.   285
Send Doctor Julio to me presently.
Uncharitable woman, thy rash tongue
Hath raised a fearful and prodigious storm.
Be thou the cause of all ensuing harm.   *Exit*
FLAMINEO
Now, you that stand so much upon your honour,   290
Is this a fitting time o' night, think you,
To send a duke home without e'er a man?
I would fain know where lies the mass of wealth
Which you have hoarded for my maintenance,
That I may bear my beard out of the level   295
Of my lord's stirrup.
CORNELIA   What? Because we are poor,
Shall we be vicious?
FLAMINEO   Pray what means have you
To keep me from the galleys, or the gallows?
My father proved himself a gentleman,
Sold all's land, and like a fortunate fellow   300

282 *his* ed. (this Q)

283 s.d. *Exit* ed. (Exit Victoria Q)

284 *Are . . . wits*? The copy text does not reveal whether Flamineo's insolent question is
     addressed to Brachiano or Cornelia. While Flamineo is clearly furious with his
     mother for spoiling the lovers' meeting, he may also be angry with Brachiano for
     not actively preventing Vittoria's departure. The choice is left to the actor.

289 s.d. *Exit* ed. (Exit Brachiano Q)

295–6 *bear . . . stirrup* be in a higher position than unmounted foot attendant to my lord;
       hence, rise above my subservient position

299–300 *gentleman . . . land* alluding ironically to a contemporary social evil

Died ere the money was spent. You brought me up,
At Padua I confess, where I protest,
For want of means (the university judge me)
I have been fain to heel my tutor's stockings
At least seven years. Conspiring with a beard   305
Made me a graduate, then to this Duke's service;
I visited the court, whence I returned –
More courteous, more lecherous by far,
But not a suit the richer – and shall I,
Having a path so open and so free   310
To my preferment, still retain your milk
In my pale forehead? No, this face of mine
I'll arm and fortify with lusty wine
'Gainst shame and blushing.

CORNELIA

O that I ne'er had borne thee!

FLAMINEO   So would I.   315
I would the common'st courtezan in Rome
Had been my mother rather than thyself.
Nature is very pitiful to whores
To give them but few children, yet those children
Plurality of fathers; they are sure   320
They shall not want. Go, go,
Complain unto my great lord cardinal,
Yet may be he will justify the act.
Lycurgus wondered much, men would provide
Good stallions for their mares, and yet would suffer   325
Their fair wives to be barren.

CORNELIA

Misery of miseries.   *Exit*

FLAMINEO

The Duchess come to court, I like not that;
We are engaged to mischief and must on.

305–6 *Conspiring . . . graduate* Flamineo earned his degree, probably by simply reaching physical (rather than intellectual) maturity or possibly by conspiring with an older man.

308 *courteous* with manners befitting the court of a prince

324–6 *Lycurgus . . . barren* According to Plutarch, Lycurgus advocated that men should share their wives with other 'worthy' men, not to fulfil the needs of barren women, but to provide the state with citizens from the best possible stock.

327 s.d. *Exit* ed. (Exit Cornelia Q)

As rivers, to find out the ocean   330
Flow with crook bendings beneath forced banks,
Or as we see, to aspire some mountain's top
The way ascends not straight but imitates
The subtle foldings of a winter's snake,
So, who knows policy and her true aspect,   335
Shall find her ways winding and indirect.   *Exit*

[ACT II, SCENE i]

Enter FRANCISCO DE' MEDICI, *Cardinal* MONTICELSO,
MARCELLO, ISABELLA, *young* GIOVANNI, *with little*
JACQUES *the Moor*

FRANCISCO

Have you not seen your husband since you arrived?

ISABELLA

Not yet sir.

FRANCISCO Surely he is wondrous kind;
If I had such a dove-house as Camillo's
I would set fire on't, were't but to destroy
The pole-cats that haunt to't – [*To* GIOVANNI] my sweet cousin–   5

---

331 *crook* crooked
     forced artificially made
334 *winter's snake* probably the mythical *amphisbaena*, symbol of the devil, whose two
     heads allowed elaborate serpentine movement and which, unlike most snakes,
     deliberately sought cold temperatures

  0 s.d.1 *MONTICELSO* ed. (Mountcelso Q)
     s.d. 2–3 *little JACQUES* the Moor A 'ghost' character with no dialogue of his own,
     perhaps (as most editors think) a trace in the manuscript of an idea that was subse-
     quently undeveloped or discarded by Webster; but Webster may have intended
     the presence of the silent young Moor among the company to hint at the sinister
     potential of apparently virtuous characters such as Monticelso and Francisco.
     Aaron, also a Moor, appears but does not speak in the first scene of Shakespeare's
     Titus Andronicus; his brooding presence casts a shadow over the apparently
     virtuous Tamora (later revealed as Aaron's mistress) as she pleads for her son's life.
  3 *such a* ed. (a such Q)
     dove-house a house for doves; here referring ironically to Vittoria, since the dove
     was traditionally a symbol of peace and innocence
  5 *pole-cats* small, foul-smelling predatory mammals; a term of abuse for a vile person
     or a prostitute

GIOVANNI

    Lord uncle, you did promise me a horse
    And armour.

FRANCISCO   That I did my pretty cousin;

    Marcello see it fitted.

MARCELLO   My lord the Duke is here.

FRANCISCO

    Sister away, you must not yet be seen.

ISABELLA

    I do beseech you entreat him mildly,   10
    Let not your rough tongue
    Set us at louder variance; all my wrongs
    Are freely pardoned, and I do not doubt
    As men to try the precious unicorn's horn
    Make of the powder a preservative circle   15
    And in it put a spider, so these arms
    Shall charm his poison, force it to obeying
    And keep him chaste from an infected straying.

FRANCISCO

    I wish it may. Be gone.

                                Exit [ISABELLA]

              Enter BRACHIANO *and* FLAMINEO

              Void the chamber;

    [*Exeunt* FLAMINEO, MARCELLO, GIOVANNI *and* JACQUES]
    You are welcome, will you sit? [BRACHIANO *sits*] I pray my lord   20
    Be you my orator, my heart's too full;
    I'll second you anon.

MONTICELSO   Ere I begin

    Let me entreat your grace forego all passion
    Which may be raised by my free discourse.

  14–16   *unicorn's horn . . . spider* In this test a spider was encircled by an extremely rare and
          expensive powder believed to come from the mythological unicorn's horn, which
          was thought to be an antidote to poison; if the horn were genuine, the spider would
          remain inside the circle.
    19   *Void the chamber* A bold stroke of staging on Webster's part: no sooner is the stage
          crowded with actors than it is suddenly cleared at Francisco's command. The stage
          picture – in which two men chastise a third for unseemly behaviour – replicates I.i,
          in which Gasparo and Antonelli reprimand Lodovico.

BRACHIANO

   As silent as i'th'church – you may proceed.   25

MONTICELSO

   It is a wonder to your noble friends

   That you have as 'twere entered the world

   With a free sceptre in your able hand,

   And have to th'use of nature well applied

   High gifts of learning, should in your prime age   30

   Neglect your awful throne, for the soft down

   Of an insatiate bed. O my lord,

   The drunkard after all his lavish cups

   Is dry, and then is sober; so at length

   When you awake from this lascivious dream,   35

   Repentance then will follow, like the sting

   Placed in the adder's tail: wretched are princes

   When fortune blasteth but a petty flower

   Of their unwieldly crowns; or ravisheth

   But one pearl from their sceptre; but alas!   40

   When they to wilful shipwreck loose good fame

   All princely titles perish with their name.

BRACHIANO

   You have said, my lord,–

MONTICELSO   Enough to give you taste

   How far I am from flattering your greatness?

BRACHIANO

   Now you that are his second, what say you?   45

   Do not like young hawks fetch a course about;

   Your game flies fair and for you.

FRANCISCO   Do not fear it:

   I'll answer you in your own hawking phrase;

   Some eagles that should gaze upon the sun

---

   31   *awful* awe-inspiring

36–7   *sting . . . tail* While the adder inflicts injury primarily with its mouth or fangs, the hindpart of its tail was also supposed to be able to sting. Monticelso may be implying that, while Brachiano's affair now primarily injures his public reputation, he will later badly regret it himself.

38–9   *fortune . . . crowns* Not a mixed metaphor but a cunning play on words: 'flower' could mean a jewel in a crown; 'crown' could mean a garland of flowers.

   42   *name* good name, reputation

   46   *fetch a course about* change direction, turn tail (as young hawks are supposed to do when directed to fly at old game)

Seldom soar high, but take their lustful ease,   50
Since they from dunghill birds their prey can seize.
You know Vittoria.

BRACHIANO   Yes.

FRANCISCO   You shift your shirt there
When you retire from tennis.

BRACHIANO   Happily.

FRANCISCO
Her husband is lord of a poor fortune
Yet she wears cloth of tissue.

BRACHIANO   What of this?   55
Will you urge that, my good lord cardinal,
As part of her confession at next shrift,
And know from whence it sails?

FRANCISCO   She is your strumpet.

BRACHIANO
Uncivil sir there's hemlock in thy breath
And that black slander; were she a whore of mine   60
All thy loud cannons and thy borrowed Switzers,
Thy galleys nor thy sworn confederates
Durst not supplant her.

FRANCISCO   Let's not talk on thunder.
Thou hast a wife, our sister; would I had given
Both her white hands to death, bound and locked fast   65
In her last winding-sheet, when I gave thee
But one.

BRACHIANO Thou hadst given a soul to God then.

---

51 *prey* ed. (pery Q)
    dunghill birds birds (such as ravens, kites and common barnyard fowl) whose prey
    is offal, contrasted to eagles, by popular belief the only bird able to look directly at
    the sun. Francisco is comparing Brachiano to an eagle sluggish enough to seize the
    contemptible, corrupt prey (Vittoria) of an inferior bird (Camillo).

52 *shift* change

53 *Happily* Perhaps

55 *cloth of tissue* a rich kind of cloth, often interwoven with gold or silver, that sump-
    tuary laws restricted to women of high birth (NCW II.i.55 n.)

59 *hemlock* poison

61 *borrowed Switzers* Swiss mercenary soldiers

67 *Thou ... then* Brachiano is acknowledging Isabella's fitness for the spiritual life.
    Does he mean this as a genuine compliment, or as an ironic comment on her unfit-
    ness for the real world? The ambiguity aptly prepares an audience for a character
    whose saintly self-sacrifice leads her to deliver vicious harangues.

FRANCISCO   True:

   Thy ghostly father with all's absolution

   Shall ne'er do so by thee.

BRACHIANO   Spit thy poison.

FRANCISCO

   I shall not need, lust carries her sharp whip   70

   At her own girdle; look to't, for our anger

   Is making thunder-bolts.

BRACHIANO   Thunder? In faith,

   They are but crackers.

FRANCISCO   We'll end this with the cannon.

BRACHIANO

   Thou'lt get nought by it but iron in thy wounds,

   And gunpowder in thy nostrils.

FRANCISCO   Better that   75

   Than change perfumes for plasters.

BRACHIANO   Pity on thee,

   'Twere good you'ld show your slaves or men condemned

   Your new-ploughed forehead. Defiance! And I'll meet thee,

   Even in a thicket of thy ablest men.

MONTICELSO

   My lords, you shall not word it any further   80

   Without a milder limit.

FRANCISCO   Willingly.

BRACHIANO

   Have you proclaimed a triumph that you bait

   A lion thus?

MONTICELSO My lord.

BRACHIANO   I am tame, I am tame sir.

---

68   *ghostly* spiritual

73   *crackers* explosive fireworks (as in modern sense); also, boasts or lies

76   *change ... plasters* i.e. exchange the sweet smells of sensual indulgence for its
     consequences, the bandages to treat venereal disease

78   *new-ploughed* deeply furrowed (with anger)
     forehead ... thee ed. (fore-head defiance, and I'le meete thee Q). Repunctuation is
     necessary to make sense of the text. 'Defiance!' is a plausible trumpet call to mark
     Brachiano's shift from contempt for Francisco to self-assertion.

80   *word it* argue, dispute

82   *triumph* a public festivity during which, in ancient Rome, lions might be 'baited', or
     taunted to fight

82–3   ed. (baite a / Lyon thus Q)

FRANCISCO

We send unto the Duke for conference
'Bout levies 'gainst the pirates. My lord Duke 85
Is not at home. We come ourself in person,
Still my lord Duke is busied; but we fear
When Tiber to each prowling passenger
Discovers flocks of wild ducks, then my lord
'Bout moulting time, I mean we shall be certain 90
To find you sure enough and speak with you.

BRACHIANO   Ha?

FRANCISCO

A mere tale of a tub, my words are idle,
But to express the sonnet by natural reason,
When stags grow melancholic you'll find the season.

Enter GIOVANNI [*in armour*]

MONTICELSO

No more my lord; here comes a champion 95
Shall end the difference between you both,
Your son the prince Giovanni. See my lords
What hopes you store in him; this is a casket
For both your crowns, and should be held like dear.
Now is he apt for knowledge; therefore know 100

---

88   *prowling* ed. (proling Q)
     prowling passenger peregrine falcon in search of prey
89   *wild ducks* prey for the falcon; prostitutes
90   *moulting time* when birds shed their plumage; when people lose their hair (as a result
     of venereal disease; cf. I.ii.27–9); i.e. when his hair begins to fall out, Brachiano will
     discover Vittoria is a prostitute – another dig at Vittoria's reputation (cf. l. 76)
92   *tale of a tub* proverbial, a cock and bull story; and punning on the sweating tub
     used in treatment of venereal disease
93   *express . . . reason* i.e. explain this little poem by common sense
94   *stags* male deer; cuckolds (like Brachiano if he discovers Vittoria is a prostitute)
     stags . . . melancholic After stags mated, they were supposed to retreat into solitary
     ditches to lie alone.
     season fit occasion or opportunity (to meet with us)
     s.d. ed. (to r. of l. 93 in Q)
95   *champion* a valiant combatant. Giovanni is now outfitted in the suit of armour
     Francisco promised him at the beginning of the scene, a living emblem of
     the chivalric ideal Brachiano should strive for (identified in Webster's time with
     Prince Henry).

It is a more direct and even way
To train to virtue those of princely blood
By examples than by precepts: if by examples
Whom should he rather strive to imitate
Than his own father: be his pattern then,   105
Leave him a stock of virtue that may last,
Should fortune rend his sails and split his mast.

BRACHIANO

Your hand boy – [*Shaking his hand*] growing to a soldier?

GIOVANNI

Give me a pike.

[*One hands him a pike*]

FRANCISCO

What, practising your pike so young, fair coz?   110

GIOVANNI

[*Tossing the pike*] Suppose me one of Homer's frogs, my lord,
Tossing my bullrush thus; pray sir tell me
Might not a child of good discretion
Be leader to an army?

FRANCISCO   Yes cousin, a young prince
Of good discretion might.

GIOVANNI   Say you so?   115
Indeed I have heard 'tis fit a general
Should not endanger his own person oft,
So that he make a noise when he's a horseback
Like a Dansk drummer. O 'tis excellent.
He need not fight; methinks his horse as well   120
Might lead an army for him. If I live
I'll charge the French foe, in the very front
Of all my troops, the foremost man.

---

106 *stock* line of descent; store, fund
108 *to a* ed. (to Q)
109 *pike* spear-like weapon used by foot soldiers; the penis
111 *Homer's frogs* from *The Battle of Frogs and Mice*, a burlesque epic attributed to
      Homer in which the frogs used bulrushes as pikes
113 *discretion* good judgement, prudence, circumspection, as in Falstaff's 'the better
      part of valour is discretion' (*1 Henry IV* V.iv.119–20). Giovanni's answer
      (ll. 116–17) suggests he takes Francisco to be playing on the latter meaning.
119 *Dansk* Danish (famous for martial music, including drums)

FRANCISCO   What, what!
GIOVANNI
   And will not bid my soldiers up and follow
   But bid them follow me.
BRACHIANO   Forward lapwing.   125
   He flies with the shell on's head.
FRANCISCO   Pretty cousin.
GIOVANNI
   The first year uncle that I go to war
   All prisoners that I take I will set free
   Without their ransom.
FRANCISCO   Ha, without their ransom?
   How then will you reward your soldiers   130
   That took those prisoners for you?
GIOVANNI   Thus my lord:
   I'll marry them to all the wealthy widows
   That falls that year.
FRANCISCO   Why then the next year following
   You'll have no men to go with you to war.
GIOVANNI
   Why then I'll press the women to the war,   135
   And then the men will follow.
MONTICELSO   Witty prince.
FRANCISCO
   See, a good habit makes a child a man,
   Whereas a bad one makes a man a beast:
   Come, you and I are friends.
BRACHIANO   Most wishedly,
   Like bones which broke in sunder and well set   140
   Knit the more strongly.
FRANCISCO [*Calling offstage*] Call Camillo hither.
   You have received the rumour, how Count Lodowick
   Is turned a pirate.
BRACHIANO   Yes.
FRANCISCO   We are now preparing
   Some ships to fetch him in.

---

125 *lapwing* proverbial type of precocity, supposed to run (if not to fly) immediately
    after hatching
137 *habit* garment (applied to Giovanni); custom, practice (applied to Brachiano)

[*Enter* ISABELLA]

    Behold your Duchess;
We will now leave you and expect from you   145
Nothing but kind entreaty.
BRACHIANO   You have charmed me.
     Exeunt FR[ANCISCO], MON[TICELSO], GIOV[ANNI]
You are in health we see.
ISABELLA   And above health
To see my lord well.
BRACHIANO   So I wonder much,
What amorous whirlwind hurried you to Rome.
ISABELLA
Devotion, my lord.
BRACHIANO   Devotion?   150
Is your soul charged with any grievous sin?
ISABELLA
'Tis burdened with too many, and I think
The oft'ner that we cast our reckonings up,
Our sleeps will be the sounder.
BRACHIANO   Take your chamber!
ISABELLA
Nay my dear lord, I will not have you angry;   155
Doth not my absence from you two months
Merit one kiss?
BRACHIANO   I do not use to kiss.
If that will dispossess your jealousy,
I'll swear it to you.
ISABELLA   O my loved lord,
I do not come to chide; my jealousy,   160
I am to learn what that Italian means;
You are as welcome to these longing arms,
As I to you a virgin.   [*Attempts to embrace him*]

---

146 s.d. ed. (placed opposite ll. 144–5 in Q for lack of text space)
152–4 '*Tis . . . sounder* The historical Isabella had a lover, but Webster was probably
    unaware of this (Boklund, p. 118); rather, Isabella's 'devotion' to Brachiano includes
    implicating herself in his transgressions (compare Desdemona's 'heaven forgive us'
    in *Othello* IV.ii.87).
 161 *am to learn* am yet to learn (am ignorant of)
    Italian i.e. characteristically Italian emotion (jealousy)

BRACHIANO [*Turning away*] O your breath!
    Out upon sweetmeats, and continued physic.
    The plague is in them.
ISABELLA   You have oft for these two lips   165
    Neglected cassia or the natural sweets
    Of the spring violet; they are not yet much withered.
    My lord I should be merry; these your frowns
    Show in a helmet lovely, but on me,
    In such a peaceful interview methinks   170
    They are too too roughly knit.
BRACHIANO   O dissemblance.
    Do you bandy factions 'gainst me? Have you learnt
    The trick of impudent baseness to complain
    Unto your kindred?
ISABELLA   Never my dear lord.
BRACHIANO
    Must I be haunted out, or wasn't your trick   175
    To meet some amorous gallant here in Rome
    That must supply our discontinuance?
ISABELLA
    I pray sir burst my heart, and in my death
    Turn to your ancient pity, though not love.
BRACHIANO
    Because your brother is the corpulent Duke, –   180
    That is the great Duke – 'Sdeath I shall not shortly
    Racket away five hundred crowns at tennis,
    But it shall rest upon record: I scorn him
    Like a shaved Polack: all his reverent wit
    Lies in his wardrobe; he's a discreet fellow   185
    When he's made up in his robes of state.
    Your brother the great Duke, because h'as galleys,

---

166   *cassia* a kind of cinnamon; in poetic usage, a sweet-smelling herb or perfume
171   *too too* ed. (to too Q)
172   *bandy factions* i.e. form conspiracies
175   *haunted out* visited frequently (with perhaps also the sense of 'hunted out': chased away)
181–3   *'Sdeath ... record* i.e. by God's death, soon I shall not be able to lose 500 crowns wagered at tennis without having it recorded as evidence (probably referring to Francisco's charge at ll. 52–3)
183–4   *I scorn ... Polack* i.e. I scorn him as of no account. Poles, according to Fynes Morison, *Itinerary*, 1617, shaved all their heads except the forehead.

And now and then ransacks a Turkish fly-boat,
(Now all the hellish Furies take his soul),
First made this match – accursed be the priest   190
That sang the wedding mass, and even my issue.

ISABELLA
O too too far you have cursed.

BRACHIANO   Your hand I'll kiss:
This is the latest ceremony of my love,
Henceforth I'll never lie with thee, by this,
This wedding ring: I'll ne'er more lie with thee.   195
And this divorce shall be as truly kept
As if the judge had doomed it: fare you well,
Our sleeps are severed.

ISABELLA   Forbid it the sweet union
Of all things blessed; why, the saints in heaven
Will knit their brows at that.

BRACHIANO   Let not thy love   200
Make thee an unbeliever. This my vow
Shall never on my soul be satisfied
With my repentance: let thy brother rage
Beyond a horrid tempest or sea-fight,
My vow is fixed.

ISABELLA   O my winding sheet,   205
Now shall I need thee shortly; dear my lord,
Let me hear once more what I would not hear:
Never.

BRACHIANO Never!

ISABELLA
O my unkind lord, may your sins find mercy
As I upon a woeful widowed bed   210
Shall pray for you, if not to turn your eyes
Upon your wretched wife and hopeful son,
Yet that in time you'll fix them upon heaven.

188 *fly-boat* pinnace or fast sailing boat
192 *too too* ed. (to too Q)
193 *latest* last
193–8 *This . . . severed* Brachiano's ceremony of 'love' is a parody or inversion of the wedding rites, when vows and rings are exchanged. In Jacobean England, one spouse
could divorce another from bed and board (*a mensa et thoro*), especially on
grounds of adultery (of which Brachiano accuses Isabella at ll. 175–7). Such
divorce did not, however, allow for remarriage.

BRACHIANO

No more; go, go, complain to the great Duke.

ISABELLA

No my dear lord, you shall have present witness   215
How I'll work peace between you; I will make
Myself the author of your cursed vow.
I have some cause to do it, you have none;
Conceal it I beseech you, for the weal
Of both your dukedoms, that you wrought the means   220
Of such a separation; let the fault
Remain with my supposed jealousy,
And think with what a piteous and rent heart
I shall perform this sad ensuing part.

Enter FRANCISCO, FLAMINEO, MONTICELSO, MARCELLO
[ISABELLA *weeps*]

BRACHIANO

Well, take your course – my honourable brother.   225

FRANCISCO

Sister – this is not well my lord – why, sister–
She merits not this welcome.

BRACHIANO   Welcome, say?
She hath given a sharp welcome.

FRANCISCO   Are you foolish?
Come dry your tears; is this a modest course,
To better what is nought, to rail and weep?   230
Grow to a reconcilement, or by heaven,
I'll ne'er more deal between you.

ISABELLA   Sir you shall not,
No though Vittoria upon that condition
Would become honest.

FRANCISCO   Was your husband loud,
Since we departed?

---

224   s.d. *MONTICELSO* ed. (Montcelso Q)
         Enter . . . MARCELLO ed. (Enter . . . MARCELLO, CAMILLO Q)
225   *take . . . course* Previous editors punctuate so that Brachiano addresses these words
         to Isabella. Without emendation, however, the line may be read as Brachiano's
         invitation to Francisco to proceed against Isabella.
230   *nought* wicked, immoral
234   *honest* chaste

| ISABELLA | By my life sir no. | 235 |

I swear by that I do not care to lose.
Are all these ruins of my former beauty
Laid out for a whore's triumph?

FRANCISCO   Do you hear?
Look upon other women, with what patience
They suffer these slight wrongs, with what justice   240
They study to requite them; take that course.

ISABELLA
O that I were a man, or that I had power
To execute my apprehended wishes,
I would whip some with scorpions.

FRANCISCO   What? Turned fury?

ISABELLA
To dig the strumpet's eyes out, let her lie   245
Some twenty months a-dying, to cut off
Her nose and lips, pull out her rotten teeth,
Preserve her flesh like mummia, for trophies
Of my just anger! Hell to my affliction
Is mere snow-water. By your favour sir –   250
Brother draw near, and my lord cardinal –
Sir, let me borrow of you but one kiss.

                              [*Kisses* BRACHIANO]

Henceforth I'll never lie with you, by this,
This wedding-ring.

FRANCISCO   How? ne'er more lie with him!

ISABELLA
And this divorce shall be as truly kept   255
As if in thronged court a thousand ears

---

236   *lose* ed. (loose Q)

243   *apprehended* conceived, fully understood

244   *I . . . scorpions* Originally a biblical reference (to I Kings 12.11: 'my father hath chastised you with whips, but I will chastise you with scorpions'), the phrase denotes punishment by a whip made of knotted cords or steel spikes.
      Turned fury Cf. Flamineo's words to Cornelia at I.ii.252; a specific style of acting may have been required.

248   *mummia* Cf. I.i.16n.

251–62   *Brother . . . repentance* Unlike Brachiano, Isabella theatricalizes her 'divorce' by drawing attention to spectators/auditors both onstage and off. His appeal to the authority of a 'judge' (l. 197) becomes her evocation of 'a thousand ears' (the theatre audience). Compare Vittoria's appeal to 'this auditory / Which come to hear my cause' at III.ii.15–16. Here Isabella is both parodying and outdoing Brachiano.

Had heard it, and a thousand lawyers' hands
Sealed to the separation.
BRACHIANO   Ne'er lie with me?
ISABELLA
Let not my former dotage
Make thee an unbeliever; this my vow   260
Shall never on my soul be satisfied
With my repentance: *manet alta mente repostum.*
FRANCISCO
Now by my birth you are a foolish, mad,
And jealous woman.
BRACHIANO   You see 'tis not my seeking.
FRANCISCO
Was this your circle of pure unicorn's horn,   265
You said should charm your lord? Now horns upon thee,
For jealousy deserves them; keep your vow
And take your chamber.
ISABELLA
No sir, I'll presently to Padua,
I will not stay a minute.
MONTICELSO   O good madam.   270
BRACHIANO
'Twere best to let her have her humour,
Some half-day's journey will bring down her stomach,
And then she'll turn in post.
FRANCISCO   To see her come
To my lord cardinal for a dispensation
Of her rash vow will beget excellent laughter.   275

262 *manet alta mente repostum* a common phrase originating in Virgil's description of
     Juno's smouldering resentments, 'It shall be treasured up in the depths of my mind'
     (*Aeneid* I, 26) and thus appropriate to Isabella. In the depths of Juno's mind lay
     hatred both for Paris, who scorned her beauty (in choosing Venus), and for the
     Trojan race, descendants of Jupiter's union with Electra, Juno's rival.
     repostum ed. (repositum Q)
266 *horns upon thee* normally, those which grow upon a cuckolded husband's forehead;
     here transferred to Isabella, whose jealousy in Francisco's view has now licensed
     Brachiano's adultery
268 *take . . . chamber* Cf. Brachiano's command at l.154.
268–9 ed. (one line in Q)
272 *stomach* pride, obstinacy; vexation, pique (*OED*)
273 *turn in post* return post-haste

ISABELLA

[*Aside*] 'Unkindness do thy office, poor heart break,
Those are the killing griefs which dare not speak.'   *Exit*

Enter CAMILLO

MARCELLO

Camillo's come my lord.

FRANCISCO

Where's the commission?

MARCELLO

'Tis here.   280

FRANCISCO

Give me the signet.

FLAMINEO

[*To* BRACHIANO] My lord, do you mark their whispering; I will
compound a medicine out of their two heads, stronger than
garlic, deadlier than stibium; the cantharides which are scarce
seen to stick upon the flesh when they work to the heart, shall   285
not do it with more silence or invisible cunning.

Enter Doctor [JULIO]

BRACHIANO

About the murder.

FLAMINEO

They are sending him to Naples, but I'll send him to
Candy; [*Seeing the doctor*] here's another property too.

276–7   *Unkindness . . . speak* a common proverb, signalled in the text by inverted commas
at the left margin. Cf. Seneca, *Hippolytus, or Phaedra* 607: 'Curae leves loquuntur,
ingentes stupent.'

279–80 ed. (one line in Q)

282–318 At this point Webster shifts to a split stage, a characteristic technique (cf. *The
Duchess of Malfi* I.ii.75–133, III.iii), which allows him to highlight visual parallels
and contrasts between different groups.

284   *stibium* metallic antimony, used as a poison
cantharides the dried beetle *cantharis vesicatoria*, or Spanish Fly, applied externally
to produce blisters as a counter-irritant (and taken internally as an aphrodisiac,
among other things), but poisonous if taken in excess

288–9 *to Candy* to Candia (now Crete), whose inhabitants were believed to live on
poisonous snakes – hence, to death

289   *property* stage accessory (for the 'play' Flamineo and Brachiano are writing);
instrument, tool
here's ed. (her's Q)

BRACHIANO

O the doctor. 290

FLAMINEO

A poor quack-salving knave, my lord, one that should have been lashed for's lechery, but that he confessed a judgement, had an execution laid upon him, and so put the whip to a *non plus*.

DOCTOR

And was cozened, my lord, by an arranter knave than myself, and made pay all the colourable execution. 295

FLAMINEO

He will shoot pills into a man's guts, shall make them have more ventages than a cornet or a lamprey; he will poison a kiss, and was once minded, for his masterpiece, because Ireland breeds no poison, to have prepared a deadly vapour in a Spaniard's fart that should have poisoned all Dublin. 300

BRACHIANO

O Saint Anthony's fire!

DOCTOR

Your secretary is merry my lord.

291   *quack-salving* characteristic of a quack doctor
291–3   *should ... non plus* i.e. he should have been whipped for lechery, but that he claimed to be under a previous sentence (for debt), was taken into custody, and in this way rendered the whip ineffectual
294–5   *And ... execution* The doctor was then tricked by a greater rascal than himself (who pretended to be the creditor to whom money was owed), and he was forced to pay out everything required by the legal judgement.
295   *colourable execution* supposed judgement
296   *shoot pills* fire bullets in the form of pills
296–7   *more ... lamprey* more holes than a cornet (wind instrument) or a lamprey (fish with numerous apertures on its head)
298–9   *Ireland ... poison* Ireland was supposed to be free of venomous beasts, because of either the properties of the soil or the influence of St Patrick.
299–300   *deadly ... Dublin* A doubly xenophobic jest: a Spaniard, Don Diego, was notorious for breaking wind in St Paul's some time before 1598; the Irish were supposed to find such smells particularly offensive.
301   *Saint Anthony's fire* or *ignis sacer* (sacred fire), probably slang for breaking wind (Dent, p. 96)
     Anthony's ed. (Anthony Q)

FLAMINEO

O thou cursed antipathy to nature; look, his eye's bloodshed like
a needle a chirurgeon stitcheth a wound with. Let me embrace
thee toad, and love thee, [*Embraces him*] O thou abhominable   305
loathsome gargarism, that will fetch up lungs, lights, heart, and
liver by scruples.

BRACHIANO

No more; I must employ thee honest doctor,
You must to Padua and by the way
Use some of your skill for us.

DOCTOR   Sir I shall.   310

BRACHIANO

But for Camillo?

FLAMINEO

He dies this night by such a politic strain
Men shall suppose him by's own engine slain.
But for your Duchess' death—

DOCTOR   I'll make her sure.

BRACHIANO

Small mischiefs are by greater made secure.   315

FLAMINEO

Remember this you slave; when knaves come to preferment
they rise as gallowses are raised i'th'Low Countries, one upon
another's shoulders.

              Exeunt [BRACHIANO, FLAMINEO *and Doctor* JULIO]

MONTICELSO

[*Hands* CAMILLO *a paper*] Here is an emblem nephew, pray
peruse it.

'Twas thrown in at your window.

303 *bloodshed* bloodshot
305 *abhominable* The common Renaissance spelling retains the false etymology of the
       word as from the Latin *ab homine*, away from man, inhuman, beastly.
306 *gargarism* gargle
       lights another word for lungs
307 *by scruples* in very small quantities
309–10 ed. (one line in Q)
312 *politic strain* cunning exigency; apparent accident
313 *engine* device, means
317–18 *they ... shoulders* improvised gallows, where one man hoists the other on his
       shoulders before stepping aside to leave the prisoner hanging
318 *another's* ed. (another Q)
319 *emblem* a picture expressing a moral fable or allegory, usually accompanied by a
       written gloss, extremely popular in Renaissance Europe

CAMILLO   At my window?   320
  Here is a stag, my lord, hath shed his horns,
  And for the loss of them the poor beast weeps:
  The word *Inopem me copia fecit.*
MONTICELSO   That is:
  Plenty of horns hath made him poor of horns.
CAMILLO
  What should this mean?
MONTICELSO   I'll tell you: 'tis given out   325
  You are a cuckold.
CAMILLO   Is it given out so?
  I had rather such report as that my lord
  Should keep within doors.
FRANCISCO   Have you any children?
CAMILLO
  None my lord.
FRANCISCO   You are the happier:
  I'll tell you a tale.
CAMILLO   Pray my lord.
FRANCISCO   An old tale.   330
  Upon a time Phoebus the god of light,
  Or him we call the sun, would need be married.
  The gods gave their consent and Mercury
  Was sent to voice it to the general world.
  But what a piteous cry there straight arose   335
  Amongst smiths, and feltmakers, brewers and cooks,

---

323 *word* motto
    Inopem ... fecit 'My plenty makes me poor' (Narcissus complaining to his shadow
    in Ovid, *Metamorphoses* III, 466). Like many of Webster's allegories, this one has
    several possible applications, all hinging on the bawdy double meaning of 'horns' as
    the sign for cuckold and penis, deprivation and potency, as well as their ambiguous
    reference to Camillo and Brachiano. Thus the motto could mean that Camillo's
    obvious status as a cuckold has made him impotent (like the weeping stag); or that
    Brachiano's ample sexual satisfaction with Vittoria has left Camillo deprived; or
    even that Brachiano's potency has left him sexually spent (cf. Lodge, *Wits Miserie,*
    Works IV, ii, 321–4: 'his horns are not yet budded, because he moulted them verie
    lately, in the lap of an Harlot', cited by Dent, p. 99).
330–51 This 'old tale' is borrowed from *The Fables of Esop in English* (1596 ed.). It appears
    first to apply mockingly either to the foolish Camillo or to the 'fiery' Brachiano,
    both of whom should be 'gelded', castrated; Francisco neatly twists it to apply to
    Vittoria at the end.

Reapers and butter-women, amongst fishmongers
And thousand other trades, which are annoyed
By his excessive heat! 'Twas lamentable.
They came to Jupiter all in a sweat   340
And do forbid the bans. A great fat cook
Was made their speaker, who entreats of Jove
That Phoebus might be gelded, for if now
When there was but one sun, so many men
Were like to perish by his violent heat,   345
What should they do if he were married
And should beget more, and those children
Make fireworks like their father? So say I,
Only I will apply it to your wife:
Her issue, should not providence prevent it,   350
Would make both nature, time, and man repent it.

MONTICELSO
    Look you cousin,
Go change the air for shame. See if your absence
Will blast your cornucopia. Marcello
Is chosen with you joint commissioner   355
For the relieving our Italian coast
From pirates.

MARCELLO   I am much honoured in't.

CAMILLO   But sir,
Ere I return the stag's horns may be sprouted
Greater than these are shed.

MONTICELSO   Do not fear it,
I'll be your ranger.

CAMILLO   You must watch i'th'nights,   360
Then's the most danger.

---

341 *bans* (banns) of marriage, called in church
348 *fireworks* fiery displays; products of fire or passion (more children); venereal
     disease; devils (NCW II.i.330–50 n.)
353 *Go . . . air* go and leave this place
354 *cornucopia* normally a symbol of fertility, the 'horn of plenty', here ironically the
     'plenty of horns' that are the cuckold's heraldry
358–9 *stag's . . . shed* Are these 'stag's horns' Camillo's or Brachiano's? Since the stag
     sprouted horns in preparation for mating, Camillo may anticipate Brachiano's
     greater sexual vigour in his absence; but since the stag commonly represented the
     cuckold, Camillo may simply fear his shameful status will become more obvious.
360 *ranger* gamekeeper

FRANCISCO   Farewell good Marcello.
   All the best fortunes of a soldier's wish
   Bring you o'ship-board.
CAMILLO
   Were I not best now I am turned soldier,
   Ere that I leave my wife, sell all she hath   365
   And then take leave of her?
MONTICELSO   I expect good from you,
   Your parting is so merry.
CAMILLO
   Merry my lord, o'th'captain's humour right;
   I am resolved to be drunk this night.

                      Exit [*with* MARCELLO]

FRANCISCO
   So, 'twas well fitted, now shall we discern   370
   How his wished absence will give violent way
   To Duke Brachiano's lust.
MONTICELSO   Why that was it;
   To what scorned purpose else should we make choice
   Of him for a sea-captain, and besides,
   Count Lodowick which was rumoured for a pirate,   375
   Is now in Padua.
FRANCISCO   Is't true?
MONTICELSO   Most certain.
   I have letters from him, which are suppliant
   To work his quick repeal from banishment;
   He means to address himself for pension
   Unto our sister Duchess.
FRANCISCO   O 'twas well.   380
   We shall not want his absence past six days;
   I fain would have the Duke Brachiano run
   Into notorious scandal, for there's nought
   In such cursed dotage to repair his name,
   Only the deep sense of some deathless shame.   385
MONTICELSO
   It may be objected I am dishonourable
   To play thus with my kinsman, but I answer,

364   *Were I not best* i.e. would not the best thing for me be
380   *sister Duchess* Monticelso is Camillo's uncle, not Isabella's brother. 'Sister' may be a
      title of courtesy, or Webster may have confused Cardinal Monticelso with Cardinal
      de' Medici, Isabella's brother in life.

For my revenge I'd stake a brother's life
That being wronged durst not avenge himself.
FRANCISCO
Come to observe this strumpet.
MONTICELSO   Curse of greatness,   390
Sure he'll not leave her.
FRANCISCO   There's small pity in't.
Like mistletoe on sere elms spent by weather,
Let him cleave to her and both rot together.

Exeunt

[ACT II, SCENE ii]

Enter BRACHIANO *with one in the habit of a Conjuror*

BRACHIANO
Now sir I claim your promise; 'tis dead midnight,
The time prefixed to show me by your art
How the intended murder of Camillo
And our loathed Duchess grow to action.
CONJUROR
You have won me by your bounty to a deed   5
I do not often practise; some there are,
Which by sophistic tricks aspire that name
Which I would gladly lose, of nigromancer;
As some that use to juggle upon cards,
Seeming to conjure when indeed they cheat;   10
Others that raise up their confederate spirits
'Bout windmills, and endanger their own necks

---

392   *Like ... weather* Cf. III.i.47–8, where Flamineo alludes to the rare medicinal
      qualities of mistletoe, here ironically associated with Brachiano.

  8   *lose* ed. (loose Q)
      nigromancer one who claims to carry on communication with the dead; wizard,
      conjuror (with a suggestion of the 'black art' contained in the prefix nigro-, from
      Latin *niger*, black)
  9   *juggle* play tricks so as to cheat or deceive
 12   *windmills* fanciful schemes or projects

For making of a squib; and some there are
Will keep a curtal to show juggling tricks
And give out 'tis a spirit: besides these   15
Such a whole ream of almanac-makers, figure-flingers,
Fellows indeed that only live by stealth,
Since they do merely lie about stol'n goods,
They'd make men think the devil were fast and loose,
With speaking fustian Latin. Pray sit down,   20
Put on this night-cap sir, 'tis charmed, and now
I'll show you by my strong-commanding art
The circumstance that breaks your Duchess' heart.

A DUMB SHOW

Enter suspiciously, DOCTOR JULIO *and* CHRISTOPHERO; *they
draw a curtain where* BRACHIANO'*s picture is, they put on
spectacles of glass which cover their eyes and noses, and then burn
perfumes afore the picture and wash the lips of the picture; that*

13   *squib* explosive firework
13–15   *some ... spirit* one of many Renaissance references to Mr Banks, who travelled
    around England and the Continent with his performing horse, which was by 1595 a
    docked bay gelding, or curtal, named Morocco. Banks trained Morocco to perform
    some marvellous circus tricks, such as dancing, playing dead, counting money and
    responding to elaborate verbal instructions. Far from giving out that his horse was a
    spirit, however, Banks frequently defended himself against charges of witchcraft –
    apparently successfully, since despite Jonson's claim that he was burned at Rome as a
    witch (*Epigrams* no. 133), he retired to be a vintner in Cheapside.
16   *ream* realm (kingdom); large quantity (of paper)
    figure-flingers casters of horoscopes, pretenders to astrology
17–18   *live ... goods* possible reference to the casting of horoscopes to find stolen goods
19   *fast and loose* a proverbial phrase meaning shifty, unscrupulous: originally, a cheating
    game (in which a string which appeared to be easily made 'fast' or tight was in fact
    'loose', easily undone)
20   *fustian* inflated, made-up gibberish (cf. Francisco to the lawyer at III.ii.46)
23   *breaks ... heart* an echo of Isabella's own last words at II.i.276
23   s.d. DUMB SHOW The first dumb show anticipates Brachiano's own death by a
    poisoned beaver in V.iii (when he fears his kiss will poison Vittoria, l. 27). It also
    recapitulates allegorically the interview between Brachiano and Isabella in II.i, by
    restaging symbolically their kiss of divorce (l. 252). Both these elaborate dumb
    shows allow Webster to represent highly dramatic action while formalizing and dis-
    tancing its emotional impact (especially important in the case of Isabella's murder).
    Each dumb show was probably staged at either side of the full stage (not in a
    discovery space) to maximize the visual spectacle.
23   s.d.1 *suspiciously* in a manner deserving of suspicion
    CHRISTOPHERO like little Jacques the Moor (II.i.0 s.d.) and Guid-Antonio (below), a
    so-called 'ghost character' who appears briefly but delivers no lines. Usually explained

done, quenching the fire, and putting off their spectacles, they depart laughing. Enter ISABELLA *in her nightgown as to bedward, with lights after her, Count* LODOVICO, GIOVANNI, GUID-ANTONIO *and others waiting on her; she kneels down as to prayers, then draws the curtain of the picture, does three reverences to it, and kisses it thrice. She faints and will not suffer them to come near it; dies. Sorrow expressed in* GIOVANNI *and in Count* LODOVICO; *she's conveyed out solemnly.*

BRACHIANO
Excellent, then she's dead.

CONJUROR   She's poisoned
By the fumed picture: 'twas her custom nightly,   25
Before she went to bed, to go and visit
Your picture, and to feed her eyes and lips
On the dead shadow; Doctor Julio
Observing this infects it with an oil
And other poisoned stuff, which presently   30
Did suffocate her spirits.

BRACHIANO   Methought I saw
Count Lodowick there.

CONJUROR   He was, and by my art
I find he did most passionately dote
Upon your Duchess – now turn another way,
And view Camillo's far more politic face,   35
Strike louder music from this charmed ground,
To yield, as fits the act, a tragic sound.

as evidence of Webster's revision, such characters may also suggest Webster's acute theatrical awareness. Not only are silent figures thus clearly individualized, they may also have been doubled for significant visual effect. For example, Julio and Christophero, the murderers of Isabella, may have been doubled with Antonelli and Gasparo, the murderers of Brachiano, to emphasize the play's retributive pattern.
s.d.2 BRACHIANO's ed. (Brachian's Q)

25 *fumed* exposed to ammonia vapour

28 *dead shadow* lifeless image

35 *face* Q4 emends 'face' to 'fate', which may be correct. However, Q may stand if 'politic face' (sagacious visage) is taken to apply ironically to Camillo (cf. Flamineo's remark about Camillo at I.ii.45–8).

36 *Strike . . . music* Webster gives no stage direction to indicate what sort of music was provided, but it would have been appropriate if it issued from beneath the stage (NCW II.ii.36–7 n.).

37 s.d.2 *vaulting-horse* For this detail Webster may have either misunderstood, or knowingly literalized, Monte Cavallo, the actual place where Francesco Peretti, Camillo's historical counterpart, was murdered. The vaulting horse may also furnish

THE SECOND DUMB SHOW

Enter FLAMINEO, MARCELLO, CAMILLO *with four more as Captains, they drink healths and dance, a vaulting-horse is brought into the room,* MARCELLO *and two more whispered out of the room, while* FLAMINEO *and* CAMILLO *strip themselves into their shirts, as to vault; compliment who shall begin; as* CAMILLO *is about to vault,* FLAMINEO *pitcheth him upon his neck, and with the help of the rest, writhes his neck about, seems to see if it be broke, and lays him folded double as 'twere under the horse; makes shows to call for help.* MARCELLO *comes in, laments, sends for the Cardinal and Duke, who come forth with armed men, wonder at the act, commands the body to be carried home, apprehends* FLAMINEO, MARCELLO, *and the rest, and go as 'twere to apprehend* VITTORIA.

BRACHIANO
'Twas quaintly done, but yet each circumstance
I taste not fully.

CONJUROR   O 'twas most apparent,
You saw them enter charged with their deep healths   40
To their boon voyage, and to second that,
Flamineo calls to have a vaulting-horse
Maintain their sport. The virtuous Marcello
Is innocently plotted forth the room
Whilst your eye saw the rest, and can inform you   45
The engine of all.

[BRACHIANO]   It seems Marcello and Flamineo
Are both committed.

CONJUROR   Yes, you saw them guarded,
And now they are come with purpose to apprehend
Your mistress, fair Vittoria; we are now
Beneath her roof: 'twere fit we instantly   50
Make out by some back postern.

    an obscene visual joke at Camillo's expense – since 'vaulting' can mean 'mounting sexually' (as in *Cymbeline* I.vi.134), Camillo's ignominious position under the vaulting horse is a visual sign of his sexual inadequacy.
38 *quaintly* skilfully, ingeniously
41 *boon* prosperous (as in 'bon voyage')
46 *engine* means, contrivance s.p. BRACHIANO ed. (MAR. Q)
47–51 The distanced perspective of the magical dumb shows is suddenly foreshortened; typically in Webster, observers are never safe from involvement in the action of the drama, as one perspective can shift into another with dizzying rapidity.

BRACHIANO   Noble friend,
>You bind me ever to you; this shall stand
>As the firm seal annexed to my hand.
>It shall enforce a payment.
CONJUROR   Sir I thank you.

Exit BRACHIANO

>Both flowers and weeds spring when the sun is warm,   55
>And great men do great good, or else great harm.

Exit

[ACT III, SCENE i]

Enter FRANCISCO, *and* MONTICELSO, *their* CHANCELLOR
and REGISTER

FRANCISCO
>You have dealt discreetly to obtain the presence
>Of all the grave lieger ambassadors
>To hear Vittoria's trial.
MONTICELSO   'Twas not ill,
>For sir you know we have nought but circumstances
>To charge her with, about her husband's death;   5
>Their approbation therefore to the proofs
>Of her black lust, shall make her infamous
>To all our neighbouring kingdoms. I wonder
>If Brachiano will be here.
FRANCISCO   O fie,
>'Twere impudence too palpable.   10

[*Exeunt*]

52–3   *this . . . hand* i.e. this token (money, a jewel, or simply, a handshake) will stand for
>   the seal attached to my signature
> 54   s.d. ed. (to r. of l. 53 in Q)
> 56   s.d. *Exit* ed. (Exit Con. Q)

>   0   s.d.1 As Francisco and Monticelso converse, their chancellor and register may be
>   setting properties in place for the arraignment: a table (III.ii.8), and probably one
>   or two raised chairs or 'states' for Monticelso and Francisco (NCW III.i.0.1 n.).
>   s.d.2 REGISTER registrar (scribe or secretary)
>   2   *lieger* resident
> 9–10   *If . . . fie* / *'Twere . . . palpable* ed. (one line in Q)

Enter FLAMINEO *and* MARCELLO *guarded, and a* LAWYER

LAWYER

What, are you in by the week? So; I will try now whether thy
wit be close prisoner: methinks none should sit upon thy sister
but old whore-masters.

FLAMINEO

Or cuckolds, for your cuckold is your most terrible tickler of
lechery: whore-masters would serve, for none are judges at   15
tilting, but those that have been old tilters.

LAWYER

My lord Duke and she have been very private.

FLAMINEO

You are a dull ass; 'tis threatened they have been very public.

LAWYER

If it can be proved they have but kissed one another—

FLAMINEO

What then?

LAWYER   My lord cardinal will ferret them.   20

FLAMINEO

A cardinal I hope will not catch conies.

LAWYER

For to sow kisses (mark what I say), to sow kisses, is to reap
lechery, and I am sure a woman that will endure kissing is
half won.

FLAMINEO

True, her upper part by that rule; if you will win her nether   25
part too, you know what follows.

[Sennet offstage]

11 *in by the week* ensnared, caught
12 *sit upon* sit in judgement on, with possibly an obscene suggestion of 'sit astride, mount'
14 *tickler* chastiser, punisher; also, provoker, inciter (cf. I.ii.88–90 where the jealous
    cuckold promotes his own betrayal)
16 *tilting* literally, jousting or thrusting as in a tournament; here, with a sexual innu-
    endo of thrusting as in copulation
17 *private* intimate; secretive, secluded
18 *public* open to general observation, conspicuous; also promiscuous (a 'public
    woman' was a prostitute: cf. *Othello* IV.ii.73: 'O thou public commoner')
20 *ferret* literally, to hunt (rabbits, etc.) with ferrets; metaphorically, to hunt down or
    question searchingly
21 *catch conies* literally, catch rabbits (as above); and punning on the senses swindle or
    dupe people; fornicate with women (a 'cony' could be applied to a woman either
    endearingly or indecently)

LAWYER

  Hark, the ambassadors are lighted.

FLAMINEO

    [*Aside*] I do put on this feigned garb of mirth

  To gull suspicion.

MARCELLO   O my unfortunate sister!

  I would my dagger's point had cleft her heart   30

  When she first saw Brachiano. You, 'tis said,

  Were made his engine, and his stalking-horse

  To undo my sister.

FLAMINEO   I made a kind of path

  To her and mine own preferment.

MARCELLO   Your ruin.

FLAMINEO

  Hum! thou art a soldier,   35

  Followest the great Duke, feedest his victories,

  As witches do their serviceable spirits,

  Even with thy prodigal blood. What hast got?

  But like the wealth of captains, a poor handful,

  Which in thy palm thou bear'st, as men hold water –   40

  Seeking to gripe it fast, the frail reward

  Steals through thy fingers.

MARCELLO   Sir–

FLAMINEO   Thou hast scarce maintenance

  To keep thee in fresh chamois.

MARCELLO   Brother–

FLAMINEO   Hear me.

  And thus when we have even poured ourselves

  Into great fights, for their ambition   45

  Or idle spleen, how shall we find reward,

---

32 *engine* instrument

    stalking-horse originally, a trained horse used by a fowler to get within easy reach of
    the game without being observed; hence, a person whose participation in an action
    is used to disguise its real design

37 *As . . . spirits* Witches were commonly supposed to nourish their spirits or familiars
    (usually beasts sent by the devil) with their own milk or blood from supernumary
    teats.

38 *prodigal* wastefully used

43 *chamois* supple leather jerkins worn beneath armour

But as we seldom find the mistletoe
Sacred to physic on the builder oak
Without a mandrake by it, so in our quest of gain.
Alas the poorest of their forced dislikes   50
At a limb proffers, but at heart it strikes:
This is lamented doctrine.

MARCELLO   Come, come.

FLAMINEO

When age shall turn thee
White as a blooming hawthorn—

MARCELLO   I'll interrupt you.

For love of virtue bear an honest heart,   55
And stride over every politic respect,
Which where they most advance they most infect.
Were I your father, as I am your brother,
I should not be ambitious to leave you
A better patrimony.

Enter SAVOY [AMBASSADOR]

FLAMINEO   I'll think on't—   60
The lord ambassadors.

---

47 *mistletoe* parasitic European plant sacred to the Druids which, when found growing
on the oak, was thought to be able to cure illness

48 *on* ed. (: Or Q) *builder* which builds itself up, or is used for building

49 *mandrake* plant with narcotic and medicinal properties whose forked root resembles a human form and attracted superstition: it reputedly shrieked when pulled
out of the ground and grew under the gallows (or the gallows-tree, the oak). The
mandrake in Webster feeds, like the witch's familiars, on blood   (cf. III.iii.107–8),
and drives men mad (cf. *The Duchess of Malfi* II.v.1–2).

50–1 *Alas . . . strikes* i.e. the most insignificant of their feigned dislikes appears to injure
only superficially but in fact it wounds deeply and irrecoverably (because it results
in loss of favour)

60 s.d. ed. (opposite l. 60 in Q)

60–1 *A better . . . on't / The . . . ambassadors* ed. (one line in Q)

61 s.d.2 *Enter French Ambassador* ed. (Enter French Embassadours Q)
Though the stage directions are slightly confusing, the procession is probably led by
Savoy, who is followed by the French ambassador, the English ambassador, the
Spanish ambassador and two more. This takes its place among processions over the
stage, by which Webster highlights pivotal events of his drama (the arraignment,
the papal election, the wedding of Brachiano and Vittoria). Typically, visual spectacle is counterpointed by verbal commentary, and perspectives are always shifting:
the ambassadors are now observed, now observers of the action (cf. IV.iii.4–32).

*Here there is a passage of the lieger Ambassadors over
the stage severally. Enter* FRENCH AMBASSADOR

LAWYER

O my sprightly Frenchman, do you know him? He's an
admirable tilter.

FLAMINEO

I saw him at last tilting; he showed like a pewter candle-stick
fashioned like a man in armour, holding a tilting staff in his   65
hand little bigger than a candle of twelve i'th'pound.

LAWYER

O but he's an excellent horseman.

FLAMINEO

A lame one in his lofty tricks; he sleeps o' horseback like a
poulter.

Enter ENGLISH *and* SPANISH [AMBASSADORS]

LAWYER

Lo you my Spaniard.   70

FLAMINEO

He carries his face in's ruff, as I have seen a serving-man carry
glasses in a cypress hat-band, monstrous steady for fear of
breaking. He looks like the claw of a black-bird, first salted and
then broiled in a candle.

Exeunt

---

63   *tilter* Cf. l. 16 above.

68–9 *he . . . poulter* 'lame' could mean 'impotent': i.e. all his attempts at (sexual) acrobat-
      ics result only in impotence; like poulterers who often fell asleep on the way to
      market. France was famous for both horsemanship and syphilis, which could lead
      to impotence.

72   *cypress hat-band* cobweb lawn or crepe used as a band for the hat

73–4 *He . . . candle* an ingenious analogy, in which the wide ruffs sported by the Spanish
      are compared to the claw of the blackbird which is spread wide when prepared for
      grilling

74   s.d. Flamineo, Marcello and the lawyer exit only to re-enter immediately in the
      larger group, thus emphasizing visually their loss of dramatic control as the
      arraignment begins.

[ACT III, SCENE ii]

THE ARRAIGNMENT OF VITTORIA

Enter FRANCISCO, MONTICELSO, *the six lieger* AMBASSADORS,
BRACHIANO, VITTORIA, [ZANCHE, FLAMINEO, MARCELLO,
SERVANT,] LAWYER, *and a* GUARD

MONTICELSO

[*To* BRACHIANO] Forbear my lord, here is no place assigned
you,

This business by his holiness is left

To our examination.

BRACHIANO   May it thrive with you.

Lays a rich gown under him

---

0 s.d.1 *MONTICELSO* ed. (Montcelso Q)

    s.d.2–3 *ZANCHE . . . MARCELLO* ed. (Isabella Q)

    The title and mass entry signal the central importance of the arraignment for readers. The third act is divided into scenes for the convenience of readers, but may be considered a single unbroken dramatic unit on the stage. In fact, the stage is probably never cleared in Act III, and the ambassadors, Flamineo, Marcello and the lawyer simply take their places, while the others enter. Judging from a title-page woodcut depicting a courtroom scene from *Swetnam the Woman Hater*, a Red Bull play staged about 1619, the original staging may have had Monticelso seated on a throne, facing the standing Vittoria (and possibly Zanche), while the ambassadors, court officials and Francisco, seated on low stools, were symmetrically placed on either side; Brachiano probably sat (conspicuously) on the floor, close to the audience (NCW, pp. 101–3).

    The entry for Isabella – who has just been killed in the previous act – is usually dismissed as an irrational slip, but may be explained by the doubling of Isabella with Zanche (omitted in the stage direction but present in the scene). An actor who had just played Isabella may still have been identified in Webster's mind with that part. When Isabella reappears as a ghost in IV.i (obviously not in the blackface required for Zanche), she may have been shrouded (Francisco replaces his 'dead sister's face' with her more general 'figure' in his imagination, IV.i.98–101) or even played by another actor. Such a doubling would serve not only theatrical economy but also aesthetic design, linking Vittoria with Isabella through Zanche and further blurring the play's black/white, good/evil polarities.

1 *assigned* ed. (assing'd Q)

3 s.d. Brachiano's action may recall I.ii.186ff., where the two lovers rest on 'fair cushions' as they embrace. If so, the lovers' adultery is recalled even as it is about to be punished.

450

FRANCISCO

A chair there for his lordship.

BRACHIANO

Forbear your kindness; an unbidden guest   5
Should travail as Dutch women go to church:
Bear their stools with them.

MONTICELSO   At your pleasure sir.
Stand to the table gentlewomen. Now signior,
Fall to your plea.

[LAWYER]

Domine judex converte oculos in hanc pestem mulierum   10
corruptissimam.

VITTORIA

What's he?

FRANCISCO A lawyer that pleads against you.

VITTORIA

Pray my lord, let him speak his usual tongue.
I'll make no answer else.

FRANCISCO   Why you understand Latin.

VITTORIA

I do sir, but amongst this auditory   15
Which come to hear my cause, the half or more
May be ignorant in't.

8 *Stand ... gentlewomen* Though many editors emend to 'gentlewoman', Monticelso may be referring to Vittoria and Zanche in these dignified terms with heavy irony, since the trial will reveal his contempt for both of them. The women are condemned together (ll. 263–4). The analogies between them that are later suggested would be strengthened by their appearing here side by side. On the other hand, if Vittoria appeared solo (requiring emendation of the text), that would strengthen parallels and contrasts with I.i and II.i, where Lodovico and Brachiano face social disapproval alone. The choice is left to the director.

10 s.p. LAWYER ed. (not in Q). The comically ineffectual lawyer may originally have been doubled with Camillo, 'thus failing twice to bring Vittoria to book' (Thomson, p. 28).

10–11 *Domine ... corruptissimam* 'Lord Judge, turn your eyes upon this plague, the most corrupted of women.'

14 *Why ... Latin* Probably a taunt, for in early modern England women rarely learned Latin. While Vittoria disdains the use of Latin, however, she pointedly uses it at l. 200.

15–16 *this ... cause* probably a reference to the theatre audience (rather than to the well-educated ambassadors), some of whom would also be sitting on the stage at the Red Bull; an early indication of the metadramatic control Webster gives Vittoria

MONTICELSO   Go on sir.
VITTORIA   By your favour,
    I will not have my accusation clouded
    In a strange tongue: all this assembly
    Shall hear what you can charge me with.
FRANCISCO   Signior,   20
    You need not stand on't much; pray change your language.
MONTICELSO
    O for God sake: gentlewoman, your credit
    Shall be more famous by it.
LAWYER   Well then have at you.
VITTORIA
    I am at the mark sir, I'll give aim to you,
    And tell you how near you shoot.   25
LAWYER
    Most literated judges, please your lordships,
    So to connive your judgements to the view
    Of this debauched and diversivolent woman
    Who such a black concatenation
    Of mischief hath effected, that to extirp   30
    The memory of't must be the consummation
    Of her and her projections—
VITTORIA   What's all this?
LAWYER
    Hold your peace.
    Exorbitant sins must have exulceration.
VITTORIA
    Surely my lords this lawyer here hath swallowed   35

---

21   *stand on't* insist on it
22   *credit* reputation
24   *give aim* in archery, to guide someone's aim by informing him of the result of a previous shot
27   *connive your judgements* a malapropism (for 'conduct your judgments'?) caused by the lawyer's pompous search for elaborate terms ('connive' means to shut one's eyes to, to be complicit in, injustice)
28   *diversivolent* wishing strife (a nonce-word, presumably inspired by the lawyer's avid search for Latinisms in place of Latin)
32   *projections* projects
34   *Exorbitant . . . exulceration* i.e. outrageous sins require punishment (ulcers must be lanced)

Some pothecary's bills, or proclamations.
And now the hard and undigestible words
Come up like stones we use give hawks for physic.
Why this is Welsh to Latin.
LAWYER   My lords, the woman
Knows not her tropes nor figures, nor is perfect   40
In the academic derivation
Of grammatical elocution.
FRANCISCO   Sir your pains
Shall be well spared, and your deep eloquence
Be worthily applauded amongst those
Which understand you.
LAWYER   My good lord.
FRANCISCO (*Speaks this as in scorn*)   Sir,   45
Put up your papers in your fustian bag –
Cry mercy sir, 'tis buckram – and accept
My notion of your learn'd verbosity.
LAWYER
I most graduatically thank your lordship.
I shall have use for them elsewhere.   [*Exit*]   50

36   *pothecary's bills* medical prescriptions, often inflated and long-winded. Cf. Webster's
'Character' of a 'Quacksalver': 'a Mountebanke of a larger bill then a Taylor; if
he can but come by names enow of Diseases, to stuffe it with, tis all the skill hee
studies for'.
      proclamations formal orders issued in the name of the sovereign, often written in
inflated prose
38   *Come up* Are vomited
      stones . . . physic 'If your Hawke by over-flying, or too soone flying, be heated and
inflamed in her body, as they are much subject thereunto, you shall then to coole
their bodies, give them stones' (Gervase Markham, *Cheape and Good Husbandry*
(1614) S3).
39   *Welsh to Latin* Renaissance dramatists often used Welsh as the prototype of an
unintelligible language (cf. *A Chaste Maid in Cheapside* IV.i.100–65, *1 Henry IV*
III.i.187–240).
40   *tropes . . . figures* in rhetoric, the figurative use of words or phrases
42   *elocution* oratory: the art of appropriate and effective expression
45   s.d. ed. (to r. of ll. 46–7 in Q)
46   *fustian* a pun: coarse cloth made of cotton and flax; inflated, bombastic language
composed of high-sounding words and phrases
47   *buckram* coarse, stiff linen traditionally used for lawyers' bags (as Francisco would
know)
49   *graduatically* a nonce-word, meaning as a graduate should

MONTICELSO

I shall be plainer with you, and paint out
Your follies in more natural red and white
Than that upon your cheek.

VITTORIA   O you mistake.

You raise a blood as noble in this cheek
As ever was your mother's.   55

MONTICELSO

I must spare you till proof cry whore to that;
Observe this creature here my honoured lords,
A woman of a most prodigious spirit
In her effected.

VITTORIA   Honourable my lord,

It doth not suit a reverend cardinal   60
To play the lawyer thus.

MONTICELSO

O your trade instructs your language!
You see my lords what goodly fruit she seems,
Yet like those apples travellers report
To grow where Sodom and Gomorrah stood: 65
I will but touch her and you straight shall see
She'll fall to soot and ashes.

VITTORIA

Your envenomed pothecary should do't.

51–3   *plainer . . . cheek* The Cardinal is invoking the misogynist stereotype of the 'painted' woman (cf. *Hamlet* III.i.143–4: 'God hath given you one face and you make your-selves another'), and claiming he will use the 'plain' style to 'paint' (show) Vittoria by contrast.

58   *spirit* courage; perhaps punning on the bawdy senses 'semen' or 'erection' (as in *Romeo and Juliet* II.i.23–4: ' 'Twould anger him / To raise a spirit in his mistress' circle')

59   *effected* brought about, produced (a weak and redundant ending to Monticelso's grand rhetorical flourish – here he sounds like the kind of lawyer Vittoria accuses him of playing); ejaculated (NCW III.ii.59 n.)

64–7   *apples . . . ashes* The original source is Deuteronomy 32:32: 'their vine is of the vine of Sodom, and of the fields of Gomorrah; their grapes are grapes of gall, their clus-ters are bitter'. This detail about apples turning to ashes is apocryphal, but frequently invoked by authors such as Sir John Mandeville (*Travels*, p. xxx), who interprets it as a sign of God's vengeance in burning up the cities.

68   *Your . . . do't* i.e. your poisonous apothecary, not you, should reduce me to ashes. Vittoria cleverly turns Monticelso's metaphor against him – his or his apothecary's touch, rather than her nature, is 'envenomed'.

MONTICELSO

    I am resolved.

    Were there a second paradise to lose   70

    This devil would betray it.

VITTORIA   O poor charity!

    Thou art seldom found in scarlet.

MONTICELSO

    Who knows not how, when several night by night

    Her gates were choked with coaches and her rooms

    Outbraved the stars with several kind of lights,   75

    When she did counterfeit a prince's court

    In music, banquets and most riotous surfeits,

    This whore, forsooth, was holy?

VITTORIA   Ha? Whore, what's that?

MONTICELSO

    Shall I expound whore to you? Sure I shall;

    I'll give their perfect character. They are first   80

    Sweetmeats which rot the eater: in man's nostril

    Poisoned perfumes. They are coz'ning alchemy,

    Shipwrecks in calmest weather! What are whores?

    Cold Russian winters, that appear so barren

    As if that nature had forgot the spring.   85

    They are the true material fire of hell,

    Worse than those tributes i'th'Low Countries paid,

    Exactions upon meat, drink, garments, sleep;

    Ay even on man's perdition, his sin.

    They are those brittle evidences of law   90

    Which forfeit all a wretched man's estate

    For leaving out one syllable. What are whores?

    They are those flattering bells have all one tune,

---

70   *lose* ed. (loose Q)

72   *scarlet* colour of a cardinal's vestments and a lawyer's robes

78   *holy?* ed. (holy Q)

80   *character* formal description of a character-type based on the classical models of Theophrastus. Webster contributed several to 2nd edn of Overbury's *Characters.*

82   *Poisoned perfumes* a fleeting verbal reminder of Brachiano's murder of Isabella, which is still undiscovered; Brachiano's unpunished crimes are recalled as Vittoria is tried simply for 'black lust' (III.i.7).
alchemy the process of transforming baser metals into gold, often requiring the investment of vast sums of money by hopefuls (cf. I.ii.138)

87–9   *Worse ... sin* At this time in the Low Countries taxes, especially those on wine, often equalled or exceeded the value of the commodity itself.

At weddings, and at funerals: your rich whores
Are only treasuries by extortion filled,   95
And emptied by curs'd riot. They are worse,
Worse than dead bodies, which are begged at gallows
And wrought upon by surgeons, to teach man
Wherein he is imperfect. What's a whore?
She's like the guilty counterfeited coin   100
Which whosoe'er first stamps it brings in trouble
All that receive it.
VITTORIA   This character scapes me.
MONTICELSO
  You, gentlewoman,
  Take from all beasts, and from all minerals
  Their deadly poison.
VITTORIA   Well what then?
MONTICELSO   I'll tell thee.   105
  I'll find in thee a pothecary's shop
  To sample them all.
FRENCH AMBASSADOR She hath lived ill.
ENGLISH AMBASSADOR
  True, but the cardinal's too bitter.
MONTICELSO
  You know what whore is; next the devil, Adult'ry,
  Enters the devil, Murder.
FRANCISCO   Your unhappy husband   110
  Is dead.
VITTORIA O he's a happy husband
  Now he owes nature nothing.
FRANCISCO
  And by a vaulting engine.
MONTICELSO   An active plot;
  He jumped into his grave.

97–9   *dead … imperfect* The Barber-Surgeons were legally allowed four executed felons a
       year for the purpose of instructing students in anatomy; others may have been
       'begged'.
 100   *guilty* probably with a play on 'gilt'
100–1 *counterfeited … it* For counterfeiting as a metaphor for illicit intercourse, cf.
       Measure for Measure II.iv.45–6.
 101   *brings* ed. (bring Q)
 109   *whore … Adult'ry* ed. (Whore is next the devell; Adultry. Q)

FRANCISCO	What a prodigy was't,	
That from some two yards' height a slender man		115
Should break his neck?		
MONTICELSO	I'th'rushes.	
FRANCISCO	And what's more,	

FRANCISCO   What a prodigy was't,
   That from some two yards' height a slender man   115
   Should break his neck?
MONTICELSO   I'th'rushes.
FRANCISCO   And what's more,
   Upon the instant lose all use of speech,
   All vital motion, like a man had lain
   Wound up three days. Now mark each circumstance.
MONTICELSO
   And look upon this creature was his wife.   120
   She comes not like a widow: she comes armed
   With scorn and impudence. Is this a mourning habit?
VITTORIA
   Had I foreknown his death as you suggest,
   I would have bespoke my mourning.
MONTICELSO   O you are cunning.
VITTORIA
   You shame your wit and judgement   125
   To call it so. What, is my just defence
   By him that is my judge called impudence?
   Let me appeal then from this Christian court
   To the uncivil Tartar.
MONTICELSO   See my lords,
   She scandals our proceedings.
VITTORIA [*Kneeling*]   Humbly thus,   130
   Thus low, to the most worthy and respected
   Lieger ambassadors, my modesty
   And womanhood I tender; but withal
   So entangled in a cursed accusation
   That my defence, of force, like Perseus   135

---

116 *rushes* commonly strewn on the floor in private houses and on the stage
117 *lose* ed. (loose Q)
119 *Wound up* wrapped in a winding-sheet or shroud
122 Vittoria is wearing a sumptuous gown.
128 *Christian* ecclesiastical; civilized (not barbarous)
129 *uncivil* uncivilized. The Tartars were infamous for barbarism and cruelty.
130 *scandals* disgraces s.d. Vittoria may curtsy here; however, kneeling seems an appropriate demonstration of her humility and courage (cf. *The Duchess of Malfi* IV.ii.230) and echoes I.ii.261.
135 *of force* of necessity
     Perseus son of Zeus and Danae. Perseus cut off the head of the Gorgon Medusa and saved Andromeda from the sea monster. In Jonson's *Masque of Queens* (1609),

Must personate masculine virtue to the point.
Find me but guilty, sever head from body:
We'll part good friends: I scorn to hold my life
At yours or any man's entreaty, sir.

ENGLISH AMBASSADOR
She hath a brave spirit. 140

MONTICELSO
Well, well, such counterfeit jewels
Make true ones oft suspected.

VITTORIA   You are deceived.
For know that all your strict combined heads,
Which strike against this mine of diamonds,
Shall prove but glassen hammers, they shall break; 145
These are but feigned shadows of my evils.
Terrify babes, my lord, with painted devils,
I am past such needless palsy, for your names
Of Whore and Murd'ress, they proceed from you,
As if a man should spit against the wind, 150
The filth returns in's face.

MONTICELSO
Pray you mistress satisfy me one question:
Who lodged beneath your roof that fatal night
Your husband brake his neck?

BRACHIANO   That question
Enforceth me break silence: I was there. 155

MONTICELSO
Your business?

BRACHIANO   Why I came to comfort her,
And take some course for settling her estate,
Because I heard her husband was in debt
To you my lord.

MONTICELSO   He was.

BRACHIANO   And 'twas strangely feared
That you would cozen her.

> Perseus, 'expressing heroique and masculine Vertue', routs the antimasque of
> witches and celebrates the virtues of twelve famous queens.

136 *personate* imitate; symbolize, emblematically represent *virtue* moral excellence;
physical courage, valour *to the point* exactly, in every detail
143 *strict combined heads* literally, the joint force of your hammer-heads; figuratively,
your closely allied military forces
148 *palsy* trembling (with fear)

MONTICELSO   Who made you overseer?   160

BRACHIANO

Why my charity, my charity, which should flow
From every generous and noble spirit,
To orphans and to widows.

MONTICELSO   Your lust.

BRACHIANO

Cowardly dogs bark loudest. Sirrah priest,
I'll talk with you hereafter, – Do you hear?   165
The sword you frame of such an excellent temper,
I'll sheathe in your own bowels:
There are a number of thy coat resemble
Your common post-boys.

MONTICELSO   Ha?

BRACHIANO   Your mercenary post-boys.
Your letters carry truth, but 'tis your guise   170
To fill your mouths with gross and impudent lies.
                              [*He makes for the exit*]

SERVANT

My lord your gown.

BRACHIANO   Thou liest, 'twas my stool.
Bestow't upon thy master that will challenge
The rest o'th'household stuff, for Brachiano
Was ne'er so beggarly, to take a stool   175
Out of another's lodging: let him make
Valance for his bed on't, or a demi-foot-cloth,
For his most reverent moil; Monticelso,

---

161 *charity* Cf. l. 71: Brachiano supplies the 'charity' which (as Vittoria remarks)
     Monticelso should show. While it targets Monticelso, the line also exposes Brachiano
     as a liar and possibly a coward, since he is providing himself with an alibi.

166 *sword* metaphoric weapon against Brachiano, which he declares he will use as a
     sword of justice *temper* referring to Monticelso, anger; referring to the sword, the
     resilient strength imparted to steel by tempering

168 *coat* clerical profession

169 *post-boys* letter-carriers

173 *challenge* lay claim to

177 *Valance* drapes around a bed canopy
     demi-foot-cloth half-length covering for a horse, used by lesser dignitaries; an insult
     (NCW III.ii.177 n.)

178 *moil* mule (traditional mount for cardinals)

Nemo me impune lacessit. *Exit*

MONTICELSO

Your champion's gone.

VITTORIA The wolf may prey the better. 180

FRANCISCO

My lord there's great suspicion of the murder,
But no sound proof who did it: for my part
I do not think she hath a soul so black
To act a deed so bloody; if she have,
As in cold countries husbandmen plant vines 185
And with warm blood manure them, even so
One summer she will bear unsavoury fruit,
And ere next spring wither both branch and root.
The act of blood let pass, only descend
To matter of incontinence.

VITTORIA I discern poison 190

Under your gilded pills.

MONTICELSO

[*Showing a letter*] Now the Duke's gone I will produce a letter,
Wherein 'twas plotted he and you should meet
At an apothecary's summer-house,
Down by the river Tiber: view't my lords: 195
Where after wanton bathing and the heat
Of a lascivious banquet – I pray read it,
I shame to speak the rest.

VITTORIA Grant I was tempted,

Temptation to lust proves not the act,
Casta est quam nemo rogavit, 200
You read his hot love to me, but you want
My frosty answer.

---

179 *Nemo me impune lacessit* 'No one wounds me with impunity.' *lacessit* ed. (lacescit Q)
   s.d. *Exit* ed. (Exit Brachiano Q)
190–1 *poison . . . pills* Apothecaries sometimes covered pills with gold in order to increase
   their prices.
193 *he* ed. (her Q)
195 At several points during the scene (ll. 57, 107–8, 119–20, 130–3, 140), the audience's attention is drawn away from the sparring combatants to the ambassadors,
   allowing a more detached assessment of the scene.
200 *Casta est quam nemo rogavit* 'Chaste is she whom no man has asked' (from Ovid,
   Amores I.viii.43). The context of the line is ironic since it occurs in a speech
   designed to persuade a woman to take many lovers.

MONTICELSO   Frost i'th'dog-days! Strange!
VITTORIA
 Condemn you me for that the Duke did love me,
 So may you blame some fair and crystal river
 For that some melancholic distracted man   205
 Hath drowned himself in't.
MONTICELSO   Truly drowned indeed.
VITTORIA
 Sum up my faults I pray, and you shall find
 That beauty and gay clothes, a merry heart,
 And a good stomach to feast, are all,
 All the poor crimes that you can charge me with: 210
 In faith my lord you might go pistol flies,
 The sport would be more noble.
MONTICELSO   Very good.
VITTORIA
 But take you your course, it seems you have beggared me first
 And now would fain undo me; I have houses,
 Jewels, and a poor remnant of crusadoes,   215
 Would those would make you charitable.
MONTICELSO   If the devil
 Did ever take good shape behold his picture.
VITTORIA
 You have one virtue left,
 You will not flatter me.
FRANCISCO   Who brought this letter?
VITTORIA
 I am not compelled to tell you.   220
MONTICELSO
 My lord Duke sent to you a thousand ducats,
 The twelfth of August.
VITTORIA   'Twas to keep your cousin
 From prison; I paid use for't.
MONTICELSO   I rather think
 'Twas interest for his lust.

---

202 *dog-days* very hot and oppressive weather when Sirius the Dog-star is high, and
   when malignant influences including lust were supposed to prevail
215 *crusadoes* Portuguese coins of gold or silver bearing the figure of a cross
223 *use* interest

VITTORIA

 Who says so but yourself? If you be my accuser   225
 Pray cease to be my judge, come from the bench,
 Give in your evidence 'gainst me, and let these
 Be moderators; my lord cardinal,
 Were your intelligencing ears as long
 As to my thoughts, had you an honest tongue   230
 I would not care though you proclaimed them all.

MONTICELSO

 Go to, go to.
 After your goodly and vain-glorious banquet
 I'll give you a choke-pear.

VITTORIA   O' your own grafting?

MONTICELSO

 You were born in Venice, honourably descended 235
 From the Vitelli; 'twas my cousin's fate –
 Ill may I name the hour – to marry you;
 He bought you of your father.

VITTORIA   Ha?

MONTICELSO

 He spent there in six months
 Twelve thousand ducats, and to my acquaintance 240
 Received in dowry with you not one julio:
 'Twas a hard penny-worth, the ware being so light.
 I yet but draw the curtain now to your picture:
 You came from thence a most notorious strumpet,
 And so you have continued.

227 *these* i.e. the ambassadors, or more broadly, the theatre audience
229 *intelligencing* spying
  long ed. (louing Q)
234 *choke-pear* rough, unpalatable pear, difficult to swallow; a severe reproof
  grafting literally, with trees and plants, the action of inserting a shoot or scion into a groove or slit made in another stock, so as to allow the sap of the latter to circulate through the former; with an obvious bawdy sense (as in *The Duchess of Malfi* II.i.148–9)
235–6 *born . . . Vitelli* The real Vittoria was descended from the Accoramboni and born at Gubbio, but Webster may have wanted to associate her with Venice, famed for its prostitutes.
241 *julio* silver coin struck by Pope Julius II (1503–13), formerly current in Italy. There may be an unintended ironic reference to 'Doctor Julio' (cf. II.ii.28) as Vittoria's real 'dowry' or gift to Camillo, especially since the word is italicized like other proper names in the copy.
242 *light* not heavy; wanton, unchaste

VITTORIA   My lord.

MONTICELSO   Nay hear me,   245
  You shall have time to prate – my lord Brachiano –
  Alas I make but repetition,
  Of what is ordinary and Rialto talk,
  And ballated, and would be played o'th'stage,
  But that vice many times finds such loud friends   250
  That preachers are charmed silent.
  You gentlemen Flamineo and Marcello,
  The court hath nothing now to charge you with,
  Only you must remain upon your sureties
  For your appearance.

FRANCISCO   I stand for Marcello.   255

FLAMINEO
  And my lord Duke for me.

MONTICELSO
  For you Vittoria, your public fault,
  Joined to th'condition of the present time,
  Takes from you all the fruits of noble pity.
  Such a corrupted trial have you made   260
  Both of your life and beauty, and been styled
  No less in ominous fate than blazing stars
  To princes; here's your sentence: you are confined
  Unto a house of convertites and your bawd–

FLAMINEO
  [*Aside*] Who I?

MONTICELSO   The Moor.

FLAMINEO [*Aside*]   O I am a sound man again.   265

---

246 *prate . . . Brachiano* – ed. (no punctuation in Q)
     prate tell or repeat to little purpose
248 *Rialto talk* talk of the Exchange, or meeting-place
249 *ballated* turned into a ballad (and thus made notorious)
     would . . . stage As many contemporary scandals were in Webster's time.
254 *sureties* persons who will make themselves liable for another's appearance in court
257 *public* Cf. III.i.18n.
262 *blazing stars* comets, considered signs of ill omen, especially for great men
263 *To . . . here's* ed. (To Princes heares; Q)
264 *Unto* ed. (VIT. Unto Q)
     house of convertites The real-life Vittoria was imprisoned in Castel Sant' Angelo in
     Rome, though a contemporary account, translated by John Florio, claims she was
     'put into a monasterie of Nunnes'. In Jacobean London the 'house of correction' for
     reformed prostitutes was Bridewell.

VITTORIA
  A house of convertites, what's that?
MONTICELSO   A house
  Of penitent whores.
VITTORIA   Do the noblemen in Rome
  Erect it for their wives, that I am sent
  To lodge there?
FRANCISCO
  You must have patience.
VITTORIA   I must first have vengeance.   270
  I fain would know if you have your salvation
  By patent, that you proceed thus.
MONTICELSO   Away with her.
  Take her hence.   [GUARD *leads* VITTORIA *away*]
VITTORIA   A rape, a rape!
MONTICELSO   How?
VITTORIA
  Yes, you have ravished Justice,
  Forced her to do your pleasure.
MONTICELSO   Fie, she's mad.   275
VITTORIA
  Die with these pills in your most cursed maws,
  Should bring you health, or while you sit o'th'bench,
  Let your own spittle choke you.
MONTICELSO   She's turned fury.
VITTORIA
  That the last day of judgement may so find you,
  And leave you the same devil you were before,   280
  Instruct me some good horse-leech to speak treason,
  For since you cannot take my life for deeds,
  Take it for words. O woman's poor revenge
  Which dwells but in the tongue; I will not weep,

266–7   *A . . . Rome* ed. (*A . . . that? / MON . . . whoores./Do . . . Rome*, Q)
269–70 *To . . . there? / You . . . vengeance* ed. (*To . . . patience / I . . . vengeance* Q)
    272 *patent* special licence
    276 *maws* throats, gullets
276–7   *Die . . . health* probably a reference to the 'gilded pills' (l. 191) or apparently pious
        words uttered by her enemies
    281 *horse-leech* literally, blood-sucker; a cunning rhetorician (as in Erasmus, *Praise of
        Folly* (1509): 'the rhetoricians of our day who consider themselves as good as gods
        if like horse-leeches they can seem to have two tongues' (trans. Clarence Miller,
        1979: p. 14))

No I do scorn to call up one poor tear   285
To fawn on your injustice; bear me hence,
Unto this house of – what's your mitigating title?

MONTICELSO

Of convertites.

VITTORIA

It shall not be a house of convertites.
My mind shall make it honester to me   290
Than the Pope's palace, and more peaceable
Than thy soul, though thou art a cardinal.
Know this, and let it somewhat raise your spite,
Through darkness diamonds spread their richest light.

Exit [*with* ZANCHE, *guarded*]

Enter BRACHIANO

BRACHIANO

Now you and I are friends sir, we'll shake hands,   295
In a friend's grave, together: a fit place,
Being the emblem of soft peace t'atone our hatred.

FRANCISCO

Sir, what's the matter?

BRACHIANO

I will not chase more blood from that loved cheek,
You have lost too much already; fare you well.   [*Exit*]   300

FRANCISCO

How strange these words sound? What's the interpretation?

FLAMINEO

[*Aside*] Good, this is a preface to the discovery of the Duchess'
death. He carries it well. Because now I cannot counterfeit a
whining passion for the death of my lady, I will feign a mad
humour for the disgrace of my sister, and that will keep off idle   305
questions. Treason's tongue hath a villainous palsy in't; I will talk

288–9   ed. (one line in Q)
   294   s.d. *Exit* ed. (Exit Vittoria Q)
319–337 Later in the scene Webster employs imultaneous staging which allows visual paral-
         lels (cf. II.i.282–318); the ambassadors silently confer with Monticelso (about the
         trial) while Francisco and Giovanni react to news of Isabella's death: thus Vitto-
         ria's 'disgrace' is juxtaposed with Isabella's 'death' (as in Flamineo's speech, ll.
         303–6), and cause and effect are reversed in the dramatic sequence
   306   *palsy* nervous disease characterized by involuntary tremors.

to any man, hear no man, and for a time appear a politic
madman.   [*Exit*]

Enter GIOVANNI, *Count* LODOVICO

FRANCISCO
How now my noble cousin, what in black?
GIOVANNI
Yes uncle, I was taught to imitate you   310
In virtue, and you must imitate me
In colours for your garments; my sweet mother
Is—
FRANCISCO How? Where?
GIOVANNI
Is there – no, yonder; indeed sir I'll not tell you,
For I shall make you weep.
FRANCISCO   Is dead.   315
GIOVANNI
Do not blame me now,
I did not tell you so.
LODOVICO   She's dead my lord.
FRANCISCO
Dead?
MONTICELSO
Blessed lady; thou art now above thy woes.
[*To* AMBASSADORS] Wilt please your lordships to withdraw a
little?   320
GIOVANNI
What do the dead do, uncle? Do they eat,
Hear music, go a-hunting, and be merry,
As we that live?
FRANCISCO
No coz; they sleep.
GIOVANNI   Lord, Lord, that I were dead—
I have not slept these six nights. When do they wake?   325
FRANCISCO
When God shall please.

319 *Blessed . . . woes* ed. (Dead? . . . Lady / Thou . . . woes Q)
322–3 ed. (one line in Q)

GIOVANNI   Good God let her sleep ever.
   For I have known her wake an hundred nights,
   When all the pillow, where she laid her head,
   Was brine-wet with her tears. I am to complain to you sir.
   I'll tell you how they have used her now she's dead: 330
   They wrapped her in a cruel fold of lead,
   And would not let me kiss her.

FRANCISCO   Thou didst love her.

GIOVANNI
   I have often heard her say she gave me suck,
   And it should seem by that she dearly loved me,
   Since princes seldom do it.   335

FRANCISCO
   O all of my poor sister that remains!
   Take him away for God's sake—

                 [*Exeunt* GIOVANNI *and* LODOVICO]

MONTICELSO   How now my Lord?

FRANCISCO
   Believe me I am nothing but her grave,
   And I shall keep her blessed memory
   Longer than thousand epitaphs.   340

                                  [*Exeunt*]

---

327   *For* ed. (GIO. For I Q) s.p. misplaced

331   *fold of lead* covering made of lead (an aristocratic addition to the more permeable winding sheet made of linen in which all corpses were wrapped); a leaden coffin moulded to the shape of the body (designed to preserve the corpse)

333   *she . . . suck* No mean boast among the English or Italian upper classes, whose infants were usually sent out to wet-nurses. Much of the domestic conduct literature recommended that mothers nurse their own children: 'How can a mother better expresse her love to her young babe, then by letting it sucke of her owne breasts?' (William Gouge, *Of Domesticall Duties* (1612) p. 509).

[ACT III, SCENE iii]

Enter FLAMINEO *as distracted* [, MARCELLO *and* LODOVICO]

FLAMINEO

We endure the strokes like anvils or hard steel,
Till pain itself make us no pain to feel.
Who shall do me right now? Is this the end of service?
I'd rather go weed garlic; travail through France, and be mine
own ostler; wear sheep-skin linings; or shoes that stink of   5
blacking; be entered into the list of the forty thousand pedlars
in Poland.

Enter SAVOY [AMBASSADOR]

Would I had rotted in some surgeon's house at Venice, built
upon the pox as well as on piles, ere I had served Brachiano.

SAVOY AMBASSADOR

You must have comfort.   10

FLAMINEO

Your comfortable words are like honey. They relish well in your
mouth that's whole; but in mine that's wounded they go down
as if the sting of the bee were in them. O they have wrought
their purpose cunningly, as if they would not seem to do it of
malice. In this a politician imitates the devil, as the devil imitates 15

---

0   s.d. *as distracted* The s.d. ('as distracted') may indicate gestures or dress befitting
    the 'distracted' person. The s.d. at V.iv.88 reads 'Cornelia doth this in several forms
    of distraction', suggesting, perhaps, such conventionalized gestures as wringing the
    hands and beating the breast.
5   *ostler* groom, stable-boy *linings* underclothing
6–7 *forty . . . Poland* The Poles were proverbially poor.
9   *built . . . piles* i.e. built on a fortune made from curing syphilis, as well as haemor-
    rhoids (with a pun on 'piles' as pillars or timbers, especially necessary as
    foundations in Venice)
12–13 *they . . . them* lines borrowed from an unidentified translation of Seneca, *Epistles*
    109, 7: 'Some there are to whom honey seemeth bitter in regard of their sicknesse'
    (trans. Lodge). Cf. Pierre Matthieu, *The History of Lewis the Eleventh* (1611):
    'Honey how sweet soever it be, is sharpe and offensive to a mouth ulcered with pas-
    sion and slander' (p. 25).

a cannon. Wheresoever he comes to do mischief, he comes with
his backside towards you.

Enter the FRENCH [AMBASSADOR]

FRENCH AMBASSADOR

The proofs are evident.

FLAMINEO

Proof! 'Twas corruption. O Gold, what a god art thou! And O
man, what a devil art thou to be tempted by that cursed   20
mineral! Yon diversivolent lawyer – mark him, knaves turn
informers, as maggots turn to flies; you may catch gudgeons
with either. A cardinal – I would he would hear me – there's
nothing so holy but money will corrupt and putrify it, like
victual under the line.   25

Enter ENGLISH AMBASSADOR

You are happy in England, my lord; here they sell justice with
those weights they press men to death with. O horrible salary!

ENGLISH AMBASSADOR

Fie, fie, Flamineo.

FLAMINEO

Bells ne'er ring well till they are at their full pitch, and I hope
yon cardinal shall never have the grace to pray well, till he come   30
to the scaffold.

[*Exeunt* AMBASSADORS]

16–17 *Wheresoever . . . you* Showing one's back is not threatening but, as with a cannon,
       one has only to turn to face someone to be a threat.
   21 *Yon* ed. (You Q)
       diversivolent Flamineo uses the lawyer's word against him (cf. III.ii.28).
       turn turn into
   22 *gudgeons* small fish much used for bait; credulous gulls
   25 *victual . . . line* food at the equator
       line ed. (live Q)
   25 s.d. ed. (*Enter English Embassador* l. margin opposite l. 27 in Q)
 26–7 *here . . . with* ironic, since it was English law which devised the *peine forte et dure*, or
       torture of the press, for those who remained mute when required to plead at trial.
       Prisoners who were thus starved and crushed under heavy iron weights died in
       slow agony, though their property could not be confiscated from their heirs
       because they could not be convicted.
   27 *salary* reward
   29 *full pitch* highest point (of a bell-tower)

469

If they were racked now to know the confederacy! But your
noblemen are privileged from the rack; and well may. For a little
thing would pull some of them a' pieces afore they came to their
arraignment. Religion; oh how it is commeddled with policy.   35
The first bloodshed in the world happened about religion.
Would I were a Jew.

MARCELLO

Oh, there are too many.

FLAMINEO

You are deceived. There are not Jews enough, priests enough,
nor gentlemen enough.   40

MARCELLO

How?

FLAMINEO

I'll prove it. For if there were Jews enough, so many Christians
would not turn usurers; if priests enough, one should not have six
benefices; and if gentlemen enough, so many early mushrooms,
whose best growth sprang from a dunghill, should not aspire to   45
gentility. Farewell. Let others live by begging. Be thou one of
them; practise the art of Wolner in England to swallow all's given
thee; and yet let one purgation make thee as hungry again as
fellows that work in a sawpit. I'll go hear the screech-owl. *Exit*

LODOVICO

[*Aside*] This was Brachiano's pander, and 'tis strange   50
That in such open and apparent guilt
Of his adulterous sister, he dare utter
So scandalous a passion. I must wind him.

33 *well may* with good reason
34 *pull . . . pieces* dismember on the rack; reduce to a state of confusion
35 *commeddled* mixed together
    policy intrigue
36 *first . . . religion* a reference to Cain's murder of his brother Abel, possibly fore-
    shadowing Flamineo's murder of Marcello (cf. V.vi.13–14)
39 *Jews* synonymous with usurers, as in *The Merchant of Venice*
44 *early mushrooms* young upstarts
47–8 *practise . . . thee* Wolner was a famous Elizabethan glutton who consumed iron, glass,
    oyster shells, raw meat and raw fish. He died of eating raw eel. Flamineo is very likely
    reiterating his cynical view of Marcello's exploitation by Francisco (cf. III.i.38–43).
49 *a sawpit* ed. (sawpit Q)
    screech-owl bird of evil omen
53 *wind* find out about

Enter FLAMINEO

FLAMINEO

    [*Aside*] How dares this banished count return to Rome,

    His pardon not yet purchased? I have heard   55

    The deceased Duchess gave him pension,

    And that he came along from Padua

    I'th'train of the young prince. There's somewhat in't.

    Physicians, that cure poisons, still do work

    With counterpoisons.

MARCELLO [*Aside*]   Mark this strange encounter.   60

FLAMINEO

    The god of melancholy turn thy gall to poison,

    And let the stigmatic wrinkles in thy face

    Like to the boisterous waves in a rough tide

    One still overtake another.

LODOVICO   I do thank thee

    And I do wish ingeniously for thy sake   65

    The dog-days all year long.

FLAMINEO   How croaks the raven?

    Is our good Duchess dead?

LODOVICO   Dead.

FLAMINEO   O fate!

    Misfortune comes like the crowner's business,

    Huddle upon huddle.

LODOVICO

    Shalt thou and I join housekeeping?

FLAMINEO   Yes, content.   70

    Let's be unsociably sociable.

    55 *purchased* obtained

    56 *pension* salary, wages

60–129 This 'strange encounter' brings the play's two tool-villains into parallel relation: both are the miserable dependants of great men, though Lodovico does not share Flamineo's complex ambivalence about his position.

    61 *gall* gall bladder, supposed source of bitterness and choler

    62 *stigmatic* branded, deformed, ugly

    65 *ingeniously* cleverly (usual sense): also used, mistakenly, to mean ingenuously, candidly

    66 *dog-days* Cf. III.ii.202 n.

        raven another bird of ill omen

    68 *crowner's* coroner's

    69 *Huddle upon huddle* 'tumbling in heaps one over the other' (Lucas, p. 235)

69–70 ed. (Huddle . . . housekeeping? / FLA. Yes, . . . content. Q)

LODOVICO

Sit some three days together, and discourse.

FLAMINEO

Only with making faces;
Lie in our clothes.

LODOVICO

With faggots for our pillows.

FLAMINEO   And be lousy.   75

LODOVICO

In taffeta linings; that's gentle melancholy;
Sleep all day.

FLAMINEO   Yes; and like your melancholic hare
Feed after midnight.

Enter ANTONELLI [*and* GASPARO, *laughing*]

We are observed: see how yon couple grieve.

LODOVICO

What a strange creature is a laughing fool,   80
As if man were created to no use
But only to show his teeth.

FLAMINEO   I'll tell thee what,
It would do well instead of looking-glasses
To set one's face each morning by a saucer
Of a witch's congealed blood.

74–5   ed. (Lie . . . pillowes. / FLA. And . . . lowsie. Q)
   75   *faggots* bundles of sticks
        lousy full of lice; filthy, vile
   76   *taffeta linings* glossy silk underclothing (supposed to protect against lice)
        gentle ed. (gentile Q)
77–8   *melancholic . . . midnight* Hares were supposed to be among the most melancholy
        beasts, sleeping all day and feeding at night (because 'their hart and bloode is cold',
        explains Topsell in *The Historie of Four-footed Beasts* (1607)).
   78   s.d. *Enter Antonelli* ed. (to r. of l. 90 in Q)
   79   *We . . . grieve* Q offers no s.d., though there is space for one. The likeliest explana-
        tion is that Antonelli's entry has been misplaced to 11 lines later (to correspond
        with his speech), and Gasparo's entry omitted. It is less likely, though possible, that
        two ambassadors have remained on stage as witnesses to the comic 'flyting', or
        exchange of insults.
        grieve probably intended ironically, given Lodovico's subsequent remark
   84   *saucer* receptacle for blood in blood-letting

LODOVICO   Precious girn, rogue.   85
  We'll never part.
FLAMINEO   Never: till the beggary of courtiers,
  The discontent of churchmen, want of soldiers,
  And all the creatures that hang manacled,
  Worse than strappadoed, on the lowest felly
  Of Fortune's wheel, be taught in our two lives   90
  To scorn that world which life of means deprives.
ANTONELLI
  My lord, I bring good news. The Pope on's death-bed,
  At th'earnest suit of the great Duke of Florence,
  Hath signed your pardon, and restored unto you–
LODOVICO
  I thank you for your news. Look up again   95
  Flamineo, see my pardon.
FLAMINEO   Why do you laugh?
  There was no such condition in our covenant.
LODOVICO   Why?
FLAMINEO
  You shall not seem a happier man than I;
  You know our vow sir, if you will be merry,
  Do it i'th'like posture, as if some great man   100
  Sat while his enemy were executed:
  Though it be very lechery unto thee,
  Do't with a crabbed politician's face.

---

85 *witch's ... blood* Witches were supposed to be melancholy (Scot, *Discoverie of Witchcraft* (1584) p. 7), hence cold and dry, which caused their blood to congeal. (Cf. *The Taming of the Shrew* Induction ii.132: '. . . too much sadness hath congeal'd your blood'.)
    girn, rogue ed. (gue Q) 'Girn' meant 'the act of showing the teeth; a snarl', and Marston's *Antonio and Mellida* contains a parallel passage; after 'setting of faces' in a looking glass, Balurdo cries: 'O that girn kills, it kills' (III.ii.125–6). Lodovico may be reacting to Flamineo distorting his visage. Altered during press correction from 'grine rogue' to 'gue', the latter (from French *gueux*, beggar), meaning 'rogue, sharper', is rarely accepted as authoritative; 'gue' (which looks like the end of 'rogue') may be the result of a botched attempt at correcting the spelling of both words. Perhaps the compositor mistook the press-corrector's transposition sign for a deletion (see NCW III.iii.82 n.).

89 *strappadoed* hoisted from the ground by the hands when tied across the back, a torture
    felly felloe or section of the rim of a wheel

90 *Fortune's wheel* The proverbial turning of this wheel might raise one to prosperity or lower one to misfortune. For this reason it was frequently conflated, as here, with a torture-wheel (cf. *King Lear* IV.vii.45–6: 'I am bound / Upon a wheel of fire').

LODOVICO
   Your sister is a damnable whore.

FLAMINEO   Ha?

LODOVICO
   Look you; I spake that laughing.   105

FLAMINEO
   Dost ever think to speak again?

LODOVICO   Do you hear?
   Wilt sell me forty ounces of her blood,
   To water a mandrake?

FLAMINEO   Poor lord, you did vow
   To live a lousy creature.

LODOVICO   Yes.

FLAMINEO   Like one
   That had for ever forfeited the daylight,   110
   By being in debt.

LODOVICO   Ha, ha!

FLAMINEO
   I do not greatly wonder you do break:
   Your lordship learnt long since. But I'll tell you—

LODOVICO
   What?

FLAMINEO And't shall stick by you.

LODOVICO   I long for it.

FLAMINEO
   This laughter scurvily becomes your face;   115
   If you will not be melancholy, be angry.   *Strikes him*
   See, now I laugh too.

MARCELLO
   [*Seizing* FLAMINEO] You are to blame, I'll force you hence.

LODOVICO [*To* ANTONELLI *and* GASPARO]   Unhand me.
                Exit MAR[CELLO] & FLAM[INEO]

107–8   *forty . . . mandrake?* Cf. III.i.49 n. Lodovico implies that Vittoria will be executed.

110   *for ever . . . daylight* i.e. been imprisoned for life

112   *break* break your covenant (cf. l. 97); become bankrupt (as in previous line)

113   *learnt* ed. (learn't Q)

114   *stick* remain in your memory; with a suggestion of 'stab, pierce' (though Flamineo clearly uses his fist, not a sword)

118   *Unhand me* Antonelli and Gasparo restrain Lodovico physically as they restrain him verbally in I.i.

That e'er I should be forced to right myself
Upon a pander.
ANTONELLI   My lord.   120
LODOVICO
H'had been as good met with his fist a thunderbolt.
GASPARO
How this shows!
LODOVICO   Ud's death, how did my sword miss him?
These rogues that are most weary of their lives
Still scape the greatest dangers;
A pox upon him: all his reputation –   125
Nay all the goodness of his family –
Is not worth half this earthquake.
I learnt it of no fencer to shake thus;
Come, I'll forget him, and go drink some wine.

Exeunt

[ACT IV, SCENE i]

Enter FRANCISCO *and* MONTICELSO

MONTICELSO
Come, come my lord, untie your folded thoughts,
And let them dangle loose as a bride's hair.
Your sister's poisoned.
FRANCISCO   Far be it from my thoughts
To seek revenge.
MONTICELSO   What, are you turned all marble?
FRANCISCO
Shall I defy him, and impose a war   5
Most burdensome on my poor subjects' necks,
Which at my will I have not power to end?
You know; for all the murders, rapes, and thefts,
Committed in the horrid lust of war,

123   *Ud's death* (By) God's death, an oath

2   *loose . . . hair* Jacobean virgin brides wore their hair loose. Loose or dishevelled hair
     was also a conventional sign for distraction or grief.

He that unjustly caused it first proceed   10
Shall find it in his grave and in his seed.

MONTICELSO

That's not the course I'd wish you: pray, observe me.
We see that undermining more prevails
Than doth the cannon. Bear your wrongs concealed,
And, patient as the tortoise, let this camel   15
Stalk o'er your back unbruised: sleep with the lion,
And let this brood of secure foolish mice
Play with your nostrils, till the time be ripe
For th' bloody audit and the fatal gripe:
Aim like a cunning fowler, close one eye,   20
That you the better may your game espy.

FRANCISCO

Free me my innocence from treacherous acts:
I know there's thunder yonder: and I'll stand
Like a safe valley which low bends the knee
To some aspiring mountain: since I know   25
Treason, like spiders weaving nets for flies,
By her foul work is found, and in it dies.
To pass away these thoughts, my honoured lord,
It is reported you possess a book
Wherein you have quoted, by intelligence,   30
The names of all notorious offenders
Lurking about the city.

MONTICELSO   Sir I do;
And some there are which call it my black book.

15–16   *patient . . . unbruised* In George Wither's *Collection of Emblems* (1635), the tortoise
       represents self-sufficient virtue: 'If any at his harmlesse person strike; / Himselfe hee
       streight contracteth, Torteis-like, / To make the Shell of Suffrance, his defence; / And
       counts it Life, to die with Innocence' (p. 86).   The application of the image in this
       context is thus highly ironic.
    19   *audit* searching inspection
    20   *fowler* hunter of fowl
    22   *from* ed. (fro Q)
  23–5   *I . . . mountain* Though Francisco's words imply that he leaves vengeance to heaven,
       his actions (perhaps gesturing towards and bowing before Monticelso) may appeal
       to Monticelso himself as that 'aspiring mountain'.
    30   *quoted* noted, set down *by intelligence* by secret information
    33   *black book* an official register bound in black; a record of those liable to censure. In
       his *Disputation* (1592), Robert Greene promised to publish a pamphlet called *The
       Blacke Booke* to expose the knaves of London.

Well may the title hold: for though it teach not
The art of conjuring, yet in it lurk   35
The names of many devils.

FRANCISCO   Pray let's see it.

MONTICELSO
    I'll fetch it to your lordship.   *Exit*

FRANCISCO   Monticelso,
    I will not trust thee, but in all my plots
    I'll rest as jealous as a town besieged.
    Thou canst not reach what I intend to act;   40
    Your flax soon kindles, soon is out again,
    But gold slow heats, and long will hot remain.

Enter MONT[ICELSO,] *presents* FRAN[CISCO] *with a book*

MONTICELSO
    'Tis here my lord.

FRANCISCO
    First your intelligencers, pray let's see.

MONTICELSO
    Their number rises strangely,   45
    And some of them
    You'd take for honest men.
    Next are panders.
    These are your pirates: and these following leaves,
    For base rogues that undo young gentlemen   50
    By taking up commodities; for politic bankrupts;
    For fellows that are bawds to their own wives,

---

35 *conjuring* the 'black art' of calling up devils to do one's bidding (cf. *Doctor Faustus*
    I.i.154, where Faustus is advised to consult books by famed magicians like Bacon in
    order to conjure)
37 s.d. *Exit* ed. (Exit Monticelso Q)
39 *jealous* vigilant
42 *heats* ed. (heat's Q)
    s.d. ed. (to r. of ll. 43–4 in Q)
45–8 The sequence of half-lines is unusual, and may indicate pauses in Monticelso's speech
    as he turns the pages and points to sections of his black book (Brown IV.i.45–8 n.)
51 *taking up commodities* To circumvent laws against high rates of interest, swindlers
    lent cheap commodities, at a highly inflated value, instead of money. Then the
    gullible borrower, required to repay the alleged value of the commodities, often
    ended up in debtors' prison.
    politic bankrupts those who feign bankruptcy in order to avoid creditors

Only to put off horses and slight jewels,
Clocks, defaced plate, and such commodities,
At birth of their first children.

FRANCISCO   Are there such?   55

MONTICELSO
These are for impudent bawds
That go in men's apparel; for usurers
That share with scriveners for their good reportage:
For lawyers that will antedate their writs:
And some divines you might find folded there,   60
But that I slip them o'er for conscience' sake.
Here is a general catalogue of knaves.
A man might study all the prisons o'er
Yet never attain this knowledge.

FRANCISCO   Murderers.
Fold down the leaf I pray;   65
Good my lord let me borrow this strange doctrine.

MONTICELSO
[*Handing him the book*] Pray use't my lord.

FRANCISCO   I do assure your
    lordship,
You are a worthy member of the state,
And have done infinite good in your discovery
Of these offenders.

MONTICELSO   Somewhat sir.

FRANCISCO   O God!   70
Better than tribute of wolves paid in England,
'Twill hang their skins o'th'hedge.

53–5 *Only . . . commodities* i.e. men who prostituted their own wives in exchange for
      goods sold at an inflated price to their wives' lovers
56–7 *impudent . . . apparel* a reference to the contemporary controversy surrounding
      women crossdressing as men, some of whom were prostitutes, all of whom were
      attacked in antifeminist tracts
57–8 *usurers . . . reportage* i.e. moneylenders who give a 'cut' to scriveners (who supplied
      those who wanted to raise money on security) in exchange for their recommenda-
      tion, their good report
  59 *antedate . . . writs* i.e. produce a phony legal document (alleging an offence) ante-
      dated so as to take precedence over, and thus displace, a genuine one (cf. II.i.291–5)
  71 *tribute . . . England* The Welsh were supposedly ordered by King Edgar (944–75) to
      pay a tribute of three hundred wolves a year as a means of controlling the wolf
      population in Wales.

MONTICELSO   I must make bold
  To leave your lordship.
FRANCISCO   Dearly sir, I thank you;
  If any ask for me at court, report
  You have left me in the company of knaves.   75

                           Exit MONT[ICELSO]

  I gather now by this, some cunning fellow
  That's my lord's officer, one that lately skipped
  From a clerk's desk up to a justice' chair,
  Hath made this knavish summons; and intends,
  As th'Irish rebels wont were to sell heads,   80
  So to make prize of these. And thus it happens,
  Your poor rogues pay for't, which have not the means
  To present bribe in fist: the rest o'th'band
  Are razed out of the knaves' record; or else
  My lord he winks at them with easy will,   85
  His man grows rich, the knaves are the knaves still.
  But to the use I'll make of it; it shall serve
  To point me out a list of murderers,
  Agents for any villainy. Did I want
  Ten leash of courtesans, it would furnish me;   90
  Nay laundress three armies. That in so little paper
  Should lie th'undoing of so many men!
  'Tis not so big as twenty declarations.
  See the corrupted use some make of books:
  Divinity, wrested by some factious blood,   95
  Draws swords, swells battles, and o'erthrows all good.
  To fashion my revenge more seriously,
  Let me remember my dead sister's face:
  Call for her picture: no; I'll close mine eyes,
  And in a melancholic thought I'll frame   100

---

80 *Irish ... heads* A bounty was paid by Elizabeth I's officers for heads in the Irish
     rebellions.
90 *leash* set of three (animals or birds used in hunting)
91 *laundress* furnish with laundresses (reputedly of easy virtue) *in so* ed. (so in Q)
93 *declarations* official proclamations
95 *wrested ... blood* i.e. stirred by some violent, seditious passion
100 s.d. *Enter* ISABELLA's *Ghost* Francisco's view of the ghost as a figment of his own
      imagination is in tension with a long stage tradition of unquestioned presentation
      of ghosts. This one is highly ambiguous, unlike the ghost of Brachiano which
      appears in V.iv.

Enter ISABEL[L]A*'s Ghost*

Her figure 'fore me. Now I ha't – d'foot! How strong
Imagination works! How she can frame
Things which are not! Methinks she stands afore me;
And by the quick idea of my mind,
Were my skill pregnant, I could draw her picture.   105
Thought, as a subtle juggler, makes us deem
Things supernatural which have cause
Common as sickness. 'Tis my melancholy;
How cam'st thou by thy death? How idle am I
To question my own idleness? Did ever   110
Man dream awake till now? Remove this object,
Out of my brain with't: what have I to do
With tombs, or death-beds, funerals, or tears,
That have to meditate upon revenge?

                         [*Exit Ghost*]

So now 'tis ended, like an old wives' story.   115
Statesmen think often they see stranger sights
Than madmen. Come, to this weighty business.
My tragedy must have some idle mirth in't,
Else it will never pass. I am in love,
In love with Corombona, and my suit   120
Thus halts to her in verse. –   *Writes*
I have done it rarely: O the fate of princes!

---

101   *ha't – d'foot* ed. (– ha'te Q) The uncorrected Q reads 'Now I – d'foot' ('by God's
      foot', an oath). The editors of NCW hypothesize (IV.i.99 n.) that the mark of inclu-
      sion for 'ha'te' led the corrector to think that 'd'foot' was being struck out. If both
      words stand, the actor can register more effectively the shock of opening his eyes to
      find a real ghost before him.
104   *quick* active, vital
105   *pregnant* fertile, imaginative
106   *juggler* conjuror, magician
108   *melancholy* During the Renaissance, melancholy was believed to be a physiological
      disease caused by an excess of black bile which often produced visual hallucina-
      tions: 'From the fuming melancholy of our spleen mounteth that hot matter into
      the higher region of the brain, whereof many fearful visions are framed' (Thomas
      Nashe, *Terrors of the Night* (1594)).
110   *idleness* folly; delirium
121   *halts* is defective in rhyme and measure (like this line)
      s.d. ed. (opposite l. 123 in Q)
      s.d. *Writes* ed. (he writes Q)

I am so used to frequent flattery,
That being alone I now flatter myself;
But it will serve; 'tis sealed.

Enter SERVANT

                Bear this   125
To th'house of convertites; and watch your leisure
To give it to the hands of Corombona,
Or to the matron, when some followers
Of Brachiano may be by. Away.
                            Exit SERVANT
He that deals all by strength, his wit is shallow: 130
When a man's head goes through, each limb will follow.
The engine for my business, bold Count Lodowick;
'Tis gold must such an instrument procure,
With empty fist no man doth falcons lure.
Brachiano, I am now fit for thy encounter.   135
Like the wild Irish I'll ne'er think thee dead
Till I can play at football with thy head.
Flectere si nequeo superos, Acheronta movebo.   *Exit*

[ACT IV, SCENE ii]

Enter the MATRON, *and* FLAMINEO

MATRON
Should it be known the Duke hath such recourse
To your imprisoned sister, I were like
T'incur much damage by it.

---

131   *When . . . follow* proverbial image for a cunning fox or snake, here applied to a man
134   *lure* i.e. train a falcon to come to the lure (a bunch of feathers held by the falconer
       resembling its prey); hence entice, tempt
136–7 The Irish were notoriously cruel and bloodthirsty.
138   *Flectere . . . movebo* 'If I cannot prevail upon the gods above, I will move the gods of
       the infernal regions' (Virgil, *Aeneid* VII, 312). This was a stock remark for villains
       in the drama.
       s.d. *Exit* ed. (Exit Mon. Q)

FLAMINEO   Not a scruple.
The Pope lies on his death-bed, and their heads
Are troubled now with other business   5
Than guarding of a lady.

Enter SERVANT [*with the letter*]

SERVANT
[*Aside*] Yonder's Flamineo in conference
With the Matrona. [*To the* MATRON] Let me speak with you.
I would entreat you to deliver for me
This letter to the fair Vittoria–   10
MATRON
I shall sir.

Enter BRACHIANO

SERVANT   With all care and secrecy;
Hereafter you shall know me, and receive
Thanks for this courtesy.   [*Exit*]
FLAMINEO   How now? What's that?
MATRON
A letter.
FLAMINEO To my sister: I'll see't delivered.
                    [*Takes the letter. Exit* MATRON]
BRACHIANO
What's that you read Flamineo?
FLAMINEO   Look.   15
                    [*Gives him the letter*]
BRACHIANO
Ha? [*Reads*] 'To the most unfortunate his best respected
    Vittoria –'
Who was the messenger?

---

    3 *scruple* very small quantity; with a play on the usual modern sense, a thought that
       troubles the conscience
    4 *Pope ... death-bed* Gregory XIII, historically responsible for Vittoria's imprison-
       ment in a monastery, died on 10 April 1585.
    10 *letter ... Vittoria* Francisco's letter to Vittoria becomes an important prop in this
       scene; passed rapidly from one character to another, it triggers explosive feeling and
       reinforces gesturally the heated verbal exchanges.

FLAMINEO   I know not.

BRACHIANO

  No! Who sent it?

FLAMINEO   Ud's foot, you speak as if a man

  Should know what fowl is coffined in a baked meat

  Afore you cut it up.   20

BRACHIANO

  I'll open't, were't her heart. What's here subscribed –

  Florence? This juggling is gross and palpable.

  I have found out the conveyance; read it, read it.

                           [*Thrusts the letter at* FLAMINEO]

FLAMINEO

  (*Reads the letter*) 'Your tears I'll turn to triumphs, be but mine.

  Your prop is fall'n; I pity that a vine   25

  Which princes heretofore have longed to gather,

  Wanting supporters, now should fade and wither.'

  Wine i'faith, my lord, with lees would serve his turn.

  'Your sad imprisonment I'll soon uncharm,

  And with a princely uncontrolled arm   30

  Lead you to Florence, where my love and care

  Shall hang your wishes in my silver hair.'

  A halter on his strange equivocation.

  'Nor for my years return me the sad willow:

---

18   *Ud's foot* (By) God's foot (see III.iii.122)

19   *coffined ... meat* i.e. enclosed in pastry or in a pie

22   ed. (Florence? / This Q)

     juggling ... palpable i.e. this deception is plain and manifest

23   *conveyance* means of communication; cunning contrivance; document by which property (i.e. Vittoria) is transferred from one person to another (NCW IV.ii.24 n.)

24   s.d. *Reads the letter* ed. (outer r. margin ll. 24–5 in Q)

24–7   *Your ... wither* Cf. III.ii.185–8, where Francisco describes Vittoria as a vine in a much less complimentary context; cf. also II.i.391–3, where in Francisco's analogy Brachiano is the vine and Vittoria the withered, rotting elm.

28   *Wine ... turn* Flamineo mockingly takes Francisco's analogy literally: wine with its dregs (lees) can be made by gathering vines.

30   *uncontrolled* ungoverned, not subjected to control

33   *halter ... equivocation* Flamineo calls for a rope with a noose (a halter) to emphasize Francisco's 'equivocation', his possibly duplicitous use of the word 'hang' (as a threat as well as a promise).

34   *willow* sign of a rejected lover

Who prefer blossoms before fruit that's mellow?'   35
Rotten on my knowledge with lying too long i'th' bed-straw.
'And all the lines of age this line convinces:
The gods never wax old, no more do princes.'
A pox on't, tear it, let's have no more atheists for God's sake.

BRACHIANO

Ud's death, I'll cut her into atomies   40
And let th'irregular north-wind sweep her up
And blow her int' his nostrils. Where's this whore?

FLAMINEO

That –? What do you call her?

BRACHIANO   O, I could be mad,
Prevent the curst disease she'll bring me to,
And tear my hair off. Where's this changeable stuff?   45

FLAMINEO

O'er head and ears in water, I assure you,
She is not for your wearing.

BRACHIANO   In you pander!

FLAMINEO

[*Facing him*] What me, my lord, am I your dog?

BRACHIANO

A bloodhound: do you brave? Do you stand me?

---

   36   *Rotten . . . bed-straw* Fruit was ripened in straw; people could grow melancholy and
        lousy by lying too long in bed (where straw served as a mattress); cf. III.iii.74–7.
   37   *all . . . convinces* i.e. all the wrinkles of age this line refutes; all the maxims of old
        this maxim confutes
   39   *atheists* Here, Francisco is an 'atheist' because he appears to deny the Christian God
        by invoking the classical gods. Flamineo again wittily reacts with shock not to
        Francisco's attempted seduction of Vittoria but to his stale analogies.
   40   *atomies* minute particles, motes
   41   *irregular* disorderly
   43   *That –?* ed. (That? Q)
44–5   *Prevent . . . off* i.e. forestall the hair loss caused by venereal disease I'll contract from
        her by tearing out my own hair
   45   *changeable stuff* inconstant whore; material such as shot or watered silk that shows
        different colours under different aspects (a sense unintended by Brachiano, played
        on by Flamineo)
46–7   *O'er . . . wearing* i.e. literally, in deep water, thus unfit to be worn (whereas watered
        silk would be); figuratively, absorbed in weeping, and thus unfit for Brachiano's
        offered destruction
   49   *bloodhound* hunter for blood (for lifeblood and for sexual passion, as in the case of
        a pander)
        brave defy
        stand withstand

FLAMINEO

    Stand you? Let those that have diseases run;   50

    I need no plasters.

BRACHIANO

    Would you be kicked?

FLAMINEO   Would you have your neck broke?

    I tell you duke, I am not in Russia;

    My shins must be kept whole.

BRACHIANO   Do you know me?

FLAMINEO

    O my lord! Methodically.   55

    As in this world there are degrees of evils:

    So in this world there are degrees of devils.

    You're a great Duke; I your poor secretary.

    I do look now for a Spanish fig, or an Italian sallet daily.

BRACHIANO

    Pander, ply your convoy, and leave your prating.   60

FLAMINEO

    All your kindness to me is like that miserable courtesy of
    Polyphemus to Ulysses; you reserve me to be devoured last. You
    would dig turves out of my grave to feed your larks: that would
    be music to you. Come, I'll lead you to her.   [*Walks backwards*]

---

  50 *run* as in the usual sense, move away quickly; also, ooze (as from a 'running' sore,
      requiring plasters)

51–2 *I . . . plasters / Would . . . broke?* ed. (I . . . kickt? / FLA. Would . . . broke? Q)

  52 *Would . . . broke?* Flamineo threateningly reminds Brachiano of his expert murder
      of Camillo (II.ii.37).

53–4 *I . . . whole* The Russians reputedly punished those who refused to pay their debts
      ('politic bankrupts') by beating them on the shins.

  55 *Methodically* in accordance with a prescribed method

  59 *Spanish fig* insulting gesture of thrusting thumb between two closed fingers or into
      the mouth; also poison; *Italian sallet* Italian salad; poisonous concoction – Italians
      being notorious in Renaissance tragedy for clever ways to kill

  60 *ply . . . convoy* i.e. get on with your business (of pandering)

61–2 *miserable . . . last* In Homer's *Odyssey* (IX, 369–70), Polyphemus, a Cyclops (a
      savage one-eyed giant), promised Ulysses a hospitable gift, which turned out to be
      the vow to eat him last. In the end, Ulysses blinded the Cyclops.

  63 *turves* pl. of turf.

62–3 *You . . . larks* i.e. you would dig grassy slabs from my grave to feed your ethereal
      birds; figuratively, you would mutilate my body to feed your soul

BRACHIANO

    Do you face me?   65

FLAMINEO

    O sir, I would not go before a politic enemy with my back
    towards him, though there were behind me a whirlpool.

Enter VITTORIA *to* BRACHIANO *and* FLAMINEO

BRACHIANO

    [*Showing the letter*] Can you read, mistress? Look upon that letter;
    There are no characters nor hieroglyphics.
    You need no comment, I am grown your receiver;   70
    God's precious, you shall be a brave great lady,
    A stately and advanced whore.

VITTORIA   Say, sir.

BRACHIANO

    Come, come, let's see your cabinet, discover
    Your treasury of love-letters. Death and furies,
    I'll see them all.

VITTORIA   Sir, upon my soul,   75

    I have not any. Whence was this directed?

BRACHIANO

    Confusion on your politic ignorance.
    You are reclaimed; are you? I'll give you the bells
    And let you fly to the devil.   [*Gives her the letter*]

---

    65 *face* stand facing; brave, defy
    67 s.d. Flamineo offers to 'lead' Brachiano to Vittoria, but the s.d. suggests that Vittoria
          enters (perhaps via the discovery space). An unsummoned entry, imitating the
          force of the 'whirlpool' (l. 67), would immediately give her dramatic control.
    69 *characters* cabbalistic or magical signs
    70 *comment* commentary, explanation (of the 'hieroglyphics')
          receiver procurer, pimp
    71 *God's precious* i.e. by God's precious blood (an oath)
    73 *cabinet* case for letters or jewels, casket
    78 *reclaimed* redeemed from a wrong course of action; (in falconry) called back,
          tamed after being let fly
 78–9 *I'll . . . devil* In falconry, bells attached to the hawk's legs aided recovery of the prey.
          In his disgust, Brachiano rejects everything associated with Vittoria.
    79 *Ware hawk* either, simply, 'Watch out for what *this* hawk might do (when she gets
          angry)' or 'Beware the officer who pounces upon rogues' (warning Brachiano against
          Vittoria's retaliation), or an imitation of the hunting call used by the falconer when
          patiently training a hawk to enjoy the rewards of its own kill (Dent, pp. 124–5;
          implying that Brachiano should reward her with his attentions?)

FLAMINEO   Ware hawk, my lord.

VITTORIA

Florence! This is some treacherous plot, my lord,   80
To me he ne'er was lovely I protest,
So much as in my sleep.

BRACHIANO   Right: they are plots.
Your beauty! O, ten thousand curses on't.
How long have I beheld the devil in crystal?
Thou hast led me, like an heathen sacrifice,   85
With music and with fatal yokes of flowers
To my eternal ruin. Woman to man
Is either a god or a wolf.

VITTORIA [*Weeps*]   My lord.

BRACHIANO   Away.
We'll be as differing as two adamants:
The one shall shun the other. What? Dost weep?   90
Procure but ten of thy dissembling trade,
Ye'd furnish all the Irish funerals
With howling, past wild Irish.

FLAMINEO   Fie, my lord.

BRACHIANO

That hand, that cursed hand, which I have wearied
With doting kisses! O my sweetest Duchess   95
How lovely art thou now! [*To* VITTORIA] Thy loose thoughts
Scatter like quicksilver. I was bewitched;
For all the world speaks ill of thee.

VITTORIA   No matter.
I'll live so now I'll make that world recant
And change her speeches. You did name your Duchess.   100

---

81 *lovely* amorous, affectionate; lovable, attractive
84 *devil in crystal* a common expression signifying self-deception, easy credulity
87–8 *Woman ... wolf* used proverbially for the relation of man to man, and applied by
     Montaigne to marriage (*Essays*, trans. Florio III, v)
89 *adamants* loadstones, magnets
92–3 *furnish ... Irish* According to contemporary accounts, the Irish hired women to
     mourn the dead; 'for some small recompence given them, [they] will furnish the
     cry, with greater shriking and howling, then those that are grieved indeede'. 'To
     weep Irish' thus meant 'to weepe at pleasure, without cause, or griefe' (Rich, *A New
     Description of Ireland* (1610), p. 13).
94–5 The gesture recalls Brachiano's divorce from Isabella by kissing her hand (II.i.192).

BRACHIANO
    Whose death God pardon.
VITTORIA   Whose death God revenge
    On thee, most godless Duke.
FLAMINEO   Now for two whirlwinds.
VITTORIA
    What have I gained by thee but infamy?
    Thou hast stained the spotless honour of my house,
    And frighted thence noble society: 105
    Like those which, sick o'th'palsy, and retain
    Ill-scenting foxes 'bout them, are still shunned
    By those of choicer nostrils. What do you call this house?
    Is this your palace? Did not the judge style it
    A house of penitent whores? Who sent me to it?   110
    Who hath the honour to advance Vittoria
    To this incontinent college? Is't not you?
    Is't not your high preferment? Go, go brag
    How many ladies you have undone, like me.
    Fare you well sir; let me hear no more of you.   115
    I had a limb corrupted to an ulcer,
    But I have cut it off: and now I'll go
    Weeping to heaven on crutches. For your gifts,
    I will return them all; and I do wish
    That I could make you full executor   120
    To all my sins – O that I could toss myself
    Into a grave as quickly: for all thou art worth
    I'll not shed one tear more – I'll burst first.
                Throws herself [face down] upon a bed [and weeps]
BRACHIANO
    I have drunk Lethe. Vittoria?

---

102   *two* ed. (tow Q)
108   *those . . . nostrils* Foxes, known for their foul odour, were commonly used in the
       treatment of the palsy (a disease characterized by involuntary tremors or paralysis).
113   *preferment* promotion
116   *I . . . ulcer* The historic Brachiano had a malignant ulcer in his leg.
116–18 *I . . . crutches* An echo of St Mark 9.45: 'And if thy foot offend thee, cut it off: it is
       better for thee to enter halt into life, than having two feet to be cast into hell'.
123   s.d. *Throws* ed. (She throws Q)
       s.d. *Throws . . . bed* The bed may be thrust out on the stage at the beginning of
       the scene, or, perhaps, upon Vittoria's entry (l. 67). Vittoria's dramatic physical
       gesture, more than her words, seems to precipitate Brachiano's abrupt change of heart.
124   *Lethe* river of oblivion, forgetfulness

My dearest happiness? Vittoria?   125
What do you ail my love? Why do you weep?
VITTORIA
[*Turns to him*] Yes, I now weep poniards, do you see.
BRACHIANO
Are not those matchless eyes mine?
VITTORIA   I had rather
They were not matches.
BRACHIANO   Is not this lip mine?
VITTORIA
[*Turning away*] Yes: thus to bite it off, rather than give it thee.   130
FLAMINEO
Turn to my lord, good sister.
VITTORIA   Hence you pander.
FLAMINEO
Pander! Am I the author of your sin?
VITTORIA
Yes: he's a base thief that a thief lets in.
FLAMINEO
We're blown up, my lord—
BRACHIANO   Wilt thou hear me?
Once to be jealous of thee is t'express   135
That I will love thee everlastingly,
And never more be jealous.
VITTORIA   O thou fool,
Whose greatness hath by much o'ergrown thy wit!
What dar'st thou do that I not dare to suffer,
Excepting to be still thy whore? For that,   140
In the sea's bottom sooner thou shalt make
A bonfire.
FLAMINEO O, no oaths for God's sake.
BRACHIANO
Will you hear me?

124–5 *I . . . Vittoria?* ed. (I . . . Lethe / Vittoria? . . . Vittoria? Q)
  127 *poniards* daggers (suggesting her anger as well as grief)
128–9 *I . . . matches* a play on 'matchless' as 'not matches'. i.e. I had rather my eyes were
       not symmetrical. Vittoria's desire to thwart an unwanted lover by mutilating herself
       recalls Celia's in *Volpone* III.vii.251–7.
  134 *blown up* shattered, as by the explosion of a mine

VITTORIA Never.

FLAMINEO

What a damned imposthume is a woman's will?
Can nothing break it? Fie, fie, my lord. 145
Women are caught as you take tortoises,
She must be turned on her back. Sister, by this hand
I am on your side. Come, come, you have wronged her.
What a strange credulous man were you, my lord,
To think the Duke of Florence would love her? 150
Will any mercer take another's ware
When once 'tis toused and sullied? And yet sister,
How scurvily this frowardness becomes you!
Young leverets stand not long; and women's anger
Should, like their flight, procure a little sport; 155
A full cry for a quarter of an hour;
And then be put to th'dead quat.

BRACHIANO   Shall these eyes,
Which have so long time dwelt upon your face,
Be now put out?

FLAMINEO   No cruel landlady i'th'world,
Which lends forth groats to broom-men, and takes use for them 160
Would do't.
Hand her, my lord, and kiss her: be not like
A ferret to let go your hold with blowing.

144 *imposthume* abscess, festering sore
144–67 Flamineo is playing his part as pander by encouraging each of the lovers to move towards reconciliation; it is unclear, however, whether his lines are asides directed at Brachiano and Vittoria in turn or delivered openly in the hearing of both. The choice is ultimately the actor's; however, given Flamineo's generally open misogyny (cf. I.ii.106–10, 180–2), the latter seems more likely.
146–7 *Women . . . back* To catch tortoises one need only turn them on their backs.
151 *mercer* merchant dealing in silks, velvets and other costly materials
152 *toused* rumpled; (of a woman) abused, roughly handled
153 *frowardness* naughtiness, perversity
154 *leverets* young hares (once thought to be all female); mistresses
stand hold out (in the hunt)
156 *full cry* full pursuit (of the hounds); open weeping
157 *quat* squat (position taken by a cornered hare)
160 i.e. who lends pennies to street-sweepers and earns interest on them
them ed. (the Q)
162 *Hand* fondle
162–3 *be . . . blowing* Blowing at a ferret forces it to let go of the thing its teeth are fixed in.

BRACHIANO

Let us renew right hands.

VITTORIA   Hence.

BRACHIANO

Never shall rage, or the forgetful wine,   165

Make me commit like fault.

FLAMINEO

Now you are i'th'way on't, follow't hard.

BRACHIANO

Be thou at peace with me; let all the world

Threaten the cannon.

FLAMINEO   Mark his penitence.

Best natures do commit the grossest faults   170

When they're giv'n o'er to jealousy; as best wine

Dying makes strongest vinegar. I'll tell you;

The sea's more rough and raging than calm rivers,

But nor so sweet nor wholesome. A quiet woman

Is a still water under a great bridge.   175

A man may shoot her safely.

VITTORIA

O ye dissembling men!

FLAMINEO   We sucked that, sister,

From women's breasts in our first infancy.

VITTORIA

To add misery to misery.

BRACHIANO   Sweetest.

VITTORIA

Am I not low enough?   180

Ay, ay, your good heart gathers like a snowball

Now your affection's cold.

FLAMINEO   Ud's foot, it shall melt

To a heart again, or all the wine in Rome

Shall run o'th'lees for't.

---

165   *forgetful* inducing forgetfulness
175   *great bridge* like London Bridge, which was impassable when tides ran high
176   *shoot* descend (a river) swiftly (in a boat or other vessel); penetrate sexually
177–8   We ... infancy ed. (prose Q)
182   *Ud's foot* ed. (Ud'foot Q)

VITTORIA

Your dog or hawk should be rewarded better   185
Than I have been. I'll speak not one word more.

FLAMINEO

Stop her mouth
With a sweet kiss, my lord.

                [BRACHIANO *embraces* VITTORIA]

So now the tide's turned the vessel's come about.
He's a sweet armful. O we curled-haired men   190
Are still most kind to women. This is well.

BRACHIANO

[*To* VITTORIA] That you should chide thus!

FLAMINEO   O, sir, your little
    chimneys
Do ever cast most smoke. I sweat for you.
Couple together with as deep a silence
As did the Grecians in their wooden horse.   195
My lord, supply your promises with deeds.
'You know that painted meat no hunger feeds.'

BRACHIANO

Stay – ingrateful Rome.

FLAMINEO

Rome! It deserves to be called Barbary, for our villainous usage.

BRACHIANO

Soft; the same project which the Duke of Florence   200
(Whether in love or gullery I know not)
Laid down for her escape, will I pursue.

FLAMINEO

And no time fitter than this night, my lord;

---

185   *rewarded* (in hunting) given part of the prey they have helped to kill (and thus encouraged to continue hunting)

191   *still* always

195   *Grecians . . . horse* The Greeks won the Trojan war by presenting a large wooden horse as a gift to the Trojans. It was taken into Troy and the Greeks hidden inside it emerged to effect a victory.

198   *Stay . . . Rome* ed. (Stay ingratefull Rome. Q) Rome was proverbially ungrateful to Romans.

199   *Barbary* land of barbarians (in northern Africa)

201   *gullery* deception

The Pope being dead; and all the cardinals entered
The conclave for th'electing a new Pope;   205
The city in a great confusion;
We may attire her in a page's suit,
Lay her post-horse, take shipping, and amain
For Padua.

BRACHIANO

I'll instantly steal forth the Prince Giovanni,   210
And make for Padua. You two with your old mother
And young Marcello that attends on Florence,
If you can work him to it, follow me.
I will advance you all: for you Vittoria,
Think of a Duchess' title.

FLAMINEO   Lo you sister.   215

Stay, my lord, I'll tell you a tale. The crocodile, which lives in the
river Nilus, hath a worm breeds i'th'teeth of't, which puts it to
extreme anguish: a little bird, no bigger than a wren, is barber-
surgeon to this crocodile; flies into the jaws of't; picks out the
worm; and brings present remedy. The fish, glad of ease but   220
ingrateful to her that did it, that the bird may not talk largely of
her abroad for non-payment, closeth her chaps intending to
swallow her and so put her to perpetual silence. But nature
loathing such ingratitude, hath armed this bird with a quill or
prick on the head, top o'th'which wounds the crocodile   225
i'th'mouth, forceth her open her bloody prison, and away flies
the pretty tooth-picker from her cruel patient.

BRACHIANO

Your application is, I have not rewarded
The service you have done me.

FLAMINEO   No my lord.

208–9   *Lay ... Padua* i.e. provide her with relays of post-horses, embark and sail with all
        speed to Padua
216–27 *Stay ... patient* Webster borrows this tale from Topsell, *History of Serpents* (1608),
        pp. 135–6, and possibly from Africanus, *History and Description of Africa* (1600).
        He invents the crocodile's motive for wanting to swallow the bird ('that the bird
        may not talk largely of her abroad for non-payment'), adding a human concern for
        reward (clearly at stake in the scene) to a story of animal savagery. Brachiano and
        Flamineo suggest different interpretations of the tale; critics have found still others.
        Its precise meaning is less important than the symbiosis among the characters it
        illuminates: all three are locked into complex relationships in which desire and
        self-interest, love and cruelty, are inextricable.
218–19 *barber-surgeon* Barbers acted as dentists in Webster's time.

You sister are the crocodile: you are blemished in your fame,   230
my lord cures it. And though the comparison hold not in every
particle; yet observe, remember, what good the bird with the
prick i'th'head hath done you; and scorn ingratitude.
[*Aside*] It may appear to some ridiculous
Thus to talk knave and madman; and sometimes   235
Come in with a dried sentence, stuffed with sage.
But this allows my varying of shapes,
'Knaves do grow great by being great men's apes.'

                                        Exeunt

[ACT IV, SCENE iii]

Enter LODOVICO, GASPARO, *and six* AMBASSADORS. *At
another door* [FRANCISCO] *the Duke of Florence*

FRANCISCO

[*To* LODOVICO] So, my lord, I commend your diligence –
Guard well the conclave, and, as the order is,
Let none have conference with the cardinals.

---

236   *sentence* aphorism, maxim
     sage culinary herb; wisdom (cf. I.ii.124)

  0   s.d. ed. (Enter Francisco, Lodovico, Gasper, and sixe Embassadours Q)
     This scene is unique in the play for its indebtedness to a single source, Hierome
     Bignon's *A Briefe, but an Effectuall Treatise of the Election of Popes*. This eyewitness
     account of a papal election in Rome in 1605 (just seven years before the first per-
     formance of *The White Devil*) furnishes many of the details in the scene, and may
     even suggest stage action Webster had in mind but failed to record fully in the
     printed text.
1–3   Webster opens the scene at a dramatic point in the papal election. Francisco inter-
     cepts Lodovico as he guards the ambassadors' passage from the conclave after they
     have solicited the cardinals on behalf of their own rulers. The conclave must
     now be completely sealed off from the outside world until a new Pope is elected
     (cf. ll. 27–32).
  2   *conclave* place in which the cardinals meet in private for the election of a Pope. In
     Rome, the conclave is in the Sistine chapel.

LODOVICO

I shall, my lord. Room for the ambassadors–

[*The* AMBASSADORS *pass over the stage*]

GASPARO

They're wondrous brave today: why do they wear   5
These several habits?

LODOVICO   O sir, they're knights
Of several orders.
That lord i'th'black cloak with the silver cross
Is Knight of Rhodes; the next Knight of S. Michael;
That of the Golden Fleece; the Frenchman there   10
Knight of the Holy Ghost; my lord of Savoy
Knight of th'Annunication; the Englishman
Is Knight of th'honoured Garter, dedicated

---

4   s.d. The theatrical spectacle of the passage of the ambassadors, magnificently
     dressed as knights of venerable orders, allows Webster to feast the eyes of the Red
     Bull audience while emphasizing by implied contrast the sinister perversion of
     honour and ceremony by Monticelso and Francisco. (I am indebted to NCW
     III.i.61 n. for identification of ambassadors with knights.)

4–17 Like Monticelso in III.ii.320–40, Francisco may be conversing with the ambassa-
     dors while they are observed by Lodovico and Gasparo from a peripheral position
     on the stage.

5   *brave* finely dressed

6   *several* various

9   *Rhodes* The order of the Knights of St John of Jerusalem, founded during the First
     Crusade, moved from Jerusalem to Rhodes, and finally to Malta, granted by
     Charles V in 1530. According to W. Segar's *Honour, Military and Civil* (1602), they
     wore 'a white Crosse upon a blacke garment' (p. 97).
     S. Michael Knights of this order (founded in 1469 by Louis XI) wore a richly
     embroidered mantle and hood of cloth of silver over white doublet, hose and shoes.

10   *Golden Fleece* Spanish ambassador. Knights of this order (founded in 1429 by
     Philip Duke of Burgundy) wore a hood and mantle of crimson velvet with a border
     of flames and fleeces; from their distinctive collar hung a fleece of wrought gold
     ('which signifieth *Iustice uncorrupted*' (Segar, p. 80)).

11   *Holy Ghost* French ambassador. Knights of this order (founded in 1578 by Henry
     III) wore mantles of black velvet embroidered with gold and silver and decorated
     with capes of embroidered green cloth of silver, lined with orange satin, over white
     doublet and hose.

12   *Annunciation* Savoy ambassador. Knights of this order (founded in 1362 by
     Amadeus VI of Savoy and the highest order of knights in Italy) wore white satin
     with a cloak of purple velvet along with the gold collar of their order.

13   *Garter* English ambassador. Knights of this order (founded in 1350 by Edward III)
     wore a mantle of purple velvet over a gown of crimson velvet; over the right

Unto their saint, S. George. I could describe to you
Their several institutions, with the laws   15
Annexed to their orders, but that time
Permits not such discovery.
FRANCISCO   Where's Count Lodowick?
LODOVICO
    Here my lord.
FRANCISCO   'Tis o'th'point of dinner time;
Marshal the cardinals' service.
LODOVICO   Sir, I shall.

Enter SERVANTS *with several dishes covered*

Stand, let me search your dish; who's this for?   20
SERVANT
    For my Lord Cardinal Monticelso.
LODOVICO
    Whose this?
SERVANT   For my Lord Cardinal of Bourbon.
FRENCH AMBASSADOR
    Why doth he search the dishes? To observe
What meat is dressed?
ENGLISH AMBASSADOR   No sir, but to prevent
Lest any letters should be conveyed in   25
To bribe or to solicit the advancement
Of any cardinal; when first they enter
'Tis lawful for the ambassadors of princes
To enter with them, and to make their suit
For any man their prince affecteth best;   30
But after, till a general election
No man may speak with them.
LODOVICO
    You that attend on the lord cardinals
Open the window, and receive their viands.

shoulder hung a hood of crimson velvet lined with white. Around their necks these
knights wore a pure gold chain worked in garters and knots, and enamelled with
white and red roses, from which hung the image of St George, worked in precious
stones. Around their left legs they wore a garter worked in gold, pearl and stones,
with the motto HONI SOIT QUI MAL Y PENSE ('Shame to him that evill thinketh').
 19 s.d. ed. (to r. of ll. 19–22 in Q)
 24 *meat* food
     dressed prepared

A CARDINAL

    [*At the window*] You must return the service; the lord cardinals   35
    Are busied 'bout electing of the Pope;
    They have given o'er scrutiny, and are fallen
    To admiration.

LODOVICO   Away, away.

                            [*Exeunt* SERVANTS *with dishes*]

FRANCISCO

    I'll lay a thousand ducats you hear news
    Of a Pope presently – hark; sure he's elected–   40

    [*The*] *Cardinal* [*of* ARRAGON *appears*] *on the terrace*

Behold! My Lord of Arragon appears
On the church battlements.

ARRAGON

    [*Holding up a cross*] *Denuntio vobis gaudium magnum.*
    Reverendissimus Cardinalis Lorenzo de Monticelso electus est in
    sedem apostolicam, et elegit sibi nomen Paulum quartum.   45

OMNES

    Vivat Sanctus Pater Paulus Quartus.

---

35   s.d. *window* probably a grating or wicket in a stage door, or perhaps a stage-level
      window (NCW IV.iii. 35 n.)

37   *scrutiny* taking of individual votes. The cardinals voted until a two-thirds majority
      elected a new Pope.

38   *admiration* adoration: means of papal election by divine inspiration. The cardinals
      turned and kneeled before the one they desired to be made Pope; when they saw that
      two-thirds had done so, the Pope was elected. Bignon comments that this method is
      not as lawful as voting, 'because by meanes of contentions, and partialities, there may
      be some fraude or violence committed therein, in that the weaker side may be
      drawne to Adoration by the example of those more mightie, and those fearful,
      induced by them more resolute' (Brown, p. 196). Papal elections (like that of the real
      Montalto) were often decided in this way.

40   s.d. ed. (to r. of ll. 39–40 in Q). *terrace* i.e. the upper stage

42   s.d. Since Webster follows Bignon closely verbally here, he may intend the accom-
      panying action: 'he shewes forth a Crosse'.

43–6 *Denuntio . . . Quartus* i.e. 'I announce to you tidings of great joy. The Most Reverend
      Cardinal Lorenzo di Monticelso has been elected to the Apostolic See, and has
      chosen for himself the name of Paul IV.' ALL: 'Long live the Holy Father Paul IV.' In
      fact, the historical Cardinal Montalto became Pope Sixtus V.

[Enter SERVANT]

SERVANT
  Vittoria my lord–
FRANCISCO   Well: what of her?
SERVANT
  Is fled the city–
FRANCISCO   Ha?
SERVANT   With Duke Brachiano.
FRANCISCO
  Fled? Where's the Prince Giovanni?
SERVANT   Gone with his father.
FRANCISCO
  Let the Matrona of the convertites   50
  Be apprehended: fled – O damnable!

                                        [*Exit* SERVANT]

  How fortunate are my wishes. Why? 'Twas this
  I only laboured. I did send the letter
  T'instruct him what to do. Thy fame, fond Duke,
  I first have poisoned; directed thee the way   55
  To marry a whore; what can be worse? This follows.
  The hand must act to drown the passionate tongue,
  I scorn to wear a sword and prate of wrong.

          Enter MONTICELSO *in state* [*in pontifical robes*]

MONTICELSO
  Concedimus vobis apostolicam benedictionem et remissionem
  peccatorum.   60

                              [FRANCISCO *whispers to him*]

  My lord reports Vittoria Corombona
  Is stol'n from forth the house of convertites
  By Brachiano, and they're fled the city.

47–9 ed. (*Vittoria . . . Lord. /* FRAN. *Wel . . . Ha? /* SER. *With . . . Giovanni /* SER. *Gone . . .*
      father. Q)
50–2 The speech illustrates the gap between public and private. Francisco's first two lines
      are spoken for the benefit of the ambassadors; the rest are addressed to Lodovico
      and the audience (NCW IV.iii.52, 53 n.).
  54 *fond* foolish; infatuated
59–60 *Concedimus . . . peccatorum* 'We grant you the Apostolic blessing and remission of
      sins.' This Latin benediction was added by Webster during press correction, perhaps
      a verbal expansion of stage business already implicit in Monticelso's entry 'in state'.
  64 *seat* technical term for the throne or office of a Pope. Monticelso may be carried on
      and offstage in the 'great and high Pontificall Chayre' described by Bignon.

Now, though this be the first day of our seat,
We cannot better please the divine power   65
Than to sequester from the holy church
These cursed persons. Make it therefore known,
We do denounce excommunication
Against them both: all that are theirs in Rome
We likewise banish. Set on.   70

        Exeunt [all except FRANCISCO *and* LODOVICO]

FRANCISCO
Come dear Lodovico.
You have ta'en the sacrament to prosecute
Th'intended murder.

LODOVICO   With all constancy.
But, sir, I wonder you'll engage yourself,
In person, being a great prince.

FRANCISCO   Divert me not.   75
Most of his court are of my faction,
And some are of my counsel. Noble friend,
Our danger shall be 'like in this design;

         Enter MONTICELSO

Give leave, part of the glory may be mine.   [*Bows*]
                          Exit

MONTICELSO
Why did the Duke of Florence with such care   80
Labour your pardon? Say.

LODOVICO
[*Kneeling*] Italian beggars will resolve you that
Who, begging of an alms, bid those they beg of
Do good for their own sakes; or't may be
He spreads his bounty with a sowing hand,   85
Like kings, who many times give out of measure
Not for desert so much as for their pleasure.

MONTICELSO
I know you're cunning. Come, what devil was that
That you were raising?

79 *Exit* ed. (Exit Fran. Q)
80–1 Cf. III.iii.92–6.
  85 *sowing* scattering (like seed); presumably, in hope of reaping
  86 *out of measure* excessively
  88 *cunning* sly, crafty; possessing magical skill (to raise or conjure devils)

LODOVICO   Devil, my lord?

[MONTICELSO]   I ask you
  How doth the Duke employ you, that his bonnet   90
  Fell with such compliment unto his knee
  When he departed from you?

LODOVICO   Why, my lord,
  He told me of a resty Barbary horse
  Which he would fain have brought to the career,
  The 'sault, and the ring-galliard. Now, my lord,   95
  I have a rare French rider.

MONTICELSO   Take you heed:
  Lest the jade break your neck. Do you put me off
  With your wild horse-tricks? Sirrah you do lie.
  O, thou'rt a foul black cloud, and thou dost threat
  A violent storm.

LODOVICO   Storms are i'th'air, my lord;   100
  I am too low to storm.

MONTICELSO   Wretched creature!
  I know that thou art fashioned for all ill,
  Like dogs that once get blood, they'll ever kill.
  About some murder? Was't not?

LODOVICO   I'll not tell you;
  And yet I care not greatly if I do;   105
  Marry with this preparation. Holy Father,
  I come not to you as an intelligencer,
  But as a penitent sinner. What I utter
  Is in confession merely; which you know
  Must never be revealed.

MONTICELSO   You have o'erta'en me.   110

---

89   *MONTICELSO . . . you* ed. (I aske you / MONT. How . . . bonnet Q)
93   *resty* restive, intractable, stubborn
     Barbary horse small, swift and hot-tempered horse from Barbary
94   *career* a gallop at full speed brought up short
95   *'sault* leaps and vaults
     ring-galliard a mixture of bounding forward and lashing out with the heels
96   *French rider* The French were supposed to be excellent horsemen and promiscuous
     lovers (hence prone to syphilis).
97   *jade* ill-tempered horse; woman (used pejoratively)
98   *horse-tricks* exercises in the horse's manage; horseplay
101 *I . . . storm* Lodovico refers both to his social status and (perhaps) to his physical
     position as he kneels before Monticelso.
107 *intelligencer* spy, informer
110 *o'erta'en* i.e. caught, ensnared (with an unexpected event)

LODOVICO

    Sir I did love Brachiano's Duchess dearly;

    Or rather I pursued her with hot lust,

    Though she ne'er knew on't. She was poisoned;

    Upon my soul she was: for which I have sworn

    T'avenge her murder.

MONTICELSO   To the Duke of Florence?   115

LODOVICO

    To him I have.

MONTICELSO   Miserable creature!

    If thou persist in this, 'tis damnable.

    Dost thou imagine thou canst slide on blood

    And not be tainted with a shameful fall?

    Or, like the black, and melancholic yew-tree,   120

    Dost think to root thyself in dead men's graves,

    And yet to prosper? Instruction to thee

    Comes like sweet showers to over-hard'ned ground:

    They wet, but pierce not deep. And so I leave thee

    With all the Furies hanging 'bout thy neck,   125

    Till by thy penitence thou remove this evil,

    In conjuring from thy breast that cruel devil.   *Exit*

LODOVICO

    I'll give it o'er. He says 'tis damnable:

    Besides I did expect his suffrage

    By reason of Camillo's death.   130

Enter SERVANT *and* FRANCISCO [*standing apart*]

FRANCISCO

    Do you know that count?

SERVANT   Yes, my lord.

---

118   *slide* slip

119   *tainted* injured; convicted, proven guilty

120   *yew-tree* Cf. I.ii.236. For the audience, the image may connect Lodovico with his victim, Brachiano (the yew/you of I.ii).

125   *Furies* Cf. I.ii.252 n.

127   s.d. ed. (to r. of l. 128 in Q)
       s.d. *Exit* ed. (Exit Mon. Q)

129   *suffrage* support, assistance; prayers, liturgical intercessory petitions

130   s.d. ed. (to r. of ll. 130–1 in Q)

FRANCISCO

    Bear him these thousand ducats to his lodging;

    Tell him the Pope hath sent them. Happily

    That will confirm more than all the rest.   [*Exit*]

SERVANT [*Giving money to* LODOVICO]   Sir.

LODOVICO

    To me sir?   135

SERVANT

    His Holiness hath sent you a thousand crowns,

    And wills you if you travel, to make him

    Your patron for intelligence.

LODOVICO   His creature

    Ever to be commanded.

                                [*Exit* SERVANT]

    Why now 'tis come about. He railed upon me;   140

    And yet these crowns were told out and laid ready

    Before he knew my voyage. O the art,

    The modest form of greatness! That do sit

    Like brides at wedding dinners, with their looks turned

    From the least wanton jests, their puling stomach   145

    Sick of the modesty, when their thoughts are loose,

    Even acting of those hot and lustful sports

    Are to ensue about midnight: such his cunning!

    He sounds my depth thus with a golden plummet;

    I am doubly armed now. Now to th'act of blood;   150

    There's but three Furies found in spacious hell;

    But in a great man's breast three thousand dwell.   [*Exit*]

---

   134   s.d. Francisco may exit or withdraw to observe (NCW IV.iii.135 n.).

   137   *wills* ed. (will Q)

   138   *intelligence* secret information or news

138–9   *Your ... commanded* ed. (one line in Q)

   141   *told out* counted out

   142   *art* ed. (Art Q)

   143   *form* customary method; outward appearance

144–8   Lodovico's simile anticipates the wedding that opens Act V.

   145   *puling* weak, sickly

   146   *loose* unchaste

   149   *plummet* ball of lead attached to a line to measure depth (here, money)

151–2   *There's ... dwell* These lines turn Monticelso's own words (ll. 125–7) back on himself.

[ACT V, SCENE i]

A passage over the stage of BRACHIANO, FLAMINEO,
MARCELLO, HORTENSIO, [VITTORIA] COROMBONA,
CORNELIA, ZANCHE *and others*

[*Exeunt all but* FLAMINEO *and* HORTENSIO]

FLAMINEO
In all the weary minutes of my life
Day ne'er broke up till now. This marriage
Confirms me happy.
HORTENSIO   'Tis a good assurance.
Saw you not yet the Moor that's come to court?
FLAMINEO
Yes, and conferred with him i'th'Duke's closet;   5
I have not seen a goodlier personage
Nor ever talked with man better experienced
In state affairs or rudiments of war.
He hath by report served the Venetian
In Candy these twice seven years, and been chief   10
In many a bold design.
HORTENSIO   What are those two
That bear him company?
FLAMINEO
Two noblemen of Hungary, that living in the emperor's service
as commanders, eight years since, contrary to the expectation
of all the court entered into religion, into the strict order of   15

---

0 s.d. This is probably a wedding procession, with Brachiano and Vittoria splendidly
dressed (the latter with her hair flowing loose and sprinkled with arras powder).
Though Lodovico's final speech in IV.iii, on the hypocrisy of apparently virtuous
brides, must cast a shadow over this procession, the presence of Marcello and
Cornelia – and possibly, among the 'others', the ambassadors (ll. 55–60), still
dressed in magnificent robes – emphasizes the lovers' new stature, despite their
excommunication in the previous scene. Typically in Webster, a formal public
moment rapidly gives way to private commentary.

2 *up till* until

10 *Candy* Crete, and, by ironic metaphoric extension, death. Flamineo's apparent
obliviousness to the pun he himself made earlier (I.i.288–9) suggests his new loss
of linguistic and thus dramatic control.

Capuchins: but being not well settled in their undertaking they
left their order and returned to court: for which being after
troubled in conscience, they vowed their service against the
enemies of Christ; went to Malta; were there knighted; and in
their return back, at this great solemnity, they are resolved for   20
ever to forsake the world, and settle themselves here in a house
of Capuchins in Padua.

HORTENSIO

'Tis strange.

FLAMINEO

One thing makes it so. They have vowed for ever to wear next
their bare bodies those coats of mail they served in.   25

HORTENSIO

Hard penance. Is the Moor a Christian?

FLAMINEO

He is.

HORTENSIO

Why proffers he his service to our Duke?

FLAMINEO

Because he understands there's like to grow
Some wars between us and the Duke of Florence,   30
In which he hopes employment.
I never saw one in a stern bold look
Wear more command, nor in a lofty phrase
Express more knowing, or more deep contempt
Of our slight airy courtiers. He talks   35
As if he had travelled all the princes' courts
Of Christendom; in all things strives t'express,
That all that should dispute with him may know:
Glories, like glow-worms, afar off shine bright
But looked to near, have neither heat nor light.   40
The Duke.

16 *Capuchins* order of monks established in 1528 to restore the original austerity and
    simplicity of the Franciscans. The pun on the name of the Duke of Florence, here
    submerged, surfaces at V.iii.38. Capuchins derived their name from their long,
    pointed hoods, a useful disguise for Gasparo and Lodovico. This circular account of
    the career of the supposed Capuchins, with its alternation of militarism and religious
    devotion, is probably designed to arouse suspicion in the minds of the audience.

26–7 *Hard . . . is* ed. (ued . . . penance/Is . . . is. Q)

31 no s.d. ed. (Enter Duke Brachiano Q)

39–40 *Glories . . . light* Fond of this phrase (borrowed from Alexander's *Alexandrean
    Tragedy*), Webster reused it in *The Duchess of Malfi* (IV.ii.141–2). Here, Flamineo

Enter BRACHIANO, [FRANCISCO, *Duke of*] *Florence disguised*
like Mulinassar; LODOVICO, ANTONELLI, GASPARO
[*all disguised*]; FERNESE *bearing their swords and helmets;*
[CARLO *and* PEDRO]

BRACHIANO

You are nobly welcome. We have heard at full
Your honourable service 'gainst the Turk.
To you, brave Mulinassar, we assign
A competent pension: and are inly sorrow,   45
The vows of those two worthy gentlemen
Make them incapable of our proffered bounty.
Your wish is you may leave your warlike swords
For monuments in our chapel. I accept it
As a great honour done me, and must crave   50
Your leave to furnish out our Duchess' revels.
Only one thing, as the last vanity
You e'er shall view, deny me not to stay
To see a barriers prepared tonight.
You shall have private standings: it hath pleased   55
The great ambassadors of several princes

again misses the dramatic irony of his own words on the deceptiveness of outward appearances. Since Alexander's lines are a comment on the futility of princely ambition, the irony may also encompass Francisco as well as Brachiano (a 'glow-worm' or 'proud fool' was applied contemptuously to persons after 1624), as they both enter while Flamineo speaks.

41 s.d.4 CARLO . . PEDRO While it is possible (and some editors maintain) that Carlo and Pedro (who appear in speech prefixes at ll. 61 and 63) are names taken by Lodovico and Gasparo in disguise, it is more likely that they are separate characters, members of Brachiano's court who are of Francisco's faction (IV.iii.76). Thus the 'moles' welcome Francisco and his travelling companions at l. 63 (with 'all things ready' for the murder), witness Marcello's death – possibly bearing his body to Cornelia's lodging (V.ii.69) – and appear in the final masque and murder to 'strike [Flamineo, Vittoria and Zanche] with a joint motion' (V.vi.227–8) and taste the justice of Giovanni (V.vi.288). The presence of conspirators inside Brachiano's own court may emphasize his self-destruction; in *Antony and Cleopatra*, Caesar plants defectors in the front lines 'That Antony may seem to spend his fury / Upon himself' (IV.vi.9–10).

54 *barriers* Cf I.ii.27. In January 1610 and again in January 1612 (probably just before the first performance of *The White Devil*), Prince Henry fought at barriers at Whitehall (carefully staged by Ben Jonson and Inigo Jones in 1610). Webster composed an elegy (*A Monumental Columne*) for Prince Henry after his sudden death in 1612, mourning the loss of this popular chivalric hero...

In their return from Rome to their own countries
To grace our marriage, and to honour me
With such a kind of sport.

FRANCISCO　　　　　　　I shall persuade them
To stay, my lord.

[BRACHIANO]　　Set on there to the presence.　　　　　　　60

　　　　　　Exeunt BRACHIANO, FLAMINEO *and* [HORTENSIO]

CARLO [*To* FRANCISCO]
Noble my lord, most fortunately welcome,

　　　　　　　　　　The conspirators here embrace

You have our vows sealed with the sacrament
To second your attempts.

PEDRO　　　　　　　　And all things ready.
He could not have invented his own ruin,
Had he despaired, with more propriety.　　　　　　　65

LODOVICO
You would not take my way.

FRANCISCO　　　　　　　'Tis better ordered.

LODOVICO
T'have poisoned his prayer book, or a pair of beads,
The pommel of his saddle, his looking-glass,
Or th'handle of his racket – O that, that!
That while he had been bandying at tennis,　　　　　　　70
He might have sworn himself to hell, and struck
His soul into the hazard! O my lord!

60　ed. (To . . . Lord / Set . . . presence Q) Most editors assign the final command to
　　Brachiano, but Webster may want to suggest Francisco's control in Brachiano's
　　court.
　　presence presence chamber
　　s.p. *BRACHIANO* ed. (not in Q)
　　s.d. *HORTENSIO* ed. (Marcello Q). Unless Marcello remains silent, he probably
　　passes over the stage and exits with the rest at the opening of the scene. The exit is
　　probably intended for Hortensio, who has spoken, rather than Marcello.
61　s.d. ed. (to r. of ll. 63–5 in Q)
68　*pommel . . . saddle* Edward Squire, a Catholic conspirator, was hanged in 1598 for
　　poisoning the pommel of the Queen's saddle. The contemporary allusion strength-
　　ens Webster's association of Brachiano with legitimate power and his enemies with
　　popish heresy.
70–2　*bandying . . . hazard* Brachiano has earlier been identified with the aristocratic
　　game of tennis (II.i.53). Here Lodovico, like Hamlet, is bent on destroying his

I would have our plot be ingenious,
And have it hereafter recorded for example
Rather than borrow example.
FRANCISCO   There's no way   75
More speeding than this thought on.
LODOVICO   On then.
FRANCISCO
And yet methinks that this revenge is poor,
Because it steals upon him like a thief;
To have ta'en him by the casque in a pitched field,
Led him to Florence!
LODOVICO   It had been rare. – And there   80
Have crowned him with a wreath of stinking garlic.
T'have shown the sharpness of his government,
And rankness of his lust. Flamineo comes.

> *Exeunt* LODOVICO, ANTONELLI [*and*
> GASPARO, FERNESE, CARLO, PEDRO]

> [FRANCISCO *stands apart*]
> *Enter* FLAMINEO, MARCELLO *and* ZANCHE

MARCELLO
Why doth this devil haunt you? Say.
FLAMINEO   I know not.
For by this light I do not conjure for her.   85
'Tis not so great a cunning as men think
To raise the devil: for here's one up already;
The greatest cunning were to lay him down.
MARCELLO
She is your shame.

---

enemy's soul as well as his body. In the image, Brachiano's soul is a tennis ball
struck into the 'hazard' (an opening in the inner wall of the royal tennis court; also
risk or peril).
79 *ta'en ... field* i.e. seized him by the helmet in a field planned for battle; the honor-
able military alternative
83 ed. (And ... lust/Flamineo comes. Q)
s.d. ed. (to r. of ll. 82–4 in Q)
87–8 *raise ... down* The joke is Flamineo's bawdy attempt to defend his mistress (cf.
Romeo and Juliet II.i.23–9): the 'devil' is not (as first appears) Zanche, but
Flamineo's own erection, which must be laid down through his mistress's 'cunning'.

FLAMINEO   I prithee pardon her.
In faith you see, women are like to burs;   90
Where their affection throws them, there they'll stick.

ZANCHE
[*Motioning towards* FRANCISCO] That is my countryman, a
    goodly person;
When he's at leisure I'll discourse with him
In our own language.

FLAMINEO   I beseech you do—

                      Exit ZANCHE

How is't brave soldier? O that I had seen   95
Some of your iron days! I pray relate
Some of your service to us.

FRANCISCO
'Tis a ridiculous thing for a man to be his own chronicle; I did
never wash my mouth with mine own praise for fear of getting
a stinking breath.   100

MARCELLO
You're too stoical. The Duke will expect other discourse from you.

FRANCISCO
I shall never flatter him, I have studied man too much to do that.
What difference is between the Duke and I? No more than
between two bricks; all made of one clay. Only 't may be one is
placed on the top of a turret; the other in the bottom of a well by   105
mere chance; if I were placed as high as the Duke, I should stick
as fast; make as fair a show; and bear out weather equally.

FLAMINEO
If this soldier had a patent to beg in churches, then he would
tell them stories.

MARCELLO
I have been a soldier too.   110

FRANCISCO
How have you thrived?

---

  94   s.d. (to r. of l. 93 in Q)
103–7   *What ... equally* These apparently egalitarian remarks, borrowed from Stefano
        Guazzo's *Civil Conversation* (trans. Pettie 1581), mask a deeper irony: there is in
        fact no difference in class between the two dukes, and both are, literally, 'fair' or
        white-skinned.
  108   *soldier ... churches* Beggars often claimed to be soldiers without employment
        (cf. ll. 130–2); without a licence, they could be arrested and whipped as vagabonds.

MARCELLO

Faith, poorly.

FRANCISCO

That's the misery of peace. Only outsides are then respected: as ships seem very great upon the river, which show very little upon the seas: so some men i'th'court seem Colossuses in a 115 chamber, who if they came into the field would appear pitiful pigmies.

FLAMINEO

Give me a fair room yet hung with arras, and some great cardinal to lug me by th'ears as his endeared minion.

FRANCISCO

And thou may'st do – the devil knows what villainy. 120

FLAMINEO

And safely.

FRANCISCO

Right; you shall see in the country in harvest time, pigeons, though they destroy never so much corn, the farmer dare not present the fowling-piece to them! Why? Because they belong to the Lord of the Manor; whilst your poor sparrows that belong 125 to the Lord of heaven, they go to the pot for't.

FLAMINEO

I will now give you some politic instruction. The Duke says he will give you pension; that's but bare promise: get it under his hand. For I have known men that have come from serving against the Turk; for three or four months they have had 130 pension to buy them new wooden legs and fresh plasters; but after 'twas not to be had. And this miserable courtesy shows as if a tormentor should give hot cordial drinks to one three-quarters dead o'th'rack, only to fetch the miserable soul again to endure more dog-days. 135

113–17 *misery ... pigmies* a common sentiment. Cf. *Measure for Measure* I.ii.14–16: 'There's not a soldier of us all, that in the thanksgiving before meat, do relish the petition well that prays for peace'.

116–17 *pitiful pigmies* ed. (pittifull. Pigmies. Q)

   118 *arras* tapestry adorning rooms at court (behind which one might hide unsuspected, as in *Hamlet* III.iv.7)

122–5 *pigeons ... Manor* Pigeons, though considered pests, were raised for their ready value on the open market.

   132 *miserable* compassionate; miserly; wretched

   135 *dog-days* Cf. III.ii.202.

Enter HORTENSIO, *a* YOUNG LORD, ZANCHE *and two more*

How now, gallants; what, are they ready for the barriers?

[*Exit* FRANCISCO]

YOUNG LORD

Yes: the lords are putting on their armour.

[HORTENSIO *and* FLAMINEO *stand apart*]

HORTENSIO

What's he?

FLAMINEO

A new upstart: one that swears like a falc'ner, and will lie in the
Duke's ear day by day like a maker of almanacs; and yet I knew   140
him since he came to th'court smell worse of sweat than an
under-tennis-court-keeper.

HORTENSIO

Look you, yonder's your sweet mistress.

FLAMINEO

Thou art my sworn brother, I'll tell thee – I do love that Moor,
that witch, very constrainedly: she knows some of my villainy; I   145
do love her, just as a man holds a wolf by the ears. But for fear
of turning upon me, and pulling out my throat, I would let her
go to the devil.

HORTENSIO

I hear she claims marriage of thee.

FLAMINEO

'Faith, I made to her some such dark promise and in seeking to   150
fly from't I run on, like a frighted dog with a bottle at's tail that
fain would bite it off and yet dares not look behind him. [*To*
ZANCHE] Now my precious gipsy!

135   s.d. Flamineo's cynical commentary on the court is punctuated by the arrival of the
        young lord, who epitomizes the sycophancy which Flamineo both desires and despises.
137   s.d. All except Flamineo and Hortensio are very likely setting up the barriers on
        stage (NCW V.i.134.I n.).
140   *maker of almanacs* fortune-teller, astrologer
146   *holds . . . ears* common proverb. Cf. Philip Sidney, *Arcadia, Works* II, 12: 'like them
        that holde the wolfe by the eares, bitten while they hold, and slaine if they loose'.
153   *gipsy* Like Cleopatra, Zanche is 'with Phoebus' amorous pinches black' (*Antony and
        Cleopatra* I.v.28) – as dark-skinned as the gipsies, who arrived in England in the
        early sixteenth century and were thought to come from Egypt.

ZANCHE

Ay, your love to me rather cools than heats.

FLAMINEO

Marry, I am the sounder lover – we have many wenches about   155
the town heat too fast.

HORTENSIO

What do you think of these perfumed gallants then?

FLAMINEO

Their satin cannot save them. I am confident
They have a certain spice of the disease,
For they that sleep with dogs shall rise with fleas.   160

ZANCHE

Believe it! A little painting and gay clothes
Make you loathe me.

FLAMINEO

How? Love a lady for painting or gay apparel? I'll unkennel one
example more for thee. Aesop had a foolish dog that let go the
flesh to catch the shadow. I would have courtiers be better diners.   165

ZANCHE

You remember your oaths.

FLAMINEO

Lovers' oaths are like mariners' prayers, uttered in extremity; but
when the tempest is o'er and that the vessel leaves tumbling, they
fall from protesting to drinking. And yet amongst gentlemen
protesting and drinking go together, and agree as well as   170
shoemakers and Westphalia bacon. They are both drawers on:
for drink draws on protestation and protestation draws on
more drink. Is not this discourse better now than the morality
of your sunburnt gentleman?

---

154   *cools* abates, declines (as used by Zanche); allays, cools down (implied by Flamineo)
155   *sounder lover* ed. (sounder, lover Q)
156   *heat* become sexually aroused; contract venereal disease
158   *satin* with a pun on 'Satan'
161–2   *A little . . . me* i.e. women who wear makeup and dress well attract you, and lead
      you to reject me
164–5   *Aesop . . . diners* i.e. a bird in the hand is worth two in the bush; only a fool gives up
      what he has for what he desires
165   *diners* ed. (*Diuers.* Q)
168   *tumbling* tossing and rolling about (as a ship in a storm; as in sexual intercourse)
170–1   *agree . . . bacon* Bacon draws men on to drink, and shoemakers draw shoes on to feet.
173   *morality* ed. (mortality Q)

Enter CORNELIA

CORNELIA

Is this your perch, you haggard? [*Strikes* ZANCHE] Fly to th'stews.   175

FLAMINEO

You should be clapped by th'heels now: strike i'th'court!

[*Exit* CORNELIA]

ZANCHE

She's good for nothing but to make her maids
Catch cold o'nights; they dare not use a bedstaff
For fear of her light fingers.

MARCELLO   You're a strumpet.

An impudent one.   [*Kicks* ZANCHE]

FLAMINEO   Why do you kick her? Say,   180

Do you think that she's like a walnut-tree?
Must she be cudgelled ere she bear good fruit?

MARCELLO

She brags that you shall marry her.

FLAMINEO   What then?

MARCELLO

I had rather she were pitched upon a stake
In some new-seeded garden, to affright   185
Her fellow crows thence.

---

174 s.d. *Enter* CORNELIA Flamineo's complacent misogyny is abruptly and dramatically
       disturbed by Cornelia's violent entrance, which recalls her interruption at I.ii.252
       and signals the disruption of the apparent harmony of the wedding procession, in
       which Cornelia and Zanche appeared together.
175 *haggard* wild female hawk, often applied to a promiscuous, intractable woman
       stews brothel
176 *clapped . . . heels* put in irons or in the stocks
       strike . . . court Striking and drawing blood at court was severely punished: offend-
       ers might be imprisoned for life or have their right hands chopped off.
178–9 *they . . . fingers* Bed-staves were either slats supporting the bedding or sticks used in
       making beds, well known as ready weapons; Zanche's bed-staff is a potential
       weapon or a warm male companion. She dare not use either because (she implies)
       Cornelia covets both.
181–2 *Do . . . fruit?* The source from which Webster lifted this common proverb reads: 'A
       woman, an asse, and a walnut tree / Bring the more fruit, the more beaten they bee'
       (Pettie III.39). The same text counters it with this: 'He God offendes, and holy love
       undoes / Which on his wife doth fasten churlish bloes'.
184–6 *pitched . . . thence* Marcello conflates images of Zanche as a witch ('upon a stake')
       and a crow (the black scavenger so hated by English farmers).
185 *new-seeded garden* Cf. I.ii.258

FLAMINEO You're a boy, a fool,
  Be guardian to your hound, I am of age.
MARCELLO
  If I take her near you I'll cut her throat.
FLAMINEO
  With a fan of feathers?
MARCELLO And for you, I'll whip
  This folly from you.
FLAMINEO Are you choleric? 190
  I'll purge't with rhubarb.
HORTENSIO O your brother–
FLAMINEO Hang him.
  He wrongs me most that ought t'offend me least.
  [To MARCELLO] I do suspect my mother played foul play
  When she conceived thee.
MARCELLO Now by all my hopes,
  Like the two slaughtered sons of Oedipus, 195
  The very flames of our affection
  Shall turn two ways. Those words I'll make thee answer
  With thy heart blood.
FLAMINEO Do like the geese in the progress;
  You know where you shall find me – [Exit]
MARCELLO Very good.
  And thou beest a noble friend, bear him my sword, 200
  And bid him fit the length on't.

186 *You're* ed. (Your Q)
189 *fan of feathers* appropriate to the courtier Marcello has become, not the soldier he has been
190 *choleric* Choler was one of the four humours of early physiology, hot and dry, and supposed to cause irascibility. Flamineo here treats it as a digestive malady, attended with bilious diarrhoea and vomiting, remedied by purging. Rhubarb was a commonly prescribed purgative (cf. *The Duchess of Malfi* II.v.12–13, 'Rhubarb, O for rhubarb / To purge this choler').
195–7 *two ... ways* After the two sons of Oedipus, Eteocles and Polinices, were killed in combat for their father's throne, their bodies were burnt together; the flames miraculously parted, showing that death did not end their mutual hatred.
198 *geese* ed. (gesse Q) prostitutes. The word 'gesses' is a technical term for the stopping places on a royal progress, and may be intended (Lucas, p. 251). But prostitutes plied their trade during progresses, and Flamineo's bawdy remark is typical. The syntax is ambiguous, however, and so the line may read 'Do as the prostitutes do in a progress, who know where their victims are to be found', or 'Do – I shall be found as easily as prostitutes in a progress'.
201 s.d. ed. (to r. of ll. 222–3 in Q)

YOUNG LORD   Sir I shall.

                                [*Exeunt all but* ZANCHE]

      Enter FRANCISCO *the Duke of Florence* [*disguised*]

ZANCHE

   [*Aside*] He comes. Hence petty thought of my disgrace –
   [*To* FRANCISCO] I ne'er loved my complexion till now,
   Cause I may boldly say without a blush
   I love you.
[FRANCISCO] Your love is untimely sown;   205
   There's a spring at Michaelmas, but 'tis but a faint one –
   I am sunk in years, and I have vowed never to marry.
ZANCHE

   Alas! Poor maids get more lovers than husbands. Yet you may
   mistake my wealth. For, as when ambassadors are sent to
   congratulate princes, there's commonly sent along with them a   210
   rich present; so that though the prince like not the ambassador's
   person nor words, yet he likes well of the presentment. So I may
   come to you in the same manner, and be better loved for my
   dowry than my virtue.
[FRANCISCO]

   I'll think on the motion.   215
ZANCHE

   Do, I'll now detain you no longer. At your better leisure
   I'll tell you things shall startle your blood.
   Nor blame me that this passion I reveal;
   Lovers die inward that their flames conceal.
[FRANCISCO]

   [*Aside*] Of all intelligence this may prove the best,   220
   Sure I shall draw strange fowl, from this foul nest.

                                          Exeunt

205, 215, 220 s.p. *FRANCISCO* ed. (FLA Q)
  206–7 ed. (Ther's . . . sunck / In . . . marry. Q)
     206 *spring . . . one* Michaelmas is 29 September.
     215 *motion* offer, proposal

[ACT V, SCENE ii]

Enter MARCELLO *and* CORNELIA [*and a* PAGE]

CORNELIA

    I hear a whispering all about the court,
    You are to fight; who is your opposite?
    What is the quarrel?

MARCELLO   'Tis an idle rumour.

CORNELIA

    Will you dissemble? Sure you do not well
    To fright me thus – you never look thus pale,   5
    But when you are most angry. I do charge you
    Upon my blessing; nay I'll call the Duke,
    And he shall school you.

MARCELLO   Publish not a fear

    Which would convert to laughter; 'tis not so –
    Was not this crucifix my father's?

CORNELIA   Yes.   10

MARCELLO

    I have heard you say, giving my brother suck,
    He took the crucifix between his hands,
    And broke a limb off.

CORNELIA   Yes: but 'tis mended.

Enter FLAMINEO

FLAMINEO

    I have brought your weapon back.

FLAMINEO *runs* MARCELLO *through*

CORNELIA   Ha, O my horror!

MARCELLO

    You have brought it home indeed.

---

   2 *You* ed. (Your Q)
  10 *crucifix* Cornelia wears this around her neck, probably from the beginning of the play, immediately identifying her (along with the Cardinal) as a guardian of traditional Christian values.
  13 s.d. ed. (to r. of l. 12 in Q). The sudden violence of Flamineo's entrance and subsequent assault imitates precisely Cornelia's attack on Zanche (V.i.175). Thus Flamineo makes clear that his action is a direct response to his mother's rigid morality.

CORNELIA	Help – O he's murdered.	15

FLAMINEO

Do you turn your gall up? I'll to sanctuary,
And send a surgeon to you.   *[Exit]*

Enter CARL[O,] HORT[ENSIO,] PEDRO

HORTENSIO   How? O'th'ground?

MARCELLO

O mother now remember what I told
Of breaking off the crucifix: farewell –
There are some sins which heaven doth duly punish   20
In a whole family. This it is to rise
By all dishonest means. Let all men know
That tree shall long time keep a steady foot
Whose branches spread no wider than the root.

CORNELIA

O my perpetual sorrow!

HORTENSIO   Virtuous Marcello.   25

He's dead: pray leave him lady; come, you shall.

CORNELIA

Alas he is not dead: he's in a trance.
Why here's nobody shall get anything by his death. Let me call
him again for God's sake.

CARLO

I would you were deceived.   30

---

16   *turn . . . up* probably a witty extension of Flamineo's earlier remark about purging Marcello's choler (supposed to have its seat in the gall). Since bloodletting was a remedy for choler (like purgation), Flamineo may be humorously expressing surprise that Marcello's irascibility is increased by being stabbed. He then offers to send a doctor to complete the cure.

17   s.d. ed. (to r. of ll. 19–20 in Q). The entrance of Carlo and Pedro, 'moles' in league with Francisco, as witnesses to Flamineo's fratricide emphasizes the self-determination of Brachiano and his allies; the revenge plot is unexpectedly superseded in the final act.

23–4   *That . . . root* Cf. I.ii.233–7, where the 'yew' of Vittoria's dream strikes Isabella and Camillo dead with one of its branches.

24   *wider* ed. (wilder Q)

26   Carlo, Pedro and Hortensio force Cornelia away from the body of Marcello, and she struggles to free herself.

CORNELIA

O you abuse me, you abuse me, you abuse me. How many have
gone away thus for lack of tendance; rear up's head, rear up's
head; his bleeding inward will kill him.

HORTENSIO

You see he is departed.

CORNELIA

Let me come to him; give me him as he is, if he be turned   35
to earth; let me but give him one hearty kiss, and you shall put
us both into one coffin. Fetch a looking-glass, see if his breath
will not stain it; or pull out some feathers from my pillow,
and lay them to his lips – will you lose him for a little pains-
taking?   40

HORTENSIO

Your kindest office is to pray for him.

CORNELIA

Alas! I would not pray for him yet. He may live to lay me
i'th'ground, and pray for me, if you'll let me come to him.

Enter BRACHIANO *all armed, save the beaver, with* FLAMINEO,
[LODOVICO *disguised and* FRANCISCO *disguised*
as MULINASSAR]

BRACHIANO

Was this your handiwork?

FLAMINEO

It was my misfortune.   45

CORNELIA

He lies, he lies, he did not kill him: these have killed him, that
would not let him be better looked to.

BRACHIANO

Have comfort my grieved mother.

CORNELIA

O you screech-owl.

36–9   *earth . . . lips* Webster is borrowing from *King Lear* (V.iii.262–6): 'She's dead as
        earth. Lend me a looking-glass, / If that her breath will mist or stain the stone, /
        Why then she lives . . . This feather stirs; she lives!'

  39   *lose* ed. (loose Q)

  43   s.d. ed. (to r. of ll. 45–7 in Q)

  49   *screech-owl* bird of ill-omen. The line is addressed either to Brachiano, who has
        attempted to comfort her, or to Flamineo.

HORTENSIO

   [*Restraining her*] Forbear, good madam.   50

CORNELIA

   [*Shaking him off*] Let me go, let me go.

> *She runs to* FLAMINEO *with her knife drawn and*
> *coming to him lets it fall*

   The God of heaven forgive thee. Dost not wonder
   I pray for thee? I'll tell thee what's the reason –
   I have scarce breath to number twenty minutes;
   I'd not spend that in cursing. Fare thee well –   55
   Half of thyself lies there: and may'st thou live
   To fill an hour-glass with his mouldered ashes,
   To tell how thou shouldst spend the time to come
   In blest repentance.

BRACHIANO   Mother, pray tell me

   How came he by his death? What was the quarrel?   60

CORNELIA

   Indeed my younger boy presumed too much
   Upon his manhood; gave him bitter words;
   Drew his sword first; and so I know not how,
   For I was out of my wits, he fell with's head
   Just in my bosom.

PAGE   This is not true madam.   65

CORNELIA

   I pray thee peace.
   One arrow's grazed already; it were vain
   T'lose this: for that will ne'er be found again.

BRACHIANO

   Go, bear the body to Cornelia's lodging:

---

51   s.d. ed. (to r. of ll. 51–5 in Q)

61   *younger boy* Marcello. Younger brothers were frequently angry about their disen-
   franchised position (cf. Orlando in *As You Like It*); Cornelia may be capitalizing on
   the choleric reputation of younger brothers.

67   *grazed* probably 'grassed' (lost in the grass) with the secondary meaning 'grazed' (to
   cut the surface of, as in a wound). The idea of shooting a second arrow to find the
   first was a common metaphor for ambition.

And we command that none acquaint our Duchess   70
With this sad accident: for you Flamineo,
Hark you, I will not grant your pardon.

FRANCISCO   No?

BRACHIANO

Only a lease of your life. And that shall last
But for one day. Thou shalt be forced each evening
To renew it, or be hanged.

FLAMINEO   At your pleasure.   75

> LODOVICO *sprinkles* BRACHIANO*'s beaver with a poison*

Your will is law now, I'll not meddle with it.

BRACHIANO

You once did brave me in your sister's lodging;
I'll now keep you in awe for't. Where's our beaver?

FRANCISCO

[*Aside*] He calls for his destruction. Noble youth,
I pity thy sad fate. Now to the barriers.   80
This shall his passage to the black lake further,
The last good deed he did, he pardoned murder.

                                        Exeunt

74–5   *But . . . pleasure* ed. (But . . . it, / or . . . pleasure Q)

75   s.d. *beaver* lower portion of the face-guard of a helmet. The poisoning of
Brachiano's mouthpiece recalls the dumb show in II.ii.23, when Dr Julio washed
the lips of Brachiano's picture in order to poison Isabella when she kissed it.

77   Cf. IV.ii.48–9.

81   *black lake* probably Acheron, black river of the underworld

[ACT V, SCENE iii]

Charges and shouts. They fight at barriers; first single pairs, then three to three

Enter BRACHIANO *and* FLAMINEO *with others*
[GIOVANNI, VITTORIA, *and* FRANCISCO
disguised as MULINASSAR]

BRACHIANO
An armourer! Ud's death, an armourer!
FLAMINEO
Armourer; where's the armourer?
BRACHIANO
Tear off my beaver.
FLAMINEO   Are you hurt, my lord?
BRACHIANO
O my brain's on fire,

Enter ARMOURER

the helmet is poisoned.

ARMOURER
My lord upon my soul–   5
BRACHIANO
Away with him to torture.

[*Exit* ARMOURER, *guarded*]
There are some great ones that have hand in this,
And near about me.
VITTORIA   O my loved lord, poisoned?
FLAMINEO
Remove the bar: here's unfortunate revels –
Call the physicians;

---

0 s.d. The fight at barriers, a spectacle for the Red Bull stage, was a highly formal ceremonial combat (frequently allegorized as, for example, Truth vs. Opinion) rapidly disappearing from courtly life. Here, it gives Webster the opportunity to juxtapose chivalric courtly ideals with the Machiavellian revenge plot. The scene opens with six combatants jousting in full armour (probably Brachiano and five of the ambassadors; cf. l. 12); they may be observed (perhaps, from the upper stage) by an audience which includes Francisco, Lodovico, Gasparo, Vittoria, Zanche, Giovanni and Flamineo (so NCW V.iii.0.1–2 n.).
4 *O . . . poisoned* ed. (O . . . fire / The . . . soule Q)
9 *bar* probably the barrier, still on the stage

Ent[er] 2 PHYSICIANS

                    a plague upon you; 10
  We have too much of your cunning here already.
  I fear the ambassadors are likewise poisoned.
BRACHIANO
  O I am gone already: the infection
  Flies to the brain and heart. O thou strong heart!
  There's such a covenant 'tween the world and it, 15
  They're loth to break.
GIOVANNI   O my most loved father!
BRACHIANO
  Remove the boy away.
                  [GIOVANNI *is led offstage*]
  Where's this good woman? Had I infinite worlds
  They were too little for thee. Must I leave thee?
  What say yon screech-owls, is the venom mortal? 20
PHYSICIANS
  Most deadly.
BRACHIANO   Most corrupted politic hangman!
  You kill without book; but your art to save
  Fails you as oft as great men's needy friends.
  I that have given life to offending slaves
  And wretched murderers, have I not power 25
  To lengthen mine own a twelvemonth?
  [*To* VITTORIA] Do not kiss me, for I shall poison thee.
  This unction is sent from the great Duke of Florence.
FRANCISCO
  Sir be of comfort.
BRACHIANO
  O thou soft natural death, that art joint-twin 30

---

20 *screech-owls* the physicians, who can foretell, but not prevent, death
21–3 *Most . . . friends* This is addressed to Death, here envisaged as a schemer who kills by
      rote (without book), but lacks the ability to save life as great men lack friends. This
      speech reveals that, while Brachiano knows he is Francisco's victim (in a revenge
      tragedy), he nonetheless sees himself as the great victim of Fate (in a *de casibus*
      tragedy), and thus ignores the disguised Duke of Florence to focus on larger forces.
24–5 *I . . . murderers* Cf. V.ii.82.
  27 *Do . . . me* Brachiano protects Vittoria from the poisoned kiss which, in picture,
      killed Isabella (II.ii.23).
30–1 *death . . . slumber* Sleep is 'death's second self, that seals up all in rest' (Shakespeare,
      Sonnet 73).

To sweetest slumber: no rough-bearded comet
Stares on thy mild departure: the dull owl
Beats not against thy casement: the hoarse wolf
Scents not thy carrion. Pity winds thy corse,
Whilst horror waits on princes.   35

VITTORIA

[*Wailing*] I am lost for ever.

BRACHIANO

How miserable a thing it is to die,
'Mongst women howling!

[*Enter* LODOVICO *and* GASPARO *disguised as Capuchins*]

What are those?

FLAMINEO   Franciscans.

They have brought the extreme unction.

BRACHIANO

On pain of death, let no man name death to me,   40
It is a word infinitely terrible.
Withdraw into our cabinet.

Exeunt [*all*] *but* FRANCISCO *and* FLAMINEO

FLAMINEO

To see what solitariness is about dying princes. As heretofore
they have unpeopled towns, divorced friends, and made great
houses unhospitable, so now, O justice! where are their flatterers   45
now? Flatterers are but the shadows of princes' bodies, the least
thick cloud makes them invisible.

FRANCISCO

There's great moan made for him.

FLAMINEO

'Faith, for some few hours salt water will run most plentifully

---

31–3   *rough-bearded . . . casement* a series of prodigies associated with the fall of kings
35–6   ed. (one line in Q)
   38   *Franciscans* a wonderful pun: the murderers are both disguised Franciscan friars
        and servants to Francisco.
   39   *extreme unction* both the anointment of the faithful before death and the most
        powerful poison of the murderers
   42   *Withdraw . . . cabinet* Brachiano, Vittoria and the disguised assassins may retreat into
        the curtained discovery space at the rear of the stage, where they are discovered at l. 81.

in every office o'th'court. But believe it; most of them do but   50
weep over their stepmothers' graves.

FRANCISCO

How mean you?

FLAMINEO

Why? They dissemble, as some men do that live within compass
o'th'verge.

FRANCISCO

Come, you have thrived well under him.   55

FLAMINEO

'Faith, like a wolf in a woman's breast; I have been fed with
poultry; but for money, understand me, I had as good a will to
cozen him, as e'er an officer of them all. But I had not cunning
enough to do it.

FRANCISCO

What did'st thou think of him? 'Faith speak freely.   60

FLAMINEO

He was a kind of statesman that would sooner have reckoned
how many cannon bullets he had discharged against a town, to
count his expense that way, than how many of his valiant and
deserving subjects he lost before it.

FRANCISCO

O, speak well of the Duke.   65

FLAMINEO

I have done. Wilt hear some of my court wisdom?

Enter LODOVICO [*disguised*]

To reprehend princes is dangerous: and to over-commend
some of them is palpable lying.

FRANCISCO

How is it with the Duke?

LODOVICO   Most deadly ill.

He's fall'n into a strange distraction.   70
He talks of battles and monopolies,

53–4   *compass . . . verge* within twelve miles of the king's court, under the jurisdiction of
the Lord High Steward

56–7   *wolf . . . poultry* The 'ulcerous wolf' (*The Duchess of Malfi* II.i.57), common par-
lance for a cancerous ulcer, was fed with fresh meat so that it would not consume
human flesh. The ulcer in the thigh of the real-life Brachiano was treated with raw
meat. There may also be a pun on 'poultry' and 'paltry' (rubbish, trash).

Levying of taxes, and from that descends
To the most brain-sick language. His mind fastens
On twenty several objects, which confound
Deep sense with folly. Such a fearful end   75
May teach some men that bear too lofty crest,
Though they live happiest, yet they die not best.
He hath conferred the whole state of the dukedom
Upon your sister, till the Prince arrive
At mature age.

FLAMINEO   There's some good luck in that yet.   80

FRANCISCO

See here he comes.

Enter BRACHIANO, *presented in a bed,* VITTORIA *and others*
[*including* GASPARO, *disguised*]

There's death in's face already.

VITTORIA

O my good lord!

These speeches are several kinds of distractions and in the
action should appear so

BRACHIANO   Away, you have abused me.
You have conveyed coin forth our territories,
Bought and sold offices, oppressed the poor,
And I ne'er dreamt on't. Make up your accounts;   85
I'll now be mine own steward.

FLAMINEO   Sir, have patience.

---

81 *See . . . already* ed. (See . . . comes / There's . . . allready Q)

81 s.d. ed. (to r. of l. 81 in Q) The bed recalls that in the house of convertites in IV.ii.123, upon which Vittoria threw herself earlier; now Brachiano, like Vittoria in the earlier scene, is the accuser. The bed may have been thrust out onto the main stage and remained for the rest of the scene.

82 s.d. ed. (to l. of ll. 83–90 in Q). This s.d. suggests that distraction was signalled by conventionalized gestures (cf. V.iv.88 s.d.): perhaps beating the breast or wringing the hands (see Thomson, p. 31). Brachiano is clearly feeling the effects of the poison.

83 *conveyed . . . territories* The export of money was a serious offence; Henry VIII published a statute forbidding it.

BRACHIANO
 Indeed I am too blame.
 For did you ever hear the dusky raven
 Chide blackness? Or was't ever known the devil
 Railed against cloven creatures?
VITTORIA   O my lord!   90
BRACHIANO
 Let me have some quails to supper.
FLAMINEO   Sir, you shall.
BRACHIANO
 No: some fried dog-fish. Your quails feed on poison –
 That old dog-fox, that politician Florence –
 I'll forswear hunting and turn dog-killer.
 Rare! I'll be friends with him: for mark you sir, one dog 95
 Still sets another a-barking: peace, peace,
 Yonder's a fine slave come in now.
FLAMINEO   Where?
BRACHIANO   Why, there.
 In a blue bonnet, and a pair of breeches
 With a great codpiece. Ha, ha, ha,
 Look you his codpiece is stuck full of pins   100
 With pearls o'th'head of them. Do not you know him?
FLAMINEO
 No my lord.
BRACHIANO Why 'tis the devil.
 I know him by a great rose he wears on's shoe
 To hide his cloven foot. I'll dispute with him.
 He's a rare linguist.

88–9 *raven ... blackness* 'The raven chides blackness' is proverbial, like the pot calling the kettle black. Ravens were considered malignant: Brachiano may refer either to the dark-haired Vittoria or the dark-skinned Zanche. Francisco, disguised as Mulinassar, is a more appropriate, though unintended, target for this remark.

91 *quails* birds supposed to feed on venomous seeds, and considered a culinary delicacy; courtesans

92 *dog-fish* a small shark; applied opprobriously to persons

93 *dog-fox* male fox (symbol of sly cunning and craft)

95–6 *one ... a-barking* It is proverbial that if one dog barks, they all do.

100–1 *codpiece ... them* Codpieces, out of fashion in 1612, were in Henry VIII's time very prominent and highly decorated.

103–4 *rose ... foot* Large, expensive silk rosettes on shoes became fashionable at the end of the sixteenth century.

105 *linguist* polyglot; eloquent speaker

VITTORIA   My lord here's nothing.   105

BRACHIANO

Nothing? Rare! Nothing! When I want money,
Our treasury is empty; there is nothing,—
I'll not be used thus.

VITTORIA   O! Lie still my lord —

BRACHIANO

See, see, Flamineo that killed his brother
Is dancing on the ropes there: and he carries   110
A money-bag in each hand, to keep him even,
For fear of breaking's neck. And there's a lawyer
In a gown whipt with velvet, stares and gapes
When the money will fall. How the rogue cuts capers!
It should have been in a halter.   115
'Tis there; what's she?   [*Points to* VITTORIA]

FLAMINEO   Vittoria, my lord.

BRACHIANO

Ha, ha, ha. Her hair is sprinkled with arras powder, that makes
her look as if she had sinned in the pastry. What's he?
                   [*Points to* GASPARO *or* LODOVICO]

FLAMINEO

A divine my lord.

BRACHIANO

He will be drunk: avoid him: th'argument is fearful when   120
churchmen stagger in't. Look you; six grey rats that have lost
their tails crawl up the pillow; send for a rat-catcher.
I'll do a miracle: I'll free the court
From all foul vermin. Where's Flamineo?

FLAMINEO

I do not like that he names me so often,   125

---

110   *ropes* tightropes
113   *whipt* trimmed
114–15   *rogue . . . halter* Flamineo is the rogue cutting capers, or dancing; the rope on which
           he dances should have gone around his neck.
117   *hair . . . powder* As a new bride, Vittoria's hair would have been sprinkled with
           powdered orris, or iris root, commonly used for whitening and perfuming hair.
118   *pastry* place where pastry is made
121–2   *six . . . pillow* possibly a reference to witches, who often turned themselves into
           animals, like the witch in *Macbeth*, who promises 'Like a rat without a tail, / I'll do,
           I'll do, and I'll do' (I.iii.9–10)
122–4   *send . . . vermin* a possible allusion to the Pied Piper of Hamelin

Especially on's death-bed: 'tis a sign
I shall not live long: see he's near his end.

BRACHIANO *seems here near his end.* LODOVICO *and*
GASPARO *in the habit of Capuchins present him in his bed with a
crucifix and hallowed candle*

LODOVICO
Pray give us leave; *Attende Domine Brachiane–*
FLAMINEO
See, see, how firmly he doth fix his eye
Upon the crucifix.
VITTORIA   O hold it constant.   130
It settles his wild spirits; and so his eyes
Melt into tears.
LODOVICO
*(By the crucifix) Domine Brachiane, solebas in bello tutus esse tuo
clypeo, nunc hunc clypeum hosti tuo opponas infernali.*
GASPARO
(By the hallowed taper) Olim hasta valuisti in bello; nunc hanc   135
sacram hastam vibrabis contra hostem animarum.
LODOVICO
*Attende Domine Brachiane si nunc quoque probas ea quae acta
sunt inter nos, flecte caput in dextrum.*
GASPARO
*Esto securus Domine Brachiane: cogita quantum habeas meritorum
– denique memineris meam animam pro tua oppignoratam si quid*   140
esset periculi.

---

127 s.d. ed. (to r. of ll. 120–30 in Q). For the crucifix as a significant property cf. V.ii.10.
     The 'hallowed candle' may recall the dumb show (II.ii.23) when Dr Julio and his
     assistant burned perfumes in the 'fire' before Brachiano's picture.

128 *Attende . . . Brachiane* 'Listen, Lord Brachiano.' The fraudulent Capuchins begin the
     Commendatio Animae, the commending of the soul to God, which follows the
     extreme unction in Roman ritual: in this ritual, candle and crucifix are symbols of
     hope and comfort to the dying (McLeod, *Dramatic Imagery*, p. 66).

133 s.d. ed. (to l. of ll. 133–5 in Q)

133–43 i.e. LODOVICO 'Lord Brachiano, you were accustomed to be guarded in battle by
        your shield; now this shield [the crucifix] you shall oppose against your infernal
        enemy.' – GASPARO 'Once with your spear you prevailed in battle; now this holy

LODOVICO

Si nunc quoque probas ea quae acta sunt inter nos, flecte caput in loevum.

He is departing: pray stand all apart,

And let us only whisper in his ears   145

Some private meditations which our order

Permits you not to hear.

Here the rest being departed LODOVICO *and* GASPARO
discover themselves

GASPARO   Brachiano.

LODOVICO

Devil Brachiano. Thou art damned.

GASPARO   Perpetually.

LODOVICO

A slave condemned and given up to the gallows

Is thy great lord and master.

GASPARO   True: for thou   150

Art given up to the devil.

LODOVICO   O you slave!

You that were held the famous politician;

Whose art was poison.

GASPARO   And whose conscience murder.

spear [the hallowed taper] you shall wield against the enemy of souls.' – LODOVICO
'Listen, Lord Brachiano, if you now also approve what has been done between us,
turn your head to the right.' – GASPARO 'Rest assured Lord Brachiano: think how
many good deeds you have done – lastly remember that my soul is pledged for
yours if there should be any peril.' – LODOVICO 'If you now also approve what has
been done between us, turn your head to the left.'

The whole passage is based on Erasmus, *Funus*, an account of the death of
Georgius Balearicus, a corrupt and wealthy man, whose death is described by
Erasmus as 'the last acte of the comedy'. After purchasing papal remission of sins
(and justifying all his goods 'goten by extorcyon and robbery'), Georgius himself,
'lyke a man of warre', delivers the first two speeches which Webster gives to the
assassins. Erasmus emphasizes the corruption and hypocrisy of the dying man;
Webster uses the same ceremony to highlight the villainy and hypocrisy of the
dying man's assassins.

135   s.d. ed. (to l. of ll. 135–7 in Q)

144–65 The revengers parody the *Commendatio*, by dismissing witnesses (who normally
participated in prayers for the dying one's soul), and by commending Brachiano
not to God but to the devil (NCW V.iii.144–7, 148–64 n.).

147   s.d. ed. (to r. of ll. 146–8 in Q)

153   *conscience* inmost thought

LODOVICO
That would have broke your wife's neck down the stairs
Ere she was poisoned.   155
GASPARO
That had your villainous sallets—
LODOVICO
And fine embroidered bottles, and perfumes
Equally mortal with a winter plague—
GASPARO
Now there's mercury—
LODOVICO   And copperas—
GASPARO   And quicksilver—
LODOVICO
With other devilish pothecary stuff   160
A-melting in your politic brains; dost hear?
GASPARO
This is Count Lodovico.
LODOVICO   This Gasparo.
And thou shalt die like a poor rogue.
GASPARO   And stink
Like a dead fly-blown dog.
LODOVICO   And be forgotten
Before thy funeral sermon.   165
BRACHIANO
Vittoria! Vittoria!

154–5   ed. (prose in Q)
        broke ... poisoned probably an allusion to the notorious Earl of Leicester's alleged
        attempt to poison his wife, Amy Robsart, before having her thrown down the stairs
        at Cumnor Place in 1560, when she finally died. Leicester wanted to be free to
        marry Queen Elizabeth; according to the 1584 pamphlet *Leicester's Commonwealth*,
        the Earl employed a poisoner named Dr Julio as well as two 'atheists' for 'figuring
        and conjuring'. Renaissance Italy was thus not so different from Renaissance
        England.
156   *sallets* salads
157   *And ... perfumes* ed. (And ... bottles / And perfumes Q)
158   *winter plague* A plague which flourished during the cold months was considered
        most pernicious.
159   *mercury ... quicksilver* Mercury *is* quicksilver (unless the poisonous plant,
        Mercurialis perennis, or wild mercury, is meant); Gasparo is trying to 'terrify him at
        the last gasp' (l. 211) through sheer emphasis. Copperas (sulphate of copper, iron
        or zinc) is fatal only when taken in quantity.
164–5   ed. (one line in Q)

LODOVICO   O the cursed devil,
  Come to himself again. We are undone.

Enter VITTORIA *and the* ATTEND[ANTS]

GASPARO
  [*Aside to* LODOVICO] Strangle him in private.
  [*Aloud*] What? Will you call him again
  To live in treble torments? For charity,   170
  For Christian charity, avoid the chamber.
                    [*Exeunt* VITTORIA *and* ATTENDANTS]

LODOVICO
  You would prate, sir. This is a true-love knot
  Sent from the Duke of Florence.

BRACHIANO *is strangled*

GASPARO   What, is it done?
LODOVICO
  The snuff is out. No woman-keeper i'th'world,
  Though she had practised seven year at the pest-house,   175
  Could have done't quaintlier.

[*Enter* VITTORIA, FRANCISCO, FLAMINEO, *and* ATTENDANTS]

             My lord he's dead.

OMNES
  Rest to his soul.

167–76 Thomson (pp. 33–4) argues that the bustle of mass entries and exits risks bringing
       the scene close to farce on the stage; the visual movement of Vittoria with her
       attendants on and off the stage certainly emphasizes by contrast Brachiano's isola-
       tion and stillness in death.
   170 *charity* a word that echoes throughout the arraignment (cf. III.ii.71, 161)
   172 *true-love knot* the noose used to strangle Brachiano (perhaps Lodovico's waistcord
       or rosary: so NCW V.iii.171 n.). The word-play links Brachiano's death with his
       love affair, and recalls Francisco's feigned courtship of Vittoria.
   174 *snuff* proverbial: to die is to go out like a candle in a snuff (possibly punctuated by
       Lodovico snuffing out the hallowed taper)
       woman-keeper female nurse, often suspected of killing off patients
   175 *pest-house* a hospice for those sick of the plague. One was erected in London in 1594.
   176 *quaintlier* more skilfully
   177 s.d. *Exit* ed. (Exit Vittoria Q)

VITTORIA   O me! This place is hell.
                          Exit [with ATTENDANTS and GASPARO]
[FRANCISCO]
   How heavily she takes it.
FLAMINEO   O yes, yes;
   Had women navigable rivers in their eyes
   They would dispend them all; surely I wonder   180
   Why we should wish more rivers to the city
   When they sell water so good cheap. I'll tell thee,
   These are but moonish shades of griefs or fears,
   There's nothing sooner dry than women's tears.
   Why here's an end of all my harvest, he has given me nothing –   185
   Court promises! Let wise men count them cursed
   For while you live he that scores best pays worst.
[FRANCISCO]
   Sure, this was Florence' doing.
FLAMINEO   Very likely.
   Those are found weighty strokes which come from th'hand,
   But those are killing strokes which come from th'head.   190
   O the rare tricks of a Machiavellian!
   He doth not come like a gross plodding slave
   And buffet you to death: no, my quaint knave,
   He tickles you to death, makes you die laughing
   As if you had swallowed down a pound of saffron.   195
   You see the feat, 'tis practised in a trice –
   To teach court-honesty it jumps on ice.

178–205, 217 s.p. *FRANCISCO* ed. (FLO Q)
181–2 *Why ... cheap* Sir Hugh Middleton's artificial New River, which was designed to
       supply London with water, was begun in 1608 and under way at the time of the
       play's first performance.
183   *moonish* changeable (like the moon)
187   *he ... worst* i.e. he who runs up a score or debt on credit (like him who depends on
       promises) pays dearly for it
191   *Machiavellian* ed. (Machivillian Q, with a pun on 'villain')
193   *buffet* strike, beat
       quaint ingenious
195   *saffron* in moderation, supposed to quicken the senses and make men merry; fatal
       when taken in excess
197   *To ... ice* i.e. to teach court intrigue that it is precarious and dangerous. In *The
       Duchess of Malfi*, courts are 'slippery ice-pavements' on which 'men may break their
       necks' (V.ii.328–9).
       court-honesty honesty as practised at court – deception, intrigue

[FRANCISCO]
    Now have the people liberty to talk
    And descant on his vices.
FLAMINEO   Misery of princes,
    That must of force be censured by their slaves!   200
    Not only blamed for doing things are ill,
    But for not doing all that all men will.
    One were better be a thresher.
    Ud's death, I would fain speak with this Duke yet.
[FRANCISCO]
    Now he's dead?   205
FLAMINEO
    I cannot conjure, but if prayers or oaths
    Will get to th'speech of him, though forty devils
    Wait on him in his livery of flames,
    I'll speak to him and shake him by the hand,
    Though I be blasted.   *Exit*
FRANCISCO   Excellent Lodovico!   210
    What? Did you terrify him at the last gasp?
LODOVICO
    Yes; and so idly, that the Duke had like
    T'have terrified us.
FRANCISCO   How?

Enter [ZANCHE] *the Moor*

LODOVICO   You shall hear that hereafter.
    See! Yon's the infernal that would make up sport.
    Now to the revelation of that secret   215
    She promised when she fell in love with you.

199   *descant* comment, enlarge
210   *blasted* stricken by supernatural agency
      s.d. *Exit* ed. (Exit Flamineo Q)
      s.d. ed. (to r. of l. 211 in Q)
      Lodovico, in his hooded Capuchins' robe, has been a silent witness to the preceding
      dialogue; his presence on the stage is a constant visual reminder of Francisco's
      hypocrisy.
214   *infernal* Zanche is considered devilish because she is black (the s.p. 'Moor' draws
      attention to her colour); Francisco, here in blackface as Mulinassar, may exemplify
      the proverb 'The white devil is worse than the black' (Tilley D310).
      make up sport make our fun complete

[FRANCISCO]

    You're passionately met in this sad world.

[ZANCHE]

    I would have you look up, sir; these court tears

    Claim not your tribute to them. Let those weep

    That guiltily partake in the sad cause.   220

    I knew last night by a sad dream I had

    Some mischief would ensue, yet to say truth

    My dream most concerned you.

LODOVICO   Shall's fall a-dreaming?

FRANCISCO

    Yes, and for fashion sake I'll dream with her.

[ZANCHE]

    Methought, sir, you came stealing to my bed.   225

FRANCISCO

    Wilt thou believe me sweeting? By this light

    I was a-dreamt on thee too, for methought

    I saw thee naked.

[ZANCHE]   Fie, sir! As I told you,

    Methought you lay down by me.

FRANCISCO   So dreamt I,

    And lest thou shouldst take cold, I covered thee   230

    With this Irish mantle.

[ZANCHE]   Verily I did dream

    You were somewhat bold with me; but to come to't.

LODOVICO

    How? How? I hope you will not go to't here.

FRANCISCO

    Nay, you must hear my dream out.

[ZANCHE]   Well, sir, forth.

FRANCISCO

    When I threw the mantle o'er thee, thou didst laugh   235

    Exceedingly methought.

[ZANCHE]   Laugh?

218–64   s.p. ZANCHE ed. (MOO or MOORE. Q)

221–68   This scene both illustrates visually Flamineo's words about the Machiavellian (here, Francisco) who 'tickles you to death' (1.198) and clearly recalls I.ii.228ff., where two lovers embrace and Vittoria recounts her dream, which is to lead to murder.

    231   *Irish mantle* blanket worn by rustic Irish in all weathers as the only covering over their naked bodies

FRANCISCO And cried'st out,
 The hair did tickle thee.
[ZANCHE] There was a dream indeed.
LODOVICO
 Mark her, I prithee: she simpers like the suds
 A collier hath been washed in.
[ZANCHE]
 Come, sir; good fortune tends you; I did tell you 240
 I would reveal a secret – Isabella
 The Duke of Florence' sister was empoisoned
 By a fumed picture and Camillo's neck
 Was broke by damned Flamineo, the mischance
 Laid on a vaulting-horse.
FRANCISCO Most strange!
[ZANCHE] Most true. 245
LODOVICO
 The bed of snakes is broke.
[ZANCHE]
 I sadly do confess I had a hand
 In the black deed.
FRANCISCO Thou kept'st their counsel.
[ZANCHE] Right.
 For which, urged with contrition, I intend
 This night to rob Vittoria.
LODOVICO Excellent penitence! 250
 Usurers dream on't while they sleep out sermons.
[ZANCHE]
 To further our escape, I have entreated
 Leave to retire me, till the funeral,
 Unto a friend i'th'country. That excuse
 Will further our escape. In coin and jewels 255
 I shall, at least, make good unto your use
 An hundred thousand crowns.
FRANCISCO O noble wench!

---

238 *simpers* with a play on 'simmers'
239 *collier* coal-carrier or coal-miner (blackened by coal dust, which would then appear
  in the soap suds)
243 *fumed* perfumed
245–6 ed. (Laid . . . strange! / MOO. Most . . . broke. Q)
246 *bed . . . broke* literally, the intertwined nest of snakes is untangled; figuratively, the
  mystery is revealed

LODOVICO

Those crowns we'll share.

[ZANCHE]   It is a dowry,

Methinks, should make that sunburnt proverb false,

'And wash the Ethiop white'.

FRANCISCO   It shall, away–   260

[ZANCHE]

Be ready for our flight.

FRANCISCO   An hour 'fore day.

                          Exit [ZANCHE] *the Moor*

O strange discovery! Why till now we knew not

The circumstance of either of their deaths.

Enter [ZANCHE *the*] *Moor*

[ZANCHE]

You'll wait about midnight in the chapel.

FRANCISCO   There.

                          [*Exit* ZANCHE]

LODOVICO

Why, now our action's justified.

FRANCISCO   Tush for justice.   265

What harms it justice? We now, like the partridge,

Purge the disease with laurel, for the fame

Shall crown the enterprise and quit the shame.

                         Exeunt

259–60 *sunburnt . . . white* The proverb is based on Jeremiah 13:23: 'Can the Ethiopian change his skin, or the leopard his spots?'

    261 s.d. ed. (to r. of l. 262 in Q). Zanche's exit and immediate re-entry realistically suggest her anxious over-insistence, as well as the precarious position of the villains in Brachiano's court (cf. l. 167).

    264 *You'll . . . There* ed. (You'le . . . midnight / In . . . There. Q)

266–8 *like . . . shame* According to Pliny, partridges purged themselves by eating laurel (or bay leaves), also a symbol of fame; Francisco declares that they will rid their crimes of any taint by the glory they will achieve.

    268 *quit* clear, pay off

Enter FLAM[INEO] *and* GASP[ARO] *at one door, another
way* GIOVANNI *attended*

GASPARO

The young Duke. Did you e'er see a sweeter prince?

FLAMINEO

I have known a poor woman's bastard better favoured. This is
behind him. Now to his face – all comparisons were hateful.
Wise was the courtly peacock, that being a great minion and
being compared for beauty, by some dottrels that stood by, to   5
the kingly eagle, said the eagle was a far fairer bird than herself,
not in respect of her feathers, but in respect of her long tallants.
His will grow out in time – [*to* GIOVANNI] My gracious lord.

GIOVANNI

I pray leave me, sir.

FLAMINEO

Your Grace must be merry: 'tis I have cause to mourn, for wot   10
you what said the little boy that rode behind his father on
horseback?

GIOVANNI

Why, what said he?

FLAMINEO

'When you are dead, father' (said he) 'I hope then I shall ride
in the saddle.' O, 'tis a brave thing for a man to sit by himself: 15
he may stretch himself in the stirrups, look about, and see the
whole compass of the hemisphere. You're now, my lord,
i'th'saddle.

GIOVANNI

Study your prayers, sir, and be penitent.
'Twere fit you'd think on what hath former bin,   20
I have heard grief named the eldest child of sin.

Exit [*with others*]

---

   5 *dottrels* a variety of plover, supposed to be easy game because of their stupidity;
      term often applied to simpletons
   7 *tallants* talons (with a possible pun on 'talents', natural disposition or abilities, as in
      Love's Labour's Lost IV.ii.63–4)
  21 *grief . . . sin* Cf. cardinal in *The Duchess of Malfi* (V.v.53–4): 'I suffer now for what
      hath former bin / *Sorrow is held the eldest child of sin*'.
      s.d. *Exit* [*with others*] ed. (Exit Giou. Q)

FLAMINEO

> Study my prayers? He threatens me divinely. I am falling to
> pieces already – I care not, though, like Anacharsis, I were
> pounded to death in a mortar. And yet that death were fitter for
> usurers' gold and themselves to be beaten together to make a   25
> most cordial cullis for the devil.
>
> He hath his uncle's villainous look already,
> In *decimo-sexto*.

Enter COURTIER

> Now, sir, what are you?

COURTIER

> It is the pleasure, sir, of the young Duke
> That you forbear the presence, and all rooms   30
> That owe him reverence.

FLAMINEO

> So, the wolf and the raven are very pretty fools when they are
> young. Is it your office, sir, to keep me out?

COURTIER

> So the Duke wills.

FLAMINEO

> Verily, master courtier, extremity is not to be used in all offices.   35
> Say that a gentlewoman were taken out of her bed about
> midnight and committed to Castle Angelo, to the tower yonder,
> with nothing about her but her smock. Would it not show a

---

23 *Anacharsis* Scythian philosopher noted for his wisdom, actually killed by his
    brother with an arrow. Webster's source confuses him with Anaxarchus, pounded
    to death in a mortar with iron pestles because he challenged the authority of
    Nicocreon, tyrant of Cyprus. Anaxarchus was famous for jesting at death.

25–6 *usurers' . . . devil* A cullis, or fortifying broth, could be made by simmering together
    bruised chicken bones and pieces of gold (supposed to have medicinal value).

28 *decimo-sexto* a very small book, in which a page is one-sixteenth of a full sheet; a
    diminutive person
    s.d. ed. (to r. of l. 27 in Q)

30 *presence* presence-chamber

37 *Castle Angelo* i.e. the Castel Sant'Angelo at Rome, in which the real-life Vittoria was
    imprisoned
    tower yonder The Red Bull audience would doubtless have understood by this the
    Tower of London, where King James had recently imprisoned Arbella Stuart, his
    cousin, for marrying for love without royal permission.

cruel part in the gentleman porter to lay claim to her upper
garment, pull it o'er her head and ears, and put her in naked?   40

COURTIER

Very good: you are merry.   [*Exit*]

FLAMINEO

Doth he make a court ejectment of me? A flaming firebrand
casts more smoke without a chimney than within't. I'll smoor
some of them.

> *Enter* [FRANCISCO, *Duke of*] *Florence*
> [*disguised as* MULINASSAR]

How now? Thou art sad.   45

FRANCISCO

I met even now with the most piteous sight.

FLAMINEO

Thou met'st another here, a pitiful
Degraded courtier.

FRANCISCO   Your reverend mother

Is grown a very old woman in two hours.
I found them winding of Marcello's corse,   50
And there is such a solemn melody
'Tween doleful songs, tears, and sad elegies,
Such as old grandames watching by the dead
Were wont t'outwear the nights with, that believe me
I had no eyes to guide me forth the room,   55
They were so o'ercharged with water.

FLAMINEO   I will see them.

FRANCISCO

'Twere much uncharity in you, for your sight
Will add unto their tears.

FLAMINEO   I will see them.

---

42   *flaming firebrand* a piece of wood kindled at the fire; one who kindles strife or
     mischief; one who deserves to burn in hell. Flamineo is playing on his own name.
43   *smoor* smother, suffocate
50   *winding of . . . corse* wrapping Marcello's corpse in a shroud or winding-sheet (the
     face was usually left uncovered)
53–4 *old . . . with* The practice of watching all night over the deceased, with candles
     burning, was increasingly disappearing in seventeenth-century England, but
     persisted in rural Ireland until the twentieth century.

FRANCISCO
> They are behind the traverse. I'll discover
> Their superstitious howling.   [*Draws the traverse*]   60

>   CORNELIA, [ZANCHE] *the Moor and three other Ladies*
>   *discovered, winding* MARCELLO's *corse. A song*

CORNELIA
> This rosemary is withered, pray get fresh:
> I would have these herbs grow up in his grave
> When I am dead and rotten. Reach the bays;
> I'll tie a garland here about his head:
> 'Twill keep my boy from lightning. This sheet   65
> I have kept this twenty year, and every day
> Hallowed it with my prayers – I did not think
> He should have wore it.

[ZANCHE] [*Seeing* FLAMINEO] Look you; who are yonder?
CORNELIA
> O, reach me the flowers.

[ZANCHE]
> Her ladyship's foolish.

WOMAN   Alas! Her grief   70
> Hath turned her child again.

CORNELIA (*To* FLAMINEO)   You're very welcome.
> There's rosemary for you, and rue for you,
> Heart's-ease for you. I pray make much of it.
> I have left more for myself.

59 *traverse* a curtain at the rear of the stage. The tableau thus discovered has almost
     emblematic visual significance (recalling, perhaps, as at *King Lear* V.iii.257 s.d., the
     pietà); it is held in place during the 'song'.
61 *rosemary* evergreen herb, symbol of immortality and remembrance, customary at
     weddings and funerals
63–5 *bays . . . lightning* Laurel wreaths were both tokens of fame and glory, and reputed
     to protect one from lightning.
65 *sheet* i.e. winding sheet
68–76 s.p. ZANCHE ed. (MOO. Q)
72–4 Cornelia may distribute real flowers, or be sufficiently unhinged to use imaginary
     ones (NCW IV.iv.60 ff. n.).
71 s.d. ed. (to r. of l. 72 in Q)
72–3 *rue . . . Heart's-ease* Rue, a perennial evergreen shrub, symbolized sorrow, repen-
     tance or compassion; the heart's-ease, or pansy, represented tranquillity.
72–4 *There's . . . myself* an obvious echo of Ophelia in *Hamlet* IV.v.175 ff.: 'There's rose-
     mary, that's for remembrance; pray you, love, remember. And there is pansies, that's
     for thoughts . . . There's rue for you, and here's some for me.'

FRANCISCO   Lady, who's this?

CORNELIA

  [*To* FLAMINEO] You are, I take it, the grave-maker.

FLAMINEO   So.   75

[ZANCHE]

  'Tis Flamineo.

CORNELIA

  Will you make me such a fool? [*Takes his hand*] Here's a white
    hand:

  Can blood so soon be washed out? Let me see:

  When screech-owls croak upon the chimney tops

  And the strange cricket i'th'oven sings and hops,   80

  When yellow spots do on your hands appear,

  Be certain then you of a corse shall hear.

  Out upon't, how 'tis speckled! H'as handled a toad sure.

  Cowslip-water is good for the memory: pray buy me three
    ounces of't.

FLAMINEO

  I would I were from hence.

CORNELIA   Do you hear, sir?   85

  I'll give you a saying which my grandmother

  Was wont, when she heard the bell toll, to sing o'er

  Unto her lute–

---

  75 *grave-maker* grave-digger. In this case, Flamineo, as Marcello's murderer, is literally
     his 'grave-maker'.

77–8 *Here's . . . out?* Cf. Lady Macbeth in *Macbeth* V.i.43: 'What, will these hands ne'er be
     clean?'

79–82 *When . . . hear* In popular superstition, these were all signs that a death was imminent.

  83 *how . . . speckled* Thomas Adams, author of *The White Devil or the Hypocrite
     Uncas'd* (1612), a sermon, praises his patron for being 'free from the aspersion of
     these speckled stains' – the sins which he is about to expose.

  84 *Cowslip-water* medicinal extract from the cowslip flower, reputed to be good for the
     head and sinews

84–5 ed. (Couslep . . . oun / ces . . . sir? Q)

87–8 ed. (Was . . . lute / Doe . . . doe. Q)

  88 *lute* Ophelia is playing on the lute when she enters in a distracted state in Q1 of
     Hamlet IV.v.20; perhaps Cornelia has one too.
     s.d. ed. (to r. of ll. 91–3 in Q). The gestures of madness called for by the stage direc-
     tion are in tension with the elegiac, melodic strain of the dirge itself; the discordant
     effect is appropriate to the play's increasing fragmentation and despair.

FLAMINEO   Do, and you will, do.

CORNELIA *doth this in several forms of distraction*

CORNELIA
  'Call for the robin-red-breast and the wren,
  Since o'er shady groves they hover,   90
  And with leaves and flow'rs do cover
  The friendless bodies of unburied men.
  Call unto his funeral dole
  The ant, the field-mouse, and the mole
  To rear him hillocks that shall keep him warm   95
  And (when gay tombs are robbed) sustain no harm,
  But keep the wolf far thence that's foe to men,
  For with his nails he'll dig them up again.'
  They would not bury him 'cause he died in a quarrel
  But I have an answer for them.   100
  'Let holy church receive him duly
  Since he paid the church tithes truly.'
  His wealth is summed, and this is all his store:
  This poor men get and great men get no more.
  Now the wares are gone, we may shut up shop.   105
  Bless you all good people.
                Exeunt CORNELIA [, ZANCHE] *and Ladies*

FLAMINEO
  I have a strange thing in me, to th'which
  I cannot give a name, without it be
  Compassion. I pray leave me.

                      Exit FRANCISCO

---

  89   *robin-red-breast . . . wren* allusion to the widespread belief that robins (and wrens,
       believed to be female robins) covered up and tended dead bodies
  93   *dole* rites of funeral
97–8   *keep . . . again* According to popular superstition, the wolf was a minister of God's
       revenge, sent to dig up the corpses of those who had been murdered; cf. *The
       Duchess of Malfi* IV.ii.303–5: 'The wolf shall find her grave, and scrape it up; / Not
       to devour the corpse, but to discover / The horrid murther'.
 103 *summed* reckoned *this . . . store* Cornelia may indicate the area of the stage on
       which Marcello lies or the winding sheet itself.
 105 *shut . . . shop* Having perhaps retreated into the discovery space to sing her dirge
       (after talking to Flamineo), Cornelia now closes the curtains.
 109 Flamineo's request that Francisco leave the stage is visual confirmation of his new
       interiority.

This night I'll know the utmost of my fate: 110
I'll be resolved what my rich sister means
T'assign me for my service. I have lived
Riotously ill, like some that live in court;
And sometimes, when my face was full of smiles
Have felt the maze of conscience in my breast.   115
Oft gay and honoured robes those tortures try:
'We think caged birds sing, when indeed they cry'.

Enter BRACHIA[NO'*s*] *Ghost. In his leather cassock and breeches,*
boots, a cowl [*and in his hand*] *a pot of lily-flowers with a*
skull in't

Ha! I can stand thee. [*The Ghost approaches*] Nearer, nearer yet.
What a mockery hath death made of thee? Thou look'st sad.
In what place art thou? In yon starry gallery   120
Or in the cursed dungeon? No? Not speak?
Pray, sir, resolve me, what religion's best
For a man to die in? Or is it in your knowledge
To answer me how long I have to live?
That's the most necessary question.   125
Not answer? Are you still like some great men

---

115 *maze* labyrinth; state of confusion
116 i.e. often those who wear gay and honoured robes (i.e. courtiers) experience those
     tortures
117 s.d. ed. (to r. of ll. 118–24 in Q). This spectacular vision fulfils Flamineo's earlier
     vow to shake Brachiano 'by the hand' (V.iii.209), and confirms his private vision of
     the truth underlying appearances. It is highly emblematic: the lily symbolizes that
     which is fair in show but foul in smell, beneath which is buried the horrible symbol
     of mortality, the skull (revealed at l. 128).
     s.d.1 *leather cassock* A cassock was a long coat or cloak worn by soldiers; a leather
     cassock was worn by ghosts in tragedies.
     s.d.2 *cowl* monastic hood or robe. In Renaissance Italy, men were commonly buried
     in the habit of a Franciscan friar, in the hope that it would procure a remission of
     their sins.
118 *stand thee* Flamineo's defiance of Brachiano here recalls IV.ii.48–9.
119 *mockery* counterfeit, shadow; object of ridicule
120–1 *starry . . . dungeon* probably theatrical terms: the gallery or upper stage; the dun-
     geon or the area below the stage, accessible by trapdoor, from which, in other plays,
     devils ascended
121, 126 The ghost's silence and ominous gestures are a powerful contrast (and perhaps
     rebuke) to Flamineo's rapid and desperate speech (cf. ghost in *Hamlet* I.i.50, whose
     silence suggests that 'it is offended').

542

That only walk like shadows up and down
And to no purpose? Say–

The Ghost throws earth upon him and shows him the skull

What's that? O fatal! He throws earth upon me.
A dead man's skull beneath the roots of flowers.   130
I pray speak, sir. Our Italian churchmen
Make us believe dead men hold conference
With their familiars, and many times
Will come to bed to them and eat with them.

Exit Ghost

He's gone; and see, the skull and earth are vanished.   135
This is beyond melancholy. I do dare my fate
To do its worst. Now to my sister's lodging
And sum up all these horrors: the disgrace
The Prince threw on me; next the piteous sight
Of my dead brother; and my mother's dotage;   140
And last this terrible vision. All these
Shall with Vittoria's bounty turn to good,
Or I will drown this weapon in her blood.   *Exit*

[ACT V, SCENE v]

Enter FRANCISCO, LODOVICO, *and* HORTENSIO
[*overhearing them*]

LODOVICO

My lord upon my soul you shall no further:
You have most ridiculously engaged yourself
Too far already. For my part, I have paid
All my debts, so if I should chance to fall

127 *shadows* insubstantial persons
128 s.d. ed. (to r. of ll. 130–4 in Q)
136 *This . . . melancholy* i.e. this ghost is more than a figment of imagination (unlike
     Isabella's ghost in IV.i.100, which Francisco believes is produced by his melan-
     choly). According to contemporary theories, beyond melancholy lay spiritual
     despair (NCW V.iv.136 n.).
143 *this weapon* Flamineo rushes off the stage waving, probably, a poniard.

My creditors fall not with me; and I vow   5
To quite all in this bold assembly
To the meanest follower. My lord, leave the city
Or I'll forswear the murder.
FRANCISCO   Farewell Lodovico.
If thou dost perish in this glorious act,
I'll rear unto thy memory that fame   10
Shall in the ashes keep alive thy name.
                    [*Exeunt* FRANCISCO *and* LODOVICO]
HORTENSIO
There's some black deed on foot. I'll presently
Down to the citadel and raise some force.
These strong court factions that do brook no checks
In the career oft break the riders' necks.   [*Exit*]   15

[ACT V, SCENE vi]

Enter VITTORIA *with a book in her hand,* ZANCHE; FLAMINEO
following them

FLAMINEO
What, are you at your prayers? Give o'er.
VITTORIA   How ruffin?
FLAMINEO
I come to you 'bout worldly business:
Sit down, sit down. Nay stay, blouze, you may hear it,
The doors are fast enough.

6   *quite* repay, requite
11   s.d. Lodovico and Francisco probably enter through the same door (while
     Hortensio enters through the other); here, they exit through opposite doors, having
     said their farewells. The staging thus anticipates the fracturing of the villains' plot.
12   *presently* immediately
15   *career* short gallop at full speed; charge in tournament or battle *oft* ed. (of't Q)

0   s.d. ed. (to 1 of ll. 1–6 in Q). Flamineo's first line indicates that the 'book' is devotional
     (perhaps a bible). One of Webster's sources claims that the murderers 'stabbed her
     where they found her at prayer'. On the stage, the reading of a book was a conven-
     tional sign of melancholy or guilt (cf. *The Duchess of Malfi* V.v.0 s.d.). Flamineo
     probably brandishes his poniard threateningly here, or otherwise menaces the women.
1   *ruffin* devil
3   *stay . . . it* Flamineo's words suggest that Zanche attempts to flee, a gesture of open
     rejection from his former 'sweet mistress' (V.i.143), and yet another rebuff in a series.
     blouze fat, red-faced wench (here ironic)

VITTORIA   Ha, are you drunk?

FLAMINEO

Yes, yes, with wormwood water – you shall taste   5
Some of it presently.

VITTORIA   What intends the fury?

FLAMINEO

You are my lord's executrix and I claim
Reward for my long service.

VITTORIA   For your service?

FLAMINEO

Come therefore, here is pen and ink, set down
What you will give me.   10

                                         She writes

VITTORIA

There.

FLAMINEO Ha! Have you done already?
'Tis a most short conveyance.

VITTORIA   I will read it.

[*Reads*] 'I give that portion to thee and no other
Which Cain groaned under having slain his brother.'

FLAMINEO

A most courtly patent to beg by.

VITTORIA   You are a villain.   15

FLAMINEO

Is't come to this? They say affrights cure agues.
Thou hast a devil in thee: I will try
If I can scare him from thee. Nay, sit still:
My lord hath left me yet two case of jewels

---

5   *wormwood* plant with a bitter taste; emblem of what is bitter and grievous to the soul

6   *fury* Cf. I.ii.252, II.i.244 and III.ii.278; normally used of an angry woman, here used
     ironically by Vittoria, perhaps turning Flamineo's description of Cornelia and gen-
     eral misogyny back on himself.

8   *service?* ed. (service Q)

10   s.d. ed. (outer margin, l. of l. 11 in Q)

11   *already?* ed. (already, Q)

13–14 *I . . . brother* Cf. Genesis 4:11–12: to Cain who slew his brother Abel, the Lord said:
       'And now art thou cursed from the earth, which hath opened her mouth to receive thy
       brother's blood from thy hand; when thou tillest the ground, it shall not henceforth
       yield unto thee her strength; a fugitive and a vagabond shalt thou be in the earth'.

15   *courtly . . . by* Cf. V.i.108.

16   *They* ed. (the Q)

19   *case* pair (two pairs of pistols or four pistols: cf. ll. 92–5)

Shall make me scorn your bounty; you shall see them.   20

[Exit]

VITTORIA
Sure he's distracted.
ZANCHE   O he's desperate –
For your own safety give him gentle language.

He enters with two case of pistols

FLAMINEO
Look, these are better far at a dead lift
Than all your jewel house.
VITTORIA   And yet methinks
These stones have no fair lustre, they are ill set.   25
FLAMINEO
I'll turn the right side towards you: you shall see
How they will sparkle.
VITTORIA   Turn this horror from me!
What do you want? What would you have me do?
Is not all mine yours? Have I any children?
FLAMINEO
Pray thee good woman, do not trouble me   30
With this vain worldly business; say your prayers.
I made a vow to my deceased lord
Neither yourself nor I should outlive him
The numb'ring of four hours.
VITTORIA   Did he enjoin it?
FLAMINEO
He did, and 'twas a deadly jealousy   35
Lest any should enjoy thee after him
That urged him vow me to it. For my death,
I did propound it voluntarily, knowing

22 ed. (to r. of ll. 21–3 in Q)
23 *at . . . lift* in a sudden emergency (derived from pulling a heavy, or 'dead' weight),
     with an obvious play on 'dead'
27 *they* ed. (the Q)
31 *worldly* ed. (wordly Q)
35–7 A possible reference to King Herod, who ordered that his adored wife Mariam be
     killed upon his death; Lady Elizabeth Cary, the first woman playwright in England,
     dramatized the story from Mariam's point of view in *The Tragedy of Mariam, Fair
     Queen of Jewry*. Cary's play, published in 1613, circulated in manuscript, and may
     be Webster's source here.

If he could not be safe in his own court
Being a great Duke, what hope then for us?   40
VITTORIA
This is your melancholy and despair.
FLAMINEO   Away!
Fool thou art to think that politicians
Do use to kill the effects of injuries
And let the cause live. Shall we groan in irons
Or be a shameful and a weighty burden   45
To a public scaffold? This is my resolve:
I would not live at any man's entreaty
Nor die at any's bidding.
VITTORIA   Will you hear me?
FLAMINEO
My life hath done service to other men;
My death shall serve mine own turn. Make you ready.   50
VITTORIA
Do you mean to die indeed?
FLAMINEO   With as much pleasure
As e'er my father gat me.
VITTORIA [*Aside to* ZANCHE] Are the doors locked?
ZANCHE
Yes madam.
VITTORIA
Are you grown an atheist? Will you turn your body,
Which is the goodly palace of the soul,   55
To the soul's slaughter house? O the cursed devil,
Which doth present us with all other sins
Thrice candied o'er: despair with gall and stibium,
Yet we carouse it off – [*Aside to* ZANCHE] cry out for help –
Makes us forsake that which was made for man,   60

42   *Fool* ed. (Foole, Q)
47–8   *I . . . bidding* An echo of Vittoria's lines during her arraignment (III.ii.138–9): 'I
     scorn to hold my life / At yours or any man's entreaty, sir'.
54–5   *body . . . soul* Perhaps revealing her sensual nature, Vittoria inverts the usual image of
     the body as the soul's *prison* (cf. *The Duchess of Malfi* IV.ii.127–31: 'didst thou ever
     see a lark in a cage? such is the soul in the body: this world is like her little turf of
     grass, and the heaven o'er our heads, like her looking-glass, only gives us a miserable
     knowledge of the small compass of our prison'.)
58   *candied o'er* sugared over
58–9   *despair . . . off* i.e. despair (unlike other sins) is flavoured with gall (bile; venom)
     and stibium (the poison antimony), yet we drink it down (commit suicide)

547

The world, to sink to that was made for devils,
Eternal darkness.

ZANCHE   Help, help!

FLAMINEO   I'll stop your throat
With winter plums—

VITTORIA   I prithee yet remember
Millions are now in graves, which at last day
Like mandrakes shall rise shrieking.

FLAMINEO   Leave your prating,   65
For these are but grammatical laments,
Feminine arguments, and they move me
As some in pulpits move their auditory
More with their exclamation than sense
Of reason or sound doctrine.

ZANCHE [*Aside*]   Gentle madam   70
Seem to consent, only persuade him teach
The way to death; let him die first.

VITTORIA
[*Aside*] 'Tis good, I apprehend it.
[*Aloud*] To kill oneself is meat that we must take
Like pills, not chew't, but quickly swallow it –   75
The smart o'th'wound or weakness of the hand
May else bring treble torments.

FLAMINEO   I have held it.
A wretched and most miserable life,
Which is not able to die.

VITTORIA   O but frailty!
Yet I am now resolved: farewell, affliction!   80
Behold Brachiano, I, that while you lived
Did make a flaming altar of my heart
To sacrifice unto you, now am ready
To sacrifice heart and all. Farewell, Zanche.

62–3   *stop . . . plums* i.e. gag you with hard fruit (stop your mouth with bullets); so NCW
       V.vi.63–4 n.

  65   *mandrakes* Cf. III.i.49n.

66–7   *grammatical . . . arguments* i.e. laments composed according to formal rules, weak
       arguments

  69   *exclamation* formal declamation; emphatic speech

82–3   *flaming . . . you* A continental emblem book (Rollenhagen's *Nucleus Emblematum*,
       Cologne, 1611–13) shows a flaming heart on an altar as an image of sacrifice to
       God.

ZANCHE

    How, madam! Do you think that I'll outlive you?   85

    Especially when my best self Flamineo

    Goes the same voyage?

FLAMINEO   O most loved Moor!

ZANCHE

    Only by all my love let me entreat you:

    Since it is most necessary none of us

    Do violence on ourselves, let you or I   90

    Be her sad taster, teach her how to die.

FLAMINEO

    Thou dost instruct me nobly. Take these pistols,

    Because my hand is stained with blood already;

    Two of these you shall level at my breast,

    Th'other 'gainst your own, and so we'll die,   95

    Most equally contented. But first swear

    Not to outlive me.

VITTORIA *and* [ZANCHE] Most religiously.

FLAMINEO

    Then here's an end of me. Farewell daylight

    And O contemptible physic! That dost take

    So long a study only to preserve   100

    So short a life, I take my leave of thee.

    These are two cupping-glasses that shall draw

    All my infected blood out –

    Are you ready?

VITTORIA *and* ZANCHE Ready.   *Showing the pistols*

FLAMINEO

    Whither shall I go now? O Lucian thy ridiculous purgatory!   105

---

   91 *taster* a servant whose duty it is to taste food and drink before they are served to his master, in order to ascertain their quality or detect poison

92–5 Flamineo offers each woman a case or pair of pistols; each of them points one at Flamineo, one at the other woman.

   97 s.p. ed. (VIT. & MOO. Q)

 102 *cupping-glasses* cup-shaped surgical vessels applied to the body, then heated to create a vacuum and thus draw off blood

 104 s.d. ed. (to r. of ll. 102–3 in Q)

       VITTORIA *and* ZANCHE ed. (BOTH Q)

 105 *Lucian . . . purgatory* Lucian's *Menippos* includes different examples of the ignominious fates of great men, such as King Philip of Macedon cobbling shoes.

       purgatory! ed. (Purgatory Q)

To find Alexander the Great cobbling shoes, Pompey tagging
points, and Julius Caesar making hair buttons, Hannibal selling
blacking, and Augustus crying garlic, Charlemagne selling lists
by the dozen, and King Pippin crying apples in a cart drawn
with one horse.   110
Whether I resolve to fire, earth, water, air,
Or all the elements by scruples, I know not
Nor greatly care – Shoot, shoot,
Of all deaths the violent death is best,
For from ourselves it steals ourselves so fast   115
The pain once apprehended is quite past.

They shoot and run to him and tread upon him

VITTORIA

What, are you dropped?

FLAMINEO

I am mixed with earth already: as you are noble
Perform your vows and bravely follow me.

VITTORIA

Whither – to hell?

ZANCHE   To most assured damnation.   120

VITTORIA

O, thou most cursed devil.

ZANCHE   Thou art caught–

VITTORIA

In thine own engine. I tread the fire out
That would have been my ruin.

---

106 *Alexander ... shoes* Cf. Hamlet's different musing on the fate of Alexander
     (V.i.203–4): 'Why may not imagination trace the noble dust of Alexander, till 'a
     find it stopping a bunghole?'
106–7 *tagging points* fixing metal tags on the laces or points which held together
       Elizabethan clothing
107–10 *Julius ... horse* Flamineo increases the absurdity of his examples by giving them
        wittily appropriate activities: bald Caesar makes hair buttons, black Hannibal sells
        black polish, King Pippin (also a variety of apple) calls out the price of his apples,
        etc. (Dent, p. 165).
108 *lists* strips of cloth
112 *by scruples* by small degrees or portions
116 s.d. ed. (to r. of ll. 115–18 in Q)
120 ed. (Whither to hell, Q)
122 *engine* device

FLAMINEO

Will you be perjured? What a religious oath was Styx that the
gods never durst swear by and violate? O that we had such an   125
oath to minister, and to be so well kept in our courts of justice.

VITTORIA

Think whither thou art going.

ZANCHE   And remember
What villanies thou hast acted.

VITTORIA   This thy death
Shall make me like a blazing ominous star –
Look up and tremble.

FLAMINEO   O I am caught with a springe!   130

VITTORIA

You see the fox comes many times short home,
'Tis here proved true.

FLAMINEO   Killed with a couple of braches.

VITTORIA

No fitter offering for the infernal Furies
Than one in whom they reigned while he was living.

FLAMINEO

O, the way's dark and horrid! I cannot see –   135
Shall I have no company?

VITTORIA   O yes, thy sins
Do run before thee to fetch fire from hell
To light thee thither.

FLAMINEO   O I smell soot,
Most stinking soot, the chimney is a-fire –

---

124   *Styx* in Greek myth, a river in the underworld. The gods swore their oaths upon its
        honoured waters (*Iliad* XV, 36 ff.).
127   *Think . . . remember* ed. (Iustice . . . remeber Q)
129   *blazing . . . star* an ominous prodigy foreshadowing the fall of princes (cf. the
        'rough-bearded comet' of V.iii.31). Using light imagery (cf. the 'diamonds' of
        III.ii.294), Vittoria prophesies her own triumphant revenge.
130   *springe* snare for trapping small game and birds
131   *fox . . . home* i.e. even the cunning fox can come home without his tail (i.e. dead)
132   *with . . . braches* i.e. by a couple of bitches
133   *Furies* Cf. IV.iii.125, 151, where first Lodovico, then Monticelso, is supposed to be
        inhabited by the Furies.
138–9   *O . . . a-fire* ed. (one line in Q)
139   *stinking* ed. (sinking Q)
        chimney is ed. (chimneis Q)

My liver's parboiled like Scotch holy-bread;   140
There's a plumber laying pipes in my guts, it scalds;
Wilt thou outlive me?

ZANCHE   Yes, and drive a stake
Through thy body; for we'll give it out
Thou didst this violence upon thyself.

FLAMINEO
O cunning devils! Now I have tried your love   145
And doubled all your reaches.

Riseth

I am not wounded:
The pistols held no bullets: 'twas a plot
To prove your kindness to me and I live
To punish your ingratitude. I knew
One time or other you would find a way   150
To give me a strong potion. O men
That lie upon your death-beds and are haunted
With howling wives, ne'er trust them – they'll remarry
Ere the worm pierce your winding sheet, ere the spider
Make a thin curtain for your epitaphs.   155
How cunning you were to discharge! Do you practise at the
Artillery Yard? Trust a woman? Never, never. Brachiano be my
precedent: we lay our souls to pawn to the devil for a little
pleasure and a woman makes the bill of sale. That ever man

---

140   *liver* seat of the passions
      Scotch holy-bread according to Cotgrave's *Dictionarie of the French and English Tongues* (1611), a sodden sheep's liver
142–3 *drive ... body* traditional treatment of suicides, who were then buried at crossroads
146   *doubled ... reaches* i.e. matched your plots or contrivances
146   s.d. ed. (to r. of ll. 146–7 in Q)
      s.d. *Riseth* ed. (Flamineo riseth Q)
147   A metatheatrical joke; as Flamineo rises, Webster makes his audience (which has shared the women's illusions) conscious of the reality of the theatre, in which death is always feigned.
151–3 *men ... wives* possibly a deliberate allusion to Brachiano's cry at V.iii. 37–8: 'How miserable a thing it is to die / 'Mongst women howling!'
157   *Artillery Yard* In 1610 the weekly exercise of arms and military discipline for citizens and merchants was revived in the Artillery Gardens at Bishopsgate.
158   *precedent* ed. (president Q)

should marry! For one Hypermnestra that saved her lord and   160
husband, forty-nine of her sisters cut their husbands' throats all
in one night. There was a shoal of virtuous horse-leeches.
Here are two other instruments.

Enter LOD[OVICO], GASP[ARO, *disguised*], PEDRO, CARLO

VITTORIA   Help, help!

FLAMINEO
What noise is that? Hah? False keys i'th'court!

LODOVICO
We have brought you a masque.

FLAMINEO   A matachin it seems   165
By your drawn swords. Churchmen turned revellers.

CONSPIRATORS
Isabella, Isabella!

                          [*They throw off their disguises*]

LODOVICO
Do you know us now?

FLAMINEO   Lodovico and Gasparo.

LODOVICO
Yes, and that Moor the Duke gave pension to
Was the great Duke of Florence.

160–2   *For ... night* Hypermnestra's father, Danaus, was warned by an oracle that he
        would be killed by one of his brother's sons. He then persuaded his fifty daughters
        to marry his brother's fifty sons, and instructed them to murder their husbands
        on the wedding night. Only Hypermnestra disobeyed her father and spared her
        husband.

162   *horse-leeches* bloodsuckers; double-tongued rhetoricians (cf. III.ii.281)

163   *two ... instruments* i.e. two more weapons (perhaps poniard and sword, with
        which he may have intended to attack Vittoria and Zanche) probably wrested from
        his grasp by the four assassins. Alternatively, this could be a contemptuous refer-
        ence to Vittoria and Zanche as 'instruments' of death like Hypermnestra's sisters.
        Help, help! Vittoria may be appealing to the masked conspirators to save her from
        Flamineo (NCW V.vi.163–4 n.).

165   *masque* ritualistic dance of masked revellers, who invited those already present to
        participate; often used by Jacobean dramatists as a means to bring on disguised
        conspirators for a final massacre, to which the formality of the masque offers a
        striking contrast (cf. *The Revenger's Tragedy* V.iii)
        matachin sword-dance in masks and fantastic costumes

166–7   ed. (By ... swords. / Church-men ... Isabella, Q)

VITTORIA   O we are lost.   170
FLAMINEO
   You shall not take justice from forth my hands –
   O let me kill her! I'll cut my safety
   Through your coats of steel. Fate's a spaniel,
   We cannot beat it from us: what remains now?
   Let all that do ill take this precedent: 175
   'Man may his fate foresee, but not prevent'.
   And of all axioms this shall win the prize:
   ' 'Tis better to be fortunate than wise'.
GASPARO
   Bind him to the pillar.
VITTORIA   O your gentle pity!
   I have seen a blackbird that would sooner fly   180
   To a man's bosom, than to stay the gripe
   Of the fierce sparrow-hawk.
GASPARO   Your hope deceives you.
VITTORIA
   If Florence be i'th'court, would he would kill me.
GASPARO
   Fool! Princes give rewards with their own hands,
   But death or punishment by the hands of others.   185
LODOVICO
   Sirrah you once did strike me – I'll strike you
   Into the centre.
FLAMINEO
   Thou'lt do it like a hangman, a base hangman,
   Not like a noble fellow, for thou seest
   I cannot strike again.
LODOVICO   Dost laugh?   190
FLAMINEO
   Wouldst have me die, as I was born, in whining?

173–4   *Fate's ... us* Webster probably borrows this phrase from Nashe's *Lenten Stuffe* (1599), which explains: 'the more you thinke to crosse it, the more you blesse and further it'. Spaniels were reputed to fawn on those who beat them.
175   *precedent* ed. (president Q)
179   *Bind ... pillar* either a freestanding stage post or one of the two pillars supporting the heavens
181   *stay* wait for
187   *centre* i.e. heart or soul
188   *hangman* executioner

GASPARO

    Recommend yourself to heaven.

FLAMINEO

    No, I will carry mine own commendations thither.

LODOVICO

    O, could I kill you forty times a day

    And use't four year together 'twere too little: 195

    Nought grieves but that you are too few to feed

    The famine of our vengeance. What dost think on?

FLAMINEO

    Nothing, of nothing: leave thy idle questions;

    I am i'th'way to study a long silence.

    To prate were idle – I remember nothing.   200

    There's nothing of so infinite vexation

    As man's own thoughts.

LODOVICO   O thou glorious strumpet,

    Could I divide thy breath from this pure air

    When't leaves thy body, I would suck it up

    And breathe't upon some dunghill.

VITTORIA   You, my death's-man;   205

    Methinks thou dost not look horrid enough,

    Thou hast too good a face to be a hangman;

    If thou be, do thy office in right form:

    Fall down upon thy knees and ask forgiveness.

LODOVICO

    O thou hast been a most prodigious comet   210

    But I'll cut off your train: kill the Moor first.

VITTORIA

    You shall not kill her first. Behold my breast.

    I will be waited on in death; my servant

    Shall never go before me.

GASPARO

    Are you so brave?

196   *grieves* ed. (greeu's Q)

198   *Nothing . . . nothing* This secular response is later echoed by the Duchess in *The Duchess of Malfi* before her death (IV.ii.16). *idle* foolish, useless

208–9 It was conventional for executioners to beg a perfunctory pardon before going to work: cf. *Measure for Measure* IV.ii.49–51: 'I do find your hangman is a more penitent trade than your bawd; he doth oft'ner ask forgiveness'.

211   *train* tail of a comet, with a pun on 'attendants' (Zanche)

214–17 ed. (Shall . . . brave. / Yes . . . death / As . . . weapon / halfe . . . tremble Q)

VITTORIA   Yes, I shall welcome death   215
   As princes do some great ambassadors:
   I'll meet thy weapon halfway.
LODOVICO   Thou dost tremble –
   Methinks fear should dissolve thee into air.
VITTORIA
   O thou art deceived, I am too true a woman:
   Conceit can never kill me. I'll tell thee what –   220
   I will not in my death shed one base tear,
   Or if look pale, for want of blood, not fear.
CARLO
   Thou art my task, black fury.
ZANCHE   I have blood
   As red as either of theirs; wilt drink some?
   'Tis good for the falling sickness: I am proud   225
   Death cannot alter my complexion,
   For I shall ne'er look pale.
LODOVICO   Strike, strike
   With a joint motion.

[They strike]

VITTORIA   'Twas a manly blow.
   The next thou giv'st, murder some sucking infant
   And then thou wilt be famous.
FLAMINEO   O what blade is't?   230
   A Toledo or an English fox?

215   *Conceit* idea or imaginative apprehension (of death); vanity or pride (proverbially
     feminine); physical conception of a child

220   *Conceit* idea or imaginative apprehension (of death); vanity or pride (proverbially
     feminine); physical conception of a child

221   An echo of Vittoria during the arraignment (III.ii.284–6): 'I will not weep, / No I
     do scorn to call up one poor tear / To fawn on your injustice'.

223–4   *I . . . theirs* Red blood was a sign of courage.

225   *falling sickness* epilepsy

227–8   *Strike . . . motion* This is group tragedy, as the three are stabbed simultaneously:
     Flamineo by Lodovico, Vittoria by Gasparo, and Zanche by Carlo.

228–30   In the 1991 National Theatre production, Josette Simon as Vittoria met Lodovico's
     dagger thrusts 'as though they represented a tempestuously flattering act of copula-
     tion', and completed the bitter self-parody with a 'cool pretence that she is
     congratulating him on his sexual prowess [which] ironically deflates his vengeful
     achievement' (Paul Taylor, *The Independent*, 20 June 1991).

231   *Toledo . . . fox* different types of short swords (the latter inscribed with a wolf, com-
     monly mistaken for a fox)

I ever thought a cutler should distinguish
The cause of my death rather than a doctor.
Search my wound deeper: tent it with the steel
That made it.   235

VITTORIA

O my greatest sin lay in my blood.
Now my blood pays for't.

FLAMINEO   Th'art a noble sister –
I love thee now. If woman do breed man
She ought to teach him manhood: fare thee well.
Know many glorious women that are famed   240
For masculine virtue have been vicious
Only a happier silence did betide them.
She hath no faults, who hath the art to hide them.

VITTORIA

My soul, like to a ship in a black storm,
Is driven I know not whither.

FLAMINEO   Then cast anchor.   245
'Prosperity doth bewitch men seeming clear,
But seas do laugh, show white, when rocks are near.
We cease to grieve, cease to be Fortune's slaves,
Nay cease to die by dying.' [To ZANCHE] Art thou gone?
[To VITTORIA] And thou so near the bottom? False report   250
Which says that women vie with the nine Muses
For nine tough durable lives. I do not look

---

232 *cutler* one who deals in knives and cutting utensils
234 *tent* i.e. use a tent or plug to search or clean my wound; with a pun on *tend*, care for
     (with a possible reference to miraculous cures effected by wounds)
234–5 ed. (one line in Q)
236–7 *blood . . . blood* Cf. I.i.274. Usually interpreted as conventional penitence, however
     uncharacteristic: 'My greatest sin lay in my sexual passion; now my life-blood pays
     for it'. (An actor, of course, could deliver even this meaning ironically.) However,
     the first 'blood' could also mean simply 'high temper, mettle', so Vittoria maintains
     her spirited self-defence; it could also mean 'kindred, family', so Vittoria targets
     Flamineo.
238, 240 *woman; women* (woemen Q) The unusual spelling here may just indicate a pun:
     woman as 'woe-to-man'.
245 *I . . . whither* Sinners proverbially died not knowing where they were going.
246–7 Webster's source (Alexander's *Croesus* I.i.65–73) clarifies this image: 'Vaine foole,
     that thinkes soliditie to find / . . . The fome is whitest, where the Rock is neare / . . .
     The greatest danger oft doth least appeare'.
250–2 *False . . . lives* Proverbially, nine lives are attributed to women and *cats*, not Muses.

Who went before, nor who shall follow me;
No, at myself I will begin and end:
'While we look up to heaven we confound   255
Knowledge with knowledge'. O, I am in a mist.

VITTORIA

O happy they that never saw the court,
'Nor ever knew great man but by report'.

Dies

FLAMINEO

I recover like a spent taper for a flash,
And instantly go out.   260
Let all that belong to great men remember th'old wives'
tradition, to be like the lions i'th'Tower on Candlemas day, to
mourn if the sun shine for fear of the pitiful remainder of
winter to come.
'Tis well yet there's some goodness in my death,   265
My life was a black charnel. I have caught
An everlasting cold. I have lost my voice
Most irrecoverably. Farewell, glorious villains.
'This busy trade of life appears most vain,
Since rest breeds rest where all seek pain by pain.'   270
Let no harsh flattering bells resound my knell,
Strike thunder and strike loud to my farewell.   *Dies*

ENGLISH AMBASSADOR

[*Within*] This way, this way, break ope the doors, this way.

---

258   s.d. *Dies* ed. (Vittoria dies Q)

261   *wives'* ed. (wides Q)

261–4   *Let . . . come* Proverbially, 'If Candlemas day [2 February] be fair and bright, winter
will have another flight'. Like the lions (kept in a small zoo in the Tower), the
courtier who anticipates gloomy weather even in bright sunshine 'will keepe him in
such humilitie and lowlynesse as Princes like of' (Pettie II.211).

266–8   *I . . . irrecoverably* another metatheatrical joke, since an actor with a long part like
Flamineo's might well be in danger of losing his voice at the end of the play

269   *trade* habitual course of action; passage to and fro; profession practised as a means
of livelihood

272   *Strike thunder* a prodigious sign associated with the fall of great men (cf. *The
Revenger's Tragedy* V.iii.44: 'Duke's groans are thunder's watchwords'); also, of
course, a theatrical directive (or a reference to the offstage pounding of the doors
by the ambassadors: NCW V.vi.270 n.)

LODOVICO
    Ha, are we betrayed?
    Why then let's constantly die all together,   275
    And having finished this most noble deed,
    Defy the worst of fate, not fear to bleed.

Enter AMBASSAD[ORS] *and* GIOVANNI [GUARDS *follow*]

ENGLISH AMBASSADOR
    Keep back the Prince – shoot, shoot–

[GUARDS *shoot at conspirators*]

LODOVICO   O I am wounded.
    I fear I shall be ta'en.
GIOVANNI   You bloody villains,
    By what authority have you committed   280
    This massacre?
LODOVICO   By thine.
GIOVANNI   Mine?
LODOVICO   Yes, thy uncle,
    Which is a part of thee, enjoined us to't.
    Thou know'st me I am sure, I am Count Lodowick,
    And thy most noble uncle in disguise
    Was last night in thy court.
GIOVANNI   Ha!
GASPARO   Yes, that Moor   285
    Thy father chose his pensioner.
GIOVANNI   He turned murderer!
    Away with them to prison and to torture.
    All that have hands in this shall taste our justice,
    As I hope heaven.

275 *constantly* resolutely
277 s.d. ed. (following l. 273 in Q)
281 *This . . . uncle* ed. (This . . . Mine? / LOD. Yes, Q)
285–6 ed. (Was . . . Ha! / Yes, . . . pentioner. Q)

LODOVICO   I do glory yet
    That I can call this act mine own: for my part,   290
    The rack, the gallows, and the torturing wheel
    Shall be but sound sleeps to me. Here's my rest –
    'I limbed this night-piece and it was my best'.
GIOVANNI
    Remove the bodies. See, my honoured lord,
    What use you ought make of their punishment.   295
    'Let guilty men remember their black deeds
    Do lean on crutches, made of slender reeds.'

                                      [*Exeunt*]

Instead of an Epilogue only this of Martial supplies me:
Haec fuerint nobis praemia si placui.

For the action of the play, 'twas generally well, and I dare   300
affirm, with the joint testimony of some of their own quality
(for the true imitation of life, without striving to make nature a
monster), the best that ever became them: whereof as I make a
general acknowledgement, so in particular I must remember
the well approved industry of my friend Master Perkins, and   305
confess the worth of his action did crown both the beginning
and end.

FINIS

292   *rest* peace of mind; final resolution; remaining hope
293   *limbed* limned (painted, portrayed) with a possible pun on 'limbed' as 'pulled limb
     from limb, dismembered' (though the *OED* records the earliest use of this verb in
     1674)
     night-piece painting representing a night-scene; tragic composition (used later by
     Webster himself to describe his elegy upon the death of Prince Henry (*A
     Monumental Column*, dedication))
295   *ought make* i.e. ought to make
299   *Haec . . . placui* 'These things will be our reward, if I have pleased' (Martial II, xci, 8).
301   *quality* profession
305   *Master Perkins* Richard Perkins was the leading player of Queen Anne's Men, well
     known for both his experience and his versatility; he probably played the part of
     Flamineo.

NOTES ON THE TEXTS

THE SPANISH TRAGEDY

The sole authoritative text of the play is the 1592 octavo, the basis for this edition. The Stationers' Register for 1592 records a dispute settled on 18 December that year when Edward White, the publisher of the 1592 text, was fined for 'having printed the spanishe tragedie belonging to Abell Jeffes'. White claimed on his title page that his version was 'Newly corrected and amended of such grosse faults as passed in the first impression'. The version by Jeffes has not survived. The one copy of White that has survived shows it was set by two compositors, one inexperienced, who used wrong founts perhaps from his own distribution of used type. Only sigs. A, C, H and L are free from such errors.

Other early editions copying their predecessors followed in 1594, 1599, 1602 (with the 'Additions'), 1603, 1610, 1615, 1618, 1623 and 1633. Most early copies were evidently read to pieces, because only one of the first and three of the first four editions have been found. The frequent reprinting adds a second testimony to its high popularity besides the constant quotations. The punctuation with its heavy end-stopping registers the rhetorical effects required from the words. Critics have found imperfections in the final scene, IV.v, offering a variety of conjectures to explain them. Philip Edwards, for instance, argues that the manuscript behind the 1592 text up to III.xiv was far better than the rest, where inconsistencies in the action suggest revision and abridgements made to Kyd's original copy. Some of these inconsistencies are registered in the footnotes.

In accordance with the general policy of this series, departures from the copy-text in substantive readings are recorded. Earlier editorial changes are not acknowledged except under the general designation 'ed.' Punctuation is made convenient for the modern reader through the wish to present a text an actor might use on stage. The punctuation has been lightened somewhat by the removal of commas, making colons commas, and excising a number of unnecessary full stops. Occasionally punctuation has been added when the meaning seems obscure though not deliberately ambiguous. When foreign languages are quoted a form of the language recognizable by present-day linguists is used, though there is no certainty that Kyd originally got them 'right' by modern standards. The speech prefixes and names in stage directions have been modernized and standardized throughout.

J.R. MULRYNE

THE REVENGER'S TRAGEDY

The play was first printed in 1607 by George Eld; in the following year sheets of this edition were made up and issued under a variant title page. The present edition has been based on the copy of the second issue (British Museum 644 c 80) and with it I have collated the 1607 issue (British Museum C. 34. e. 11). I have also collated editions by Allardyce Nicoll and Richard Harrier and, for the 1990 edition, that by R. A. Foakes. The press-work for the first printing has been analysed by George Price (see *The Library* vol. xv). Price accounts for the high incidence of variants in sig. H. More recently McD. P. Jackson in his Introduction (1983) to a facsimile of Q1, lists the stints of two compositors in setting the text. These compositors worked for the printer Eld in 1607–8 on a number of plays by several dramatists; Jackson believes that since they followed known orthographical preferences when setting the plays of other dramatists, he can be confident that the 'linguistic pattern of *The Revenger's Tragedy* is not a product of the printing house'. The quarto has many detailed stage directions, one or two for actions not indicated by the dialogue (e.g. III.v.155, IV.ii.44). Speech prefixes are generally clear and specific, except for such instances as the attendant Gentlemen, Nobles and Lords in Act V. Some exits and entrances are not marked.

In producing the present modernized critical edition I have regularized, simplified or added stage directions and speech headings where necessary. The collation at the foot of the text-pages records substantive changes from Q; modernization of spelling, non-substantive corrections and expanded abbreviations have been made silently. Many verse lines divided between speakers are printed in Q as successive short lines; in the present edition these are arranged as verse. A number of scenes are partly in verse, partly in prose; the compositors seem sometimes to have had difficulties in distinguishing verse from prose and despite the best efforts of editors there remain difficulties about the verse/prose status of some passages. The problem is associated with the more supple rhythms of dramatic dialogue in early Jacobean drama – somewhat similar lineation problems are seen in, for example, III.ii of Shakespeare's *Measure for Measure* of 1604.

BRIAN GIBBONS

'TIS PITY SHE'S A WHORE

The control-text for any modern edition of *'Tis Pity She's a Whore* is inevitably the Quarto of 1633 (Q) printed by Nicholas Okes for Richard Collins. Since it contains a dedication signed by Ford, it is generally taken to be an authorized edition printed from an authorial manuscript. The play was not reprinted in the seventeenth century, although in 1652 a copy of Q was bound with six other Ford Quartos, with a general printed title page, to produce a collection of Ford's *Comedies, tragi-comedies; & tragaedies*. All subsequent editions derive their text either directly or indirectly from Q.

Q is a book rich in bibliographical interest, providing much material for speculation about printing-house mishaps and even a visit to the press by the author. However, there is little to pose any major textual difficulty: a few words are misprinted and verse and prose are often confused or mis-lined (sometimes because the copy was wrongly marked up into pages, forcing the compositor to squash and stretch material to fit the space available). A number of surviving copies contain sheets printed after press correction, which introduce a total of forty-five variants; in this edition the corrected reading has been silently adopted in all substantive instances. The notes record all emendations and significant changes to the lineation of verse passages (including prose erroneously set as verse in Q); but changes to the division of prose passages and verse lines split to accommodate them within the margins of the Q page are not recorded. Q divides the text into five acts, and I have followed the usual convention of marking a new scene every time the stage is completely cleared. Q supplies a list of 'The Actors' Names', which provides some interesting hints about how Ford conceived the characters and their relationships, but which requires interpretation and, obviously, does not address itself to the needs of the modern reader; in this edition the list of the persons of the play has been compiled afresh, while the 1633 list appears as an appendix.

Speech prefixes have been silently expanded and all Latin stage directions silently translated into English, with the exception of the now-conventional *exit* and *exeunt*. Although it is possible that some of Q's stage directions were written for the seventeenth-century reader rather than for the playhouse, there are a number of points where necessary stage action is unclear, or where the reader is obliged to infer actions from subsequent dialogue references to them; stage directions (or parts thereof) which appear in square brackets have been added to resolve such issues. A number of directions to enter are given late in Q, presumably to indicate the point at which the characters concerned enter the action, rather than the stage; with one problematic exception (on which, see the note to II.iii.28 s.d.), such stage directions are repositioned in this edition to indicate the point at which those characters become visible to a theatre audience, and to other characters already on stage.

Spelling and punctuation are modernized throughout in accordance with New Mermaid series conventions. No previous editor has attempted a full modernization of Q's light, rhetorical punctuation, which is eccentric (and sometimes mystifying) in its use of dashes, and tends to use commas and semi-colons to separate entirely distinct syntactic units. This edition uses heavier, grammatical punctuation in an effort to guide the reader through the syntax.

Perhaps the greatest challenge which the play offers its editor lies in the deceptive simplicity of some of its language: a number of its unadorned and unspecific lines are open to irreconcilable alternative interpretations. This is quite a different matter from the deliberate, meaningful ambiguity celebrated by the critical school of William Empson (and which is also present in some parts of the play), where the multiple senses of a word coexist and interact to create a richer matrix of significance; I refer rather to cases which might be seen as the literary equivalent of Schrodinger's cat, where the process of realizing the text forces you to choose one meaning and exclude all others. The less virtual the play becomes, the more these possibilities will cease to exist: an edition with modernized spelling and (especially) punctuation will have closed down some, and a production all of them. In preparing this edition, I have tried to be alert to this issue, to avoid imposing one possible stage realization at the expense of another, and to discuss the more clear-cut interpretative options in the notes.

Like all editors, I owe much to the work of my predecessors. After Q, the play next appeared in print as part of Robert Dodsley's *Select Collection of Old Plays* (1744), which was later revised by Isaac Reed in 1780. From Dodsley onwards, the editorial history has been one of progressively introducing emendations to Q, and more recently rejecting them in favour of the original Q readings; this edition continues the latter trend. I have been especially indebted to the important contributions to the play's bibliographical and textual history in the editions of N.W. Bawcutt (1966) and Derek Roper (1975), and to the thorough modernization of the spelling in that of Marion Lomax (1995). I have also found useful the editions of Henry William Weber (1811), William Gifford (1827), Alexander Dyce (1869), A.K. McIlwraith (1953). Brian Morris (1968), Keith Sturgess (1970), Colin Gibson (1986), and Simon Barker (1997).

MARTIN WIGGINS

THE WHITE DEVIL

The White Devil was first printed in 1612 by Nicholas Okes, and is free from major textual obscurity. I have taken as my copy text the authoritative first quarto (British Museum shelfmark C.34. e.18). Press corrections have been supplied from John Russell Brown's list ('The Printing of John Webster's Plays (II)', *Studies in Bibliography* 8 (1956), 113–17); substantive press variants indicate that Webster himself may have been involved in proofreading and correcting. Recently, Anthony Hammond has distinguished three main compositors, whom he calls A, B and N, the latter (who set B1r–E4v) being the least experienced and most prone both to commit error and to follow his copy in matters of punctuation.

The manuscript which Webster supplied to the printer was probably based on his 'foul papers' rather than on a text adapted for use in the theatre, judging from the irregular speech headings, misplaced entries and complete absence of act and scene divisions in the copy, as well as the truculent attitude he adopts in the preface towards the playhouse. As his afterword commending the players indicates, Webster was acutely sensitive to performance; indeed, he attempted to supplement the necessarily incomplete experience of a *reader* of the play by adding a number of stage directions to the second part of the text, perhaps while the first part was already being set by the printer. In the published text, these added stage directions occur in the margins after F3v. Since they are not different in kind from other stage directions, which the compositors usually squeezed into available text space, they are treated as accidental features of the printer's copy, and both marginal and other stage directions are incorporated into the text at appropriate points in the dialogue, though all changes to their position are recorded in the notes.

I have modernized spelling (unless the original spelling allowed for a play on words), eliminated both capitalized nouns and italicized proper names, regularized speech prefixes and expanded elisions such as final syllable apostrophes. Because there is reason to doubt compositorial consistency (Brown lxx), I have used quotation marks for all gnomic pointing in the copy (normally indicated by either italics or inverted commas). I have added the customary act and scene divisions in square brackets. In accordance with the policy of this series, I have followed the lineation of the copy text except when verse is obviously set as prose to save space, in which case the change is indicated in the notes. Blank verse lines are staggered when they are shared by two or more speakers. The light punctuation of Q has been followed wherever possible, though it has been necessary in some cases to add commas, semi-colons and dashes to capture, without arresting, Webster's fluid language.

CHRISTINA LUCKYJ

APPENDIX

Francis Bacon's essay 'Of Revenge' from his
Essayes or Counsels (1625 edition)

REVENGE is a kind of wild justice; which the more man's nature runs to, the more ought law to weed it out. For as for the first wrong, it doth but offend the law; but the revenge of that wrong, putteth the law out of office. Certainly, in taking revenge, a man is but even with his enemy; but in passing it over, he is superior; for it is a prince's part to pardon. And Solomon, I am sure, saith, It is the glory of a man, to pass by an offence. That which is past is gone, and irrevocable; and wise men have enough to do, with things present and to come; therefore they do but trifle with themselves, that labour in past matters. There is no man doth a wrong, for the wrong's sake; but thereby to purchase himself profit, or pleasure, or honour, or the like. Therefore why should I be angry with a man, for loving himself better than me? And if any man should do wrong, merely out of ill-nature, why, yet it is but like the thorn or briar, which prick and scratch, because they can do no other. The most tolerable sort of revenge, is for those wrongs which there is no law to remedy; but then let a man take heed, the revenge be such as there is no law to punish; else a man's enemy is still before hand, and it is two for one. Some, when they take revenge, are desirous, the party should know, whence it cometh. This is the more generous. For the delight seemeth to be, not so much in doing the hurt, as in making the party repent. But base and crafty cowards, are like the arrow that flieth in the dark. Cosmus, Duke of Florence, had a desperate saying against perfidious or neglecting friends, as if those wrongs were unpardonable. You shall read (saith he) that we are commanded to forgive our enemies; but you never read, that we are commanded to forgive our friends. But yet the spirit of Job was in a better tune. Shall we (saith he) take good at God's hands, and not be content to take evil also? And so of friends in a proportion. This is certain, that a man that studieth revenge, keeps his own wounds green, which otherwise would heal, and do well. Publiç revenges are for the most part fortunate; as that for the death of Caesar; for the death of Pertinax; for the death of Henry the Third of France; and many more. But in private revenges, it is not so. Nay rather, vindictive persons live the life of witches; who, as they are mischievous, so end they infortunate.